BOOKS BY W. A. SWANBERG

DREISER

CITIZEN HEARST

JIM FISK:
The Career of an Improbable Rascal

FIRST BLOOD
The Story of Fort Sumter

SICKLES THE INCREDIBLE

Dreiser

Dreiser

BY W. A. SWANBERG

CHARLES SCRIBNER'S SONS · New York

1 3 5 7 9 11 13 15 17 19 K/C 20 18 16 14 12 10 8 6 4 2

PRINTED IN THE UNITED STATES OF AMERICA
Library of Congress Catalog Card Number 75–35060

ISBN 0–684–14552–9

813
D771zswd

PERMISSIONS

The author thanks the following for kind permission to quote extracts from the copyrighted works listed.

The World Publishing Company for *The Financier* (1912), *The "Genius"* (1915), *A Hoosier Holiday* (1916), *Twelve Men* (1919), *A Book About Myself* (1922, republished in 1931 as *Newspaper Days*), *Dreiser Looks at Russia* (1928), *A Gallery of Women* (1929), *Dawn* (1931), and *Moods* (1935), all by Theodore Dreiser; the same company for *My Life With Dreiser*, by Helen Dreiser (1951); Putnam's & Coward-McCann: *Author Hunting by an Old Literary Sportsman*, by Grant Richards (1934); Mrs. George Jean Nathan: *The Intimate Notebooks of George Jean Nathan* (Knopf, 1932); Harcourt, Brace & World, Inc.: *Harlan Miners Speak* (1932); Houghton Mifflin Company: *Dorothy and Red*, by Vincent Sheean (1963); Alfred A. Knopf, Inc.: *Letters of H. L. Mencken*, edited by Guy J. Forgue (1961); Mrs. Sherwood Anderson and Harold Ober Associates: *The Portable Sherwood Anderson* (Viking Press, 1949); and Simon & Schuster, Inc.: *My Life*, by Claude Bowers (1962).

LW/98857

TO THE MEMORY OF

H. L. Mencken
who knew Dreiser
at his best and worst,
and fought for the best

Contents

Illustrations

Dreiser

Book One

INDIANA GOTHIC

I. On the Wabash

Terre Haute, Indiana, summer, 1871—a hot, smoky town on the Wabash River with a steel mill, a distillery, coal mines, a huge railroad car works and a score of other enterprises from tanneries to foundries. The post-Civil War era of ruthless industrial exploitation was in full career. Terre Haute had its "best people"—its minority of the wealthy who had been foresighted or aggressive, had launched themselves in business and built gabled homes with sweeping lawns on Wabash Avenue. There was one authentic millionaire, Chauncey Rose, who had amassed a fortune in land and railroads and now in his old age was giving it to charities and dispensing an average of ten dollars a day to beggars at his door. But easily 90 per cent of the 17,000 inhabitants were the twelve-hour-a-day workers and their families who lived in a condition not called poverty because it was commonplace and accepted.

Among the poorest were the Dreisers on South Ninth Street, a family that seemed dogged by misfortune. Already the unschooled parents had eight living children. Another was on the way—the one who would be Theodore Dreiser—and the prenatal atmosphere was more suggestive of a gypsy tribe than an Indiana household. The parents, hearing nocturnal noises, were convinced that spirits haunted the place. Bearded, forty-nine-year-old John Paul Dreiser at last asked the help of Father C. N. Gällweiler of St. Benedict's German Catholic Church, who came and sprinkled holy water around the house.[1]

Both Dreiser and his wife Sarah had a firm belief in apparitions and portents. Had not Sarah, years earlier when she had only three sons, seen three phosphorescent lights bobbing erratically toward her across a meadow?

"Right away," she said, "I knew that those were my three children and that they were going to die!"[2]

Within three years, the three sons *had* died.

Now Father Gällweiler was confronted by spirits of more than ordinary mettle. When Sarah was in labor with the child who would become Theodore, she said she saw three graces "garbed in brightly colored costumes" trip into the house, pass silently around her bed, then dance out the back door and vanish. The pretty trio was seen also by her husband and their eldest daughter, Mary Frances (called Mame), or so they said thereafter.

When Herman Theodore Dreiser was born at 8:30 on the morning of

3

August 27, 1871, he was such a scrawny infant that his days seemed numbered. He was "puny beyond belief" a fortnight later when he was baptized into the Roman Catholic Church he would come to detest.³ So fearful was Sarah that she did something she had done before and would do again: she secretly disobeyed her fanatically religious husband.

In a hovel across Ninth Street lived a German crone believed to have occult powers not sanctioned by the church. One night when Theodore seemed about to die, Sarah sent ten-year-old Mame running to fetch the sorceress. But the woman, knowing of John Dreiser's strict religious views, refused to come.

"If your mother wants help," she said, "tell her to take a string and measure your brother from head to toe and from finger-tip to finger-tip. If the arms are as long as the body, bring the string to me."

Mame hurried to comply. When she brought back the string, the German woman smiled and sent for Sarah Dreiser.

"Your child will not die," she said. "But for three nights in succession, you must take him out in the full of the moon. Leave his head and face uncovered, and stand so that the light will fall slantwise over his forehead and eyes. Then say three times: '*Wass ich hab, nehm ab; wass ich thu, nehm zu!*'"⁴

Sarah, overjoyed, followed these instructions faithfully. Thereafter she was convinced that her son's life was saved by a string, an incantation and the light of the moon.

Theodore Dreiser was reared in superstition, fanaticism, ignorance, poverty and humiliation. Though he would be permanently hurt, he was not crushed, thanks to his own powerful spirit and the warm, sheltering love of his earthy, illiterate but great-hearted mother. Sarah Dreiser could not write her own name. She believed in fairies. She was so passionate, so pagan, that Theodore himself in later years thought it quite possible that occasionally she had taken a lover. "She did if she wanted to, I'm certain of that," he said, adding that he was satisfied of his own legitimacy because he had inherited some of John Paul Dreiser's traits.⁵

To the later, free-loving Dreiser it made no difference whether she took one lover or a dozen. To him she was perfect, a lovely combination of pagan and poet, so artlessly tender that utter strangers were drawn to her instantly and mere acquaintances called on her for help, always getting it even though she needed help far more than they. Plump, handsome, smiling Sarah had an irresistible maternal warmth of the kind the old Greeks worshipped in Demeter.

The daughter of prosperous Mennonites of Czech ancestry, Sarah Maria Schänäb grew to girlhood on a farm near Dayton, Ohio. She was seventeen when she met John Dreiser. To her—a girl with no schooling who had never seen a town bigger than Dayton—he must have brought an engulfing air of sophistication, the romance of far places and large affairs. In 1844, at twenty-three, Dreiser had left his birthplace in Mayen, Germany, to escape conscription, lingered briefly in Paris, then gone to America to follow his trade as a weaver. He had worked at woolen mills in New York and Connecticut, then moved to a mill at Dayton. Slight of build but a prodigious worker, he spoke halting English and had the piercing gaze of a zealot.

Sarah's parents, militant anti-Catholics, forbade the match. But she and the twenty-nine-year-old Dreiser celebrated New Year's Day of 1851 by running off to nearby Piqua and getting married.[6] Sarah, still four months short of eighteen, was disowned by her family for this iniquity. The young couple moved to Fort Wayne, Indiana, where Dreiser worked in a small woolen mill, then by 1858 to Terre Haute, where he had a supervisory position in a larger mill.

He was ambitious, a driver, seeking success and gradually achieving it. In 1867 there were six children when he moved his family twenty-five miles south to Sullivan and went into debt to become a wool manufacturer on his own. His dream crumbled in 1869 when the factory burned to the ground. Although the building itself was owned by Chauncey Rose, the Terre Haute capitalist, Dreiser had invested heavily in machinery and in tons of farmers' fleece, unpaid for and uninsured.[7]

This reverse visited on the family two decades of hell hardly to be rivaled by the hereafter. To top it off, John Dreiser was injured so severely by a falling timber that the hearing in one ear was destroyed and he was in bed for weeks. By the time he recovered, moved his family back to Terre Haute and found work there, he was a man almost crazed by the sin and shame of debt. Every dollar he owed had to be paid off. The ambition that once drove him seemed to be replaced by a wild need to placate the fates. Although he was in his prime, an expert in wool-buying and fabrication, he gave up hope for the future, turned his thoughts solely to the debts of the past and hoarded pennies and nickels for salvation, determined that he would save his family and himself from eternal torment even if it meant privation. "Never have I known a man more obsessed by a religious belief," Theodore later recalled.[8]

II. SIN ON ALL SIDES

When Theodore was born in 1871, his father was only sporadically employed and still in debt. The birth of the last child, Edward, two years later, made a family of twelve, with five sons and five daughters, and although the oldest of them picked up what work they could, poverty had now become accepted and the only hope was to ward off outright destitution. In Terre Haute the Dreisers gained a reputation as a chaotic, hard-pressed clan, often behind in their bills, whose older sons were wild and whose older daughters were flirty. Theodore, called Theo or by the Germanic nicknames of Dorsch or Dorse, was sensitive and emotional. A clinger to his mother's skirts, he noticed the ragged slippers she wore, and stroked her feet in sympathy.

"See poor mother's shoes?" Sarah said. "Aren't you sorry she has to wear such torn shoes? See the hole here?" [9]

He wept in pity for her, and she caught him in a loving embrace.

Each morning the family knelt around the father as he asked a blessing for the day, and each evening for a similar blessing for the night. His earnest German prayers were a household ritual. Stern, free with the strap, he was losing touch with his rebellious children. He intended his oldest son, musically inclined Paul, for the priesthood, but Paul was always in trouble, even being jailed briefly on suspicion of robbery. He tried to interest his second son, Marcus Romanus, known as Rome, in the wool business. Rome, a wild one, preferred petty jobs away from the Teutonic eye. He acquired a taste for whiskey and gambling in his teens, and liked to lounge in lordly fashion in front of the town's grandest hotel, the Terre Haute House on Wabash Avenue, picking his teeth to give the impression that he had just eaten there, which he had not.

"Loafers!" John Dreiser snapped in his imperfect English. "Idle, good-for-nothings!" [10]

Later, when Paul forged a note in his father's name, Dreiser let the law take its course. Paul stayed in jail despite his mother's pleas that something be done for him.

The Dreiser family became the center of a quiet maternal conspiracy. Sarah, believing that love might succeed where tyranny failed, shielded her children from Dreiser's wrath to hold her family together. With three of the younger children in the throes of measles, and Dreiser out of work again, the family moved to a bigger house at Sixth and Mulberry Streets and Sarah took in boarders. The older daughters, Mame and Emma, were primping now, cultivating spitcurls. To Dreiser, this was a prostitute's lure, and he would stalk the floor, his hands behind his back, railing at Sarah for letting the girls go straight to damnation, then would retire, muttering, to his prayer book.

Luckily, he did not know all. A prominent Terre Haute attorney took a lustful fancy to Mame Dreiser, then a pretty blonde of sixteen and less than half his age. Seeing her stare wistfully at a shop window crammed with Easter finery, he said, "Mary, wouldn't you like that hat?"

"Indeed I would," she replied.

"Then you take this ten dollars and see if you can't get it." [11]

She took it—the first of a series of benefactions. Sarah, not knowing where the next meal was coming from and never fastidious in such matters, let her take the gifts and used some of the money for food. The lawyer seduced the girl and became her lover. He later appeared in court for Paul and got him out of jail. Paul, twelve years older than Theodore, was a character too vital to hold in check, friendly, uproarious, already hatching sentimental ballads. He invented comic names for each of his brothers and sisters, Theodore being Frossus, and Ed, Fitus. Sang the troubadour Paul:

> *Fitus and Frossus were fighting for flies;*
> *Fitus gave Frossus a pair of black eyes.*[12]

He felt his father's strap fairly regularly until at last he was sent to St. Meinrad's Seminary near Evansville in the hope that he would straighten out and become a priest.

John Dreiser worked intermittently at low wages as a wool-sorter, a spinner, even as a laborer. A beaten man, he relied more and more on God and less and less on himself. The boarding-house venture failed because Sarah fed her guests too well and could not keep the accounts straight, so the Dreisers moved again, this time to something little better than a shack.

Theodore, a skinny, tow-haired weakling, often had to make do with fried mush and milk for dinner, sometimes minus the milk, which was too dear. There was no money for coal. By the time he was five, he went out with his older brother Alphonse to pick coal along the tracks of the Terre Haute & Evansville Railroad, occasionally being driven away by cursing workmen. There were times when the Dreiser children went to bed both cold and hungry. Once, unable to pay the rent and threatened with eviction, Sarah was so desperate that at Rome's urging she let a younger daughter go over to Wabash Avenue and beg from a prosperous lumber dealer known for his generosity. Touched, the merchant handed her $50—and Rome, waiting outside, took all but $15 of it and squandered it on cards and liquor.

Sarah took in washings. She found work scrubbing and cleaning at the Terre Haute House, known locally as the Terrible Hot House—the hostelry where Rome was wont to swagger—and when she came home exhausted she did not take kindly to John's lectures about the children's descent to hell. Let him first make a decent living, she said. Then it might be time to talk of hell.

Although she had adopted his religion, she felt him unreasonable in thinking that heaven had to be bought at the price of near-starvation. It was all very fine for Paul to go to St. Meinrad's, but it cost money. There were free public schools in Terre Haute, yet the children had to go to St. Benedict's Parochial School, which cost money. Dreiser exploded when she ventured to protest about this.

The family quarrels became more frequent. Rome, disgusted, ran off to become a train butcher, selling peanuts and newspapers. The older girls, passionate as all the Dreisers were passionate, sick of their father's lectures, were enjoying affairs with men. At St. Meinrad's, Paul tired of the discipline and ran away. He knew better than to go home, made his footsore way to Indianapolis and joined up as a minstrel with a covered-wagon medicine show, booming Dr. Hamlin's Wizard Oil—guaranteed to cure all ills.

The sensitive Theodore grew up among tensions. For a time he developed a nervous stutter. He cried easily. Among his earliest reflections was the realization of the sharp schism between his mother's way of life and his father's, the schism between the pagan and the puritan. There was never any question as to whose side he was on.

III. THE IRON DEER

At six, Theodore was taken to the parochial school by his eight-year-old sister Claire. He was terrified by the nuns with their flaring bonnets and by the sense of discipline that pervaded the place, the catechism, the rules. When he met the priest, he lifted his cap and said, "Praised be Jesus Christ," the priest lifting his hat and responding, "Amen!" [13]

To Theodore the school was an extension of his father into nuns and priests who censored the joys from his life and said the same things but with even more authority—the must-nots, the avoid-evils, the hell-awaits-the-sinners. Hell was a frightening place, and yet his father and the church seemed preoccupied with it. But not his mother! She showered him with love, showing a natural favoritism toward the only weakling in the family.

Theodore was homely, with protruding teeth and a cast in one eye. Poor at sports, bullied by other boys, he had little choice but to be a solitary child. The Dreisers, he saw, were different from other people—poorer. They were looked down upon. It was humiliating to wear ragged clothing and disintegrating shoes, to sneak coal from the tracks. He sometimes stared enviously through iron fences at the homes of the wealthy on Wabash Avenue, marveling at the flowers, the lawns, the iron deer.

He dreamed that he had a house like those. He envisioned nickels, dimes and quarters strewn on the ground. One of his few friends was an old railroad gateman who would pass the house and give him a jawbreaker or an apple—gifts so splendid that Theodore always greeted him with delirious shouts of "Mr. Watchman! Mr. Watchman!" The gateman died one day and Theodore was taken to the house nearby where he lay in his coffin. Each eye was covered by a nickel. Theodore, fascinated, reached out and would have taken them had he not been restrained by his mother.[14]

Always the Dreisers were moving—never because they wanted to, never to a better house, always because they had to, because they were evicted or to save on rent. In Theodore's seven years in Terre Haute they lived in five different houses. Tradesmen hounded them about unpaid bills. In the spring of 1879, John Dreiser, after a period of unemployment, found work at a local rug factory and enlisted his older daughters as loomworkers.

Years earlier, Sarah had befriended a frivolous Terre Haute girl named Susan Bellette. Sue, now the wife of a fire captain in Vincennes, wrote inviting Sarah to come, offering gratis a small apartment over the fire house. While in some ways it was a thoroughly impractical scheme, it offered the adventure of renewing an old friendship and at least facing poverty in a different milieu, and it would end the incessant quarrels with Dreiser and remove the younger children from this unpleasantness.

It was arranged that Sarah, then forty-six, would go to Vincennes with six-year-old Ed, seven-year-old Theodore and nine-year-old Claire. Eleven-year-old Al was sent to work at a relative's farm. Paul and Rome were gone, no one knew where. The four older daughters, Mame, Emma, Theresa and Sylvia, would stay in Terre Haute with John Dreiser and would send what help they could.

Reaching Vincennes with her three youngest, Sarah gratefully took over the apartment on a floor otherwise given over to firemen's sleeping quarters. Theodore was thrilled by red-coated firemen sliding down brass poles as well-trained horses trotted out to stop under suspended harness in answer to an alarm. He saw workmen install the first telephone he had ever seen, a device the captain let him listen to, and he actually heard a scratchy voice saying, "Hello." But Sarah, at first puzzled by the arrival of painted women at odd hours, discovered that marriage had not slowed the racy Susan. She was running a firemen's bordello. Theodore himself, peering in an open door, saw "a corn-haired blonde, her pink face buried in a curled arm, lying in a bed allotted to one of the firemen serving on the night shift." [15]

Flexible as Sarah's morals were, they would not stretch that far. After some five weeks in Vincennes, she told Sue that they must leave.

2. On the Move

Clearly avoiding a return to Terre Haute, Sarah instead packed the children off to Sullivan, halfway between Vincennes and Terre Haute—the town where Dreiser had started on his own, where his courage had crumpled after the fire. There the four lived with an Irish family they had known in better times, until they found a cottage on the edge of town at seven dollars a month. They borrowed a couple of straw mattresses, some dishes, an iron cooking pot. There was almost no furniture. But this was summer, 1879, there were roses and trumpet vines around the house, and the childlike Sarah was as charmed as if she were entering a mansion.

"See all the nice roses!" she exclaimed. "Aren't the fields about here beautiful now? It's just like the country." [1]

Theodore was happier in Sullivan than he ever had been before, largely because his father came only for occasional visits. Since his brother Ed enjoyed games with other boys, the non-athletic Theodore resorted to other pleasures. He often rose before dawn to sit by the window with a mongrel pup in his lap, marveling at the sun as it rose over a neighboring field of clover, then watching the swallows skim the blooms. He was a wondering observer, a spectator rather than a participant. While other boys played mumbledepeg or swam in the nearby Busseron River, Theodore investigated the habits of turtles and crayfish.

In Terre Haute, the four older girls quarreled with their father, one by one quit the rug factory to find work as housemaids, and seized every opportunity to visit Sullivan and the mother they loved. Sarah was the magnet who drew all the children, whatever their delinquencies. Even Rome, strapping and handsome after an absence of a couple of years, appeared unannounced in Sullivan to greet his mother with an enthusiastic kiss, then demand a meal and let it be known that he was broke. He had drifted as far west as Texas, and he told tall tales of mining and cowpunching. Now that he had visited Chicago, he scorned Sullivan as a hick town.

"These yokels around here don't know anything!" he said. [2]

But he found Sullivan's whiskey potable, got drunk and caused his mother great embarrassment and chagrin before he left for another protracted adventure.

With John Dreiser out of work again, Sarah did washings and took in several laborers from the local coal mine as boarders, one of them a drunken, sinister gorilla who terrorized the household until the police came and arrested him on an old murder charge. That winter, Theodore and Ed were sent home from the parochial school because they had no shoes—a problem Sarah finally solved by doing washings for Solomon Goodman, a local clothier, who in return supplied the shoes. Theodore carried bundles of washing all over town, ashamed of the chore, just as he was of the frequent trips he made with Ed to pick coal at the yards and sometimes steal it from cars.

At night, with Claire, he had a project he loved. They worked patiently with their mother, taught her the characters, until at last she satisfied a lifelong ambition. She learned to write.

Then Mame Dreiser arrived, but not on a routine visit. Weeping, she told her mother that she was pregnant, that her lawyer lover had given her $50 and the name of a country doctor who was believed to perform abortions. The doctor had refused her. What was she to do?

Sarah's answer was that she must marry the man, of course. But the lawyer refused to marry Mame, disapproved of the Dreiser clan, and Mame was too awed by his importance and his violent temper to appeal to him again. So Sarah went to Terre Haute to see him, found him obdurate, and faced the crisis with her usual fortitude.

"Well, never mind now," she told the tearful Mame. "I will see you through this. You will be alright [*sic*]. You will be a better girl for it. Don't cry." [3]

Possibly she recalled that in her extremity she had allowed Mame to accept money from the man in the first place, and that this might have been unwise. In any case, it was another secret to be kept from John Dreiser and from the Sullivan neighbors. For some weeks Mame stayed inside the cottage to keep her condition from becoming known—a situation of which Theodore, then nearing nine, was at least partially aware. When the baby was born in April, Mame was attended by an old family doctor who kept the matter confidential. The child, a boy, was stillborn. At midnight Sarah dug a grave near the house, performed a quick burial, and later showed Mame the grave.

In the Dreiser family, disasters were never far apart. The following winter the Sullivan mine closed and several of Sarah's boarders left without paying their keep. She owed such bills at the nearer markets that the proprietors cut her off and it became urgent to find other markets, ever farther away, where she might be trusted for a few potatoes, a loaf of bread. That Christmas, Theodore had only one present, a gimcrack sent by the good-hearted, rattle-brained Mame, who had no sooner survived the Sullivan ordeal than she had run off to Chicago to take up with another admirer. He dreamed of Rome now—the swashbuckler who knew Chicago, knew Texas, knew cowboys and Indians. But the dreams collapsed before the reality of his empty stomach and his wretched mother. "For years," he later recalled, "even so late as my thirty-fifth or fortieth years, the approach of winter invariably filled me with an indefinable and highly oppressive dread. . . ." [4]

There came a day in February, 1881, when Sarah was beside herself. There was not a scrap of food in the house. The rent was long overdue. It seemed certain that they would be evicted, thrown out into the snow, without even money to make the twenty-five-mile trip to Terre Haute, where Dreiser himself was almost destitute.

What happened then was pure melodrama.

There was a knock on the door and Paul Dreiser strode in, plump, well-fed, beaming, wearing a silk hat, fur coat and brandishing a gold-headed cane. Paul, whom they had not seen for several years, radiated such an aura of cheer that they all shouted with joy and Sarah could not repress tears as he embraced them in turn with the affection that was so much a part of him. "He was like the sun," Theodore said later, "or a warm, cheering fire." [5] Paul had passed through Terre Haute, learned that his mother was in Sullivan and had taken the first train down. Now he produced a thick wallet and peeled off greenbacks.

His success had been meteoric, as he freely admitted. With the Wizard Oil troupe he had enacted blackface roles and composed comic songs that put the rubes in stitches. He had jumped the troupe to join a Cincinnati minstrel show, had moved to New York and appeared in minor roles at Harry Miner's Bowery Theater, and now he was end man for Thatcher, Primrose and West's famous minstrel show, drawing a handsome salary. Now twenty-three and growing fat, he was no longer Paul Dreiser but Paul Dresser, an easier name for his public to remember. He gave the children copies of the Paul Dresser Songster, a gaudy pamphlet of his own songs which was sold to audiences for a dime. He left money for food, rent and clothes before he had to catch up with his show in Terre Haute. He promised that he would be back. When he left, in Theodore's eyes Paul had displaced Rome as the greatest man in the world.

II. EVANSVILLE

Paul Dresser, one of the most sentimental and sensual of men, was so appalled by his mother's poverty that he altered his own career to help her. He quit his show in Evansville, embarked on an affair with Sallie Walker, alias Annie Brace, a woman with jet-black hair who was the prosperous madam of a high-class brothel on Main Street, and moved into Sallie's splendid apartment in the establishment. He easily landed the job of leading man at Evansville's Apollo Theater stock company. In the spring he sent his mother money for rail fares and met her at the Evansville station when she arrived with the three children.

Evansville had at least 30,000 people, and the broad Ohio beside it made Terre Haute's Wabash River seem like a creek. The group boarded a horse-car—the first Theodore had ever seen—and Paul maintained a beaming air of mystery until he escorted them up the walk of a neat brick cottage at 1413 East Franklin Street, made a sweeping gesture and said it was theirs. Sarah stared at the flower-wreathed porch, at the new furniture and shiny cook-stove inside, and wept, while Paul, wet-eyed himself, put a fond arm around her. Sallie Walker sent groceries and later, clad in striking black, called in her glittering carriage. Sarah soon understood that she was Paul's mistress but was unaware that she was the town's reigning courtesan, that a part of Paul's prosperity came from the profits of her twenty girls and that he sometimes entertained her clients at the piano.[6]

John Dreiser, in Terre Haute, had no idea that his wife and three youngest were being subsidized by harlotry.

Theodore, though freed from poverty for the first time in his life, still had to go with Ed and Claire to Holy Trinity Parochial School on Vine Street, where a martinet "Herr Professor" smote the knuckles of laggard students with a ruler, and where Father Anton Dudenhausen predicted that Robert Ingersoll would go to hell and drag many erring souls with him. Hell, however tiresome, was real to Theodore. Even when he had the envied job of pumping the church organ, behind the arras where no one could see him, he dropped to his knees when the host was elevated lest he be struck dead and cast into flame. He lost himself in books he found in his attic—Ouida's *Wanda*, Goldsmith's *The Deserted Village* and Bulwer's *Ernest Maltravers*—tales charged with a suspense lacking in the *Catholic Eclectic Reader*.

At least now he could take pride in his brother Paul—Paul, rich and famous, whose picture appeared on sheet music he wrote, whose round face beamed from Main Street billboards advertising the next production at the Apollo. Paul could do *anything*. He wrote a humorous column for the *Evansville Argus* called "Plummy's Pointers." He knew everybody in town. Paul would arrive at the house, kiss his mother, delight everybody with his shouting good humor, then sit down at the piano and play his own ballads—some of them funny, some so sad that he would weep over the keys—doubtless the same songs he played at Sallie's bordello. Paul would bring candy for his mother, balls and bats for the boys, a gift for Claire. Paul brought tickets for his minstrel show, the first stage spectacle Theodore had ever seen. With his brother Ed he sat in the gallery, bursting with pride as Paul—the interlocutor, the head man—asked funny questions and got answers that made the crowd roar. After the show Paul took the boys backstage, introducing them to the actors and the glamorous world of greasepaint. On the Fourth of July, Paul came to the house laden with firecrackers and rockets. On Christmas, he staggered in with an armload of presents, seemingly unconcerned about hell, always enjoying life and delighting in bringing happiness to others.

At eleven, Theodore was ignorant of Sal Walker's reputation and of Paul's relationship with her until one day when Sarah sent him with a basket of preserves for the lady. A Negro servant escorted Theodore up a handsomely carpeted stairway to a lavish apartment with awninged windows that over-looked the river. There was Paul in light trousers and a silk shirt, making his morning toilet, and with him was raven-haired Sal in a beribboned pink dressing gown. Paul, not in the least disconcerted, made much of Theodore and gave him spending money as the boy stared in awe at the thick rugs, the wicker furniture, the big piano and the silver toilet articles.

On his way out, he passed down a corridor where half-open doors disclosed tumbled beds, and in one room a "yellow-haired siren half naked before her mirror . . . her arms and breast exposed, 'making up' her cheeks and eyes." Theodore's impression that there was something excitingly sinful here was magnified when a friend, Harry Truckee, stopped him to say, "Hey, Thee! What's the name of that woman your brother lives with downtown?"

Theodore, flushing, said he did not know.

"Never heard of Sallie Walker!" Harry scoffed. "Why, everybody knows her. She keeps a fast house down on the waterfront. You ask your brother sometime, he'll tell yuh. They say she's stuck on him and he lives there." [7]

John Dreiser, still working in Terre Haute, came down occasionally to make sharp inquiries about church attendance. Al Dreiser came for a visit, as did the older daughters—a scattered brood drawn always by the magical Sarah. And out of the blue came strapping Rome, after a two-year absence, to cry bitterly on his mother's shoulder over his wasted life, then to go downtown, get drunk, advertise himself as Paul's brother, pass several bad checks and land in jail. Paul, annoyed, used his influence to get Rome out, whereupon Rome drowned his sorrows at the nearest saloon, stole a buggy to visit other saloons, abandoned the buggy and staggered home. To Sarah's humiliation, policemen arrived in the early hours to arrest him again. Once more Paul interceded for his brother, this time on condition that he leave town immediately, which he did.

Theodore was snarled in a confusion of values. While his father and the priest demanded utter rectitude, his indulgent mother was satisfied with much less. And there was Paul, whom Father Dudenhausen would certainly call a sinner, yet who went to mass, counted himself a good Catholic and was indubitably a great man. It was not surprising that the boy puzzled over such problems instead of joining in rough games he played poorly. His mother, pitying his frail physique and imperfect eyes, babied him. "I was a great coward, mortally afraid of being hurt," he later confessed. [8]

Although the Dreisers did not know it, their stay in Evansville depended not only on Paul's bounty but also on the serenity of his mistress, which fluctuated with Paul's own wavering affections. When he became involved with one of Sallie Walker's girls, the black-haired madam dismissed the wench in a fury. He promptly became interested in another Evansville woman, causing a tempest so violent that he left Sallie and put up at the St. George Hotel. Always a free spender, he was now deprived of free board and room and other perquisites accompanying Sallie's favor which enabled him to maintain the Franklin Street cottage.

He had a conference with his mother. It was decided that Sarah and the children would move to Chicago, where the three oldest Dreiser girls were now established.

Paul left to rejoin Thatcher's touring minstrels. It was not easy for him to forget Sallie, whom he later immortalized in his song "My Gal Sal," which let millions know that she was "a wild little devil, but dead on the level"—millions who never dreamed he was referring to an Evansville madam.

III. CHICAGO—HOUSE NO. 10

The Chicago sisters—Mame, Emma and Theresa—secured a third-floor apartment at West Madison and Throop Streets, a respectable middle-class neighborhood. It was at least the tenth dwelling the rootless Theodore had lived in during his twelve years, and the fifth town. He was denied familiar friends and exposed to constant change, aggravating his uncertainty, shyness and withdrawal. Like all the Dreiser moves, this one in the early summer of 1884 was impelled by need rather than by desire or careful plan, and was less sensible than most.

Theodore was excited by Chicago. What size! What activity, noise and color! Madison Street was a melting pot of Poles, Germans, Jews, Swedes, Irish and other races. Across the street from the Dreiser apartment was an open-air beer garden from which music and applause drifted up to the boy's ears. He was delighted by this new arena of spectatorship. When he faced the hard necessities of life, he failed immediately.

He got a summer job as cash boy in a nearby Madison Street dry-goods store. But he found it hard to concentrate on his work, and although he was almost thirteen he was so confused by the noise and bustle in the store, and the demands made on him, that he wanted to cry. He told his mother, who promptly decided that he was too young to work and let him quit, much as she needed every penny.

He then ran head-on into a mystery that would convulse, torment, preoccupy and delight him for the remainder of his long life—that would drive him physically and mentally, profoundly influence his career, afflict him with insomnia, cost him the best job he ever had, break up his first marriage and cause him to be indicted for adultery and to become an object of some curiosity as a literary rake. This was the mystery of sex.

He fell so madly in love with a Throop Street girl that, as he put it, "for days after my first glimpse of her, I could scarcely sleep." [9] It was the purest of loves, since it existed only in his fantasy. Too shy even to approach her, he mooned about at a distance, silently jealous of a well-dressed neighborhood boy who openly flirted with her. One day the boy, annoyed at Theodore's peripheral yearning, walked up and struck him on the mouth, cutting his lip. Theodore fled, then seethed with humiliation at his cowardice, his failure to live up to the ideal role of the fearless hero he had read about in books and treasured in his imagination.

For years he would follow this same pattern, finding success in reverie that he was unable to translate into fact.

The Chicago venture lasted only a few months because John Dreiser now sank into one of his longer periods of unemployment and joined his family on Madison Street, too discouraged to make any energetic effort to find work. His presence created an immediate problem. Mame Dreiser had taken up with Austin Brennan, a traveling dry-goods man from Rochester who was four-teen years her senior; Emma was being courted by an elderly architect, and Theresa was pursued by a wealthy manufacturer, a widower. These affairs were hidden from Dreiser—something that could be accomplished only by considerable intrigue in which Sarah joined. Yet Dreiser was not without misgivings, and he gave vent to diatribes which got scant attention now that he was jobless.

To this unpleasantness was added the growing realization that they could not afford to live in Chicago. The $35 monthly rent was a burden to which was added a $25 monthly payment on some $600 worth of furniture bought in a rash surge of confidence. Paul, with troubles of his own, was unable to contribute as much as had been hoped. By the summer's end, it was apparent that Sarah would have to move to a cheaper place with her younger trio.

Her father had not forgiven her transgression in marrying a Catholic until he died, when he left her five acres of land in Benton, Indiana. To this land she had resolutely clung, in the naïve hope that someday she might farm it, and perhaps in the sheer joy of *owning* something. Now, for some vague reason of her own, she decided to move closer to this tract, and rented a house in Warsaw, a placid county-seat town in northern Indiana. The move was not made without a Dreiserian tragedy. According to law, the furniture could not be moved out of Illinois until it was wholly paid for, but the older daughters scoffed at this, saying it could be shipped to Warsaw and the remaining payments made there. The furniture was packed for shipment and trucked to the freight house, when the instalment-collector arrived at the apartment, flew into a rage, shouted, "Don't you try to come any game over me!" threatened to call the police, and repossessed the furniture at the railroad platform.[10]

The Dreisers arrived in Warsaw in the fall of 1884 sans a table to eat from or a bed to sleep on.

3. Convention

John Dreiser found work again in Terre Haute, carrying his gloom away with him; Paul sent money, contributions from the Chicago sisters made possible the purchase of second-hand furniture, and Warsaw turned out to be a lovely town with a green-carpeted public square and a stately courthouse with a tall tower clock that struck pleasant chimes. Located on the Tippecanoe River and ringed by three pretty lakes, the town seemed to welcome the wandering Dreisers. Their comfortable home (eight dollars a month) had a large leftover garden with vegetables waiting to be picked, apple trees loaded with fruit, and beyond them a fine grove of ash trees.

But Warsaw was chiefly glorious for the battle fought there, a battle in which Sarah withstood the pious assaults of her husband and sent Theodore, Ed and Claire to the free public school. Although Theodore entered the seventh grade of the West Ward School with the old trepidation, he found it a joy from the first day because instead of a "gloomy nun" there was a winsome, chestnut-haired, twenty-one-year-old girl, May Calvert, as his teacher. He fell in love with her immediately. "Her eyes, her pretty mouth, her hair, her pink cheeks!" he exulted.[1]

Miss Calvert took an interest in the shy, wall-eyed, poorly clothed boy with the wistful smile—sensed that he needed encouragement. She formed a habit of patting his head or pinching his ear as she passed his desk—gestures that made him melt with pleasure—and occasionally she complimented him on his work.

"I can't tell you how beautifully you read, Theodore," she said one day.[2]

He went into reveries over her beauty, thinking, "Love me; love me, love me, please!" Here, girls and boys were placed together in the same classrooms. Near him, almost close enough to touch, were Myrtle Trego, Maud Tuttle and other girls, each of whom had a mystery and allure that obsessed him. "I dreamed constantly of their hidden physical lines," he recalled, and "my blood ran hot and cold." Magazine pictures of semi-nude women inflamed him. His thoughts grew so lustful that he became alarmed and confessed them to the kindly priest, who cautioned him against "mortal sins of the flesh that dragged one to hell." The warning did no good, for the boys he knew talked constantly of sex, of "breasts, thighs, underwear. . . ."[3]

His debauchery, while it made him lag in grammar and arithmetic, was entirely cerebral. At a Halloween party at Myrtle Trego's he remained almost

17

wordless, worrying about his homeliness, his shabby clothing. When they played post office and it was his turn to kiss Myrtle, he was so paralyzed with fright that he could hardly plant a tremulous kiss on her cheek.

Miss Calvert urged that he use the library—a suggestion that induced him to read Kingsley's *Water Babies*, Hawthorne's *The House of the Seven Gables* and works by Irving, Longfellow, Cooper and Poe. His father, on a visit from Terre Haute, was so impressed by his thoughtful conversation that he bought him cheap sets of Dickens and Scott. Theodore was malicious enough to bait him, saying that in the public school they taught that Martin Luther was a heroic figure, and that the Catholic Church had punished Galileo for insisting that the earth was round.

"Scoundrels! Liars!" Dreiser exploded. "That such things should be allowed to be taught in these public schools. . . . No separation of girls and boys as there should be in any well-regulated state of society! The shamelessness of these American boys and girls!"

He turned on Sarah: "It is you, with the way you think and the excuses you make for them, that are the cause of all our trouble with our children!" [4]

At the end of the school year, Theodore knew that he was failing in grammar and feared that he would have to stay back. Instead, Miss Calvert gave him a sunny smile.

"I'm going to pass you just the same," she said. "Grammar isn't everything." Then she added, "Shy boy. I hope you'll have a happy future." And she kissed him, leaving him flushed to the roots of his hair. [5]

Although Warsaw in summer was a paradise of boating and swimming, Theodore remained the observer. He had no close friends. Other boys must have noticed that his thoughts were far afield and laughed at him. He liked his brother Ed, but athletic Ed was busy with his own world, and as for his sister Claire, Theodore thought her insufferable. Alone, he tended the garden his mother had planted, or climbed a tall ash tree to gain a splendid view of a broad cat-tailed swamp and the winding Tippecanoe beyond, swaying with the wind on his high perch.

In the fall he attended the eighth grade in the high-school building just off the square. He envied the sons of prosperous local merchants who had snappy suits and polished shoes—some even owning canoes or ice boats. Yet Warsaw was friendly and he felt that he came closer to social acceptance here than in any other place he had ever lived—a feeling he treasured, particularly when it became threatened in his third year there.

The first cloud arrived in the form of Rome, who appeared after one of his long absences, having worked for railroads in odd places—upper Michigan, Kansas, western Canada. Immediately he got drunk, lurched around the public square, buttonholed staid citizens and bragged of his exploits. Sarah reproached him tearfully when he came home intoxicated.

"Why do you come down here now, Rome, and spoil everything?" she said. "Here I have planned for years to get to a place where the family could at least appear respectable, and now you come again and do this!" [6]

But Rome stayed for a fortnight, continued his drinking, begged his mother for money and finally looted a toy bank for liquor before he cleared out, calling Warsaw a "rube town."

The second cloud was John Dreiser, arriving in Warsaw because the Terre Haute mill had closed down again—out of work and ailing with bladder trouble.

Then Emma Dreiser, who had left her architect lover, and her younger sister Sylvia, who had lost her Chicago job, picked this time to pay Warsaw a visit. In the evenings they would apply rouge, array themselves in finery including patent-leather shoes with white tops and broad-brimmed hats with sweeping ostrich plumes, and head for the public square to dazzle male loungers. Their father would look up from *Der Wahrheit Freund* in outrage.

"Such a bold, shameless way to dress!" he stormed. [7]

But his authority had dwindled. The girls made friends with local sports and had a flurry of dates—parties, dances, boat rides, the opera house. Conventional Warsaw took note of this: the Dreisers not only had a drunken son but two brazen daughters. When Theodore heard his chums make knowing remarks about his sisters' morals, he knew that again he had lost that universal hope of youth to be conventional, respected, like everyone else. His father's ascending tirades puzzled as well as disturbed him, for normally he disagreed with the old man on principle, yet here he felt that his father had at least some justice on his side.

Dreiser's rage boiled over one night when the girls had not returned by midnight.

"This thing is not going to go on any longer!" he shouted to Sarah. "Here I sit if I have to wait up all night! . . . Who knows where they are? Who knows what they do?" [8]

When they returned at two, he locked them out. There was a scene between him and Sarah, who insisted that it was her home, not his, and finally let them in. The quarrel then became a four-party affair, climaxed when Dreiser shouted, "You strumpet!" and advanced on Sylvia as if to choke her, causing both Sylvia and Emma to scream at the top of their voices. Sarah eventually restored order, but Theodore was embarrassed the next day when neighbor children asked what all the screaming was about. The problem was resolved when Emma returned to Chicago to find work while Sylvia remained in Warsaw, the theory being that she would behave better alone.

In Chicago, Emma took an assumed name and embarked on more bizarre adventures. She fell in love with L. A. Hopkins, the suave, fortyish cashier of Chapin & Gore, a fashionable downtown bar, then discovered that he was already married. But she eloped with him to Montreal, where he admitted that while drunk he had stolen $3,500 from the Chapin & Gore safe. The police, he knew, were on his trail. Possibly it was this reflection that made him repent the theft, return all but $800 in a letter to his late employers and beg them not to prosecute him. They did not, but the scandal made headlines in the Chicago papers, in which the Dreisers escaped mention only because Emma had taken another name. Fearful of returning to Chicago, she cast her lot with the absconder and the couple went to New York, where they supported themselves by renting rooms to women of easy virtue.[9]

A few months later, Sylvia, still in Warsaw, tearfully admitted to Sarah that she was pregnant and that her lover, the son of a wealthy family in town, now refused to marry her. Luckily, Dreiser was again working in Terre Haute. Sarah made a forlorn effort to take legal action against the young man, then sent Sylvia off to have her baby at her sister's in New York.

For weeks the back-fence talk in Warsaw centered around the Dreiser girl who had run off to have an illegitimate child.

II. THE DREISER SCANDAL

Convention, that mass judgment which Theodore later would publicly defy, found him defenseless in Warsaw. Boys made wisecracks about his sister. Girls eyed him askance. He was no longer invited to parties. His sister Claire, though entirely virtuous, was reduced to a single girl companion. Local opinion had ostracized the Dreisers as trash, and Theodore, who needed few friends, nevertheless was badly hurt by his exclusion. Even a visit by Paul, that infallible joy-dispenser, failed to give the usual lift although Paul had recently written "The Letter That Never Came," a ballad so popular that it was being sung in Warsaw.

But high school, where he was a freshman, became a refuge because of one of his teachers, a tall, gentle spinster in her thirties named Mildred Fielding. Kindly and attentive, Miss Fielding helped him after school with his algebra and told him that he had latent abilities which he should develop. "You must study and go on," she said, "for your mind will find its way. I know it!"

He went on solitary walks, contemplating the flight of blackbirds and the instinct that sent them southward in armies. He read, deriving a wicked thrill from the sexual exploits of Tom Jones and Moll Flanders. At Morris' bookstore on the square he found pamphlets that went into astonishing detail about sex. At the opera house one night he was thrown into ecstasies by his first view of an actress in tights. "About this time," he later recalled, "I fell into the ridiculous and unsatisfactory practice of masturbation. . . ."[10]

This brought new fears, for he had read that total collapse often followed such indulgence. When his face broke out in a temporary rash of pimples, he was certain that this advertised his vice to the world and that he was nearing dissolution. His nervousness increased. He began walking in his sleep, one night falling out of a second-floor window and luckily suffering only bruises. He noticed a ringing in his ears, had occasional dizzy spells and felt himself evil. Although convinced that he would die, he was unable to stop his erotic stimulation. Later he took a less drastic view, believing that he would only ruin himself sexually for life but feeling that he must confide in someone. He went to the priest and confessed some of his mental lewdness. He received only a stern warning to desist which increased his dread because he could not desist and felt that he would certainly roast in hell.

One evening Theodore passed a bakery opposite the courthouse where he had often bought bread and was greeted by the stocky fifteen-year-old girl who worked there. She pushed him archly, said, "I'll bet you can't catch me," and raced down the alley with him following. She turned into a high-fenced yard, where he seized her playfully and, to his bewilderment, discovered that she was not resisting but tempting him. They fell down together. As he put it, "I found her . . . suddenly and swiftly assisting me in a relationship which, while I had contemplated the same in many ways with so many others in my imagination in the past, I had never so much as dreamed of in connection with her." [11] He left in a daze, excited and yet unnerved. The experience he had envisioned had not, in reality, come up to his expectations and, instead of feeling relief at this proof that he was not yet sexually crippled, he yearned for other girls he really admired and worried about contracting a disease.

After Sylvia had her baby in New York, the inevitable happened. She found a job and left the infant with Sarah Dreiser in Warsaw, the mother who could never refuse an appeal. No longer could the secret be kept from Dreiser, who was out of work and back in Warsaw again, and he was bitter about the sin of it, blaming Sarah. Theodore sometimes had to mind the tot—the living symbol of the Dreiser disgrace—and now people were gossiping more than ever.

In his misery, Miss Fielding was a comfort. Reared in a small town herself, she knew the Warsaw talk about the Dreiser scandal and pitied Theodore's inner hurt.

"You mustn't mind my saying this, Theodore," she said, "because I am fond of you and want you to succeed in life. . . . I know how small people can be and how they talk. But please don't let it affect you. You will soon grow up and go away and then all that has happened here will seem as nothing to you. . . ." [12]

He nearly wept with gratitude, unaware that Miss Fielding later would have a profound effect on his life. Inspired, he worked at his lessons and did well. But when summer came, his two best friends, the Misses Fielding and Calvert, were away on vacation, and he suffered humiliation at a nearby farm where he found a job weeding onions. Within an hour his muscles ached, the sun seared him and he fell into non-productive meditations about the repulsiveness of farm labor until his boss growled, "My God, this will never do," paid him fifty cents and fired him.

His mother exclaimed over the half-dollar, "You really earned all that?" she cried.

Yet he realized that he had failed. As always when confronted by such a reverse, he conjured up idyllic circumstances where his abilities would be appreciated, his employers would admire him and he would sweep on irresistibly to success. What did Warsaw mean now but economic and social failure? Sick of failure, he understandably dreamed of success, which meant money, fine clothes, social acceptance, admiring girls—all the things he had longed for and never had. Success was impossible in Warsaw. Chicago was just the place, a city of miraculous opportunity and no onion fields. When he read a Sunday-supplement account of Chicago's wonders, it brought the dream close.

"Ma," he said one day, "I am going to Chicago. . . . I don't want to sit around this place any longer. We can't get anywhere here. People only talk about us." [13]

Sarah had misgivings, but she reflected that he could easily come back. She scraped up six dollars for him and he was off alone on the afternoon train to Chicago, three hours away.

4. A Waif Amid Forces

The story of Theodore's struggle with reality, so ridiculous in its externals (as he later candidly acknowledged), has all the tragedy of wounded, confused, maladjusted boyhood. He was almost sixteen, skinny and gangling, in that summer of 1887 as the train whirled him through cornfields toward Chicago, which he visualized as being like "an Aladdin view in the Arabian nights." Indeed he would need a magic lamp. He was physically incapable of heavy labor and his inexperience would make it hard to get any other kind of work.

His sisters Mame and Theresa lived in Chicago, but as his train puffed into the depot he was so imbued with the drama of his adventure that he decided to find work on his own and then surprise them with his success. He took a cheap room on West Madison Street not far from where he had formerly lived and next morning started his search, envisioning himself as an efficient clerk in a handsome office. He walked miles, applying wherever he saw a "boy wanted" sign, but the proprietors eyed his scrawny frame and turned him away. He chased down want ads in the *Daily News* but always found a dozen boys ahead of him. He was relieved when he was taken on as a car washer in a South Side railroad yard, but this was far from his idea of success and he was so inept at the job that he was fired after a half-day without pay.

He grew frightened at the bigness of the city, its impersonal cruelty. After several days he was down to $1.90. A ticket back to Warsaw would cost $1.75, and perhaps he would have taken that escape except for a letter from his mother (*he* had taught her how to write!) containing two dollars and news that cheered him. Sarah herself was tired of hostile Warsaw, and she wrote that if he got work, and if Mame and Theresa would help a bit, she would move to Chicago with Claire and Ed and make a home there.

At last he was hired as dishwasher in an odorous restaurant on Halstead Street run by a Levantine named John Paradiso, at five dollars a week plus free meals. Here he labored with his arms immersed in dirty dishwater, emptied slops and tended fire, all but retching at the smells. But Paradiso was cheerful even in his orders.

"Little bucket coal, Theodore!" he would sing out. "Quick! Some wood, too! Muss make quick fire, now!" [1]

Theodore now visited his sisters, telling them that he was a haberdashery clerk making seven dollars a week. This was the job and salary he dreamed of, so it seemed not improper to say that. This handsome salary and its augury of

23

good fortune (the Dreisers always being subject to superstition) increased the sisters' enthusiasm about their mother's projected move to Chicago. Twenty-year-old Al Dreiser, who was working in Milwaukee, approved the idea and agreed to join them. With everybody working, and Paul occasionally sending money, how could they fail? In September, the Warsaw detachment of the Dreisers—Sarah, eighteen-year-old Claire, fourteen-year-old Ed and the illegitimate grandchild—arrived in Chicago and joined the rest in an apartment on Ogden Avenue near Robey Street.

"Well, Dorse," Sarah said warmly to Theodore, "I thought maybe you'd have to come back, but you didn't, did you?" [2]

He was delighted by her praise for the substantial clerkship he said he had, and more than ever revolted by the rancid horrors of Paradiso's. His brother Al, joining them, also was impressed by his job and asked the address of the haberdashery, planning to apply there himself. Poor Theodore, trapped, had to confide in him that he was really a dishwasher but was looking for something better, which he was not. He continued to picture himself in the dignity and ease of selling neckties and gloves in a soft-carpeted store. He worked at Paradiso's during the three daily rush hours, with a couple of hours off in mid-morning and mid-afternoon which would have been an ideal time to seek other work. But he put this off, still smarting so keenly from his rebuffs that he preferred even the Paradiso smells to job-hunting. One day he rebelled and quit Paradiso, then spent more than a month without work.

He and his family thereby lost twenty precious dollars plus scores of free Paradiso meals. Meanwhile, Al found no immediate work and Sarah grew distrait at the high cost of living, with no home-grown vegetables and fruit to help, wondering if the Chicago adventure had been foolhardy.

No haberdashery wanted Theodore. When he finally found work at a nearby hardware store, cleaning second-hand stoves, he resented it when he was put in a dirty loft with two ill-clad men, one of whom said gruffly, "Brush and polish these here stove-legs!" Downcast at the thought of a young man of his endowments being forced to such demeaning labor under men he felt inferior, he let his stove-polishing slacken and his two partners decided that he was a shirker. When one of them barked at him to help move a heavy stove, Theodore was offended by the surly tone, appalled at the size of the stove and convinced that this was a trick to humiliate him.

"I can't lift this," he protested.

"The hell you can't!" snapped his burly mate. With a sudden stride, he booted Theodore painfully on the backside. Outraged, Theodore seized a stove-leg to protect himself as he backed swiftly away, then ran to complain to his employer, who fired him after only a few hours on the job. [3]

Next door to the Dreiser apartment lived a commercial artist named Davis who was courting blonde Theresa Dreiser. To strengthen his suit with Theresa, he hired Theodore as studio flunky at seven dollars a week—a dazzling salary for easy work, which consisted mainly of applying sizing to fresh canvases on which Davis would then paint advertisements for theater attractions. Davis admired Walt Whitman, and the lonely Theodore, seeing in him a kindred spirit, talked incessantly of the books he had read. Shy as he was with strangers, he could loose a flood of language on those who understood him. Davis became so wearied after some ten days of this that he gently told Theodore he was not needed any longer. Theodore was humbled a few days later when his younger brother Ed was hired in his place and he learned from Theresa the cause of his downfall. Then began the distressing hunt for work again, interrupted this time by the arrival of Rome, the seasonal monsoon of the Dreiser family, whose coming was now dreaded even by his mother.

Rome was half drunk, as usual, seeking to borrow money. But he talked grandly of his intimacy with officials of the C., B. & Q. Railroad, and to everyone's surprise succeeded in steering Theodore to a $45-a-month job as a boxcar tracer at the Burlington yards in suburban Hegewisch.

"For God's sake," Theodore thought, "that's almost eleven dollars a week!" [4]

Thinking of new clothes and other luxuries, he began work with an enthusiasm that cooled when he saw the great plexus of tracks over which he was expected to trace cars. Where was Track 32? Where was Track 9? He was so lacking in practical sense that the work seemed impossibly complicated. He clambered over cars and around the ends of trains, fearful that he would be run down, sometimes getting lost between endless rows of boxcars. In the afternoon he saw men clustered around the body of a worker killed by a train. By the day's end he was thinking less of his glorious $45 than of the dangers of the job and the fact that most railroad workmen seemed to be unshaven foreigners, inferior to him in intelligence and station. On the second day it rained, soaking him to the skin. He caught a cold, whereupon his mother kept him home and decided that the work was too hard for him, to which Theodore unhappily agreed.

II. THE ROLLTOP DESK DREAM

Theodore, the most imaginative member of the family, was also the most unemployable. Ed, Claire, Al and Theresa were all working steadily while he failed at five successive jobs. The family had moved to a cheaper apartment at 61 Flournoy Street by the time he walked the streets again in late October. One reaction to his humiliations was to conjure a compensating picture of himself as a superior person, and he envisioned himself behind "a great rolltop desk" in a "large enclosed office" dictating important letters to an attentive secretary. Instead, he found employment as stock boy at five dollars a week in the huge wholesale hardware firm of Hibbard, Spencer, Bartlett & Company at Wabash and Lake Streets.

He was bored at his job of sorting pots, pans and coal scuttles. He disliked his boss, whom he considered a spy. The other stock sorters seemed to him ignorant, and he was angered to learn that some got twice his salary. But he found companionship with one fellow worker, an emaciated, big-domed, forty-five-year-old Dane named Christian Aaberg. An intellectual and a debauchee, Aaberg would come to work red-eyed, exclaiming, "My Gott! My Gott, how drunk I was yesterday!" and adding bitterly, "These devils of women!" He was an omnivorous reader and free-thinker whose mind roved history and the arts. He worshiped Voltaire, Ibsen, Goethe, Wagner and Schopenhauer, and could describe the golden age of Greece, the character of Peter the Great or the campaigns of Napoleon. He laughed at Theodore's Catholicism, shocked him by saying that the cross was originally a phallic symbol, and scoffed at the delusion of liberty even in liberty-talking America.

"Liberty is in here!" he said, tapping his forehead. "As for the rest, priests and the strong drive people like horses. The dumb pay tribute to everyone who can think faster than they can. Liberty! Pah!" [5]

He was the first rationalist who at once saw talent in the boy and could talk with him by the hour as man to man. Theodore's hunger for knowledge so impressed him that he remembered it thirty-three years later. Aaberg encouraged him to read again, startled him with the observations of a skeptical, independent mind and exposed him to the excitement of the intellect. But the immediate effect, as Theodore later acknowledged, was to reinforce his sense of superiority, swell his plans for a future of wealth and power and to fill him with disgust at having to wait for these things: "What, me a bin-cleaner and case-opener, and for five dollars a week. . . !" [6]

Not surprisingly, he was an inefficient stock boy. On Christmas Eve he received his pay and with it a blue slip telling him he would not be needed after December 31—this while others were getting raises in pay. Frantically he realized that he *needed* this job. On his way out he plucked up his courage, stopped at one of those "large enclosed offices" and spoke to a kindly looking executive of the firm.

"I have been here since October," he said. "I thought I was going to get a raise tonight, but I have been discharged. I don't want to be discharged now because the family . . ." He dissolved in tears. The executive hesitated, then patted his back, said he was reinstated and wished him a merry Christmas. [7]

In 1888 he had a job he loathed, but he did not dare quit to look for another because looking for work was the worst ordeal of all.

Chicago was in a ferment of strife and growth. The bloody Haymarket riot had occurred only the year before he arrived, and the fate of several of the anarchists involved was still being debated in the courts and the headlines. McCormick, Pullman, Field, Swift and Armour were gathering prodigious wealth. A cheerful corruptionist named Charles Tyson Yerkes was gobbling up the city's traction lines. Critical social issues surrounded Theodore, but he matured slowly and seemed unaware of them as yet. Chicago to him was a great spectacle, stirring his imagination but denying him practical success. Unaware of the nature of his own talents, Theodore Dreiser at seventeen and eighteen drifted along with the hardware job.[8]

He gave three dollars of his weekly five dollars to his mother, which left him little for entertainment. He lived for those rare occasions when he and Al could afford to go to the great ten-story Chicago Opera House, where they saw such extravaganzas as *Ali Baba and the Forty Thieves* and *The Crystal Slipper*—views of an enchanting world which he felt must exist somewhere and which he could enter if he could only find the key. For the rest, his morale sank. Still indulging in auto-erotic stimulation, as he would for years, he no longer had any doubt that he had ruined himself sexually. His stomach troubled him so that he could scarcely eat—an ailment he blamed on Paradiso—and he grew emaciated. He developed a chronic cough caused by his inhalation of dust from excelsior-filled packing cases. He noticed blood in his sputum. Fearful of "consumption," he loafed when the boss was not watching.

In the summer of 1889 he was inevitably on his way out at the hardware firm when he was summoned to the front office, where a caller waited. It was tall, smiling Mildred Fielding, his former Warsaw teacher, now principal of a Chicago high school.

No life-preserver could have come more opportunely, for Theodore was in the depths. Was she impelled by that confiding, wistful quality in him, so appealing to maternal sympathy? Surely not entirely. She had seen promise in him, had carried him in her mind for two years while hundreds of other students passed under her instruction, had thought him more deserving than any of these other hundreds, and now wanted to do something for him. She wanted him to go to Indiana University—at her expense.

"Theodore, work of this kind isn't meant for you, really," she said. "It will injure your spirit. I want you to let me help you go to school again."[9]

Conscious of his overalls, ashamed of his job, he tried to save face. He talked of the great opportunities in the hardware business. Miss Fielding saw through his bumbling embarrassment. She had her way after talking with Sarah Dreiser, who had worried about his health and regretted the end of his education. Miss Fielding wrote to the university and arranged that Theodore, although he had only one year of high school, be accepted as a freshman. The total cost for one year at Bloomington was enormous, about $300, and she supplied it all.

5. Temptations

I. THE FRESHMAN

Tall and shambling, wearing a cheap new suit, Theodore arrived in Bloomington in the fall of 1889 with a battered trunk and some romantic notions of college life gained from a quick reading of *Four Years at Harvard* and *Tom Brown at Rugby*. The university seemed huge, having some six hundred students, every one of them a stranger. But the campus, on a rise just east of town, its half-dozen buildings shaded by trees and bordered by a brook, was a place of warm autumn beauty after the hardware bins.

At eighteen, he had no practical aim in life. He was astonished by other students who knew clearly that they wanted to become teachers, lawyers or merchants and unhesitatingly signed for courses that set them toward their goal. Theodore, taking Miss Fielding's advice, registered for courses which would presumably make him think: Latin, geometry, English literature and history. Indeed he rather scorned those who were content to channel themselves into narrow specialties while he was free to explore knowledge itself.

His intelligence seems not to have been greatly above average. What made him unique was a combination of qualities beyond mere mentality—a passionate and genuine emotion, fierce ambition warring with girlish tenderness, a basic innocence of outlook and an amazing eye for detail.

At once his eyes were on coeds, alluring in frilled blouses and floor-sweeping skirts. Taking a room in the vine-embowered home of a widow in town, he sat down to study, looked across the lawn and saw that a blonde girl was studying at a window opposite. As he watched, she removed hairpins so that her hair cascaded over her book and he was transfixed by the beauty of it. As he recalled it, she evoked "such a nervous disturbance in me as was scarcely endurable. . . ." Studies forgotten, he spied on her, was convinced that occasionally she looked across the yard at him, even smiled. The dream was glorious, the reality dismal. A few days later she came over to ask if he could help her with her Latin. Tongue-tied with shyness, he sat down with her, mumbling that he knew little Latin, ecstatic when her hair brushed his cheek but blushing painfully until she said, "Oh, well, I think I can get along now," and left. Next day his roommate arrived, sociable Bill Yakey, whose prime interests were football and girls. No sooner did Yakey see the coed across the way than he cried, "Say, she's a cute little bitch, that!" He strode outside, got her in conversation, and soon was chasing her around the yard and seizing her in a kiss, after which she retired with a pout of mock anger.[1]

No roommate could have dramatized Theodore's ineffectuality more than

28

the handsome extrovert Yakey. Yakey soon had friends by the score. He went out for football and became the best halfback on the team. He was tapped for a fraternity. His muscles bulged. One morning he looked critically at Theodore's figure, scrawny in underwear.

"Good God, man," he exclaimed, "a fellow of your height ought to have at least a four-inch chest expansion! You're terrible!"

Thereafter Yakey dragged him out on the open lawn every morning and led him in setting-up exercises, shouting, "Come on now, Bones! Move and get strong!" [2]

Theodore felt that with his homely face and poor clothing it would take more than a four-inch chest expansion to bring him social success. When winter came, he wore a cut-down overcoat formerly belonging to his fat brother Paul. No fraternity sent him a bid, and he reflected bitterly on the snobberies of society and the advantages given to some simply because they were prosperous. He found it hard to concentrate on his studies, for he was not really stimulated by any of his courses.

Despite the cast in his eye, his buck teeth and feeling of inferiority, he was not unattractive. He had a sense of humor (always subject to sudden descents into gloom), his mother's warm smile and a most considerate interest in those few friends he had. Even the popular Yakey liked him, offered to arrange dates with girls and brought noisy groups of fraternity and football men to the room in bull sessions of which Theodore was a part. Indeed, Yakey was too helpful, too obviously intent on making a new man of him, so that he recoiled and found friends almost as poor as himself. One was Howard Hall, an earnest young man from Michigan who was determined to become a lawyer despite a speech defect which, aping Demosthenes, he tried to correct by lone sessions of speaking with a pebble in his mouth. Best of all was Russell Ratliff, a chubby sophomore who had an intellectual maturity and a realistic acceptance of life that drew Theodore to him.

Ratliff paid his way by collecting students' laundry, striding cheerfully about the campus with a wicker basket, showing no apprehension that this might be considered demeaning by more prosperous collegians—a serenity Theodore admired, knowing that the same chore would humiliate him. The two took to discussing philosophy and reading Tolstoy together in Ratliff's room. Ratliff's inquiring mind, his efforts to bring intelligence to bear on reality, soon made Theodore regard him as more of a mentor than his professors—more even than Aaberg had been. There was one drawback. Ratliff's room overlooked a fraternity house which was always blazing with gaslight, full of music and revelry. He saw Theodore's expression of longing.

"It is hard, isn't it?" he said.

Theodore, knowing precisely what he meant, shrank from any admission that he was socially unsuccessful.

"What is hard?" he asked. [3]

So hurt was he by his feeling of exclusion that he even considered leaving college. He was unassuaged by proofs of his engaging qualities such as his friendship with Day Allen Willy, a sophomore law student whom he met at an interclass rush and who took an immediate fancy to him. Willy, a fraternity man, the son of a prosperous upstate judge, had money to burn, wore costly clothing, smoked cigars, had a bachelor apartment of his own and was intelligent in the bargain. He treated Theodore to a dinner at Bohmer's, a Bloomington restaurant where liquor could be had and where the university smart set gathered. Theodore accepted the favor, but when Willy suggested it again he was forced to admit his poverty.

"I can't go your pace," he said, "and there's no use my trying it." [4]

But the law student was understanding. They became fast friends, Willy dropping in at Dreiser's room and in return inviting him to his fraternity for dinner, with Theodore thoroughly enjoying the companionship except for his need to be miserly and to refuse Willy's proposals for larks in Indianapolis or Louisville. The crisis came when Willy arranged a double date with two town girls for dinner one night at his apartment. Although ashamed of his clothes, Theodore got along well enough while there were three others to carry the conversation. Later, to his horror, Willy and his lady went out, leaving him frighteningly alone with his own companion, a girl named Eva whom he thought stunning. His terror grew when Eva's knee touched his own and she leaned languorously against him. Certain of his own impotence, he sought desperately to avoid the issue, but he was lured into an intimacy during which he was so nervous that his fears of sexual depletion were realized—a catastrophe that left him burning with shame. He could not sleep that night, thinking that Eva must be telling her friend of his ignominy, that the friend would tell Willy, that the news would fly so that the sole topic of gossip at Indiana University would be that he, Theodore Dreiser, was impotent.[5]

He was relieved when Willy later showed his old cordiality. No one eyed him scornfully on campus. Evidently his shame had somehow escaped detection. Yet he was so shaken, so determined not to risk such humiliation again, that he decided he must get away from Willy and Yakey, the two who often tried to arrange dates for him. He moved to another room just south of the campus, resolving to concentrate on his studies and forget about sex. No sooner was he established there than he noticed the daughter of a physician living nearby and conceived an immediate infatuation for her. He watched her secretly, gazing through French windows to see her playing the piano, meeting her often on the street but afraid to speak to her, neglecting his studies for weeks over her, composing notes to her which he tore up in despair. Finally he mustered the courage to hand her a note as he passed her, and she took it wordlessly.

The note suggested that she meet him near her home. She did not do so, and in this inglorious fashion his year at Indiana ended. He passed his courses with fair grades except for a condition in geometry. On the last night, the students followed annual custom and burned their books in a campus bonfire—a revelry he refused to attend.

"They can all go to hell!" he said, meaning the fraternities, the clubs, the dances, the flirtations, the upper crust of college society to which he had dreamed of belonging but which had excluded him. He bade his friends good-by, then late at night sneaked over to the doctor's house, haunted by the moonlight and the fragrance of spring, gazing at the darkened windows, thinking that *she* was inside, and murmuring, "Darling." [6]

This hopeless romance would linger in his memory for years. Now he realized that he loved the university, that his year there had given him bright experiences despite the glamor that had been denied him, and that he would miss Ratliff, Yakey, Willy and Hall. He was actually reluctant to leave this vernal college town, a feeling abetted by the knowledge that now he must face Chicago, the reality that had defeated him before. When he boarded the train he was in a funk.

II. AUTUMN LEAVES

Theodore found his family more solvent than usual. True, his father was there, jobless again and brooding, but the children were working and Paul had written another resounding song hit, "I Believe It for My Mother Told Me So." Paul, who had quit the minstrel show and become an actor, soon arrived in Chicago as leading comedian in *The Tin Soldier*, stayed with the Dreisers on Flournoy Street and played his new song for his mother, for whom he had written it, with such feeling that Sarah wept and so did Theodore.

Nearly nineteen and still skinny as a rail, Theodore had nevertheless profited from his setting-up exercises and the Bloomington air. His cough and stomach trouble were gone. Although he thought his college year almost wasted, and he declined Miss Fielding's offer to subsidize him further, he later called it "one of the most vitalizing years of my life." [7]

He found a job at the newly opened Ogden Avenue real estate office of pious Asa Conklin, a white-haired Civil War pensioner who promised him three dollars a week plus commissions which might bring it to $12 depending on business. He set out in Conklin's snappy buggy and showed real enterprise in getting listings. However, he discovered that Conklin, though kindly and well-intentioned, had no business ability or initiative, merely warming a swivel chair in his office and waiting for big deals to enter uninvited. Theodore found himself doing all the work and still getting only $3 a week. As the summer wore on, Conklin bewailed his meager income and by fall Theodore was getting no pay at all.

Having learned something of the business and shown vigor as a canvasser, he might have landed a job with another real estate firm. He could not face the humiliations of job-hunting, fearing that other employers would be more demanding than Conklin, and besides, as he later admitted, "I had a buggy to ride in, a good horse to drive. . . ." The appearance of success—a neat office, business clothes, a handsome rig—was so pleasant that he did not even insist on his minimal three dollars a week. He scored a success in another category when a flirtatious Italian girl entered the office to inquire about an apartment, stopped to dally, went into the back room with him and enabled him to prove that he was not impotent. This feat quelled for a time a fear that had haunted him for almost five years, but it also disclosed his characteristic, nagging self-doubt; for soon he was puzzled that the girl did not pay him another uninvited visit and attributed this to his own unattractiveness.[8]

He was concerned because his mother, although only fifty-seven, had been listless all summer and by fall was definitely ill. Since he was getting no pay, he had no compunctions about using Conklin's rig outside the line of strict duty, and he took her for occasional buggy rides.

"You know," she said on one of them, "I feel so strange these days. I hate to see the leaves turning. I'm afraid I won't see them again."

"Oh, Ma, how you talk!" he protested. "You're just feeling blue now because you're sick." [9]

But the superstitious Sarah told him of a dream in which she had seen her late mother and father beckoning to her. Theodore, himself a believer in portents, was frightened. As she grew worse and took to her bed, the whole family, so prone to quarrel, became unified in fear for the mother they all loved. John Dreiser, now sixty-nine, took refuge in prayer as doctors came and went. Theresa waited on her mother hand and foot. On November 14, Theodore came home for lunch to find her feeling enough better so that she wanted him to help her sit up. Although he demurred, she insisted, and as he embraced her heavy body he felt her go limp, saw her eyes light momentarily in a preternatural brilliance and then fade to blankness.

"Mamma!" he cried, terrified.

Theresa came running, to find that the pulse was gone. John Dreiser sank to his knees beside the bed, weeping. "Oh, I should have gone first!" he sobbed.[10]

Al, Claire and Ed were summoned. Paul arrived after a matinee performance and burst into tears. Dreiser's first thought was of the church, and a Bavarian priest came, spoke with him in German and grew doubtful as he learned the circumstances. Sarah Dreiser had not received absolution. In her illness she had not been to mass or confession for months. Despite Dreiser's servile explanations, the priest felt that this barred her from churchly ceremonies.

"If this is the religion of this place," he said, eyeing Sarah's corpse, "then let someone else attend her now. The church keeps its services and its sacraments for those who deserve them—not for those who ignore them until it is too late!" And he left as the weeping Dreiser begged him to forgive these lapses,

Theresa, long alienated from the church because of her father's dogmatism—more than ever so now because Davis, her fiancé, was an unbeliever—was white with anger.

"To think that that fat little beast of a priest should dare to come in here and talk and strut around like that!" she raged.[11]

But John Dreiser was pursuing the priest, who eventually relented, and Sarah was buried in St. Boniface Cemetery on the North Side. Engraved in Theodore's memory was that dreadful tableau—his mother dying in his arms, his father weeping, the priest refusing absolution. Bitter against the priest, he was not yet ready to break with the church. Most of all, he felt so terribly alone that he would never quite get over it.

III. THE OVERCOAT DREAM

"If a man cannot keep pace with his companions," Thoreau had written, "perhaps it is because he hears a different drum." Theodore had not yet heard the drum that would later come to his ears alone. Now he sat penniless at the office, infected by the defeatism of Conklin, who owed him $21—seven weeks' pay—and could do nothing about it until his father intervened. Dreiser was trying to collect extra weekly payments from each of his children, not only for doctors' and undertakers' bills but for masses to be said, at $2.50 each, to help Sarah through purgatory. When he learned that Theodore could not contribute because Conklin had not paid him, he was incredulous.

"This man must be a scoundrel!" he exclaimed.[12]

He went to Conklin, who sadly admitted that he could not pay and that Theodore might as well seek other work. In lieu of salary, Conklin let him use his credit at a department store, where Theodore bought a cheap suit and a few accessories. His mood soared as he eyed his natty, mirrored reflection, then crashed against the necessity to find another job. Again he walked the West Side streets, peering into offices filled with what seemed hostile people, turning away without applying, sometimes merely walking and surveying the Chicago scene.

It was through a "help wanted" advertisement that he finally found work as a driver for Munger Brothers, a Madison Street laundry. This was a descent after his white-collar status, but it had the advantage of paying eight real dollars per week, and he could observe human phenomena and let his imagination rove as his horse drew him along crowded streets. He was still delivering laundry in the summer of 1891, when he was twenty.

Meanwhile the Dreiser family circle, held together so long by Sarah's love, flew apart. As John Dreiser waved the bills that had to be paid, the children argued about their respective contributions. Theresa, no longer a Catholic and indignant at the cost of the masses, quarreled outright with Claire, who was now a department store clerk. At length Claire arranged a defection, she,

Ed and Theodore taking a small apartment a few blocks south on Taylor Street. With Emma and Sylvia in New York, Paul on the road and Rome God alone knew where, it left the aging father with only Mame, Theresa and Al.

"Well, you're going, are you?" he said sadly to Theodore. "I'm sorry, Dorsch. I done the best I could. The girls, they won't ever agree, it seems. . . ." [13]

Theodore pitied him, but he left. Sorely missing his mother, he began dating a demure Scottish cashier at Munger's, Nellie Anderson. He enjoyed his long drives in the laundry wagon through colorful streets, and was observant when liveried servants let him into mansions on fashionable Washington Boulevard that kindled visions of making a marriage that would give him entree into this splendor. These thoughts reduced his estimate of Nellie, although she was a temporary comfort and he was buying new haberdashery to impress her and was trying to make love to her, much annoyed by her virgin resistance. Still intimidated by Catholic teachings, it seemed to him that he was a mental lecher, convulsed with passion by every pretty girl he saw. He had opportunities. Complaisant women invited him inside, but always his romantic ideal made him hurry away. They were not really beautiful, or they had "wholly unaesthetic minds," or their households were slatternly, and, as he put it, "it was of youth and beauty of almost unrivaled perfection that I was really thinking and dreaming." [14]

Now, as he pursued Nellie Anderson, he discovered that her younger sister Lily was more desirable, felt certain that Lily was attracted to him, and cursed the ill luck that had committed him to Nellie. He still called occasionally on Miss Fielding, and at her urging he began reading again and attending Sunday lectures by liberals and free-thinkers at Central Music Hall and by Ethical Culturists at the Grand Theater. Badly though he wanted to get ahead and make money, he could do nothing about it. But he found a better-paying job when a woman customer who liked his manner of delivering laundry referred him to her husband.

This man was pint-sized Frank Nesbit, who operated a cozy enterprise from an office at 65 East Lake Street. Nesbit sold the cheapest of gewgaws—lamps, clocks, rugs, albums—at exorbitant prices to working-class families, always on the instalment plan, with payments spread out over as much as a year, at thirty-five cents a week. Dreiser became a collector for him at $14 a week, the best salary he had ever made. [15]

He loved the job. It was easy and it took him into the Hogarthian slums south of Madison Street where he saw life at its rawest, sometimes collecting from "dancing or singing, or even naked or doped, whores and their paramours." Although he disliked to threaten delinquents who were poor or unemployed, he did it. They were hopelessly ignorant, he reasoned, and if they did not pay him they would spend money on some other folly—and did he not need money himself to pay for the continuing masses for his mother and the new clothes that always lured him?

He enjoyed Eugene Field's column, "Sharps and Flats," in the *Daily News*, filled with comment and verse about Chicago. As he made his rounds on foot, he began to compose rhapsodies about the city, wrote them down at night, sent a batch to Field and was hurt not to get even an acknowledgment. He found that by working fast he could finish his collecting by two, go down-town and spend a few pleasant hours in a hotel lobby or the Art Institute before delivering his cash to Nesbit. Chicago's old Water Tower and new skyscrapers thrilled him. He took to blowing himself to a sixty-cent meal at Rector's just for the grandeur of it, and he haunted the lobby of the huge, Florentine-towered Auditorium Hotel, dreaming that he was a part of this splendor. But the glittering displays at the big State Street department stores were constant reminders that even $14 a week was not enough.[16]

He was now sharply dressed except for a shabby overcoat, and he saw a satin-lined garment in a store window that fairly bewitched him. If he could get that overcoat, plus new gloves and a cane, he felt that he would be irresistible to women and would cut a fine figure in the hotel lobbies. He could not afford it. The overcoat preyed on his mind, became a necessity.

Because some of his clients paid him in a lump sum to eliminate tiresome weekly calls, he often had $50 or more to hand over to Nesbit at the day's end. Why not hold out $25 of this, unknown to Nesbit, and repay it by the week?

He capitulated in November, bought the clothes and felt himself sartorially perfect. All went well until mid-December, when a woman whose money Dreiser had kept went to Nesbit to complain about a defective clock, showing her receipt that she had paid for it in full. Nesbit confronted Dreiser that afternoon.

"Theodore," he said, "there is a little matter here which seems to be mixed up somewhat." And he displayed the receipt.

Quaking, envisioning himself in jail, Dreiser admitted borrowing the money with the intent to pay it back.

"Are there any more like this?" Nesbit asked.

"Two or three," Dreiser said, although there were more than that.

"Theodore, I'm dreadfully sorry about this. You're a bright boy, and I don't think you're naturally dishonest. My wife picked you on your looks alone. But if you're going to begin anything like this, you know, you're on the straight road to hell, and I can't keep you."[17]

Dreiser was out of work, with Christmas only ten days off.

6. Newspaperman

"I seethed to express myself," Dreiser recalled.[1] Certainly the artist in him was awakening, although in his own memoirs he stressed motives of ambition: his impression that newspaper reporters were men of importance and dignity who interviewed the great in politics, business and society and were on a par with them all. Answering a "want ad" saying that the *Chicago Herald* needed help in the "business department," he was chagrined to learn that what they wanted was men to hand out free toys and gifts to the poor during the Christmas holidays—a *Herald* promotion scheme. He took the job, hoping it would lead to a reporter's berth. He was sick with worry over his $25 defalcation, fearful that at any moment a policeman's hand would fall on his shoulder.

On Christmas Eve, Claire, who worked at the Fair Store, brought home a fellow clerk, Lois Zahn. When Dreiser saw her blue eyes and warm smile, and heard her play the banjo, Nellie Anderson faded out and he was in love with Lois.

"Oh," he thought, "if I could have a girl like this. . . ."[2]

To impress Lois, he told her that he was a *Herald* reporter, doing very well. Instead, he was doling out cheap dolls and toy wagons to an endless queue of the poor, and when Christmas was over he was out of work again. Yet at last he had a goal, knew what he wanted to do. He canvassed the newspaper offices energetically, and although he got only curt refusals his glimpses of newsmen at work seemed to confirm his impression that they were men of greatness moving among the great. "Those who interested me most," he later wrote, "were bankers, millionaires, artists, executives, leaders, the real rulers of the world."[3] He ran out of money even as he dreamed of millions. This was frightening now that he was on his own, "going steady" with Lois and making a show of prosperity. He landed with another time-pay firm as collector, still fearful that Nesbit would suddenly materialize to denounce him, still telling Lois of his adventurous work as a reporter. Collecting, so enjoyable before, now seemed a vulture's work when placed beside a bright newspaper career. The World's Fair was abuilding, the Democratic National Convention would be in Chicago that summer, and he ached to get at the heart of these activities as he felt a reporter would. When he saw an accident or street incident, he wrote it up in a practice news story, polished it, compared it with stories published in the papers and reasoned that his own was fully as good. He quarreled with his sister Claire, whose cooking he

36

thought abominable, and finally he and Ed moved away to take a room together.

He scrimped to buy a spring outfit he felt befitting a newspaperman—checked trousers, blue jacket and yellow shoes—and in April, having saved $65, he quit his collecting job and canvassed the newspapers again. He was pleased to catch a glimpse of Eugene Field at the *Daily News*, but he found there was no chance for an inexperienced man at the better papers so he applied at the fourth-rate *Daily Globe* on Fifth Avenue. "There's not a thing in sight," the city editor told him. He did not say "never," so Dreiser haunted the *Globe* office daily, taking a chair in a corner, hoping that something would turn up. Finally the copy editor, fat, cynical John Milo Maxwell, took notice of him.

"Why do you pick the *Globe?*" he asked. "Don't you know it's the poorest paper in Chicago?"

"That's why I pick it," Dreiser said innocently. "I thought I might get a chance here."

Maxwell laughed. "Hang around," he advised, adding that the *Globe* might need an extra man when the Democratic convention opened.[4]

After a fortnight, the city editor, a frustrated writer named Sullivan, broached a proposition. He had collaborated on a novel which was selling poorly. If Dreiser would go out and sell 120 copies at $1 each, he would get a ten-cent commission per copy and a try-out on the *Globe*. Dreiser, although thinking this an odd qualification, spent a hard ten days selling the books and was taken on temporarily at $15 a week.

Naïve though he was, for the first time in his life he had moved with determination toward a goal until he attained it. He was nearing twenty-one, tall and spindling, in June of 1892 when Sullivan told him to watch the convention committee rooms at the Palmer House, Auditorium, Grand Pacific and Richelieu Hotels. "Cover the hotels for political news," he said.

Dreiser suddenly realized that he did not know what political news was, nor how to get it. Visiting the hotels, he was irritably waved away by minor politicians. At the day's end, having secured no interviews, he wrote nine pages of "impressions" of the convention preliminaries as he felt George Ade or Brand Whitlock would do. Maxwell scowled as he read it.

"This is awful stuff!" he said, tossing it into the waste-basket. But he gave Dreiser daily lectures on whom to see, what to look for, how to cram the basic facts of a story into the lead paragraph. As Dreiser submitted other items, Maxwell wielded a savage blue pencil, hacking away Dreiser's beautifully fleshed-out thoughts, leaving only the bones.

"Now you probably think I'm a big stiff, chopping up your great stuff like this," he said, "but if you live and hold this job you'll thank me."

Through sheer luck Dreiser picked up information indicating that Grover Cleveland would be nominated, a scoop that won praise even from the critical Maxwell, who rewrote Dreiser's story for two full columns. But when

Dreiser, grateful for his help, ventured to lay a friendly hand on Maxwell's shoulder, the copy editor froze him.

"Cut the gentle con work, Theodore," he snapped. "I know you. You're just like all other newspapermen or will be: grateful when things are coming your way. . . . Life is a goddamned, stinking, treacherous game, and nine hundred and ninety-nine men out of every thousand are bastards." [5]

Cleveland was nominated and Dreiser was kept on. He cut his last tie with his family, leaving Ed and taking a room alone on Ogden Place overlooking Union Park—a spot where he later placed *Sister Carrie*. Top reporters for big newspapers got as much as $70 a week and were sent far away to cover important newsbreaks, to Washington—even to Africa to find lost explorers. The future looked bright, although the *Globe* itself was disillusioning. Its reporters, far from being intellectuals, were poorly paid, hard-bitten cynics who cursed each other and regarded Dreiser's bright world of politics and society as a cesspool of sham and self-seeking. One was a drunkard, another boasted that he was curing his syphilis with mercury, and a third was a regular brothel patron. Dreiser's Catholic belief in a firm moral order was further shaken by Maxwell's insistence that all politics was corrupt, that heroes were really only successful crooks.

Yet Dreiser saw the *Globe* as a stepping stone, and he was buoyed by a discovery: he loved to write. Since his spelling and grammar were shaky and his prose execrable, probably only his eagerness to write and rewrite, his willingness to work all hours, saved his job. Maxwell swore as he toiled over Dreiser's copy, but he saw that the young man was improving, that he had an unusual depth of inquiry. When Dreiser began doing features for the Sunday paper—"color" pieces that conveyed a mood and did not require the condensation of news stories—he was more in his element. In the dark hours he strode Chicago's vilest slums, between Halstead Street and the river, mingling with drunkards, dope fiends and prostitutes and coming up with a feature from which Maxwell viciously excised whole paragraphs but which he grudgingly praised.

"You know, Theodore," he said, "you have your faults, but you do know how to observe." [6]

"No common man am I," Dreiser kept telling himself. His stock rose when a new city editor came in, forty-five-year-old John T. McEnnis, a brilliant newspaperman from St. Louis who had skidded on saloon sawdust. Always half drunk without showing it, he read Dreiser's features, encouraged him and usually borrowed a dollar.

"Don't settle down anywhere yet," McEnnis advised, "don't drink and don't get married, whatever you do. A wife will be a big handicap to you." [7] Then he borrowed another dollar.

Early in the fall he was impressed when Dreiser wrote a series of articles exposing a chain of fake auction shops selling bogus jewelry, forcing the laggard police to close them. But here Dreiser endangered his success with a piece of gross naïveté. He was accosted by an auction swindler still operating who begged him to "lay off," stuck a diamond stickpin in his cravat by way of inducement and said, "Be a nice young feller now. I'm a hard-workin' man just like anybody else. I run a honest place."

Dreiser took the stickpin back to McEnnis, who exploded.

"Why did you do this?" he shouted. "If I didn't think you were honest I'd fire you right now!" [8]

There was danger that the transaction had been witnessed and that the *Globe* might get into trouble. McEnnis solved the dilemma by swearing out a warrant for attempted bribery against the dealer, thus giving the *Globe* an "exclusive" on a Dreiser-written exposé of the incident. Although McEnnis never returned any of the dollars he borrowed, he took a liking to Dreiser and was working through a colleague to get him a job on the respected *St. Louis Globe-Democrat*.

In his off-hours Theodore took Lois for walks in Jackson Park, where enormous World's Fair buildings were being erected, and exaggerated his importance and his salary. He was indeed something of a liar. She would clap his hand under her arm and talk delightedly of a cottage she planned for them on the South Side near the lake, then would sense his reservations.

"Oh, Dorse," she said once, "if we could just be together always and never part!"

"We will be," he said, guiltily aware of his own deception.[9] Much as he liked her, Lois the unattainable had been more enchanting than Lois the reality, the stationery clerk, the fiancée. They had a trivial quarrel or two. "Ah, if I could just marry a really rich girl," he told himself, "one truly rich and truly beautiful!" [10] Yet one of the last imaginative pieces he wrote for the *Globe*, called "The Return of Genius," showed him recognizing that day-dreaming was useless without action.

It told of a genius, remarkably like Theodore Dreiser, who suffered poverty in his youth and uttered a prayer for fame and riches. The god of genius granted his wish, but with one stipulation: that the genius would never hear the world's praise. The genius agreed and was transported to a glittering palace where his every whim was granted but one. No one spoke of his fame. He protested to the god, who reminded him of his bargain, saying that if he mingled with the world his fame would vanish. "I will mingle with men and be of them," the genius finally replied. "They are dearer to me than silver or jewels. . . . I will again seek mankind." [11]

Early in November he received a telegram from the *Globe-Democrat:*

YOU MAY HAVE REPORTORIAL POSITION ON THIS PAPER AT TWENTY DOLLARS
A WEEK, BEGINNING NEXT MONDAY. WIRE REPLY.[12]

He wired an acceptance, went to say good-by to Lois, found her gone, became irrationally jealous, and left for St. Louis after writing her a curt note.

II. IN SEARCH OF SUCCESS

The Theodore Dreiser who arrived at the Poplar Street station in St. Louis was 6 feet 1½ inches tall but almost translucent, weighing only 137 pounds. He had inherited traits from each of his conflicting parents—his mother's paganism and human sympathy, his father's ambition, seriousness and pig-headedness—that left him in inner strife. He wanted to be good but great, a rake and a saint, a poet and a tycoon. There were two Dreisers, one a gentle spirit who looked at the ruthless other self with alarm.

But success was the highest goal. The boy who had picked coal from the tracks was determined to make life pay him back. "Where the crash of mighty things were, at their very apex, life could place you," he reflected.[13] He kept telling himself that he was "destined for a great end." [14] The dream was so powerful that he had manic-depressive tendencies, sometimes exalted by the certainty of his own genius, sometimes sunk in despair at his own inferiority.

The moment he hit St. Louis he was homesick. The city of 450,000 people looked dreary on a Sunday afternoon—much smaller than Chicago, with no real skyscrapers. He so needed love and admiration that he had to resist an impulse to write Lois and beg her to join him, not as his wife—that would never do—but perhaps as his mistress. He rented a hall bedroom at Fifth and Pine Streets. On Monday morning he went to the substantial eight-story *Globe-Democrat* building at Sixth and Pine and reported to the editor, short, cigar-chewing Joseph B. McCullagh, who had been a correspondent with Sherman during the Civil War and whose corrosive editorials were famous throughout the Midwest.[15]

"Um, yuss!" McCullagh grunted. "See Mr. Mitchell in the city room. . . ."

Dreiser, expecting a warm welcome, was hurt. The city editor, fat Tobias Mitchell, sent him off to investigate an "altercation" at an address that proved to be a vacant lot, where Dreiser prowled until he realized that he was a victim of the wild-goose assignment trick often played on cubs. A friendly reporter, Bob Hazard, asked him where he had worked in Chicago.

"At the *Globe* and *News*," Dreiser replied.[16] He had never worked at the *Daily News*, but the *Globe* was such a poor thing that he needed the prestige that the *News* would give him.

Mitchell curtly assigned him to cover evening activities at the North Seventh Street police station, a grimy place. The *Globe-Democrat*, a morning Republican paper despite its name, was the biggest in town, but Dreiser felt himself unappreciated, lonely, cowardly, and so ugly that no lovely girl would look at him. His broodings were almost suicidal until he met the two staff artists, Peter B. McCord and Richard Wood, both sophisticates and bohemians. McCord, a bearded, twinkling-eyed tobacco-chewer, had a shining brass cuspidor which he kept spotless by spitting on the floor at a safe distance from it, protecting it from more conventional spitters by shouting, "Hold! Out—not in—to one side, on the mat!" [17] Wood, a languid aesthete, wore a pastel shirt, a flowing tie and a boutonniere of violets.

Dreiser felt inferior to them both. So uncertain were his ambitions that he repented becoming a writer, wishing that he were an artist so that he could be on equal terms with them. He was delighted when they became friendly. Wood invited him to his "studio" at Broadway and Locust, where Dreiser drank beer and admired Wood's prints, his collection of curios and Chinese coins and the bohemian air of it all. Dreiser, the writer who wished he were an artist, missed the irony in the fact that Wood, the artist, yearned to be a writer and had collected an assortment of rejection slips. If Dreiser envied Wood, he became devoted to McCord, a self-made philosopher who took life as it came, enjoyed every minute of it and would have a lasting influence on his thinking. McCord took him on walks through the slum-and-vice district on Chestnut Street beyond Twelfth, once stopping with him at a Negro brothel where the girls greeted McCord as a friend. McCord, a fair musician, played a flute while someone else rattled a tambourine, and several girls executed a sinuous dance. Dreiser was fascinated at the same time that his Catholic rearing warned that he was infecting himself with evil.

A letter came from Lois, sad but friendly, implicitly acknowledging that he had jilted her, asking him to return her letters and adding a postscript:

"I stood by the window last night and looked out on the street. The moon was shining and those dead trees over the way were waving in the wind. I saw the moon in that little pool of water over in the field. It looked like silver. Oh, Theo, I wish I were dead." [18]

He felt himself an utter scoundrel. The pathos of the postscript cut him so deeply that he used it almost verbatim in his novel The "Genius," published twenty-three years later. He even considered marrying Lois. Absently he began scribbling loose verse in an effort to dramatize his predicament poetically. The predicament dwindled as he became absorbed in improving his lines. As he later put it, "I became so moved and interested that I almost forgot [Lois] in the process." [19]

Important as women were, the artist and his career came first.

III. THE INJUSTICES OF GOD

How could Dreiser, with his cumbersome style, ever make the grade as a reporter? One explanation is the unhurried attitude of the Nineties, when journalism had not yet adopted the fact-piled-on-fact ideal and some rambling was permissible.

He was abstemious, a hard worker enjoying his job. He observed aspects of news events that escaped more orderly writers. Even if he did snarl the facts, a rewrite man could make something of them. He did best on the semi-imaginative "feature" yarn where terse journalese was not wanted—where indeed his poetic speculations were an asset—and it was to this type of story that his editors steered him when they could. He never did attain real proficiency on the strict news side, for when at last he came to meet his supreme journalistic challenge he would fail.

Revolted when his dowdy landlady paid him coy attentions, he packed his bag and sneaked away to another room at Tenth and Walnut, a loft area he felt was bohemian enough to win the approval of McCord and Wood. By now the hated city editor, Mitchell, had accepted him and handed him a daily column called "Heard in the Corridors" in addition to his regular chores. This had previously been handled by W. C. Brann, now famous as editor of the *Iconoclast*. How could he possibly fill Brann's shoes? He visited the hotels—the Southern, Lindell and LaClede—hunting for celebrities who would say remarkable things for his column. He found few celebrities, and those he found spoke mostly dullness, but he knew that Brann had solved the problem by inventing interviews with fictitious people. He continued the practice, gaining fictional enjoyment and interspersing the fiction with an occasional genuine celebrity.

One of these was John L. Sullivan, whom he interviewed in his suite at the Lindell. Sullivan, who had recently lost his title to Jim Corbett in New Orleans, was sparkling with diamonds and happily drunk. Dreiser asked him his favorite question: What did he think of life?

"Aw, haw! haw! haw!" the Strong Boy guffawed. "You're all right, young fella, kinda slim, but you'll do. . . . Sit down and have some champagne. Have a cigar. . . . Write any damned thing you please, young fella, and say that John L. Sullivan said so." [20]

Dreiser regretted Sullivan's refusal to discuss questions troubling his own mind, questions always centering on God, creation and justice. Why did God permit the viciousness he saw everywhere—the ignorance, the slums, the vice? Why did God condemn him, Dreiser, to grow up in poverty while Day Allen Willy had everything he wanted? Why was he given a weak frame, buck teeth and a cast in one eye while Bill Yakey and John L. Sullivan had handsomeness and strength? Then there was the problem of the Rabelaisian Peter McCord, a Catholic who had lost his religion and now had a humorous tolerance of all beliefs but himself believed in none, unless one counted his agnostic wonder at the inscrutability of nature, his conviction that everything in nature—even the prostitutes on Chestnut Street—had some benign usefulness in a grand scheme no one could hope to understand. Dreiser knew that his father would have condemned McCord as an infidel headed straight for hell, yet he felt McCord the most civilized and humanitarian man he had ever met. He interviewed the theosophist Annie Besant when she came to town to lecture. Poverty, she told him, was an outrage from which the rich suffered as well as the poor.

"You do not recognize, then," Dreiser asked, "a controlling principle—a God?"

I. THE HABERDASHERY DREAM

"No, we do not. If there is a God, the order of this life is then manifestly unjust. Some things are born with ability and strength, some with dulled sense, with weaknesses and deformities. . . . Instead of accusing a divine being with being partial, we turn to the individual himself and find a solution of the apparent discrepancy in reincarnation." [21]

She also spoke of Nirvana, which Dreiser had to look up when he returned to the city room. For all of Annie Besant and Peter McCord, he was not ready to dump his religion, reasoning that the world's ills might not be attributable to God but to man's inability to understand God. While on his hotel beat, he liked to loaf in the lobby of the Lindell, teetering in a rocking chair, observing. One evening, clad in a rented dress suit, he covered a public ball at the stock exchange, awed by the grandeur of the decorations and the beauty of the women, fearful that the guests discerned that this was the first time he had ever worn a clawhammer. On his return he was rushed away to cover a triple murder in South St. Louis. Still in evening clothes, he entered a hovel—the antithesis of the perfumed splendor he had just left—and saw on the floor the bloody bodies of two children and their mother, slain by the husband and father in a fit of insanity that seemed an unjust act of God.

Dreiser could have cried over the senseless tragedy. Yet he went back to the office and forgot his pity as he finished his accounts of the ball and the murders with high satisfaction over his work.

On Saturday morning, January 21, 1893, he got a lucky tip on a railroad wreck across the river near Alton, Illinois. Mitchell was not in, so Dreiser, sensing a big story, left a note for him and boarded an east-bound train. Getting off at Wann, Illinois, three miles north of Alton, he saw a crowd of several hundred watching a half-dozen wrecked and burning boxcars. It happened that seven oil tank cars stood on a siding near the fire. As Dreiser hurried up the tracks toward the crowd, one of the tank cars exploded from the heat, touching off another in thunderous reverberations. He saw flaming oil spray everywhere, drenching dozens of onlookers.

People were ablaze, screaming in torment. A flaming man ran toward him, shrieking hoarsely, and fell into a ditch, twisting like a worm. Dreiser tore off his own coat to smother the man's burning clothing, but saw that he was unconscious, terribly seared.

Then he was transformed from the horrified observer to the calculating reporter. This was the biggest story of his career, and he was the only newspaperman there. He walked about, counting the dead, questioning victims who were still able to talk.

"Oh, can't you let me alone!" groaned one man whose body was raw with blisters. "Can't you see I'm dying?"

"Isn't there someone who will want to know?" softly asked reporter Dreiser.

"You're right," the man said. He gave his name and gasped out an account of his experience. Dreiser did the same with others. Later, in the Alton hospital where charred survivors were brought, he talked with witnesses, surgeons, railroad officials. He returned to St. Louis and wrote from 7 P.M. to 1 A.M.—the only eyewitness account of a disaster that took some thirty lives, and a clear scoop for the *Globe-Democrat*, which gave it four columns on the front page and almost two more on page two. McCullagh called him in.

"A fine piece of work," he said. He gave Dreiser a $20 bonus and raised his salary to $25 a week.[22]

Dreiser bought new clothing of a flashy design he considered bohemian. He at least impressed his new landlady, this one a trim widow from the Balkans, who also paid him marked attentions. One night, covering a church affair on Pine Street, he met a girl who allowed herself to be persuaded to spend the night with him. Although he described it as "a delicious contest, made all the more so by [her] real or assumed bashfulness," he was again so terrified about his imagined sexual enfeeblement that when she left in the morning he feared he had failed. Now his landlady, finding hairpins on his pillow, grew arch. They became lovers, and she often joined Dreiser when he arrived home around 1 A.M. While this affair at last settled his doubts about his prowess, he entertained, as he put it, a "growing feeling that she was . . . very much beneath me mentally and in every other way," and he escaped by moving to a room on Chestnut Street.[23]

His own memoirs portray him as being entangled with so many women that one might suspect exaggeration if his subsequent career had not followed the same pattern. And a later *Globe-Democrat* man wrote, "Office gossip had it in 1896 that Dreiser had been active in obtaining feminine relaxation for [city editor] Mitchell. . . ."[24]

IV. DISASTER

Emboldened by his railroad scoop, Dreiser applied for and was given the vacant post of dramatic critic of the *Globe-Democrat*. He pictured himself as the cool arbiter of the stage, writing powerful dramas himself, mingling with the social élite, with actors, and above all with famous actresses. However, the *Globe-Democrat* did not take drama seriously, covering several plays in one article giving only a paragraph or two to each. Dreiser was also expected to handle regular assignments at the same time. But St. Louis had eight theaters, he had free tickets to everything, and nightly he squirmed in suspense over cliffhangers. Fascinated by cardboard scenery and fragile heroines, he was so carried away by a heart-wrenching love scene in a totally spurious play at the Olympic that his review was a hosanna and he was startled, but not convinced, when an older staff man told him sourly it was rot.

Yearning to write a play himself, he lacked confidence until McCord shouted, "Why don't you try?" Had not such famous writers as Augustus Thomas, Eugene Field and William Marion Reedy started out as St. Louis newspapermen? Dreiser got on with it, sketching out the plot of a comic opera he called *Jeremiah I*, the story of an Indiana farmer who accidentally struck a magical Aztec stone on his farm, was transported to Mexico of the Aztec era, acclaimed by the amazed natives as their ruler, and became a despot until the love of a glamorous Aztec maiden turned him into the most benevolent of kings.[25]

Jeremiah I was a précis of Dreiser's fantasies of power, justice and sex, but McCord was so enthusiastic that he began designing costumes and settings for the extravaganza. Meanwhile, Dreiser was reviewing as many as three plays in an evening, taking in one act at one theater and rushing off to the next. Uncritically he admired De Wolf Hopper, Richard Mansfield, Eddie Foy and Frank Daniels, but it was the soubrettes—vivid young things, including Della Fox, Edna May and Mabel Amber—who excited him most. When he was introduced to E. S. Willard, star of *The Professor's Love Story*, he barely saw the famous Willard because he was eyeing his leading lady and thinking, "Could anything be so lovely?" He reveled in the world of Pinero and Wilde. Then, when he hit the chill street outside, he was downcast by the realization that he was, after all, only a miserable reporter. He felt, at twenty-one, that he was growing old, that fame was passing him by, that fortune was opposed to him personally and would not give him a chance, that "the dice were loaded."

His luck went sour. In reviewing a performance at Exposition Hall by the Negro singer Sisseretta Jones, billed as "the black Patti," he went into rhapsodies, writing in small part that her singing "reminds one of the beauty of nature and brings back visions of the still, glassy water and soft swaying branches of some drowsy nook in summer time." [26]

In St. Louis, one did not praise Negroes with such abandon. McCullagh had enemies because of his bitter pen, and rival papers seized on the review as proof that he was a "nigger-lover," the *Post-Dispatch* calling him "the great patron of the black arts." Dreiser was rebuked for this, but later in April he stumbled into real trouble.

On an evening when there were three new openings at the Grand, the Havlin and Pope's Theater, he was enraged when Mitchell at seven o'clock sent him to cover a picayune street-car holdup on the far west side that would keep him from attending the plays. He wrote hurried reviews of the three productions from advance press-agent material, thinking that he would return in time to look in at the theaters. It was far too late when he got back. In the morning he was stricken to see a story in the *St. Louis Republic* saying that none of the three shows had reached town, train service having been disrupted by floods and washouts.

He perspired as he read his own reviews in the *Globe-Democrat*, saying that "A large and enthusiastic audience received Mr. Sol Smith Russell" at the Grand and commenting likewise on the performances at Pope's and the Havlin.

"Oh, Lord!" he groaned.[27]

This was the end. He sneaked into the city room, left an apologetic note of explanation for McCullagh, gathered his few belongings and left. That afternoon he found the other papers making merry, not at his expense but McCullagh's. The editor had shown some interest in psychic phenomena, and the *Post-Dispatch* and *Chronicle* agreed that here was undeniable proof of his clairvoyance. "Great, indeed, is McCullagh," said the *Post-Dispatch*. "[This is] one of the finest flights of which the human mind or the great editor's psychic strength is capable. . . . This latest essay of his into the realm of combined dramatic criticism, supernatural insight, and materialization, is one of the most perfect things of its kind. . . ."[28]

Dreiser thought he was ruined, the laughingstock of St. Louis. He became a hermit, slinking out of his room to eat in remote restaurants. He avoided Hackett's bar, the newsmen's hangout—shunned even his good friends Mc-Cord and Wood, unable to face their imagined contempt. He thought of fleeing to Chicago, but he had not saved enough money. Alone, he sank into terrible depression.

7. Involvement

Dreiser remained in hiding for more than a week. When his funds were almost gone, he called at the second-rate morning *Republic*, whose rattletrap building was at Third and Chestnut. The city editor, swarthy H. B. Wandell, chuckled over the incident of the reviews.

"Yes, that was very funny—very," he said.

He took Dreiser on at $18 a week, a comedown but good enough for a failure. Dreiser was surprised to find, however, that his disgrace was largely in his own mind, that the *Republic* men said nothing of it and that Wandell, who favored sex and scandal stories, gave him good assignments and liked his work, urging him to emulate Zola and Balzac.

"Get in all the touches of local color you can," he counseled. "And remember Zola and Balzac, my boy, remember Zola and Balzac."[1]

Dreiser, a sketchy reader, did not get around to Zola and Balzac, but he gathered courage to call on Wood and McCord. "Where the hell have you been keeping yourself?" Wood demanded, and McCord immediately began discussing *Jeremiah I*. The world was good again except for the contemptible $18 salary. Dreiser came to like a *Republic* reporter named Clark, a man of great charm and ability who vanished one day, no one knew where, until Dreiser met him weeks later on a slum street, filthy, bedraggled, shaking from drink and begging him for a dollar—an experience so unnerving that Dreiser ran into the Southern Hotel bar and had a quick one himself. Another reporter, a poetic fellow named Rodenberger, alternated between periods of admirable efficiency and drunken debauchery and brothel-haunting, once going on an almost fatal morphine binge. How could one explain the impulses that moved men to their own ruin, or the inscrutability of a Creator too remote or indifferent to care about the individual?

Dreiser was troubled also by the ferocious, story-at-any-price newspaper code and his own willingness to exploit it for his own advancement. On one occasion he broke his promise to a mayoralty candidate and published an unguarded statement he had made, losing him the election. After office hours he seemed unable to avoid involvement, for now his Chestnut Street landlady proved too attractive and flirtatious to resist.

Under Wandell, he became a valued feature man on the *Republic*. He got no raise, for the 1893 panic was paralyzing business, but in the summer he was given a reward of a different kind. To promote circulation, the *Republic* staged a popularity contest among Missouri schoolmarms, selecting the

47

twenty who got the most votes and paying their way to the Chicago World's Fair, now going full blast. Dreiser was picked to accompany them and write about their activities on the excursion, never failing to puff the *Republic*.

Although delighted at the opportunity to visit Chicago, he dreaded the chore of shepherding twenty homely spinsters until he boarded the Pullman and found most of them young and attractive in summery frocks. Painful timidity engulfed him until the train was rolling through Illinois, when his roving eye settled on one of his charges, a demure young lady whose white dress set off her girlish figure, almond eyes and rich coils of sunny red hair. She was Sara Osborne White, who would be a factor in his life for the next forty-nine years. She admitted that she had never been to Chicago.

"I've never been anywhere, really," she said. "I'm just a simple country girl, you know." [2]

This gave him an edge, and he talked to her as an old Chicagoan. Sallie White was twenty-four, two years and three months older than Dreiser. She came from Montgomery City, seventy-five miles west of St. Louis, but taught in Florissant, a St. Louis suburb. He was enchanted both by her allure and an air of virginal serenity he had never found in any landlady, and by the time they reached Chicago he was half in love with her, murmuring, "What a delightful girl!" [3]

Next day they walked through splendor that realized his Arabian Nights dreams—the Fair, with its splendid Court of Honor, its magnificent avenues, its lagoons and gondolas, its music, its fairyland of electric lights. He took Sallie's hand; she quietly retrieved it. She had studied at a seminary in O'Fallon, Missouri, and until now she had never seen any city other than St. Louis. She had five sisters and two brothers, and she spoke of her farm-people parents with evident affection. Despite her rustic background she had achieved a poise he could not muster, based on a family tranquillity he had never known and expressing standards she accepted and practiced—an attitude that must have made him envious since he was groping blindly for standards, sure of nothing, least of all himself. Although he later enjoyed passionate kisses on a secluded bench with another Missouri school teacher, a Miss Ginity, he could not get the maddeningly chaste Miss White out of his mind. He went to the West Side and visited his father, now seventy-two—a meeting that made them both burst into tears.

"Tell me, Dorsch," the old man said almost at once, "do you still keep up your church duties?" [4]

He took his father to the Fair, where the old man was delighted by the German Village, strolling about in a derby hat so mildewed that Theodore gave him for a new one. He accepted the money, not for a new hat but for a mass for the repose of Sarah's soul. Theodore also visited his brother Al, now an electrician, and Ed, who was driving a delivery wagon, and he rashly urged them to join him in St. Louis, forgetting that times were hard and thousands were unemployed. Then he rushed back to the Fair to find Sallie, discovering that her younger sister, laughing, freckle-faced Rose White, had come from Missouri to join her. Within minutes he was captivated by Rose's vivacity, wondering if he did not like her even better than Sallie. "One of the things which troubled and astonished me," he noted, "was that I could like two, three, and even more women at the same time. . . ."[5] After two weeks at the Fair, he returned to St. Louis in romantic confusion.

II. BETROTHAL

Dreiser's advice that Al and Ed come to St. Louis reflected his sincere liking for them and also his weakness for embroidering on his own success. Impressed by his talk, both brothers quit their Chicago jobs and moved in with him at his Chestnut Street room. It was pleasant until they discovered that the panic had made work almost unobtainable, and Theodore's own hospitality cooled when he had to help them financially. Al became aware of his affair with the landlady, who openly called him "Dearie," and warned, "Look out she don't hand you a disease."[6] Theodore was relieved when they returned to Chicago, nor did it occur to him that he was responsible for a set-back to them both and that they might have trouble finding work again in Chicago.

Soon afterward he broke with his landlady and moved to Morgan Avenue, not because of Sallie White or Al's warning but because he became unreasonably jealous when he learned that the woman was carrying an another simultaneous affair.

He ran into his old chief, McCullagh, at the Southern Hotel and found him cordial.

"I want you to know," McCullagh said, "that if you are ever free and want to come back you can."[7]

Dreiser was elated. Here was an invitation to return to the best paper in town, and at a better salary. Yet he vacillated, temporized, thought of his dislike of city editor Mitchell, and ended by staying on the *Republic*, disgruntled though he was at the poor pay. One assignment, however, excited him. The clairvoyant J. Alexander Tyndall came to town and arranged a promotion scheme with the *Republic*, Tyndall being blindfolded and taking the reins in a buggy while Dreiser sat beside him, silently giving him directions by telepathy alone. The unseeing Tyndall drove at a smart clip through crowded downtown streets, narrowly missing other vehicles while Dreiser hung on for dear life. Yet Tyndall followed his thought-waves without error, turned several corners and pulled up correctly at a destination on Broadway which he knew only from Dreiser's unspoken thoughts—a demonstration that permanently influenced Dreiser's thinking, clouded as it already was by superstition.

Lonely again, he wrote Sallie White, and she replied pleasantly that she would come to St. Louis in mid-September when school began. He could not eat or sleep normally, worrying about the impression he would make on her. He bought a new fall suit of "startling pattern," patent leather shoes, a pearl gray hat and other accessories. When the day came he went by trolley to meet her at her aunt's home in the West End, carrying flowers, candy and theater tickets, lamenting that he could not afford a carriage. He waited in the parlor, and when she came in she stood framed for a moment in a white doorway, her red hair and lovely figure making a picture so stunning that it became ever more vital to impress her with his importance. He took her to see Chauncey Olcott at the Grand Opera House, telling her that he was no ordinary reporter but a "traveling correspondent" for the *Republic*.

Thereafter he saw her every two weeks, for Sallie—known since childhood as Jug—spent the intervening weekend with her family in Montgomery City. He wrote her interminable letters, longing for their next meeting, finding that St. Louis took on a new glamor because of his love. He was sickened when he covered a hanging at the prison, but a letter came from Sallie and the victim was forgotten.

His purpose was quick seduction. He later admitted that it was "her charming physical self that I craved." But Sallie White, a virginal Methodist, repulsed him. He was racked by "an intense ache and urge," so frustrated that thirty years later he railed at "all the formalities, traditions, beliefs, of a conventional and puritanic region," adding, "If only this love affair could have gone on to a swift fruition it would have been perfect, blinding." Neighbors who saw him courting Sallie thought him "a big silly," saying, "He was always going about gawking and mooning." [8] He laid earnest siege, brought her roses, took her to free plays, and clothes were an obsession. For winter he bought an extravagantly long military coat, a Stetson, a cane and pleated shirts. He did not dare wear this regalia to the office, so on Saturdays when Sallie was in town he would rush to his room, execute an actor's quick change, then change again for another news assignment, sometimes changing three times a day and cursing the *Republic*'s demands on him.

Still, for all this effort, only an occasional stolen kiss.

Losing sleep, he finally capitulated. He proposed. Delirious at her acceptance, he spent his last cent on a diamond ring. Sallie gave him her photograph, which he framed in silver and hung in his room. He begged for a lock of her hair and got it—even stole a bit of blue ribbon she had worn, keeping it as a fetish, feeling that betrothal would give him privileges heretofore denied him.

It did not.

Too poor to marry, he fell into depression. In the midst of this his old mentor, John Maxwell, lost his Chicago job and appeared in St. Louis. Dreiser had some influence with Wandell and had succeeded in getting berths for other Chicago newsmen, so Maxwell called on him—and spied the photograph of Sallie.

"That's the girl I'm engaged to," Dreiser said proudly.

"Oh hell, Theodore!" Maxwell snorted. He urged Dreiser not to be a fool and tie himself down. "That girl is five years older than you if she's a day. . . . She belongs to some church, I suppose."

"Methodist," Dreiser said ruefully.

"I knew it! But I'm not knocking her; I'm not saying she isn't pretty and virtuous, but I do say she's older than you, and narrow. Why, man, you don't know your own mind yet." [9]

Dreiser was in such confusion that he did little to aid the man who had given him his start in journalism, and Maxwell, finding no work, left town without even saying good-by. Soon after, in December, Dreiser passed the Havlin Theater on South Sixth Street and was overjoyed to see a familiar face smiling at him from a billboard. His brother Paul, whom he had not seen for two years, was coming to the Havlin as star of a melodrama, *The Danger Signal*.

His affection for Paul was tinctured with deepest envy for his fame, self-assurance and utter *success*. Paul greeted him joyfully when he arrived a few days later, dispensed free tickets, and Theodore took McCord, Wood and other friends to see his brother in *The Danger Signal*, a piece of claptrap that even contained a heroine lying across the rails in danger of being minced by a locomotive. Yet Paul's humorous sallies and his singing of his own song, "The Bowery," brought down the house. He had long sensed an undeveloped genius in his incomprehensible younger brother, and during the week he stayed he urged that Theodore go to New York, where Paul himself now had an interest in a music publishing firm. But his reaction after meeting Sallie White was disturbing.

She was "charming," he said, but if he were Theodore he would not think of marrying as yet.[10]

The misogamy of Paul and Maxwell revived Dreiser's own caution. Jug, desirable as she was, was not the rich and aristocratic siren of his dreams. Although the *Republic* appreciated his talents and began sending him on frequent out-of-town assignments, his paycheck remained the same. He was dissatisfied, restless, sexually driven, allured by Paul's talk of New York but harboring a country-boy fear of the metropolis—in a disposition to give ear to almost any proposition that offered change and a dream. Such a proposal came from a young reporter friend on the *Republic*, J. T. Hutchinson, who came from Grand Rapids, Ohio (population 600), where his parents still lived. A country weekly was for sale near there which could be had for a small down payment, Hutchinson said, painting a vivid picture of the joys and opportunities of rural journalism.

Although he thought Hutchinson a mental lightweight, Dreiser built visions of success and fame in Ohio. "In my sky," he later wrote, "the latest cloud of thought or plan was the great thing," [11] but he was impelled by fear as well as hope, feeling, at twenty-two, that his youth was slipping away and he must try a cast of the dice, even though they were loaded against him, or subside into mediocrity. To Jug he outlined the plan as a calculated risk with glittering potentialities—a rosy view, when he had only about $100 and Hutchinson had no more. Late in February, 1894, Hutchinson went to Ohio, looked over the paper and sent back an enthusiastic report. When Dreiser gave notice at the *Republic*, Wandell urged him to stay and the publisher himself, Charles W. Knapp, promised him more money and an editorial post. Dreiser, disgruntled because they had not thought of these things before, took pleasure in rejecting their belated attentions.

He tore himself away from Jug despite what he called "that immense physical desire toward my beloved." On March 5, he boarded an east-bound train at Union Station, carrying a letter from Knapp:

> Any favors extended to the bearer Mr. T. H. Dreiser traveling corre-
> spondent for the St. Louis Republic, will be greatly appreciated by me on
> behalf of the Republic.[12]

As the train pulled away, this confused young man suddenly was over-whelmed by despair, a sense of failure, because successful men did not have to go "jerking about the world seeking a career." [13]

8. Jerking About the World

Theodore's persistent fear that time was running out reflected his need for quick success. Now the influence of Sarah Dreiser was in the ascendant as he abandoned a promising career in a city of a half million at a time of nationwide depression in favor of a shadowy prospect in an unknown hamlet. En route to Ohio his spirits rose as he visualized country editors as men of prestige who often moved up the political ladder to greatness. He pictured himself as State Senator Dreiser, then Congressman Dreiser and Governor Dreiser, and finally, in a fine imaginative leap, as President Dreiser.[1]

The White House dwindled when he reached sleepy Grand Rapids, twenty-five miles southwest of Toledo on the Maumee River, and was met by the optimistic Hutchinson. The countryside was bleak and wintry as they went to nearby Weston, where the *Wood County Herald* was for sale, and visited its office. Dreiser was shocked to find it a dingy loft with broken-down equipment above a feed store. Instead of a book-lined editorial sanctum where deferent political leaders came and went, this was a cobwebby shambles.

"It's horrible," he told himself. "I should die."

The paper had fewer than five hundred subscribers, its advertising was negligible and its news concerned church socials, farmers' ailments and obituaries. He was angry with Hutchinson, but the simple answer was that Hutchinson's dream of success was less exalted than his own.

"I don't see how I can go into this with you," Dreiser said. "There isn't enough in it." [2]

He had thrown over his job for a chimera. He spent a disgruntled interlude with Hutchinson at his parents' farm nearby, debating his next move. St. Louis now appeared as a city of some glamor, the only place in these hard times where he could be sure of a job, but to return there would be humiliating. He took the train to Toledo where, in a routine that became habitual, he went on a long spectator's walk, viewing the waterfront, the industries, then the mansions that excited his envy. At last he tackled the city editor of the *Toledo Blade*, a compact, creamy-complexioned man of twenty-six named Arthur Henry.

They liked each other immediately. Henry said there was nothing open but a few days' work reporting the Toledo street-car strike.

"But I'll tell you frankly, it's dangerous," he said. "You may be shot or hit with a brick." [3]

Dreiser risked it. He boarded a trolley and rode around the city, not without misgivings that strikers might seize the car and manhandle him, but he saw no violence at all. Although his sympathies were with the strikers, whom he identified with his own background of poverty, he tried for impartiality in his story. Henry was delighted with his work. He found a few more assignments for Dreiser—insisted on forsaking the fiancée he would soon marry and taking Dreiser to dinner, the two finding affinity in hours of talk, Henry aspiring to become a poet and novelist, Dreiser a playwright, Dreiser so charmed by him that he thought, "If I had been a girl I would have married him, of course," Henry thinking he had found "a perfect friend." Born in Pecatonica, Illinois, Henry as a boy had ridden a white horse from Chicago to New York to campaign for temperance at the behest of his mother, a founder of the W.C.T.U. A brilliant conversationalist, he urged Dreiser to stay on the chance that an opening would occur. But Dreiser, too low in funds to wait, moved on to Cleveland with the assurance that Henry would telegraph him if a job developed. [4]

In Cleveland he ogled the Euclid Avenue mansions of Rockefeller, Tom Johnson and Henry Flagler, then tried the newspapers. He made no use then or later of Knapp's letter of recommendation, fearing illogically that it might get him a bigger job than he could hold. Without it, he got no job at all other than some Sunday feature work at space rates for the *Leader*, whose editor uttered a criticism of Dreiser's style that many editors would later echo: "You don't want to write so loosely." He spent much of his time lobby-lounging at the splendid Hollenden Hotel, hoping for a telegram from Henry that never came, and when, after two weeks he had made only $7.50 at the *Leader*, he took a train to Buffalo.

He tried the four newspapers there, but not with real aggressiveness, still feeling a humiliation in job-hunting. Although his money was dwindling, he resumed his old role as spectator, walking the Buffalo streets and waterfront and taking the trolley to Niagara Falls. After ten days and no job, he moved on to Pittsburgh before mid-April, seeing mountains for the first time in his life. When he arrived after dark at the station across the Monongahela from Pittsburgh's business district he was excited by the walls of lamp-flecked hills on every side, by the orange flame belching from scores of stacks along the river and the incessant clanking of a hundred mighty forges.

He found a cheap room on Wylie Avenue and soon got a nibble from city editor Harry Gaither of the *Pittsburgh Dispatch*, who said he might need a man in a couple of days. Then came a wire from Arthur Henry offering Dreiser a job in Toledo at $18 a week. He felt that if he showed Gaither the telegram it would land him on the *Dispatch*, but at that same salary. Carefully he erased the "$18" on the telegram, retyped it to read "$25," and took it to Gaither, telling him he was leaving for Toledo. Gaither promptly hired him at $25, saying, "Come around tomorrow at twelve." [5]

II. CARNEGIE AND THE HUNKIES

Pittsburgh's jagged contrasts fascinated Dreiser from the start. Never had he seen such extremes, from the swarms of Hunkies, Poles, Lits and Croats in their reeking river-flat slums to the palaces of the millionaires Carnegie, Phipps, Frick and Oliver up on the hill. Coxey's Army was still on the march, the bloody riots at nearby Homestead were less than two years past, there had been violent strikes at the Connellsville mines, and the shooting of Henry Clay Frick by the anarchist Alexander Berkman was a vivid memory. Dreiser sensed a sullen tension, as if the present quiet were only a truce in the battle between capital and labor which might burst out again at any moment. One of his early assignments was to interview Congressman Thomas B. Reed, soon to be Speaker of the House, in his luxurious suite at the Monongahela Hotel and ask him what he thought of Coxey's Army.

"Why, it's the same as revolution!" Reed snapped. Orderly democratic action, he insisted, was the answer for any injustice. "Now comes along a man who finds something that doesn't just suit his views, and instead of waiting and appealing to the regular party councils, he organizes an army and proceeds to march on Washington."

"But what about the thing of which they are complaining?" Dreiser asked.

"It doesn't matter what their grievance is," Reed said testily. "This is a government of law and prescribed political procedure. Our people must abide by that." [6]

Although there seemed a superficial logic in this, Dreiser was more moved by the human logic implicit in the miserable condition of workers who got no help from such talk. He felt some contempt for the well-fed Reed, who hobnobbed with steel barons and spoke of democracy when anyone who smelled the slums of Homestead knew by his nose that this was not democracy.

Pittsburgh's inequalities brought into some organization the occasional impressions of social injustice that had affected him in Chicago and St. Louis. Everywhere one found the rich and the poor, but here the disparity between them was so wide that they seemed a different species. He saw that the local papers reported with servile admiration the hunting excursions of the steelmasters, the silver-and-damask social functions of their womenfolk and their trips to New York or Europe, while suppressing any hint of exploitation of the workers who made this luxury possible.

"We don't touch on labor conditions except through our labor man, and he knows what to say," Gaither warned him. "The big steel men here just about own the place, so we can't." [7]

The *Dispatch* labor reporter, a sad-faced young man named Martyn, told him how the steelmen's foreign labor agents lured European peasants to come to Pittsburgh and work for low wages, how labor spies and company stores operated, how even the churches used their influence to keep labor in line.

"But you can't say anything about it in Pittsburgh," Martyn said. "If I should talk I'd have to get out of here." [8]

Deplorable as all this was, when Dreiser took his mansion-viewing walks out Fifth Avenue to Schenley Park he was filled with envy at the fenced-in palaces, the carriages and footmen bought through the toil of the hovel-dwelling foreigners, still dreaming of magnificence for himself. His own toil was not excessive. For the *Dispatch* he covered the city hall across the river in Allegheny, an assignment giving him time to browse in the handsome Carnegie library opposite—another luxury sweated for by the laborers, but in a good cause. Here he saw a complete set of Balzac. Recalling Wandell's "Remember Balzac, my boy," he picked up *The Wild Ass's Skin* and became enthralled. Balzac's Raphael was much like him, a young man inhibited by his father's puritanism, who brooded over his shyness, his poverty and shabby clothing, who yearned for women and fame. Said Raphael in the novel: "How many a time, silent and motionless, have I not admired the woman of my dreams, floating through a ball-room!" Again: "Many a time, from childhood up, had I struck my forehead, saying to myself . . . 'There is something here.'. . . I, myself, have been general, emperor, Byron, even. . . ." Raphael even explained how the world rewarded "mere schemers, rich in words," while ignoring geniuses like Raphael and Dreiser.[9]

Raphael *was* Dreiser. In purest identification Dreiser suffered with Raphael, triumphed with Raphael when he realized all his dreams by using the magic skin. But Dreiser missed the moral to the story—one that would eventually apply to him. For Raphael, in being granted every wish, met disaster because his ever-mounting desires slowly killed him.

For weeks Dreiser spent a good deal of the *Dispatch*'s time reading Balzac, moving on to *Père Goriot, A Great Man of the Provinces in Paris* and others, losing himself in the narratives and traversing Paris like an old boulevardier. He went a little crazy over Balzac, reasoning that Pittsburgh, with its rivers and bridges, was much like Paris, so that when he crossed over to Allegheny he could fancy himself crossing the Pont Neuf to the Left Bank. Although he was not yet inspired to write novels of his own, he could find in Balzac social implications that echoed his own fumbling observations—the contrast between poverty and wealth, the depiction of life as amoral and heedless of the fate of the individual, the scenes of sexual license, the open criticism of Catholicism. And he understood perfectly when Raphael said, "How many a young soul of talent withers and dies in a garret for want of a friend, for want of a consoling woman. . . ."

In his own need for consolation, Dreiser resorted to prostitutes. He later listed three he patronized, wondering at the moral code that regarded such a woman as "irretrievably lost . . . but not I, who shared this sensual traffic with her." One of them, a "light chestnut type," intrigued him with her beauty and her air of absent-mindedness, almost of indifference—a demeanor that puzzled him until he saw that "her left arm, from her hand fully halfway to the elbow was dotted with a thousand, as it seemed, needle-pricks."

Shocked, he launched into a sermon on the evils of the drug habit. Why, he demanded, did she do this?

"Oh, great God!" she said wearily at last, "why do you talk? What do you know about life?"

Dreiser pitied her wretchedness. What indeed did he know of life? "My primary lust vanished on the instant," he wrote. "I sensed a kind of misery and hopelessness here, and for once in my life I did a decent thing. I had not much for myself, but I took out three dollars . . . and laid it on the nearby mantel.

" 'That's all right,' I said when she looked at me oddly. 'I'm glad to give you this. You don't want me tonight, anyhow.' And I went out in the rain and so on home, thinking of her and the old house and the bare room, and the punctured arm. . . ." [10]

While Dreiser had a remarkable capacity for getting facts twisted—a weakness he never conquered—the *Dispatch*, like his previous newspaper employers, found him effective at feature yarns wherein he could speculate, digress and dramatize. Just as Lucien de Rubempré in *A Great Man of the Provinces* wrote sketches of Paris life, Dreiser wrote essays about Pittsburgh scenes and oddities with what he felt was the Balzac touch. He could find unusual sidelights in commonplace subjects, writing about cats, the Hancock Street morgue, hoboes, the mosquito menace, dog catchers, suicides and similar topics. Proud of these pieces, he sent clippings to Paul, who was back in New York after his tour and was urging him to come there. Theodore's fear of the metropolis was countered by an attraction spurred by his reading of *Munsey's* and *Town Topics*, which told of a New York social glitter so glamorous that he yearned to go there and bag an heiress or capture a fortune on his own. Even as he wrote ardent letters to Jug, he feared that she did not measure up to his ideal and that "a brief period of pleasuring with her might be sufficient after all." [11]

Paris called him again as he read George Du Maurier's *Trilby*, then running in *Harper's Monthly*. Fascinated by the depiction of studio life with its colorful iniquities, he identified himself totally with Little Billee, bleeding for him as he searched for his beloved Trilby and stricken with tragedy at Trilby's death. Now he identified Sallie White with Trilby, fearing that he would lose her through poverty just as Billee had lost Trilby through trickery. The thought so tormented him that he got a short vacation from the *Dispatch* and boarded a train for Missouri, hypnotized by Du Maurier as Trilby had been by Svengali.

III. GOOD AND EVIL

Arch Herndon White, Jug's father, was a community leader in somnolent Montgomery City, Missouri, a white-haired man of prayer and principle who never lost his native dignity even when leading a cow in for milking. His buxom, cheerful wife Anna never questioned that peace, order and morality were the good things of life. They were the "best family" in town, and their house on the outskirts was decayed but pretty. Jug, one of eight children, was their true daughter.

When Dreiser arrived in July, her beauty, in a background of evening katydids and flowers, aroused him after almost five months of separation. Yet when he saw her younger sister Rose laughing over a silly book, he was more in love with Rose and irked that his betrothal to Jug kept Rose out of reach. Fickle as a moth, he envied the solidity and integrity of this family's conduct even though his own impulses were opposite and he felt disdainfully that they did not really know life as it was in Pittsburgh, for example. When alone with Jug he grew so importunate that she had to restrain him almost by force. There was one climactic night when the family was gone and her resistance all but collapsed. "My hand opening her dress and forcing its way to her naked breasts," Dreiser recalled, "caused her to sink in a kind of swoon . . . . Passion had at last mastered . . . every aspect of narrow, conventional training. Here in this very home, the sanctity of which was almost as impressive to me as to her, the thing might have been done."

But as he carried her toward his room, convention was not quite defeated.

"This house!" Jug gasped. "Oh, not here, not here! You are so strong. I cannot help myself, but you save me." [12]

Dreiser, touched, relented. He never got over this frustration. Years later he grumbled about it, blaming this rebuff for the wreck of his romance, writing:

> Love should act in its heat, not when its bank account is heavy. . . . Nature's way is correct, her impulses sound. The delight in possessing my fiancée then would have repaid her for her fears, and me for ruthlessness if I had taken her. A clearer and a better grasp of life would have been hers and mine. The coward sips little of life, the strong man drinks deep. Old prejudices must always fall, and life must always change. It is the law. [13]

It was not the law in Montgomery City, so unlike Balzac's Paris or the studios of Du Maurier. Indeed Dreiser's reasoning suggested that of all people the prostitute and the rake had the clearest grasp of life—an opinion he later sometimes entertained. When a letter arrived from Paul, again urging him to come to New York, he impulsively wired Paul that he was coming, said good-by to Jug and stopped in St. Louis on his way east. But St. Louis now irked him because the city was doing very well without him—proof of his own unimportance. Even his friends Peter McCord and Dick Wood, while delighted to see him, hurt him by discussing things which had occurred since he left, a further indication that he was not necessary to them. The morbidly sensitive Theodore left unhappily for New York, thinking, as he neared twenty-three, that he was growing older every hour, that he must hurry to make the world recognize instead of forget him.

Paul met him in Jersey City with a salvo of jokes and took him by ferry to

Manhattan, where Theodore was disappointed by the littered streets and small horsecars.

"My boy," Paul chuckled, "you haven't seen anything yet. . . . Wait'll you see Broadway and Fifth Avenue." [14]

Paul, on the road during the "season," spent his summers in New York, living with his sister Emma and her husband L. A. Hopkins on Fifteenth Street—the same Hopkins who eight years earlier had abstracted $3,500 from the safe of his Chicago employer, Chapin & Gore, and later returned most of the money. Paul was in clover, coining money three ways as actor, song-writer and one-third owner of a new music concern, Howley, Haviland & Company, at 4 East Twentieth Street. He took Theodore to the apartment of Emma, whom Theodore had not seen since the death of their mother four years earlier.

"Why, Theodore, I'm so glad to see you!" she cried.[15]

She was matronly, not the beauty that she once had been—another reminder of the inexorable passage of time. Her self-assured husband had sunk from his comfortable Chicago estate and now was only intermittently employed. During the few days Theodore was there, Paul took him up Broadway, stopped in at Delmonico's, and led him into the Metropole for a drink, where Theodore was amazed by the number of snappily dressed characters—actors, song-writers, pugilists, politicians—who greeted Paul delightedly as a favorite. Paul habitually kept a pocket full of sugar lumps, stopping to treat tethered horses along the street. He took his brother to a brothel famous for its "French girls," and Theodore, fearful but unwilling to admit unsophistication, had an experience which he found "wild, blood-racking, brain-scarifying," and yet which made him reflect, "I felt as though I were witnessing one of the great horrors and crimes of the soul in the world, a thing, or sin, which, once one passed out of life, might certainly cause one to be grilled in hell. . . ." Just for a look, they went on to the even more luxurious House of All Nations, where one could pick from women of any race, including Indians, Japanese and Negroes, and where the bedroom walls and ceilings were mirrored. All this debauchery was at the opposite pole from the purity exemplified by the White family in Montgomery City. Theodore characteristically was drawn both ways, admitting, "I oscillated between an intense desire to share in the pleasure which all this suggested and a kind of Christian horror of the evil involved," and his fear that "in that direction lay disease, deterioration and death. . . ." [16]

On Sunday Paul took him to Manhattan Beach, where he goggled at the splendid hotels, Pain's spectacular fireworks and the music of Sousa's band, thinking, "I've never lived at all until now!" Then his enjoyment gave way to envy at the flannels, saw-toothed straw hats and white shoes: "Look at all the beautiful women here, the comfortable, well-dressed men! There isn't one who isn't really much better dressed than I am." Finally he succumbed to despair and resentment at his poverty: "How dare so many live and be gay

and comfortable, whereas I was not or could not be so? Who had loaded the
dice in their favor and not in mine, and why?" [17] Returning to the city, he
strode Fifth Avenue, gazing enviously at the mansions of Gould, Havemeyer
and Astor. He admired the newspapers but was intimidated by their air of
authority. Paul, having an innocent faith in his genius, could not understand
what he was waiting for.

"You take my advice," Paul said, "and move down here. The quicker the
better." [18]

All unknowing, Paul doubtless was one of the reasons for Theodore's fear
of New York. What could he be here other than a mere shadow beside his
famous brother? How could he, shy and ugly and moody, compete with
Paul's vast charm? What could he be but an outsider beside Paul, the insider
who knew everyone from the headwaiter at Delmonico's to the horses on
Broadway? New York was thrilling, but it could hurt an outsider.

Theodore went back to Pittsburgh to save money so that he could stand
being hurt for a while.

IV. BLOWN TO BITS

In Pittsburgh, which now seemed a dreary hole with no flavor of
Paris, he shunned entertainment, ate fifteen-cent meals and collided against
Thomas Huxley and Herbert Spencer. He felt his lingering Catholicism drain
away as he read Huxley's *Science and Hebrew Tradition* and *Science and
Christian Tradition*. The Bible, Huxley said, was not revealed truth but
merely a record of religious experiences—erroneous ones at that. Christianity
was only one of many dogmas, and Huxley, the scientist, treated all dogma
as mere superstition.

Dreiser was still in shock when he read Spencer's *First Principles.* Spencer,
the philosopher of evolution, disposed of religion as being a concern of the
"unknowable," interesting to ponder but beyond the realm of true knowledge or facts, which alone were the domain of science. Man was simply a
stage in evolution, a creature responding helplessly to inner physico-chemical
actions over which he had no control. He was a tiny particle of energy, a
mere atom, not only bereft of any authority over his own minuscule inner
compulsions but also buffeted by larger outer forces likewise beyond his
control. Worse yet, man the mechanism was only one of a myriad agencies
through which an Unknown Cause worked via evolution to produce a state
of equilibrium in nature, with the alternating forces of love and hate, good
and evil, life and death fighting to balance each other in an endless universal
pulsation.

"[Spencer] nearly killed me," Dreiser said, "took every shred of belief
away from me; showed me that I was a chemical atom in a whirl of unknown
forces; the realization clouded my mind." [19]

This was a climactic moment in his life, one that affected him permanently.

Spencer destroyed beliefs which he held very dear—convictions not necessarily logical but essential to his happiness. The extent of his hurt showed how deeply he had cherished them. In Dreiser, as in his father, was much of the religious zealot. For all his questioning of the church, his religious rearing had left him with an urgent need for a kindly personal God who rewarded noble effort and punished transgression. Spencer snatched God away, turned him into an impersonal force.

Implicit in Dreiser's belief in God had been a faith in a moral order embodying justice. Spencer obliterated justice as Dreiser had conceived it.

Perhaps strongest of all was Dreiser's sense of individuality, of ego, of success attained through his own genius. Spencer had slain his individuality and therefore his dreams. The young man who set such store by his own inalienable selfhood discovered that he had none. How could an insignificant, will-less machine, buffeted in an inexorable complex of nature along with billions of other heedless machines, have pride or hope? His vision of fame was a bubble. His love for Jug was a humiliating "chemic compulsion."

Unread in philosophy, incomplete in his understanding of Spencer, he nevertheless grasped what struck him as the most appalling idea—the helplessness of the individual. Evidence of this was all around him. The Pittsburgh workers were impotent motes moved to their own tragedy by imponderable forces. Carnegie himself was a similar atom, actuated by chemic compulsions that now made him crush a strike, now made him donate libraries. The prostitute, moved by still another compulsion, sank the needle in her arm. There was no justice, no selfhood. No one could help himself or anyone else.

Spencer had equated him with the amoeba and the ephemerid. He never entirely outlived his dismay. The bitterness was indelible. He would continue to despair that nature or the creative force had failed to build a more perfect universe and to reward genius while heaping riches and fame on fools. And he would continue to blame the church for swindling him, leading him up a bright path of hope blocked in the end by a stone wall of fraud.

Terribly depressed, he did his work for the *Dispatch* automatically. At last he decided that one must follow his star even if it was only an involuntary compulsion, hoping it might be a lucky one like Carnegie's. Since one was hopeless anywhere, one might as well be hopeless in New York as in Pittsburgh. Late in November, 1894, having saved $240 by stern economy, he quit the *Dispatch* and went to New York.[20]

Book Two

MARRIAGE

1. The Atom in New York

1. OUTER AND INIMICAL FORCES

The tall Hoosier stayed with his sister on Fifteenth Street as he canvassed the newspapers. He was shocked to find that he could not reach the editor at any of them, being barred by gum-chewing office boys who snapped, "No vacancies." Paul was on the road with a comedy and would not be back until spring, so New York, gripped by depression, seemed utterly hostile. Meeting repulse at the offices on Printing House Square, Dreiser crossed to City Hall Park, sat among scores of down-and-outers and stared at the swirling human mass and the great buildings which defeated him—the *Tribune, Sun, Press, Times* and *World,* the latter in the gold-domed tower built by Pulitzer, who himself had started in St. Louis.

"But you mustn't worry," Emma told him when he returned. "Paul says you can write wonderfully." [1]

Dreiser later mustered all his nerve at the *World* office, brushed by two office boys who followed him with angry shouts into the editorial room, and attracted the attention of Arthur Brisbane, then a young editor on his way up.

"I want a job," Dreiser almost shouted. [2]

Brisbane, liking his determination, took him to the city editor, and Dreiser delightedly found himself on the staff of the nation's greatest newspaper, a colleague of such famous writers as David Graham Phillips, James Creelman and Reginald De Koven. But the *World* office turned out to be a madhouse, the city editor a snarling savage, and Dreiser discovered that he was working on space, getting $7.50 a column for whatever he wrote that was used. On his first day he made $1.86, a trifle less than the going rate for street sweepers. On some subsequent days he got even less. He was bewildered by the size and ferocity of the *World*'s operations, which made the *Pittsburgh Dispatch* seem like a country weekly, and depressed by the tension and hostility of his fellow workers. "The great city scared me stiff," he later admitted. [3]

A further problem was his sister's straits, for her husband was now unemployed. With Paul away there was no help from that quarter, and Dreiser had to bolster their meager income from two roomers by paying not only for his board and room but making additional payments.

At the *World* he was allowed to write up two-paragraph squibs, but when he arrived with a bang-up story he itched to handle it was given to a regular man who was well paid while Dreiser got only his expenses. The *World* quickly discovered that, whatever his feature abilities might be, he was all thumbs when it came to the curt-and-clear necessities of newswriting. Ironically, he scored a modest success when he was sent to report a tenement fight, found it to be a beer brawl not worth a hundred words, then wrote a humorous and thoroughly fictitious feature account saying that the quarrel had arisen over the noisy wee-hour efforts of a musician, pounding on his piano as he endeavored to compose a waltz. The editor liked it. He used it for a quarter-column ($1.88) and rewarded Dreiser with a follow-up assignment on an affray at the Hoffman House between the bar manager and a wealthy young society man.

Dreiser was beaten before he started by his fear of caste. Intimidated by the famous Hoffman House and its rococo onyx-and-mahogany barroom, he was squelched by the lofty bar manager who said icily that there was never any trouble in *his* bar. Instead of seeking a lesser barman who might give him the facts, he retreated, made a feeble effort to locate the society man involved, then gave up utterly. His editor was vicious about his failure. His stock sank further when he was sent to interview the millionaire Russell Sage, thought wildly, "They might as well have asked me to interview St. Peter," [4] and failed to penetrate Sage's anteroom. For a time he covered Bellevue Hospital and the nearby morgue, where he gazed gloomily at corpses in decomposition. At the city hospital he was sickened by the cynical, sadistic attitude of the staff toward their public charges as well as by the open graft practiced everywhere. When one accident victim was wheeled in, he saw two young surgeons wager over his condition. One said, "Fifty that he's dead," the other, "Fifty that he isn't!" A stethoscope was applied, the man was found dead and $50 changed hands. Forgetting that this was precisely the kind of story the crusading *World* might splash on the front page, Dreiser did nothing with it.[5]

Simultaneously he had to help his sister Emma in her growing domestic crisis. Weeping, she told him that her only income was the stipend she got from her lodgers, that she could no longer meet her expenses and that Hopkins was pressing her to rent rooms for immoral purposes. Dreiser urged her to force her husband to find work by leaving him and taking cheaper quarters—a move she feared to make until Dreiser engineered a hoax in which she reluctantly joined.

Pulling a long face, he told Hopkins he had failed in New York and was returning to Pittsburgh. Instead, he took a room at $1.50 a week on grimy Fourth Street just east of the Bowery, unaware that the place was a bedhouse and that he served as a screen against the police. From there he routed a letter to Emma through a journalist friend in Pittsburgh, telling her he was well located there and inviting her to join him, pointedly excluding Hopkins from the invitation. Hopkins took the hint, stirred himself and got a hotel job in Brooklyn. In February, Emma bade Hopkins a stagey farewell before "leaving for Pittsburgh," actually moving only a few blocks to a cheap apartment on West Seventeenth Street but moving permanently out of Hopkins' life.[6]

On Fourth Street, Dreiser, sensing that his days at the *World* were numbered, began studying the magazines with a view to writing fiction. As a
feature writer in St. Louis and Pittsburgh he had been a success. As a straight
newsman on the *World* he was a failure. He blamed it not on his own sloppy
writing but on his poor physical condition resulting from starving himself in
Pittsburgh to save money, and on the refusal of his editors, with their
"unwarranted and unnecessary airs," to give him a fair chance. The crisis
came when he brought in a story and again was told by an editor to give the
facts to another man to write.

"I don't see why I should always have to do this," Dreiser protested. "I'm
not a beginner at this game."

"Maybe . . . but we have a feeling that you haven't proved to be of much
use to us," the editor snapped.[7]

Dreiser, terribly hurt, quit before he could be fired.

II. THE SIDEWALKS OF NEW YORK

In his off-Bowery room, in an atmosphere of furtive prostitution
superintended by his landlady, Dreiser studied the fiction in *Harper's*, *Century* and the *Atlantic Monthly*, knowing that such writers as Mrs. Humphrey
Ward, William Dean Howells and Charles Dudley Warner were well paid
for their work. These stories invariably dealt with situations in which virtue,
though assailed, was triumphant. This was so different from what he had
observed in Chicago, St. Louis, Pittsburgh and New York that he was
puzzled, thinking that these writers must occupy a social world higher and
nobler than any he had been privileged to see. He wrote several yarns
imitating the nobility-requited theme, but they were rejected. Worried at his
failure, he was further depressed by the terrible squalor of the Bowery and his
fear that he would become a part of it. His funds were dwindling when he
returned home one evening to find that the place had been raided, a policeman
posted at the door.

"And where do you think you're going?" the bluecoat demanded.

Dreiser explained that he was an innocent lodger, a writer—a story the
policeman sneered at until Dreiser took him up and showed him his manuscripts. "Well, all right, pack it up and I'll let ye go," the patrolman growled.[8]

Dreiser took refuge at the Mills Hotel on Bleecker Street, where for
twenty-five cents verminous bums got a bed for the night. He ate the
cheapest meals at Childs' restaurants. He wrote more happy-ending stories
and got more rejections—even tried the newspapers again. By the spring of
1895 he had to pawn his $25 watch. The business panic was worse instead of
better, throngs of unemployed haunted the breadlines and soup kitchens, and
unless something happened he would have to join the lineup.

One day as he walked down Houston Street a pretty Italian girl standing in
front of a restaurant greeted him with a smile and a joke. He stopped to talk
with her, learned that her father owned the restaurant and rented rooms

above, and was surprised when she invited him inside. He stayed with her for a few days, finding her a charming companion after his loneliness. Her parents offered him free board and room, looking on him as a prospective son-in-law—a seductive proposal for a man flirting with starvation—but he disentangled himself for three reasons: they were Catholics, and he had turned with some bitterness against the church; he still had faith in his "grand destiny" and feared that these simple Italians would stifle his genius; and he thought of Jug, waiting for him in Missouri. He was on his uppers when he swallowed his pride and walked into the Twentieth Street offices of Howley, Haviland & Company with a proposition for Paul, who had just returned from his last tour as an actor. The partners made an odd trio. Pat Howley was a tiny hunchback (Paul, like Theodore, believed that hunchbacks brought one luck); Fred Haviland was tall and slender; and Paul's enormous girth reflected the pleasures of the table and the bar.[9]

Theodore had noticed on the stands a magazine published by the well-established Ditson music firm, containing a melange of popular songs, stories and pictures. It was selling well. If Howley-Haviland would let him edit a similar magazine, he proposed, he would make it a better one and it would help sell the company's songs.

Howley-Haviland were now prospering, one of their new songs, "The Sidewalks of New York," just becoming a smash hit. Paul and his partners agreed, although apparently with some misgivings on the part of Howley, who ran the business end, for he set Theodore's salary at $10 a week through the summer and $15 after the magazine got under way with its October 1895 issue. He resented the low salary, but it saved him from destitution.

Ev'ry Month—the name he gave his magazine—ranged from 32 to 48 pages in large format, was built around the four songs per issue that constituted its *raison d'être*, and was poorly printed, but it was dear to him at first. He selected fiction, poetry and pictures, dispensed household hints, wrote captions, did occasional interviews, wrote book reviews and—best of all—had a department called "Reflections" in which he addressed his own meditations to the reader, signing himself "The Prophet." Here, for the first time in his life, he could write with comparative freedom. He so enjoyed the privilege that he perhaps abused it a trifle. His "Reflections" were confined to no mere column but filled from two to seven whole printed pages in which he roamed ambitiously for a twenty-four-year-old, covering all creation, attacking corruption, upholding nobility of character, discussing war clouds in Europe, atrocities in Armenia, mental telepathy, the possibility of life on Mars, and the philosophy of Herbert Spencer, which had become his religion.[10]

After more than a year of wrestling with Spencer's evolutionary theories, his first shock at finding himself a will-less mechanism moved by cosmic chemical and physical forces had subsided. He had decided that Spencer's philosophy, cruel as it was, explained the world's cruelties and in its great precision and order contained real beauty if a man were strong enough to accept it, as he told himself he was. Spencer, he informed his readers, was "a great father of knowledge" whose teachings would eventually enlighten all mankind.[11] Showing his own inner need for a God, he took comfort in Spencer's acknowledgment of an Unknown Cause which if not precisely God was at any rate an awe-inspiring Thing, a Creator of wonders. And man, even if he was only one of a myriad of living creatures, could take pride in being the highest form of life, able to harness science to his aid and to produce a human specimen as inspiring as Spencer himself. It is not impossible that Haviland and Howley wished that Theodore would write less about such subjects as Spencer and more about musical topics which might help sell such songs as "Moonlight Kisses Gavotte" and "We Go to Church as Lovers—Come Back as Man and Wife."

He worked at the Twentieth Street office amid the audible banging of one or more Howley-Haviland pianos and often the tenor fortissimo of a vaude-villian trying out a new song. Paul, a simpleton when it came to business, was "outside man" for the firm, covering the Broadway spots where the clan gathered, urging composers to publish with Howley-Haviland and coaxing actors to sing their songs. Although this was pure fun for him, he was happiest when he was composing. He could rip out a tune with such speed that one commentator joked, "Paul Dresser hasn't written a new song in twenty minutes. I'm worried." Since his nationally popular "The Letter That Never Came," written while Theodore was in Warsaw, he had turned out scores of tunes, many of them ephemeral but touching springs of sentiment that put them on parlor pianos all over the country, among them "My Mother Told Me So," "Here Lies an Actor," "The Convict and the Bird," "The Blue and the Gray" and "The Pardon Came Too Late." He took his songs seriously and, like Theodore, he never forgot his mother.

"As long as the world rolls around," he said, "there will come up little petty incidents that would for the moment make us all kin. While cynics might refer to my little simple melodies as trash and [the] words as maudlin sentiment, still to me, with apologies to none, the grandest word in English or any other language is 'mother.' "[12]

He was proud of his huge scrapbook containing letters from thousands of admirers and clippings of Sunday-supplement chronicles about the amazing Paul Dresser. Money poured in and he poured it out again. He cared not a fig for Herbert Spencer, his favorite reading being Bill Nye. He lived grandly at the Gilsey House in a suite containing a great square rosewood piano over which he worked for hours in the throes of composition. Whenever he was in the office he would settle his six-foot, 300-pound bulk at a cigar-burned piano there, his rump overwhelming the bench as he worked over tunes, hunting for something new and sentimental. Theodore once watched him finger the keys, perfecting an unfinished melody, trying this, trying that, as engrossed as Mozart until at last he was satisfied.

"Listen to this, will you, Thee?" he said.[13]

He played and sang the first verse and chorus of "Just Tell Them That You Saw Me," becoming so moved that he had to stop near the end and wipe away his tears. Theodore thought it a pretty thing in its sphere, though he had a low opinion of the sphere. He was astonished a few months later, after the song had been advertised and sung in theaters, to find that the public went mad about it, orders flowing in so fast that the Howley-Haviland staff worked overtime shipping bundles of copies of the latest Paul Dresser hit all over the country.

Theodore's love for Paul contained envy that at times rose to anger. Paul was expert in his imitations of Irishmen, Jews or Germans, loving all jokes, vulgar or otherwise. When he heard a new one he insisted that Theodore accompany him along Broadway, where he would render it with gestures, sending groups into gales of laughter at a dozen saloons. He had a stage trick of hooking his derby hatbrim under his back collar so that when he nodded his head the derby would lift miraculously—a dodge he used as he sang:

> Let me tell you of a fellah, lah-de-dah!
> A fellah who's a swell, ah, lah-de-dah! [14]

At each "lah-de-dah" his hat would flip, making observers roll in merriment. Theodore, chuckling himself, was fascinated by Paul as a miracle of human chemistry but also was inclined to regard him as essentially trivial and bereft of common sense. Paul could not turn down a Broadway beggar. He was forever slipping a twenty to a broken-down actor, paying a fine for a friend, making good the deficit of his Knights of Columbus chapter or buying a coffin so that a late song-writer could have a decent burial.

"Why don't you save your money?" Theodore demanded. "Why should you give it to every Tom, Dick and Harry that asks you?" [15]

But there was no more curbing Paul's generosity than his occasional weakness for liquor or his perpetual love of women, which Theodore found amusing and a little ridiculous in such a self-proclaimed Catholic. In his songs Paul sighed over the innocence and sweetness of maidenhood, whereas in real life his aim seemed to be to obliterate all innocence. On one occasion an actor friend disguised himself with sideburns and a goatee, entered the Howley-Haviland office and clapped a hand to his hip as he shouted at Paul, "So you're the scoundrel that's been running around with my wife, are you?"

Paul retreated in fright. "Don't shoot!" he gasped. [16]

The cronies gathered there, all in on the hoax, burst out laughing. Paul sulked for a moment, then joined in the mirth.

III. THE DIAMOND-AND-SILK DREAM

By 1896 *Ev'ry Month* was a modest success. Although Theodore had to cater to his readers with fashion articles, poetry by the Duer sisters, light fiction by Amelia Barr and articles by his Toledo friend Arthur Henry, he wrote his "Prophet" column in deadly earnest. More important, he had the perception to seek out and publish a story by Bret Harte and another by Stephen Crane. Crane's "A Mystery of Heroism" was hidden between a waltz, "Bright Summer Days," and a ballad, "In Sunny Spain," but it was *there*.[17] Although no record shows how he obtained the Crane piece, or what he thought of it, its inclusion in this gimcrack journal read mostly by conventional women is significant. The young editor yearned for something better. He recognized quality and realism in writing, even though his lighthearted audience forbade more than a flavor of it.

His judgment in matters non-literary, however, was apt to be emotional rather than analytical. Distressed by the continuing business depression, he found the solution in the heady Populist cry for "free silver" that came out of the West. And although he hated the newspapers for their falsehoods (and how they had treated him), he gave ear to the yellow-journal propaganda about Spanish atrocities in Cuba, repeated them in *Ev'ry Month* and in his guise as "The Prophet" said it was high time the United States interfered. "It doesn't look as though we have a heart," he wrote.[18]

In April he made a quick trip to Missouri to visit Jug, whom he had not seen in twenty-one months and who was now teaching in Danville. Jug was no Populist, her father evidently being a conservative believer in the gold standard, but Theodore forgot politics in a renewed ardor for his red-haired fiancée that drove him almost crazy when he had to return to New York. All his doubts had been temporarily dispelled by warm Missouri kisses. He became neurotically ill if three days passed with no letter from Jug, and when he took lone evening walks in Madison Square, walled in by handsome town houses and the Fifth Avenue Hotel, Delmonico's and the Hoffman House, he dreamed of occupying a mansion with her. He would clothe her in silks, make her dazzle with diamonds. When he saw Sousa's *El Capitan* and heard the prima donna sing her love song, he identified her with Jug and melted with tenderness. Yet after Pittsburgh and years of reporting he had an awareness of a need for realism in art and he knew that *El Capitan* was largely spurious.

One of the most frankly erotic of men, he built reveries of wealth, of surrounding Jug with voluptuous Oriental splendor in which they would enjoy perpetual passionate embrace. He put her name on short pieces in *Ev'ry Month*, even managed to get her name on the cover, and sent her copies. He suffered insomnia, at times regarding himself as an invalid.

He was so ardent an admirer of the Democratic candidate, William Jennings Bryan, that he was genuinely excited when Bryan came to speak in New York. On August 12, Dreiser, the hunchback Howley and a songwriter named Theo Morse fought their way in steaming heat with 15,000 others into Madison Square Garden, only to see Bryan drop his usual spellbinding and disappoint his audience with a cautious speech read from manuscript. The next night Dreiser saw Bryan back in form as he addressed a

street throng from the balcony of the Hotel Bartholdi off Madison Square—
massive head shaking, hair disheveled, arms waving, voice booming like an
organ. Dreiser loved it. He would always be more than a little naïve politically.

Sexual delight was as essential to him as eating. Throughout his adult life he
was a libertine, and it can be said with certainty that he was not "true" to Jug.
He was not one to hoard nickels with marriage in view. His salary was
boosted with the success of his magazine, and he lived up to it. A confirmed
theatergoer, with Theo Morse he attended *Lost, Strayed or Stolen* at the
Fifth Avenue Theater, in which Paul had a leading role, and others, including
A Parlor Match, starring the kinetic Anna Held, who he enviously wrote
drew "a pitiful salary of $1,500 per week." [19] With Haviland, Howley, Morse,
Paul, the "Yellow Kid" cartoonist R. F. Outcault and others he enjoyed a stag
banquet with ten courses of food and eight kinds of wine that lasted uproariously until morning. He sometimes blew himself to a Delmonico dinner.
He went on summer outings to Atlantic City. Rubbing elbows with the
prosperous, he emulated them as best he could. Clothes as always being a
symbol of success after his ragged boyhood, he seized at the symbol, not
content with cheap ready-made suits but having himself measured by a
tailor.

Jug, economizing in Missouri and sewing on her trousseau, must have read
his letters about New York high life and wondered if he was sacrificing
anything toward their future. While she yearned for marriage, he was obsessed with wealth and was also concerned about the restraints Missouri
Methodism would place on his freedom. On her part, Jug could not forget
that in the spring she would be twenty-eight years old.

Although one of his strongest traits was this driving ambition for money
and success, he had already reached a dichotomy which enabled him to
believe the direct opposite. At almost this same time the mercurial Prophet
was writing an editorial for *Ev'ry Month* which of course Jug read—he sent
her every issue—in which he assailed hollow ambition and the worship of
pelf and adjured his readers:

> Rather in this life seek well-doing and content. To build up a fabric of
> love for others: to possess and strengthen the mind in the knowledge of right
> deeds well done, for to walk in virtue and simplicity blessed on every hand, is
> better than riches and great honor, and more to be desired than power and
> great place.[20]

One doubts that the Prophet was merely filling an empty column with
tongue in cheek. It is a safe guess that he meant this, at the time.

IV. ON THE BANKS OF THE WABASH

Bryan and silver were defeated by McKinley and gold, but Bryan
would long remain a hero to Dreiser. He took comfort in reading Darwin,

who confirmed his belief in evolution and also gave interesting theories as to why the male courted the female. Ed Dreiser arrived on a visit from Chicago, determined to become an actor, and recited hunks of Shakespeare to Theodore in a resonant stage voice. Christmas of 1896 brought a large family reunion. Austin Brennan and Mame (who apparently had married) arrived from Chicago with Claire to spend the holiday at Emma's apartment with Theodore, Paul, Ed and Sylvia Dreiser, Sylvia now living in New York and aspiring to become a song-writer like Paul.

They often still called Theodore by his Germanic family nicknames of Dorsch or Dorse. Perhaps as they gathered around the table they talked of the absent Dreisers, all in Chicago except Rome, who might be anywhere in God's creation. Father Dreiser, hale at seventy-five, was convinced that the whole world was going to hell; the still beautiful Theresa and her artist husband Davis were childless; Al, whom everybody liked, was an unsuccessful wage-earner. There must have been loving recollections of Sarah Dreiser, who Mame said "beyond doubt was one of the greatest women of all time." [21]

Claire, whom Theodore probably had not seen since the World's Fair, was ailing, soon to go to Arizona to fight tuberculosis. Paul, who had brought presents for all, was the life of the party, and Brennan, still traveling for a coffin concern, drank too much and became ill, causing Theodore to feel that he would meet an early death from overindulgence.

Still the fetishist, Theodore kept one of Jug's slippers and one glove in his room to worship. For a time during Ed's stay in New York, Theodore lived with him at Paul's roomy apartment. But Theodore, the sensualist who could not abide off-color stories and blushed at anything suggestive, was annoyed by Paul's uproarious indecency. When Paul one morning paraded in the nude, a towel draped over his prominent masculinity, Theodore left in anger and returned to his own lodgings.[22]

Ev'ry Month was displaying more advertising—Pears' Soap, Sapolio, pianos, bicycles, furniture—indicating a growing readership that must have been lured in part by the human touch of its editor. Yet Theodore was often unhappy, bitter, sharp of tongue. He detested the hypocrisies of convention, the taste of the masses for sweet nothings, the one-track Howley-Haviland aim to sell more music. The firm regarded the magazine solely as a promotion for its songs, whereas he thought the songs trivial, gagged at much of the editorial material he was forced to print and yearned for freedom to print work he could respect. There were disagreements with Howley and Haviland over this. His disgruntlement increased with a visit to New York by the light-hearted Arthur Henry, who had quit the *Toledo Blade*, served for a time as publicity man for the magician Hermann the Great, and now was sounding out the editors with story ideas. An enemy of convention himself, Henry called at Theodore's grimy office and found him disconsolate.

"I am drawing a good salary," he said. "The things I am able to get the boss to publish that I believe in are very few. The rest must tickle the vanity or cater to the foibles and prejudices of readers. From my standpoint, I am not succeeding." [23]

Henry, an incurable optimist who believed in acting on impulse and was fond of such aphorisms as "the liberty of to-morrow is never worth the slavery of today," obviously felt Theodore a needless slave. He had a high regard for Theodore's writing abilities, and his nonchalance about the morrow must have made Dreiser feel a drone chained to a desk. Henry and his young wife Maude had recently bought a fine old mansion in Maumee, south of Toledo, with a formidable mortgage that troubled him not at all. Before he returned west, he urged Theodore to join him there so that they could write together—a flyer Dreiser was not yet ready to take and which indeed would be hard to explain to the waiting Jug.

At times he was so angry at (or jealous of) Paul that he would scarcely speak to him. But one summer Sunday in 1897 the brothers were at the office, Paul improvising on the piano as usual.

"Why don't you give me an idea for [a song] once in a while, sport?" he said.

"Me?" Theodore said almost contemptuously. "I can't write those things. Why don't you write something about a state or a river? Look at 'My Old Kentucky Home,' 'Dixie,' 'Old Black Joe'—why don't you do something like that, something that suggests a part of America? People like that. Take Indiana—what's the matter with it—the Wabash River? It's as good as any other river, and you were 'raised' beside it." [24]

Paul beamed. He urged Theodore to write the words, which he would set to music. Theodore was disdainful, but at Paul's insistence he conjured up a few sentimental Hoosier thoughts and assembled them into a nostalgic ballad, reworking his lines to make them scan and to achieve the necessary rhyme. He tired of it after finishing the first verse and chorus:

> 'Round my Indiana homestead waves the cornfield,
>   In the distance loom the woodlands clear and cool;
> Often times my thoughts revert to scenes of childhood,
>   Where I first received my lessons, Nature's school;
> But one thing there is missing in the picture—
>   Without her face it seems so incomplete—
> I long to see my mother in the doorway,
>   As she stood there years ago her boy to greet.
>
> Oh, the moonlight's fair tonight along the Wabash,
>   From the fields there comes the breath of new mown hay,
> Through the sycamores the candle lights are gleaming,
>   On the banks of the Wabash far away. [25]

Although Theodore ever afterward scoffed at this poesy, there is little doubt that he was thinking tenderly of his mother as he wrote it. Paul was enthusiastic, urging him to write a second verse—something with a girl in it—but he refused. Not long afterward, in one of his thornier moods, he quarreled with Paul, then quarreled also apparently with Howley, demanded a better salary and more editorial freedom, and found himself without a job. The September 1897 *Ev'ry Month* was his last.

2. Sister Carrie

I. THE HACK-WRITER

As Freud later said, "A man who has been the indisputable favorite of his mother keeps for life the feeling of a conqueror. . . ."[1] Strong though this feeling was in Dreiser, as was his reverence for realism, his next move showed that his need for success was even stronger. He did not yet know his own powers. He became a hack-writer.

At twenty-six, after two years on *Ev'ry Month*, he had enough seasoning in a cynical game to know the first rule of survival as a writer: conform. Magazines were in business to please customers and make money. He conformed, although it must have been hateful. Already acquainted with some editors, he set to work with furious energy on factual articles and occasional verse. He dreamed up ideas, did his own legwork and sold with growing regularity to magazines ranging from *Munsey's* and *Ainslee's* to *Metropolitan* and *Cosmopolitan*. Early in 1898 he began a series of "inspirational" interviews with men of wealth and achievement for Dr. Orison Swett Marden, founder of the new *Success* magazine. Richard Duffy, an editor at *Ainslee's*, was so impressed by Dreiser's abilities that he got him on the magazine as a writer and part-time consulting editor at $150 a month. Soon he was making an average income of close to $100 a week.

At the same time he was indulging the habit of sloppy writing that would dog him through life. He had a bent for saying the same thing twice or more. His grammar was poor, he was no connoisseur of words and he could not master the art of organizing his writing so that one telling point followed another. Added to this was his fear that life was slipping away, that he must hurry, hurry, make more money so that he could realize his dream of love in a mansion. He worked on three or four articles at a time, with a poem or two thrown in, simultaneously hatching a half-dozen new ideas, always thinking of payment, not quality, since it was all trash anyway. He had no patience to toil over a script, polish it, prune away the excess. "I have an easy pen," he boasted—too easy. He got by very well because he was bursting with ideas for articles, and because amid the disorder of his writing could be found—if one had time to search—astute observation, random sentences of striking force and a powerful interest in humanity.

"By the way," Orison Swett Marden wrote him, "we shall have to charge you about ten dollars on each article for editing manuscript. . . ." And about a later article Marden complained, "We had to do a great deal of work on [it]."[2]

A rejection came from Ellery Sedgwick of *Leslie's Weekly* because "the 'average reader' . . . would wonder in reading it where the 'story' was going to begin." ³ *Cosmopolitan* wrote him, "We would . . . like permission to materially change or rewrite and condense the manuscript." ⁴ "I would have speech with thee . . . anent the Longfellow article," wrote Duffy of *Ainslee's*.⁵ "The paper is too long," wrote *Munsey's*.⁶

Despite such criticism he was doing well. "Gee whiz! What a lot of money you must be pulling in," Marden wrote.⁷ The Spencerian-Darwinian Dreiser had observed, "In the presence of [a great man] pity has no mission. . . . Nothing can withstand him, for he is working in harmony with great laws which place splendid powers in his hands and assist him to rise." He added, "It is only the unfit who fail. . . ." ⁸ He fought for money and success. Toward editors he was a trifle truculent, often setting a price on a manuscript and asking its return if the price was not met, expecting quick payment, accusing *Leslie's* of "prejudice" against him, complaining to *Success* about the payment for an article, getting a lawyer to threaten suit against *The New York Times* for failing to pay for a piece they had not used. He added to his income by selling pictures on art and other subjects to the magazines.

He left his hall bedroom and moved to the Salmagundi Club at 14 West Twelfth Street, where he hobnobbed with the painters J. Francis Murphy and Bruce Crane. Sartorially he was a cane-swinging dandy. One spring night in 1898 he heard a knot of young men singing in the street and recognized phrases about sycamores and candle light and the Wabash River. They were his words. Obviously Paul had another hit song in "On the Banks of the Wabash." Theodore was so resentful that he no longer called on Paul even though the melody was haunting enough to awaken memories of Mother and bring him close to tears.

Now he could afford to marry Jug, and indeed she was counting on a spring wedding in Missouri, with all the relatives gathered, but he was temporizing, telling her of his busy-ness, pushing back the still undeclared date. He was terrified at the thought of marriage, in part because of shyness at being the center of a solemn spectacle, in part because his affections were roving as usual. He had become friendly with Mary Annabel Fanton, a pretty and intellectual editor on *Demorest's Family Magazine*, who bought his poetry and invited him to dinner at "a big open fire." ⁹ He was more than friendly with a young woman writer—so involved that he debated breaking off with Jug and marrying the writer until he decided that her ego was as large as his own and that two such temperaments would certainly clash. His attitude toward marriage could veer from a calculating appraisal of its effect on his own happiness and his career to a sudden rush of emotional pity for Jug, who had such *faith* in him. There was also the growing feeling that the safest course was not to marry at all, take what he wanted, keep free. At times the ring and the promise to Jug took on the aspect of an I. O. U.

To her, the ring and the promise were solemn vows, pledges of holy matrimony. Reaching her twenty-ninth birthday on April 29, 1898, she was undoubtedly applying pressure and he was putting her off.

He noticed scornfully that "On the Banks of the Wabash" was being sung in theaters, played by bands and street-organs, mentioned in the newspapers—a bigger hit even than "Just Tell Them That You Saw Me." One day by chance he met Paul on Broadway, clad in a straw hat, smart summer suit and carrying a gold-headed cane.

"Ah," Theodore said sarcastically. "On the banks, I see."

Paul was cordial. "On the banks," he agreed. "You turned the trick for me, Thee, that time. What are you doing now? Why don't you ever come and see me? I'm still your brother, you know. A part of that is really yours."

"Cut that!" Theodore snapped, and walked on coldly after a few more words.[10]

He loved and hated his brother, wrote furiously for money and scorned his own commercialism, pursued women as he felt pangs of remorse over the waiting, virginal Jug, and paid for these emotional clashes in periods of nervousness and insomnia. With a young soprano, who would later appear in *The "Genius"* as Christina Channing he enjoyed a round of intimacies in a rural Virginia retreat, so fascinated by her lovemaking that he was hurt to discover that she had no desire to marry him, being dedicated to her voice. He was plagued by his old neurosis, his feeling of impermanence in a world where time rushed on, his fear that his "grand destiny" was escaping him as death drew closer.

He found that rocking steadily in a rocking chair gave him some relief. A non-smoker, he developed a habit of pleating his handkerchief carefully, then folding it into a cube, finally flinging it out like a flag and starting the folding process all over again—a routine he could continue for hours and which calmed him somewhat. He sought relief by visiting a female "thought healer," finding wry humor in learning that his publisher friend, Dr. Marden, the apostle of cool and successful thinking, was himself a nervous wreck from overwork and was consulting the same healer. Once, seated at his desk, Dreiser was seized by a strange feeling that he was *unable to move*. He managed to reach his telephone and call the healer, who commanded him over the wire to concentrate mentally on her imagined presence with him, which he did until he gratefully recovered the power to get up and walk.[11]

II. THE PALE FLAME OF DUTY

What with his own problems and his conviction that he was crumbling physically, Dreiser did not enlist in the war in Cuba and contented himself with writing a patriotic poem about it. His sister Claire was in Phoenix, writing him, "I hate to think I am a consumptive and doomed to end my days in that slow, miserable way. . . ."[12] His sister Theresa only the previous fall had been struck by a train in Chicago and instantly killed. His sister Sylvia had given up her song-writing and recently married Hide Kishima, a Japanese-born photographer of Newark. His sister Mame and Austin Brennan now lived in Rochester, and old John Dreiser with them. His brother Ed had arrived in New York once more for the big stage gamble, and while Theodore liked Ed and was glad to see him it was of course Paul who took Ed in hand, introduced him to Clyde Fitch and other theater celebrities, so that Ed soon had a part in a road show.[13]

Theodore worked hard when he was not sunk in depression. He went to Long Island to gather material for a story about oysters and clams for *Leslie's* and another about William Cullen Bryant's home for *Munsey's*, then hurried on to New Haven, Bridgeport and Stamford to research an article about cartridge factories for *Cosmopolitan*. He described the Harlem River Speedway for *Ainslee's*, explained the use of carrier pigeons in wartime for *Demorest's*, interviewed the artist Irving Wiles for *Metropolitan*, did a piece on "The Harp" for *Cosmopolitan*,[14] supplied poems for *Munsey's* and *Cosmopolitan* and was planning a trip to Chicago for *Success* and other magazines. Pressing for money, he was sometimes careless, sometimes apparently not averse to lifting easy copy. *Ainslee's* complained that he botched the captions on a group of pictures he sent them. A later Dreiser article caused trouble, *Ainslee's* wiring him:

WARD DENYING SCULPTURE ARTICLE WANTS RETRACTION BY US COME DOWN TO-MORROW.

Concerning still another *Ainslee's* article, about the sculptor Henry Shrady, Duffy wrote, "It is most unfortunate that the *World* on p. 25 of the supplement yesterday, had the same article almost verbatim. . . ."[15] Dreiser was caught by a sharp reader of his cartridge-factory article in *Cosmopolitan*, who wrote the publisher, "I find matter copied bodily, without credit, from the catalogue of the Winchester Arms Co."[16]

Insomnia plagued him. His new status as a successful writer and man of the world dramatized Jug's limitations—a puritan, a Methodist, a country schoolmarm whose greatest fling was one trip to the Chicago World's Fair. Yet he still yearned for her in his vacillating way, and the events of June shook him. On June 14 he boarded a train for St. Louis to visit Jug, since he had work to do in Chicago. The mere thought of seeing her had brought the vision of her close again. He had four days with her, days that had precisely the same effect as his visit two years earlier. He left for Chicago almost weeping.

In a fog of adoration he strode Chicago, getting material for a half-dozen articles. He interviewed the highly successful Philip D. Armour for *Success*—then the equally prosperous Marshall Field for the same magazine. He visited Robert Lincoln, son of the Great Emancipator and president of the Pullman Company, who aided Dreiser in his article about Pullman for *Ainslee's*. He called on Alexander Revell, the furniture millionaire, and on Dr. Frank Gunsaulas, the president of Armour Institute. He took notes on the Chicago drainage canal for another *Ainslee's* piece.[17] He went to Jackson Park to see the remnants of the World's Fair where he and Jug had met. He stayed at the Palmer House, dined at the Athletic Club, and made frequent trips to the post office to see if there was a letter from his beloved.

But there was no constancy in him. Already he was pondering the terrible finality of marriage and the fidelity the chaste Jug would expect. On the train homeward July 1, he had as his seat partner the eminent Dr. Gunsaulas, who was scheduled to lecture in New York and who, like Dreiser, was an admirer of Bryan. Apparently at this time Dreiser moved from the Salmagundi Club to 232 West Fifteenth Street, where he was exposed to refreshing new stimuli. Through open rear windows visible from his own he saw young women recklessly shedding garments in the summer heat. In September he traveled to Ilion, New York, to do a story on a typewriter factory there. Returning on the night boat from Albany, with moonlight bathing the deck, he saw a blissful young couple enter their stateroom and was filled with combined delight and envy. He eavesdropped at their window. He had put much thought on his nuptial night with Jug, which had to be perfection, and now he had it—they would marry in Jersey City, then take the best stateroom on that same boat.

He was doing a sketch for *The Saturday Evening Post* and a story on the Haverstraw brickworks for someone else, he was off to Maine for material about Longfellow and Blaine, there were other women, the image of Jug faded, and September and October were gone. Then came a letter from Rose White, the younger sister Dreiser sometimes thought he liked better than Jug—a very private letter reminding him of his promises and of Jug's despair, so much like the letter Dreiser later put in his "fictional" account of this odd affair, *The "Genius."* [18]

This was reality, and it shocked him. True, he loved Jug—or did he? He could never make up his mind because he was forever weighing the factors: sincere affection and sincere doubts, his desire to have the advantages of both estates and the disadvantages of neither, the pleasures of wifely admiration and home cooking plus the perfect freedom of the artist, philosopher and rake.

Unable to face a family wedding, he arranged to meet Jug in Washington. She arrived with her sister Rose (for whom he still had a secret passion) and on December 28, 1898, Theodore Dreiser and Sara Osborne White were married on Massachusetts Avenue by a Methodist clergyman named J. W. Duffy. Jug was four months shy of thirty. Dreiser, four months over twenty-seven, later described the event as "the pale flame of duty." [19]

III. RELUCTANT NOVELIST

The semi-young couple took a New York apartment and enjoyed connubial joy marred temporarily by difficulties of adjustment which Dreiser later in *The "Genius"* described with apparent deadly accuracy. Jug was hardly in the position of a bride who had been swept off her feet by an urgent lover. She had waited six years for him, during the last two of which he had been prosperous but elusive. Forced at last to apply pressure, she had been in a nervous, despairing condition by the time they were married. On top of this, the ceremony took place in seclusion, unattended by any of her relatives except Rose or any of his—a secrecy he laid to his shyness but which also might imply lack of pride. When they took up housekeeping, she discovered that he had not told his relatives and friends, who exhibited astonishment when they called and found him married. A few of his bohemian acquaintances, some of them women, apparently were not warmly cordial at first, annoyed by Dreiser's failure to tell them and regarding Jug as something of a backwoods interloper. His lack of subtlety and tact in such matters was disastrous. The whole effect was hardly flattering to Jug, who was hurt and upset.

But she loved him dearly, waited on him with devotion and called him Honeybugs. He called her Kitten, discovering that she was as passionate as any non-Methodist. As he described it, "she had come to the marriage bed with a cumulative and intense passion," and he found her "astonishing and delightful." [20]

In July they heeded Arthur Henry's summons and went to Maumee, Ohio. The Henry home there, a handsome old fourteen-room riverfront pile fronted by four two-story Doric pillars, was in part a monument to the earning capacities of his peppery wife, Maude Wood Henry. Since he had left the Blade, his income had been irregular, but Mrs. Henry had recently finished thirty-six weeks in charge of publicity for the Theodore Thomas orchestra. The Henrys had had fun in Maumee, writing, putting out a paper called the Maumee Liar and assembling a group of actors for an outdoor production of As You Like It, but Mrs. Henry was not so oblivious of their large mortgage as was her husband.

Henry escorted Dreiser to the basement study, a wood-paneled room with fireplace, a bearskin rug and even a comfortable rocker with a broad arm for copy paper, providentially designed for the rocker-loving Dreiser. Jug, an excellent cook, took over the kitchen while Mrs. Henry kept house. It was an idyllic spot, for in the morning the two men would trot across the back yard, plunge into the river, return for a hearty breakfast and then fall to their writing. On one occasion they traveled to Battle Creek, returning with a box of health food on which they proposed to live while they collaborated on an article, "How to Live on Eight Cents a Day," but a chicken dinner prepared by Jug ended that.

In the evenings the men would don white ducks, the women full-skirted frocks, and sit on the back porch to talk and sing snatches of ballads—possibly even "On the Banks of the Wabash"—as bullfrogs croaked in the moon-bathed river. Dreiser and Henry, artists and philosophers both, were devoted to each other. Only once was Mrs. Henry able to promote a visit to friends in Toledo—a party at which Jug, obviously a happy bride, amused the guests by singing a comic song. Dreiser even forgot his nerves. Forty-six years later, Mrs. Henry recalled him as tranquil: "Chewing slowly and meditatively, with closed eyes, the great American novelist-to-be rocked back and forth, singing a bit in a hoarse voice." [21] In 1894 Henry had been the city editor who might or might not give Dreiser a job. Now Dreiser had forged ahead of him, was listed in the 1899 *Who's Who* as an editor, poet and author, contributor to such national journals as *Cosmopolitan* and *The Saturday Evening Post*. Dreiser, the pessimist, was stimulated by the light-hearted Henry, by Henry's admiration for his writing, by Henry's insistence that he should get busy on a novel or at the very least some short stories. "I never had the slightest idea that I would ever be a novelist," Dreiser said later. Henry gave him the encouragement he needed. He did not yet start a novel, but at Henry's urging he did finish an eerie tale which emerged as "The Shining Slave Makers," in which one Robert McEwen, lost in dreams, becomes a member of an ant colony in mortal struggle with other ants, and is saved from destruction only by awakening to reality.

"[Henry] insisted on my going on," Dreiser recalled, "that it was good— and I thought he was kidding me, that it was rotten. . . ." [22]

Maude Henry did the worrying for all four. Until the Dreisers came the Henrys had lived cheaply, but now, with farm-bred Jug in charge of the menu for almost two months and Dreiser eating like a horse, Mrs. Henry's nest egg shrank so low that she warned her husband.

"He at once looked so injured and abused," she recalled, "that one would think I had produced this disaster with malice aforetent. What he did was to tell Dreiser who, no doubt thinking this was a great way to entertain visitors . . . loaned him a hundred or two dollars, and without my knowledge or consent, Arthur promptly made over a half-interest in the House of Four Pillars to him." [23]

So they each owned half of the mortgaged house, a transaction that seemed to seal their *Blutbruderschaft*. When the Dreisers left for New York in September, Arthur went with them, leaving Maude Henry to resume her own labors. Henry for a time lived at the Dreiser apartment at 6 West 102nd Street, where he and Theodore continued their writing, collaborating on magazine articles, delighting in their companionship as they knocked ideas back and forth. "He is the most generous—the least self interested of men," Henry wrote of Dreiser. "The ideas I caught seemed to him larger than his own." [24]

Henry had started a novel, *A Princess of Arcady*, and now he implored Dreiser to begin a novel himself so that they could work together. "Finally," as Dreiser described it, "I took out a piece of yellow paper and to please him wrote down a title at random—Sister Carrie. . . ." He later insisted that he had no plot in mind. "My mind was a blank except for the name," he said. "I had no idea who or what she was to be. I have often thought there was something mystic about it, as if I were being used, like a medium." [25]

One can accept this account of the conception of *Sister Carrie* or not, but if

Dreiser had no idea of the story when he wrote the title, he soon did. He had often pondered the tragedies of his youth, the injustices which ignorance and passion and circumstance had played on some of his sisters. Now, as he began work in earnest on the novel that would make him at once famous and infamous, his own sister Emma, who in 1886 had eloped from Chicago with the absconding Hopkins, became, with fictional changes, Sister Carrie. Hopkins became George Hurstwood, and Chapin & Gore, the "truly swell saloon" where Hopkins rifled the safe, became Fitzgerald & Moy's. Much of his plot came ready-made. It was not his plot, however, but his treatment of it that made this winter of 1899–1900, as he worked on *Sister Carrie* with Arthur Henry working beside him on *A Princess of Arcady*, a momentous one.

In *Carrie* for the first time of importance, Dreiser translated his own experience into the desperate, hopeless yearnings of his characters. *Ev'ry Month* had held him in a tight little strait-jacket. His magazine articles were pot-boilers conforming to editors' wishes. Now the reluctant conformist was free to write as he pleased about life as he saw it. He let himself go far, far into unconformity, apparently not realizing the extent of his divagation, but surely there was unconscious rebellion against the restraints that had curbed him for four years. Although he had read Hardy with admiration and he was not forgetting Balzac, what came out of his pen was pure Dreiser tinctured with Spencer and evolution. He was simply telling a story much as he had seen it happen in life. If one can trust his own account, he did not take it seriously at first, and after a month or so he put it aside in disgust. "I thought it was rotten," he recalled.[26] Henry thought it was great and coaxed him to resume it.

He seems to have had no inkling that he was creating a revolutionary work. He wrote with a compassion for human suffering that was exclusive with him in America. He wrote with a tolerance for transgression that was as exclusive and as natural. His mother, if not immoral herself, had accepted immorality as a fact of life. Some of his sisters had been immoral in the eyes of the world. In his own passion for women he was amoral himself, believing that so-called immorality was not immoral at all but was necessary, wholesome and inspiring, and that conventional morality was an enormous national fraud.

Thus the man who wrote *Sister Carrie* that winter was, by standards then prevailing, a greater potential menace to pure American ideals than Emma Goldman, who was preaching anarchism across the land, or her lover Alexander Berkman, who had shot Henry Clay Frick in Pittsburgh.

Dreiser's easy pen rolled. Now and then he would drop into Maria's restaurant on West Twelfth Street, a hangout of his good friend Richard Duffy and other literary bohemians. "The fecundity of the man was amazing," Duffy recalled. "Every few days he could make the breezy announcement that since he last came into view he had written as many as ten or twenty thousand words." [27] Jug was helping him with grammar and structure although she disapproved of some of the story's "immoralities," [28] but for a time he got stuck, unable to hit on a satisfactory way for Hurstwood to steal the money from the safe. He put the novel aside and turned to magazine work. For *Harper's Monthly* he did an article, "The Railroad and the People," for *Ainslee's* "The Trade of the Mississippi," and for *Atlantic Monthly* a piece about Fall River. The summer in Maumee had curtailed his production, as had the time spent on *Carrie*, and he was worried about money. *Harper's* had rejected his first short story effort, "The Shining Slave Makers," so he sent it on to *Century Magazine*, whose associate editor, Robert Underwood Johnson, likewise rejected it as implausible. Dreiser blew up, wrote Johnson to criticize *Century's* editorial methods, charged that his story had been read only by underlings and added, "I assert that the Editors of the Century have never seen my story. . . ." [29]

Johnson, replying that the editors *had* read it, was annoyed enough to suggest an apology, which Dreiser, doubtless recalling that he could not afford to alienate a good market, reluctantly gave. In February, 1900, he was in Washington for at least five days, probably gleaning article material from government agencies and suggesting to Johnson an article about teacher training, writing sweepingly, "I have investigated the school systems of St. Louis, Kansas City, Chicago, Buffalo, Philadelphia, Boston, Wilmington, Providence and New York and I know whereof I speak." [30]

While one suspects that most of this investigation was done via government reports, these activities stopped *Sister Carrie* in mid-career. Another delay was caused by the temporary desertion of the coaxing, magnanimous Henry. Dreiser, though never doubting his own genius, had already developed a need for a literary helper, a friend and critic to offer constant sympathy and advice—a need that would follow him through life and would eventually number his assistants by the score. He had his manuscripts typed at the establishment of Anna Mallon, who employed a battery of typists in her office high up in the Mutual Reserve Building at 309 Broadway. When Henry went there to have a short piece typed and set eyes on the sparkling Miss Mallon, he forgot about *Sister Carrie*, *A Princess of Arcady*, his wife Maude and the mortgaged House of Four Pillars. Dreiser did not see him for some time. Annoyed by Henry's defection, he was unable to get on with the novel. But finally Henry returned and the two fell to work again.

Dreiser solved the Hurstwood theft with a facile twist. Hurstwood, the trusted manager, flushed with wine and driven by his own crisis, finds the safe unaccountably open, takes out $10,000 and is tempted to decamp with it. After an inner struggle he realizes that this would be folly and is about to replace the money when the safe door accidentally closes and locks. Since he cannot open it, there is no way to explain the incident to his employer and he becomes an embezzler in spite of himself, his moral victory ironically nullified by mere chance—a victim of fate as, in Dreiser's mind, every living creature was a victim of fate.

Dreiser hurried on, encountering two other fictional problems that stopped him momentarily and worrying more and more about money. From *Harper's* he got an assignment to do an article about fruit growing and used his material to triple effect, selling not only the *Harper's* piece but also an article to *Pearson's* on apples and another to the Success Library on marketing fruits. He was careless again, for *Pearson's* editor W. Arthur Woodward received a letter from the editor of a fruit growers' periodical saying that Dreiser was all wrong about apples. Then came a swarm of complaints, Woodward writing Dreiser, "I have been waiting with some anxiety for your report on your article on 'Apples,' in connection with which we are still receiving letters of criticism." [31]

He suffered bouts of insomnia that caused the solicitous Jug a concern that some felt amusing. "When he could not sleep and paced the floor," one friend noted, "I hear the little wife trotted up and down after him." [32]

With Henry calling regularly, reading the *Carrie* script and cheering him on, he finished the book and was dissatisfied with the ending. "The note, the exact impression that I sought," he said, "evaded me." In mid-April he crossed over to the Palisades with his notebook and pen. For two hours he lay on a ledge in the sun, letting his thoughts wander. "Then suddenly," he recalled, "came the inspiration of its own accord." [33] Carrie must be left alone at the end, dimly aware of the vanity of her hopes, yet still hopelessly hoping: "Oh, Carrie, Carrie! Oh, blind strivings of the human heart! . . . Know, then, that for you is neither surfeit nor content. In your rocking chair, by your window dreaming, shall you long, alone. In your rocking chair, by your window, shall you dream such happiness as you may never feel." [34]

He later said he had no great interest in the novel until he was writing the final chapters, but one doubts him. By now he had tasted some success and was driving hard for money and fame. It seems unlikely that he would have sacrificed time for a dozen profitable articles in order to write a novel about which he was indifferent, chiefly to please Arthur Henry. The man who had fussed over just how to have Hurstwood steal the money—who had gone to the Palisades to wrestle with his last few paragraphs—had put his heart into his work and he knew the work was good.

He had started *Carrie* in mid-September, finishing it seven months later. Easily three months of that time had been devoted to article chasing, so his first novel took him only four months' writing time. Henry helped him prune away some 40,000 words of excess verbiage, his friend Mary Annabel Fanton of *Demorest's* also did some editing, and *Sister Carrie* was ready for a publisher—if anybody would publish it.

IV. L'AFFAIRE DOUBLEDAY

Dreiser submitted the script to Harper's through Henry Mills Alden, editor of *Harper's Monthly*, to whom he had sold material. Harper's rejected it May 2, calling it "a superior piece of reportorial realism" despite uneven writing, but feeling that it would not sell.[35] Alden himself was doubtful that

any publisher would accept it because of its realism. He suggested that
Dreiser try Doubleday, Page & Company, possibly because that firm in the
previous year (then Doubleday, McClure) had been brave enough to publish
Frank Norris' violent *McTeague,* and Dreiser did so.

At that very time Jug's sister Rose was visiting the Dreisers, reading
McTeague and praising it so highly that Dreiser read it and, as he put it, "I
talked of nothing else for months." [36] By a most marvelous coincidence, the
brilliant young Norris had made such a hit with Doubleday that the publisher
snatched him away from *McClure's Magazine* and hired him as reader-
editor for the firm. Thus it happened that Norris, a literary rebel, was first to
read *Sister Carrie* for Doubleday. He knew at once that he had found a great
book.

"It is a wonder," he said to the writer Morgan Robertson, who dropped
into his office. And he wrote Dreiser that he had passed it on to the members
of the firm with a glowing report which he repeated in part:

> I said, and it gives me pleasure to repeat it, that it was the best novel I had
> read in M.S. since I had been reading for the firm, and that it pleased me as
> well as any novel I have read in *any* form, published or otherwise. [37]

Dreiser was overjoyed. All his worries seemed gone when on June 9
Walter Hines Page, a partner in the firm and the boss during Frank N.
Doubleday's absence in Europe, wrote to congratulate him on "so good a
piece of work" and later signed an agreement to publish it—this despite the
fact that Henry Lanier, the junior partner, had misgivings. Dreiser, after
finishing a magazine article, left with Jug for a writing sojourn at her parents'
place in Montgomery City. He was in high elation over *Carrie* and in disgruntlement about his marriage. Jug was too possessive, too conventional,
too much the Methodist moralist. In a later memoir, obviously autobiographical although ascribed to another, he wrote, "For me marriage was a mistake.
Either mine was not a temperament which lent itself to marriage, or I had
erred in selecting the mate with whom it might have proved a success." [38]

In Missouri, nevertheless, he basked in the praise of Jug's relatives and
friends. Always naïvely proud of his work, he had often sent his friends
copies of his magazine articles and poems, and now he had let his old
newspaper colleagues in St. Louis and Pittsburgh know of the acceptance of
Carrie. As he received letters of congratulation he looked on himself in his
new estate as a novelist, happy that he had found his true medium, deciding to
write a novel every year and then and there beginning his second one. In lush
Missouri he also risked a secret flirtation with a teen-aged girl who "affected
[him] like fire" and made him mourn, "God! To be cribbed, cabined,
confined! Why had I so early in life handicapped myself in the race for
happiness?" [39] He took comfort in his dearest friend, Arthur Henry, who had
likewise placed his *A Princess of Arcady* with Doubleday and had remained
in New York to attend to details on both books. "I am busted," he wrote

Dreiser on Anna Mallon's engraved stationery, and later he echoed Dreiser's sincere regard for him:

> I too wish with all my heart we could be constantly together, walking, talking and writing of what seems great and worthy to us. I am not able to get either inspiration or comfort from others I meet. Half the time in talking even to [Frank] Norris I get no real response. He does not feel nor see very deep. . . . The fact is that you are the only inhabitant of the same world with me—I feel like a stranger with others.[40]

The superstitious Dreiser had a growing presentiment that all was not well with his novel and was half inclined to visit a fortune teller. "I went so far," he wrote, "as to ask the negroes working for us here where a seeress lived, but neglected to seek the 'Old Mammy' pointed out." [41] This was only one of many occasions when he felt his premonitions authenticated, for trouble was truly brewing.

Frank Doubleday had returned from Europe with his wife Neltje, listened to Norris' praise of *Sister Carrie*, and taken proofs home to Bay Ridge to read. The fact that Doubleday (while associated with McClure) had published *McTeague,* and that one of his missions in Europe had been to secure American publishing rights for Zola's novels, suggests that he was not so squeamish as squeamishness was reckoned in 1900. Employed in the book business ever since he started as an office boy for Scribners, he was primarily a salesman, interested in books that would sell and make a profit. He was also an Episcopalian with a lively moral sense. He read the story of Carrie Meeber, who contracted a liaison with the drummer Drouet, then left Drouet for a longer illicit excursion with the embezzler Hurstwood, and objected strongly on two grounds: the book was immoral and it would not sell. He showed it to Mrs. Doubleday who, since she spoke French, had been active in the Zola negotiations and could scarcely have been the most strait-laced of her sex. Although she had not objected to *McTeague,* she agreed whole-heartedly with her husband that *Carrie* was evil.[42]

Indeed, in that stiff-necked era the surprise was not that the Doubledays found *Carrie* offensive. The surprise was that the cautious Walter Page had accepted the book in the first place, and one suspects that he did so in part because of the infectious enthusiasm of Frank Norris, who had achieved sudden fame and was much admired by Doubleday.

Carrie was a direct affront to current mores at a time when the sedate Howells had pushed realism as far as the public conscience would permit and Crane's *Maggie* had been shunned at the book stores as shocking. The books that were selling were the glittering, virtuous costume romances—*When Knighthood Was in Flower, Janice Meredith, Soldiers of Fortune.* Lust and vice were allowable only if punished in the end—as they had been in *McTeague*—to furnish the reader a wholesome moral lesson. Carrie, far from being punished, played fast and loose with two sinners and wound up in luxury, a successful actress, with audiences' cheers ringing in her ears as she collected a huge salary—a denouement that could be construed as advocating unchastity as a way of life. In 1900 Dreiser's novel also could be indicted on the following charges:

It dealt with uneducated people who spoke colloquially, with none of the niceties of Charles Major's ladies and gentlemen. It was vulgar.

Dreiser obviously *liked* these characters, compounding his crime by showing great sympathy for these vulgarians in their sordid tribulations.

Carrie, Hurstwood and all the rest appeared almost as helpless creatures adrift on chips in a stormy sea, devoid of will, unable to steer any course, able only to seize whatever comfort was washed their way (precisely as Dreiser had intended). This flew in the face of the moral doctrine of free will that each individual could choose his own path for good or evil.

Sister Carrie was steeped in a pessimism that offended the national taste for sweetness.

Arthur Henry called at Frank Norris' Washington Square apartment one evening and found him seething. His boss had vetoed *Sister Carrie*.

"Doubleday thinks the story is immoral and badly written," Norris said. "He simply don't think the story ought to be published by anybody, first of all because it is immoral." [43]

Henry hurried to write Dreiser in Missouri:

> Dear Teddie—It has dazed me—I am amazed and enraged—Doubleday has turned down your story. . . . [44]

On the same day, July 19, Walter H. Page wrote Dreiser in painful explanation, saying, "The more we have discussed it, I am sorry to report to you, the more uncertain do we feel about it. The feeling has grown upon us that, excellent as your workmanship is, the choice of your characters has been unfortunate. . . . To be frank, we prefer not to publish the book, and we should like to be released from my agreement with you. If you have suffered any injury, we stand ready, of course, to make amends." [45]

Page placatingly added that the Doubleday firm was interested in Dreiser's future work and invited him to contribute to a new magazine the company was planning, *The World's Work*. But Arthur Henry counseled battle:

> Dear Teddie—Hold Doubleday and Page to their agreement. I have talked with Norris several times and I am convinced that this is the best thing for you to do. They admit that they are bound to publish it, if you say so, and Norris agrees with me that if they do so Doubleday will soon get over his kick and that it will be a great seller. Norris, who attends to the newspapers, critics &c, will strain every nerve for the book and I know that he will be glad if the house publishes the book after all. [46]

Dreiser, after a sleepless night, had come to the same conclusion. He wrote Page politely that *Carrie*'s forthcoming publication was now expected by his relatives, friends and by many editors on whom he depended for his living, and its rejection would not only be humiliating but "will work me material injury." [47] Page replied that this was surely an exaggeration—that the book was not likely to be a financial success—and showed a tender solicitude for Dreiser's career:

> Our wish to be released by you is quite as much for your own literary future as for our good; we think we can say even more for your benefit than ours. If we are to be your publishers, as we hope to be, we are anxious that the development of your literary career should be made in the most natural and advantageous way. But we are sure that the publication of *Sister Carrie* as your first book would be a mistake. It would identify you in the minds of the public with the use of this sort of material. . . . [48]

Still polite despite that last affront, Dreiser asked Page to proceed with publication, writing in part:

> I appreciate your kindness in consulting the advancement of my literary career as well as your own commercial interests, and would like to feel that the development of my literary life depended, as you say, upon a "natural and advantageous way" involving the elimination of *Sister Carrie*, but I cannot. I do not have much faith in the orderly progression of publication as regards novels. A great book will destroy conditions, unfavorable or indifferent, whether these be due to previous failures or hostile prejudices aroused by previous error. Even if this book should fail, I can either write another important enough in its nature to make its own conditions and be approved of for itself alone, or I can write something unimportant and fail, as the author of a triviality deserves to fail. Therefore I have no fear on this score.
>
> As to the choice of material—I am willing to abide by your first spontaneous judgment of that. If the public will only make the same general error I shall be highly gratified.

As if reflecting that Doubleday, as his publisher, could do either well or ill by his book, Dreiser closed with the most courteous of sentiments: "I hope that always in the future I may be able to avail myself of your personal judgment and good feeling toward me and that I may live to win your complete approval and friendship." [49] Perhaps a more accurate reflection of his mood was a line he wrote to Henry: "Fortune need not forever feel that she must use the whip on me." [50]

There was a further exchange in which Page tried a new tack, asking if Dreiser would relent if Doubleday could arrange for the fall publication of *Carrie* by any one of five other reputable publishers—Appleton; Macmillan; Dodd, Mead; Stokes, or Lippincott. Dreiser declined.

The persistence of Page's efforts showed the strong aversion of Frank Doubleday (and his wife) toward the book. *Carrie* was raising a high wind in the Doubleday offices on Union Square. Of the four leading members of the firm in ascending order of seniority, Frank Norris had been enthusiastic; Henry Lanier had disliked the book and yet appreciated its power and felt that it should be published (by someone else); Walter Page had praised it and agreed to publish it; and only Frank Doubleday himself had been revolted.

Lanier's judgment remained substantially unchanged. Page, the later ambassador, obviously followed the line of diplomatic expediency and knuckled under to the boss. Only Norris still argued, but vainly. And even Norris, reflecting on Doubleday's opposition, realized that it would be better for some other publisher to bring out the book.

"Page—and all of us—Mr. Doubleday too—are immensely interested in Dreiser," Norris wrote Henry, "and have every faith that he will go far. Page said today that even if we waited till T. D. got back it would yet be time for Macmillan or some other firm to get out Sister Carrie as a fall book." [51]

This was the heyday of Anthony Comstock, and Doubleday was even fearful that the book would be seized as indecent and raise a scandal. He kept up his efforts when Dreiser returned to New York in August.

Dreiser visited the Union Square office and listened to Doubleday's arguments. The book would not sell, he said. The firm aimed at public libraries as customers, but few would allow a novel of this nature on their shelves. Church people and the conservative householders who normally bought books would shun it. Dreiser, who had been so correct in his letters, grew stubborn and then angry. As Thomas H. McKee, the Doubleday attorney, recalled it years later, he lost his temper entirely.

"He got 'tough,' " McKee wrote, ". . . declaring that the written contract would be fulfilled, 'or else.' " Doubleday's offer to sell the plates to Dreiser at cost was "peremptorily" rejected. As a last resort, Doubleday offered to *give* him the plates. When Dreiser refused and warned of his legal rights, Doubleday threw up his hands.

"All right," he snapped. "You stand on your legal rights and we'll stand on ours. . . . I see that a man of your stamp will have trouble with any publisher you deal with and it will please me if you never set foot in this office again." [52] According to Dreiser's own recollection, Doubleday also said, "We publish one edition as to contract, but we won't do as we would by a book we liked." [53]

Thus *Sister Carrie*, a literary waif that needed careful nursing, was brought into the world by a publisher who detested both the book and its author.

V. THE MYTH

Dreiser later admitted that it was a mistake to force an antagonistic publisher to bring out his book. He did so for four reasons. Excited over his first novel, he wanted it published that fall and feared that negotiations with another house would delay publication. Arthur Henry urged him to insist on publication, believing the book would succeed on its merits. After quarreling with Doubleday, Dreiser in sheer bull-headedness held him to contract. And Dreiser himself had a firm belief that he had written a great book which the public could not fail to recognize. "If the book is worthy it will be honored with the public's approval and our mutual profit," [54] he had written Page. And to Henry he wrote, "I am much of a fatalist . . . and consider my career secure." [55]

What happened thereafter—the "suppression" of *Sister Carrie*—has become a part of literary legend, some of it erroneous and much of the error traceable to Dreiser himself. His carelessness with facts was already evident. He was in such emotional distress about his marriage and his trouble with Doubleday that his instability was moving toward irrationality. The propaganda that he spread industriously for decades about the suppression of *Carrie* contained inaccuracies shown by papers in his own possession.

While Doubleday's fulfillment of the contract was less than enthusiastic, he might have done worse. The company printed sheets for at least 1,250 books and had 1,000 of them bound in red cloth with black lettering at $1.50 a copy. Had Doubleday been truly vengeful, he could have let the book go with only perfunctory promotion or none at all.

Instead, he gave Norris a free hand in publicity. He was sporting enough to let the reviewers have their say. Norris, convinced that he had made a literary find and concerned over the unfavorable publication atmosphere, truly "strained every nerve" to push the book. An interested observer of this strange affair was young McKee, the Doubleday attorney. Bearing in mind Dreiser's threats, McKee was taking steps to make sure that Doubleday would not be legally liable for nonperformance of contract.

Norris sent out 127 review copies to leading newspapers and magazines. This was a large effort in behalf of an unknown novelist, the more so because these 127 copies were accompanied by promotional material and evidently by personal letters from Norris, a shining literary light whose praise meant something. Norris in fact appointed himself a one-man *Carrie* claque. He wrote enthusiastic letters to literary people and sang the book's praises so generously that one observer said, "Apparently he was more eager for Dreiser's *Carrie* to be read than for his own novels." [56]

The book was published November 8, 1900, and soon Dreiser's and Norris' spirits sank. Dreiser was ahead of his time. *Carrie* was widely reviewed—a tribute to Norris' efforts—but some reviews appeared as much as three or four months after publication and a majority of the critics condemned the book's "immorality," dreariness and philosophy of despair. [57] A minority recognized that Dreiser was no exploiter of the bedroom, that despite the "immorality" in the novel there were no explicit scenes of passion, and that he had an unerring eye for truth and a feeling for his characters that was moving in the extreme. A few even saw greatness in him.

Yet even those reviews which praised him were "good—but" reviews. The *New York Commercial Advertiser* noted his "extraordinary power" *but* called his heroine "a very frequent and commonplace type." The *Newark Sunday News* also recognized "Mr. Dreiser's power" and his evocation of "the terrible inevitableness of fact" *but* complained of his "inelegancies" and admitted, "The effect is depressing."[58] The *Seattle Post-Intelligencer* said, "It comes within sight of greatness" *but* quenched its own praise with remarks about "Mr. Dreiser's antiseptic style" and the observation that it was "a most unpleasant tale, and you would never dream of recommending [it] to another person to read."[59]

Not a critic in the nation realized that this was a novel so transcendent in its realism and its humanity that it stood alone, that its imperfections deserved forgiveness, that it called for a new standard in criticism and a fight for recognition. No such enthusiasm was possible in 1900 over a heroine who not only sinned but spoke ungrammatically. Perhaps no one of a stature less than William Dean Howells' could have saved *Carrie* by resolute championing. But the aging Howells, who had fought his own battle for realism decades earlier and won it, demurred at this newer brand of realism. Dreiser, who had once interviewed Howells for a magazine article, met him one day at the *Harper's Monthly* office. Howells said coldly, "You know, I don't like *Sister Carrie*," and hurried on.[60]

Norris, dejected at the reception, asked Doubleday for paid advertising. No, no! This was not in the contract. Doubleday said the reviews were adverse (as they were) and he would not "send good money after bad"—a stand which, as an admitted merchandiser, he might have taken even had he liked Dreiser and his book. His commercial sense was vindicated. Dreiser's innocent belief that the public would unerringly seek out a worthy book was exploded. Meanwhile, Lawyer McKee took protective steps. He saw to it that *Carrie* was displayed at the Doubleday salesroom where wholesalers came to buy.

"I had the book bought occasionally," he related, "usually ordered and delivered later—at Macy's, Brentano's and the like, a record being kept and prompt delivery always made. In short, no request for the book was ever delayed or turned down, and I was prepared to prove it."[61]

Four hundred and fifty-six copies were sold, giving Dreiser royalties of $68.40[62]—a disaster that all but crushed him.

To be sure, *Carrie* received a token publication. If Doubleday had been as enthusiastic as Norris—if he had advertised the book—would it have been a success?

In view of the prevailing national climate, the kind of books the public was then buying, and the reaction of the critics, it seems likely that *Carrie* still would have been a commercial failure. The reviewers killed the book. The public simply did not want *Sister Carrie* in 1900.

Dreiser's dream of success and fame crumbled. In his despair, his feeling that the dice were loaded, that fortune was using the whip on him, swelled into a delusion and caused him to stray from strict truth. Having heard from Norris about Mrs. Doubleday's aversion to the book, he became convinced that she was the real editor-in-chief of a petticoat-ridden house. He later declared that Doubleday, to satisfy her that *Sister Carrie* would not corrupt the public, never did distribute the book for sale but instead threw all copies into the cellar and that "no copies were ever sold." [63] Again he wrote, "Doubleday stored all of the 1,000 copies printed . . . in the basement of his Union Square plant, and there they remained. . . ." [64] In after years he told this story to H. L. Mencken, Floyd Dell, Edgar Lee Masters, Frank Harris, Dorothy Dudley, William C. Lengel and scores of others.

His hurt was real and understandable. Yet all the while in his files were Doubleday statements dated February 1 and August 1, 1901, and February 1, 1902, reporting 456 copies sold. Also in his files was a letter from the J. F. Taylor Company, a publisher which in 1901 considered reissuing *Carrie*, saying in part:

> It is going to be next to impossible to get the book stores to consider *Sister Carrie* at present under the old name. Doubleday sprinkled enough of the book around the country to leave a few copies on many shelves. They still remain on those shelves, and when our salesmen tried to talk Sister Carrie to those who had bought the book, they said, "Well, we gave it a trial, and still have the books we ordered." [65]

3. The Crack-up

Dreiser suffered as only the rejected artist can suffer. In him despair could sink to fearful depths. On Christmas Day, 1900, his seventy-nine-year-old father died at Mame's home in Rochester and his gloom increased. His friend Richard Duffy wrote him:

> It has seemed to me that you are lately inclined to ponder sadly. . . . But you must school yourself to a habit of cheerful thinking, especially now that the encouraging reception of *Sister Carrie* impels you to write another novel . . . if I may be so bold, I would suggest that you incorporate a truly humorous character in your next novel. Infuse a solution of humor into the book entire. There is much of it even in the most sordid lives. . . .[1]

Encouraging reception! Sordid lives! Evidently even Duffy thought *Carrie* sordid, and his inane advice, however well meant, must have rankled. When Dreiser met Amelia Barr, who had contributed to *Ev'ry Month,* she grew impatient with him, later writing, "I have no sympathy with complaining men." [2] There is a legend that magazine editors now were hostile because he had written a dirty book. While it is true that he found it increasingly difficult to sell articles, the editors were friendly enough. Dreiser himself, in his despair, was more prickly than ever to deal with. He complained to John S. Phillips, editor of *McClure's,* about a payment of $100 for his sketch of Jug's father, "A True Patriarch," Phillips replying, "I don't like this dickering . . . and my first impulse . . . would be to return the story. . . ." [3] He complained to Woodward of *Pearson's* about a $100 payment for his article, "The Trolley," although Woodward had protested that a map of trolley lines Dreiser had supplied was "positively inaccurate." [4] Dreiser received cordial letters from Ida Tarbell at *McClure's,* Hjalmar Boyesen at *Cosmopolitan* and Ellery Sedgwick at *Leslie's,* and he had a ready market with his good friend Duffy at *Ainslee's.*

The editors had not changed but Dreiser himself had. In writing *Sister Carrie* he had achieved a new respect for himself as an artist rather than a hack. He no longer cared to write pot-boilers. The pieces he was producing now, such as "Whence the Song" and "Color of Today," had realistic quality and were harder to write and to sell.[5]

Arthur Henry was now deeply involved with Anna Mallon, which meant that Dreiser was deprived of Henry's stimulating literary companionship. Occasionally the Dreiser couple went picnicking with Anna and Henry, a situation that troubled Jug, who disliked sin and admired Maude Henry. But Jug had found that marriage to Dreiser meant marriage on Dreiser's terms, and even Henry remarked on how well she had managed, "in some mysterious fashion, to reconcile her traditional beliefs with his unorthodox thoughts and ways." Anna, who had a sizable income and a widowed mother with a comfortable estate, owned a cabin on Dumpling Island off Noank, Connecticut—a place Henry used as his writing studio in the summer of 1901 while his sweetheart worked in New York and came out for weekends. Anna's mother, suspicious of the affair, traveled out to Noank to spy on the island with field glasses. Despite these gaudy proceedings, the Dreisers went to Noank for a vacation stay with the couple, Dreiser arriving a few days before Jug to "get things arranged."

Henry was amazed at the change in the man who had written him, "Surely there were never better friends than we." Dreiser got off the boat and greeted him warmly, but his face clouded at the rusticity of the cabin with its unpainted flooring; he said at mealtime, "Why, these dishes are greasy," disapproved of the wild vegetation surrounding the cabin because he had expected a lawn, and was appalled by lumpy mattresses and damp bedclothing. Though matrimony galled him, he was helpless without Jug.

"If she were here," he said, "I could stay forever. I cannot do housework. I cannot look after my things. She has spoiled me, and I am lost without her."

His grouch was so pervasive that at one point the two friends wrangled bitterly until Dreiser's eyes filled with tears and he said, "Come now, let's not quarrel." He did not know that Henry was taking notes for a book about the delights of life close to nature and would use him as an example of how one could bring his miseries into sylvan surroundings and destroy all joy for others. Later the pair sailed to Noank to pick up Jug, hallooing at her as she sat on the wharf with her back turned, in mock anger because they had not met her train. Dreiser was so relieved by her arrival and the attendant relaxation of his own cares that he "beat her publicly," after which she kissed them both and they sailed back to the island with a cheer engendered solely by her radiance. When she spied the cabin and said, "It's beautiful," it seemed to spell an end to gloom.

Jug's acceptance of the light-hearted Henry suggests an adaptability Dreiser never gave her credit for. Had Henry felt her censure he would hardly have described her as "one of the sweetest and truest of women," "a being of affectionate impulses and stubborn fidelity, devoted to the comfort of her husband. . . ."

Anna Mallon arrived that same evening for her summer vacation, and Dreiser's mood was so improved that there was an interval of gayety during which he and Henry enjoyed philosophical discussions or traveled to Noank for article material. Frank Norris had sent a copy of *Carrie* to the British publisher William Heinemann, who in May had been so impressed that he contracted to bring it out in England in a curtailed version to fit his Dollar

Library of American Fiction—a cutting job Henry was eager to execute. If *Carrie* had failed in America, Dreiser at any rate had the gratifying assurance of international recognition before he was thirty. But the blackness descended again, for the possessive Dreiser now regarded Anna jealously as a woman who had stolen his comrade. He sniped at Anna with enough savagery to hurt her, criticized her preparation of fish, complained of damp night breezes and exuded a discontent that settled like a fog over Dumpling Island, reducing Anna to a rage. She then quarreled with Henry and suggested that they ask the Dreisers to leave, while Jug tried brightly to restore cheer but succumbed to nervousness herself and the usually placid Henry was beside himself with irritation. When the Dreisers left at the end of July, long before they had intended, Anna and Arthur Henry were not sorry.[6]

For economy the Dreisers had given up their pleasant apartment near Central Park, and now they took a cheaper one on East End Avenue at Eighty-second Street. Dreiser had to make a decision. Should he work on novels, after deriving $68.40 in revenue from four months' work on *Carrie*, or concentrate on magazine work, for which he had averaged $100 a week before his marriage?

There seemed only one practical answer. Yet, to his credit, he did not take the easy-money route—indeed could not. He believed in himself even if no one else but Norris, Henry and Heinemann did, and he so loved the sweep of the novel that he resumed work not on one novel but two, *The Rake* and *Jennie Gerhardt*,[7] still writing articles on the side.

But his suffering soon developed into neurosis. His window overlooked the busy East River and Blackwell's Island, which brought him gloomy thoughts of the island's institutions housing the city's sick, the criminal and insane. He also blamed his malaise on "irregular hours" and "various physical indiscretions such as unreasonable sexual connections,"[8] not specifying whether these involved his wife, other women or both. He was upset by three more rejections, all kindly, from Sedgwick at *Leslie's* and one from *Broadway Magazine*. Although his production was declining badly, he did sell his first short story, "The Shining Slave Makers," to *Ainslee's* and articles to *Ainslee's*, *Pearson's* and *Harper's Weekly*.

In September came tidings of the British reception of *Sister Carrie*—an acclaim showing the greater maturity of English criticism. Finding no immorality, the *Manchester Guardian* said *Carrie* "should belong to the veritable documents of American history," the *London Daily Chronicle* called Dreiser "a true artist," the *Athenaeum* compared *Carrie* with Zola's *Nana*, and other journals praised the novel's simplicity and power. Heinemann innocently (or did he know the truth?) wrote Doubleday, "I think [*Carrie*] without any doubt the best book we have recently published, and are likely to publish for many a long day. . . . I look on Mr. Dreiser as an author of exceptional merit. . . . I congratulate you very heartily in having discovered him. You should make a great fuss of him. How about his next and future work?" [9] Doubleday, who was *not* making a great fuss of Dreiser, forwarded the letter to him without comment.

Jug happily pasted press clippings in a scrapbook. Dreiser, correctly seeing the British reviews as a vindication, launched an effort that he would continue persistently during the next decade—to get *Carrie* reissued in America. In view of its recent failure and the copies still going begging on booksellers' shelves, it is not surprising that he got rejections at Appleton's, Stokes, Scribners, Dodd, Mead, A. S. Barnes and others. At the smaller firm of J. F. Taylor & Company, however, he found a friend in the editor, Rutger B. Jewett, who admired *Carrie* and wrote, "I believe in you and in your work and intend to make it possible for you to finish that second book. . . ." [10] Joseph Taylor, the president, agreed to buy Doubleday's plates and stock of *Carrie* but demurred at reissuing the book for a time because of its recent American failure. What he and Jewett really wanted was *Jennie Gerhardt*, and he arranged to give Dreiser advances of $15 a week on his promise to finish the novel within a year.

Although this was little enough, he had written *Carrie* in seven months with no advance at all and had sandwiched numerous articles in between. The modest conformist Jug thought he was getting recognition, that prospects were good. Dreiser saw defeat everywhere. Despite the British praise, sales of the cheap English edition seemed likely to bring him little more than $100 in royalties. [11] No longer would Arthur Henry help him as he had on *Carrie*. And his chronic worries about money now began to have real foundation. Since his marriage, what with the vacations at Maumee, Montgomery City and Noank and the time spent on the novel, not to mention his growing depression, his income had sagged far below the prosperous 1897–98 level—a loss which his superstitious nature may well have caused him to blame on Jug. He could also link Jug with Mrs. Doubleday in the forces of prudery, for had she not demurred at some of the "bad parts" in *Carrie?*

To William Marion Reedy, the Falstaffian editor of *Reedy's Mirror* in St. Louis and one of the few who had praised *Carrie*, Dreiser wrote so despairingly that Reedy replied, "You must not let the despondent mood overcome you. If life wears the aspect which you endeavor to reflect in your letter of the 9th, the whole thing is hardly of enough importance to worry about it. Every thing is for the best. . . ." [12]

Jug, the moralist, also stood in the way of his sexual freedom. With his need for recognition, a succession of women in some measure supplied the admiration the world denied him. He also found carnality poetic and stimulating, writing, "The whole matter of the sexes, their contacts, the sense of beauty and color and romance that surrounds the physical lure each has for the other, is to me more beautiful than I can say, the quintessense [*sic*] of beauty." [13]

Early in November he decided to leave the dreary East Side neighborhood and head south with Jug in the hope of improving his spirits. He paid a last call on Rutger Jewett at Taylor's, so gloomy that the kindly Jewett urged him to laugh once in a while "just for the sake of relief." [14] Well aware of his grammatical and stylistic weaknesses, he arranged with Mary Annabel Fanton—now Mrs. W. Carman Roberts—to serve in New York as his editor and critic. Then with Jug he left for Virginia to find a place where he could recapture the creative mood.

II. FLIGHT

Around November 10, the couple found room and board at a home in Bedford City, a quiet town east of Roanoke. He could see the mountains from his window, and for a time he was cheered, writing Mrs. Roberts, "Here I be, full of glee, rich as, rich as—rich can be," and adding, "I feel as if my malarial feelings were certain to quickly leave me and be replaced by a desire to work." He urged her to be fearless in cutting his copy: "Pull it together close—everything can go except the grip. That I must have in it." [15]

"Especially is it good news that you are in recreated spirit for the novel," Duffy wrote him. "Push ahead steadily now—not forgetting to allow yourself exercise in the open. . . ." [16]

He became friendly with J. E. Bowler, a young Negro pants-presser, probably meeting him on his daily walks—a friendship that resulted in a thirteen-year correspondence between them. Dreiser, doubtless stressing the survival of the fittest, encouraged Bowler to learn the tailor's trade and showed a kindness as warm as his estrangements could be chill. "Our frequent conversations," Bowler later wrote him, "have shown you to be a man of . . . large sympathy . . . and [I] highly appreciate the time you condescended to spend with me. Your various lectures to me (I may term them) have certainly caused me to see Life & Things in general different to what I did." [17]

But depression seized Dreiser again. The story of Jennie Gerhardt, based as it was experiences of two others of his sisters, opened old wounds. From Jeremiah MacDonald, a Binghamton astrologer to whom he sent for his horoscope, he received explicit warnings:

> You have stomach and bowel troubles, nervousness and cannot eat when excited or angry . . . rest and sleep are all you require when sick or exhausted. You were destined to travel and see strange things, and if cautious, sincere and faithful, you will be successful in life. You will be most fortunate by moving about. Never stay too long in one place or you will meet with disappointment. . . . You have a strong love nature; with you, to love is to worship. . . .[18]

He had made only slow progress on the novel by mid-December when he left with Jug for Missouri to spend the holidays at the White farm. Here he received a gift from Duffy, a volume of Whitman's poems, and felt guilty that he had forgotten Duffy, writing him, "I wish I knew of something that you liked—and yet I will not attempt a present this year." [19] Did he read Whitman, find in him a poetic father, a rebel who had suffered similarly? One wonders, for he never had much to say about him.

His in-laws knew he was nervously unstrung and needed a "rest." They accorded him increased respect now that he had been "written up in the papers," that infallible sign of greatness. But he was irritable, annoyed by Jug, feeling that she preened herself among the bucolic Missourians on the strength of her cosmopolitan experience as the wife of a "famous novelist."

"Married, married!" he later wrote. "The words were as the notes of a tolled bell." [20]

Of course they were incompatible. No woman could have been compatible with Dreiser. Jug was passionate, keen-witted and cheerful, but—she was conventional. She had submerged her life in his, had no independent existence, and for this he pitied her. She lacked the magic essential to keep him permanently charmed—the ability to change daily from redhead to brunette to blonde, to change physical lineaments, color of eyes, timbre of voice, tenor of mind and imagination. He wanted other women, change, the "holy grail of beauty." It is quite likely that he took the astrologer's advice about travel seriously. With Jug he took a trip to the Gulf coast, hoping to recover his calm, and failing. Early in February, 1902, they put up in Hinton, in southern West Virginia, evidently because of the curative springs near there.

Hinton was another way station in his flight from himself. He stayed there some seven weeks, collecting his payments from Taylor and trying miserably to work on *Jennie*. Jug's presence apparently was not comforting, for he wrote Jewett, "Have been going through a very sad period of entanglement for three weeks." [21] Duffy, who knew all about the Dreiser troubles, wrote, "I enclose 'Under Difficulties' which I think you and Mrs. Dreiser ought to learn by heart and recite privately. You take the first stanza & let her take the second. I shall expect to find you both letter-perfect on your return." [22] Dreiser, willing to turn an honest dollar in any direction, tried to dispose of some wildcats trapped by a local man, but got a rejection from the New York Zoological Society: "We are not in need of any more wild cats, at present, as we have some very fine specimens. . . ." [23] Another kind of rejection came from Duffy at *Ainslee's*, who sent back his article, "Problems of Distribution."

Jewett tried to josh him out of his dumps: "You are simply hopeless. The last time I saw you I told you that if you did not learn how to laugh some times just for the sake of relief, you would go crazy, or die of grief. . . ." [24]

By this time Dreiser feared he *was* going crazy. Late in March he moved to Lynchburg, Virginia, with Jug for some reason staying behind for a few days and writing him from Hinton March 26, "Will leave here Friday A.M. on No. 4. Meet me.—Juggie." [25] When her postcard reached Lynchburg he had already moved on to Charlottesville. One gets a picture of her alighting in Lynchburg, the worried, red-haired wife, looking forlornly for her Honeybugs and not finding him—a minor annoyance but symbolic of the failure of these two to find happiness in one another. There is no further mention of her at this time. Apparently soon thereafter she decided to return home and face the Missouri questions: What was wrong with her husband? Why was she not with him?

In Charlottesville, where he stayed throughout April and May, Dreiser heard from Arthur Henry in Noank. Henry's House of Four Pillars had been foreclosed by the mortgage holder, a man named Hiett, Henry writing, "I have written to Hiett to pay the balance to you." [26] Dreiser would get back perhaps only $100 but needful now. In his travail he had been able to write only ten short chapters of *Jennie* in the six months since he left New York.

"I finished chapter 10 with a strong sense of eagerness for chapter 11," Jewett wrote encouragingly. "Chapter 3 is a gem! . . . You have slashed courageously, but there will need to be still more cutting . . . where you reinforce a point by illustrating and then reillustrating." Dreiser's copy evidently was messy, for Jewett later urged, "Edit your chapters before sending to the typewriter; it will save time in the long run." [27]

But by June Dreiser was balked, unable to write. He had fits of high elation followed by despondency. His nerves now developed physical symptoms, causing pain in the tips of his fingers. Walking had always soothed him, so he quit Charlottesville and hiked northward, tall, skinny, haunted, in a trek that would cover more than three hundred miles through Virginia, Maryland and Delaware. In mid-June he lingered for a week at the beach town of Rehoboth, Delaware, hearing there from Jewett, who was concerned about having received no more copy: "What, and where is the delay? . . . We must get this book started if it is to be out by September 1st." A fortnight later Jewett bowed to the inevitable: "If the book cannot mature in time for September publication it will be better to postpone the issue until the following February. . . . Do not get discouraged." [28]

Even Jewett's kindliness did not help. Certainly one of the thoughts that obsessed Dreiser was his knowledge that the story of Jennie contained precisely the elements that American critics had so assailed in *Carrie*. Did he have to go through all that again? Could he stand it? Was there any point in battering his lone head against the solid wall of critical stupidity?

He headed north again, apparently without real aim, walking day after day, finishing a few more chapters along the way. Before July 14 he reached Philadelphia, took a room at 3225 Ridge Avenue and put aside the novel to work on a sketch, "A Samaritan of the Backwoods," which he sent to Henry Alden at *Harper's Monthly*. Another blow—Alden wrote crustily, "It is not the kind of material we want in whatever shape it may be put." [29] In Dreiser's mental state his copy was probably poor. He was further depressed by a report from Jewett on his later chapters of *Jennie:* "It is in this art of condensation, of striking a ringing blow with a few tense phrases, that I feel your limitation. You elaborate certain parts of a narrative to excess; the reader becomes confused and wearied. . . ." [30]

His old friend of St. Louis days, Peter McCord, had come east and, after a stint at the *Philadelphia North American*, was now an artist with the *Newark News*. Evidently McCord journeyed to Philadelphia to visit him, and must have been shocked by his hollow-eyed defeatism. "A Samaritan" was also rejected by *McClure's* and *Cosmopolitan*. Subject to suspicions, feeling that his name was now anathema to magazine editors, he sent the piece to *The Atlantic* under McCord's name, but it came back just the same.

Before the summer's end Jug rejoined him in Philadelphia to supply needed mothering. Probably through McCord's good offices the *North American* gave him assignments at $20 each for the Sunday supplement, and he did a few pieces for two local periodicals, the *Era* and the *Booklover's Magazine*. Although he found a sympathetic friend in Joseph Hornor Coates, one of the *Era's* editors, he sank further into despair. The fate of *Carrie* preyed on him like a bereavement, and his bitterness, as well as his comprehension of the insoluble literary problem that faced him, cried out in a piece he did for the *Booklover's Magazine*:

> Immoral! Immoral! Under this cloak hide the vices of wealth as well as the vast, unspoken blackness of poverty and ignorance; and between them must walk the little novelist, choosing neither truth nor beauty, but some half-conceived phase of life that bears no honest resemblance to either the whole of nature or to man.[31]

Graustark by then had sold almost 300,000 copies. *Mrs. Wiggs of the Cabbage Patch* sold 170,000 in 1902 alone. *Sister Carrie* had sold 456.

Duffy, receiving a despondent letter, went to Philadelphia to offer encouragement and suggest that he read Mill's autobiography, especially the fifth chapter, "A Crisis in My Life." Dreiser worried about the payments he was still getting from the Taylor company on his agreement to finish the book within a year. His year was almost up and he had hardly come to grips with the story. "Open the door," Jewett urged, "and sweep out the rubbish of distrust. . . . I know that when the book is finished it will be good." [32]

Jug, too, must have plied him with encouragement as well as pills. By now his thoughts were so morbidly self-centered that he made not a mention of Jug in a long account of his ordeal written soon afterward. Insomnia racked him, as did the pain in his fingertips. He imagined that his hair was falling out. At times he could hardly keep from weeping. Although his stomach troubled him, he had a voracious appetite which he quelled for economy's sake. Remembering Spencer, and gripped also by superstition, he felt himself a human atom like Hurstwood, so dominated by malign forces that it was almost useless to struggle. "I [thought]," he wrote, ". . . that there was an element of fatality about my troubles, that they were foreordained—worked out by invisible and adverse powers." Fate or not, he tried several nerve specialists, one of whom nodded at his recital and said, "The usual symptoms. . . . Try to overcome that [depression] as best you can by seeking amusing and companionable society and go to the theatre as much as you can." [33] The fee was $10 but Dreiser was too far gone to profit from the advice. He wrote Jewett that he was giving up *Jennie* and would try to repay his advances later, Jewett replying in part:

> Brace up, stop worrying, and rest your head as well as your body. You exaggerate greatly the obligation under which you think you are staggering. I gambled on a manuscript, and when the manuscript is finished, I believe that the result will justify my plunge. Until you are in better condition than at present, however, you cannot do good work.[34]

Although he sold a sketch, "Christmas in the Tenements," to *Harper's Weekly*, he received rejections from *Pearson's* and *McClure's*. By December he decided he must send Jug back to Missouri and go it alone. He even asked (in McCord's name!) for a special low fare due to hardship, but the Pennsylvania Railroad replied, "We are not permitted to make reductions in rates except in cases of absolute destitution." The parting must have been a sad one, with Jug fearing for her Honeybugs' actual sanity.

III. THE HORRORS

In February, 1903, after seven months in Philadelphia, Dreiser took a train to New York, arriving there with $32. If he could nurse that sum and write a few magazine articles, the fates might relent. He took the Twenty-third Street ferry to Brooklyn, where rents were cheaper and no friends would see him, found a $2.50-a-week room with tattered wallpaper at 113 Ross Street, and sighed, "To be compelled to come to this." [35]

For a few days he lashed himself into effort, called on magazine editors and even got a few assignments. "I am . . . still in the dumps in regard to *Sister Carrie*. . . ." he wrote Ripley Hitchcock, a friendly editor at *Harper's*. "In fact I seem to be just emerging from a long siege of bad weather and am only now looking to my sails again." [36] But with article assignments that would have saved his financial position, he found himself unable to write them: "Day after day I would get up and sit at my desk a little while feeling that this morning surely some ray of inspiration would arrive, but finding that it did not I would get up and go out. . . ." [37] A job seemed his only salvation, but as a "successful writer" listed in *Who's Who* he evidently could not bring himself to admit defeat by applying for an editorial post at magazines which had published his articles. He did write Arthur Henry, asking him to scout around for jobs for him, but this came to nothing. He applied fruitlessly for work at the newspapers in New York and Brooklyn, where he was not known. Then, since he could not write, he decided to find manual work at the car-barns, a sugar refinery or a factory, all of them near his room.

Yet when he approached these places he shrank at admitting his need to cynical clerks: "I would say to myself, 'They see what I am coming for,' and would turn off." His last fifteen dollars had dwindled to ten. His brother Paul was in New York, as was Ed, now a successful actor. Mame had moved from Rochester and now lived with her prosperous drummer husband Brennan on Washington Square. Even his sister Emma, despite her troubles, would gladly have aided him. To none of them would he turn—in fact, none even knew he was in Brooklyn—and as for an appeal to Jug and the Missouri relatives, that was unthinkable.

Now came the horrors in earnest. To save money he moved into an eight-by-six cell in the same house—$1.25 a week. Nightly he tossed, fearful even of snatches of sleep because of the ghastly dreams that accompanied them. "My insomnia," he wrote, "seemed to [be] racking the soul out of me." During the long night watches he heard stealthy footfalls, felt his scalp prickle as he sensed that a hand was reaching for him, leaped out of bed to light his gas lamp and find no one there, then sank into his chair in a cold sweat, staring out his window into the darkness, waiting dully for the dawn. He developed a torpor in which he was neither asleep nor awake but in a zone between that brought a new hallucination. He saw himself divide into two persons, one a tall, selfish individual, the other a silent philosopher who watched his struggles with calm detachment. "I marveled at him," he wrote, "thinking this was truly the oversoul in me—this was the thing that would last and be extant when I in my corporeal form was no more." [38] He came to regard this oversoul as a steadying influence which might save him. His chief effort now being to husband his few remaining dollars, he had cut himself down to two cheap meals a day, then to one, and finally to a daily five-cent bottle of milk and five-cent loaf of bread divided into three meals. He lost more weight. Finding a poem he had written several years earlier, he mustered the energy to send it to a magazine. When he was down to three dollars, he achieved another decision. He went to the Brooklyn charity office.

Even in his extremity he kept clean-shaven and neat despite his threadbare clothes. The charity officer was sympathetic, but when he learned that Dreiser had two brothers and two sisters within a few miles, he said with finality, "You ought to go to them." He did give Dreiser two letters of recommendation to firms which he was sure would give him temporary work. Dreiser walked out with them, then saw that they bore the letterhead of the charity office which would be seen by those to whom he presented them. "I had a horror of that," he wrote. "I tore them into bits and flung them into the gutter." [39]

When he was down to his last dollar, a letter arrived—a $10 check for his poem. This was momentarily cheering, but he had wasted from 159 to 130 pounds, his clothes hung loosely on him and he was weakening physically. The pain in his fingertips now assailed his toes, causing blisters. Things formerly square and straight—a newspaper, his table, the walls of his room—now appeared crooked, out of line. He knew this was a hallucination but could not conquer it. When he went out to calm his nerves, he walked down a street that veered crazily from its former alignment, and discovered a new aberration: he had an almost irresistible impulse to *walk in a circle*, "which," he observed, "was nothing more nor less than pure insanity." [40]

Unlike Hurstwood, he would not beg, but he did hit on a stratagem to stretch his funds. Daily he walked to the great Wallabout market a few blocks down the street—a place teeming with wagons and barrows loaded with produce—and invariably he would find an apple or an onion that had fallen from a wagon, or a potato still good enough to take home and roast over his smelly oil stove.

This was the man whose *Sister Carrie* had won him an "international reputation."

IV. STARVATION

After some seven weeks in Brooklyn, he made another effort, walked miles around by the bridge to save the three-cent ferry fare to Manhattan, tried three newspapers on Printing House Square without success, then thought of his sister Mame. Washington Square was an easy walk. He had not seen the big, cheerful Mame for three years. He had last written her from Philadelphia, and she knew nothing of his plight. Gripped by a yearning for warmth and love, he obeyed the impulse. Mame had no sooner kissed him than she said, "You're not well, are you?" [41]

He admitted having had a bout with neurasthenia but said he was recovering and doing well. The hearty Brennan, fourteen years Mame's senior, insisted that he stay for dinner, and Dreiser wolfed a Lucullan spread—soup, fish, a roast, salad, dessert—while Mame recommended a patent medicine costing a dollar a bottle which he must use liberally along with frequent draughts of rich eggnog laced with whiskey, and Dreiser thought of the $3.31 left in his pocket and his daily ten-cent limit for food, a bottle of milk and a loaf of bread. He would starve rather than admit need. When he left, and Mame asked his address, he recoiled at having any relative find him at his sordid Ross Street diggings. "Four-fourteen Willow Avenue," he lied. As he walked to the ferry, a howling wind sailed his fedora away beyond recall in the darkness—a mishap that seemed to symbolize the malevolence of fate. Raging, he spent fifty precious cents for a workman's wool cap that looked ridiculous but was warm, and returned to Brooklyn.

". . . I tested every misery to which want can compel," he wrote. Resuming his vegetable life, he imagined that small boys jeered at his workman's cap, pondered suicide, planned to break a store window so that he would be arrested and fed, then again felt certain that the tall, quiet individual—his Doppelgänger—would see him through. He received a letter from Paul which had been redirected to his correct address. Paul had talked with Mame, knew that Theodore had been ill and begged him to call on him at the Imperial

Hotel. Dreiser, still angry at Paul, did not deign to answer. But he could no longer postpone some ultimate decision. In mid-April, with eviction staring him in the face because he had less than the $1.25 due for another week's rent, he fought his impulse to walk in a circle and wandered down to the East River wharves, gazing dully at the dark waters that could so easily swallow him and his misery. But as he watched, a gleefully drunken Scotsman came up, flipped his coat-tails and did a jig for his benefit, singing (as Dreiser later recalled it with some possibly imaginative trimmings), "Ah, we're feeling verra low today, but we'll be better by and by." [42]

In turning Dreiser from possible suicide, the Scotsman unwittingly permitted the creation of *Jennie Gerhardt* and other novels. Dreiser, amused, felt his whole mood change. He walked home firmly believing that the turn had come, and was even able to get some sleep that night. In the morning he recalled hearing that the maintenance superintendent of the New York Central Railroad often gave jobs to indigent literary people. With only a few coins left, he clutched a half-loaf of bread in one hand and his bag in the other, went to Manhattan, applied at the railroad office, got the promise of a job, and walked out into a better world. His elation increased when he thought for the first time of his $100 gold watch and pawned it for $25. [43] Now, after eating a thirty-five-cent meal, his first thought was of the accursed wool cap, so symbolic of his defeat. The cap took on an extravagant significance, marking him as a laborer. He could not wait to buy a face-saving hat. He walked up Broadway to find a hat store, and as he passed the Imperial Hotel he was appalled to see Paul Dresser and Pat Howley stroll out, both of them splendidly dressed.

He did not want to see them in any case—above all now, wearing that silly cap, looking so thin and beaten. He tried to brush by unseen. Paul's hand clapped him on the shoulder.

"Theodore," he said.

"Hello, Paul," Dreiser growled, feeling "a kind of hatred of [Paul's] prosperity and of him."

Paul was shocked at his appearance. Tears came to his eyes as he asked Dreiser what was wrong, told him he had looked for him vainly at the fake Brooklyn address, told him he had money coming from "On the Banks of the Wabash," and saw his gaunt younger brother eye him in anger, eager only to get away.

"For God's sake, don't let your pride stand between us," he begged. He was just leaving for Buffalo, and he had to use all his persuasion before Theodore would accept a roll of bills and promise to meet him at the Imperial on Monday. Through it all, Theodore treated Paul with superiority and hostility, and yet when Paul hurried away Dreiser admitted, "Secretly, I felt as if I could throw my arms around his neck and hug him. . . ." [44]

Finding more than $75 in the roll Paul gave him, he resolved not to use a penny of it. He bought a two-dollar hat and spent that night and the next at the malodorous Mills Hotel on Bleecker Street. On Monday he was talking with Paul again at his luxurious hotel suite, telling him of his plan to work for the railroad.

"You'll do nothing of the sort," Paul said. "Why, man, you're not able to work. . . ." He produced a telegram from his friend William Muldoon, the former champion wrestler who now operated what he called a "repair shop" for wealthy human wrecks, mostly alcoholics, at an estate in Westchester. The telegram said that a room was awaiting Dreiser. Two years earlier the free-living Austin Brennan had spent a session at Muldoon's, describing it as sheer torture. Dreiser protested, but Paul won him over with a humor combined with tender concern that was irresistible, took him out and bought him expensive clothing from the skin out, then next day, April 21, escorted him to the Muldoon establishment three miles northeast of White Plains where Paul would pay the $35 weekly fee.[45]

Muldoon, a human tiger despite his sixty-odd years, had a contempt for weakness and a conviction that the way to cure it was with exercise and an army discipline that bordered on savagery—a regimen he got away with because his patients were in mortal terror of him and because the system worked. He liked Paul, who told him that Theodore was a writer, a genius. It made no difference. The spindly Dreiser was caught up in a hurricane of six o'clock medicine-ball workouts, calisthenics, one-minute showers and seven-mile dogtrots that had him limp. Austin Brennan wrote in vivid memory, "I think I endured more pain during the three weeks I spent [at Muldoon's] than at any like period of my life . . . it was a sort of premonition *Dante's Inferno*." [46]

"Don't stand there, Dreiser," Muldoon bellowed, hurling the medicine ball at him viciously. "If you can't do the work, get out." He showered curses on them all, including several millionaires. During a riding session, when the weary Dreiser sagged on his horse, Muldoon humiliated him before the entire group.

"Look at him," he sneered, "he thinks he is very wise. He thinks he is a philosopher. Let a selfish ass get that bee in his bonnet and there is nothing under the sun that will get his mind off himself. Now you sit up, you long legged ignoramus, and pay attention. . . ."

Though livid with embarrassment, Dreiser reflected, "I had sense enough to see that what he said was true. I was long legged and I was selfish, and I had thought I was somewhat of a philosopher. . . . Anyhow, my mind was riveted on myself and I was having a hard time getting it off." [47]

The realization was a sign of improvement. If he ached in every limb, he forgot his impulse to walk in a circle, found that the landscape looked almost level, was freed of pain in fingers and toes, gained weight and slept better. There were times when he yearned to quit the sulphurous Muldoon at all costs, times when self-pity mastered him. Once he burst into tears on hearing the song of a thrush. But Paul's cheery telephone calls buoyed him. He stuck it out for six weeks, and when he left on June 2, he felt considerably improved, shook Muldoon's hand warmly and was thankful that Paul paid the entire bill of $256.75. He applied again at the New York Central and was put to work at the Spuyten Duyvil shop on the Hudson. He had been frank about his condition, and the company letter to the foreman described him as "completely run down mentally." [48]

He took a room in nearby Kingsbridge, began piling lumber at fifteen cents an hour, and discovered how pathetically soft he was despite the Muldoon repair job. Dreiser's coordination was always poor. He was clumsy, slow at learning the many subtle shifts by which workmen attain efficiency while sparing their muscles, and the railroad must have been in dire need of help to keep him. An hour of plank-piling almost killed him, but always, when he was on the verge of exhaustion, he was given lighter work such as removing shavings. Not until now did he realize the extent of his debilitation. The workmen knew his condition, gossiped about it and doubtless waggled meaning fingers at their heads on occasion. At times he had recurrences of his mental-optical illusion that the world and everything in it was askew, and he could still sink into moods of blackest self-absorption, soliloquizing, "To be driven about this way like a slave—to be whipped and scourged!" After three weeks he was raised to seventeen and a half cents an hour. For a time he had an easier job as pile-driving inspector and was ordered, "See that [the piles] are driven full length and keep the usual record as to the weight of hammer, average length of drop, number of blows struck, distance piles are driven into the ground. . . ." [49]

Paul, who went occasionally to the Mudlavia sanitarium in Indiana and boasted that it took three carloads of mud to cover him, regaled Theodore with letters such as only Paul could write:

> Remember the future of the great N. Y. Central system, must not weaken. . . . the d-d weather gives me the *botts*. . . . I hope to hear of your advancement as general all around Supt of the tie lifting gang of Gorillas. . . .
>
> "Women like tea, sometimes is weak," . . . And tomorrow sir, I leave in a *Closed Carriage* with a *double veil* closely drawn over my face. . . . Enclosed find V [$5].
>
> Mr. Theodore Dreiser, Supt. Vice Prest, Master Mechanic, Pile Driving Overseer—& Associate of Guineas. . . . Liquor and I are strangers since Sept. 20th. . . . I have been living on milk alone, for over two weeks & am losing flesh fast. . . . [50]

Paul, who had been keenly hurt by Theodore's long estrangement, was overjoyed that they were friendly again.

As for Theodore, his celibacy was ended by a local affair or two—always a tonic to him. By September, however, Jug joined him in Kingsbridge and he would have to be more careful. Now he could not get along on his $1.75 a day so another letter came from Paul: "I am enclosing check for fifty dollars." And another, dated "Oct. umpsteen":

> Now you cut out giving opinions & views to every rube who writes & wishes to know something about God, Jeff Davis & Roosevelt—You have been working long & hard to get yourself in condition to write, so when you do write, let it be on your book.[51]

On the job, Dreiser gazed with wonder at the roaring planers, lathes and power saws, the locomotives switching, the work gangs coming and going—hundreds of men submerged for sixty hours a week in a corporation which they could not see, feel or understand—and speculated, "What a profit there must be in the control of labor. . . . This vast sway and sweep of elemental energy—how does it come that the few have put their hands on it and control it while the many serve and [wait]?" And he could still lapse into despair: "Oh, God, if I could only get back into life. If I could forget this thing. . . . Give me individuality, my old belief in the reality of things, and I will be happy again." And he could turn bitterly against life: "Evolution! Evolution to what? To where? . . . Nature is against you. She will not play fair. . . . "[52] In this frame of mind, a letter from Paul saying, "Well old sport Good luck & God bless you—Get Your hammer out & just knock h——l out of things, I am fondly Yours," probably annoyed him.

But on Christmas Eve, 1903, after three years of despair, he resigned from the railroad, sure enough of himself to write:

> After a long battle I am once more the possessor of health. . . . All that is, now passes before me a rich, varied and beautiful procession. I have fought a battle for the right to live and for the present, musing with stilled nerves and a serene gaze, I seem the victor.[53]

4. The Road Back

Dreiser got a bread-and-butter job as assistant feature editor of Frank Munsey's *New York Daily News*, he and Jug took a cheap apartment at Mott Avenue and 144th Street in the Bronx, and he began a self-rehabilitation that was both grim and aggressive. His claim of "stilled nerves and a serene gaze" was an exaggeration, for his nerves would always be jumpy and he was bitter about his three wasted years and the fate of *Sister Carrie*.

He had soured on Arthur Henry, who had divorced his first wife and married Anna Mallon, whose mother had disinherited her as a result. And when he read Henry's newly published *An Island Cabin*, he was incensed. In it the foursome at Dumpling Island had been given fictitious names, concealing from outsiders but not from Dreiser himself that he was represented as a complainer who blighted the summer outing there. Had not Dreiser dramatized his own sister in *Carrie?* It made no difference. When Henry called on him in February, they quarreled bitterly, Henry later writing him in part:

> I have . . . just gone over carefully the chapters in *An Island Cabin* that have offended you, and, as I read them now . . . it is very clear to me that this book is not responsible for the interruption of our friendship. That was doomed before the book was written, and the doom of it lay in the fact that you could listen to what other people might insinuate . . . concerning me, and say nothing to me about it, but allow these things, nevertheless, to influence your conception of me; in the fact that you could pour into Anna's ears things which should have come directly, and at once, from you to me; in the fact that, in spite of our long intimacy . . . you could form such a vulgar and undiscriminating, undiscerning conception of my attachment for Anna, and in the fact that you could tolerate in yourself such a gratuitous animosity toward her.
>
> When we were on the island, I had no idea of the extent of these evil elements in you, and I can't yet believe that you will not still eliminate them before they have perverted your whole being.[1]

Aware of great gaps in his knowledge, Dreiser resolved to educate himself from the beginning in history and philosophy. He read Kant, and somewhere along the line he studied Greek and Roman history, but his education was fated to remain spotty because he was not a steady reader and he had too many irons in the fire. He was writing Sunday features for the *News*, applying vainly for a job at *McClure's*, and sending out manuscripts based on his recent experiences, almost always unsuccessfully. In turn, *McClure's*, *Scribner's*, *Harper's Monthly*, *Harper's Weekly*, *Leslie's* and *Pearson's* rejected his "The Toil of the Laborer." *McClure's, Scribner's, The Saturday Evening Post* and *Harper's Monthly* rejected his "The Mighty Burke." *McClure's, The Post* and *Harper's Monthly* rejected his "The Cruise of the Idlewild." Again his trouble was that he was asserting his own artistic individuality. He was not doing factual pot-boilers cut to order, but sketches he wanted to write, which had only a slight story line and were therefore hard to place.

In the fall, on a tip from his friend Richard Duffy, he moved over to Street & Smith under the aegis of the huckstering Ormond G. Smith, whose motto was, "The worse the swill the better you can sell it." At $15 a week Dreiser edited the firm's sanguinary dime novels, later declaring that when he got an extra-long script he simply chopped it in two, devising a new ending for the first half and a new beginning for the second, thereby increasing output. He later called his experiences there "a riot, a scream," but as he toiled over the indomitable sheriff who tracked down the outlaw and drilled him full of holes, and knew that thousands would read it breathlessly, he must have been reminded bitterly of *Carrie's* selective sale.

Apparently he had no time to work on *Jennie Gerhardt,* but the dream of writing novels persisted. To one of his editorial colleagues, Charles De Camp, he talked with such certainty of his future that years later De Camp wrote him, "I remember the days we used to walk up town from 7th av & 15th St and how confidently you predicted what you have done." [2] But now he was not only pinched but in debt, still owing Joseph H. Taylor $750 for advances on *Jennie.* Working steadily, he wrote poetry and articles on the side, mostly for his friend Duffy, now an editor of *Tom Watson's Magazine.* Since it was apparent that Taylor was not going to reissue *Carrie,* he was determined to buy the plates and rights from him. At Street & Smith's he became friendly with Charles Agnew MacLean, a Smith subaltern, and his talents were rewarded by a raise in pay and the editorship of a new popular journal, *Smith's Magazine,* which the firm launched early in 1905. [3]

Always he thought of *Carrie.* To MacLean he talked so persuasively that the pair made plans to form a publishing house of their own, and MacLean himself bought the plates back from Taylor for $500. Meanwhile, brother Paul, still keeping a fond eye on Theodore, wrote him with an enthusiasm suggesting that he had forsaken his milk diet:

> Dear Broth Just been looking over "Smith's Mag" for *June*—Great—*fine exstatic—imperishable   Genius art thou—*
>
> *ode*
>
> > *On the shores of the Jirsey Central Rale Road*
> > *Scented by the marshes sweetund breze*
> > *I see a littul tendur footud maden*
> > *Where the tranes go flying thru like Rokefurt chese*

The balance follows later on a freight train— Yours *Broth* [4]

Paul, fortune's jack-a-dandy, was not as gay as he sounded. Late in 1903 he and Pat Howley had bought out Fred Haviland, continued in business as the Howley-Dresser Company, and failed a year later. Although Paul at this time wrote "My Gal Sal," which would later make a fortune, it was only a moderate hit at the start. Ed Dreiser, wanting to help Paul and seeing a commercial value in his name, deserted the stage, borrowed money and founded the Paul Dresser Publishing Company on West Twenty-eighth Street, an enterprise in which the improvident Paul was firmly barred from any business authority but was paid $25 a week largely for the use of his name. Now the Paul Dresser Company was losing money fast and Paul himself was on the skids, declining in health as he succumbed to gloom.

If Theodore was worried about Paul, he was often downright distraught about his own marital status. In Jug he had a helpmate who cooked, sewed, mended his clothes, gave him the medicine and pills he constantly felt he needed, and made him so comfortable that the arrangement would have been satisfactory but for her fatal flaw: she could not abide his infidelities. His marriage, he later said, "had become a torture. It was a binding state and I was not to be bound." [5] Jug, remembering her own large and happy farm family, wanted children, thinking also that this might curb her Honeybugs' wander-lust. Dreiser forbade children and took steps on his own to prevent concep-tion.[6] They were too poor, an infant would frazzle his nerves, and by this time he felt that their marriage was doomed. Jug, while conceding that they could not yet afford a child, was nearing thirty-six and anxious not to wait too long. Ironically, the whole question was futile, for Dreiser, unknown to them both, was sterile.[7] While he admired some aspects of Jug's character, and there were moments of tenderness between them, there was always the undercurrent, the conflict between the puritan wife and the husband of enormous appetites and talents.

It was not long before Paul made the ultimate admission of defeat by leaving his beloved Broadway and moving in with his sister Emma at 203 West 106th Street, where he tried and failed to knock out new hit tunes on his old rosewood piano. Theodore, visiting him occasionally, had a firm presentiment that Paul's days on earth were numbered.

In *Smith's Magazine*, printed on shaggy pulp though it was, he had a medium more satisfying than cowboy thrillers, and he worked at it seriously. Needing material, he wrote Robert Underwood Johnson at *Century* offering to buy manuscripts which he had shelved—a letter on which Johnson or a colleague scribbled, "A new magazine—I wouldn't help it a bit." [8] Although Dreiser was forced to run fluffy serials, he found space for informative articles and formed a lasting friendship with one of his contributors, a mad-brained free-thinker named Charles Fort. If *Smith's* was a literary con-fection, it could also be a stepping stone to a better magazine, a better job, more money. Believing implicitly that evolution and the survival of the fittest was the law of mankind, he aimed to be hard, to drop friends who bored him and cultivate those who stimulated him or could advance him, to push and jostle his way to the top. He warned his readers in an editorial that hardness was essential:

> *Success* is what counts in the world, and it is little matter how the success is won. . . . No matter how fine our conceptions of art or ethics, we can never see the world as it actually is, until we look this fact in the face. . . .[9]

He had made this discovery, as he made many others, with the naïve feeling that he was one of the first to discover it.

He fancied himself a cool intellectual, whereas he was unlearned and emotional, a believer in omens and fortune tellers unapproved by Darwin. He was too soft, or too dependent, to tell Jug candidly that their marriage was a failure. When Jug turned from Methodism to Christian Science in a search for comfort, Dreiser likewise seized on Christian Science, as he seized on many "new" ideas, with an air of discovery, then dropped it for the next. He could be cruel to individuals, but he was usually tender toward humanity in the mass, when he became the Dreiser who could watch in awe the throngs of male and female workers pour from the sweatshops at closing time, pinched, bedraggled, overworked, underpaid, hopelessly caught in the commercial trap, incapable of anything but grinding labor until death, and who could yet nurture the one thing they did not have, hope—the Dreiser who could write wonderingly in his own magazine:

> A long day in the shops has made them keen for the life outside, and this close of the evening with the promise of night and a modicum of pleasure puts a touch in their faces which is indescribably encouraging. It puts hope in the hearts of the most dispirited. It lifts the mind in the most exalted . . . way. You cannot move in the crowd and not feel the ancient faith of the world that life is good and something comes of this opportunity of existing. What is it, who can say? You only feel it, and it renews your youth.[10]

The other Dreiser was a nickel-nurser who would fight for every penny, even from his best side-money market, his friend Duffy at *Tom Watson's Magazine*. "I'm very sorry you feel you had to protest," Duffy wrote, "against the price paid for 'A Cradle of Tears.' " In response to a later Dreiser complaint, Duffy wrote, "I'll do the best we can in the matter of price." [11] He valued Dreiser's friendship despite his thorny moods, and the Duffys, now proud parents, exchanged visits with the childless Dreiser couple.

Smith's prospered under a Dreiser regime that included careful instructions to Charles Fort on how to inject life into his straggly writing, but a coolness developed between Dreiser and Charles Agnew MacLean causing them to drop their plan to collaborate as publishers—a circumstance Dreiser later blamed partly on himself, saying, "I was always difficult to deal with." [12] This raised again his perpetual problem: Who would reissue *Sister Carrie? Carrie* had won a cadre of avant-garde admirers who rebelled against prim American standards and regarded Dreiser as the liberator who would lead the nation into literary honesty. Edna Kenton, the Chicago critic, had bought ten remaindered copies as gifts and had taken the trouble in 1905 to write Dreiser of her admiration and hope that the book would be reissued. New York admirers included Hamlin Garland, Albert Bigelow Paine and Morgan Robertson—not Frank Norris, sadly, for he had died too young in 1902. Dreiser himself had spread the story of its "suppression" by Mrs. Doubleday, and there was a considerable feeling that he was indeed the victim of a bigoted woman. "The book is now better known and its champions quite a company in themselves," Dreiser wrote Miss Kenton.[13]

He was calling on Paul almost daily, watching him die. Most of Paul's old friends had deserted him. He saw ominous portents on sighting a broken horseshoe or a number 13, and once, when someone left a hat on his bed, he was stricken with fear at this certain death-sign. On January 30, 1906, he died at forty-eight of a heart attack at Emma's home. "When I arrived," Dreiser wrote, "he was already cold in death, his soft hands folded over his chest, that indescribable sweetness of expression about the eyes and mouth—the empty shell of the beetle." [14] The newspapers said that Paul's sister, the twenty-four-year-old actress Louise Dresser, was about to go onstage at Proctor's 58th Street Theater when she heard the news and collapsed. Louise was not his sister but a young lady born Louise Kerlin for whom Paul had taken a liking, introduced her as his sister so that she could use his famous name, and promoted her with some success.

All Broadway packed St. Francis Xavier Church on Sixteenth Street when Father Van Rensselaer celebrated the requiem mass for the man whose music—he had written some 160 songs—had stirred sentimentalists grouped around a million pianos across the land. "If he sinned, he always repented," the priest said trustfully. Paul died flat broke except for a fortune in music not yet negotiable. The Paul Dresser Publishing Company had already collapsed and Ed had returned to the stage. The family was shocked to discover that Paul left not a dime for his own funeral expenses, which were defrayed by Ed's mother-in-law. Dreiser took Paul's rectangular rosewood piano as a keepsake that he would treasure all his life.

II. POETIC LICENSE

In April, on the strength of having pushed *Smith's* to a sale of 125,000, Dreiser snapped up a job as editor of the *Broadway Magazine* at $40 a week with the promise of a raise if he boosted circulation. A majority interest in *Broadway* had been purchased by small, dapper Benjamin Bowles Hampton, a success fiend from Illinois who had prospered in the advertising business, and a lesser interest was owned by Thomas H. McKee, the former Doubleday attorney who was, like Hampton, an alumnus of Knox College. Dreiser's job was to transform a "spicy" magazine that had sunk to 12,000 circulation into a home publication presenting a bright but decent picture of city life. Hampton later claimed that he discerned Dreiser's genius instantly, saying, "I said to myself, 'Jesus, here's a wow,' and hired him on the spot." [15]

Still fearful, doubtless recalling his three lost years, the iconoclast Dreiser took the helm of a magazine vowing to be pure. The muckrakers were having a holiday. *McClure's, Collier's, The American Magazine*—even the *Ladies' Home Journal*—were exposing political corruption and social injustice, and Lincoln Steffens, Burton Hendrick, Ida Tarbell, Samuel Hopkins Adams and others were turning out copy roasting the crooks and chiselers in high places, forcing President Roosevelt to call for reforms. That same year Upton Sinclair's *The Jungle* was published—and by Doubleday, Page! Dreiser turned his back on the muckrakers and donned a Mother Hubbard. In his June issue appeared a manifesto perhaps written by him:

> It is, to all intents and purposes, a new publication, blessed right now with entirely new and refreshing ideals and rid once and forever, of the cheap, the vulgar, and the commonplace policy which once guided it. No one need to work here any longer for anything but that which is sweet and refreshing, and clean.[16]

Mr. and Mrs. Frank Doubleday would have enjoyed reading that.

After the gloomy Street & Smith diggings on Seventh Avenue, Dreiser now had a neat office at 7 West Twenty-second Street and a generous budget that enabled him to buy work from such writers as Channing Pollock, O. Henry and Rudyard Kipling. Ben Hampton devoted himself mostly to his advertising business, so the job of dictating policy on the magazine was handled by McKee, who knew all about Dreiser as the storm center of the Doubleday controversy of 1900. But since McKee had worked behind the scenes in that quarrel, Dreiser did not know of his part in it nor did McKee enlighten him. From the first, McKee, a perfectionist, admired Dreiser as a writer and idea man but complained of his inability to handle detail, to delegate duties systematically to his staff.

Dreiser's first move was to buy the plates and sheets of *Carrie* from MacLean for $550. He felt secure enough to move with Jug in the fall to a better apartment at 439 West 123rd Street overlooking Morningside Park, but he still owed J. F. Taylor $750 and he had to borrow $500 for his bond while acting as administrator of Paul's estate.[17] He tried to sell a play, *The Boomerang*, on which Paul had collaborated with Robert H. Davis, and also Paul's last song, "Marching Through Georgia to the Tune of Dixie Land."

But most of all he worked on *Broadway*, his best editorial job so far and—who could tell?—possibly the means to an even better one.

He formed a staff including Ethel M. Kelley and a bright, bitter young man from Missouri, Harris Merton Lyon, for whom he took an instant liking, possibly because Lyon admired *Sister Carrie* and was trying to write fiction with the same adherence to truth. Lyon was fascinated by his contradic-

tions—his kindliness, nervousness and morbidity—and noticed a sense of per-
secution. "I think," he observed, "this slight morbidity may have ramified out
into delusions of animosities in the world around him. . . ." [18] Dreiser's old
friend Peter McCord, still with the *Newark News*, was doing art work for
Broadway, as were James Montgomery Flagg and John Edwin Jackson. A
cultivated young man from Cedar Rapids, Carl Van Vechten, found Dreiser
uncouth but likable and contributed a piece about *Salome*, soon to appear at
the Met. Under Dreiser, *Broadway* became a handsome magazine with a
veneer of quality, devoted to the low- and middle-brow audience who
revered glitter, replete with departments such as "Beautiful Women of New
York Society" and "Summer Hostesses of Society." Dreiser contributed
occasional poetry himself, one of his offerings, "The Poet's Creed," a colossal
bromide:

> *I would not give the bells that ring*
> *For all the world of bartering,*
> *Nor yet the whispering of the leaves*
> *For all the Gold that Greed conceives.*
> *To me, the grass that grows in Spring*
> *Is sweeter than Fame's offering—*
> *And Ah! the smile of kindly worth*
> *Than all the wealth of all the earth.* [19]

Poetic license, to be sure—Dreiser was fighting tooth and nail for Gold and
Fame. On the June, 1907, issue, 140 pages long, he splashed a proud blurb on
the cover: "In one year the NEW Broadway Magazine has won place among
the highest-grade magazines in America. . . ." There were 35 pages of
profitable ads—Victrola, Prudential, Murad, White Rock, many others, and
one newspaper called Dreiser's work "the prettiest piece of transformation
work seen in New York for many a day. . . ." But McKee, who wanted even
greater things, peppered him with critical memos about his lack of discipline:

Mr. Dreiser:—You are one of the best fellows in the world, and no man
could be more faithful to his job or more sincerely in earnest or work harder.
. . . And yet you make the most exasperating errors of omission of any intelligent man I ever worked with. . . . It's simply a lack of mental discipline. . . . I don't know how many times I have spoken of bad headings on
fiction. . . . One can acquire the ability to boss details if he wants to.

Mr. Dreiser:—Just another effort to make things clear. . . . At no time
have I been satisfied with you as managing editor. You do not dig up writers
that I want, you do not run the inside work properly. Every number that has
gone to press since October has been put through with tremendous labor—
largely because you do not direct your own assistants right. . . . From my
point of view you have a lot of ability . . . and if you choose to use that
ability as I suggest you can easily hold your job and more than likely work
on your fiction at the same time. . . . If you don't want to do it my way,
you will of course want to take a job elsewhere. . . . [20]

The survival of the fittest! Yet when Dreiser found Paul's affairs in such chaos that he needed an attorney, he consulted McKee, possibly thinking that his fee would be low to a fellow Broadwayite. Paul had drawn royalties from music publishers "over the counter" as he needed them, keeping no records other than occasional scraps of paper, so the problem of determining what was due the estate from different sources seemed insoluble—and the publishers were not helpful. Dreiser, in telling McKee of the non-cooperation of Paul's publishers, was reminded of the derelictions of publishers in general and Doubleday in particular, and he launched into a long account of the "suppression" of *Sister Carrie*.

"I held my face straight," McKee recalled, "for . . . I wanted to hear his tale with all the trimmings. Then I quietly said, 'I know all about it, Dreiser. I am that rascally lawyer who you say helped to gyp you.'

"He was astounded. His face reddened and he stared at me open-mouthed. . . . But at last the ridiculous side of the scene came uppermost and we laughed long and loud. Then followed eager debate, for this topic was an obsession with him, and, I should say, he was not entirely rational about it." McKee listed the facts:

"You were strenuously urged," he told Dreiser, "to take the plates to some other publisher in the beginning, were offered the plates at cost, then even as a gift and you refused. Both you and Frank Norris were sure that the book would sell readily if shown to the public. It didn't. You made a blunder and now try to blame it on somebody else. 'Fess up now!" [21]

Dreiser argued that Doubleday was publishing authors like Norris, Kipling and Andrew Carnegie, that he wanted the prestige of such company, that he had a contract and why should he cancel it? He finally conceded that *Carrie* was not entirely suppressed but "practically suppressed." At later talks with McKee he launched into tirades against Mrs. Doubleday, saying that authors should rightly take their scripts to her at the Doubleday home rather than to the office on Union Square, that he was warning author friends of this and that, as a result, Brand Whitlock, who was much sought by Doubleday, had taken his wares elsewhere. "There was so much of this venomous kind of talk," McKee recalled, "that I began to suspect that the man was a little off his base." [22]

At the office Dreiser was often moody and depressed. The light-hearted Ben Hampton liked to josh him, shaking his head and saying, "And he looks like a normal fellow too. . . . I hate to say such things about anybody but actually he writes all that poetic hog-wash he puts into the magazine." [23] As the staff tittered, Dreiser would smile painfully, flush and muster no word of repartee. But in his assistant, Ethel Kelley, he found a sympathetic listener. He told Miss Kelley he was embittered, discouraged, through as a writer. No one would believe in him. Always he was able to confide in women more than in men, and Miss Kelley was only one of many women who would help him.

III. CARRIE REBORN

Ethel Kelley consulted with her friend Flora Mai Holly, one of the first of New York's literary agents, who had recently started in business at 156 Fifth Avenue, just around the corner from *Broadway*'s Twenty-second Street offices. Could she find a publisher brave enough to reissue *Carrie* and restore Dreiser's faith in himself? This simple step proved a turning point in his career.

Miss Holly knew Ben W. Dodge, a stocky, lovable alcoholic formerly with Dodd, Mead and an able bookman when he kept his elbow straight. Dodge, with a colleague, Charles W. Doscher, was trying to gather funds to form his own publishing house. In January, 1907, Miss Holly negotiated with Dodge, found that both Dodge and Doscher were impressed by *Carrie*, and brought Dreiser into the talks. Dreiser, while delighted, mistrusted all publishers. This time he was determined to make sure, personally and with authority, that *Carrie* got the promotion and advertising she deserved. He did it by sinking $5,000 into the corporation—$1,000 in cash and the balance later—and becoming secretary and editor of B. W. Dodge & Company, an investment suggesting that he must by then have received some returns from Paul's music.[24] He lent the plates and donated the sheets to the firm, but he would also receive a salary of $35 a week for his spare-time editorial services. During these negotiations he was a guest at the Doscher home in New York, where he told again the story of *Carrie*'s "suppression" in 1900 with such feeling that Mrs. Doscher almost a half-century later recalled, "It just seems as if I should never forget his bitterness at Mrs. Doubleday." [25]

His new enterprise was unknown to Hampton, carried on in his off hours. The Dodge office was at 24 East Twenty-first Street, only a block from the magazine. The publication of *Sister Carrie* was scheduled for May 18, and Dreiser worked furiously to send it off with a splash. He got blurbs from Reedy, Brand Whitlock, Hamlin Garland, Albert Bigelow Paine and others, urged Edna Kenton in Chicago to wheedle a good word from Henry B. Fuller—even sought to get a testimonial from President Roosevelt in the White House. The Dodge Company beat the drum, circulated leaflets bearing American praise plus the British encomiums of 1901, offered free posters in color and bought newspaper advertisements headed, "The Curtain Raised / on a generally unwritten / Phase of Life," suggesting that the book's daring realism was justified by its great art.[26] Deep strategy had been exercised in an effort to attract lowbrows interested in sex without offending highbrows demanding literature.

As a result the book was reviewed even more widely than in 1900. The returns showed that American criticism had matured somewhat in seven years, also doubtless being influenced by the British garlands. While there were still angry assaults on *Sister Carrie* as "harmful in the hands of the young," and a book "to be shunned," the *New York World* praised it as "of uncommon quality," the *San Francisco Call* said it was "a work of genius," and the *New York Sun* exclaimed, "Amid the thousands of anemic novels that come out like a flood, written by ladies for ladies of both sexes, here is a book written by a man. . . ." Dreiser was interviewed by *The New York Times.* He was the subject of a flattering editorial in the *Sun*.[27] He was vindicated. Let Frank and Neltje Doubleday read the papers now!

Carrie got off to a brisk sale. Dreiser's Negro friend, J. E. Bowler, with whom he was still corresponding, visited New York and could not locate Dreiser but later reported, "I noticed your book *Sister Carrie* on display in the store windows. . . ." [28] Dreiser was not ready to quit the literary boon-docks and climb the high peak of purity. He let it be known privily among the editorial fraternity that he was looking for a better job, and in June he got an exciting nibble:

> Dear Mr. Dreyser:
>   If you would call at this office to see me tomorrow (Friday) morning at or about eleven o'clock you would be doing me a courtesy that I would very much appreciate.
>
> Very truly yours,
G. W. Wilder [29]

George Wilder misspelled Dreiser's name and did not bother to sign his own on his typed message, but he could afford to be careless because he was president of the Butterick Publishing Company, one of the nation's biggest, publishers of dress patterns and prim magazines bought by millions of strait-laced women. Dreiser lumbered downtown to the huge, fifteen-story Butterick Building at Spring and MacDougal Streets. Two weeks later he left Hampton and was installed as top editor of the Butterick "Trio" at a starting salary of $5,000 a year plus a bonus for circulation gains.

It was the literary joke of the century—Dreiser the apostate, the libertine, the enemy of prudery, the fighter for realism, the author of *Sister Carrie*, becoming the high arbiter of dainty stories for dainty women, the iconoclast turned hymn-singer.

5. Fame and Gold

The Butterick Trio consisted of the *Delineator*, the *Designer* and *New Idea Woman's Magazine*, all of them big but *Delineator* the biggest with "almost a million" circulation, all of them devotedly commercial. They served as bait for the immensely profitable Butterick patterns. You read the magazine, you saw the dress, you bought the pattern. ("All New Butterick Patterns are 10¢ and 15¢. NONE HIGHER.") In the July, 1907, *Delineator*, 148 pages long, the first seven features—up to page 52—were devoted to fashions and contained 150 careful drawings of dresses, nightgowns, underwear, bathing suits and other garments for which Butterick would supply the patterns. Thirty-six more pages were devoted to such allied subjects as cookery, homemaking, society and children, leaving only 21 pages for fiction and eight for articles. The dark hand of profit was visible even in the Jenny Wren Club, a monthly *Delineator* feature. Jenny Wren Clubs had been organized among little girls in cities all over the land, and *Delineator* shamelessly sold them patterns for doll clothing. In the Butterick Building labored 2,000 underpaid workers, mostly on patterns. Its underground floors contained what was said to be the biggest printing plant in the world, mostly turning out patterns.

Lost among the fashion displays in Dreiser's new magazines were a few obscure fiction pieces and articles that would entertain, instruct—and never offend—women who embodied the spirit of puritanical recoil from truth which he despised. In them were permitted no slang, coarseness, lust, seduction, cigarette-smoking, drinking—not even an illustration showing wine on the table at Thanksgiving. In them life was moral, beautiful, inspiring.

Theodore Dreiser, unable to find literary success in the world of 1907, had gone into the pattern business.

If he had been a lowly literary street-walker at Smith's and a better-fed prostitute at *Broadway*, he was now one of the nation's greatest whoremasters of letters. He opened his house with an announcement headed "A BIGGER DELINEATOR":

> A magazine's greatness is determined by one thing alone, its message. *The Delineator*'s message is human betterment. Its appeal is to the one great humanizing force of humanity—womanhood. To sustain it, to broaden it, to refine it, to inspire it, is our aim. Our theme is one that a woman may carry into her home, her church and her social affairs—the theme of the ready smile, the theme of the ungrudged helping hand.

> This, then, is *The Delineator*'s broadened purpose—to help every woman in this land to live better by teaching her practical home-craft, . . . by strengthening her in her moral fight for righteousness in the world. . . .[1]

Dreiser must have roared at the irony of it. But he had endured three years of mental terror in the cause of honesty and wanted no more of that. Now he enjoyed the realization of one of his most persistent reveries, the Paneled Office Dream.

What an office! Vast, luxurious, with fumed-oak furniture, rich window hangings and a desk the size of a billiard table, it was the sort of place he would have trembled to enter a dozen years earlier. Being on the twelfth floor, he had lordly views of Brooklyn, the harbor, the Statue of Liberty and Jersey. He had 32 underlings to do his bidding—a staff he immediately began to improve by luring Charles Hanson Towne away from the *Smart Set* as his fiction editor. George Wilder was unaware that his new top man was an officer and stockholder in B. W. Dodge & Company, spending his spare time on this, even using *Delineator* stationery to write to such people as Henry L. Mencken, a Baltimore newspaperman with whom he discussed a proposal that Mencken edit a popular edition of Schopenhauer for Dodge.[2]

In despair a few months earlier, Dreiser now was as happy as a misanthrope could be, cynically playing the commercial world for all it was worth, revelling in his important editorship, his sub rosa partnership in a corporation and the fact that *Sister Carrie* was almost if not quite a best seller. He was not short-changing Wilder in the least—simply doing two men's work. He had been on the job only three weeks when his appendix flared and he went to St. Luke's Hospital to have it out, causing Flora Mai Holly, evidently aware of his predilections, to cheer him by writing, "The nurses [there] are the nicest in New York." [3] At that time an appendectomy was a grave affair. Dreiser went with Jug to recuperate at Avon-by-the-Sea, New Jersey. His bill for one week there ($51.80) included twenty-five cents for cigars—an item that gives one pause. Had Dreiser, always a non-smoker, decided that a slender perfecto would furnish the final touch of distinction in that splendid office? If so, he gave it up because he could not smoke without choking.

Although he was away for about a month, he had so carefully laid out his first issues that his staff proceeded without trouble. While he was away, Augusta Prescott, a Butterick assistant who had formerly worked under him on *Broadway*, wrote him almost daily about the progress of the Trio and also conferred with Jug, who was helping with liaison. Jug evidently regarded the Butterick job as the pinnacle of respectable success. This was one of those times when Dreiser, who could reverse himself astonishingly depending on mood, saw admirable qualities in the woman he often considered a drag on his genius. Miss Prescott wrote him:

> She [Jug] is, as you told me, good & true. I wonder if she knows how steadily you sing her praises, or how you say: "It isn't because she is Mrs.

Dreiser that I praise her, but because she is such a clever little woman!"

Oh, Mr. Dreiser, you are like all men who are in love. Only you happen to have found the right woman.[4]

Back on the job in August, he gave each of his three magazines a staff of its own to encourage individuality, brought in Katherine Leckie, an experienced newspaperwoman, to head the *New Idea*, brought in Sarah Field Splint to take charge of an enlarged children's department, redesigned the covers, brought in Flora Mai Holly as a part-time adviser, reorganized the cooking and beauty departments and dragooned Wilder into authorizing a correspondence department to give fast answers to readers' queries about baking apple pandowdy or combating excessive perspiration, giving readers an image of Butterick as their prompt, loyal ally in all problems.

Almost at once there was a crisis. Since President Roosevelt had gone to Colorado to shoot bears, the Teddy bear had blossomed into a national craze. Grown women were toting Teddy bears into shops and theaters. Far worse, little girls formerly satisfied with dolls now caressed Teddy bears that grunted when punched in the stomach—a clear threat that could seduce many little Jenny Wrens away from their dolls and therefore away from Butterick doll-clothes patterns.

Editor Dreiser met the challenge with an editorial praising Roosevelt but blasting the fad as immoral and suicidal. "An adult woman . . . who . . . goes about with a Teddy bear hugged to her heart, is a spectacle so silly that it must be seen to be believed," it read. But it pointed out that the real danger was to children and in fact to the nation itself: "Take away the little girl's dolly and you have interfered with the nascent expression of motherhood. . . . You have implanted the race suicide idea where it will work the most harm—in the very hearts of the babies themselves.

"Bring your babies back to dollies, or you will have weaned the grown-ups of the future from the babies that will never be." [5]

In the big-selling *Delineator*, Dreiser was so begrudged space for fiction by a fashion department that thought only of patterns that he introduced short-short stories. He brought in more poetry. Remembering his *Ev'ry Month* days, he published sentimental songs, some with lyrics by his old friend Arthur Henry. But he knew that he needed a smasher, a crusade that would attract attention and boost circulation, and he thought he had it when Mabel Potter Daggett brought in an article, "The Child Without a Home," a tearful piece about orphans at the New York Foundling Hospital and similar institutions.[6]

Probably many *Delineator* readers were childless, or could care for another child. Why not let the magazine become a clearing house for the placing of orphan children? Dreiser, always susceptible to ideas—often without realizing their ramifications—got George Wilder's blessing and worked furiously on the project. Undoubtedly he was sincere about it, feeling that here he could accomplish genuine good for humanity in the midst of the nonsense he was forced to dispense, and at the same time build a crusade that could be publicized from the housetops. The wheels turned. Foundling homes, it was learned, were anxious to place their charges to make room for more.

In the November issue, nine full display pages were snared away from patterns to trumpet the appeal of the *Delineator* Child-Rescue Campaign— "for the child that needs a home and the home that needs a child." The *Delineator* undertook to bring them together. As sponsors (and valuable publicists), Dreiser snagged sixteen prominent women, including Mrs. Edith Rockefeller McCormick, Mrs. Frederick Dent Grant and Mrs. William Jennings Bryan, Mrs. Bryan being quoted as saying, "The *Delineator* is undertaking a most worthy work in which I am glad to be of assistance." There were large, though faked, photographs of Bobby, "The First *Delineator* Boy," and Evelyn, "The First *Delineator* Girl"—both extraordinarily appealing—along with the pathetic history of each. *Delineator* readers were urged to give or find them homes. Publicity material went out to newspapers and women's clubs over the land, and the show was on the road.

The Child-Rescue Campaign, which continued for three years, was an emotional crusade to which the emotional Dreiser gave much time and energy. He loved children in the abstract so long as he did not have to cope with them in his own household. Doubtless in this extravaganza he found some atonement, some alleviation of his feelings of guilt in having deserted to the fleshpots.

Atonement was discernible also in his improvement of the milk-and-water Butterick articles, always within the limitations of his pallid medium. He urged women to *do* something. Such *Delineator* pieces as "What Jane Addams Has Done for Chicago" suggested that women everywhere could improve their communities; a symposium, "Does a Clever Man Need a Clever Woman?" stimulated domestic thought; and a series on "What's the Matter With the Public Schools?" [7] said plenty was the matter and that housewives could demand better standards. A Long Island architect, William Neil Smith, whom Dreiser would come to know well, contributed a series on efficient, low-priced houses. The medical articles became more practical. There was a visible effort to encourage women to think, to understand national issues and come to grips with reality. Dreiser had enough to atone for, since he could by no means eliminate the sweet sentiment, the moral sermonizing, the ghastly collections of "bright sayings of children," the articles on "The Joys of Motherhood."

Indeed, the Jenny Wren Club was so successful, with chapters in more than 200 cities buying Butterick doll patterns by the thousands, that the thought arose that boys also wore clothing even if they did not favor dolls. Hence the formation of *Delineator*'s Boy Knights of the Round Table, with the admonition, "While you can't rescue princesses or fight real battles, perhaps you can rescue a poor little kitten that is being teased by some cruel boys. . . . So, dear boys, I want you to be the kind of boys that King Arthur would have liked." [8] This message and many others was signed by Sir Launcelot. The boys were lured by pins commissioning them as pages, squires and finally knights of the Round Table, by colored pennons lettered B.K.R.T., and by communications with Sir Launcelot. This parfit gentil knight had an office at Butterick and was reincarnated in the person of Sarah Field Splint, head of the children's department, salary ten dollars a week.

Charles Hanson Towne was impressed by his boss. "Every department of the organization was under the control of Mr. Dreiser," he wrote. "Not a detail escaped his vigilant eye. He O.K.'d every manuscript that we accepted—read them all, in fact, and continuously gave out ideas to the entire staff, and saw that they bore fruit." He was no longer the disorganized *Broadway* editor who could not lead, for Towne noted, "People moved in and out of his presence, and he settled the problems they presented to him in the briefest possible language. He never quibbled; his mind was made up almost immediately." [9]

Perhaps McKee's nasty memos, or the paneled office, had helped to make a tartar out of him. Nervous, moody, he kept popping his ribboned pince-nez off and on, or fiddling with his handkerchief. He was tough, sarcastic, even cruel, driving his staff and himself, demanding ideas that would sell more magazines and thus more patterns, holding weekly editorial conferences that sometimes lasted into evening, usually quiet and considerate but sometimes wounding in his sarcasm. He was consciously advancing his destiny in accordance with his conviction that life was a struggle in which one either was a leader who drove others or was one of the driven. One day he wandered into Sir Launcelot's office to compliment her on her progress and also to do a little driving.

"You seem to have ideas," he said. "I just want to tell you that you can stay on as long as you have ideas. But once you stop you'll have to leave. I don't want any hard feelings."

"Oh, there won't be any hard feelings," Miss Splint said, but after he left she burst into tears. [10]

She was earning her ten-dollar salary. Now and then one of the nearby Knights of the Round Table clubs would visit the Butterick Building, which was a downtown showplace. The knights naturally wanted to see Sir Launcelot. Miss Splint, to avoid disillusioning them entirely, always got Towne or some other male editor to impersonate Launcelot. [11]

II. ENTER H. L. MENCKEN

By September, *Carrie* had sold 4,617 copies and Dreiser collected $813.82 in royalties plus $420 for twelve weeks' salary from Dodge, plus his juicy Butterick salary. [12] But he was not one to splurge. In 1906 he had begun repaying in small instalments the $750 he owed Taylor in advances on *Jennie Gerhardt*—a debt dating back to 1902—and he was continuing these instalments. He also had his remaining $4,000 investment in the Dodge firm to think about. In November Paul's body was moved to Chicago for burial in St. Boniface Cemetery next to the graves of his mother and father. Though Dreiser bore part of this expense, he did not feel he could yet afford a headstone for Paul, so the composer of "On the Banks of the Wabash" lay in an unmarked grave.

Dreiser loved the amiable Ben Dodge, did his best to keep him sober and with the aid of Jug spent his nights soliciting and reading manuscripts for the firm by John Kendrick Bangs, Reginald Wright Kauffman, Charles Fort and others. To some, Fort, with his exotic ideas about science and life, was an arrant crackpot, but to Dreiser he was a genius only in need of guidance. "Mrs. Dreiser is a great admirer of your work," he wrote Fort about his novel, *The Outcast Manufacturers*, "yet when she read this story she said that she found it a little difficult, and I know that I did. . . . You use very little the art of luring your readers on. . . ." [13] Jug, convinced that Dreiser's greatness was truly coming into flower, subordinated herself to him and his success even to the point of regarding his philanderings as inevitable. Sociable herself, feeling that he needed a socializing influence, she saw to it that they exchanged visits with the Dreiser clan in New York and with Peter McCord in Newark, now a happily married man. She often held open house at the 123rd Street apartment for Butterick editors, contributors and other literary people. Some found her entirely admirable, a stabilizing influence her restless husband needed, and wondered at her wifely forbearance. She was attractive, tastefully dressed, hospitable, intelligent. Others, while liking her, felt her lacking in one way or another. She was opposed to liquor, a trifle small-townish, had failed to grow with her husband. Some found her devotion to him cloying and felt that her Honeybugs nickname for him was ridiculous. He was a hypochondriac, always taking pills, and Charles Hanson Towne for one was jarred when at a dinner gathering Jug sang out, "It's time for your pill, Honeybugs." [14]

Yet no one mentioned that Dreiser, who liked to be babied, seemed annoyed by these attentions. With his quick temper he could easily have put a stop to them had he wished, and he would hardly have signed at least one note to her "H-B" for Honeybugs had the name truly pained him. There should have been no mystery as to what doomed their marriage, since he was essentially opposed to all aspects of marriage save its comforts.

In H. L. Mencken, he found a writer so forceful and cogent that he began using him regularly in *Delineator*, among other things as ghost-writer for Dr. Leonard K. Hirshberg, also of Baltimore, on a series about the care and feeding of babies. That Dreiser and Mencken could become engrossed in such a topic was only one of the miracles of commercialism. Dreiser, deadly serious, discussed the first article with George Wilder, the father of four. Then he sent it back for a rewrite, the childless Dreiser lecturing the childless Mencken on pediatrics, warning him that he must "get down to the brass tacks" and "tell all about crying," that babies employed subtly different cries for different needs "and . . . the various kinds of crying should be indicated and the mother urged to understand just what each form means." [15] Mencken consulted Dr. Hirshberg and came through gloriously:

> The cry of habit is much like the normal cry of every baby. The wails are long drawn out and have a sort of rising and falling cadence. They are still at once if the baby gets what it wants. If it does not, they gradually grow less loud and so cease.
>
> The cry of pain, on the contrary, is a short, quick, gasping cry. The baby commonly draws up its legs and gives other evidences of serious disturbance. . . . The prudent nurse . . . will make a diligent search for tight napkins and loose pins.
>
> The cry of hunger is a quick, sharp, staccato cry, with high, shrill notes. . . . It should cease at once on feeding.
>
> The cry of temper—and temper is exhibited by very young children—is long, sharp and high-pitched. It indicates that the youngster is enraged. . . . Some children have such violent tempers that they throw back their heads, grow blue in the face and seem to cease breathing. . . . The best way to deal with such recalcitrant little folks is to lay them in bed and let them cry. They will quickly observe the futility of their efforts and so cease.
>
> When children grow older they acquire what might be called the "insulted" cry. A child of six months is sensitive to sharp words and gives voice to the humiliation they produce. This cry consists of a short sob, followed by a longer one, and slowly rising in volume, though not in pitch. Indeed, it is not unlike the cry of a woman.[16]

It is funny, but it is more sad than funny, to contemplate these future literary giants donning rompers for Butterick money because there was very little else to do. There was virtually no market for the realist. One had to make a living somehow.

In the next instalment, Mencken (as proxy for Dr. Hirshberg) discussed the problems of nursing mothers, saying in part, "It is rarely safe to keep a child at the breast for more than ten or fifteen minutes." Dreiser and Mencken did the job they had to do, and they never forgot that they had to do it. It influenced their thinking permanently. Pot-boiling was less painful to Sinclair Lewis, just out of Yale, a client of Dreiser's agent Flora Mai Holly. To *Delineator* Lewis contributed a poem, "The Death-a-Cold," beginning:

> *When I stay out and slide till late*
> *I hear my Nursey scold:*
> *"O R-r-obin! You come in, right straight!*
> *You'll catch a death-a-cold!"* [17]

But Dreiser and Lewis remained only nodding acquaintances. In the summer of 1908 Mencken called at the Butterick office and for the first time the squat, aggressive, cigar-chewing Baltimorean, then twenty-seven, met the tall, wall-eyed, slack-mouthed, shambling Dreiser, nine years older. It was a meeting that would deeply influence American literature. Dreiser was amused and charmed.

"Well, well," he chuckled, "if it isn't Anheuser's own brightest boy out to see the town." [18]

Mencken affirmed that he was indeed the son of Baltimore's richest brewer—didn't his vivid necktie and yellow shoes prove it? Thus began a remarkable friendship between two individualists who had little in common except their mutual disgust at the pusillanimous state of American letters. Dreiser, delighted by the younger man, used friendly influence to get him the spare-time job of book critic for *Smart Set* magazine, the pair had convivial meetings at Luchow's or the Lafayette when Mencken came to New York, and he sometimes dined with the Dreisers.

Mencken talked like a phonograph. Dreiser was a good listener. Mencken swore vividly, studding innocent conversation with a volley of billingsgate. Dreiser swore rarely and gently. Mencken told uproariously dirty stories. Dreiser *never* told one. Mencken was quick, Dreiser slow. Mencken was well-read. Dreiser was far behind in his reading and would never catch up. Mencken believed in science. Dreiser was abysmally superstitious. Both were hypochondriacs, but with a difference: Mencken satirized his own ills, whereas Dreiser was utterly serious about his. These two opposites had one area of enthusiastic agreement, a contempt for dull, bourgeois, nicey-nice American culture as represented, for example, by the Butterick magazines. At this time Dreiser, though quieter, was the tacit leader of the pair—a relationship that would change gradually as the years went on.

Mencken found Dreiser prowling in a "forest of intrigue" because of his romantic affairs, trying to keep them under cover each from the other, and also from Jug. One night when Mencken was at the Dreiser apartment, Dreiser excused himself after dinner, saying he had some business and would be back in an hour—a fair illustration of his disregard for the amenities. Although one friend of Jug's said that "Never did she speak ill of [Dreiser]," apparently this was one occasion when her forbearance buckled. No sooner had he gone that she bewailed the difficulties of living with him.

"Do you know where he's gone?" she demanded.

"I have no idea," Mencken said, although he could guess.

"He's gone around to that Jewish girl." [19]

Mencken was sorry for her, but he was rather contemptuous toward women in general and he suspected that she had literary pretensions and was jealous of her husband's work. A Christian Science magazine on the table also reduced his regard for her. He could not wait for Dreiser, whose business took him longer than expected, and although he left with the feeling that sexually Dreiser was in a category with chimpanzees—an opinion he held many years later—he was inclined to be on Dreiser's side rather than Jug's. His disdain for Dreiser's furtive affairs did not alter his admiration for Dreiser the man and the artist, the rebel who fought the philistinism both of them hated—or *had* fought it. To Mencken, as to many other insurgents now growing in number, *Sister Carrie* was the manifesto of the rebellion and Dreiser was its prophet even as he fussed over the crying of babies. Mencken would prove his friendship.

III. TRULY UPLIFTING

That Dreiser, who seemed lacking in the editorial faculty and always needed several editors for his own writings, should have become one of New York's most successful and highest-paid editors, is only superficially surprising. The mystery is in how he got by at *Smith's*, where he actually had to wield the pencil. He could hardly have been skillful at taking a story or article and sharpening it into the simple, swift-moving prose Butterick readers wanted, but this did not bother him since it was done by subalterns. In the wider and more important aspects of editing—the sense of "feel" of the whole magazine, the ability to anticipate the wants of readers, the shrewd eye for publicity, the discussions with writers and artists, and above all the hatching of ideas that would sell magazines—Dreiser was not merely competent but exceptionally able. "He was a damn good editor," said Arthur Sullivant Hoffman, who worked closely with him as managing editor of *Delineator*.[20]

As the top editor, the man of prestige and power, the ruler of a large staff, the executive who took persistent long-distance telephone calls and was approached respectfully by such writers as Rupert Hughes, Richard Le Gallienne, Samuel Hopkins Adams, F. Marion Crawford and Ella Wheeler Wilcox, the overseer who boosted circulation and won George Wilder's regard along with a salary increase, he fought furiously for Butterick. The legend that he suffered at Butterick is not wholly correct. The artist in him languished, but the materialist in him had a whale of a time. He could write the following instructions to Charles G. Ross, a Missouri journalism instructor later to become a presidential press secretary:

> In fiction the *Delineator* buys things of an idealistic turn. We like sentiment, we like humor, we like realism, but it must be tinged with sufficient idealism to make it all of a truly uplifting character. Our field in this respect is limited by the same limitations which govern the well regulated home. We cannot admit stories which deal with false or immoral relations, or which point a false moral, or which deal with things degrading, such as drunkenness. I am personally opposed in this magazine to stories which have an element of horror in them or which are disgusting in their realism and fidelity to life. The finer side of things—the idealistic—is the answer for us. . . .[21]

Few could blame him, after his troubles, for relishing a good salary, for accepting the world as it was. Yet he should have been generous enough to forgive the Doubledays for making the same—indeed a less conscious—

acceptance. He never forgave them. He kept telling the misleading story of Mrs. Doubleday's "suppression" of *Carrie* and would continue to tell it for the rest of his life, the latest auditors being Mencken and Charles Hanson Towne, who in turn would repeat it to thousands of their own readers.

To lighten his editorial load in his moonlighting connection with the Dodge company, Dreiser handed some of this work to Fremont Rider, one of his Butterick assistants. He became interested in land promotion, buying two lots near Nyack from Rider and apparently sinking $1,000 in a 150-acre tract near Nanuet in which other Dodge associates also invested. He had somewhat patched his friendship with Arthur Henry, who had meanwhile gone with his wife Anna to North Yakima, Washington, to join his older brother Albert in promoting apple orchards there and had persuaded Dreiser to invest in instalments on a 10-acre orchard.

Projects were humming, for in 1908 Grosset & Dunlap contracted with Dodge and Dreiser for a new cheap edition of 10,000 copies of *Sister Carrie*, which got off to a good sale. Perhaps it was this success that made Dreiser find time to write twenty more chapters of *Jennie Gerhardt* and try the unfinished story on the English publisher Grant Richards, who encouraged him to complete it and also urged that he visit England.[22] With a Butterick adviser, Judge James E. West, Dreiser traveled to Washington and on October 10, 1908, had that final testimony of fame, a conference with President Theodore Roosevelt, persuading the President to take an interest in *Delineator*'s campaign for orphans that ultimately resulted in the organization of the National Child Rescue League with West as its secretary.[23]

Dreiser won praise for his editorial drive for Santa Claus associations in United States communities. He started a prize contest for the best story about pet animals, causing a flood of thousands of manuscripts that were heaped on the desk of a new assistant from Missouri, Homer Croy, who has never forgotten the ordeal of reading them.

Dreiser quarreled so bitterly with Louis Dempsey, head of the fashion department, over the use of space that he and Dempsey refused to speak to each other and Arthur Sullivant Hoffman had to serve as go-between for them. In his efforts to improve the editorial content, Dreiser also had rows with the advertising and business departments, whom he called "the God-damned hyenas on the eighth floor."[24] Subject to sudden hunches about reader interest, he sometimes threw the whole staff into panic by tearing a magazine apart at the last moment before deadline and redesigning it, sometimes developing black moods in which he found fault with everybody. But he lightened the Trio with humor, launched another contest offering prizes ranging from $300 to $2,000 for fiction that brought 15,000 manuscripts pouring in, sent a writer named Ann Forsyth to hire out as a servant for the J. P. Morgan family and then relate her experiences, introduced "daring" articles on such topics as spiritualism and Emma Goldman, and by his tender editorial approach he wheedled women readers into regarding the Butterick magazines as their friend and tutor so that more than 9,000 readers' letters a month came into the beauty department alone. Circulation kept rising, as did his salary, and he had his great office painted green and bronze with hangings and furnishings to match.[25]

At times he strained at the puritan leash. Once he summoned the entire *Delineator* staff to his office. He sat at his desk working, never looking up, as they filed in nervously. At last he looked up, frowning, taking off his pince-nez and popping them on again, then reading aloud a passage from a story recently purchased in which a woman character smoked a cigarette.

"How did that get by?" he demanded.

There was an uneasy shuffling of feet. "We can change it," one editor suggested.

"If that could be done I would not have called you in. The whole story depends on the woman smoking. If the cigarette is edited out, there is no story."

Homer Croy, who was present, later recalled that there was a serious discussion which Dreiser ended with finality.

"The point is far bigger than this matter of a cigarette," he said. "All the women's magazines are too 'nice'; they don't meet life squarely. If we want really to touch the lives of our readers, we've got to get down to vitals and stop being prissy. The woman in this story is going to smoke." [26]

Everyone quailed at this decision, which might easily cause the magazine to be condemned by women's organizations and by preachers in their pulpits. The business office howled about the story, and Dreiser had to fight another battle with the "God-damned hyenas," but he won. Yet this was the extent of his revolt. Although Grosset & Dunlap's *Sister Carrie* sold 5,248 copies by the end of 1908, continued a good sale in 1909 and might have encouraged Dreiser to resume writing, he did not do so. Rather than quitting magazines, in July of 1909 he joined with William Neil Smith and spent $1,000 to secure control of a bankrupt periodical, the *Bohemian*, keeping the deal secret from his Butterick employers, and became a publisher himself.

"You belong by nature and ability," he wrote Mencken, urging him to contribute. "Won't you come across with something real snappy.* I am going to make it a live one and *talk* plain." [27]

IV. GENIUS, I SUPPOSE

Although Dreiser was boss of the *Bohemian*, he kept his name out of it and hired Fritz Krog, a moody young German from the University of Missouri, to serve as front-man editor at the small office on West Thirty-third Street. He so enjoyed secretive operations that he might have found a promising career in espionage. Just as he kept his secretary-editorship of the

* Dreiser seldom bothered to put in question marks where they belonged.

Dodge company secret, so he took pains to keep his magazine from upsetting George Wilder at Butterick. "I want you to promise," he wrote Mencken, "not to write anything appertaining to the *Bohemian* to me care of the *Delineator* but address it instead either to me here at my apartment (429 W. 123rd) or c/o The Editor of the *Bohemian*, 40 W. 33rd Street, but don't put my name on the outside of the envelope. . . ." [28] He got his Butterick assistant Fremont Rider—already working with him sub rosa on the Dodge books—to help him on the *Bohemian*, so that his life became a labyrinth of intrigues both commercial and romantic.

The *Bohemian* had been a flimsy gazette catering to theater buffs and getting some of its photographic material gratis for publicity purposes. Whereas Dreiser was paying $5,000 for some *Delineator* serials, he paid as little as $50 for contributions to his new enterprise.

"I want to make it the broadest, most genial little publication in the field. . . ." he wrote Mencken. "I don't want any tainted fiction or cheap sex struck articles, but I do want a big catholic point of view, a sense of humor, grim or gay and an apt realistic perception of things as they are." [29]

Although he announced, "The *Bohemian Magazine* has gone into new hands—been reborn, is full of new red blood," the transfusion was slight. The magazine was brightened by amusing short essays by Mencken—"The Psychology of Kissing," "In Defense of Profanity." There was fiction by such writers as Morgan Robertson, Fritz Krog and James L. Ford. There were skits by Homer Croy, O. Henry and Clare Kummer. There were two of Dreiser's own minor pieces, "The Flight of Pigeons" and "The Cruise of the Idlewild." But the signs were plain that he was doing it more for fun and possible profit than literary revolt, that he was hampered by a scrawny budget, a lack of real plan and too little time of his own. The *Bohemian*'s full-page stock shots of stage favorites were continued, as were its one-line "reviews" of current plays. In articles it ran a bewildering gamut not likely to appeal to any special segment of readership, topics ranging from spiritualistic mediums and probation officers to animal trainers and the Russian spy system. Typographical errors abounded. The president of the Bohemian Publishing Company was announced in three successive issues as W. N. Smith, then Rider, then Krog.

The church-hating Dreiser had a deep sense of wonder at the Spencerian world in which he had mysteriously risen from degradation to fame and prosperity, as he showed in his criticism of a Mencken article, "The Decay of the Churches," which he felt wrongly placed science in opposition to religion:

> Isn't seeking knowledge (scientific) a form of prayer. Aren't scientists & philosophers at bottom trully [*sic*] reverential and don't they wish (pray) ardently for more knowledge. . . . the truth is men are not less religious— they are religious in a different way—and that's a fact.[30]

In October, 1909, the Butterick Company took over the Ridgway Company and its thriving *Everybody's Magazine*. Into the Butterick skyscraper moved Erman J. Ridgway and a large staff including John O'Hara Cosgrave, editor of *Everybody's,* and writers Lincoln Steffens and Walter Lippmann. The Butterick Trio had risen to a combined circulation of 1,400,000, with the *Delineator* being published in four languages, so that *Everybody's* with its 500,000 circulation hardly posed a threat to Dreiser. The difficulty came in Ridgway's assumption of the editorial supervision of all the magazines, leaving George Wilder to concentrate on business and advertising.

Wilder had given Dreiser a fairly free rein. Ridgway did not. "He put on airs," said Ann Watkins, an associate on *Everybody's,* "whereas Dreiser was the soul of simplicity and directness." [31] Ridgway, a meticulous dresser, took a twelfth-floor office near Dreiser's, had a dozen fresh red roses on his desk each day, and began to supervise Dreiser. A family man and a firm Methodist, he may have been offended by Dreiser's reputation as a profligate, which was a subject of gossip in the editorial fraternity, although he was not averse to a flirtation himself. "He struck me as a man training to be an ogre," Homer Croy recalled.[32] He insisted on starting his own column in the *Delineator,* piling saccharinity high with such observations as, "Life is so much sweeter when we can attune our spirits to the Great Spirit; when we can join our fellows in inspiring antiphony with the morning stars singing in glory. . . ." [33] As yet Dreiser had not sung to the morning stars. He had trouble with Ridgway, and there was friction over budget allotments with the ambitious *Everybody's* staff. Indeed, difficulties suddenly abounded, for the B. W. Dodge Company was in financial straits and Dreiser's *Bohemian* proved a money-loser so that he dropped it after four months, the December, 1909, issue being the last. Yet at Butterick Dreiser was highly regarded, and undoubtedly he could have held his job but for Mrs. Annie Ericsson Cudlipp and *l'affaire Honeypot.*

Mrs. Cudlipp, a handsome widow from Richmond, was an assistant editor at Butterick and a frequent guest at the literary soirées at the Dreiser apartment. She had a beautiful and talented seventeen-year-old daughter, Thelma, a brunette beginner at the Art Students' League who she hoped would rise to success. Jug was fond of the charming widow, and the Dreisers paid visits to the Cudlipp apartment at New Brighton, Staten Island, sometimes accompanied by a few of Dreiser's protégés, including Fritz Krog, Homer Croy and the artists Robert Amick and Franklin Booth.[34] When Dreiser met Thelma in the fall of 1909, he saw in her a freshness and beauty that he could only compare with dewy roses.[35]

That winter the irrepressible Croy and a few of his young friends formed a group called the Fantastic Toe Club which met for dancing at a genteel hall on 125th Street. Thelma joined the group, as did Dreiser, who lived only a few blocks away and who conceived a hitherto unknown enthusiasm for dancing as he pirouetted with the lovely young art student. Mrs. Dreiser, who was ailing, took no part in these gatherings, but she and Mrs. Cudlipp soon became aware of Dreiser's interest in Thelma and both women began working to break up the attachment.[36] At the same time Dreiser became friendly with a wealthy New York attorney of literary inclinations, Elias Rosenthal, who admired *Sister Carrie* and held open house Sundays for intellectuals at his huge apartment at 608 Riverside Drive. Here Dreiser, looking very sad, was wont to show up and hobnob with Rosenthal and the artists and musicians he liked to encourage.

In the spring of 1910, William C. Lengel, a twenty-one-year-old lawyer from Kansas City, deserted the law to come to New York and break into the theatrical world, finding instead a job at Butterick as Dreiser's private secretary—the beginning of a lifetime friendship. He was unaware of the brewing crisis. He was fascinated by Dreiser's misshapen face, his two-way gaze, his constant pleating of his handkerchief, his moodiness and rudeness to the staff. Seeing in the office a copy of *Sister Carrie*, unknown to him before, Lengel concluded that it was a story about a nun and that Dreiser was a religious zealot. He took the book home over a weekend, began reading it on a bench in Central Park and became so enthralled that he had to move under a lamp to finish it in growing darkness.

"And when I finished the volume," he recalled, "I sat stunned and shaken at this chronicle of the pitiful Carrie Meeber and the more pitiable Hurstwood and I thought of his man who had written this book. His harshness dropped from him. The cruel arrogance of his manner was gone. These were but a shield, a protection against his own softness. He was a human being whose heart was filled with pity, whose sympathy and understanding were deep and profound."

Dreiser immediately became his literary god, and on Monday he told him so.

"Why, you must have written that novel before you were thirty," he said. "How could a man so young have such a knowledge of life, such pity and understanding?"

Dreiser shrugged. "Genius, I suppose," he said in a matter-of-fact tone. Lengel, at first taken aback, reflected that this was not so much conceit as it was Dreiser's sincere appraisal of powers which had been given him through an accident of nature for which he was not responsible.

"How can you waste your time editing a woman's magazine when you can write like that?" Lengel asked.

Dreiser smiled. "One must live. Don't you know the history of that book? Well, someday I'll tell you." [37]

Depend upon it, he did tell Lengel.

Lengel noticed how he enjoyed his prestige and the trappings of success. He wore Knox hats and Johnston & Murphy shoes and urged Lengel to do the same, saying, "You know, the label gives you a certain standing." [38] Although one side of him still yearned to write, his years at Butterick were among the happiest of his life.

He took a liking for Ann Watkins, the young *Everybody's* assistant, and confided in her his despair over his love for Thelma which both his wife and

Mrs. Cudlipp were trying to thwart. "He was a tremendously physical person," Miss Watkins recalled, "without conventional morals, almost ugly, and yet he had a kindliness and warmth that were magnetic." [39] Taking pity on him, she invited him and Thelma to tea occasionally at her apartment on West Ninety-seventh Street. The couple also went dancing that summer at Palisades Park in New Jersey and the Staten Island Yacht Club, planning a book of nonsense jingles for which Dreiser would write the verse and Thelma would supply the illustrations. "Of course Theo was anything but handsome," Thelma later recalled, "but there was a kind of grandeur about him." [40] She was a child, just turning eighteen, utterly unschooled in sex.

"Thelma," Dreiser said to her, "you must wonder about Mrs. Dreiser. She loves me with a great devotion but she has always known I cannot give it back—I wish I could. . . . I am happy after all these dead years. . . ." [41]

And he kissed her, Thelma recalled, very gently—the greatest liberty he ever took with her.

Simultaneously the short, unprepossessing Fritz Krog had introduced new complications by falling in love with Thelma. Feeling his love unrequited and hopeless, and unaware of Dreiser's yearnings in the same direction, he went for advice to Dreiser, for whom he had a high regard. Dreiser, keeping his own secret, gravely advised Krog to forget the girl and visit his dentist brother in Indianapolis, which Krog did, while Dreiser turned to his spare-time composition of jingles for the book he and Thelma planned, one rhyme reading:

> *Hip, hip, hop, and skip,*
> *Every poet is a "dip,"*
> *Every writer is a scrub,*
> *Rub, dub, dub-a-dub!* [42]

Nervously aware of his own approaching forties, Dreiser was so charmed by this girl less than half his age that he fell easily into doggerel. Mrs. Cudlipp, who had been hired by Dreiser and had admired him both personally and as an editor, grew frantic. Since her husband's death she had endured privations to see her three children educated, and for comfort had taken occasional nips from a whiskey bottle hidden in her closet. The present crisis did not decrease her trips to the closet. She visited Dreiser's office several times to issue warnings, and Dreiser later admitted to Lengel that he could not sleep nights.

"I get up and walk about," he said, "or I dress and go out and sit through the night in Morningside Park. Sometimes I sit under a street light and write poems." [43]

He gave some of them to Lengel to copy. One differed strongly in tone from his efforts for the jingle book, its first line reading, "The street of whores, oh wondrous street it is." At last the conflict came to a climax. Jug, ill with rheumatic fever, resolutely refused to give Dreiser a divorce. Mrs.

Cudlipp by this time had learned something of Dreiser's previous affairs—very possibly Jug listed them for her—and she took melodramatic steps. She told Thelma that her signature was needed for the sale of a house the mother owned in Richmond. Thelma innocently went with her, discovered the deception after reaching Richmond, insisted on returning to New York and boarded a train with her mother which she believed was returning northward. Instead it took them to Saluda, North Carolina, where Thelma was placed in the home of a relative, without money and virtually a captive. Mrs. Cudlipp then returned to New York and issued an ultimatum to Dreiser: If he did not give up Thelma she would lay the whole matter before the executives at Butterick.[44]

He risked the job he treasured, and refused. "He must have hypnotized himself," Thelma later reflected. To Mencken, Dreiser wrote a one-line note: "I have discovered that this is a very sad world." He went to the apartment of Ann Watkins, where he railed against his fate and threatened suicide with such apparent sincerity that Miss Watkins said, "I was afraid that he would do it then and there."[45]

Sometime in September Mrs. Cudlipp told all to Wilder and Ridgway. If Dreiser was not discharged, she said, she would give the story to the newspapers. It also happened that Mrs. Cudlipp knew of an office romance being carried on by Ridgway and let him know privily that unless Dreiser was fired she would tell about *that* too. Ridgway and Wilder were both fearful about the Dreiser affair getting into the papers and making a dreadful impression among Butterick's sedate female readers. There was a flurry of summit meetings.

Fritz Krog, who seemed determined to inject comic relief into the drama, now returned from Indianapolis, learned of Dreiser's infatuation, felt that he had been double-crossed and decided to thrash Dreiser—if possible, murder him. Krog was unstable mentally, although at the time he was thought merely eccentric. One Sunday morning he picked up his fellow Missourian, Homer Croy, and went with him to the Dreiser apartment, muttering threats. Croy nervously went up the elevator first to warn his boss that Krog was in an ugly mood—might even be armed. Dreiser, writing at his desk, looked on it as a mere annoyance.

"I'm working," he said, as Croy recalled it. "Tell him I don't want to see him."

Croy went downstairs, found Krog lurking in the park shrubbery across the street, and was relieved to hear him say, "I've decided to forget about the whole thing. I'm letting him live."[46]

One day late in September, George Wilder, Erman Ridgway and James Birmingham, the Butterick treasurer, strode into Dreiser's office.

"How are you, Wilder?" Dreiser said.

"Dry-sir," Wilder punned. Everybody laughed but Dreiser. Lengel was asked to leave the room. In the ensuing talk, Dreiser was fired as of October 1, with the face-saving announcement that he was taking a year's leave of absence.[47]

V. PROXIMITY IS ESSENTIAL

Leaving his wife without saying good-by, Dreiser took a room on October 3 at the Park Avenue Hotel, Fourth Avenue and Thirty-third Street, where Lengel brought him his mail and personal effects from the office and found him sitting bleakly on the bed, pleating his handkerchief. He was furious at Jug for denying him his freedom, dying of loneliness for Thelma, exhausted from prolonged tension, nervous, unable to eat or sleep well, losing weight.

Despite his irascibility, and this passion for an eighteen-year-old, most of his colleagues at Butterick were on his side, sorry to see him go. Charles Hanson Towne, Arthur Sullivant Hoffman, William C. Lengel, Sarah Field Splint, Homer Croy, Katherine Leckie, Fremont Rider and others who had felt his wrath and received precious little praise later spoke and wrote admiringly of him. He received many notes of regret, one of them from Flora Mai Holly, who wrote without intentional irony that he had made the *Delineator* "a greater moral power" and hoped that he would now resume his writing in earnest.[48]

He *was* writing in deadly earnest, but all of it was going in the form of letters to Thelma in Saluda, who of late had written him one curt letter saying she was "tired of the rumpus." Mrs. Cudlipp, in her fear of the half-crazed Dreiser, was deceiving him. Still on speaking terms with him, she insisted that Thelma was too young but gave him some hope of eventual marriage if the pair would first agree to a long separation. Actually her intention was to separate them forever. To Thelma, for whom one of his nicknames was Honeypot—a surprising variation on Jug's nickname for him—he wrote in a variety of moods, at first hopeful:

> Certainly things have been stormy enough this past month. . . . I don't wonder you got tired of the rumpus. I got tired myself but your mother certainly did cut up high jinks. She has calmed down more under the prospect of divorce and marriage and is quite friendly to me—in fact I think she is very desirous that things should come out right.

He grew doubtful:

> But why don't you write me, Honey pot? Are you changing your mind? Has all the row made you see things differently? . . .

He resorted to baby-talk:

> Are you getting well & strong and are you just as sweet as ever?— what! Do ju lub me? Had you sweet doe eyes? Or are dey dough eyes? (Oooh what a slam) And will jus always love me? What!"

He opened the floodgates of yearning:

> Flower Face, you are so sweet. Dear God how sweet you are & how memories of you hurt. If I lose you well & good, but oh the ache—the ache. Don't you feel any of this? Won't you ever say? Why so silent? Why so voiceless?
>
> Thelma Sweet! Honey pot! Little Blue Bird! Divine Fire—I love you, love you! love you! See how you have filled my days with mental misery and stress but oh it has all been worthwhile. You are worth it all—my worry, my position, the danger of publicity—everything—I gladly pay the price & would pay it again. Strange isn't it and wonderful. But it is exactly so—
>
> Theo [49]

He wrote her daily but vainly, for Mrs. Cudlipp's relatives were intercepting every letter and Thelma received none of them. Suspecting as much, he put twelve cents in stamps on each of them with the notation: "Personal Delivery Only—Return Reciept [sic] Demanded." It did no good. He sent Thelma a telegram, paying double rates for a message requiring personal delivery and immediate acknowledgment or a return of the message. When neither came he wrote the general manager of the telegraph company threatening suit and demanding an investigation, which later imperiled the job of the Saluda agent.[50] Mrs. Cudlipp was actually fearful of him in his desperation.

Jug, still ailing at her apartment, was being cared for by her older sister Ida, whom Dreiser had hired as a Butterick circulation specialist, and by one of Dreiser's sisters, probably Mame. Being almost penniless, and having no idea where Dreiser was, she called in Thomas H. McKee to discuss the problem with him—the same McKee who in 1900 had represented Doubleday and in 1907 had advised Dreiser.

"With embarrassment evident," McKee recalled, "she . . . unfolded a tale of marital distress, giving details which were strange even to my accustomed ears and of which I cannot speak." [51]

Although she asked how she could require financial help from Dreiser, she ruled out any legal action, saying it might harm his career, and insisted that McKee's call be kept confidential. She had shared long tribulations with Dreiser, she said, and felt it unjust that now in prosperity he should leave her. She felt that he needed her, for he was subject to fits of high elation followed by deepest depression, and in both moods was inclined to say and do unwise things.

"I am slower and steadier," she said. "I can see further ahead than he can. I have been the balance wheel. I have had to keep up restraints on him, but I have done it gently and tactfully but now that he is financially free he has of late been resentful of all interference." [52]

Dreiser, she said, had forbidden her to have children on the ground that child-bearing would spoil her figure. "I had thought that with a baby to interest him he would value a home and I could hold him. But, not now."

She added something that surprised McKee.

"I have been interested in watching you as you have sat by my bedside. You have not tried to touch me. Theo could no more have done that than he could have stopped breathing. All his life he has had an uncontrollable urge when near a woman to lay his hand upon her and stroke her or otherwise come into contact with her. I have often wondered if Theo was queer that way. The fact is that I have known few men in my time, so few that I hardly know how men generally act. During all our married life I have had to lean backward in an effort to fence myself in when men were about me. Theo had no confidence in the fidelity of any woman or man—not even me. He thought himself typical." [53]

Since she barred any legal action, McKee could give her nothing but sympathy. Meanwhile Thelma, after several weeks in Carolina isolation, was permitted to return to the Cudlipp apartment in Staten Island. Somewhat tardily Dreiser made financial provision for his wife.

Although Thelma was now only a few miles away, Dreiser was forbidden to see her and he suspected that Mrs. Cudlipp was deceiving him. He wrote:

Thelma—Honeypot:

I did not sleep last night. Fear of this thing fairly sets me beside myself. I am so worried and harassed I scarcely know which way to turn. Sweet you don't seem to understand that it is proximity that is essential to me—nearness to you. I can endure a reasonable period between sights of [you] but when it means weeks and months and nothing but brief letters I suffer untold agony. Ah, honeypot, if you really love me you won't do this. You will make some compromise which will make an occasional sight of you possible. I cannot live otherwise [.] Your mother is so anxious to get you away from me: She wants you to go to Richmond or somewhere where social life will divert your mind and make you indifferent. She tells me she wants me to marry you but at bottom and after all I don't think she does. But Honey pot I *need* you. Do you understand that fully? I *NEED* you. You are the breath of life to me. All my life I have longed for this. I can work at a number of things and do well if you will only stay somewhere within reach. But if you go away and a long distance intervenes—this yearning that pulls and pulls in your direction will keep me restless and so mentally wrought up that I can scarcely do anything at all. And I must write. I want to finish my book & other things. But don't you see how it is. . . . I admit there is some point to your mother's contention of compromise—but Mrs. Dreiser is going away & there will not be so much. I am entitled to live a roving visiting life in New York in her absence. Ordinary custom sanctions that aside from the actual separation which has taken place. Some compromise can be effected [.] I will accept almost anything in the place of your going away—even a mere sight of you once in two weeks. But oh, sweet! if you love me don't go away—please don't. I love you so terribly and I need you. Can you actually leave me when I *BEG* you not to—when I have fought so hard to get you here. Oh, Honeypot be kind—be kind to me. You said once you would once [*sic*] be mother & sister and sweetheart to me [.] I am a little pleading boy now in need of your love your mother love. Won't you help me. Please do Honey-pot—please do. I beg of you—oh, I beg of you! I will make it up to you in a thousand ways all my life. Don't leave me to stay here alone. Please don't.

                                                        Theo.[54]

His world was crumbling, for B. W. Dodge & Company, in which he had sunk $5,000, was taken over by creditors [55] and Ben Dodge himself had gone on a tremendous drunk. Mrs. Cudlipp was keeping Thelma at a distance, and Thelma herself had cooled. Dreiser kept writing her impassioned letters ("Personal Delivery Only—Return Reciept Demanded"). Late in October he rented a room with private bath for $50 a month in the huge apartment at 608 Riverside Drive of the Elias Rosenthals. He was in a frenzy when Mrs. Cudlipp decided to send Thelma to spend a year with an uncle in London, and he begged her not to go. "Oh, sweet, I am so lonely," he wrote her. ". . . I love you, love you, love you, past all words to describe." [56]

Mrs. Cudlipp, shaken and fearful, was given a leave of absence at Butterick's. Late in November she and Thelma sailed for England. Dreiser was not given their London address—was forbidden to communicate with Thelma for a year.

Book Three

THE FREE-LANCE

I. *Jennie Gerhardt*

I. ONE-MAN LITERARY FACTORY

Exhausted, Dreiser took osteopathic treatment and planned to visit Thelma in England in exactly a year, not forgetting that Grant Richards, the British publisher, had invited him over. The fact that he was not prostrated by his ordeal showed a hardening since the days when an earlier upset had him walking in circles and imagining hands reaching for him. For almost a year he had wrestled with tensions, yearnings, enmities, gossip, embarrassments, insomnia and feelings of guilt. He had been defeated at every turn. He had lost home, wife, Honeypot, job, income, prestige and his splendid green-and-bronze office, and in the bargain he must have realized that he looked silly.

But he did not lose his wife, quite.

Jug's status in his life would remain in doubt for more than three years. She still loved him, hoped that he would return. The decision was up to Dreiser, who seemed unable to decide. Their crises over other women had become routine. They were like temporary fits of madness, with Dreiser always returning to sanity and coming back to the fold. As Jug saw it, this crisis was no different from the others except in its duration and violence and she saw no reason why their marriage should not be resumed. As for Dreiser, he was fond of her in a pallid way and was dependent on the wifely comforts she supplied so well and also the aid she gave in smoothing his lumpy grammar and criticizing his writing. Although he was living separately, he was preparing to send her to Europe and the pair were in amicable communication. He did not tell Mencken of any break, and Mencken's Baltimore friend Dr. Hirshberg, who always gave a big Thanksgiving party, invited both Dreisers to his 1910 gathering. To Fremont Rider Dreiser wrote:

> By the way there is a silly report abroad, due I suppose to the fact that I'm working alone for a few months, that I have deserted Mrs. Dreiser & am going to marry some one else. There's nothing in it. If [you] hear anyone say so contradict it from me.[1]

On the same day he wrote Flora Mai Holly a similar letter.

Obviously he was in confusion. Meanwhile he was exchanging letters with Louise-Ann Miller, a tiny young lady from Pittsburgh who had traveled widely in Africa, written for *Delineator* and signed her notes, "Sincerely-yours-in-crime, *L'Africaine*," asking his aid in marketing her writings.

He had a decision to make other than about his marriage. What to do for a living?

He wanted badly to finish *Jennie*. He feared the low income that he knew would be his lot as a writer. He made a decision that of itself took courage: He would take a job if he found an important one; rather than accept a picayune post he would risk writing again. He contemplated a position with the Wildman News Service, and wrote Mencken, "I am considering several good things," but he admitted, "My conscience hurts me a little . . . for first off I should finish my book." [2]

The big job did not materialize. He began writing—and with staggering prolificacy. Thelma Cudlipp, whose flower face had so shaken the Butterick skyscraper, had also, like the dancing Scot, contributed in a non-measurable way to American literature. for she unwittingly forced Dreiser to become a full-time writer.

A cabinet maker had transformed Paul's old rosewood piano into a great rectangular desk which would be Dreiser's work space for the rest of his life. Now it was in his room at the Rosenthal apartment high above Riverside Drive, where he had an expansive view of the Hudson and the Jersey palisades. He worked methodically, taking time out at Christmas to attend the Anarchists' Ball in the Village. There he sat next to gangling young Sinclair Lewis, argued anarchism with stout Emma Goldman, whose scorn for convention fascinated him, and showed even more interest, Lewis noted, in a younger lady in a "close-fitting graceful gown of cerise." [3] Soon after the holidays, after almost ten years, he finally finished the first draft of *Jennie Gerhardt*.

Jennie, a daughter of poverty, seduced by a United States Senator who intended to marry her but suddenly died, mother of an illegitimate child, fleeing from Columbus to Cleveland to hide her shame, meeting rich Lester Kane, becoming his mistress, concealing her child from him—and then what happened?

The story had a happy, moral ending, with Lester becoming reconciled to the child and bringing wedded joy to Jennie. [4]

Was Dreiser selling out, or had three years at Butterick pulled his teeth?

One of the first to read the script was Jug, who had seen *Jennie* born in 1901 and come near dying several times since. Now she thought it a great story—greater than *Père Goriot*—but she candidly criticized parts of it as overlong, in need of condensation. [5]

Dreiser gave the script to Elias Rosenthal, whose criticism is not recorded. He next gave it to one of Rosenthal's daughters, the pretty, precocious Lillian Rosenthal who was soon to leave for Europe to further her musical education. Lillian, like all the Rosenthals, had read widely. She praised *Jennie* but found fault with the ending, writing in part, "It occurs to me that if Lester had married Lettie, the tragedy of Jennie would have been greater. Poignancy is a necessity in this story, and it can only be maintained by persistent want on the part of Jennie. The loss of Lester would insure this." [6]

Dreiser, who was beginning to feel the same way, was at once delighted and amused by this sharp opinion from one so young.

"What do you know about life?" he demanded.

Lillian replied that at any rate she had read the English, French and Russian masters and the falsity of his denouement struck her keenly.[7] Dreiser meanwhile had sent another copy to Fremont Rider, whose editorial judgment he valued. Rider's opinion of the ending was similar to Lillian's, and he wondered if Dreiser had written it that way to avoid the criticism he had suffered over *Sister Carrie*. He wrote Dreiser that the denouement as it stood was weak and implausible, to which Dreiser agreed, replying, "I am convinced that one of the reasons of lack of poignancy is the fact that Lester marries Jennie."[8] If he had momentarily compromised his standards, he saw his error. He revised the story, making Jennie lose Lester, lose her daughter, lose all for a hopeless but unselfish love. He even let Jug do some of the cutting herself.[9]

Jennie became one of the best-read of unpublished novels. He continued a routine that would become habitual with him and which demonstrated at once his realization of his technical shortcomings and his proud conviction that his work was important to the world. He showed the revised *Jennie* script to about a dozen others whose opinions he wanted—to Flora Mai Holly, to James Huneker, to Charles B. DeCamp, now editor of *Metropolitan* magazine; to Butterick writers including Adachi Kinnosuke, Louise-Ann Miller and Madge Jennison; to Alexander Harvey and Barbara Langford; to Miss Galbraith Welch, head of the New York office of the London literary agency of Curtis Brown & Massie; and to his cherished friend Mencken.[10]

As Jug and several others said, the script was indeed repetitive and overlong—a chronic failing of Dreiser and one he would never overcome. He wrote too fast, sometimes many thousands of words a day. He became engrossed in the mass, losing sight of detail. He was egocentric in writing as he was in love, thinking less of the reader than of his own need to relate and describe, careless of diction, unselective, pushed on by impatience to get at the next chapter and the next, looking always ahead and seldom back. His writing mirrored the man—a lack of taste combined with nervousness, insecurity and his actual fear of time.

He was not forgetting the enthusiastic reception of *Carrie* in England. When Jug sailed alone in January, she carried with her a copy of the *Jennie* script, which she delivered to the Covent Garden office of Curtis Brown & Massie, later taking notes on the comments of Hughes Massie.[11] Massie, impressed despite reservations about prolixity, thereafter tried hard (and vainly) to become his agent. Meanwhile Dreiser unbent on March 22 by attending a "booze party" at the Washington Square studio of Robert Amick, a gathering also attended by Percy Cowan, Hippolyte Havel, and probably by Fritz Krog, Franklin Booth and others. It was a breezy affair judging from Amick's letter next day: "There were some damned uninteresting details about this joint this morning that had to be cleaned up. Some low swine put his lunch under my bed, ho! ho! One of the outstanding events of the night occurred when the sailor put out the anarchist Havel." [12]

In the spring he moved temporarily into an apartment at 225 Central Park West offered by Alice Phillips, immediately developing an interest in the peppery Mrs. Phillips (evidently a widow) that became mutual. "Are you quite irrevocably pledged?" she wrote him. "Can you look in Sunday afternoon?" He gave her a copy of the *Jennie* script. Mrs. Phillips, who was as frank and discerning as she was widely read, gave it to him straight:

> Really dear Mr. Dreiser when I turn these pages and pass from some magical, glorious paragraph to some inept "bromodious" I could cry. . . . And yet you could write [a great novel]. There's not the slightest doubt of it. It's sticking out all through "Jennie". But you're too corny. . . . Haven't I seen you work steadily from "rosy dawn to dewy eve"? But dear Mr. Dreiser dear dear Mr. Dreiser—you loved it and gloried in it and steeped yourself and wallowed in the pure joy of it. You were creating, that wasn't real work to you. It wasn't drudgery. And when you learn to drudge you'll *begin* to be great.[13]

She urged that he read the Bible to help develop simplicity of style. The delightfully tart Mrs. Phillips would thereafter reappear intermittently in his life as a sort of offstage voice of conscience.

The *Jennie* script, which had been longer, was still 723 pages long when James Huneker read it and found greatness in it that reminded him of the best of the Russians at the same time that he mourned its prolixity and diffuseness. "Again I say a big book," he ended, "eloquent in its humanity, *too long,* too many repetitions (you ride certain words to death, such as *big*) and the best fiction I have read since that of Frank Norris." [14]

Even more enthusiastic was Mencken, who found power and realism in the book's very bulk, wanted no cuts at all, and wrote, "I must go to Hardy and Conrad to find its like. . . . You have written a novel that no other American of the time could have written. . . . My earnest congratulations. By all means let me see that third book. . . . You have put over a truly big thing." [15]

Miss Holly, as Dreiser's agent, had submitted a copy of the manuscript to Edward C. Marsh at Macmillan, who rejected it, writing that although the novel had "some undeniable merits" and might be successful, there were "some things about it which frankly I do not like. . . . [16] Miss Holly immediately tried Ripley Hitchcock at Harper's, who accepted it by April 6 but who displeased Dreiser by agreeing with Huneker and disagreeing with Mencken: he insisted on cuts and revisions so extensive that Dreiser was charged $600 against royalties for Harper's editorial work. Calling on Dreiser, Miss Holly found him almost tearful because a man had been killed in an elevator accident in the building and he was picturing the shock and sorrow of the family when they got the news.[17]

It is not surprising that Dreiser's writing was disorderly, since he was operating a one-man literary factory, working simultaneously on three major projects, moving early in July to 3609 Broadway at 149th Street, where Jug rejoined him when she returned from Europe. It must have been an odd ménage, with Jug trying to restore the old Honeybugs-Kitten relationship and helping him with his writing. Probably Dreiser consented to the reunion partly out of considerations of thrift, for he was already worrying incontinently about money. Since he had to support them both anyway, they could live together more cheaply than apart, and Jug was a good cook and grammarian. Dreiser could not fry an egg to save his soul. At the same time that he was finishing and revising *Jennie*, he was working hard on the longer *The "Genius"* and beginning *The Financier*, switching from one to the other in a busy tangle of rewriting, creation and research. He would not be satisfied with fame if it meant a garret. "I am going to do three more books after [*Jennie*] . . ." he wrote Mencken, "then if there is no money in the game I [am] going to run a weekly. I can write a book every six months I think so I won't be so long out of the editing game unless perchance I should make a living this way." [18]

In *The "Genius"* he sought to purge his spirit of the recent ordeal involving Thelma, Mrs. Cudlipp, Jug and Butterick. The genius was himself, and at first there were no qualifying quotation marks. It was essentially the story of Theodore Dreiser, here named Eugene Witla, a young newspaperman (later changed to an artist) who survived a nervous breakdown and an unhappy marriage, fought his way to fame and wealth while seeking the fulfillment of his dreams in sex, then crashed to ruin when his passion for a young beauty brought her mother's cunning reprisal against him. Dreiser used the raw facts of his own life with little disguise—seldom the practice then. Although the real basis for the novel would of course be known, he showed no concern for his own privacy or that of the others involved, his conviction being that art should be taken from life even at the cost of personal embarrassment. The girl in the case was called Flowerface. The genius's wife, presented with alternate sympathy and disparagement, had a background similar to Jug's and was born Angela Blue—a paraphrase of Jug's maiden name of Sara White that seemed downright malicious. There were discussions of pre-marital and marital relations that could not fail to be painful to Jug. Although the book was written while Dreiser was resuming his life with Jug—actually living with her—it treated the wife as one incapable of understanding the genius, who called him Honeybun and was blindly motivated by dull considerations of propriety which meant nothing to him.

The "Genius," in short, was Dreiser's *coup de grâce* on his marriage before he officially ended it. One can be sure that he hid the script from Jug as a small boy hides cigarettes.

Possibly Harper's were frightened at the novel, for they encouraged him to follow *Jennie* instead with *The Financier*. He put *The "Genius"* aside although it was finished by August [19] and gave it to his new friend Barbara Langford. Since in his desire to write about "life as it is" he was unwilling to write "imaginative" fiction, *The Financier*, like all of his novels, was. a fictional rendering of fact. It dramatized the Philadelphia career of Charles Tyson Yerkes (Frank Cowperwood in the novel), the brilliantly corrupt plunger who later went on to take over traction lines in Chicago and London and harbored a succession of mistresses along the way. Dreiser, fascinated by power and wealth since boyhood, had had a taste of power and wealth at Butterick and had hardened in his conception of life as a blind struggle of human atoms in which only the strongest survived. He found much to admire in Cowperwood's efficient utilization of this principle.

"I should like to see a race of people," he wrote Lengel, "for once on this earth who like Niccolo Machiavelli could look life in the face." [20]

He was getting Philadelphia information on Yerkes from his old friend there, Joseph Hornor Coates. Evidently he had given Grant Richards some hope that he could publish *Jennie* in England, for Richards wrote in an aggrieved tone when he learned that Harper's were publishing the book both in America and England. Dreiser was alternately overjoyed by the flattering advance opinions of *Jennie* and tormented by his fear that it would not sell.

II. ENTER GRANT RICHARDS

When *Jennie* came out on October 19, it had been cut to a mere 425 printed pages. Dreiser, whose attitude toward publishers was never one of sweet faith, was disappointed at the start by Harper's opening newspaper announcement. He subscribed to a clipping service to keep close check on the promotion, advertising and reviews given the book. He well knew that he had to buck a national literary climate almost as frigid as that of 1900. Would *Jennie* encounter the same brutal misunderstanding as had *Carrie?* It was no wonder that he watched the reception with mingled hope and fear.

There were the inevitable critical complaints about his "immorality" and stylistic defects. The *Lexington* (Kentucky) *Herald* called the book "unutterably base" and dealing with the "baser instincts of the worst order of human animals," while the *Chicago Examiner* likened his style to that of a "proficient stenographer." [21] But many of the important reviews were laudatory. Even the puritans could reflect that Jennie, unlike Carrie, paid for her sins in bitter tragedy. Because of this edifying thought they could miss a point stressed by Dreiser—one near his heart although his own life did not exemplify it—that Jennie, in her unwavering love for Lester Kane, proved that an illicit attachment could embody more loyalty and goodness than a church-sanctified marriage.

If America as a whole had not matured, there was at least a growing cadre of rebels, now spreading westward, who were sick of the state of national culture. Among them was the group of anti-philistines in Chicago including

Francis Hackett, Floyd Dell, Edna Kenton and Sherwood Anderson.

In Chicago, Dell wound up a full-page review in the *Evening Post* with, "I may say, without saying it in vain: this is a great book." [22] The respected *Bookman* said, "Over and over the story of Jennie makes the reader's heart ache with the helpless pity of it all," and pronouncing Dreiser deserving of "the highest tribute." [23] The *New York Herald* said, "It comes near deserving that abused word 'great.'" [24] Franklin P. Adams wrote Dreiser, "*Jennie Gerhardt* is a great book and I salute and congratulate you, earnestly and reverentially." [25] In the *Smart Set* Mencken went all-out with a review headed, "A NOVEL OF THE FIRST RANK," shrugged off its "gross crudities" and compared it with Zola, Tolstoy and Conrad, saying, "A moral tale? Not at all. It has no more moral than a string quartet or the first book of Euclid." He added the final accolade by calling *Jennie* "the best American novel I have read with the Himalayan exception of *Huckleberry Finn*," [26] and he voiced similar applause in reviews he wrote for the *Baltimore Evening Sun* and the *Los Angeles Times.*

Indeed, Mencken, whose praise appeared also on the book's jacket, set himself up as a noisy publicist for *Jennie*. Dreiser's admiration grew to something near love as the Baltimorean sent him clippings of reviews along with chipper Mencken letters. Harper's was delighted with the reception—delighted too when Arnold Bennett, in New York at the time, told interviewers that he knew little about American literature except for Dreiser. "I know there is one novel called *Sister Carrie*, by a man named Theodore Dreiser. . . . I spend most of my time asking people if they have read it, and I find they haven't. When they say that, I always say, 'Well, get it.'" [27]

There could have been no more timely praise from a Briton much admired in America. Indeed, the generous Bennett did it deliberately, somewhat by way of returning a favor. Frederick G. Melcher of Boston's Charles E. Lauriat Company had praised his *Old Wives' Tale*, urged it on his friends, pushed it, and started a sales momentum in the United States. Now Bennett, appalled by the disregard for Dreiser in his own country, was doing a similar service. [28]

Dreiser, badly hurt by some of the unintelligent American reviews, dropped Bennett a grateful line. Harper's Major F. T. Leigh hastened to give Bennett a copy of the new *Jennie* and wrote Dreiser that he was arranging a meeting between him and Bennett. Dreiser felt that Harper's considered Bennett a more important writer and made the proposal simply for business advantage rather than wishing to bring the two together as equals. Wounded, he dodged the invitation although he was pleased when the Briton called him on the telephone and chatted with him. Dreiser in fact already was dissatisfied with Harper's, feeling that they had not pushed his book in several big cities. [29] He had started conversations with Rutger Jewett, the editor who had been with Taylor ten years earlier and had so kindly encouraged him with *Jennie* when he was nearing nervous collapse. Jewett, now with D. Appleton, was anxious to snag Dreiser for Appleton's if he should quit Harper's, writing, "I wish to continue our conversation as soon as you are free to go ahead with me in the matter." [30] Jewett invited Dreiser to attend another dinner for Bennett given by the Dutch Treat Club, which he also declined, possibly because Bennett would be the guest of honor and he merely one of the diners—a refusal Jewett could not understand, writing, "Your reasons are still as mysterious as the rites of Isis." [31]

Another letter came from a highly literate young lady he had never heard of before, Anna P. Tatum of Fallsington, Pennsylvania, who wrote many pages, finding some fault with the delineation of Jennie but in the main bursting with praise, writing, "It is magnificently constructed—like a great piece of music. . . . It has stupendous solidity and impetus." [32] To Dreiser, this was provocative. He replied immediately, beginning a relationship that would affect his whole career.

Yet, although he was actually being courted by publishers, he vacillated between elation and the dumps. He was pleased that Frank Harris, in the London *Academy and Literature*, had recently placed *Sister Carrie* among the twenty "best books" beginning with the Bible. "All the other [authors] dead this long time but yours truly," he wrote Mencken. "Also putting [*Carrie*] above *The Scarlet Letter* here & *Vanity Fair* in England [—] how's that? Poor old Thack. . . ." [33] He had talked Harper's into planning a new publication of *Carrie*, which would be its fifth, and promised additional income without further work. *Jennie* was off to a fair sale, but he had hoped for more. Certainly Bennett's published remarks about how little known he was in his own country swelled his resentment against American indifference.

He wanted badly to go to Europe to do research on Yerkes' activities there. As he saw it, his literary future, not to mention his reunion with Thelma Cudlipp, depended on this trip, which he thought would cost nearly $4,000. Indeed, the praise he had received from British critics had made him contemplate moving to England where he was appreciated. He had written Grant Richards, "I am, as you know, always strong for the British because of the profound admiration I have for their intellectual leadership. If I had the means I would live in England. . . ." [34] Richards arrived in New York early in November, stayed at the Knickerbocker Hotel and soon received a note from Dreiser written on Knickerbocker stationery:

My Dear Richards: I called, as witness. My house number is 3609 Broadway. My phone number is 1980 Audubon. Welcome to America. I am leaving you an inscribed copy of *Jennie Gerhardt*. . . .

I hope if you are interviewed you will say something definite about me and *Jennie*. It seems almost impossible to make my fellow Americans understand that I am alive. I am thinking of moving to London. Once there I will get at least an equal run with Robert Hichens and Arnold Bennett over here. . . . [35]

Richards, who still hoped to become his publisher in England, telephoned promptly and had breakfast with him next morning at the Dreiser apartment—one instance when Jug and her wonderful Missouri cookery were welcome. This was a meeting between opposites: Richards, the Cantabrigian, a man of the world, handsome and debonair at thirty-nine, connoisseur of art and literature, gourmet familiar of the cafés of Paris and Rome, wearer of a monocle which he liked to let drop occasionally, gay and generous if a bit driving; and Dreiser, the slow, hulking, thick-lipped Hoosier sunk in despair, endlessly pleating his handkerchief.

Richards was amazed at his gloom in view of the relative success of *Jennie*. Dreiser explained that he was planning another book based on Yerkes, and that to perfect his material it was essential for him to make a playground of Europe as Yerkes did, follow in his footsteps, meet the same kind of people and know the sort of women favored by the libertine Yerkes. Now he feared he must drop it because he could not go to Europe.

"What's preventing you?" Richards asked.

"Money—money, of course. How in God's name can I do these things without money?"[36]

To Richards, who was so careless about money that he would later go bankrupt several times, the spectacle of this literary behemoth worrying about a mere trip to Europe was ridiculous. Why, he said, Dreiser had a good chance for the next Nobel Prize for literature following Maeterlinck. Richards himself would push the idea in England and would get the Century Company in New York, with whom he was on close business terms, to do the same in the United States.

The dynamic Richards further guaranteed to plan for Dreiser a six-month tour of Europe that would cost only $1,500—*and* he promised to help raise the $1,500. "Look on it as a certainty," he said.[37]

Richards went to the Century Company on Union Square and talked so persuasively with Frank H. Scott, the president, that Scott authorized the payment of $1,000 to Dreiser as an advance on three articles he would do about Europe for the *Century Magazine* on his return. This also gave Century an option on a travel book Dreiser would write about his impressions. In fact, Richards started a commotion in the Century office, no doubt letting it be known that Dreiser was dissatisfied with Harper's. Century started angling for him with the most flattering of lures: a few evenings later, President Scott and his wife took Theodore and Jug Dreiser to dinner.[38]

Richards' talk about the Nobel Prize evidently had its effect, for on November 10 Dreiser wrote Ripley Hitchcock at Harper's a letter that must have stunned him. He asked an advance of a cool $4,000, $2,500 of it to be paid no later than November 14, and talking menacingly of "other propositions" he was considering—meaning other publishers—and demanding a speedy answer.[39] Hitchcock handed the letter to F. A. Duneka, secretary of Harper's, who read Dreiser a little lesson, writing in part, "Your letter was written, perhaps, in forgetfulness of the fact that you have already agreed in writing to deliver to us the MS. of [*The Financier*]. . . . You speak of 'two other propositions before you.' Of course, these propositions cannot refer to your next novel." [40]

However, Harper's did give Dreiser a $500 advance on *Jennie* plus $2,000 on *The Financier*. Thus, with the $1,000 Richards had wheedled out of Century, he had $3,500 cash in hand and he planned to sail with Richards on November 22. The Nobel Prize idea was alluring, for he wrote Mencken about it, adding, "[Richards] thought some American critic of prominence ought to make the [Nobel] suggestion somewhere to which he could call attention & I spoke of you. How about that?" [41] To save money he had persuaded his agent, Flora Holly, to cut her usual ten per cent commission in half on *The Financier* and now debated the idea of dealing direct with his publisher and eliminating the agent's fee entirely. "You will remember," she wrote him, "that you promised to let me handle your next book on a 5% basis. You know how much I want to do this, and I hope you are not going to throw me over." [42]

On November 20 Dreiser had lunch with Ann Watkins, Thelma's friend, now a literary agent at 366 Fifth Avenue. He hoped to get Thelma's London address from her, but he did not. Instead, she wrote Thelma to tell her that he was sailing, giving her his London address, care of Grant Richards, 7, Carlton Street, Regent Street, London, and adding, "Whether or not you feel it is best to communicate with him is a matter for you to decide." [43]

On November 22 Dreiser boarded the *Mauretania* with Richards. "I'm off," he wrote Mencken. "Wish me luck. I value your friendship above many things." [44]

For almost a year he had not seen Thelma nor heard from her, and he was hoping for a reunion with Flowerface at the same time that he was planning European liaisons like those of Yerkes. Thelma was with her mother at 40 Alma Square, St. John's Wood, working hard for a Royal Academy art scholarship. She had lost interest in Dreiser, but Mrs. Cudlipp took no chances. When she learned that he was coming, she and Thelma packed up and sailed for New York. [45]

2. Europe on the Worry Basis

I. A DOCTOR AND A HYPODERMIC SYRINGE

To Dreiser the loss of his job had brought a sense of insecurity heightening an unreasonable mistrust of which he was well aware. He warned Richards, "There's something strange in my make-up. I quarrel with my friends, I'm too suspicious. . . ."[1] But he sincerely admired the sporty Briton, and the Atlantic voyage was enriched by the presence of Richards' friend, the English actress Sarah Brooke, who in turn introduced them to the American actress Malvina Longfellow.

Richards had been everywhere. He knew everybody. Now he arranged everything, keeping in mind Dreiser's $1,500 budget. In England, Dreiser was a guest for three weeks at Richards' country place at Cookham Dean, Berks, with a side visit to Oxford, hikes along the Thames, several trips to London and an English Christmas with the Richards family. While Richards of course was eager to become Dreiser's English publisher, he genuinely liked the blunt American and stirred himself as host and mentor far more than mere business interest would have required. Richards saw that Dreiser met literary people including John Masefield and A. E. Housman, not to mention Ethel Bicknell, a British girl with whom he enjoyed a country walk. Dreiser dined with W. J. Locke and was embarrassed when Locke praised his novels effusively and he was forced to sit mute, ashamed to admit he had never read Locke's books.[2] Late in December Dreiser was at the Capitol Hotel in Regent Street in a front room arranged for by Richards, with books, an itinerary and instructions on what to wear and how much to tip, all given by Richards.

He let himself go hog-wild in the matter of clothes. At Hill Brothers, Richards' Bond Street tailor, he was measured for a suit. He bought fancy waistcoats, a striped tack coat, shoes, a hat, an expensive bag. He bought some of Hummel's costly shirts. From Anderson, Anderson & Anderson, Ltd., he bought a Chesterfield costing a staggering 25 pounds.

No word, of course, came from Thelma. The *London Nation*, reviewing *Jennie*, praised its "steady glow of mental integrity" but decided in the end that its literary flaws made it an "interesting failure." [3] These two reverses were enough to plunge him into gloom, and yet his mercurial temperament rebounded. He sent a flood of letters and cards to Mencken, one reading:

> I have found it. Its name is Beer Lane & it runs or winds for 1 block out of lower Thames St. There are a number of saloons there. If ever we are near it I will guide you safely through.[4]

151

He picked up a London prostitute and cross-examined her about life, visited the House of Commons, was sickened by the degradation of the East End slums and, after a trip to Manchester, was off on January 11, 1912, to Paris, where he was again joined by Richards. Here Richards introduced him to Meg Villars, a lovely English dancer now a news correspondent in Paris, who so charmed him that he recalled her wistfully three decades later. Abraham Flexner arrived in Paris to do research for a study of European prostitution, and the knowing Richards took Dreiser and Flexner to places of Montmartre including the notorious Palmyr's Bar, a den of perversion operated by the lady in whose arms Toulouse-Lautrec was said to have died.[5] With Richards he saw Mistinguett, the newest sensation at the Folies Bergère. Dreiser bought more haberdashery, hiking boots, and on jaunts along the Seine recalled his sainted Balzac. He enjoyed Paris and its women even when Richards left for a short whirl of business in London—until he heard from Duneka at Harper's that *Jennie* was not doing as well as expected and that the sale to the end of 1911 probably would not exceed 10,000 copies.[6] (Gene Stratton Porter's *The Harvester* was then enjoying a sale that would top a million.) In despair, Dreiser wrote Richards:

> If I were you I wouldn't be so concerned about me. I am not going to be a best seller or even a half seller. My satisfaction is to be purely critical if even that. Critical approval won't make a sale & critical indifference won't hinder one. I haven't the drag on the public—that's all.
>
> . . . Since my book isn't going to sell I want to return to America with as much money as I can. It is just possible that *The Financier* will do a little better. . . .
>
> Don't build any financial hopes on me. You see what happens.[7]
>
> Th. D.

He was equable again when Richards returned to Paris with his friend Sir Hugh Lane, art collector and director of the Municipal Art Gallery in Dublin. The three men enjoyed a fortnight's holiday at Monte Carlo and Cap Martin, with long hikes, a mild fling at the casino and discussions of art and literature. Dreiser joked and argued zestfully with the bearded Sir Hugh but was occasionally annoyed by Richards' tendency to run the show—an officiousness Richards laid with some justice to Dreiser's ignorance of Europe, his desire to save money, and Richards' own sense of responsibility in seeing that he enjoyed himself within his budget.[8] Richards had long since been astonished by Dreiser's wavering moods.

As he had in Paris, Dreiser was following the Yerkes pattern and his own by dallying with women, some of them introduced to him by Richards—a research routine he enjoyed but found expensive. He had written once to Jug, who had taken refuge with her relatives in Missouri. She replied with news of late reviews of *Jennie* and affirmations of her belief in Christian Science, regretful that he wrote so seldom but adding, "I hear from you indirectly tho' frequently—particularly thro' Mr. Mencken. He has been so nice to me this winter." [9] Dreiser also dashed off cards to Anna Tatum, who replied with literary talk, called him "the American Tolstoy" and warned him, "*Don't, don't* listen to the fools, the asses, the insane people who say you write *crudely*. I never heard anything more stupid and blasphemous." [10] He wrote to Barbara Langford and doubtless to other women friends, and to Mencken he sent a stream of cards and letters, mostly heavily jocular.

On February 9 Richards and Lane returned to England while Dreiser went on alone to the grand Continental Hotel in Rome, which he found too expensive. This hotel was not only suggested by Richards but was inhabited at the time by his mother, who stirred herself to welcome Dreiser and tell him what to see in Rome. Richards, in addition to playing host to him in England, was still devoting his efforts to making Dreiser's journeys pleasant and reasonably economical. He sent frequent letters of advice on itineraries, hotels and people to meet. He furnished letters of introduction. He handled Dreiser's finances. He discussed with Douglas Z. Doty, a Century editor then in London, a proposal whereby Century would take over the American publication of Dreiser's subsequent books and pay him an annual sum for ten years [11]—a plan which, although it did not materialize, Richards thought would have been ideal for the money-haunted novelist. Century was openly wooing Dreiser, for W. W. Ellsworth, a vice-president of the company, was going to Rome and would visit with him.

But by now he was in no mood for appreciation. He learned that *Jennie*, up to the end of the year, had sold only 7,720 copies instead of 10,000. A $1,000 payment due on his Yakima apple orchard further jolted him. Although he had yearned for this trip to Europe, and Richards had made it possible, he was now so oppressed with worry that he blamed it on his friend. In reply to a Richards letter about his finances, he wrote peevishly:

> Dear R: You figure wrong. If I spend 16 francs as I'm doing for a room the remaining 8 francs will about pay for car fare, postcards & tips—but scarcely. Which leaves exactly nothing for such vast adventures as laundry, vichy [and] an occasional forced outside meal etc. So much for high finance. Th. D. [12]

He complained to Richards about the hotel, calling the food and service "wretched."

He had a low opinion of Rome, writing Richards, "I don't care much for this noble village of Rome . . ." and adding, "if anyone ever says anything to me about Rome after this I'll bang 'em in the eye." [13]

Wearied by Richards' mother, he wrote the publisher with deliberate rudeness:

> Your mother is the soul of courtesy & attention but if you know me at all by now you know that I am bored to extinction by the conventional understanding & interpretation of life. I would rather—80 million times—live all alone and meditate as a hermit than to endure any save clever, attractive,

unconventional women. I think all of your women relations . . . have had the good fortune to be married to or associated with talented men—but they themselves—well they are not in the same class. It seems a rough thing to say but I'd say it to my own relatives quite as quickly and I'm sure I need not explain to you.[14]

The modest sale of *Jennie* had soured him entirely. He talked of cutting short his trip, writing Richards, "I am sorry to be handicapped financially & shall cut Paris after Berlin & sail from some port in England. No more Europe on the worry basis for me." [15] Inclined now to view everything acidly, he saw the Pope and described him as "a rather doleful old man," and although he was impressed by the Roman gardens and ruins, he wrote Mencken, "mechanically, hygienically and intellectually it's about 100 years behind the times." [16] Learning in a letter from DeCamp about changes at Butterick, he thought longingly of a steady salary, writing Richards, "I understand from one letter that Erman J. Ridgway has fallen out with the Butterick Company & quit. I may go back there." [17]

Richards was aghast that the novelist he was grooming for the Nobel Prize should consider returning to the Jenny Wren Club. "I lost patience with you horribly. . . ." he wrote about the Butterick idea. "I think such a suggestion at this moment is most disloyal—disloyal I mean to yourself and to your qualities. . . . The trouble with you is that you do really, you know, get cold feet. You are in streaks, as I told you that day on the Higher Corniche. You should cultivate equability. Keep some of your good spirits of Monday for Tuesday." He added, " 'Handicapped financially' indeed! I wish I had half your complaint. . . . And then: 'No more Europe on the worry basis for me.' Heavens, what are you talking about? A nice character but too temperamental. You ought to travel with a doctor and a hypodermic syringe. You really ought." [18]

II. MAD AS HELL

For all his vapors, Dreiser lingered in Rome for almost a fortnight, perhaps in part because Daphne Walters, the attractive, literary wife of an American writer, was also staying at the Grand Continental. He gave her a copy of *Sister Carrie* and discussed the Borgias with her. Apparently he had heard of this lurid family saga only since coming to Italy. Fascinated, he resolved to put the story in his travel book and—being too busy himself—he actually coaxed Mrs. Walters to write an account of the Borgias for him which she would mail him later.[19] The pleasant habit of confiding his problems to women and getting them to help him had become fixed. Barbara Langford in New York was writing for him a careful criticism of certain aspects of The *"Genius."* Jug, whom he wrote once from Rome, had returned from Missouri and taken temporary refuge at Our Lady of Peace chapel on West Fourteenth Street, to rest and try to learn French. She was still the confirmed Christian Scientist, but although her practitioner warned her that the Catholics might practice Malicious Animal Magnetism on her, she did not believe in M. A. M.[20]

Leaving Rome at last, Dreiser found Perugia lovely and was in Florence by March first. Here he made no mention of art treasures but wrote Duneka at Harper's mourning a mixup that had delayed his payment on the apple orchard and adding, "I fancy I have lost half my tract which in the face of my present munificent authorship returns is most inspiring." [21]

Then came a "streak," for from Venice he wrote Richards, "Nothing could be finer than Venice." He was taking notes for his travel book and articles, buying picture postcards to aid his memory, but his impressions of Europe were now often superficial, the impressions of a mind somewhat hostile and too harried to dig below the surface. Passing through Switzerland, he stopped at Frankfort, where he met Frau Culp, an opera-singer friend of Richards, and by March 12 was in Berlin, which he described to the Chicagoan Floyd Dell as "a second Chicago in enthusiasm & pace. . . ." [22] Though he was one of the most contentious of men, he felt that "One of the Berliners' most wearying characteristics is their contentious attitude." [23] He made a side trip to his father's birthplace at Mayen, where he enjoyed good German beer but found no Dreisers except in the graveyard, and was shaken on seeing one stone engraved, "Theodor Dreiser, 1820–1882."

Although he was riding third class to save money, his thrift did not extend to clothing, for when he returned to Berlin again he wrote Richards asking him to order another suit for him from Hill's in London. He merely specified a blue fabric and left the rest up to Richards. Richards doubtless was irked when Dreiser, having received a swatch and description, said it would never do. "As I telegraphed you the cloth is too thick—and double-breasted—never," Dreiser wrote him. "New York—all North America is terribly hot in July & August & I have to be there—lighter please & built for summer." [24] The suit was already cut but by quick work Richards had it altered.

After leaving the Riviera, Dreiser was often unhappy and at times almost irrational, unable to take full advantage of a journey which was of real value to him, experiencing flashes of enjoyment but sinking more and more into a funk about money and finding in Richards a convenient whipping boy. Richards could not understand his terrible materialistic fear. The Briton's letters were almost unvaryingly cheery and encouraging, but between the lines one could read his suspicion that Dreiser was a trifle crazy. If he was really pressed for cash, why did he order clothing like a boulevardier? How could he regard his European trip as too costly when he was getting a book and three magazine articles out of it? How could he view his literary future so gloomily when Century and Appleton's were itching to get him away from Harper's? And why so bitter, so savage?

While there was a wide gulf between the suave publisher who regarded the world as his oyster and the nervous American with his terror of poverty, Dreiser's failing here was clear: an inability to adjust to reduced but not disastrous circumstances and to make the best of it. Being unable to afford expensive women added to his woes. He wrote Richards:

> You talk very lightly of Amsterdam, Rotterdam, the Hague, Brussels, Bruges & Ghent, Paris, a walking tour of a week in England, etc. etc. I really don't know how much time you expect me to spend for you furnish no itinerary. . . . I find myself getting mad as hell at times and still, nevertheless & notwithstanding being hauled about at your convenience. You are at once a nemesis & a stoic & quite the most interesting man I have ever known. But you do play the game with too high a hand—really you do,—and you have at once a conscience and none.[25]

He was developing a hatred of the British, whom he had so admired, that would last all his life. It seemed founded in the inferiority complex that accompanied his sense of greatness. The idea of nobility offended him, but nobility was not confined to England. He had been shocked by the slums of the East End and Manchester, but similar slums existed in other countries. Sensitive as he was, one feels that Richards and other Britons had confronted him with a savoir-faire that exposed his own gaucherie. Even Richards' children had astounded him with a self-assurance apparently born in them. Self-assurance was what he yearned for and never attained—the quality his brother Paul had in such abundance that it had driven him mad with envy, and which upper-class Englishmen seemed to have en bloc. His dislike would grow into an obsession as he reasoned that the British patronized Americans and were at bottom fox-hunting royalists who wrung luxury out of the hopeless masses.

A few days later, still in Berlin, he wrote Richards about financial obligations that required "immediate adjustment," even mentioning a bill from Romeike's clipping service and another bill for $15.36 for fire insurance.[26] But on March 27 he softened momentarily. "I owe you much for a wise interpretation of my various needs," he wrote Richards, "and in spite of my temperamental divagations I think (I know) you understand that I put you first among those you [sic] have come near in a world that never comes very near at its very best." [27]

In Amsterdam Dreiser was entertained by Richards' friend Mevrouw Julia Rykens-Culp, a sister of the German Frau Culp. Although he found her "entirely charming" and he enjoyed the Low Countries, he was so obsessed by the need to get home that he rushed on to Paris, already having written Richards that he wanted a sailing date soon after April first. Richards met him in Paris, where the two foregathered at Madame Geruy's bar. The publisher urged him to relax at his Berkshire place and then join him in a week's walk through the Hardy country—Hardy, whom Dreiser so admired—but Dreiser would not be stayed. He would get the next boat.

The next boat was the *Titanic*.

There was some talk about this between the man with the monocle and the man folding his handkerchief—a little resentment on each side. Richards pointed out that the *Titanic*, being new, might be uncomfortable and that in any case if thrift was important the *Kroonland*, sailing a few days later, would be cheaper. Thrift was important. Thus did Richards join the dancing Scot and Thelma Cudlipp in making Dreiser's later works possible. The two men discussed German militarism, and Dreiser perhaps took a malicious pleasure in assuring Richards that there would be a war and that Germany would trample France and England with ease. He sailed from Antwerp April 13, providentially on the *Kroonland*.[28]

3. Living on Advances

Dreiser landed in New York April 23 to find the city in shock over the *Titanic* disaster. The *Times* and *Herald* listed the *Kroonland*'s first-class passengers but made no mention of the returning author, who came second class. He took a room at the St. Paul Hotel at Columbus Avenue and Sixtieth Street. He was in no hurry to rejoin Jug. Apparently their apartment at 3609 Broadway had been sublet during their absence and was available May first. Jug, after a short stay at the Catholic chapel, had put up at the Brevoort for a month—an extravagance that must have made Dreiser grind his teeth—then had moved to the Broadway apartment May first. Dreiser let her stay there alone and remained at his hotel. He lunched with Douglas Doty of Century, but was feeling more friendly toward Harper's despite his many complaints. For one thing, he discovered that *Jennie* had enjoyed a remarkable continuing sale—12,717 copies so far—and that *Carrie*, published in February, had sold 1,026.[1] For another, *The Financier* would run at least 500,000 words, and Harper's counseled him to divide it into three volumes, each one a story complete in itself and under different titles. If he did this—and it was the only solution—it would not be wise to change publishers in the middle of a trilogy.

From Barbara Langford, now in Massachusetts, came a yearning letter reading in part:

> I'd give the world away to creep into your enfolding arms . . . and forget everything but you and my own happiness.
> I know you probably can't come to me—you aren't free.[2]

From Louise-Ann Miller:

> Teddy Dear: Can you "chop" with me Saty at 7 P.M.? I want to see you about something.
> Now don't wait until Xmas to ans.[3]

From Daphne Walters:

> How do you do—? Are you in town—or are you not? It would be very nice of you some day to ask me for a cup of tea—would it not—? Yes?[4]

What with one thing and another, not until eleven days after he landed did Dreiser write Richards, and then did not bother to thank him. He must have known by then that he was going to let Richards down—that he would stay

158

with Harper's, which had an active British branch and would not let Richards publish him in England without paying a prohibitive price for the privilege. If he felt a trifle guilty, his tone thereafter also showed some satisfaction at giving Richards the back of his hand. "I am glad I did not leave on the Titanic," he wrote, without mentioning that Richards' urging on this point had probably saved him from the watery grave that claimed 1,517 passengers. ". . . I am profoundly glad that I am on my home ground and out of your clutches." [5]

On May 26, in response to a Richards query, he let the Briton know of the Harper plan, saying, "I have no particular quarrel with the house." [6] Richards, seeing the drift, replied:

> My Dear Dreiser, The affection I have for you and the admiration that I have for your work will both of them be obscured if you write such rotten letters; and also if you blow hot and cold. One day you press me to your bosom and tell me you are not going to take any step in regard to your literary affairs without my approval and sanction, because I am the only man who has ever made good for you; and then you go allowing Harper to "plan", and this I take to mean that they have arranged, to publish "The Financier" in three parts over a period of thirteen months. . . . You know you have a suspicious nature. It is an ugly, sinister trait. I should fight against it—that and your tendency to unjustified depression—these are rocks on which many a good ship has gone down. . . .[7]

Dreiser's tantalizing reply must have infuriated him:

> Do you really think you ought to have it? Personally I get very dubious when I think that the one financial thing I really wanted you to do you did not do and rather wilfully & inconsiderately I think. However this makes no difference in my personal feeling toward you. You might do worse & still have me like you. Harper's will pay me 20% & spend some money in advertising. You offer me no definite program . . . meantime I think you might well meditate on your sins and see how easy it is for the wicked to be punished at times.[8]

Apparently he was excited enough about the Harper plan to forget about Butterick. By early June, still avoiding Jug, he had moved temporarily to 605 West 111th Street—possibly his sister Emma's address. He was working furiously on *The Financier*, journeying to Philadelphia to consult Coates and the newspaper files there on Yerkes. Always needing someone to advise, criticize and praise him, he was lost without the aid of Mencken, himself on a brief European tour, and he was overjoyed when Mencken returned early in June.

"Lord I'm glad to know you're back," he wrote. ". . . When are you coming over here? I wish I could talk to you. I have a whole raft of things to discuss. . . . For heaven sake keep in touch with me by mail for I'm rather lonely & have to work like the devil." [9]

After two books about suffering women, he was glad to be writing about a male, a Machiavellian, an exemplar of his belief in the survival of the fittest. "Maybe I sound disloyal," he told an interviewer, "but Jenny's temperament does not appeal to me any longer." [10] Early in *The Financier* he set the theme, with young Frank Cowperwood gazing at a fish-store tank containing a lobster and a squid. The squid desperately tried to elude the attacking lobster, but eventually was caught and devoured, a spectacle that deeply impressed the boy. "That's the way it has to be, I guess," he said, reflecting that all life was like this, the strong preying on the weak. [11]

By late June Dreiser had rejoined his wife in the sense that they shared the 3609 Broadway address. The indications are that the move was motivated largely by economy and convenience. To Jug it was a supreme effort to heal the breach, to prove that he *needed* her. Had not time shown that he had been a fool about Thelma, just as she had predicted?

Dreiser made the decision to stay with Harper's, leaving Richards out in the cold. Apparently in writing Richards of this, he questioned the publisher's accounting of the expenses of the European tour, including bills which Richards had paid and for which Dreiser was to reimburse him. Richards let himself go in a little masterpiece of disgust:

My Poor Friend: When I read your letter I confess that I had a rather bad half hour. That I should have given myself so much trouble for, have given myself up, time & energy, house and friends so unreservedly to, anyone quite so mean—well, it rather turned my stomach. . . . But then I remembered how you had, even before we left America, warned me against your "suspiciousness", & other kindred ugly qualities. I should perhaps have known that there are men who can't believe that one is friendly disinterestedly or enthusiastic from conviction. You searched for a motive for all the trouble I took . . . & you found one after your own kind. Well, I wish you joy of it. You see if your letter means anything it means that you believe that in telling you what I'd spent on our joint accounts I "cooked" the figures —swindled you, directly or indirectly, in fact. And then you go on to complain . . . that during parts of your experiences your scale of expenditure was so high. Naturally one doesn't travel in the footsteps of a pleasure- & woman-loving financier from one end of Europe to the other, collecting notes, & having his experiences, without spending a good deal of money. For this I provided to the best of my ability—as I told you I should do beforehand—by reducing your expenditure to a minimum while you were in England by putting you up, & by pulling other strings later on. You wanted me to "manage" & I managed & in the result you went to many more places than you expected to go to, you took back to America a regular "trousseau," & you did see just those things you wanted to see & were introduced to just those people who I thought would be most useful to you. I could say a great deal more but I won't. I fancy you've cured me of taking people at their word. It'll be a long time before I take so much trouble for anyone as I've taken for you. Yours, Grant Richards. [12]

II. DRUNK ON HIS OWN STORY

Pressed by Harper's for early fall publication, Dreiser worked so hard on *The Financier* (the first volume of the Cowperwood trilogy) that he paid little heed to the odd political battle between Roosevelt, Taft and Wilson. He was now living on advances, having received from Harper's $1,000 on February 19 and $500 payments on April 13, April 22 and September 23.[13] He had dropped Miss Holly to save 5 per cent. Under such pressure the book, when completed late in August, was even more overlong than usual, a massive 270,000 words. He was in a sweat to trim it, admitting his own weakness at self-criticism and appealing to Mencken in Baltimore for help.

Mencken, busy as he was, wrote, "Eureka! Let me have those proofs by all means." On reading them, he criticized "irrelevant detail" but was generous in praise, writing in part:

> But all these things, after all, are but minor blemishes on a magnificent piece of work. You have described and accounted for and interpreted Cowperwood almost perfectly. . . . And you have given utter reality to his environment, human and otherwise. No better picture of a political-financial camorra has ever been done.[14]

Actually the usually blunt Mencken was babying Dreiser, finding in him a genius that needed gentle treatment if it were to flourish. He gave a franker opinion of *The Financier* to his friend Harry Leon Wilson, writing, "In brief, D. got drunk upon his own story and ran amuck," adding, "Dreiser is a sensitive fellow and easily dashed. He needs a little help over this rough place. . . ."[15] Later, to Willard Huntington Wright, Mencken wrote, "[Dreiser] is a real fellow and deserves all the help he can get. Some day, I believe, we will be glad to think that we gave him a hand."[16] To Dreiser himself, Mencken sent the praise he so badly needed: "You are gaining a definite place, by general acceptance, as the leading American novelist. I see you mentioned constantly, and always with the same respect. New serious novels are no longer compared to 'Silas Lapham' or to 'McTeague', but to 'Sister Carrie' and 'Jennie Gerhardt.' "[17] Without the warm encouragement that accompanied Mencken's sagacious criticism, Dreiser might have surrendered to the tempting idea of quitting fiction and finding a job. For years the Baltimore sage would remain a celestial Dreiser co-author by keeping him at his writing when no one else would have had enough influence to do so.

Dreiser forgot his penury when his own writing was at stake. He made such sweeping corrections in the *Financier* proofs that it cost him a staggering $726.90. When the book was published in October, no reviewers were as enthusiastic as Mencken but the reception was generally good. Dreiser's minute coverage of financial and political detail made it apparent that he was no mere sex-exploiter, and if there were complaints about his novel's length, there was praise for his eye for truth. At last he had fought his way to acceptance as the unquestioned leader in the still suspect field of realism. Arthur Guiterman's long rhymed review in *Life* wound up with both praise and reproof:

> *He moralizes somewhat more,*
> *With broodings neither wise nor weighty.*
> *The book is good, I said before;*
> *The pages number seven-eighty.*[18]

In the interval, Dreiser finished a short story that would become famous, "The Lost Phoebe," then began his travel articles and book. The Chicagoan, Edna Kenton, now living in New York, invited him to tea. "Dreiser took a physical (not romantic) interest in her," Miss Kenton's friend Carl Van Vechten recalled, "and attempted to seduce her. She refused him on the ground that he was a married man." [19] Dreiser was enjoying occasional literary discussions with Barbara Langford. Sometime that fall, Anna Tatum came to New York, where Dreiser arranged to meet her at the Plaza Hotel. Miss Tatum turned out to be slight, blonde and pretty, a Wellesley graduate, a young bluestocking of Quaker antecedents who infringed current mores by smoking cigarettes. Her first sight of Dreiser moved her to startled candor.

"I didn't know you were so homely," she said.[20]

Dreiser, cut to the quick, excused himself and headed for the door. Miss Tatum apologized so remorsefully that he forgave her and remained to dine. He was glad he had, for she was a scholar who could quote Verlaine in French, knew all the great novels (putting his own near the top), had a sure instinct for the dramatic, and now told him a long and involved story out of her own family background which she thought would make material for his own pen. If Dreiser was skeptical, he soon became enthralled, moved almost to tears. The story was that of Anna's father, a singularly devout and gentle Quaker whose nobility of character, rather than bringing him happiness, plunged him and his family into deepest tragedy. The irony of it was in perfect accord with Dreiser's own conviction—gleaned in part from his father's career—that religion, however idealistic, failed to meet reality and indeed, in its repression of "natural" impulses, led to disaster. The story, which he later called *The Bulwark*, made such an impression on him that although he was already committed to writing the second and third volumes of the Cowperwood trilogy and to finishing *A Traveler at Forty*, he began mentally to organize *The Bulwark*. He also sought to find a New York job for Miss Tatum so that she could be nearby and join the ranks of his helpers. What with all these diversions, Jug could have seen little of him.

He had the grace to regret his treatment of Grant Richards, for when the publisher made his annual visit to New York in December, 1912, Dreiser wrote him suggesting a meeting. Richards could think of nothing less pleasant. His resentment if anything had grown because of Dreiser's failure to reimburse him for a London bootmaker's bill for £3, 17S, 6D, and also because of his recent reading of the proofs for one of Dreiser's travel articles for the *Century Magazine*. In it Dreiser had made libelous remarks about the Carlton Hotel in London which might have involved the *Century* through its London edition in a lawsuit had not Richards warned the editors to tone it down. Now, about to sail, he wrote Dreiser from the Knickerbocker:

> I make friends with too great reluctance to surrender them with anything but great unwillingness and regret. But your letter of last July, both in what it said & what it implied and in its indications of what you propose to do with your books and manuscript, left me no choice. With regard to your books I write not as a disappointed publisher, you must please believe, but as a wounded admirer (of your work) to whom you had made certain almost extravagant promises of association. . . . You speak of business reasons for our meeting. I cannot imagine what they are . . . but all the same . . . I will say that I shall be here, with intervals, from 2:30 till 3:45 when I go down to the boat.[21]

Despite the rebuff, Dreiser called at the Knickerbocker. Richards described the meeting:

> After some salutation we each waited, like nervous dogs, for the other to begin, I folding my clothes and putting them away, he leaning back in his chair, interminably folding and unfolding his handkerchief. In effect, I believe, we neither of us spoke and, after a space, he departed.[22]

Years later, Dreiser said wistfully, "I would give anything not to have quarreled with him, and over money too! I owe him so much; that trip to Europe! It was like a tonic that lasted me for years. . . ."[23]

4. Chicago Again

On December 20, 1912, three days after the sad interview with Richards, Dreiser was at the Sherman Hotel in Chicago, intent on researching the further career of Yerkes for the second volume of the Cowperwood trilogy, *The Titan*. He had lost track of his wild brother Rome, and although apparently his steady brother Al still lived in Chicago—the only Dreiser left there—there seems no record that he looked up Al. He had of course left Jug in New York.

It was a different Chicago from the city he had known as a boy—from the World's Fair metropolis he had visited almost twenty years earlier with a bevy of teachers including Sallie White—not so ugly, nor yet quite beautiful, but still charged with the raw force that had always fascinated him.

And Dreiser was an astonishingly different Dreiser from the feckless boy Chicago had known. At forty-one he was still shy, still a dreamer, but the change in attitude toward his own individuality and his place in the world amounted to a transformation of character nearly miraculous. The one-time weakling had become aggressive, courageous, a bit truculent, embodying qualities that could best be described in a word that would never have described him before he was twenty: he was a fighter.

He was also a literary Samson, a slayer of philistines, to the slender, diffident Floyd Dell of the *Evening Post* and a dynamic group of Chicago rebels. Dell called on him at his hotel, already aware of his eccentricities—the handkerchief, the rocking chair and his occasional utterance, "It's a mad world, my masters!" Sure enough, Dreiser went through them all, but Dell could see that these were not affectations, that indeed the man had no affectations.[1]

Dreiser had letters of introduction to people who had known Yerkes before his death in 1905. He called on cynical Edgar Lee Masters, then a Chicago attorney little known as a poet, who had written to congratulate him on *The Financier* and who now saw Dreiser clad in an astrakhan-collared greatcoat, buck-toothed, smiling, friendly, impressive-looking. Masters told him of other Yerkes sources, and the two men went for a stroll on Michigan Avenue, where Dreiser was excited enough about Miss Tatum's story to tell him the plot of *The Bulwark*. "His mind was seething with ideas and plans," Masters recalled, "and I was astonished at its strength and fertility."[2]

To save money, Dreiser moved to the lodgings of William C. Lengel, now editor of *Building Management* magazine in Chicago but more interested in producing advanced little dramas on the side. To Lengel, his former boss was not only America's greatest living writer but a fatherly adviser. It was evening, a soft snow falling, when Dreiser reached Lengel's place at 712 Lincoln Parkway and Lengel strolled out to meet him, seeing him emerge from a cab and argue with the driver over a $3.50 fare.

"I will not pay it," Dreiser said. "It's a hold-up."

"You've got to pay it," the driver snapped.

Dreiser took off his overcoat and handed it to Lengel. "Now, try to collect it," he said to the cabbie.[3]

They compromised on a lower fare. On New Year's Eve, Lengel, still unmarried, took a girl friend to celebrate at the Great Northern Hotel. Dreiser, having nothing else to do, accompanied them, and since Lengel did not dance, Dreiser saw 1913 come in as he danced clumsily with Lengel's girl. Thereafter much of his spare time was spent with bohemian conspirators of the Chicago literary revolution rumbling around Schlogl's Restaurant and the Little Theater in the Fine Arts Building on Michigan Avenue, in which Dell was a central figure. Here he met Maurice Browne, founder of the nation's first Little Theater, who was about to produce *The Trojan Women;* Kirah Markham, the lovely, black-haired, white-skinned Andromache of the play; John Cowper Powys, the literary lecturer, an English clergyman's son who shunned church but prayed to fetishes and delighted in burlesque shows as an admitted *voyeur;* Arthur Davison Ficke, the handsome lawyer-poet from Iowa; Sherwood Anderson, writing hateful advertising copy by day and unpublished novels by night; Margery Currey, Masters, Lucian Cary, Margaret Anderson and others. To most of them, Dreiser and his best friend Mencken were literary liberators, heroes of the revolution.[4]

Mingling with the Little Theater troupe, Dreiser first was attracted by Hilda Golightly, then by a girl whose name is forgotten, and finally by twenty-year-old Kirah Markham. Miss Markham, the daughter of a wealthy Jewish father and gentile mother, was an intellectual as well as a beauty, an amateur painter as well as an actress, a former student at the Art Institute with an artist's temperament. He was fascinated, but there was a complication. Miss Markham and Floyd Dell were keeping company—and was not Dell the man who had so gloriously boosted *Jennie?*

If Dreiser interested Miss Markham, he repelled Margaret Anderson. This pretty eccentric, who had yet to found the *Little Review,* was annoyed by his handkerchief-twirling and other things, writing:

> Dreiser was never any good [at conversation] until some exchange of sex magnetism put him at his ease. . . . But even when I listened to Dreiser in conversation with women with whom he could establish a quick sex sympathy, his talk had no flavor for me. Sex display puts you at your best if you're a tempered human being—becomes responsible for wit. But Dreiser had no more wit than a cow. And as for being a tempered human being . . . he always left me with the impression that I was in the presence of nothing more than good old human nature. . . .[5]

Dreiser was feted at a tea at the Little Theater. He visited the studio of Jerome Blum and was delighted by Blum's rich use of color. Through Hamlin Garland he was extended the courtesies of the Cliff Dwellers for two weeks, and Garland wrote, "By the way, are you a speaker? Do you like to stand on your hind legs, and talk? If so, I think the members of the Club would like to hear from you. . . ." [6] The mere thought of public speaking paralyzed Dreiser, and undoubtedly he declined, but he did meet both Garland and Henry Blake Fuller and discussed with them the murder by American philistines of honest art. Fuller in 1895 had published his realistic *With the Procession,* and had been so abused for it that he had pulled in his horns. As Dreiser later recalled, Fuller admitted that "finding himself facing social as well as literary ostracism, he desisted." And Garland also, after his realistic *Main-travelled Roads,* likewise confessed, according to the same Dreiser recollection, a similar tendency to veer from realism in order to avoid "social ostracism." [7]

Dreiser, a far tougher man, was not yet intimidated.

Although cordial enough, Garland already had reservations about Dreiser. Garland's realism did not extend to sex. In his journal shortly afterward he wrote, "A claque for the pornographic has developed. It is becoming fashionable to sneer at marriage, chastity, home life, and the church. . . ." [8]

For Dreiser, all these were diversions piled on top of busy days interviewing friends of Yerkes and studying at the Newberry Library. Yerkes, he learned, was charming, a fine conversationalist, a cunning predator who pursued women who had brains as well as beauty and broke with them kindly when he tired of them. When one of them took to the law, he would hire a man to romance with her, contrive to compromise her, and Yerkes would then threaten to expose her if she persisted. On his staff he had a battery of fifteen lawyers drawing something like $150,000 a year to protect him from women and other threats—a luxury Dreiser had never needed in his own entanglements.

Possibly in part because of Miss Markham, he found in Browne's Little Theater the most shining example of Chicago's literary awakening—one that turned his own thoughts toward playwriting. He urged Browne to bring his troupe to New York. He gave a duplicate script of *The "Genius"* to Lengel to read and to pass on to Dell, Lucian Cary and Ray Long. When he left Chicago on February 10, Lengel saw him off at the station, as did Miss Markham, who, Lengel recalled, "threw herself in Dreiser's arms." [9]

II. FRONTING THE ABYSS

Back at 3609 Broadway—and more money worries. "I find," Dreiser wrote Harper's, "from your statement . . . that in 14 months beginning Oct. 20, 1911—I have actually earned about [$] 4,424.00 or roughly $316.00 per month. I had drawn as you know considerable [*sic*] more than that. . . .

And I have led the simple life. With your consent I will attempt the conclusion of this novel [*The Titan*] on $200 a month. . . ." [10]

As usual he was writing too fast, working simultaneously on *A Traveler at Forty* for Century and *The Titan* for Harper's, and trying through the agent Paul Reynolds to sell "The Lost Phoebe," which no one seemed to want at his bottom price of $400. His editors had troubles too. Doty of Century wrote him, "Yes—of course put in more about your actress acquaintances. But rather briefly I should suggest." [11] And Ripley Hitchcock of Harper's spelled out the Dreiser failings in large letters:

> I want to urge you most emphatically, to make [*The Titan*] relatively concise. I am sure that *The Financier* would have been equally effective and much more successful, if it had been shorter. Pray, let the reader infer something for himself. It is not necessary to go into all the details. Believe me, I am speaking for your interest. [12]

Thelma Cudlipp, now out of his life, was making her own way as an artist for the *New York Sun*. The strange Dreiser-Jug arrangement persisted, and when Lengel returned the *"Genius"* script from Chicago, and it vanished, Dreiser was convinced that Jug had found it and destroyed it in his absence—quite possible, since she would have considered it a public spectacle of her private life with him. [13] Her need for Dreiser (largely rationalized in her mind as *his* need for her) had assumed almost the proportions of a crusade to save him from himself. Living on $200 a month, and bound to support her in any case, he could scarcely have subsisted separately, but a trace of fondness persisted.

A sharp decline in the sale of *The Financier*, after it had sold a healthy 8,332 copies in the last two months of 1912, was hurtful. So was Floyd Dell's opinion of *The "Genius,"* Dell writing that despite his admiration for Dreiser he found it "a very bad book" and that "no amount of cutting could improve it—it would have to be rewritten from first to last." [14] So was Lengel's opinion, Lengel writing in embarrassment to the friend he cherished but admitting, "To my mind you have missed fire; and personally I feel that . . . it would do more to damage your career than to help it." [15] So was the opinion of Ray Long, editor of *Red Book*, which Lengel had solicited and who wrote Dreiser that the story was too detailed, "could not possibly grip a reader" and indeed was hardly worth the telling. [16] Lucian Cary also was adverse. Although Dreiser did not resent such criticism, he was beginning to discount the judgment of professionals and to rely more on admiring women, remembering that both Barbara Langford and Anna Tatum praised the book. Still he did not go ahead with publication, probably because both *A Traveler* and *The Titan* were on the stocks and it would not do to clutter the market with three Dreiser books in quick succession.

But—money! From Ben Dodge, who had been hauled forcibly away from liquor and had spent months at a relative's bone-dry Vermont farm, came an offer. Temporarily rehabilitated, he was set up in the publishing business on West Twenty-eighth Street by a wealthy banker, and wanted to make Dreiser a member of the firm.

"Am strictly sober & on the wagon," he wrote hopefully. ". . . We are both much taken with the idea of having your name on the title page either as Theodore Dreiser & Co. or linked with mine fore or aft." [17]

The idea of having a hand in a truly liberal publishing house, as well as a fixed salary for very little work, was attractive. But Dreiser, having reservations about Dodge's will power, and also concerned about his own name and reputation, as always sought the advice of Mencken, whom he had already asked to be his literary executor in case of his death. "Would you advise this at any price?" he wrote Mencken. [18]

It was as well that he decided against it, for a few months later Dodge had been drawn irresistibly into a series of saloons and was back at the Vermont farm to dry out. Dreiser, now deeply in debt to Harper's, was in a position where he could not recoup unless one or both of his upcoming books sold excellently. Characteristically, he was fed up with Harper's and was dickering with the publisher George H. Doran over a plan whereby Doran would take him over after *The Titan* and also arrange for his debts. His brush with Maurice Browne and Kirah Markham had renewed his dream of Dreiser the dramatist. When seized by an idea he liked, no amount of debt could stop him from putting it on paper. Although he was far behind schedule both on *A Traveler* and *The Titan*, he took time during the summer to rip out a one-act play, "The Girl in the Coffin," which he sent to Mencken, who liked it so well that *Smart Set* snapped it up at $150. [19] Dreiser also was seized by one of his impulses, contemplating a voyage to India, apparently with the idea of writing another travel book. But Doty at Century wrote:

> I believe it would be wiser to wait until this book [*A Traveler*] is out so that we can see what sort of reception it gets, before we decided on the nature of your next travel book. [20]

Doty was appalled when Dreiser gave him the completed *Traveler* script, for according to Grant Richards' possibly exaggerated estimate it was almost a million words long, the length of ten ordinary novels. Moreover, it dealt with sizzling frankness with street-walkers and other women Dreiser had encountered, not to mention respected persons whose identities were only thinly disguised. Doty "objected . . . like hell," as Dreiser described it. [21] When Richards arrived in New York on his annual visit, Doty asked him to go over it and tone it down.

Dreiser held no grudge, for in the narrative he often spoke flatteringly of Richards, the "Barfleur" of the chronicle—in fact dedicated the book to him. Yet Richards' eyes popped as he waded through the script, just as Jug's must have when she read *The "Genius."*

"What would have happened to me," Richards wrote, "if Dreiser's frank descriptions of my friends to whom I had introduced him, and to whose homes I had been allowed to take him as a guest, had been permitted to stand, I tremble to think! To the reflections on my own character and morality I attached no particular importance, but where others were concerned I had to think and to act. Reticence on any matter and Theodore Dreiser were as far apart as the poles. As I read I discovered that George Moore at his frankest was, compared with Dreiser, the essence of discretion. No confidence was sacred, no actual, or imagined, secret respected." [22]

Richards made wholesale cuts, as doubtless did the Century editors—so much so that when Mencken later read the proofs he found the story overly reticent in places although he praised parts of it as showing "the best writing you have done since *Jennie Gerhardt*." [23] Indeed the narrative as published was often terse and lively—in short, unlike Dreiser—and one suspects that it represents his thoughts much condensed and recast rather than his own writing. He did not, however, fail to get into it a reference to his favorite atrocity, the "suppression" of *Sister Carrie*. Mencken did what for him was a sentimental thing, showing his deep regard for Dreiser. He took the proof sheets of *A Traveler*, had them bound into a book and then illustrated the book with the scores of postcards Dreiser had sent him from Europe.

By October Kirah Markham had come to New York and taken an apartment where Dreiser made himself at home, telling her that he had broken finally with Jug. To Willard Huntington Wright, now in town as editor of *Smart Set*, he wrote:

> Note this in your memory. At 23 W. 58th St, Miss Kirah Markham . . . maintains an interesting drawing room Sunday evenings. Interesting people come and it is expected that next Sunday evening there will be a number. . . . [24]

Floyd Dell had quit his Chicago job and also come to New York, puzzled as well as irked that Dreiser had interested Miss Markham. "Dreiser," he later said, "was hardly the young man's notion of a knight-errant—somewhat pudgy, no great talker." He had learned that while in Chicago Dreiser had also romanced with a pretty secretary connected with the Little Theater, had written her to arrange for her to come to New York and serve as his helpmate and literary assistant, then had dropped her cold. Wounded, she had told Dell about it and showed him the letters. "They were long, thoughtful letters," Dell recalled, "considering her problems in the most detailed and kindly way. This capacity for entering into a woman's situation was certainly one trait that endeared him to them, although in this instance he could walk out on the girl quite brutally." [25]

Dell, although nettled, called at the Markham-Dreiser apartment for a chat and later was instrumental in getting Dreiser elected to membership in the Liberal Club on MacDougal Street. Despite his political skepticism, Dreiser was numbering radicals among his friends, among them Emma Goldman, who invited him and Miss Markham to a New Year's Eve party "to kick out the old year and meet the new."

Pressed though he was, Dreiser gave money to Ben Dodge and succored the mentally wavering Fritz Krog. Krog, who had sold a few stories through the agent Ann Watkins, had fallen madly in love with Miss Watkins—an infatuation she firmly discouraged. One day he called at her Fifth Avenue office, waving a pistol. "Come with me," he ordered. "I have a hansom outside." Miss Watkins, knowing him to be unstable, obeyed in considerable fear. Krog talked of taking her off to some island paradise, whereupon, thinking fast, she pointed out that she would need money for such an extended journey and persuaded him to let her off at the Corn Exchange Bank on Forty-second Street. While Krog waited, she escaped through another door.[26] Krog then conceived the idea of becoming police commissioner because "it would raise me in her esteem," took a suite at the McAlpin Hotel, wrote letters booming himself for the commissionership, wrote Mayor John P. Mitchel threatening him if he did not make Krog commissioner, gave the hotel a rubber check and was jailed. Dreiser's friends Franklin Booth and Robert Amick had started a "Krog Relief Fund."

"Could you send me say about a hundred sheets of paper and a quantity of Bull Durham tobacco?" Krog wrote Dreiser from the Tombs.[27]

Touched, Dreiser wrote Judge George C. Nott, before whom Krog would appear, offering to testify for him and saying, "I admire him and have faith in him, not as a normal, conventional, well balanced, commercial minded man, but as an artist, creative, imaginative, complex, enigmatic. He ought to be warned, frightened, perhaps, and then set free. But do not please, as you value the artistic temperament in life, send him to prison. It is not necessary. He will be a better man—much—for a lecture and the sensible, helpful mercy of the law." [28]

Krog was placed on probation. Meanwhile Dreiser was incensed at his publishers for curbing his own artistic freedom by eliminating sex episodes in his new work. "After I am dead," he wrote Mencken, "please take up my Mss of *The Financier, Titan* & Travel book & restore some of the woman stuff. . . . I am afraid I shall have to go to Doran on a try for freedom." [29]

Money. . . . *A Traveler at Forty*, published November 25 and given a cordial if not enthusiastic reception in the press, sold only 2,745 copies by the year's end. Knowing he could not get another nickel out of Harper's, he wheedled $550 out of Century on December 6 and asked for more. He gave his manuscript of *The "Genius"* to Century as security, then dragged out a chaotic and unfinished script he had written almost ten years earlier about his period of mental travail—*An Amateur Laborer*—and handed that to Doty. But Doty could give him nothing on that, and the best Century would do was to give him a $300 cash loan on January 12.[30]

"Do you suppose I will ever reach the place where I will make a living wage out of my books," he queried Mencken, "or is this all a bluff & had I better quit. I am getting ready to look for a job. Yours—fronting the abyss." [31]

Mencken—the one man who kept Dreiser going—wrote soothingly:

> Certainly you'll reach the place where your novels will keep you. I think it is just ahead. *The Titan*, with its melodrama, ought to make both a popular and artistic success. And once you escape from Harpers [*sic*] all of the books will pick up. . . .[32]

III. THE ARTISTIC IDEAL

Needing money, Dreiser advertised in the *Herald* for it, outlining his abilities and his needs. He got a nibble from one E. Alton of the Eothen Corporation, who replied, "If you will give me some notion of the work for which you wish aid and the amount of capital essential to complete it, I may be able to assist you. While not a Mycaenas, I am interested in good literature. . . ." [33] Apparently he failed to get a loan from Alton, but the effort illustrates his feeling that society should subsidize artists—one to which he would return.

Having long since formed a necessary habit of deception with women, he had not been truthful with Miss Markham. Helpless in matters of cookery and detail, still dependent on Jug and somewhat fond of her, he could not bring himself to make the final break with the woman he had disparaged in *The "Genius,"* and he was spending part of his time with her at the Broadway apartment. When Miss Markham learned this, she returned to Chicago. But Anna Tatum was still in New York, serving there as his unpaid secretary, when he made another research trip to Chicago early in March, 1914, putting up at the Bradley Hotel on Rush Street.

Here he besought Miss Markham again. He also renewed his acquaintance with Edgar Lee Masters, two years older than himself, who also detested literary and moral convention but was more fortunate in having a law practice to sustain him while he wrote poetry so repugnant to the American credo of sweetness that publishers shunned him. He had written his long, free-verse poem, *Spoon River Anthology*, which would soon begin publication, probably without payment, in *Reedy's Mirror* in St. Louis because no one else wanted it. Although it was printed there under a pen name, Masters' authorship of this relentless exposure of small-town hypocrisy would become known and would damage his law business.

Masters took Dreiser downstate to Oakford to spend an evening with the colorful Jack Armstrong, son of the Armstrong whom Lincoln had defended on a murder charge and who himself could dimly remember Lincoln. Masters was "impressed with the power of [Dreiser's] mind, and with the vast understanding that he has of people, of cities, of the game of life. I have never seen anyone who knew as much of these things as Dreiser does. . . ." He was as struck by Dreiser's capacity for sudden, inexplicable rudeness: "He can be the most boorish, the most unfeeling of men, just as on this occasion when he . . . treated my father . . . with unexplainable discourtesy." [34]

Dreiser was incensed by the activities of Major Funkhouser, the Chicago book-and-art censor who had once been duped by a press agent into arresting a dealer for selling a print of "September Morn," with the result that it sold millions of copies.

"How in the name of all that is logical," he asked an interviewer, "all that is art, can a man like this Bunkouser or Funkhouser come to be empowered as he is to censor and condemn? But that is the terrible thing that is overtaking this whole country, appointing someone . . . to tell you and me what is right for us to think—mind you, think! Why the pygmy, illiterate minds of these vested creatures would fall to pieces if their owners undertook to read a book on philosophy. What do they know about life, its workings, or its real religion?" [35]

After two years of work on Yerkes (the Cowperwood of his novels), Dreiser had come to admire Cowperwood, to identify himself with Cowperwood, and to proclaim a philosophy which he would later denounce with the same passion with which he now advanced it. Yes, Cowperwood was a crook—but how strong, how able, how he got things done! If he was cruel, he was also the fittest and therefore entitled to survive. To be sure, he was Machiavellian—but what a heroic Renaissance man, what an artist! Thus implied Dreiser-Cowperwood as he delivered a blast against the petty reformers who promoted measures aimed at protecting the weak against such predators as Cowperwood:

> A big city is not a little teacup to be seasoned by old maids. It is a big city where men must fight and think for themselves, where the weak must go down and the strong remain. Removing all the stumbling stones of life, putting to flight the evils of vice and greed, and all that, makes our little path a monotonous journey. Leave things be; the wilder the better for those who are strong enough to survive, and the future of Chicago will then be known by the genius of the great men it bred.[36]

While in Chicago, Dreiser was assailed by carbuncles and underwent surgery while anesthetized by laughing gas. Miss Markham was at his bedside as he burst into hysterical laughter and shouted, "I've got it . . . the secret of the universe, the same thing over and over. . . ." [37] The experience would later result in a Dreiser play. Recovering, he received amazing news from Miss Tatum in New York. Harper's, after advertising *The Titan* and printing 8,500 sets of sheets, suddenly decided not to publish the book after all.

The reason given was that its realism was too uncompromising. True, it was a shocker in the number if not the explicit treatment of seductions, relating Cowperwood's affairs with Rita Sohlberg, Antoinette Nowak, Stephanie Platow, Cecily Haguenin, Florence Cochrane et al. When Ford Madox Ford later read the book he called it "revolting" and complained that he could go no farther than the eleventh seduction. Yet Harper's had long ago read the manuscript and had invested in production and advertising, and the question remained why they had not discovered the realism sooner. There were rumors that they had become fearful that the portrayal of ruthless financiers would incense capitalists controlling the firm; also that Dreiser's delineation of Berenice Fleming could be libelous in its similarity to Emilie Grigsby, Yerkes' last mistress, who was still a fashionable personage in London.[38]

There was a flurry of telegrams between Dreiser and Miss Tatum. It happened that William C. Lengel had recently returned to magazine work in New York. In response to Dreiser's plea, he took charge of the find-a-new-publisher campaign, with Miss Tatum as his assistant—one of the many times when Lengel would work devotedly in his behalf. Proofs of *The Titan* were sent to Century, George H. Doran, the John Lane Company and to Alfred A. Knopf, then associated with Mitchell Kennerley. Knopf was keenly interested but was forced to withdraw because of indignation expressed by Kennerley, who had known Yerkes and Emilie Grigsby and felt that Miss Grigsby had reason to sue and would. Century said no, possibly also fearful. Doran, with whom Dreiser already had parleyed and whom Mencken had written in Dreiser's behalf, seemed a good bet but now he likewise got cold feet.[39]

"Dear Dodoi," Miss Tatum wrote, using her pet name for Dreiser, "I had a talk with Doran this P.M. He finally rejected the book. We don't want him anyhow. He's a 'gentleman' and a conventionalist. He said in so many words that he considers the book *unsaleable* entirely apart from the question of *morale*. He indicated that it was a pity you ever got started on Yerkes—whom he says he considers a very abnormal American. You ought to have seen me stand up to him—in attitude rather than in speech!" Miss Tatum closed with more than secretarial loyalty: "Oh, Dodoi, how I love you. And how I love, even more, the artistic ideal. . . ."[40]

"An eternal pox upon the Harpers," Mencken, who was keeping in close touch with developments, wrote Dreiser from Baltimore. "And Doran be damned for his flight."[41]

But Lengel had better luck with the John Lane Company, a British firm which had recently established a New York branch on West Thirty-second Street under the direction of J. Jefferson Jones.

"PROUD TO PUBLISH TITAN . . ." Jones wired Dreiser.[42]

"Oh, Dodoi," Miss Tatum wrote, "—if the book is just once published & put before the public in the right way nothing else matters to me. . . . I have put so much of myself into it. . . . And I don't care for any repayment. I've done it for truth and art—and principally, I admit, for affection. That brings its own reward."[43]

Mencken, who always did his reading while comfortably supine on a couch, had speedily read an unbound copy of *The Titan* sent him by Miss

Tatum. He wrote Dreiser that it was "the best thing you have ever done, with the possible exception of *Jennie Gerhardt,*" and scoffed at the idea that censors might suppress it. "There is not one word in the book that will give Comstock * his chance. He must go into court with some specific phrase—something that will seem smutty to an average jury of numskulls." [44]

Dreiser, returning to New York on March 23, wrote gratefully to the man who served without stint as his editor, critic, adviser, backslapper and public megaphone, "your view of [*The Titan*] cheers me because I have such implicit faith in your honesty—intellectual & every other way." Later, he tendered Mencken a reward that he indeed deserved: "I hereby offer you the original pen copy of any one of my mss. . . ." [45]

"In plain truth, you overcome me," Mencken replied. ". . . I am filled with suspicions that you have taken to heroin, Pilsner, formaldehyde. Purge your system of the accursed stuff—and then offer me *Sister Carrie.* And see me jump!" [46]

Dreiser immediately obliged, and Mencken became the owner of a manuscript that would later become enormously valuable.

The friendship between these two warriors was at its height. Dreiser's publishers had cut hundreds of pages of "woman stuff" and other matter from *The Financier, A Traveler* and *The Titan,* and in fact he had had to scratch to find a publisher for the last book. By now he felt that the lines were drawn: he was America's leading fighter for literary freedom, and Mencken was his blood brother.

"Don't despair," he wrote Mencken. "The philistines will never run us out as long as life do last. Given health & strength we can shake the American Jericho to its fourth sub-story." [47]

IV. NATURE IS UNSCRUPULOUS

Possibly to save money and to escape Jug, Dreiser on returning from Chicago put up temporarily with his sister Mame and her husband Brennan, now living in New Brighton, Staten Island. His finances were all in red ink. Harper's had given him $2,000 in advances on *The Titan.* The Lane Company in turn gave him a needed $1,000 advance on the same book. This meant that he would not earn a penny in royalties until the $3,000 had been repaid the two publishers—a dark prospect unless the book sold well. He still owed the Century Company some $600 which would never be entirely repaid by the sale of *A Traveler.* He had not yet bothered to repay Grant Richards the £3, 17S, 6D for the London-made boots.

Jug's status, long so ambiguous, at this point became both pathetic and ridiculous. William Lengel married in April, 1914, and, believing the Dreisers still living together, he and his bride soon went over to the apartment at 3609

* Anthony Comstock, the New York censor whose name had become symbolic of all bluenosery.

Broadway to visit them. He cannot recall that Dreiser was there, and thinks that Jug, who *was* there, gave some excuse for his absence.[48] In any case there was as yet no announcement of any break. One gets a picture of Jug, staying sadly on at 3609, giving Dreiser aid and comfort when he chose to live there and trying to perpetuate the fiction that they were still cohabiting. One also gets a picture of Dreiser using 3609 as a convenient hotel and mailing address when handy and enjoying Jug's cookery on those occasions, but always the free agent. At times he took a juvenile pleasure in keeping his domestic status a close secret from his best friends. During this time he was paying Jug $100 a month, and he later dated his separation from her officially as October 1, 1910,[49] although he was with her on the intermittent "hotel" basis for almost four years after that.

Apparently the last time he used the 3609 address was on April 7, 1914. However, on this date he was actually living at 4142 Parkside Avenue in Philadelphia, staying there for some three weeks while Kirah Markham appeared at the Adelphi Theater in that city, and writing Mencken with characteristic furtiveness, "Don't give this address to anyone." [50] Returning to New York, he fell back briefly on a post-office box—something he occasionally did when he was on the move or wished to keep his whereabouts secret. By late May he was in Staten Island again, but this time not at his sister's address, writing Mencken, "It's nice where I am—a splendid view of the bay—but I'm going to move back into town or over to Phila. I have many schemes or plans but only one pen hand—and meanwhile my allotted space ticks swiftly by. Greetings—and let's pray we keep good stomachs and avoid religion. The ills that afflict man are truly mental and not material." [51]

He had had six different addresses in three cities in two months—a sign of his restlessness and also of his romantic complications. But when he quit 3609 Broadway he had at long last separated from Jug permanently, in so doing leaving a large quantity of letters which for years he would try to recover.

By mid-July he was at Address No. 7, 165 West Tenth Street in Greenwich Village, which would be his home for an amazing five years. Now Miss Markham, persuaded of his fidelity, was with him. Their apartment, two doors from newly cut-through Seventh Avenue, was in a shabby three-story brick building—two barren first-floor rooms with gimcrack furniture and no rugs but blessed by a fireplace and the great desk made from Paul's piano. An upstairs tenant, an Italian gentleman, was industriously turning out counterfeit currency until the police came for him.

Soon thereafter, Jug moved to the apartment of her spinster sister Ida, who was still with Butterick, on Waverly Place just around the corner from the Dreiser-Markham menage. Ida, furious at Dreiser, wrote him that she would do violence to Miss Markham on sight. "It was quite amusing," Miss Markham later observed, "to stand next to Mrs. Dreiser in the meat market and not have her know me." [52] She had no sympathy for Jug, feeling (from Dreiser's analysis) that she was narrow, conventional and ambitious.

Dreiser's imagination was captured by the possibilities of *The Bulwark*. "We were going for one of our week-end hikes along the old Morris and Essex Canal," Miss Markham recalled. "Theo started to tell me about [*The Bulwark*] on the Hudson tube. We got out at the end of the line in Newark and walked to the trolley and Theo never stopped talking, telling me this tale he was going to write. The trolley was crowded and he hung over me on a strap while I was seated, still going on. Eventually . . . we got off and were suddenly walking along beside the slow moving water, a completely tranquil scene, and Theo was still pouring out to me the soul agony of this Quaker." [53]

But a strange succession of circumstances would block *The Bulwark*. Meanwhile his lobster-and-squid philosophy emerged when he was interviewed by Margaret Mooers Marshall for the *World*.

"Each of us is an expression of the will-to-power," he said. "But in America business is still the swiftest, surest method of attaining great power. . . . It never occurred to anybody that greatness could be achieved as a writer, a musician, an artist. Therefore all the potentially great men poured into business. . . .

"I am certain that the mind of the great merchant is conscious of the poetry of his work. . . . The romance of it is tremendous. . . . It takes mind, and a fine quality of mind, to think out and build up the industrial enterprises of this country. . . ."

When Miss Marshall asked if such business titans as Cowperwood were not frankly unscrupulous, Dreiser raised a protesting hand.

"Nature is unscrupulous!" he exclaimed. "She takes her own way, regardless of the suffering caused, and the fittest survive. And in each one of us lingers this instinct of nature. In the weak it is mostly drowned under the rain of ethical exhortations poured on them from the beginning. In the strong unmorality triumphs. And today America is great not because of, but in spite of, her pieties and her moralities. . . .

"Because of our narrow-minded intolerance, the men who might have given us an American art have followed the line of least resistance and gone into business. There they could do as they pleased and yet conform to all the prejudices of the community. . . .

"But on the whole these men have been a blessing to the rest of us. . . . It's because of Vanderbilt that we can now ride to Chicago in eighteen hours. It's because of Rockefeller that we get oil at the present price. . . . It's as foolish to attempt to judge these men by the ordinary code as to apply that to a thunderstorm or any other natural phenomenon. Each did what he had to do. If he had faltered a stronger man would have ridden over him. Despite all the muckraking, most of us have a secret admiration for these business giants." [54]

Certainly Dreiser did. He saw society as a jungle in which unscrupulousness equalled strength and morality equalled weakness—the precise opposite of the teachings of convention and the church. If the Carnegies, the Vanderbilts and Cowperwoods had been ruthless, they could not help it, that was nature's way, and their ruthlessness in any case had borne good fruit. Similarly, he saw no hope in politics and reform, which were expressions of a vain desire to change a world which could not be artificially changed and where such changes as did occur were not the work of politicians or reformers but merely the slow process of evolution. And of war, which now threatened to inflame all Europe, he asked: "Do I believe in the peace movement? I would, if life were peaceful, but is it?" [55]

Thus he scoffed at the ideals of others, since life was meaningless, controlled by inscrutable forces and beyond alteration by mere individuals. Not so when his own ideals were involved. "I may talk pessimism," he could write, "but I never cease to fight forward." He attacked censors and conventionalists. He had joined Mencken in a war on "the American Jericho." He was committed to a struggle for freedom of letters when his own philosophy argued the futility of such a struggle. Despite his earlier enthusiasm for the *Delineator* Child-Rescue Campaign, and his own inexperience as a parent, he assailed the average American mother as unfit and the average American home as a "fetish," injurious to children in surrounding them with sentiment instead of reality. "Within a century," he said, sounding unlike a man who saw no hope in reform, "I believe we will have turned to the idea of making the child the property of the state, which will exercise supervision over the homes, taking the children away when they find surroundings bad." [56]

But if logicians could pick apart his reasoning, the critics should have seen in his new novel the work of a unique if uneven genius. *The Titan*, published by Lane on May 10, received high praise from Huneker and Mencken but a mixed reception otherwise. There was criticism of Dreiser's prolixity and some discussion of Cowperwood's wholesale immorality, as in one stanza of Arthur Guiterman's rhymed review in *Life:*

> *Your hero's morals must be lax*
> *To make a novel realistic,*
> *But when the ladies come in packs*
> *It's getting much too Mormonistic.*[57]

The Titan sold more poorly than *The Financier*—6,601 copies in the first two months and only 8,016 by the end of the year, proving Mencken wrong in his prediction of commercial success. It fell considerably short of paying Dreiser's $3,000 debt to Harper's and Lane's, so he got no royalties at all and was still in the red.

He must have been terribly hurt. He was forty-three, and *Titan* was his fourth published novel. Where at one time Mencken had been almost his only trumpeter, he had now gathered a following that included Reedy, Masters, Dell, Anderson, John Cowper Powys and Ben Hecht. The newspapers had found him interesting copy, so that he was better known than ever before. Furthermore, *The Titan* had carried on the exploits of Cowperwood and should have attracted many readers of *The Financier*. Instead, *Titan* had the poorest sale of his last three novels and his vogue, rather than gaining, appeared to be dwindling. He owed money to Harper's, Lane's and Century—still owed for a pair of boots, getting a tart letter from Grant Richards:

> . . . I should be very glad if you would let me have a cheque for the amount you owe me personally—£3, 17S, 6D. It goes very much against the grain with me to remind you of these debts but there seems no reason why they should run on from year to year.[58]

It was not surprising that Dreiser took stock and dropped temporarily (in effect for 30 years) the third volume of the Cowperwood trilogy. In his financial and artistic dilemma he turned to a bewildering variety of writing, some of which he could hardly have expected to be highly profitable.

He recast *The "Genius"* with an ironic ending in keeping with his own failure to win Thelma Cudlipp. This he planned as his next published novel, hoping that it would bring him enough of an advance so that he could finish *The Bulwark* in the winter. At the same time he gave William Lengel a copy of the *"Genius"* script to cut to 100,000 words in the hope that it could be sold serially for magazine publication.

He became fascinated by the 1899 case in which the New York clubman Roland Molineux was accused of murdering Henry Barnet with poison because of rivalry for the charms of an actress. Through his lawyer friend Elias Rosenthal he arranged to see the court records in the case, envisioning it as a novel.

He wrote five more eerily imaginative one-act plays—"The Blue Sphere," "In the Dark," "Laughing Gas," "The Spring Recital" and "The Light in the Window"—all illustrating Dreiser's theories of life and death. He planned to make what money he could by selling the plays first to magazines, then to have them published by Lane in book form.[59]

He finished a scenario, "The Born Thief," adapted from a Greek folk tale, which he hoped to sell both to a magazine and a motion picture company, writing Mencken with excessive confidence, "It has practically been accepted by Pathé Frères. . . ." [60]

He wrote a philosophical essay, "Saving the Universe," embodying the theories that had become so important to him, and hoped to sell it to a magazine.

He confirmed the seriousness with which he took himself by getting halfway through the first volume of a contemplated three-volume autobiography, *A History of Myself*, portraying himself and his family with a candor that left few secrets unexposed.

Although he apparently made little headway with the Molineux story, he did the rest of this work—nine separate projects—between the time he finished *The Titan* and late summer of 1914, a period of about eight months. At times he worked on several at once, switching from one to the other as the mood took him. Far from being harassed by this method, he seemed to enjoy it, and he often followed the practice thereafter out of choice. But he was writing too much too fast. As Alice Phillips had said, he enjoyed the creative process, took a boyish pleasure in it, and disliked the drudgery of going back over his copy, editing, condensing, reorganizing. Although a moderate drinker, at times he found that liquor aided the creative flow. "Underneath my table," he wrote Mencken, "is a bottle of Gordon Gin & a syphon of seltzer. Life is difficult & I must keep up. . . ." [61]

5. The Village

Greenwich Village in 1914 was a residential backwash stretching from lovely Washington Square through crazy-quilt streets to the North River and inhabited largely by people unusual in divergent ways but united in a dislike for convention. This was doubtless one reason Dreiser lived there, another being the cheap rents. Times Square uptown was jumpy with electric signs, automobiles now vied with horses on the avenues, jazz and the turkey trot were coming in, the new Woolworth Building dwarfed everything, but the Village remained an island of determined bohemianism.

Yet the Village itself was subtly changing, becoming more self-conscious and militant. The Armory Show had given Village artists new courage in the fight against stuffy tradition. The Ashcan School—and Dreiser's own Eugene Witla in the yet unpublished *The "Genius"* was a member—was in full flower. The Paterson strike had given Village radicals a rallying point in their war against capitalism. The reactivated Liberal Club on MacDougal Street, with Polly Holliday's free-and-easy cellar restaurant below it, provided a new focus for dissident thought, and *The Masses* was its mouthpiece. The Village teemed with atheists, socialists, cubists, anarchists, violinists, poets, free-thinkers, free-lovers, birth-control advocates and women who bobbed their hair and smoked cigarettes, and, if some were crackpots or phonies, others were sincere enough and some were genuinely creative artists or intellectuals. Most of them were conscious rebels. Indeed, the spirit that created the Village as an entity was precisely the spirit that made Dreiser what he was—revolt against mildewed American concepts and proprieties, a yearning for a freer and better life along with great confusion as to how to attain it.

He "belonged" in this atmosphere. Here lived some of his friends, among them Floyd Dell, Franklin Booth, Edna Kenton and Homer Croy. Among Village familiars were Max Eastman, Lincoln Steffens, Berkeley Tobey, Margaret Sanger, John Reed, Harry Kemp, Sinclair Lewis, Bill Haywood, Art Young, Waldo Frank, Hutchins Hapgood and Louis Untermeyer, some of whom Dreiser would come to know and respect. Over on the Fifth Avenue side of the Village—the genteel side—Mabel Dodge's bizarre salon was flourishing, but Mabel was an heiress and Dreiser resented people who came by luxury easily. Carl Van Vechten, who had rather lost touch with Dreiser and thought him not sufficiently housebroken, was a regular at Mabel's but never saw Dreiser there. Dreiser preferred the baggy-kneed freemasonry of Polly Holliday's when he had the time. He took a special liking for Polly's "man" and helper, the seedy, profane, wild-haired anarchist Hippolyte Havel, possessor of odd scraps of knowledge and famous for his withering, "Goddamned bourgeoisie!"

"Havel is one of those men who ought to be supported by the community," Dreiser said to Hutchins Hapgood. "He is a valuable person for life, but can't take care of himself. If I ever have any money, I'll certainly settle some of it on Hippolyte." [1]

He forgot it when he did come into money. But the remark underlined his fascination with the unconventional—whether it be Havel or Cowperwood—as an aspect of life that he felt himself specially qualified to perceive. Always his friends had been noncomformists (his mother, Aaberg, Arthur Henry, Charles Fort, Mencken) and his adversaries the bourgeois (his father, his wife, the Doubledays, Major Funkhouser). In one side of his dual nature his beliefs had crystallized into a formula that might be called Dreiser's Law, and which could damage him as an artist if it took him over completely. Stripped to its fundamentals, Dreiser's Law read:

Beliefs held by the multitude, the bourgeois and their leaders, are likely to be wrong per se.

An important corollary of the Law read:

Beliefs held by unconventionalists which fly in the face of orthodoxy are in all probability right.

As extensions of these principles, he viewed the philistine as a blockhead who accepted his whole pattern of beliefs as handed down to him by elders, and who therefore did not think; and, conversely, saw the rebel as the splendid individualist, the independent thinker, the only truly creative person.

While Dreiser's Law largely ruled his thinking and his personal life, there were chinks in it, for he still had a bourgeois yearning for success and wealth—illogically, since the unconventional artist, by his very failure to please mass taste, could not hope to be popular or well-paid.

Miss Markham had that wonderful thing, an allowance from her parents, whose unhappy marriage had given her a contempt for decorum. Less than half Dreiser's age, she later felt that he taught her a lifelong lesson about the sanctity of honest art at the same time that she had to smile at his own lapses in taste and his wild craving for money and show. "Few realize how the man suffered over Life," she recalled. "Many nights we walked the streets, Theo holding my hand in the pocket of his overcoat while the tears poured down his face." She saw him grow ecstatic at the beauty of a flight of pigeons. Yet—"He wanted to be the best dressed man in New York," she noted. "Although I was still getting an allowance from my father, Theo loved to think that I never had a new costume that he did not pay for. It was always the occasion for a celebration . . . at the old Waldorf where the dining room was on the level with the street. We had to be in a window where other men could see us and envy him. Sometimes he was astoundingly naive." [2]

Once they dined at the Lafayette with Miss Markham's sister, a Vassar student, who noted Kirah's outfit as one her father had furnished a year earlier and said, "That jacket has certainly worn well, hasn't it?" Dreiser was outraged. "He never forgave her," Miss Markham said. "She was casting reflections on his care of me, on his economic status." [3]

But the couple got on splendidly at first, for there was a rapport lacking in the Jug-Dreiser relationship. Kirah was amused at his handkerchief-folding: "I bought him a lovely string of amber beads that he could pass through his fingers like a rosary, but it did not take the place of actively trying to make corners meet. . . ." [4] Kirah, when not busy on an acting role, helped him solve plot problems in the revised "*Genius*," wrote the eerie songs he used in his play, "The Spring Recital," and did typing for him. Dreiser wrote steadily from 9 to 4 and was not hospitable to callers who interrupted him. Hutchins Hapgood, who came to know him well, knew better than to call before late afternoon, when he had finished his work. For all his yearning for money, both Hapgood and Floyd Dell found him unswerving in his determination to write the unpopular truth as he saw it.

Occasionally he and Kirah could be found at Polly Holliday's restaurant on MacDougal Street enjoying the anarchist Havel. Once Dreiser, with Dell, Eunice Tietjens, the painter Bror Nordfeldt and several girls played "Up Jenkins" at Polly's until finally at 1 A.M. Polly asked them *please* to go home as she wanted to close. Again, Orrick Johns found Dreiser with a group at Polly's, writing, "I remember his telling, with contempt and indignation, his impressions of the slums of London." [5] But he was no barfly or café-haunter and he did not become widely known although this was a time when all Village "regulars" knew each other intimately. Louis Untermeyer, then a literary light of *The Masses*, seldom saw Dreiser at the Village hangouts and once was surprised to see him at a *Masses* meeting at the office on Greenwich Avenue, where the staff had beer and cheese as they discussed the publication. Dreiser, Untermeyer recalled, seemed so "unhappy, uncomfortable and yet pontifical" that the fun-loving *Masses* staff thought him a wet blanket.[6] Most Villagers, prizing their sophistication, found him naive. Although he was the unquestioned leader in the literary revolution, he remained on the periphery rather than at the center of this neighborhood circle of rebels.

Miss Markham, often annoyed by his colossal ego and his extreme jealousy, was strongly attached to him nevertheless. Almost a half-century later, she found it difficult to define his attraction. His moods of sweetness were infrequent. She described him as an "emotional steam-roller" who had a tremendous "animal magnetism" rather than personal charm or lovableness, plus a powerful will and an "utter sense of loneliness." Louise-Ann Miller sometimes dropped in at the Dreiser apartment. This lady of African adventure was a tiny hunchback, and Dreiser would take her on his knee like a child. "Again his animal magnetism," Miss Markham observed. "She would demand to sit there." [7] One wonders whether his superstitious regard for hunchbacks led him to think this might bring him luck.

Waldo Frank was an occasional caller, admiring Dreiser as the one real American novelist, amazed at his naïveté, his incapability of intellectual concentration—flaws that did not get in the way of his genius. "America is *some* place for a novelist," he said to Frank. "If only my name was Dreiserevsky, wouldn't they just love me!" He read very little and could not join in conversation about other novelists, in whom he was not really interested. Frank found him not merely egocentric but solipsistic, and yet with a feminine quality, a sweetness that balanced his ferocious preoccupation with himself. Frank could even forgive the dreadfully lurid canvases on the walls.[8]

After the Armory Show, Dreiser had little use for academic art. Earlier in New York he had admired the Ashcan painters and had used externals of Everett Shinn's career in his delineation of Witla in The "*Genius*." In Europe he had been enchanted by Picasso as well as the Flemish artists. Now, true to Dreiser's Law, he favored the impressionistic Village painters who were bucking convention as he was. And the verse he wrote thereafter was always free.

II. THE PRO-GERMANS

As German troops drove into France, Dreiser and Mencken exchanged enthusiastic *hochs*.

"I am now engaged in leading the German army on to Paris," Dreiser wrote, and later, "I think it would be an excellent thing for Europe and the world—tonic—if the despicable British aristocracy—the snobbery of English intellectuality were smashed and a German Vice-Roy sat in London." [9]

Mencken replied with successive huzzas for German victories, poured scorn on the British, and at Christmas time devoutly suggested cheers for the Redeemer.[10]

They were in accord about the Germans and the English, if not about Christ, but other differences developed. In August, 1914, the ailing *Smart Set* changed hands and Mencken and George Jean Nathan took over full editorial control. The magazine was in debt, fighting for survival. Dreiser would do what he could to help Mencken, but he was in one of his gloomier periods and he did not take to the pixie-faced Nathan, doubtless in part because Nathan, like the British, was so confoundedly self-assured, owning 14 walking sticks and 38 overcoats and caring not a fig for war or anything outside of literature and the stage. Dreiser had already sent Mencken—only for reading and comment—the three one-act plays, "The Blue Sphere," "In the Dark" and "Laughing Gas," all of them interesting departures from conventional drama. Mencken wrote him of the editorial change, saying that he would continue to work in Baltimore while Nathan looked after the New York office, and added:

> Both of us want at least two of your plays. In fact, we simply *must* have something from you. . . . What will you take for "The Blue Sphere"? Make

it as cheap as possible, if you have a heart. . . . Give us a lift now, if you can, and I think there will be good times ahead.[11]

Dreiser immediately sent him his two other one-acters, "The Spring Recital" and "The Light in the Window," but he stretched the facts in his evaluation of the first three:

> . . . It is very plain from one or two tentative opinions I have secured that I could get about $1,000 for [them] from the Century or Metropolitan. After hearing from you I sent them to Doty & DeCamp *—not as mss. offered for sale but for an opinion [.] Both have indicated that they think their respective magazines ought to be allowed to consider them—which is neither here nor there so far as the final disposition is concerned. . . .[12]

Doty's appraisal of the plays is not in the record, but Dreiser's old friend Charles "Deacon" DeCamp sounded quite unlike a man ready to pay $1,000 for the three. He wrote Dreiser that he had "a prejudice against this sort of mechanism," did not think the medium "native" to Dreiser, and although he found much to praise, he thought "The Blue Sphere" was "too long" and that "Laughing Gas" was "somewhat pretentious." [13]

At the same time, Dreiser sent Mencken "The Lost Phoebe." This story had lived a two-year saga in the mails, had been handled by two agents—Paul Reynolds and Galbraith Welch—and had been rejected at the asked price by *The Saturday Evening Post, Ladies' Home Journal, Red Book, American, Metropolitan, Scribner's, Woman's World, Century, Good Housekeeping, Collier's* and *The Atlantic*. Dreiser had successively reduced his asked price from $600 to $400 to $200 and even less. Finally, in August, 1914, Ray Long of *Red Book* without real enthusiasm agreed to take the little tragedy for $125. It was at this point that Dreiser received Mencken's appeal for copy. Doubtless moved in part by Long's lack of warmth and the fact that he could get almost as much from *Smart Set* along with better publicity, Dreiser got the script back from Long and sent it to Mencken. Mencken had told him he could pay only $100 per script, a price agreeable to him with one reservation: "That the ten per cent which I shall have to pay my dear, useless agent be added—otherwise I should only clear 90.00 [*sic*] & I need such cash as I can get." [14]

A few dollars meant much to him now. Mencken, unaware that Dreiser had been offered $125, first pronounced the story "fine stuff," then reconsidered. He rejected both the story and the last two plays, writing, "Nathan is so full of the notion that this 'Lost Phoebe' lies far off of the Dreiser that we want to play up that I begin to agree with him. . . . Those plays are fine stuff, but they involve, as it were, winning a new Dreiser audience. What we ought to have . . . is a return to C major—that is, to the Sister Carrie-Jennie Gerhardt-The Titan style. Is any such stuff in sight?" [15]

Dreiser, affronted, saw Nathan as the enemy who had queered the deal and

---

* The editors of *Century* and *Metropolitan*.

was understandably upset over the loss of a sure $125. He now demanded the return of the three earlier plays which Mencken had accepted, one of which was already in type, writing:

"Unless I am a poor reader of signs there is a distinct disagreement as to my material between you and Nathan." He explained the recall of "The Lost Phoebe" from *Red Book* and went on with some exaggeration:

> In regard to the three plays I asked both the Century & Metropolitan to drop further consideration of them when there was strong chance that I would get $900 from one or the other. . . . My whole feeling in turning them over to the *S.S.* was that you . . . really wanted them and would give them definite publicity of an intelligent, critical character. Evidently for some reason I cannot have that. Now in going as far as I have I think I have done my whole duty. I have lived up to friendship in this matter and in your private conscience you will have to absolve me. Therefore I think that under the circumstances I am justified in calling this deal off and asking that the three plays be returned. I base it on a failure of understanding between us—but there is absolutely no personal animus behind this. . . .[16]

Mencken, believing that Dreiser had made more of a sacrifice than he had in coming to *Smart Set*'s aid, was soothing.

"I take all the blame and offer my apologies," he replied. Well aware of Dreiser's thin skin, he explained patiently that the old *Smart Set* appealed to a middlebrow audience and that he and Nathan had to move slowly in using more thoughtful material lest they lose circulation with the magazine already in a precarious condition. He now offered to buy "The Lost Phoebe" and urged Dreiser not to press his demand for the return of the three plays already accepted: "Believe me, I appreciate your goodness in letting us have them, and if there was money in the drawer I'd cheerfully pay a lot more for them." [17]

Dreiser, relenting, told him to keep the plays and forget about "The Lost Phoebe." "Someone will want it and I am sorry I spoke. It was the surprise of its return after I had manipulated matters to get it free that irritated me. . . ." [18]

Again he sent "The Lost Phoebe"—which now seemed truly lost—out on its rounds. Mencken, in addition to his friendship for Dreiser, was appalled by the abysmal lack of appreciation for him in philistine America. Three prominent Englishmen—W. J. Locke, Arnold Bennett and Frank Harris—had called him America's greatest living novelist and yet American readers mostly shunned him and so far not a single American critic had attempted a serious appraisal of his work. Meanwhile, the recently published *The Eyes of the World*, by Harold Bell Wright, a literary absurdity, had sold 750,000 copies in two months and was continuing at the rate of 8,000 copies a day—the same number *The Titan* had sold in its first year. The recently published *Tarzan of the Apes*, by Edgar Rice Burroughs, would enjoy even a greater sale than

Wright's book. One can understand Mencken's disgust, and his desire to help Dreiser. He wanted to write a literary appraisal of Dreiser himself, if he could find a magazine interested enough to publish it, and he broached the idea a fortnight later to his friend Ellery Sedgwick, now editor of *The Atlantic*, writing Sedgwick, "The poor fellow [Dreiser] is now in the dumps, and talks of giving up." [19] But Sedgwick, who remembered Dreiser from the *Leslie's* days, disliked *The Titan* and turned down the idea.

For all his financial pinch, Dreiser refused to deny himself a few basic luxuries without which he felt that an artist's life would cease to exist. When Mencken arrived on his weekly visits to New York, they dined together at Luchow's, the Lafayette or the Brevoort, all expensive places. At Christmas, he and Kirah Markham spent a week at the country place at Malden-on-Hudson of Poultney Bigelow, who had contributed to *Delineator*. But his income had dwindled badly. Mencken had paid him $330 for the three plays, of which his agent got $30 and Dreiser $300—apparently the only sale of any consequence he made for several months. He was working on *The Bulwark*, a long project with no immediate returns. The loyal Lengel, out of sheer friendship, had cut the huge *"Genius"* script to 100,000 words and tried to sell the condensed version for magazine serial publication. But *Metropolitan, Red Book, Cosmopolitan, Collier's* and doubtless others had turned it down. Mencken had likewise rejected it for *Smart Set* and his opinion of *The "Genius,"* given orally to Dreiser, was certainly adverse.

Dreiser could not keep up his $100 monthly payments to Jug. Evidently he had a meeting with her at which a temporary settlement was made, for she signed the following statement:

> In consideration of the fact that my husband, Theodore Dreiser, has regularly contributed to my support since October 1910 at which time we separated, & also of the uninterrupted use & now free gift of all the furniture, books, piano, including library & dining room sets . . . which cost, originally, 8 years ago $1100.00, also in consideration of the free gift of two building lots at Grandview on Hudson, Rockland Co. N. Y. the assessed value of which at this time is $600.00 & also the previous making over to me for my private use & support of the 10 acre orchard in North Yakima, Wash. the aggregate payments on which totaled over 3,000.00 [*sic*] with taxes, I now hereby agree to release my husband Theodore Dreiser, from any further financial obligations of any kind or consideration in connection with myself for a period of eighteen months, beginning Feby. 1st, 1915.
>
> Sarah [*sic*] White Dreiser [20]

Among the things that kept Dreiser going during this interval was an advance (certainly no more than $1,500) from Lane on the book publication of *The "Genius,"* scheduled for fall, 1915; a smaller advance on his *Plays of the Natural and Supernatural;* and such small change as a $42.50 review for the *New Republic* of Maugham's *Of Human Bondage,* which he praised as a "social transcript of the utmost importance. To begin with, it is un-moral. . . ." [21]

The "Genius," started late in 1910 and revised in 1913–14, had been delayed almost five years in publication by Dreiser's preoccupation with other books and probably also by Harper's disinclination to publish it. Barbara Langford and Anna Tatum, who were not professional writers or critics, had praised it. Dell, Lucian Cary, Lengel, Ray Long and Mencken had not merely disliked but assailed it. Dreiser mistakenly thought it his greatest novel.

The script was enormously long and there is disagreement about its cutting. One investigator, Vrest Orton, later said that Frederic Chapman, English reader for the Lane firm, cut about 50,000 words from it, after which Floyd Dell made wholesale cuts in proof.[22] Chapman indeed worked so hard on it as to become exhausted, writing Dreiser careful letters about his corrections and elisions, adding in one of them, "I have everywhere that it was possible to do so eliminated the word 'sex,' with which your story is positively peppered and which is in 90 cases out of 100 wholly unnecessary. . . . The passages in which you 'call a spade a spade' I have to the best of my ability toned down. . . . You must remember that in the particular plot you have set out to cultivate spades have hitherto not even been called 'agricultural imple-ments'—they have been politely ignored altogether." [23]

Dreiser, although he admitted "I am such a poor editor," for once did not hand a script to Mencken to edit, because of the sage's low opinion of *The "Genius."* Dell, now an editor of *The Masses,* had somewhat warmed up to the story. When Chapman returned it, Dell took the "mountainous manu-script" home to work on, parts at a time, and penciled out sizable portions. "And when I returned for more, there sat Dreiser, with a large eraser, rescuing from oblivion such pages, paragraphs and sentences as he felt could not be spared. Yet," Dell noted, "he had no narrow vanity of authorship; it wasn't because they were *his* sentences that they were so precious, but only that he thought they were needed." [24]

Dreiser himself, in one of his many later errors, insisted that Chapman found only "eight or ten verbal changes" needed and that Dell had had trouble cutting as much as 3,500 words.[25]

He was too much the serious artist to turn to money-making articles which once had supported him so well. In January, 1915, he applied for a study room at the New York Public Library to read up on physics and chemistry—probably an effort to learn more about the "chemisms" that so fascinated him. He would return again and again to science, but always the dilettante, the ingenuous seeker of quick cosmic answers. And, out of friendliness and respect for their talent, he tried to find publishers for four men—Masters, Sherwood Anderson, Harris Merton Lyon and Charles Fort.

Except for Fort, none of the four was hard up. Masters had his law practice in Chicago. Anderson, whom he had met only casually in Chicago but who was being loyally put forward by his friend Floyd Dell, had a steady salary as an advertising copywriter. Lyon, living with his wife at North Colebrook, Connecticut, had a small salary as story scout for Thomas Ince of the movies. Yet Dreiser spoke for them all. He tried Masters' *Spoon River Anthology* on J. Jefferson Jones at Lane's, and was refused. He made no headway with either Lyon or Fort, but kept trying. He helped place Masters and Lyon pieces in Mencken's *Smart Set*. He urged Anderson's first novel, *Windy McPherson's Son*, on Jones but was held up because the script was then being read by Macmillan. Meanwhile, William Lengel's wife had a baby daughter who lived only three days, and Lengel still recalls how Dreiser came to the hospital to sit with him for hours, gentle and comforting, "just like a father." [26]

Yet he could turn churlishly on Mencken, whose low opinion of *The "Genius"* had wounded him. Also, he seemed jealous of the glossy George Jean Nathan's influence over Mencken, just as Anna Mallon had spoiled his friendship with Arthur Henry years earlier. On April 6, Mencken, laboring to put *Smart Set* on a paying basis, begged him for a blurb:

> If you have ever given the resurrected Smart Set a glance, and can do it without injury to your conscience, and have no scruples otherwise, I wish you would dash off a few lines saying that it has shown progress during the past six months and is now a magazine that the civilized reader may peruse without damage to his stomach. This for chaste publication in refined announcements, along with the statement that you are a high-class novelist, a faithful Elk and a swell dresser on and off the stage. We are turning the corner and a help will actually help. But if the lie is too vast for you, say Nix in a loud tone and no one will hear it save myself. Meanwhile I continue to pray for your conversion to orthodox Swedenborgianism and Lake Mohonkery.[27]

Dreiser said Nix: "I wish I could say whole-heartedly that I liked the Smart Set. . . . Under you and Nathan the thing seems to have tamed down to a light, non-disturbing period[ical] of persiflage and badinage, which now and then is amusing but which not even the preachers of Keokuk will resent seriously. It is as innocent as the *Ladies' Home Journal*. Really the thing is too debonair, too Broadwayesque. . . . Everything, apparently, is to be done with a light, aloof touch, which to me is good but like a diet of soufflé. I like to feel the stern, cool winds of an *Odessey* [*sic*] now and then."

He went pitilessly over the contents of the April issue, item by item, finding fault with most and delivering judgments such as, "only fair," "trivial," "fairly clever," "truck—uninspired," "mediocre," "suitable for Godey's Lady Book." He urged a more serious point of view—articles such as those in revolutionary publications like *The Masses*. He criticized a Nathan piece on the drama. He complained that he had recommended Masters but Mencken had passed him over in favor of third-raters. (Mencken had bought a Masters poem, yet unused.) Significantly, he feared Nathan's influence, writing, "Once I was on the point of writing you. I felt that you were helplessly in tow of the Broadway-bebraided George Jean, for whom I have some respect as a lighter touch." He wound up:

> Does this sound severe? I don't mean it to. Frankly I think you are infinitely better than the paper you produce. Why is this? [28]

The serious artist here seemed shaded with petulance. Mencken, a mighty smiter, could easily have cuffed him. Was he forgetting the Butterick days, the Jenny Wren Clubs, the concern over babies' cries? But Mencken replied amiably, listing difficulties Dreiser knew or should have known: *Smart Set's* slim budget could not afford *Odysseys*. Running highbrow stuff meant risking a loss in circulation and resulting disaster. "As it stands, of course, it represents a compromise between what we'd like to do and what the difficulties that we face allow us to do." As for Dreiser's urging of a more serious point of view and the use of critical pieces such as appeared in *The Masses* and other Village publications, Mencken replied that he had received material from the "red-ink boys" including Benjamin De Casseres and Floyd Dell but found it "inexpressibly empty." "The whole red-ink bunch . . . is hollow-headed and childish." And to Dreiser's complaint about lightness, he replied logically, "But the light touch you protest against is what we want. The Smart Set—consider its title!—is no place to print revolutionary fustian. . . ." [29]

But Dreiser had a chip on his shoulder. Possibly he and Mencken had disagreed on the same subject in a personal conversation. In his reply he took offense as if Mencken had linked him with the "red-ink boys," which Mencken in his letter had in no way done:

"You make a mistake in regard to my supposed interest in 'the red ink fraternity', as you call them. I hold no brief for the parlor radical." And later: "I sometimes think that because I have moved into 10th Street and am living a life not suitable to the home streets of Baltimore that you think I have gone over to the red ink family and 'the brothers of the hollow skull'. Give yourself one more guess. I have never had a better line on myself than at present. . . ." He insisted, "I am genial—not angry," but he did not sound genial.[30]

"Pish!" Mencken replied in small part. "What slush is this about 'living a life not suitable to the home streets of Baltimore'? Do you take me for a Methodist deacon—or a male virgin? For far less insults I have had gentlemen killed by my private murderer, a blackamoor but a deft hand at the garrote." [31]

III. KNOCK DOWN THE STEEPLES

That incurable traveler, "The Lost Phoebe," after its rejection by *Smart Set,* had gone on another urban tour, being rejected in turn by *Semi-Monthly, Everybody's, Woman's Home Companion, McClure's, Pic-*

torial Review and *Lippincott's*. This made 19 rejections, but 20 was a lucky number. When Douglas Doty became editor of *Century*, he read it, wrote Dreiser, "I am very much charmed with your story," and bought it for $200.[32]

Did this mean that Dreiser had $200 in pocket? No. He still owed Century $334.48, so the sale merely reduced his debt to $134.48.[33] Yet when Edgar Lee Masters visited New York in August, Dreiser (and Miss Markham) entertained him royally. These two literary realists saw each other almost every day, and Floyd Dell, dropping in on them at Tenth Street, found them reading Sophocles aloud: "O ye deathward-going tribes of men, what do your lives mean except that they go to nothingness?" Though he liked Dreiser, Dell thought him a strange combination of dunce and genius and was amused by his deeply sentimental undercurrents and his habit of keeping clippings of his own work and of newspaper items about him. Once, reading a Dreiser scrapbook, Dell had delightedly come upon that bromide, "The Poet's Creed," and chuckled when Dreiser, discovering what he was reading, snatched the book away. Dell, who had a good memory, maliciously declaimed:

> *I would not give the bells that ring*
> *For all the world of bartering*
> *Nor yet the whispering of the leaves*
> *For all the Gold that Greed conceives.*

Dreiser, the realist, sulked at this exposure of his earlier poesy.[34]

For Masters, whom Kirah found snappish, Dreiser did what he would have done for almost no one else—gave a party. Since Charles Fort was also to be a guest, and Dreiser was trying to find publishers for them both, he got in some good work by inviting two publishers, Ben Huebsch, who had his own firm, and Rutger Jewett of Appleton's. Jewett had been trying to snag Dreiser for years. Recently, when Dreiser had sent a hopeful author to him, name unknown, he had written, "do not forget that you and I should get together ourselves on a publishing proposition before we give a job to the grave diggers." Now, apparently sensing another ploy, he wrote, "I know Mr. Masters' 'Spoon River Anthology,' and regret that I am not to be in town," and on that note the Jewett letters to Dreiser ceased.[35]

Huebsch, who was present, knew Dreiser only slightly and felt that he was there in his capacity as a publisher. A *New York World* reporter noted that there were almost no chairs and wrote, "The Dreiser establishment does not run much to rugs. . . . So all the guests squatted here and there on the pine parquet. . . . To begin with, there was Miss Kirah Markham, Mr. Dreiser's secretary, who presided at the punch bowl." [36] It was a typical Village literary function—floor-sitting by candlelight—and among about twenty guests, mostly unconventionalists and "red-ink boys," were Dell and his colleague on *The Masses*, Berkeley Tobey. Franklin Booth, the long-haired pianist Alex

Raab, the socialist Courtenay Lemon, the illustrator Willy Pogany, stage
manager Will Pennington of the Washington Square Players, a ukelele player
and a few actresses and bobbed-haired models.

Dreiser proved that he could relax among friends, for Masters noted,
"Dreiser walked the floors laughing and joshing. His immense humor fairly
boiled over. His teeth stuck out, his face was red from health and excitement" [37]—doubtless aided by the punchbowl, though Masters did not say this.
Masters had to strain his eyes in the dimness to read *Spoon River* to the
gathering as Dreiser pleated his handkerchief. In part because of Dreiser's
ceaseless promotion, Macmillan would publish this landmark in poetry in
1916 with astonishing success.

During the evening, Dreiser talked with Franklin Booth, also from Indiana,
now a prosperous advertising illustrator who owned a Pathfinder touring car.
Dreiser had known the tall, quiet Booth since 1904, when he had done
illustrations for the *Daily News* Sunday supplement on which Dreiser
worked. Booth proposed an idea which Dreiser seconded and the John Lane
Company soon approved—a book about a motor trip to Indiana which Dreiser
would write and Booth illustrate. Dreiser was convinced that this journey was
preordained when he met a "kindly little Jew" whom he had first known at
Muldoon's. He wrote in all seriousness:

> For a period of over fifteen years in my life, at the approach of every
> marked change—usually before I have passed from an old set of surroundings
> to a new—I have met a certain smug, kindly little Jew, always the same Jew,
> who has greeted me most warmly. . . . I have never known him any more
> intimately than that. Our friendship began at a sanatorium, at a time when I
> was quite ill. Thereafter my life changed and I was much better. Since then,
> as I say, always at the critical moment, he has never failed. I have met him in
> New York, Chicago, the South, in trains, on shipboard. It is always the
> same. . . . I am not theorizing; I am stating facts.[38]

So, although he still had not found a publisher for Masters or Fort, he had,
through the little Jew's intercession, found a new book to write.

He and Booth set out in mid-August. Such a trip was a stirring adventure in
1915, but he was spared the discomforts of tire changes because Booth
employed a chauffeur. In Indiana he grew alternately nostalgic and bitter as
he visited Warsaw, Terre Haute, Bloomington, Sullivan, Vincennes and
Evansville, the scenes of his childhood and youth. He stayed one night at the
Terre Haute House where his mother had once scrubbed floors—where Paul
had been tendered a great banquet because his song about the Wabash had
stirred a state-wide nostalgia. In Indiana, Paul was known to everyone who
had a piano or hummed a tune. A town had been named after him—Dresser,
Indiana, near Terre Haute, population 800—but Dreiser's own fame was
small.

Here he recalled his stern, conventional father, saw Indiana men and women imprisoned by these same proprieties, living a lie as they itched to get away from the "prying eyes of Terre Haute" so that they could drink deep of life as they secretly wanted to do and as they should do, instead of only sipping. The mere sight of a church was enough to set him off on a tirade against a clergy which in recoil from plain truth had condemned Carrie Meeber, Jennie Gerhardt and Frank Cowperwood:

> Out on them for a swinish mass! Shut up the churches, knock down the steeples! Harry them until they know the true place of religion,—a weak man's shield! [39]

Indeed, Dreiser, who had often infuriated the ardent socialist Floyd Dell by his Spencerian belief in the futility of human effort, was as inconsistent as ever. Dell had shouted at him, "Look, this world is changing. You might as well point to the clouds and say they will remain as they are forever. It's changing before your eyes—changing because of human effort." [40]

Dreiser had stubbornly shaken his head. Now he wrote:

> I refuse to think that it is either necessary or inevitable that I, or any other man, should work for a few dollars a day, skimping and longing, while another, a dunce, who never did anything but come into the world as the heir of a strong man, should take the heavy profits of my work and stuff them into his pockets. It has always been so, I'll admit, and it seems that there is an actual tendency in nature to continue it; but I would just as lief contend with nature on this subject. . . . We are not sure that nature inevitably wills it at that. [41]

At his boyhood town of Sullivan, he noted the fertile soil and robust people and commented, "It made me think that governments ought to take starving populations off unfertile soils and put them on land like this." [42]

He seemed unaware that in admitting that man might contend with nature and that starving peoples should be removed to richer land, he was denying his own determinism, opening a flood of possibilities, implying that life was not meaningless but could be gloriously meaningful, that man could act, that the socialists were right after all in believing that intelligent action could improve humanity's lot. Yet he did not see the implications of his own reasoning and for years thereafter (with his inevitable occasional switches) he clung to his stand that life was meaningless and yet somehow beautiful. Pushed one way and another by emotion, he was alternately a cynic and a believer, admiring ruthless capitalists but indignant at their exploitation of the masses, shocked by man's depravity and inspired by his goodness, wishing to be a spectator and yet to reform the world, worshiping science but seeing an omen in the "kindly little Jew." [43]

6. The "Genius"

I. A TOMCAT FOR A HERO

Returning to New York in September, Dreiser was sufficiently fed up with his difficulties to embrace a dream of becoming a film mogul. Lengel was now editor of the *Hoggson Magazine*, published by Hoggson Brothers, a building construction firm on Fifth Avenue. The Hoggsons, noting the growth of the moving picture industry, planned to gather capital and form their own company, Mirror Films, and were looking for a scenario director. Lengel immediately suggested Dreiser for the job. Apparently Dreiser had an interview with the president, W. J. Hoggson, for he became so enthusiastic that although the new firm was not organized he all but donned puttees. Hoggson's plan was to produce films of quality, and Dreiser saw in it not only a handsome income but a chance to spread his crusade for honest art in the new medium. Prematurely he wrote Lyon, Richard Le Gallienne and "Deacon" De Camp, suggesting that they might work for him. He wrote Mencken:

> Fairest Mencken: I am thinking of accepting a directorship in a new and . . . imposing film corporation. Can you recall a story which would make a suitable film offering for my first. I cant [*sic*] begin by ramming naturalism down their throats—not at least until I get my hand in. . . .[1]

Mencken must have chuckled at this confession of expediency in catering to his anticipated audience when Dreiser had so recently belabored Mencken for the same expediency in *Smart Set.*

But the great event of the fall was Lane's publication, early in October, of the long-awaited *The "Genius,"* price $1.50.

This was the weakest of Dreiser's five novels, the most vulnerable on purely literary grounds. In its preoccupation with sex it never could have found a publisher in 1900—probably not in 1915, had he not paved the way and won solid standing—and thus was proof in itself of his large individual part in forcing a gradual retreat of the puritans, who were nevertheless still armed and dangerous. Despite the book's sensational later misadventures at the hands of the censors, a sampling of newspaper reviews indicates that most of the journalistic critics kept reasonably calm:

The New York Times, which reviewed Sinclair Lewis' *The Trail of the Hawk* in the next column, said, "Once more Theodore Dreiser has chosen an abnormal character and written an abnormally long novel about him. . . . It is all very realistic—and very depressing and unpleasant. . . . the author relates [Eugene's] experiences at interminable length and with wearisome iteration. . . ." *The Times* called Lewis' book "straightforward, clear, good art. . . ."[2]

Harper's Weekly said, "Mr. Dreiser, chronicler of vulgar American types, has failed dismally with his Genius. . . . Mr. Witla is about as witty as an opera librettist . . . 'Nix' is his favorite negative. . . ."[3]

The *Brooklyn Eagle*, under the heading "A GENIUS AND ALSO A CUR," said, "The first section called 'Youth' [is] pretty nearly an orgy of lust. The thing that saves it from . . . condemnation . . . is the emphasis which Dreiser puts on the mental side of Witla's various fascinations. . . ."[4]

The *New York Herald:* "It is all very sordid, but unquestionably true. . . . Mr. Dreiser is an extremely observant writer. . . . Of humor, satire, the spiritual or poetic quality, there is no trace whatever. . . ."[5]

The *Boston Transcript:* "His attitude is utterly pagan. He seems to have no thought of himself as a moral or even as an artistic influence. . . . [But it] is with exceptional dexterity that Mr. Dreiser visualizes both the people in his story and the scenes of which they are a part."[6]

The *Chicago Herald:* "The evil of the tremendous tale too markedly predominates. . . . But the depressing book in many ways is a great one."[7]

There were exceptions. Dreiser's friend John Cowper Powys, who saw him as the only free American voice, described The *"Genius"* as "the American prose-epic" in the *Little Review*.[8] The *Lusitania* had been sunk, anti-German feeling was reaching hysteria, and the strait-laced Mrs. Elia W. Peattie of the *Chicago Tribune*, who had contributed to the *Delineator* when Dreiser was editor, rose up in wrath at Powys' words. In a review headed "MR. DREISER CHOOSES A TOM CAT FOR A HERO," she assailed his opposition to "the righteous forces of the will" and spitefully hinted at his German ancestry: "I repudiate it as the American prose-epic. I have not yet lost my patriotism and I will never admit such a thing until I am ready to see the American flag trailing in the dust dark with the stains of my sons, and the Germans completing their world rule by placing their Governor general in the White House. . . ."[9] Mrs. N. P. Dawson of the *New York Globe* also made shrewish though oblique mention of the author's background: "We hope that The *'Genius'* will immediately appear in a German translation. That's how kindly we feel toward the Germans!"[10] More cleverly malicious was the snappy three-paragraph review in the *New York World:*

> The *"Genius,"* by Theodore Dreiser, the story of an artist who goes in for advertising and the pursuit of women, is 736 pages long, weighs nearly a pound and three-quarters, and contains approximately 350,000 words.
>
> It would be better if it were less by about 350,000 words, lighter by nearly a pound and three-quarters, and shorter by 736 pages.
>
> Mr. Dreiser should get over the idea that because he was successful with two novels of sex, he can keep on, world without end, filling thick volumes with the emptyings of passion.[11]

Dreiser, who liked to picture himself as unmoved by critical blasts, was on the contrary excruciatingly hurt by them. He sent the *Globe* and *World* reviews to Mencken, asking if he had ground for libel suits. Mencken told him to forget it, saying the reviews were unimportant and commenting on the English reverse at the Dardanelles.[12] Dreiser at the moment could take no comfort in the English reverse at the Dardanelles. He was also wounded because Masters in the *Chicago Evening Post* had praised the book and then ruined it all by adding, "But [Dreiser] has not reached the climax whither his genius inevitably tends." [13] He wrote to Masters about this but got no balm there either, Masters replying, "I do like The 'Genius.' . . . Yet somehow you don't seem to work up to the maximum of your gift. . . ." [14]

But he did find one new, unequivocating, whole-souled admirer. This was Harold Hersey, a young poet who worked for the Library of Congress in Washington and who so venerated all of Dreiser's books that he not only wrote him to say so but also wrote the *New York Globe*, the *Chicago Tribune* and others to protest their reviews and defend *The "Genius."* Dreiser sent Hersey a grateful note. He ended it with a strangely self-dramatizing suggestion:

> And I give you one kindly bit of advice. Never bother to know me, personally. Remain illusioned, if you can[.][15]

But later, in *The Nation*, came the most formidable of all onslaughts against Dreiser and his writings. Typical of the critical spirit of the times, it was the first full-dress magazine attempt to assess America's greatest living novelist, who had produced seven books in 15 years, and it was sheer attack. Thus far the "major" critics had ignored Dreiser because he offended the genteel tradition not on one count but two—content and style. Now young, ambitious Stuart Pratt Sherman, professor of English at the University of Illinois and a friend of Mrs. Peattie's, set out to demolish him in a three-page essay, "The Barbaric Naturalism of Mr. Dreiser."

With some skill Sherman satirized Dreiser's stylistic and philosophical weaknesses, denied him any standing as a realist because he worked from "a theory of animal behavior" rather than human behavior, complained of "jungle" courtships in which "Mr. Dreiser's leonine men but circle once or twice about their prey, and spring," and suggested that a writer coming from such a mixed ethnic background was incapable of higher spiritual values. Unlike Mrs. Peattie, whom Mencken described as one of the "ovarian school" of criticism, Sherman realized that moral platitudes were not enough and sought to scuttle Dreiser on intellectual grounds. His essay's length, its appearance of plausibility and its publication in a liberal magazine of standing helped to fix Dreiser's position as a writer to be shunned by the genteel.[16]

Dreiser was outraged. He bought extra copies of *The Nation* and opposite Sherman's remark about "animal behavior" he wrote, "Animal behavior being evil of course," while next to the mention of human behavior he wrote,

"Good conduct of course," and sent them to his friends. His new ally, Harold Hersey, promptly sent a reply to *The Nation*, attacking Sherman's attack. He praised Hersey for it, wishing only that he had pounced on the differentiation between human and animal behavior, believing this the most vulnerable point.

"These moonbeam chasers are attempting to make a devil of me," he wrote Hersey. "As they did to the very sane Machiavelli so they would do to me. I am now being tied up with all the evils which the Germans are supposed to represent. I am anti-christ."

He was accused of emphasizing the sordid when he had written sincerely of reality, things which had actually happened to his sisters, himself, his wife, Yerkes, and appeared every day in the newspapers. "I [am] feeling," he added to Hersey, "like saying 'gentlemen, here is the morning paper. Read it. Is this a picture of devils or angels or just men[?]' " [17]

II. THE SOCIAL WHIRL

At Emma Goldman's uptown apartment on Lenox Avenue, Dreiser and Kirah attended a party and enjoyed Russian food and wine, cheering the plump, forty-five-year-old Emma as she executed Russian folk dances. Alexander Berkman was there, and Ben Reitman, who spied the madonna-like Kirah and pursued her from room to room until finally she took refuge with Dreiser, who put an arm around her.

"Don't be afraid of Ben," he said. "He may ask you to sleep with him but you can just tell him that you are sleeping with me." [18]

They dined at the Twelfth Street apartment of John Cowper Powys and his sister Marion, who scrutinized Dreiser's palm and shrieked, "Oh, this is terrible! Wherever you go there is tragedy and disaster!" Not long thereafter, Kirah and Dreiser, walking down Greenwich Avenue, saw a careening ambulance run down an old man before their eyes. An interne jumped out, said, "Shove him in beside the other one," and the vehicle drove on. On another occasion they saw an express truck roll into Fifth Avenue and sideswipe a speeding fire truck, throwing firemen into the air, "arms and legs outspread so that they fell to the pavement like dead frogs." Dreiser and Kirah helped minister to unconscious men and later to get them into ambulances. Then they went to Allaire's for dinner, where Kirah went to pieces: "As I cried and Theo sat across the table holding my hand, the thick, German waiter came up and demanded that we leave as we were drunk and disorderly!" [19]

But Kirah grew incensed at his secret affairs and his unreasoning jealousy. He might preach the beauties of free love for both sexes, but not when it came to his own woman. Here Dreiser's Law broke down badly and he became thoroughly conventional because this brand of unconventionality wounded his pride. "If a man so much as sat by the fire with me," she recalled, "while he was off of an evening with another woman there were horrible scenes the next morning. . . . With his own promiscuous code, he could not believe in my faithfulness." Once, being uptown and remembering he had told her he would dine with his publisher, she waited at Lane's door until he came out—alone. He flew into a rage, upbraiding her for "spying" on him. She realized then that his dinner date was not with the publisher but with another woman.[20]

Although The "Genius" got off to a respectable sale, he was still dickering with Hoggson, soliciting ideas from more of his friends—Hersey and Arthur Davison Ficke among them—for his hypothetical film venture. "I would like this place for a change," he wrote Hersey, "but only if freedom to do something different and better were included. These details—full control for instance—are not yet completed." [21]

Inspired by German victories, he wrote Mencken, "Hoch Hindenburg! Von Besselen! Von Mackensen! Von Tirpitz! Hoch!" He obviously admired Mencken's epistolary horseplay and occasionally tried to imitate it, usually with elephantine results. He was no match for the blasphemous Baltimorean who satirized all convention. Hard at work during the week on The Bulwark and his account of the Indiana jaunt, called A Hoosier Holiday, Dreiser felt a need for more human companionship. Ben Huebsch and Mary Fanton Roberts were among those who received a card hand-lettered by Kirah:

Friends can always find
Kirah Markham
and
Theodore Dreiser
at home on Sunday evenings
November–March
165 West 10th St.   Chelsea 7755 [22]

Freud was sweeping the Village, Floyd Dell was being psychoanalyzed, and when Dell dropped in Dreiser asked to be instructed on the subject. "I did my best to do so," Dell recalled. "He listened patiently, thoughtfully, doggedly, but he was perfectly incapable of taking in these ideas." Mencken called with his lady friend Marion Bloom and hammered at the piano.[23] Eugene O'Neill, as yet unknown by Dreiser or the world, was spending the winter in sodden drunkenness at the Hell Hole saloon a few blocks away. Dreiser drank sparingly—when nervous he would take a dram of whiskey in water—but offended some by the voracity with which he attacked his food. There was a phonograph in his rugless studio on which he liked to play lugubrious Russian records, and there was a ouija board which provided some of the Dreiser-Markham winter entertainments. Dreiser professed little faith in ouija boards, but in view of his interest in tea-leaf readers and hunchbacks he should have had no bias against the lettered board. About hunchbacks he wrote:

The appearance of a certain person in my life has always been heralded by a number of hunchbacks who came forward, passed—sometimes touching my elbow—and frequently looking at me in a solemn manner, as though some subconscious force, of which they were the tool, were saying to me, "See, here is the sign."[24]

Once or twice he and Miss Markham gathered around the board with guests including Harry Kemp, De Camp, Powys and his British friend Louis Wilkinson. Dreiser was interested enough to take notes. While the board told Miss Markham that the Kaiser would no sooner win the war than his cook would poison him, Dreiser learned that there was no master intelligence over the universe, no such thing as evil and no reason for one to follow so-called morality.[25]

He gave up these Sunday soirées because they became too noisy and quarrelsome, possibly because of the tender subject of the war. He could be the most genial of hosts, but was subject to sudden indignation. He asked stand-and-deliver questions. His prejudice against the English was settled, as was his evolutionary philosophy, and he was apt to flare at disputants on these points. He was still corresponding with Mevrouw Rykens-Culp in Holland, and it enraged him (as it did others) to find his mail from Holland opened by British censors. "We are a political appendage of John Bull," he wrote Mencken, and he complained to the Postmaster General without effect.

His mistrust of publishers mounted when he received Lane's report of the sale of 6,577 copies of The "Genius" to the end of 1915. What with the controversy over the book he had expected a larger sale, and he suspected that Lane's—an English firm—were deceiving him, paying him for fewer copies than they sold. It was his policy, even had it not been necessary, to ask large advances on the theory that the publisher would then work harder and advertise more extensively. Now he made a quiet check at local bookstores and felt his suspicions confirmed. He wrote Mencken, Masters and perhaps others, asking them to make a similar canvass at bookstores in their own cities. "I may be mistaken," he wrote Mencken, "but my private advices from dealers indicate more sales than I have been paid for." [26]

Masters, as though a trifle irked at the errand, replied, "I'll see what I can do. . . ." [27] Mencken pointed out that there were a dozen bookstores in Baltimore and there was no guarantee that the dealers would not exaggerate their sale, adding that it was quite possible that Lane's sales figures were perfectly accurate.[28]

At the same time, Dreiser was haggling with Mencken over seven poems he had sent Smart Set, three of which Mencken had quickly rejected as "hopelessly commonplace" but finding the other four "truly excellent" and offering $30 for them.

"Thirty dollars is little enough for that group," Dreiser wrote. "Don't let your German war-time thrift get the best of you." [29]

"If this seems too little," Mencken replied, "I can only return your four poems. . . . In any event, I shall surely not abandon my daily supplication for your salvation." [80]

III. WHY IS A GULL?

Early in 1916 Dreiser was in such low spirits that he felt ill. His prostate was troubling him—a terrible worry, bringing fears of ultimate impotency. He was upset because of entanglements with several women who he feared would learn of his duplicity. Deeply attached to Miss Markham, and insisting on her absolute fidelity to him, he employed juvenile wiles in his efforts to hide his other affairs, but without complete success. There were times when he became so romantically involved that he could escape exposure and unpleasantness only by fleeing. Doubtless this was a factor, along with his sinking morale, that made him decide on a boat trip to Savannah late in January while Miss Markham stayed in New York to appear in the cast of Hauptmann's *The Weavers*, at the Garden Theater.

Characteristically, on the day of his departure he bought a health belt and some pills. He took Miss Markham to lunch at the Brevoort, furious because the waiter insisted on reserving the two best tables at the front. He sweated in fear that one or more of the other girls might see him off at the boat and thus compromise him. He tried to telephone one of them but failed to reach her, and gave up on another. "Too dangerous to phone her at her family," he wrote in the sloppy but detailed diary he kept of this journey.[31]

His relief was vast when he said good-by that evening, January 26, to Kirah at the North River pier and no other woman arrived to embarrass him. He sailed out the river with a glorious view of the lighted Woolworth and Singer towers, and the diary he kept was a revelation of the morose Dreiser temper and the troubled Dreiser mind—a mind that saw everything through the wondering eyes of a child, seeking the eternal, refusing to accept things as they were.

"The travellers on this line are a scrubby lot, I must say—horrible American bourgeoisie," he wrote. ". . . Eat—but the food is bad—a wretched ship's cook. . . . Have a brandy & soda. The Scotch on this boat is horrible." In the morning, the sight of some gulls provoked an introspective binge:

> There are about 24 of them—gray white, trailing the ship. They had a rusty squeal and kept craning their necks & looking from side to side and up & down, watching each other. Some seemed old—wise old hawks that clung close to the ship in easy postures. . . . Others younger or more active were constantly moving from side to side in wide sweeps, dropping back, coming forward, dropping to the water for food—a restless crew. What brooding spirit of life generated them? What thing is it, in nature, which wants to be a gull, haunting the gray sea, or is it a curse—but I do not see any form of life as a curse. I never did[,] not in my darkest, most unhappy hours[.] Change in life—not less life or no life was what I craved.

Avoiding other passengers, he satisfied his incessant creative urge by writing a free-verse poem about the sea, then another about the clouds. The psychiatrist Clemens E. Benda might have been writing about Dreiser years later when he noted that "visual curiosity and the infantile urge to ask questions persist in the artist and philosophical thinker, that the artist continues in an infantile fixation, instead of living like ordinary human beings and taking for granted what life has to offer." The artist "reveals by his endless doubting, searching, struggling that he is never done with the primary problems and suffers from them all his life." [32]

Next Dreiser pondered the fickleness of his moods: "I have watched my moods shift chameleon like from grave to pleasant [sic], but with never a word to me from anyone. The sea has fascinated me. I have smiled. My stomach has felt a little upset—immediately I have been disgusted with life. On everybody present I have passed judgment, weighing them lightly—perhaps most unfairly—in my hand. This man is a fool, this woman a silly, that one a strumpet, this man a wolf or a dull materialist. Scarcely a person have I approved of in my mind and yet I know that, coming in contact with them I would more or less like them all. That is the way with me. In silence I condemn and condemn—in verbal control, I explain away my dislikes and take them as they are and as life is—with a shrug and a smile, making the best of a world that I cannot improve upon." [33]

In the diary were glimpses of his greatness and weakness as a novelist—a simple but deep amazement at life, an intensive observation of detail and an inability to exclude minutiae that was like no one but Dreiser. Shunning company, he read and liked Hutchins Hapgood's *An Anarchist Woman*, and another glimpse of the sea prompted: "I thought how wonderful it would be to create a new world out of the faultless sea." Landing in Savannah January 29, he found the citizens "a dull crude lot" and was only momentarily cheered when he made a beeline for the nearest bookstore and found three copies of *The "Genius"* on sale. He bought cheap used copies of *The Voyage of H.M.S. Beagle* and *Crime and Punishment*, found a furnished room on East Liberty Street, then gave the whole South the back of his hand:

> Segregation of blacks an odd but necessary custom. Character of Southerners—peaked, whiney, suspicious, jealous, touchy—an offensive company. All this is due to the perversion of naturalness following upon a promoralistic atmosphere. The result of sex suppression is jealousy, suspicion, envy, false witness, false pretense, a better than thou viewpoint; women going about like saints craving subconsciously what they sniff at openly—sex. It is a horrible case of race or national perversion which will end in disaster. The South as it stands today will be destroyed. It will pass away.

Two days later he was actually ill because he had not received letters from *any* of his women, sleepless, frantic. He needed a woman—a mother—to pet and pamper him. "Almost sick with worry," he wrote. "Arise—headache, sick stomach. Pain in vitals. . . . Go to P.O. No letters. Can't eat. One and one half crullers. . . . Go home. Try to write. Can't. Try to read can't."

Then he received a telegram from Miss Markham:

SWEETHEART HAVE WRITTEN EVERY DAY SINCE FRIDAY LOVE. KIRAH.[34]

She would have been delighted at her therapeutic powers, for Dreiser wrote after receiving the message: "Relief. Headache subsides. Pain goes."

She would have been less pleased at the continuing entry: "Go to P.O. See chief clerk. He gets two letters—one from K—— one from L——. K's letter OK. Feel much better. Come to room. Write K—— long letter—also L—— also B.H.M."

Next day he was in the dumps again: "I dispise [sic] life without a woman. . . . A wasted day. Room is cold and am lonely in spirit. It is a bad thing being an intellectual—one is too distant & people do not draw to one." He found a better room on Taylor Street, bought more pills and confided to his diary, "massaged prostate." He was also taking hot baths to succor that vital gland. He worked miserably on *A Hoosier Holiday*, his nerves so jumpy that he had to stop and take long walks. By mail he tried vainly to interest Ben Huebsch in Fort's book—Huebsch, who was about to sail with Henry Ford's Peace Ship. He had written Hoggson about the film job. Hoggson, still trying to raise capital, replied vaguely, "The matter of the Mirror Films is one of policy, which, as soon as adjusted and put through, I will again take up the subject of your connection with the company." [35]

On his walks he bought picture postcards and kept a sharp eye for such lucky omens as horseshoes. February 9 was a better day, for he not only found a horseshoe but received letters from three women, and next day he heard from Mencken, who demanded:

What are you doing in Savannah? Acting in the movies? If so, I shall cheerfully risk a nickel to see you in your young beauty.[36]

The two had had a continuing dispute about the payment for the four poems, which Dreiser now settled with a sweeping gesture: "Let us have no more correspondence over the poems. They are yours as a Christmas present." From his best friend on earth, the hearty Mencken, he concealed the anguish he recorded in his diary, suggesting that he was having a whale of a time: "While I read reports of men dying in blizzards . . . I sit on my balcony, watch ambling negroes with buckets on their heads selling apples and look at palm trees and flowers. . . . It's like throwing off a big, material load." [37]

Dreiser believed love to be a force so powerful that it could send waves through long spaces, but the waves emanating from New York seemed weak or unsatisfactory in Savannah. In his diary he mentioned interest in six women: "K——" (Miss Markham), "A.P.T." (doubtless Anna P. Tatum) and four others unknown: "L——," "C——," "B.H.M." and one called simply "Muriel," but to only half of them did he send valentines, noting: "Went and bought 3 Valentines—one to K—— one to L—— one to C——." He kept watching for horseshoes, mentioning them a dozen times in his diary along with the suggestion that a whole horseshoe meant good while a broken one presaged evil. "See 1 more broken horse shoe," he wrote on February 14. "Then whole one again. My spiritual guardian & enemies are fighting. Meet old broken down hunch backed cripple on crutches. Give him 1 dollar." [38]

Despite the luck a hunchback should bring, he was tormented by a feeling that Miss Markham was growing indifferent. He was so relieved when *The Weavers* closed and she joined him in Savannah that his diary ended abruptly.

But he did not meet her with warm affection. "Although he wanted me to join him," she wrote, "he was resentful when I came, making snide remarks about my interfering with his life." [39]

With her help he finished *Holiday* and resumed work on *The Bulwark*, meanwhile perhaps concealing from her letters from L——, C—— and the rest, including the following from a young New York woman:

> What can be more human than love, and I love you with all my heart and soul. . . . You have the keenest of eyes, milord, for everything (excepting only my love for you). . . . May God kiss your eyes and keep your vision clear. I love you as I love Truth itself, with an overwhelming love. . . .[40]

From Savannah he sent a copy of his *Plays of the Natural and Supernatural*, published February 18, to W. J. Hoggson—a futile effort to stir him, for Hoggson was unable to raise enough capital and soon dropped the film project. Dreiser had sent Fort's script to Waldemar Kaempffaert of *Popular Science Monthly* for advice, Kaempffaert commenting, "A vast amount of reading has been done which has not been correctly applied. . . . When a man says that there is no such thing as objective reality and then utilizes scientific experiments on objective realities to prove a point, surely something must be wrong." [41] Unconvinced, Dreiser sent the script to Alfred Knopf, now a publisher on his own, only to have it rejected again. He had never stopped publicizing Sherwood Anderson, admiring his contempt for the American idea of financial success, and at last Lane's accepted Anderson's *Windy McPherson's Son* for fall publication.

Early in April Dreiser returned to New York with his *Hoosier* script. First envisioned as a 50,000-word travelog, this book in his large hand had swelled to 200,000 and was far more a criticism of American mores than a travel book. He shoved it at Mencken for editing. While Mencken freely offered his services, Dreiser had come to take them somewhat for granted, writing him, "Do me the favor to read it carefully and advise me as to policy. . . ." Again, asking Mencken to make a full-page correction: "If you want to do me a favor typewrite & paste it in—you expert editor. . . . Make three copies and send me the other two, please." Again, "Jones [J. Jefferson Jones of Lane's] wants 150 or 200 words . . . concerning *A Hoosier Holiday* as well as *The Bulwark* to put in a trade circular. . . . Could you possibly dope these out for me?" [42] Mencken always obliged.

Dreiser had also left with Jones the first volume of his autobiography, which contained such intimate revelations of his sisters' sexual adventures that immediate publication was impossible. He wrote Mencken, "I am instructing Jones to this effect: that in case anything happens to me this manuscript is to be turned over to you and your judgment as to its disposition followed. In case anything should happen to you kindly arrange further for its care. You can guess why of course. If it ever fell into the hands of Mrs. Dreiser or some of my relatives I am satisfied that they would destroy it at once[.]" [43]

Mencken agreed but pointed out that another literary executor might be advisable: "It is conceivable that we may enjoy the felicity of dying to-gether—for example, in battle for the Republic." Although he found *Holiday* too long and repetitious, and containing some of Dreiser's inevitable errors, he wrote, "The book is full of excellent stuff. . . . I am constantly outraged, however, by banalities. . . . My hands itch to get at the job." [44]

Although supposedly a "liberated artist," Dreiser was so attached to Kirah Markham that he gave lip service to fidelity. Fearing to lose her, he inhabited that same "forest of intrigue" Mencken had noticed when he was living with Jug—elaborate lies, secret telephone calls, quick, clandestine meetings. Miss Markham knew all about it. She had regarded herself as married to him in a manner holier than one involving churchly ceremonies. Though terribly fond of him, she could stand his duplicity no longer. A few weeks after their return from Savannah, she left him and moved into the Twelfth Street household of her good friend Augustin Duncan, brother of Isadora, and his wife. Dreiser, stricken with loneliness, soon learned where she had gone and kept calling at the Duncan home to beg her to come back. Refusing, she soon went to Provincetown to join George Cram Cook, Susan Glaspell and others of the Village stage innovators who founded the Provincetown Playhouse with Eugene O'Neill.

In July came another kind of blow that threatened Dreiser's very survival as an artist. The New York Society for the Suppression of Vice banned *The "Genius"* as blasphemous and obscene.

"The book was selling the best of any and now this cuts me off right in midstream," he wrote Mencken. "Don't it beat hell." [45]

IV. COMSTOCK THE LESS

"In [1915]," wrote Floyd Dell, "the infamous Anthony Comstock died and went to hell, and an obscure person named John S. Sumner took his place as the hired agent of a private organization which, in cahoots with a corrupt police force, exercised an unofficial Censorship over American thought, and art, and literature; and a cowardly and hypocritical American public allowed this tyranny to go on." [46]

Comstock in his day had destroyed enough books, plates and spicy magazines to fill 16 boxcars. Sumner, known as Comstock the Less, was working on his first carload. Forty years old, the son of a Navy admiral, he had been shocked by obscene pictures passed around at his high school in Brooklyn and had never got over it. He had not gone to college but had studied law at night, passed the bar, joined the Y.M.C.A. and had come into his job of literary sanitation with a mind that had no understanding of literature but was filled with alarm at the threat to public morality posed by "obscene" books, films, magazines and postcards. A mild, polite little man, desperately in earnest, he spent his time reading suspect matter, and the storeroom at his Nassau Street office was crammed with a choice collection of dirty literature.

But little Sumner's shadow loomed large across the desk of every New York editor. They feared his power to arrest, to confiscate, to cause personal discomfiture and great monetary loss. They deleted "damns" and rewrote love scenes to eliminate any suggestion that sex might be a human phenomenon. Probably one reason the frank *"Genius"* was published at all was that it was approved by Lane's English reader, Frederic Chapman, who was accustomed to the greater British freedom and less aware of the New York shadow.

It was not Sumner who first detected Dreiser's enormities. This occurred a week earlier in Cincinnati when the Rev. John Herget of the Ninth Street Baptist Church got a telephone call from an indignant parishioner about *The "Genius,"* read it himself and passed it on to F. L. Rowe, secretary of the Western Society for the Prevention of Vice. Rowe found it "filled with obscenity and blasphemy," had it removed from Cincinnati bookstores, complained to the Post Office Department in Washington and also warned Sumner in New York.[47]

Strangely, Sumner had just been mailed a batch of pages torn from a public library copy of the book by an angry New York reader who underlined "obscenities." Sumner now read the book carefully and spotted 17 profane and 75 lewd passages. On July 25 he visited Lane's New York office on West Thirty-second Street and confronted J. Jefferson Jones with the charges.

The New York Society for the Suppression of Vice had a semi-official status, being chartered by the state to assure enforcement of anti-obscenity laws. The effect was that Sumner, like Comstock before him, was the state's top spy and censor. He knew the laws, worked in harmony with the district attorney, and had a high record of convictions against those brave enough to go to court. Jones, intimidated, agreed to withdraw the book pending a legal contest. He was further concerned when two postal inspectors called to inquire about *The "Genius."* He showed them favorable reviews, and although the federal government took no further action Jones was so fearful of being charged with sending obscene matter through the mails that he recalled all copies from bookstores throughout the country.

"Well, hell," Masters wrote Dreiser on hearing the news. "Get a lawyer if you have to and fight 'em." [48]

Charles Fort was fascinated by the charge of lewdness. "High-priest of Evil:" he wrote, "What shall I do to be lewd? . . . I write of the attractions of the planets, and of the affinities of atoms. These are lusts. Yet, to save me, I can not convey evil notions of astronomic and chemic obscenities." [49]

To Dreiser the case united, in the figure of Sumner, the moralists who had assailed him for 16 years and whose latest voices were those of Mrs. Peattie and Stuart Sherman. In actual sales the suppression suppressed little, for the book had been published for ten months and despite Dreiser's statement that it was "selling the best of any," its sale of 6,202 copies in the last three months of 1915 had dwindled to 1,685 in the first six months of 1916. At 20 per cent the total sale netted Dreiser $2,366.10, but about $1,500 of this was an advance repaid to Lane's so that he got a payment of about $866.10. A fair estimate would be that the book might have sold 1,000 more copies in the last half of 1916, so that Sumner actually deprived him of some $300 in royalties over that period. He was now living chiefly on an $1,800 advance Lane's had given him on *The Bulwark*. Although he was poor enough so that the loss of $300 was hurtful, the real issue here was the principle of artistic freedom, and he recognized this.

"Jones' first scare has passed," he wrote Mencken, "& I am doing my best to pump him up to a fighting point. . . . Am perfectly willing to . . . go to jail myself. It will save me my living expenses this winter." Later he repeated, "A fight is the only thing & I want Lane to fight. I hope & pray they send me to jail." [50]

But neither he nor Jones would go to jail unless one of them flouted the ban by publicly selling a copy of *The "Genius"* and inviting arrest. This Jones refused to do, on understandable commercial grounds, for Lane's New York office was not prosperous and the cause of literary freedom stood a poor second to the figures in the ledger. Why make a costly fight for a book whose sale was mostly finished? Dreiser did not go out on Union Square to hawk a copy either—an omission he later regretted. Had it been a question of only a few "illegal" passages he would have been willing to compromise with Sumner, but he flatly refused to compromise on 92 alleged infringements.

As always he turned to Mencken, who seemed to know what to do in any crisis. Mencken had edited two spicy magazines for Warner—*The Parisienne* and *Saucy Stories*—whose whole purpose was to make money and avoid legal involvement with the censors. He had therefore familiarized himself with the obscenity laws. Although he heartily disliked *The "Genius"* and had said so in print, he knew that Dreiser had written it in absolute good faith. It was a bad example over which to make a fight for freedom—what a pity the Comstocks had not swooped down on *The Financier* or *The Titan* instead! Yet Sumner had forced the issue. His Society had imposed a shameful censorship on serious letters, among the books already banned being *The Decameron* and unexpurgated editions of *The Three Musketeers*, *The Wandering Jew* and Horace's odes. If he succeeded in killing *The "Genius"* it meant that America's outstanding novelist was muzzled. The blow would not only hurt Dreiser but would discourage promising younger realists and assure the nation of a steady diet of literary treacle.

"On with the machine guns!" Mencken wrote Dreiser. "Forward the Zeppelins! I am planning a general offensive." [51]

Sumner, as Mencken wrote later, had gone through the book with "the terrible industry of a Sunday-school boy dredging up pearls of smut from the Old Testament. . . . When young Witla, fastening his best girl's skate, is so overcome by the carnality of youth that he hugs her, it is set down as lewd. On page 51, having become an art student, he is fired by 'a great warm-tinted nude of Bouguereau'—lewd again. On page 70 he begins to draw from the figure, and his instructor cautions him that the female breast is round, not square—more lewdness." He felt that Sumner had become so fascinated in finding 75 lewdnesses that he had spotted only 17 less interesting profanities and had actually missed a few: "On page 191 I find an overlooked *by God.* On page 372 there are *Oh, God, God curses her,* and *God strike her dead.* On page 373 there are *Ah, God, Oh, God,* and three other invocations of God. On page 617 there is *God help me.* On page 723 there is *I'm no damned good.* . . . But I begin to blush." [52]

Yet Mencken, an eminently practical man, knew that he had not only an inferior novel to defend but an angry, bull-headed author. Dreiser was a genius bereft of common sense, gifted at giving offense to philistines. He was unpopular among many conservatives on one ground or another—his pro-Germanism, his belligerence and his bizarre sex life. The problem, as Mencken instantly understood, was to enlist the aid of the very philistines Dreiser despised and displeased—the Joyce Kilmers and the William Lyon Phelpses—who far outnumbered the rebels in number and influence. This was impossible unless done by a strategy of indirection. Mencken would defend *The "Genius,"* yes, but he would put more emphasis on defending the principle of literary liberty itself.

This required a fine line of diplomacy. It also meant that the blundering Dreiser must be kept quietly in the background while *Feldmarschal* Mencken commanded the troops.

"After all, we are living in a country governed by Puritans," he cautioned Dreiser, "and it is useless to attempt to beat them by a frontal attack. . . . I see very clearly that the Puritans have nearly all of the cards. They drew up the laws now on the statute books and they cunningly contrived them to serve their own purposes. The only attack that will ever get anywhere will be directed—not at the Puritan heroes but at the laws they hide behind. In this attack I am full of hope that schrapnel will play a part." [53]

V. A LITERARY SEWAGE DISPOSAL PLANT

No one could reasonably question Mencken's sincerity or accuse him simply of helping a friend, since he had belittled *The "Genius"* in *Smart Set*. He immediately drafted Harold Hersey, Dreiser's admirer who had become assistant to Eric Schuler, secretary of the executive committee of the Authors' League of America. Dreiser had refused to join the League, lampooning it in 1913 as being controlled by "the pseudos, reactionaries and pink tea and chocolate bon bon brotherhood of literary effort"—a scorn he perhaps now regretted, since the League was the only recognized writers' organization, the obvious one to fight censorship, and now he had to beg aid of the philistines he ridiculed. He was lucky that Hersey, whose regard for him approached worship, was there to pull out his chestnuts. While Mencken and John Cowper Powys drafted protests for writers to sign, Dreiser met on August 24 with the executive committee of the League.

Members of this group, which included Ellis Parker Butler, Rex Beach, George Creel, Louis Joseph Vance, Kate Jordan, George Barr Baker and others, were not unanimous in their admiration of the book or its author. Yet they passed a resolution declaring that *The "Genius"* was "not lewd, licentious or obscene," that the tests applied by the Society for the Suppression of Vice were "narrow and unfair" and urging the League to take action to prevent the suppression of the book. The League itself followed with an official protest, noting that "Some of us may differ from Mr. Dreiser in our aims and methods, and some of us may be out of sympathy with his point of view," but praising his "manifest sincerity" and "high accomplishments," attacking the effort to "condemn a serious artist under a law aimed at common rogues" and urging amendments of the laws to prevent such persecutions.[54]

Despite its brave declaration, the League was half-hearted on this issue which should have closed its ranks in united battle. Its members were not even unanimous in their condemnation of Sumner as censor or of the principle of censorship itself. The League president, Winston Churchill, had grown prosperous on at least two best-sellers, *Richard Carvel* and *The Crisis*. He signed the protest but remained aloof from the skirmish although he was busy planning a committee to meet "distinguished guests from Europe." The vice-president, former President Theodore Roosevelt, was unheard from, being preoccupied with politics and the war in Europe. Brander Matthews felt that the Comstocks, if occasionally fanatical, did good work in suppressing filth. Ellis Parker Butler had reservations, writing Mencken, "Today I am inclined to believe that some books can be so rotten they should be destroyed in some literary sewage disposal plant. Things are not necessarily truthful because they stink nor strong because they smell so."[55] Mark Sullivan thought that *The "Genius,"* being tasteless and vulgar, was a poor thing to make an issue of. Rupert Hughes and others objected to wording in the protest according Dreiser praise. Hamlin Garland, a former rebel turned mossback, opposed any League aid for Dreiser, whom he accused unfairly of "a piece of very shrewd advertising." The turbulent Briton, Frank Harris, who had come to New York to edit *Pearson's Magazine*, was so irate at the League's milksop attitude that he resigned in disgust and assailed Sumner in *Pearson's*.

Meanwhile Mencken was launching Zeppelins, sending out 25 letters daily asking editors and writers to sign the protest. Hersey was doing the same. Mencken devoted most of his time to authors of such standing or popularity as to carry influence, among them Robert Frost, Rex Beach, Earl Derr Biggers and Henry Sydnor Harrison. He labored at his typewriter far into the night. When he got a refusal he often sent out a second amiable but cogent plea, one such to Harrison numbering some 1,300 words. He shunned radicals and crackpots and warned Dreiser to do the same, feeling that help from them would alienate the "respectable" support so much needed. Dreiser had already issued unwisely bellicose statements to the press, one of them appearing in the *New York Tribune:*

> I don't know what action the John Lane Company will take, but they have been asked to destroy the plates of the book. . . . But I can say there will be no suppression of the book nor will the plates be destroyed, because if the publishers should wish to accede to the demands, which I don't believe they will, I will get out an injunction to prevent them.[56]

"Why did you deliver such a crack at Jones in the *Tribune* article?" Mencken asked. "Surely this is a bad way to keep him on the track." [57]

But Dreiser, with some reason, suspected that Jones was backing down and had threatened him to his face. From Jones, however, he got the *"Genius"* plates and shipped them to New Jersey to prevent their destruction. Anxious to make publicity use of the hubbub over The *"Genius,"* he was busy sending out letters and printed leaflets to some 240 booksellers urging them to display and push unsold copies of his other books. Mencken meanwhile egged on Jones to solicit British help, which resulted in a cable signed by Arnold Bennett, Hugh Walpole, E. Temple Thurston, William J. Locke and H. G. Wells reading:

> WE REGARD THE GENIUS AS A WORK OF HIGH LITERARY MERIT AND SYMPATHISE WITH THE AUTHORS LEAGUE OF AMERICA IN THEIR PROTEST AGAINST ITS SUPPRESSION.[58]

The lukewarm League needed some such bucking up, for some of its more conservative members misunderstood Dreiser's aims or disliked his work and were irked that Hersey was spending so much of his time in Dreiser's behalf. By fall the suppression had stirred up a small storm. The *New York Tribune* attacked unintelligent censorship, saying, "It retards the development of our art. . . ." The *Des Moines Register* said, "[Dreiser] is an analyst of the

human mind through realism, and appeals only to readers of adult mentality." [59] Frank Harris in *Pearson's*, Ezra Pound in *The Egoist*, Felix Shay in
the *Era* and Alexander Harvey in his rebel weekly *The Bang* denounced the
suppression. Even a *Saturday Evening Post* editorial commented on its folly.
Dreiser's old lawyer friend Elias Rosenthal at his own expense published a
pamphlet, "Theodore Dreiser's 'Genius' Damned," describing Sumner as "a
lawyer of no particular distinction" and declaring that censorship was in the
hands of "priests, ministers, young men who have been secretaries of religious
societies [but who have no sound judgment] of literature in the broad and
sensible meaning of that word." [60] Dreiser and Mencken were invited to speak
against censorship at the Liberal Club, and when Dreiser relayed the invitation Mencken was angry. He had a settled prejudice against the "red-ink
boys," had twitted Dreiser about his friendship with some of them and felt
that in the eyes of the puritans their support was equivalent to support from
immoralists and cranks.

"For God's sake," he urged, "don't start making speeches at the Liberal
Club. This organization consists of all the tinpot revolutionaries and sopho-
moric advanced thinkers in New York. . . . These jitney liberals are forever
trying to get advertising by hooking on to better men." [61]

To his good friend, the Irishman Ernest Boyd, now a British consul in
Spain, he wrote, "Meanwhile, Dreiser . . . plays the fool. It seems impossible
for him to shake himself free from the Washington Square mountebanks.
. . . The plain truth is that he is a fearful ass and that it is a very difficult thing
to do anything for him." [62]

He was outraged when Dreiser enlisted Max Eastman, editor of *The
Masses;* Floyd Dell, Alexander Harvey and Rose Pastor Stokes, the fiery
reformer recently sentenced to prison. "Let me say once more," he wrote
Dreiser, "that I think this is damnably silly, perverse and dangerous policy.
You are making it very hard for Hersey, who has already imperilled his job in
your behalf, and spitting into the eyes of the rest of us. . . . All of these
jitney geniuses are playing you for a sucker. They can't advance your
reputation an inch, but you make a very fine (and willing) stalking horse for
them." [63]

"I do not get the reason for the unnecessarily harsh & dictatorial tone of this
letter," Dreiser replied. ". . . Recently, on several occasions you have gone
out of your way to comment (and before others) on my supposed relationship to this band of 'jitney radicals and tenth-rate village geniuses. . . .' I am
not in touch with the life of this section. I do not go out with or receive here
any radicals of any sort—or village characters—not any. Although I have
privately said to myself and here and now state to you that it is really none of
your business . . . still you persist. Have I tried to supervise your private life
or comment on any of your friends or deeds? What's eating you, anyhow? . . . Your letter smacks of something I do not like. . . ." [64]

To Boyd in Spain, Mencken wrote in part, "Dreiser, as usual, is playing the fool. . . . [He] insisted upon adding the names of a lot of Washington Square jitney geniuses. The result is that the Authors League men in charge of the matter are violently enraged. . . . The old ass is ruining his case by his folly. These frauds flatter him and so make use of him. . . . Dreiser's association of his case with the names of mountebanks advocating birth control, free verse, free love and other such juvenile propaganda is hurting him very severely. . . ." [65]

But to Dreiser himself he wrote soothingly, although repeating his warnings, and the campaign went on. He and Hersey sent 50 copies of the protest each to willing workers including Alfred A. Knopf, Ben Huebsch, Willard Huntington Wright, Francis Hackett, Harvey O'Higgins and Powys, asking that they circulate them and contribute a dollar to the postage fund. Such conservatives as Nicholas Murray Butler, Joyce Kilmer and William Lyon Phelps preferred not to link their names with Dreiser's, but signatures were coming in by the score. At the same time it was evident that Jones, perhaps offended by Dreiser's threats, was delicately withdrawing from the battle and that the Lane firm would not risk a legal defense of The "Genius."

That fall, Dorothy Dudley, the daughter of a wealthy Chicago family, a graduate of Bryn Mawr and a friend of Edgar Lee Masters, arrived in New York to begin a lifelong friendship with Dreiser. A striking young rebel, she had shocked Chicago by posing for a portrait with a cigarette in her hand. Bringing Masters' greetings, she called at the Tenth Street studio. As an emancipated woman she approved of Dreiser's romantic affairs and thought it typical of a culture-barren country that few thought of him as a great novelist but asked only, "Do you know what woman Dreiser's living with now?" [66] Miss Dudley was scornful of the spectacle of America's greatest writer—a man who should have been accorded national veneration—instead being harried and impoverished by cranks and puritans.

Mencken, who spent $300 of his own money in the fray, and Hersey labored on at a job made harder by Dreiser's unpopularity in some quarters, his German ancestry and his own tactical blunders. Yet most of the writers approached understood the principle involved. "I think Mr. Dreiser is one of the most over-rated writers in America," William Rose Benét wrote Mencken, "sincere as he may be. . . . I sign the document you send merely because I believe in your side of the greater issue you state—the freedom of American letters." [67]

Before the year's end, Mencken and Hersey had secured some 500 signers including many of the nation's most respected creative artists and editors, from Percy MacKaye, Robert Frost and Channing Pollock to Ed Howe, Mary Wilkins Freeman and Ellery Sedgwick; from Jack London, William Allen White and James Lane Allen to Gelett Burgess, Douglas Z. Doty and David Belasco. The list included others famous or soon to win fame, among them Sinclair Lewis, Amy Lowell, Willa Cather, John Reed, Rex Beach, Max Eastman, Rachel Crothers and Edwin Arlington Robinson. From Chicago, Sherwood Anderson, whose first novel had just been published in part through Dreiser's intercession, wrote in disgust that the issue of freedom was the most important of all: "Jesus Mariar [*sic*] the question of whether America goes to war or not is secondary." [68]

Sumner was not impressed. "Authors taken as a whole," he wrote Alexander Harvey, "may be very good judges of the . . . literary merits of any particular writing, but as judges of the tendency of that writing on the manners and morals of the people at large they are no more qualified than are an equal number of mechanics of ordinary education. The term 'indecent' is a word of common significance. . . . It is not for any limited group of individuals to attempt to force upon the people in general their own particular ideas of what is decent or indecent." [69]

Under this last sentence, when Harvey forwarded the letter to him, Dreiser logically wrote, "What about the group Mr. Sumner represents?"

"Through the story," Sumner wrote George T. Keating, "there are very vivid descriptions of the activities of certain female delinquents who do not, apparently, suffer any ill consequence from their misconduct but, in the language of the day, 'get away with it.' It is wholly conceivable that the reading of such a book by a young woman would be very harmful. . . ." [70] And in Chicago Father James Gillis said amen in condemning *The "Genius"*: "Unless I fundamentally misunderstand the American public, it will guard the morals of the people even at the sacrifice of the liberty of the individual. In other words, we do believe in censorship." [71]

The issue could not have been more clearly stated. It was Sumner and Gillis not so much against Dreiser as against any mature expression of American art. Dreiser, far from being crushed, was enjoying the battle, confident of victory. He saw enough humor in the situation to write a burlesque menu for a dinner apparently held at his apartment for his allies, writing in not flawless French, "*Oeufs Jennie Gerhardt. . . . Mouton Bouillé oaux Oeuvres Suppressées. . . . Pommes de Terre a la Soeur Carrie. . . .*" [72]

VI. THE HAND OF THE POTTER

The suppression hurt Dreiser in other ways—his loss of valuable writing time in the fight and his inability for some weeks to recapture the creative mood. Women as always took much of his time. He went walking with Miss Dudley. He was urging Mencken to help Anna Tatum find an editorial job. His current secretary was a young woman named Estelle Kubitz, whom he playfully called Gloom, but it is doubtful that Gloom was getting a regular salary. There were others. Thelma Cudlipp, now a successful artist for *Vanity Fair*, once encountered him by chance. She spied Dreiser across the room in a Village restaurant, and wrote:

> [He looked] oh, so down-at-heels with, oh, so drab a woman, and I had heard stories about the utterly abandoned life he was leading and his utter cruelty to women—I should have asked myself, "Was he ever cruel to you?" [73]

Two of his good friends had recently died—the young Harris Merton Lyon of a kidney ailment, and Ben Dodge by suicide. (Dodge, who for a time had been reduced to labor on a Jersey chicken farm, had returned to New York and to temptation. Ben Huebsch one day was saddened to see Dodge stumble into his office, red-eyed, seedy, "looking as if he had rolled in the gutter," to ask Huebsch for a loan. Huebsch gave him a few dollars. Shortly thereafter the despairing Dodge jumped into the East River and ended up at the same morgue Dreiser had once covered for the *World*.)

Dreiser, mourning them both, felt that puritanism had defeated Lyon and would later write a sketch about him. To Dorothy Dudley he spoke disgustedly of puritanism, declaring that among other things it had made prudes of the nation's women, shorn them of sexual passion, and that without passion there could be no art. Almost the only vital, passionate women left, he said, were prostitutes and actresses.

Yet he did not succumb to the despair that almost drove him mad after the *Carrie* debacle in 1900. Now he was sure of his own standing and validity and was fighting for it. For Waldo Frank of the *Seven Arts Magazine* he wrote an attack on censorship tyranny titled "Life, Art and America," and characteristically tried to jack up the payment on it. "There is a mistake in the count of your words . . ." he wrote Frank. "It must be nearer $85 than $70." [74] He could no more avoid seeking an extra $15 than he could resist seeking a woman or the first piece of cake. Once Frank and a few others were his evening guests. There was a cake, and Frank observed with fascination his host's insensate lust to get at that cake:

> Dreiser licked his lips. . . . Dreiser's eyes bulged, his hands thrummed. She cut a slice. Dreiser tipped his chair, sprawled forward. . . . Then, the lady noticed his behavior. Swiftly, as if working against a possible crisis, the good lady put a piece of cake on the plate and handed it to Dreiser. He fell to, rolling his eyes. The lady proceeded to serve Theodore Dreiser's guests. . . . [75]

Badly though he needed money, Dreiser in November worked on a piece unlikely to be profitable but sure to offend all the Sumners and Gillises.

This was a four-act play, *The Hand of the Potter*, whose central character was sexually depraved young Isidore Berchansky. Isidore, sensing himself a victim of impulses he fears but cannot control, moves from temptation into violence, attacking and killing an eleven-year-old girl, realizes the enormity of his own act and says helplessly, "I didn't make myself, did I?" before he commits suicide. It was an attempt at dramatic exposition of Dreiser's main theme—the inscrutability of life. Working furiously at night, he finished the play in three weeks and sent it on to Mencken for free criticism, particularly on the German accent of one character.

He seemed to have no suspicion that his subject, daring for 1916, sexual abnormality, might be indiscreet at this time of censor alertness. Or did he?

Did he, consciously or unconsciously, write *The Hand of the Potter* as a nose-thumbing directed at the Sumners? One can only guess.

Mencken, who had recently sent him a prayer book and a wall plaque labeled "Jesus," exploded in vivid protest:

> Frankly, the play seems to me to be hopeless, not only because the subject is impossible on the stage, but also and more especially because the treatment is lacking in every sort of dramatic effectiveness. . . . The whole thing is loose, elephantine and devoid of sting. It has no more dramatic structure than a jelly-fish.
>
> . . . It is all very well enough to talk of artistic freedom, but it must be plain that there must be a limit in the theatre, as in books. You and I, if we are lucky, visit the bowel-pot daily; as for me, I often have to leave a high-class social gathering to go out and piss; you, at least, have been known to roll a working girl on the couch. But such things, however natural, however interesting, are not for the stage. . . . Nothing is more abhorrent to the average man than sexual perversion. He would roar against it in the theatre.
>
> I see you getting into an understandable but nevertheless unfortunate mental attitude. Resisting with justice the imbecilities of the Comstocks, you unconsciously fly to an extreme, and demand a degree of freedom that is obviously impossible. I have no patience with impossibilities. . . .
>
> If the thing were possible, I'd advocate absolutely unlimited freedom in speech, written and spoken. I think the world would be better off if I could tell a strange woman, met at a church social, that I have diarrhoea . . . if novels and other books could describe the precise process of reproduction, beginning with the handshake and ending with lactation, and so show the young what a bore it is. But these things are forbidden. The overwhelming weight of opinion is against them. The man who fights for them is as absurd as the man who fights for the right to walk down Broadway naked, and with his gospel pipe in his hand. Both waste themselves upon futile things while sound and valuable things remain to be done.
>
> . . . Surely you don't want to get into the position of a mere bad boy of letters—shocking the numskulls for the mere sake of shocking them. Consider the politics of the situation. Imagine the play printed tomorrow. The moralists would pounce upon it with cheers. And remember that not only your own artistic freedom, but also the freedom of many other men depends upon the issue.[76]

Dreiser reacted as if in surprise:

> For the life of me I cannot discover what there is in the subject *matter* of this play to have evoked this tirade. . . . Admittedly the idea may be badly worked out—a botch. But the subject! . . . What pray is there about this that is so low and vulgar? . . .
>
> . . . When you . . . tell me what I can or cannot put on the stage, what the artistic or moral limitations of the stage are and what the American people will stand for . . . my answer is that I have more respect for my own judgment in this matter than I have for yours. . . .[77]

He asked Mencken not to mention it to others, or to review it in advance, since his adverse opinion might influence others. Mencken, seeing that he intended to go ahead with it, resumed the attack:

> I still think it rotten politics to come out with a play on sexual perversion at such a time. . . . If you had anything to say on the subject, I'd be for saying it. But you actually say nothing. . . . Fully half the signers of the Protest, painfully seduced into signing by all sorts of artifices, will demand that their names be taken off. You fill me with ire. I damn you in every European language. You have a positive genius for doing foolish things. Put the ms. behind the clock, and thank me and God for saving you from a mess. . . . In brief, apply to this business the elementary reasoning powers of a streptococcus.
>
> . . . The play is a piece of pish—clumsy, banal, unnatural, almost idiotic. Its publication would lose your case, forfeit the respect of all intelligent persons, and make every man who has labored on the protest look like an ass.

He urged that Dreiser show the play not to women but to competent judges such as Huneker, Louis Wilkinson or Masters before rushing into print.[78]

Dreiser, to be sure, had discussed the play with women, as he admitted in his next—with Gloom, Daphne Walters and one other. But he had also talked it over with Hutchins Hapgood and with Masters, both of whom had praised the idea. Furthermore, he had shown the completed play to a lawyer friend, who was enthusiastic, and to "a leading movie producer" who said he was "crazy to produce it." Surely, he pointed out, if the play was as bad as Mencken claimed, there was no danger because no one would want it. He suggested that Mencken was growing as stuffy and moral as the Pope. And he added a paragraph expressing perfectly the Dreiser credo:

> I deny your ruling in connection with perversion and its place on the stage. Tragedy is tragedy and I will go where I please for my subject. If I fail ridiculously in the execution let the public and the critics kick me out. They will anyhow. But so long as I have any adequate possession of my senses current convention will not dictate to me where I shall look for art—in tragedy or comedy. My inner instincts and passions and pities are going to instruct me—not a numbskull mass that believes one thing and does another.[79]

He felt that Mencken, of all people, had broken Dreiser's Law—sided with the moralists, abandoned freedom, slipped into bed with Sumner. But the quarrel proved academic since no one was willing to produce or publish the play at the time. Dreiser tried it on others—on Lengel, who wrote that it started out strongly, then slumped, and that he was "utterly out of patience with courtroom scenes. . . ."[80] And on Jones at Lane's, who rejected it, advising Dreiser "not only as your publisher but also as a friend . . . [that] it would do you immeasurable harm."[81]

Right as he may have been on this score, Jones or his firm had failed Dreiser in the *"Genius"* crisis, meekly obeying Sumner's edicts, refusing to advertise or sell the book unless it was judicially determined that it did not violate the law.

With the case at an impasse, Dreiser, through his old friend Robert Davis at *Munsey's*, got the aid of John B. Stanchfield, an able attorney who agreed to represent him without charge. At the Authors' League, young Harold Hersey had been working so devotedly at $15 a week in getting signers for the protest that conservative members demanded sourly whether he was working for Dreiser or the League. The League's busiest censorship-fighter was asked to resign, which he did. When Dreiser heard that Hersey was in such straits that he had sent his wife and small child to Washington to live with her relatives, he tided him over with a loan, which Hersey acknowledged gratefully, writing, "It literally saved my life." [82]

Dreiser's own funds must have been slim. *A Hoosier Holiday*, published in the fall at $3, had sold only 1,665 copies by the year's end, and since Booth got half the royalties Dreiser netted only $373.12. The *Plays* had sold only 698 copies to the end of 1916—royalties about $130. There were no royalties from the frozen *"Genius,"* and from Harper's at the end of 1916 his combined royalties on sales of *Carrie, Jennie* and *The Financier* amounted to $73.84.

Although his estimate of Mencken was reduced, the two enjoyed a beer party at Luchow's in December. And Mencken, soon to leave for a short stint as a war correspondent, sent his usual Christmas blasphemy. [83]

7. The Philistines

Harassed by money worries, conferences with lawyers, meetings with censorship-fighters and the usual romantic complications, Dreiser in early 1917 faced the threat of extinction as a writer. He could look back over 17 years of stuggle that had shown distinct signs of victory since the *Carrie* disaster in 1900—the warm reception of *Jennie* in 1911, the praise for *The Financier* and *The Titan*—only to meet catastrophe again with *The "Genius."*

One of Sumner's achievements was the suppression of several possible Dreiser novels that might have enriched literature. Now it was patently impossible for him to write other novels that might be suppressed, even if he could have afforded the luxury, and a full decade would elapse between *The "Genius,"* which impoverished him, and his next novel, which would make him rich. Who knows what might have come from his pen had he been encouraged instead of banned?

Recognizing the Sumner stand as a threat not only against him but against all liberty, he gave freely of his time in resisting the Comstocks. On January 5 he met with Hersey, the lawyer Theodore Schroeder, Karl Karsten and Frank Harris at Harris' diggings at 3 Washington Square. Many proposals were aired—propaganda against censorship, lobbying against it in the legislature, the establishment of a fund to aid suppressed authors—but nothing came of it. The immediate question was one of law. After many discussions with Jones and with Stanchfield and his colleagues, it was agreed that Dreiser would press a "friendly suit" against the Lane firm to enjoin them from violating their contract on the ground that the book did not violate the law. But when would the slow-moving courts get around to it?

Now Dreiser was forced to write short material—stories, articles, moneymakers. In the circumstances he should not have risked further feminine involvement, but when Mrs. Louise Campbell of Philadelphia wrote him in February to rebut disparaging remarks he had made about Pennsylvania in *A Hoosier Holiday*, he did what came natural to him. He urged her to drop in when she next came to New York, which she did. Petite and vivacious, Mrs. Campbell was terrified by a mouse which he had trapped, found uninjured and put in a cage at his seedy studio. He found money to take her to lunch at the Brevoort. She was astonished when he gave her—an intelligent, well-read but totally inexperienced young woman—a short story he had written and asked her to analyze it.[1] He had so soured on professional critics that he

216

sought a fresh, undoctrinaire point of view. Thereafter Mrs. Campbell traveled occasionally between Philadelphia and New York, beginning what would be an intermittent but lifelong stint as Dreiser's part-time literary adviser and—at uncertain pay—as his part-time typist.

President Wilson had severed relations with Germany over the U-boat issue and the papers had little space to devote to an eccentric Tenth Street novelist's battle for liberty. They took only back-page note of the Public Forum meeting on March 18 at Dr. Percy Stickney Grant's Church of the Ascension at Fifth Avenue and Tenth Street, where John S. Sumner was the chief speaker.

Dreiser evidently attended the meeting with Joseph S. Auerbach, another lawyer who had volunteered to advise him. Dr. Grant was one cleric he truly admired, for he was *unconventional*. He wrote poetry. He was concerned with live issues. He flirted with socialism and sometimes outraged his own parishioners by working for such sordid things as the rehabilitation of prostitutes. But chiefly Dreiser admired Grant because he had written about *The "Genius,"* "The book in no way should be considered, in my opinion, injurious to public morals. It is practically a sex-hygiene pamphlet in the form of fiction. If I were the President of Vassar College, I should regard every girl who read the book as more strongly fortified for the dangers and adventures of her own career." [2]

"Knock down the steeples!" Dreiser had written; but Dr. Grant's steeple was safe.

Unknown to Sumner, who had twice arrested Margaret Sanger, three young women distributed copies of her *Birth Control Review* outside the church while he spoke within of his determination to enforce the laws against the dissemination of information about contraception. Things grew stormy as other speakers then attacked or defended Sumner. John Cowper Powys attacked him as an "amateur detective" for suppressing Dreiser's book, which had been hailed as a work of art by those who knew art. [3]

Sumner, undeterred, within a few weeks struck out twice again for purity. He raided the Union Square offices of Frank Harris' *Pearson's Magazine* (which had attacked him), served a warrant on Harris and seized all copies of the May issue of *Pearson's* which contained an "offensive" article about the New York night court. And he swooped down on David Graham Phillips' novel *Susan Lenox*, declaring it contained some 100 obscene pages. The Authors' League took no stand on *Susan Lenox*, but Phillips' publisher, unlike Dreiser's, prepared to go to court and fight.

Dreiser later said he was living on some ten dollars a week and was hard put to buy coal. When Mencken returned from Europe, he and Nathan occasionally taxied to Tenth Street to fill Dreiser's mailbox with oddities—letters from President Wilson urging him to come to the White House, Black Hand threats, frankfurters tied with colored ribbon and booklets on sex hygiene. Unequal to this jocose pair in horseplay, he could think of no better reposte than to send Mencken a paper novel by Bertha M. Clay. Harry Kemp, the strapping "Byron of the Village," lived a block away with his beautiful, violet-eyed wife, Mary Pyne. Kemp was even poorer than Dreiser—actually had borrowed money from him—and seldom had any coal at all. So Mary would leave her freezing flat to warm herself at Dreiser's grate, discuss Dostoyevsky with him and fix lunch for him.[4] Apparently he kept a discreet distance from her—a self-restraint so remarkable that one wonders whether he was bearing in mind the powerful, jealous Kemp, or more likely the fact that Mary was tubercular. He observed, however, that Hutchins Hapgood was befriending her and he took note of the details as material for a story, "Esther Norn," which later would infuriate Hapgood because of alleged misinterpretation of his platonic motives.

But now he was friendly with the hard-drinking Hapgood, who cultivated anarchism while he drew comforting help from his family's capitalistic fortune. Hapgood saw that Dreiser's prime preoccupation was the difficulty of writing against the mores of his time.

"The only other absorbing interest he had," Hapgood wrote, "was sex; and that took decidedly a second place." He was struck by Dreiser's use of his women as typists and literary assistants: "Dreiser . . . always combined his work and his love. The women he lived with . . . always helped him very definitely in his work. I do not believe that the love of any woman ever, even for a short time, stood first in his interest."[5]

Hapgood was jolted occasionally by Dreiser's crudeness. One weekend, when Dreiser and his then mistress visited the Hapgood couple at Spring Lake, New Jersey, "he introduced [the] young woman to Neith [Mrs. Hapgood] with a jocular allusion to his relations with her, making the girl blush up to her hair."[6]

Another practical use he made of these women in his work would become evident years later with the publication of his *A Gallery of Women* and "This Madness"—stories based so faithfully on his own romantic affairs as to bring embarrassment and anger to some. There were those who felt that his erotic exploits were merely calculated research to give him literary material from real life. The painter John Sloan, for one, "disliked Dreiser's carelessness about women whose hearts were wrecked by an 'artist's' desire for 'experience.' "[7] There was a fallacy here. Dreiser would have pursued women had he been a plumber, but since he *was* a writer he gladly used all that vivid material. The man whose writings would win fame for their expression of warm human pity could himself at times be quite inhuman.

II. SILK SHIRTS

At this point Dreiser had difficulty in selling even his shorter material. The magazines declined *The Hand of the Potter.* Seeking to capitalize on the publicity given *The "Genius"* by its suppression, he had Lengel busy offering the condensed version to the magazines again, with no takers. He was working steadily on new material, but not until February 26 did he make a sale, an article about New York to *Hearst's* for a needed $500. He must have been overjoyed on March 30 when he received $800 more from *Cosmopolitan* for his story "Married"—an account of Jug's failure to understand him which had been removed from *The "Genius."* He was unable to leave a story alone. When he got the proofs of "Married" from *Cosmopolitan*, he went through them and changed the hero from a painter to a musician—a change *Cosmopolitan* changed right back, because "The pictures have already been made showing him in his studio—one with a painting on the easel." [8]

Although the immediate financial pressure was off when he sold his story "Free" to *The Saturday Evening Post* for $500, he was depressed by the coolness shown toward most of his fiction. His story "Will You Walk into My Parlor?" was rejected in turn by *The Saturday Evening Post, Ladies' Home Journal, Harper's, Cosmopolitan* and four others. His play "The Dream" was rejected by *Hearst's, Century, The Saturday Evening Post* and others. More than ever he was aware of the prejudice against material not conforming to the Butterick standard of sweetness and he was pondering methods that might assure some sympathetic reception of serious art. One of them, quite visionary, was to form a new publishing house, a combination of Alfred Knopf, Frank Shay and the Boni brothers—all of them fighters against the treacle tradition—where honest writing would get intelligent consideration. [9]

Manna came from heaven that spring when the anti-treacle Arthur Hopkins, a producer who liked plays that made audiences think, paid him $1,000 for an option on *The Hand of the Potter*. On top of that royalties had at last wiped out his debts to Harper's and Century, so that his only large outstanding debt was an $1,800 advance he had received from Lane's for *The Bulwark*. He had never relinquished his ownership of the plates and rights to *Carrie*, and Frank Shay, the Washington Square bookseller, now contracted to put out an edition of 1,000 copies of *Sister Carrie*, offering Dreiser a 25 per cent royalty.

Mencken wrote Boyd, "[Dreiser] has more money than he ever saw before, and is wearing silk shirts." [10] He was able to give financial help to his sister Mame, who lived nearby on Eleventh Street and whose husband, Brennan, now seventy, was ill and out of work.

"I thank you dear for your goodness to me . . . " Mame wrote. "I think of you every day and ask a blessing for you." [11]

In June he left New York with Gloom as companion, for a month at a farm near Westminster, Maryland, where he was at last free to work on the second volume of his autobiography and on *The Bulwark*. He had the privacy of a lone cabin in the woods. As usual when leaving New York, he left a key to his apartment with William Lengel, who would forward his mail and also act as his unpaid agent, sending rejected manuscripts on to other magazines. Lengel, one of those who had watched with indignation the philistine efforts to thwart him, was glad to accommodate him. From his rustic cabin Dreiser wrote Mencken, "Do me a favor. Look up Admiral Perry in your Encyc and give me the details of his visit to Japan—the year, what fort, what the Japs said, whether he fired on the defenses before he was admitted—or not. I am making a reference to it." [12]

Mencken obliged: "Commodore Matthew Perry arrived at Kurahama, on the Bay of Yedo, July 7, 1853, with 4 ships and 530 men," going on with a careful listing of facts. Now the owner of an automobile, he wrote that he would be out for a visit, saying, "I'll bring the alcohol" and adding, "I am at work upon my autobiography, and have just finished the chapter describing my baptism and seduction." [13] Actually, he was just polishing off his *A Book of Prefaces*, which contained a wounding discussion of Dreiser.

Enraged at President Wilson for his part in America's entry into the war, and at the widespread tales of Hun atrocities, Dreiser had committed a literary indiscretion by writing a pro-German, anti-English essay, "American Idealism and German Frightfulness." Waldo Frank, in an unguarded moment, had tentatively accepted it for *Seven Arts*, and from Maryland Dreiser haggled with him over a $100 price-tag. Leaning ever more toward his idea of somehow getting subsidization, he suggested to Frank that someone like the "pro-German" banker Herman Baehr might bolster the payment out of his own pocket—an idea Frank emphatically rejected. And he received a letter on a personal subject that must have made him goggle.

It was from a reader, Mrs. Amanda Jefferson of Chicago, who praised *The "Genius"* as an "impressive sermon" but added that she had heard something about him so disturbing that she was "almost unable to sleep":

> A few days ago I mentioned to my pastor that I had read The Genius. He had not read it himself, so could not say anything against it, but he told me something that . . . distressed me not a little. That is, he told me that you are a man of loose life and that you are at present living in carnal sin. Will you not be good enough to give me a line saying this is not so? I admire you so much that I cannot bear to think of you as turning aside from the straight path of rectitude. Surely our good Lord, by endowing you with your great talent, has given into your keeping a trust that you must cherish. . . . [14]

Dreiser, cherishing the trust in his own way, let Mrs. Jefferson go sleepless. Returning to New York by the end of July, he found that Lengel had tried "American Idealism" on Douglas Doty of *Century*, hoping for a better price. America was at war, the lid was down and Doty recoiled at the article's anti-English spleen.

"It strikes us as neither sound nor convincing," he wrote Lengel, "and, frankly, I think it comes clearly under the head of those proscribed writings that 'give aid and comfort to the enemy,' " adding, "I strongly advise Mr. Dreiser not to publish this article. I am very much afraid it would injure—temporarily at least his literary career." [15]

Public sentiment being what it was, the article probably would have put him under surveillance as a possible German spy and caused his books to be removed wholesale from the libraries and burned. The *North American Review* rejected it and even the liberal *Seven Arts*, on a second look, got cold feet, Frank urging Dreiser earnestly not to publish it. Dreiser considered printing and distributing it himself—as he had already done with "Life, Art and America"—but fortunately gave up the idea. He managed to sell his story "The Second Choice" to *Cosmopolitan* for $800 and "St. Columba and the River" to *The Saturday Evening Post* for $750. He complained vainly to *The Post* about the $750 price, winning George Horace Lorimer's heavy disapproval.

The six-foot-one, 190-pound Dreiser was taking pills for nervousness, rundown condition and low blood pressure and occasionally consulted a tea-leaf reader named Mrs. Spafford who he felt had amazing powers of divination. Nervous or not, when his good friend John Cowper Powys went to Post-Graduate Hospital for a gastroenterostomy, Dreiser accompanied him, put on a white gown in the operating room and, Powys said, "described the whole thing to me later and told me that he actually held in his hand at one moment some important portion of my guts." [16]

III. THE SNUFFLING PEASANT

The *"Genius"* had now been banned for more than a year, the laggard courts had not yet got to the case, and Sumner in effect had won. The fight was costing Dreiser time, distraction and money. Had he been an expedient man, willing to adjust himself to the world as it was, he would have dropped it.

But he was as determined as Sumner. His mettle was so disputatious that he could find principles in trivialities. He took time to write indignantly to the president of the Pennsylvania Railroad because an information clerk had been impolite over the telephone. And he sent several angry letters to the Pullman Company over a muffler he had lost in a car en route to Atlantic City, a loss he blamed on the porter.[17] In the *"Genius"* case he took pleasure in fighting a whole nation's prudery, but above all he believed deeply, and truly, that he was right. He knew there was something sacred in an honest account of human experience, and that Sumner, not he, was the corrupter, the obscene. Perhaps he was unaware that in his violent reaction against convention he was in danger of losing the quality so appealing in his earlier works—his status as spectator of life as it was. Now he was becoming the critic of life, the super-moralist attacking moralists, the pamphleteering self-justifier, the preacher of Dreiser's Law. The artist in him suffered so that it might be questioned whether he could ever achieve the detachment to produce anything of the first rank again.

Shortly after his return from Maryland, Dreiser was pleased by a visit from a tall, cadaverous young man with a beautiful smile—Horace Liveright. Liveright, thirty-six, a born gambler from Pennsylvania, was quitting the Wall Street brokerage business to join with Albert Boni in the publishing firm of Boni & Liveright. Boni, though he disliked Dreiser personally, admired his fiction and had suggested that Liveright sound him out.[18]

To Herbert Spencer and Theodore Dreiser, life was *force*. Dreiser was attracted by people with force. Liveright had force expressed in enthusiasm and charm. He proposed that B & L take over the publication of *Carrie* begun by Frank Shay, who had been drafted into the army, but he suggested a great deal more than that.

Both Boni and Liveright were gifted and energetic, believers in good literature, scornful of the strait-laced bookmen of the day and eager to let fresh air into the musty publishing parlors. Dreiser and B & L were made for each other. They wanted at least to double Shay's issue of 1,000 copies of *Carrie*. In addition they wanted to take over *all* of Dreiser's works—those owned by Harper's, by Century and by Lane's, including *The "Genius."* They were not afraid of censors and they would fight to get *The "Genius"* back in circulation. And there was talk of a new, uniform edition of all of his works.

This was precisely what Dreiser had been hoping for. It was bad enough to have his eight books scattered among three different publishers, but none of the three were now particularly interested in them. This was an era when authors of standing were distinguished by "complete works," and he was not only flattered by the thought of *Carrie, Jennie* and all the rest appearing in uniform bindings but he knew that the publisher would have to *sell* a complete set. Nobody was selling them now. Yet his suspicion of publishers—especially a newcomer in the field—made him suspend judgment. He gave B & L permission to go ahead with *Carrie*, its sixth publication, just to see what they could do.

Meanwhile he became a bookseller and advertiser himself. He had 5,000 five-by-seven cards multigraphed listing his books published by the three firms and reading:

> Mr. Dreiser's works have been continuously attacked by Puritans solely because America is not yet used to a vigorous portrayal of itself. If you will examine these books for yourself you will discover the reason for his present high position in American letters. If your local book dealer will not get any one of these for you, address the publishers direct, or George C. Baker, 165 West Tenth Street, New York City.[19]

This of course was his own address, and Dreiser, alias George C. Baker, doubtless had his current secretary busy sending out cards. His disgust with censorship mounted when an issue of the pacifist *Masses* was pronounced subversive by federal investigators—a charge that would soon bring his friends Dell, Eastman and Art Young into court. And his resentment at Mencken boiled over with the appearance in the fall of 1917 of his *Book of Prefaces.*

In it, Mencken honored Dreiser with the first long, understanding, critical examination of his writings—the *first* after five major novels and numerous other works in 17 years. He was generous in his praise. He raked the puritans and the Comstocks. He gave the back of his hand to Phelps and other professors who had written recent literary surveys which could take approving note of Richard Harding Davis and Robert W. Chambers without so much as a mention of Dreiser. He exposed what amounted to a national conspiracy on the part of the Brahmins to scuttle Dreiser by utterly ignoring him, if not by methods more overt.

Being Mencken, however, he paused also to pillory Dreiser's own literary sins.

"One-half of the man's brain, so to speak," he wrote, "wars with the other half. He is intelligent, he is thoughtful, he is a sound artist—but there come moments when a dead hand falls upon him, and he is once more the Indiana peasant, snuffling absurdly over imbecile sentimentalities, giving a grave ear to quackeries, snorting and eye-rolling with the best of them."

And he let himself go on Dreiser's favorite, *The "Genius."* This, he wrote, was "as gross and shapeless as Brünnhilde. . . . The thing rambles, staggers, trips, heaves, pitches, struggles, totters, wavers, halts, turns aside, trembles on the verge of collapse. . . . The book is an endless emission of the obvious. . . . It runs to 736 pages of small type; its reading is an unbearable weariness to the flesh. . . ." And he touched on what had come to be a Dreiser sore spot when he added, "It somehow suggests the advanced thinking of Greenwich Village." [20]

Although the essay was a moving tribute, the whiplash on style and on Dreiser's growing didactic point of view was searing. Ever since the *Potter* quarrel, Dreiser, who would compromise on nothing, had felt that Mencken was subtly compromising with the Comstocks—that Mencken indeed was growing a trifle passé, that he failed to understand Dreiser's new aims.

The letters and meetings between the two ceased, an estrangement each regretted after nine years of literary and beer-hall camaraderie.

"Dreiser, it appears, is subtly outraged by certain passages in my prefaces," Mencken wrote Boyd, later admitting, "I suddenly find myself very lonely in New York." [21]

When Arthur Hopkins gave up his plan of producing *The Hand of the Potter,* Dreiser's indignation rose. He blamed Hopkins' move on "the nosy interference and criticism of Mencken and Nathan talking to Hopkins behind my back." [22] Now he decided to publish *Potter* as a book, seeing in it an opportunity to test Liveright's courage. He submitted the script to B & L.

A few days later Liveright telephoned in some embarrassment. "I'm advised it's too strong," he said. "Why not wait and give us something else first?"

Dreiser growled that he could forget about being his publisher, and hung up. Within a half-hour Liveright called back to say that they would publish the play.[23]

Liveright wanted Dreiser, but he did not want Charles Fort, whose book X Dreiser was urging on him. The problem of finding a publisher for Fort was almost insoluble—as Dreiser saw it, another indictment of American shallowness. The big, shaggy-haired Fort had become a recluse in his dingy West Forty-third Street apartment, surrounded by thousands of notes gathered from papers all over the world telling of strange phenomena which he used as evidence for a series of books (all unpublished) intended to demonstrate that science was unscientific. He believed life to be a "superdream," a phantasmagoric existence hovering between the two poles of Order and Chaos. He could produce proof that there had been rains of frogs, rains of blood, that people had been mysteriously swished off this planet and that strange people from other planets had visited here in hordes. Orthodox scientists, he said, denied the evidence because of their enslavement to dogma. Fort had no formal technical education and no laboratory other than the public library, where he haunted the periodical room for data. A likeable eccentric, he poked fun at logic, reality and himself. To read a Fort book was to enter a frantic universe where anything could happen and did, to find one's brain reeling in a welter of shrewd observation mixed with utter buffoonery.

Despite Dreiser's interest in the sciences Fort assailed, he had known and befriended Fort since 1905. He saw courage and validity in Fort's unconventionality, his plunge into fields of arcane speculation which formal science shunned. Fort saluted Dreiser's efforts in his behalf with a Fortean invention, writing:

> It's a meatless cocktail.
> You take a glass of beer, and put a live goldfish in it—instead of a cherry or olive or such things that occur to a commonplace mind.
> You gulp.
> The sensation of enclosing an organism is delightfully revolting.
> I think it's immoral. I have named it the Dreiser cocktail—[24]

Meanwhile the Dreiser-Mencken rift so disturbed the kindly Ben Huebsch, who knew them both, that he offered his services as mediator. Dreiser replied gratefully, but insisted that there was no personal quarrel:

> Where we diverge, and only there (and there is no personal feeling in this), is in regard to my own work. His profound admiration, apparently, is only for *Sister Carrie*, and *Jennie Gerhardt*, works which to me represent really old-line conventional sentiment. For *The "Genius"*, The Hand of the Potter, "Laughing Gas," "Life, Art and America," and a somewhat newer vein, he has, apparently, no eye. . . .

Since he is slowly but surely drifting into position where he feels it incumbent upon him as a critic to place me in a somewhat ridiculous light, I have felt that this close personal contact might as well be eliminated, for the time being anyhow. . . .

I wish it were different, but for me, apparently . . . there is only strenuous diverging work ahead.[25]

The issue between the two was clear. Dreiser felt that he had grown artistically and intellectually, that he had moved beyond Mencken. But Mencken, whatever his critical failings, was right in his main argument: The innocent, wondering Dreiser of the earlier novels was an artist, whereas the new, disturbed, contentious "intellectual" was something less.

IV. REJECTIONS, REJECTIONS

Even then Dreiser was writing "Hey Rub-a-Dub-Dub" and other "intellectual" essays that would bore Mencken stiff. Although never a joiner, he was moving closer to the "Greenwich Village group" who approved heartily of his rebellion and seemed to understand him. He wanted to be liked. His friend Powys, who admired him enormously, admitted that he was "very susceptible to praise." [26] Villagers were excitedly discussing the Russian revolution, some seeing in it new hope for the world, and Hapgood was even contemplating a trip to Russia.

In Edith De Long, Dreiser had a radical friend beautiful enough and forceful enough to influence his thinking. A stunning brunette, she had left her rich, philistine husband in Colorado and come to New York to plunge into left-wing, bohemian activities. Reckless and intense, she had evidently taken an interest in Dreiser and appropriated him as her escort at radical meetings at the Liberal Club and elsewhere. At her Riverside Drive apartment, where she held avant-garde gatherings, Dreiser had met Edward H. Smith, a Kansan who had been educated at the University of Jena and was now a writer for the *Sunday World*. Smith had fallen in love with Edith, but could not marry her until she divorced her Western husband, who made himself unpleasant by hiring detectives to spy on her. Smith had become one of Dreiser's admirers and was trying with little success to get publicity in the *World* about the fight against Sumner.[27]

Dreiser was now deeply involved with the red-ink crowd which Mencken held in almost pathological contempt. ". . .The man is such a hopeless ass that he falls for any flatterer," Mencken wrote Boyd. "Let some preposterous wench come in in a long blue smock, and call him 'Master', and he is immediately undone." Again he wrote Boyd, "He is doing little writing but devotes himself largely to the stud. I haven't seen him for six months, but hear of him indirectly." [28]

Although Dreiser was taking osteopathic treatments for his prostate condition, Mencken was wrong about the writing. He was writing short material steadily but without success. Editors were finding him almost unpublishable. The catalog of his rejections in 1918 is staggering.

His story "Love" (later called "Chains") was rejected by *The Atlantic, Century, Cosmopolitan, Harper's, Red Book, The Saturday Evening Post, Hearst's, Pictorial Review, Metropolitan* and *Smart Set.*

"The Hand" was rejected by *The Post, Collier's, Scribner's, Red Book, Pictorial Review, Harper's, Metropolitan* and *The Atlantic.*

"Khat" was rejected by *The Post, Scribner's, The Atlantic, McCall's, Chicago Tribune, Everybody's, Metropolitan, Collier's* and *Century.*

Others of his pieces were rejected at least by the following number of magazines, probably more: "Phantasmagoria," six; "Old Rogaum and His Theresa," six; "Phantom Gold," nine; "Rural America in War Time," five; and "Vanity, Vanity," four. Since Charles Hanson Towne and William Lengel worked as agents for some of his stories, the total number of rejections is difficult to find. But the records show that during this same 1918 period Dreiser's "The Country Doctor," "A Story of Stories," "Equation Inevitable," "War and Peace," "The American Financier," "More Democracy or Less," "The Village Feudists," "A Mayor and His People," "The Court of Progress," "Hey Rub-a-Dub-Dub," "Change," "The Old Neighborhood" and "Neurotic America and the Sex Impulse" were rejected at least a total of 33 times.

During 1918 he had a grand total of at least 76 rejections of short material—probably an all-time record.[29]

It is true that some of these pieces were rejected because they were of poor quality (such as "Khat") or because they represented Dreiser's new "intellectual" phase and were confused and boring (such as "Equation Inevitable"). Even his old friend Mary Fanton Roberts, now editing *Touchstone*, to whom he would send material when better-paying markets turned it down, complained that his offerings were "too complicated and weird."[30]

Yet even his better stories had poor luck. Particularly now that the country was at war, editors sought cheerful fiction and frequently praised his offerings but found them too tragic or shocking for their readers. *Red Book* rejected "Old Rogaum" "because the characters are Germans."[31] Three comments on his story "Chains" disclosed the widespread editorial desire for sweetness and safety.

"It is one of the best things you've done," wrote Douglas Doty, now with *Cosmopolitan*, but he rejected it because "I am afraid it would . . . be extremely dissatisfying to the average reader."[32]

"Perhaps . . . the finest piece of short fiction . . . that you have accomplished," wrote Thomas R. Smith of *Century* as he turned it down with the observation, "We are the ones who have to face the Philistines."[33]

"It really is a beautiful sketch," wrote Arthur T. Vance of *Pictorial Review*, rejecting it because "We like [our stories] with some meat in them, but not too much."[34]

The Saturday Evening Post, after bravely publishing his non-inspirational "Free," had received "dozens of telegrams and hundreds of letters" from readers who condemned the story.[35] Dreiser felt that market closed to him as a result, and although he was prone to imagine editorial pusillanimity, in this case he was evidently justified. *The Post* was afraid to publish his "St. Columba," which it never used, and thereafter he got only rejections from Independence Square.

He could well throw up his hands at the state of American culture. For him 1918 was a year of terrible failure and frustration—one that only his enormous toughness and vast ego could have survived. Sinclair Lewis, after a few moderately successful novels, made $8,000 that year on short stories alone, most of them popular confections. Dreiser by now was incorruptible out of principle—also perhaps because he could not produce a marshmallow if he tried. He received a measly $300 from *Metropolitan* for "The Old Neighborhood," $300 from *Scribner's* for "Rural America in War Time" (which he had to rewrite) and $300 more from *Munsey's* for "The Hand." The censors had wrecked him in his true medium, the novel, and he could not afford to finish *The Bulwark* although Lane's had already announced its coming publication.

A few windfalls saved him from insolvency. From Boni & Liveright he got $246.75 in royalties from *Carrie*, and also a $500 advance on *Free*, a book of short stories. And in August Mr. and Mrs. Charles D. Coburn paid him $1,000 for an option on *The Hand of the Potter*, which they planned to produce at the Greenwich Village Theater.[36] This play was already being printed by B & L, and Dreiser now asked them to hold up on publication until its production—a request Liveright was only too happy to grant.

Planning a trip to Pittsburgh, Dreiser headed for the station with his bag, then began to feel uneasy about the journey. Some inner voice suggested that it was not safe. He postponed the trip, and was glad he had when he read in the papers next day that the train he would have taken had jumped the track at Horseshoe Curve, sending many cars into the river and causing death and injury to passengers. He had no doubt that a kind spirit had saved him.[37]

There were few such gentle spirits among his critics. When Dreiser in the pro-German *New York Evening Mail* praised Adreas Latzko's book *Men in War*, which blamed war in part on women's desire for heroes, Mrs. Peattie of the ovarian school bared her patriotic claws:

"Latzko does a thing which Dreiser himself might have done. He takes all of the honor away from women's courage. He makes them willing to send their husbands and sons to the battle front because it is the fashion to do so. . . . Inevitably Dreiser would approve. He is not at the front—any front— and he insults, with every book he writes, the integrity of women." [38] The Latzko book was promptly suppressed by the post office.

Now, at long, long last—after two years of suppression—Dreiser's "*Genius*" case was coming to court. His friend Edward Smith of the *World* wanted to raise a hoopla about it: "I and some friends . . . want to get up a dinner for you when your 'Genius' matter is adjudicated. . . . If you win, jubilation; if you lose, protest." [39] He planned to invite Huneker, Mencken, Powys, Masters, Abraham Cahan and many others. David Karsner of the socialist *New York Call* fell in with the idea, writing Dreiser, "We Socialists have suffered much from such people that persecute you," and suggesting that radicals including Max Eastman, Art Young and John Sloan be invited. [40] Mencken got wind of it and wrote Boyd, "You may be sure that I shall not be present at this convention of frauds. The newspapers will poke fun at it, and do D. a lot of damage." [41]

The dinner, which did not come off, would have been in protest. In May Joseph Auerbach argued for Dreiser before the Appellate Division, asking that The "*Genius*" be cleared of the charge of obscenity and that the John Lane Company be required to fulfill their contract to advertise and sell the book. Auerbach felt it necessary to say:

> Consider that The "*Genius*" is not written with a moral! . . . A creative book is not necessarily . . . the occasion for some ethical or moral or religious ruminations of the author. [42]

Throughout his argument his anxiety was evident that the learned judges might feel—as Sumner did—that a book to be permissible must be uplifting, that all fictional sinners must be punished before the last page. It did no good. After two more months had passed, the judges threw out the case on a technicality. There had never been any formal charge against the publisher or writer, since Lane's had withdrawn the book voluntarily on Sumner's mere threat, and the court was not empowered to render "advisory opinions." [43]

The big mistake had been made when neither Jones nor anyone else had publicly sold the book and been brought up on criminal charges. The case was left in a legal vacuum. Dreiser got no relief although his lawyers tried other maneuvers for several years more. The Authors' League had lost interest in the matter, turning now to expelling the pro-German George Sylvester Viereck from membership. All this, as Dorothy Dudley observed, at a time when American soldiers were fighting in France to the battle cry of freedom.

V. ILL-ADVISED AND CALAMITOUS

After seven months of estrangement from Mencken, Dreiser broke the ice with a short note as he submitted his playlet "Phantasmagoria" to *Smart Set*. [44] Mencken replied cordially. He was tactful enough to call "Phantasmagoria" "fine stuff" and to have Nathan reject it—at least its fourth rejection. The Dreiser-Mencken correspondence resumed, each happy that the quarrel was over. There was warm affection between them. There was also mutual respect heightened by their knowledge that they understood the strangling power of philistinism better than anyone else alive, though they disagreed about methods of attacking it, and that together they might achieve some kind of literary revolution.

Dreiser was still torn between sloppy haste and a desire for perfection. The stories he gave to Liveright for the collection *Free* were a copy-editor's nightmare, and when he received the proofs he covered them with corrections that cost him heavily in printer's fees.

"For Heaven's sake don't let us have a lot of more corrections!" Liveright wrote him. ". . . You have practically rewritten the whole book. Not only will it probably be cheaper to reset this whole book, but on account of the poor copy provided in so many of the stories, extra charge will be made for composition. Of course, you are the doctor so far as costs are concerned, but as a decent, conscientious publisher, I must ask you to give us clean copy at the start, both for your own interest and ours." [45]

Dreiser's concern about art did not extend to fact. When Mencken read a bound copy of the book in August, he was upset over gross medical errors in the lead story, "Free."

"Who in hell was your medical consultant in 'Free'?" he demanded. "Some 3rd Ave. abortionist, I do suspect. Know ye that blood transfusion is not done for leaky heart valves, that the blood cannot be brought in a bottle, that the person giving it must go to bed beside the patient (often a charming business, and responsible for most public offers), that horse blood is not thicker than human blood, that horse blood would poison the patient, etc., etc. Come to the old reliable Doctor Mencken when you want pathology. Forty years uninterrupted practise in private diseases. . . . No publicity." [46]

Softer voices came to Dreiser out of the past. As a result of an article about him by Frank Harris in *Pearson's*, he heard from his first Chicago journalistic tutor, John Maxwell, now an Indianapolis newspaperman. And a letter came from May Calvert—of all people—the fair-haired beauty who had taught him seventh-grade lessons in Warsaw in 1884. Miss Calvert, now Mrs. May Baker, was teaching school in Huntington, Indiana. She had read *A Hoosier Holiday* by her pupil of 34 years earlier and had been delighted to find herself named therein as an inspiration and veritable life-saver by Theodore, who had become famous after a fashion although he was not highly regarded in Indiana.

"Your book hurts me because of your evident disappointment," she wrote. ". . . Thank you for the beautiful story of your first term in Warsaw. I am glad I was that teacher. . . ." [47]

"[Your letter] pleased me so much that I was happy all day long," he replied. ". . . I have thought of you for years, always with pink cheeks and a warm girlish smile and kind eyes—haloed by the affection and the fancy of youth. . . . Do you recall that I couldn't learn grammar? I don't know a single thing about it yet." [48]

To renew such an old acquaintance, free from contention and enshrined in nostalgia, was to him one of the wonders of a life that could be brutal. He urged that she visit him in New York, and when she arrived in July to see other friends as well, he spent much of a day strolling along the Hudson with her, reliving old times in Warsaw.

Nearing sixty, Mrs. Baker was graying, plump and charming, a childless divorcee after an unhappy marriage. Dreiser liked her so much that two months later he planned to visit her in Indiana. In his dependence on women he had the poor taste to ask if she could put up his secretary as well as himself, to which she replied regretfully, "I wish I had room for your secretary but there are five in family now. . . ." [49] Mrs. Baker lived with her sister, who had children. This trip fell through, probably for lack of funds, but he promised to make it later, adding, "I have many things in hand and as usual the critics discuss me most savagely, but I can stand it. I'm used to it. And besides they become more ridiculous every year." [50]

He had written some new personality sketches to add to those done years before about his brother Paul, Muldoon and others, and now intended to collect them in a book called *Twelve Men*. To Dorothy Dudley, who worshiped the mass effect of his writings but deplored his style, he gave several of the sketches to edit. She worked at it fondly, correcting stylistic lapses and simplifying turgid sentences. "Always he agreed gratefully to the changes," she recalled, "but in the midst of the work he made an excuse of my slowness and finished the revision himself." [51] He placed more reliance on Louise Campbell, who was typing the first volume of his autobiography in Philadelphia. No longer could he entrust editorial work to Doctor Mencken, who was willing but who had ruled himself out because of his unkind remarks in the *Prefaces*.

In November the Germans collapsed, New York exploded with victorious whistles and bells, and Dreiser began work on an idea for the resurrection of free art by intelligent subsidization.

This was a brain-child long in gestation. He envisioned forming a board of able, unfettered critics who would pass on new works and pay for those whose realism prevented their sale to the venal magazines and other marketplaces corrupted by popular taste. Probably he was remembering how the philanthropic Philadelphia soap manufacturer, Joseph Fels, had subsidized Harry Kemp and others. Money seemed to be no problem, for Liveright had a wealthy friend (perhaps it was Otto Kahn) who he thought would put up $100,000, and the lawyer Joseph Auerbach felt that August Belmont would give $500,000 to such a cause. [52] Dreiser outlined his plan in a letter to his admirer, Harold Hersey, soon to be released from a Louisiana army camp. Hersey enthusiastically agreed to do the legwork, writing, "I want to jump right in as soon as I get back . . . [and help in] the formation of a real society to help authors." [53]

So Dreiser, whose conviction that man was helpless had so exasperated Dell, was out to help. In his mind was the ideal of encouraging the new, the gifted, the sincere. He arranged a meeting at his apartment January 8, 1919, preparing his guest list with care. He eliminated Frank Harris, one of the most vocal of the censorship-fighters, because he was annoyed by Harris' sketch of him and he distrusted the Briton. He decided against inviting Max Eastman and similar radicals who were clearly on his side but who he feared would lose the organization conservative support. He came up with a list of members of various arts, among them Mencken, Nathan, Edward H. Smith, George Luks, Nina Wilcox Putnam, George Bellows, Dr. Percy Stickney Grant, Liveright, John Cowper Powys, Lawrence Gilman, Douglas Doty, Ludwig Lewisohn and Hutchins Hapgood. Hersey was present to take notes, but Dreiser was already growing annoyed with Hersey.

Mencken of course stayed away. "Dreiser is trying to organize a society to save the national letters from the Baptists," [54] he jeered to Boyd. But many of those invited came, for when Nathan arrived he found men "packed like soda crackers" in the small Dreiser living room, which was dimly lighted and thick with tobacco smoke. Since there were few chairs, most of the guests sat on the floor. Nathan knew only a few of those present, but Dreiser merely announced "Nathan" as he came in and suggested, "Find yourself a seat on the floor." Nathan did so, to discover himself cemented to "a small sticky piece of cake that had evidently been lying there for a couple of days." [55] Dreiser folded his handkerchief nervously. He dreaded addressing a group of any kind, and he made it short.

"There are a lot of . . . geniuses in America," he said, as Nathan recalled it, "who are so poor that they can't go ahead with what they've got in them and who need help. Unless they get help, these geniuses, so far undiscovered, will never be heard of. It's my idea that what we all ought to do is to go around and try to interest rich men in these geniuses and get them to subsidize them. Let me hear your opinions." [56]

According to Nathan's satirical account, Luks, the bibulous painter, took a nip from his flask and hooted, "Who are these great neglected geniuses?" Nathan himself, being an editor of Smart Set who was obliquely accused of buying popular material instead of quality, denied that really good writers could not get published. Luks complained, "This floor is damned hard and my backside is getting sore." But there was a considerable discussion, with Powys, Lewisohn, Bellows and others supporting Dreiser's proposal before the group disbanded. [57]

The plan was idealistic, fraught with practical problems. Yet Dreiser was so hopeful that he set Hersey to work, giving him $15 as a starter. To this Hersey added $125 collected from well-wishers, hired a secretary, sent out 275 letters and called personally on some 50 people to urge their cooperation in Dreiser's society. He worked for five weeks, getting so little response that he grew utterly discouraged.

Dreiser's own enthusiasm cooled. He began to fear the organization might develop into a parcel of cranks with axes to grind, and he differed with

Hersey on strategy. They both gave up the campaign. But when Hersey set out on his own to publish an account of this losing effort to bolster honest art as well as the story of the *"Genius"* suppression, Dreiser suspected his motives. He wrote his young admirer a tart letter in employer-to-employee terms, accusing him of "persistent and self-interested use of my name." [58]

Hersey was wounded, an idealist whose literary hero had turned on him. He recalled that he had lost his job at the Authors' League because of his championing of Dreiser, and he resented Dreiser's reference to him as an employee after contributing only $15 to his five weeks of work. He wrote Dreiser bitterly, in part:

> All my connections with you have been ill-advised and calamitous. . . . Your idea is wrong, Dreiser, you think that everyone works to make something out of a personal contact with you. . . . I'll bet you are also forgetting [Mencken's] efforts in your behalf . . . and yet he has done more for you than any living man. . . . Do you remember years ago that you said in your first letter to me that you knew that I would be disillusioned in you[?] Clever guess, clever guess. . . . You are not growing old gracefully and I certainly do not want to be a pallbearer. [59]

That last reference was distressing, for Dreiser hated to be reminded of his age. He was already promoting another idea to succor the arts. This was a book-magazine, tentatively called *The American Quarterly*, which would print only realistic writing, including that of such radicals as Emma Goldman, Eugene Debs and Bill Haywood. He had discussed it with Liveright, who agreed to publish it, and with Merton S. Yewdale, an editor at Lane's. Yewdale was eager to do the editing under the supervision of Dreiser, who would be editor-in-chief.

Dreiser was enthusiastic, writing Mencken, Masters and William Marion Reedy among others about it and planning an advisory council that would include these three along with Lewisohn, H. B. Fuller, George Sterling, Robert Frost, Powys, Hapgood and others. Then Yewdale was forced to withdraw because his new employer, Harper's, did not want him involved in so elaborate a side-enterprise. Dreiser could find no one as satisfactory as Yewdale. It would take too much of his time if he assumed the editorial burden himself. He regretfully dropped his second save-the-arts project after giving it much of his own effort and stirring up several hundred other people. [60]

His motives were laudable. Yet this double defeat underlined weaknesses that all but guaranteed failure in any Dreiser-sponsored group movement: his impulsiveness, his inability to foresee practical difficulties, and his manic-depressive subjection to moods of unreasonable assurance that could suddenly plunge into unreasonable despair.

8. *Enthusiasms and Disgusts*

I. FIRE BURNS, WINE INTOXICATES

Not surprisingly, Dreiser had become a Village curiosity. He was bohemian enough to suit anyone, but devoid of sophistication. For days he might shut himself in his lair, writing or listening to recorded music, refusing to answer callers or the telephone, then suddenly embark on what for him was a riot of sociability at Polly's. When he was gay he could laugh at an inane remark until the tears rolled, but when he was depressed he was unfit for human society. Normally so penurious that he would fight for a nickel, he splurged now and then on a deluxe dinner or a striped shirt. Ordinarily temperate, he was on rare occasions so troubled that he got very drunk. He would stoop to pick up a pin for luck, then discourse on science. He was secretive about trivialities—his whereabouts or his telephone number—but could make astonishingly intimate revelations of his own frailties. For a determinist who professed a disbelief in causes, he became inconsistently involved in causes of his own.

His magnetic power over women was composed of something more than sex attraction. For as long as his interest lasted, it was often intense, kindly, flattering, truly sympathetic and wonderfully understanding—indeed, perhaps too powerful to last very long.

To men who appreciated his genius he could be so charming that they went to unusual effort in his behalf—Lengel, Edward Smith, Powys, Hapgood and David Karsner among them. To the intellectuals he was a lowbrow.

Albert Boni thought him a terrible bore with a "schoolboy mentality." [1]

James Oppenheim felt him "naive about many things. . . . A poor thinker." [2]

Floyd Dell said, "There were certain respects in which Dreiser could be called stupid." [3]

In Louis Untermeyer's opinion, "Dreiser became so pleased with the role of dissident and nonconformist that he automatically took the attitude of the objecter." [4]

John Cowper Powys wrote, "He is fantastic, queer. . . . Nothing with him follows any tradition. All is abnormal, sub-normal, super-normal." [5]

Ernest Boyd saw him as a primitive, full of platitudes, an "interesting personality without a single personal idea." [6]

Ludwig Lewisohn wrote, "When Dreiser tries to think he writes like a child." [7]

Waldo Frank was impressed by his naïveté, his conviction that skepticism was profundity: "Like a child, he is intellectually active—discovering that fire burns, and that pain is not pleasant. Like a child, he is furiously busy, piling up evidence of the physical world: such as the facts that women are sexually attractive, that monogamy is not a natural state, that business men love power, that wine intoxicates, that all the ladies who go to church are not saints. . . ." [8]

Yet all these men saw his native genius, a creative power that seemed to emerge like water from a spring. All would have agreed with Mencken that Dreiser the artist was in some danger of defeat by Dreiser the foggy intellectual. Merton Yewdale, who had been observing him with friendly fascination, wrote him candidly:

> You are a peculiar man in this respect: you have, in order to bring yourself into action, either to defend or attack something or somebody. You are an immense and powerful force yourself, and therefore you need an equal force exerted upon you to realize your life. . . . Of course, there never will be a time when there is not some force to oppose you, but if there could be, you would lose your power immediately . . . if the moment should come when all the world acclaims you as its true spokesman, you will be horribly disappointed and disillusioned. . . . [9]

II. TAKE TEA WITH ME

Meanwhile the dashing Edith De Long had finally secured a divorce from her Colorado husband and in the fall of 1918 had married Edward H. Smith. Dreiser apparently served as best man. Edith had made a deep impression on him as a woman of *force* who lived life to the hilt, wrote poetry, plunged into radicalism and surrounded herself with interesting people. The Smiths took an apartment on West 182nd Street, and it was here that Dreiser met jovial, Austrian-born Dr. Abraham Arden Brill.

Brill had studied under Jung, translated Freud into English and was largely responsible for the growing popularity of psychoanalysis in New York. Dreiser promptly read one of his books—probably *Psychoanalysis: Its Theories and Practical Application*—and sank into depression because of its description of mental abnormalities. He wrote Brill twice, telling him of the dark mood his book had induced. Brill replied soothingly:

> That my book should have produced that depressing effect on you is not bad. Such depressions are usually very transitory. You will find ways of rationalizing the depressing ideas, and the result will undoubtedly be even a greater penetration of human life than you have given to the world thus far. . . . [10]

Dreiser soon had dinner with the Brills—the beginning of a long friendship. Influenza was stalking the land, a jingle of the day being, "I opened the winda / And influenza." His short story "Khat" was rejected by *The Atlantic*, "Love" by *Smart Set*, and "Sanctuary" by *The Post*, *Cosmopolitan* and the *New York Tribune*. Two editors' comments on "Sanctuary" were familiar:

Ray Long of *Cosmopolitan* wrote, "This is a very exceptional piece of work but I do not believe it is a story which we should print." [11]

Burton Rascoe of the *Tribune* praised it as "forcible and crushingly truthful" but admitted that it "might get me scalped if I published it in this polite family journal." [12]

Dreiser's fiscal affairs were growing even more chaotic. At the end of 1918 he received from Lane's $21.84 in royalties on *The Titan*, $7.13 on the *Plays*, $5.18 on *A Hoosier Holiday* and nothing at all on the suppressed "*Genius*." But he was deeply in the red with Lane for the advance on *The Bulwark* and other charges, owing them a total of $2,143.06. He was fed up with Lane and was living chiefly on advances from Liveright, who had given him $500 on *Free* in 1918 and added another $500 on *Twelve Men* in January, 1919, and a second $500 in February. Although *Free* sold fairly well for a book of short stories—2,742 copies to December 1, 1918—he still owed Liveright $148 on the advance and the extra printing charges.

Liveright, who had great intuitive faith in Dreiser, still wanted to take over all his books and above all was anxious to publish *The Bulwark*, which he felt would be a success. With Dreiser's permission he was dickering with Jones of the John Lane Company over details of the change-over. Yet Dreiser was already quarreling with Liveright and questioning his reports on sales, convinced that he kept a double set of books. Liveright was an aggressive merchandiser, interested in new ideas, anxious to publish radical and "shocking" books, and he had proved it by publishing Dreiser and others such as the pacifist Latzko book and the first book of Eugene O'Neill's plays. Dreiser never trusted him, although Liveright made many concessions to please him, as in the case of Charles Fort.

Fort had put aside his unpublished *X*, a later manuscript called *Y*, and in the spring of 1919 produced a new effort, *The Book of the Damned*, an extravaganza assailing dogmatic science's refusal to accept phenomena Fort took perverse pleasure in accepting. For this book Fort had gathered 40,000 notes under 1,300 headings, culled from newspapers and semi-scientific journals in Fort's chaotic, speculative way. It told of floating luminous objects, again of rains of blood, showers of caterpillars and dead birds. Although Fort's own tongue was partly in his cheek, Dreiser apparently took him with some seriousness. He was delighted by *The Book of the Damned*, writing Fort:

> Wonderful, colorful, inspiriting—like a peak or open tower window commanding vast realms. . . . My hat is off. All of your time has been admirably spent. This book will be published and I offer my services to that extent as a tribute[.] [13]

He went to Liveright with an ultimatum: Either he would publish Fort or he would lose Dreiser. Liveright, with what must have been great misgivings, gave in and published a small edition of *Damned* the following year.[14] A month later Dreiser, spurred by a growing interest in the science of human behavior, wrote to a man who did not believe in rains of blood—the great Dr. Jacques Loeb of Rockefeller Institute, the socialistic, atheistic master of the mechanistic theory of life.

"It was, naturally, a gratification to me," Loeb replied in part, "that you should take an interest in my work, which, as a rule, is not relished by the majority of literary people on account of the frankly materialistic or chemical conception of life expressed in my writings." He directed Dreiser to two of his books, adding, "It would give me great pleasure to meet you personally, since I have followed your literary career with special interest. Needless to say, I am not a romanticist in literature." [15] However, Loeb was at Woods Hole, where Dreiser's letter had followed him, and events would postpone the meeting of these two for three years.

"If it hadn't been for short stories I'd be out in the snow sure enough," Dreiser wrote Mencken. "Personally, at this age I have concluded that literature is a beggar's game. . . ." [16]

He was having trouble enough with his short stories. He tried hard to sell "Love," "Khat" and "Phantom Gold," which had been unanimously rejected by the better-paying magazines, to Burton Kline, who had succeeded Rascoe at the *New York Tribune*. He wrote Kline with unconscionable hard-sell:

"Any of these stories if sold by me to the Post would bring $1,000.* From the Cosmopolitan I could extract $800. Hearsts the same . . . and I do not expect the Tribune to pay as much as the Post, Hearst's or Cosmopolitan." [17] Three days later he was offering Kline the three stories in a lump for $650. Kline took him up on it. He started out by publishing "Love," by which time his boss found out about it and Kline lost his job with the *Tribune*, which wanted no such advanced fiction and which not long before had conducted a virulent campaign against pro-Germans. The *Tribune* sent the other two stories back.[18]

Indeed this was a period when the gods, as Dreiser often imagined, seemed to be thrusting him into odd situations and chuckling at his discomfiture. It was no wonder that when he attended a small stag dinner given by Tom R. Smith of *Century* at the Beaux Arts restaurant, he was far from sober. The wonder was that he was gay. He played Swiss music on glasses with his knife, he pulled chairs out from under guests, he proposed toasts to Jehovah and mussed the sleek hair of his table companion, George Jean Nathan.

"So here you are again, by God!" he shouted as Nathan recalled it. "So here you are again. Well, well, well! Look who's here, fellows. It certainly is an awful sight. Yes sir, it certainly is!" And all this, Nathan observed, "to the accompaniment of . . . chuckles of self-satisfaction over his great sardonic humor." [19]

He corresponded with Milton Goldberg, residing at California's San Quen-

* $750 was the best payment he had received from *The Post*.

tin Prison, who wrote that *The Financier* and *The Titan* were the most popular books among inmates. Goldberg astonishingly admitted certain financial irregularities: "I'm guilty, admit it, admit the validity and reasonableness of my punishment. . . ." [20] Freed at last, he came to New York, called with his wife at the Tenth Street studio, got a job with General Motors and would remain for years a friend.

Dreiser, always intrigued by stimuli to the creative, tried several narcotics—ether, heroin, dentist's gas and hasheesh among them—to test the effect on his imagination. One day Lengel walked in to find him sniffing from a bottle of ether. "It does something to me," he said. [21] But he gave up drugs as valueless and unpleasant and returned to his traditional addiction. At a gathering in the spring he met Bettina Morris, a blonde young woman to whom he wrote immediately afterward:

> My, My—What a masterful maid! And a fighter, that's plain. . . . I like your searching blue eyes and above all the snap and force and the yellow hair. . . . I like your mother, too.
> Take tea with me some time. Or go with me to dinner or to a show. Or make some suggestion of your own. I'd like to know you better. [22]

Forceful women who kept their distance could reduce him to erotic frenzy. Miss Morris, who replied politely but remained aloof, did this, and he continued to write her although he did not set eyes on her again for years.

A week later, on May 11, as he was crossing Columbus Circle, he was knocked down by a touring car, one wheel passing over his body. Certain he was fatally hurt, he dimly heard a girl passerby exclaim, "Oh, the poor old man!"—a comment as wounding as his injuries. [23]

He was taken to Roosevelt Hospital, where three stitches closed his scalp; he was treated for shock, two broken ribs, contusions of the left arm, right hand and right side, and sent home next day. He refused to make a charge against the driver.

Evidently he recuperated for a few days at the Lenox Avenue apartment of Estelle Kubitz, where Liveright addressed a consoling note. Mencken wrote:

> I surely hope your beauty is not spoiled by the accident. There is a good lawyer in Essex Street, by name Irving Noblestone. Mention my name. He takes only 50% and expenses. Let me know what the x-ray shows. Don't let them flash it on your seeds. Ten seconds exposure will shrivel them. [24]

Dreiser's lacerated right hand kept him from writing for almost three weeks. His *Twelve Men*, published March 25 and praised by most critics, was not selling well. Early in June, Edith Smith was hospitalized by influenza. Dreiser took her flowers, comforted the terrified Edward Smith and was almost as appalled as he when Edith died a few days later. He postponed for five days a trip he planned to Indiana, evidently so that he could be with Smith.

"I truly don't know how we might have weathered this shock without the aid of a few friends," Smith wrote him, "conspicuously you and one or two others. . . . We buried our poor girl out in Boulder, in the shadow of her mountains." [25]

III. BACK HOME IN INDIANA

On June 15 Dreiser boarded an Indiana-bound Erie train, *solus*, still feeling aches from the accident. He was met at Huntington by May Calvert Baker, who put him up at her home and was utterly charmed by her former pupil. Like so many women, she could not help mothering this big, sad, fate-haunted man. He loved to be mothered even though Mrs. Baker was sure that his melancholy came from his refusal to seek comfort in God. She doted on Billy Sunday, whose mere name made his hackle rise. Worse yet, while she admired Dreiser's writings she felt him wrong in hewing to hurtful realities when he could as easily soar into the inspirational. "That your books are true I never doubted," she had written him, "but we have to see so much of tragedy in real life, why not give us some nice idealistic things to read about." [26]

In short, Mrs. Baker was a grassroots Indiana philistine of the variety he hated and fought. She, multiplied by millions, was the force behind John S. Sumner, the force Dreiser had catered to at Butterick, the force that now made Ray Long, George Horace Lorimer and Tom Smith reject his stories and keep him poor. But while he remained on distant terms with God and Billy Sunday, he still loved Mrs. Baker, never forgetting what she had done for him as a boy.

With her he enjoyed a round of porch-sitting and socializing, a visit to Culver Academy and Lake Maxinkuckee, cake-and-coffee talks with local businessmen. He never failed to draw them out about their history, regarding them as potential characters in future novels. Interviewed by the Huntington Press, he loosed a blast against Wall Street that would have delighted Floyd Dell and made Mencken snicker. He urged government control of utilities, jeered at the "myth" that anyone might rise to be a Rockefeller, and said that the "money class" was so in control that any ordinary man who did original thinking was jailed as a Bolshevik.

"In order for this ordinary man to climb in life," he said, "he must agree with the powers that be or he is ostracized in the business world." [27]

He met J. L. Swihart, a teaching colleague of Mrs. Baker's and a former resident of Warsaw who had read *A Hoosier Holiday* and knew the people named in it. With Mrs. Baker and the Swiharts, Dreiser made the 35-mile trip to Warsaw in the Swihart Interstate Six, filled with the nostalgia of remembered youth. "He was soft-spoken, modest, unassuming, congenial," Swihart recalled, "and . . . seemed to be thoroughly enjoying the simple pleasures of the country and the company." [28] With Mrs. Baker he discussed the fact that no one was selling his books in his native Indiana. She had an idea. Why not assemble a number of sets of Dreiser books from the various publishers, send them to Indiana bookstores and let her spur the sale by visiting the towns in the summer, spreading posters and stirring local interest? He agreed to broach the idea to Liveright, which he later did.

Relaxed though he seemed, the diary he kept showed him to be inwardly tense as usual, worried about his work, money and women. He sent $25 to Miss Kubitz. He received letters from a girl named Muriel. He was exhausted, unable to sleep well, writing, "To bed very tired & have dreadful dreams." [29] At midnight on June 30 the nation would implement the Eighteenth Amendment outlawing liquor—a puritanical step he deplored—but the strait-laced Hoosiers had already voted their own state dry law. In the cellar of a local country club he enjoyed his first scofflaw drink, seeing here his favorite theme, the hypocrisy of American mores, the establishment of rules meant to be broken in secrecy.

After a week in Huntington, he took the interurban car to Indianapolis to meet his 1892 Chicago friend John Maxwell. Maxwell, bald at fifty-five, worked for the *Indianapolis Star* and was preoccupied with two ideas—a hatred for Prohibition and a conviction that Shakespeare was a fraud. He had spent seven years and $10,000 of his own money to prove that the works attributed to the Bard had actually been written by Robert Cecil, first Earl of Salisbury, and was setting forth this contention in an exhaustive book that would run about five volumes.

"I shall knock Shakespere of Stratford off his pedestal in Stratford church just as surely as I sit here. . . ." [30] he had written Dreiser.

Dreiser was fascinated. It was rebellious and unconventional—a stirring application of Dreiser's Law—to unfrock Shakespeare and smite musty scholars. But he also experienced the wonderment and approval he always felt when witnessing enthusiastic creative effort. He was discovering another potential genius. His average was high—Masters, Anderson, Lyon—but with Charles Fort and John Maxwell the flame flickered a trifle. Maxwell sensed a quiet conspiracy against exposing the Shakespeare hoax. "Every trashy book possible to conceive," as he put it, "from thimble brained professors of one kind or another have been published in connection with Shakespeare— greedily grasped at by publishers. Yet when the real, one manuscript appears, letting real light into the situation, it is very likely that they will refuse to publish it." [31]

Dreiser agreed to help combat the conspiracy, and would later work hard in his behalf. Staying at the home of Maxwell's sister, he visited the *Star* office for an interview that might sell a few of his books. Seeing his name in print always delighted him. As was his habit, he secured extra copies of the issue containing the interview and mailed them to his friends. In his diary he recorded the minutiae that obsessed him, writing at intervals:

> I get hat cleaned, buy an umbrella. It rains. Take a taxi . . . 3.00 for 5 miles. . . . Buy a pair of shoes, a razor strop & drink. . . . Go to Claypool [Hotel]. Sit about & study crowd. Get a shave.[32]

With Maxwell he visited a palmist, noting, "She reads my palm. Future looks good. Am to live to be 80." [33] He interested Maxwell in the idea of starting a campaign to move Paul Dresser's body from Chicago to Terre Haute with suitable ceremonies, and through Maxwell's influence he sat for a portrait by a local painter, Simon P. Baus, which later was exhibited at an Indianapolis art store.

But the state of Indiana was cool toward Theodore Dreiser, who had not flattered it in *A Hoosier Holiday*, had attacked the churches and was said to be sinful. People here were enthusiastic about those other Indianians, Gene Stratton Porter (whose *Laddie* had sold almost 1,500,000 copies) and George Barr McCutcheon, Booth Tarkington and Meredith Nicholson. The presence of the author of *Sister Carrie* went almost unnoticed. No literary group urged his appearance before them. No invitation came to visit his home town of Terre Haute. Probably he would not have been interviewed by the *Star* had not Maxwell worked there.

Mrs. Baker felt differently. "I miss you dreadfully," she wrote him, "and to think of you going back to New York without another glimpse of you gives me the horrors. Won't you please come back this way . . . ?" [34]

Dreiser had a magic with women of all ages. But he declined and on July 1 he took a train for Toledo, noting, "The girl who flirts with me until we reach Bellefontaine." His mission was to meet Charles E. Yost, editor of a weekly newspaper at Fayette, west of Toledo. Yost had read all of his books and had written, "God, how I would love to meet you not that I could do you any good but the pleasure of personally knowing a man whose writings I enjoy so much would do me good." [35] At the Yost home he sat almost wordless while his host made much of him. He did admit by inference that Witla of *The "Genius"* was himself, and he told Yost with considerable exaggeration that his copy of that suppressed book was worth more than $100. Having few such all-out admirers, he cherished each one of them and would continue an almost lifelong correspondence with Yost.

En route home, he had a stopover in Toledo, which was already crowded with sports eager to see the July fourth heavyweight fight between 195-pound Jack Dempsey and the 245-pound champion, Jess Willard, both of whom were sparring daily before cash customers. Dreiser's diary, vague here, indicates that he went to see either Willard or Dempsey slug with sparring partners. Was he impressed by the champion or the challenger? Apparently not, for he mentioned neither. What interested him was some hunchbacks he saw, those harbingers of change or good luck. All he wrote was, "Buy ticket. Go out & see the fight Coliseum. The hunch backs. Return. Go to train." [36]

On the train he switched to science, reading Jacques Loeb's *Physiology of the Brain* as he rode back to New York.

9. Helen

I. COMBUSTION AND ANNIHILATION

Let no one shrug at hunchbacks. Change was coming.

Dreiser was then at one of his lowest ebbs. A love affair had gone sour, as they always did. He was angry at Boni & Liveright, calling them "almost worthless" because, he wrote Mencken, "They did nothing with Twelve Men. . . ." [1] The Coburns had finally given up the idea of producing *The Hand of the Potter*—an event he had longed for—so B & L were at last bringing it out as a book. *The "Genius"* was still outlawed and copies were being "booklegged" at $12.50. He was trying to sell two of his original manuscripts—one of them *Jennie Gerhardt*—to raise money.

"Dreiser, I hear, is in a hell of a fix financially," Mencken wrote Boyd. "His 'Twelve Men' has not sold enough to keep him, and he has no other means." [2] Dreiser himself wrote an autobiographical note with more than usual fustian: "The drag and almost despair of a dreary interlude was upon me. At best one feeds so much on husks. Affairs begin and affairs end. . . . My soul was really sick of this malaise that concerns the black lees of once sparkling cups." [3] He was putting together his philosophical essays into a book called *Hey Rub-a-Dub-Dub*, suggesting the meaninglessness of life, and was thinking of giving it to Knopf to publish.

However, fate was preparing for him the most protracted, searing and significant romantic attachment of his life in the person of Oregon-born Mrs. Helen Patges Richardson. Stage-struck, fame-struck Helen Patges had married an actor, Frank Richardson, at sixteen. The couple had gone broke after landing only a few parts in West Coast theatrical productions, and ultimately had separated. Coming to New York, Helen studied stenography and became secretary to William E. Woodward, the handsome Carolinian who was an executive with the Industrial Finance Company on William Street and would later gain some fame as the "debunker" of history. Helen was tall, shapely, sinuous, sensual, with a smiling face framed by a mass of gold-chestnut hair. That anyone with such physical attributes could also be an efficient secretary was astonishing, and Woodward grew very fond of her.

It happened that Helen was Dreiser's second cousin, her grandmother having been a sister of Dreiser's mother. Helen called on Ed Dreiser and his wife Mai and learned that they seldom saw Theodore any more. She read *The "Genius"* and *Twelve Men* and mentioned to her boss that she wanted to meet Dreiser. "If you want to meet him just write him a note and say so," Woodward said. [4]

Woodward himself had been so impressed by Dreiser's writings that he had telephoned him one day and taken him to lunch at the Brevoort. He noticed an air of suspicion about Dreiser as they met. No sooner had they sat down than he asked bluntly, "What do you want?" Not until Woodward had sworn himself free of any ulterior motive had Dreiser relaxed.[5]

In mid-September Helen went to 165 West Tenth without bothering to write. She had heard something in the meantime about Dreiser the moody, the unpredictable. Probably she heard about his "varietism" also, but if so this did not trouble her, for she was not strait-laced herself. Yet she was nervous as she reached the door of the red-brick apartment—with reason, for she was letting herself in for 26 years of what she later described as alternating ecstasy and torment but which the average woman would have likened more simply to hell.

Dreiser, in a terrible mood, had not answered his bell or telephone for days as he grappled with *Hey Rub*. This time he relented. Being in shirtsleeves, he donned a blue Chinese smock. As he recalled it, "I noticed I had slipped on the coat wrong side out—a most drastic and inescapable and invariable sign of change. I had never known it to fail." [6] When he opened the door, the omen was already working.

"Are you Ed's brother?" Helen stammered inanely.

"Yes, I am," he replied.

"Well, I am his cousin."

He laughed. "Well, if that is so, then you are my cousin, too." [7]

Inviting her inside, he was kindliness itself, but he was sending out such powerful Dreiserian waves that Helen reflected with gross understatement, "Something was happening." They talked family. He inscribed a copy of the newly published *Hand of the Potter* to his "little Oregon cousin" and gave it to her. He also gave her a promotional brochure put out by John Lane several years earlier of which he was quite proud, containing sketches of him by Harris Merton Lyon and John Cowper Powys and a poetic description of Dreiser by Edgar Lee Masters beginning:

> *Soul enrapt, demi-urge*
> *Walking the earth,*
> *Stalking life.*
> *Jack o'lantern, tall shouldered,*
> *One eye set higher than the other,*
> *Mouth cut like a scallop in a pie,*
> *Aslant, showing powerful teeth,*
> *Swaying above the heads of others. . . .*[8]

By the time Helen left she was enchanted—overjoyed next morning when he telephoned her at 8 to say, "I haven't slept all night. I must see you." [9] She joined him for breakfast at the Pennsylvania Roof, where he puzzled her by asking if she was religious and charmed her with a quality so many others had noticed—a complete, sympathetic absorption in her as he drew her out about her own career. He insisted on a third meeting at his studio, where he mixed cocktails while she gazed at the peculiar Dreiser art treasures, among them a voluptuous reclining nude and a study of Egyptian dancers composed of triangles. Waldo Frank had thought them ghastly. To Helen they were great art.

They dined at Polly Holliday's, where he pointed out people he knew—Hippolyte Havel, Edward H. Smith and Harry Kemp, whose beautiful wife Mary Pyne was dying of tuberculosis. "Each time I looked around I noticed Edward Smith studying me," [10] Helen recalled. One can imagine Smith's thoughts: Who was this latest flower in Dreiser's interminable daisy chain? If her own account is true, it was not until they returned to his studio that he took her in his arms. He was forty-eight, she twenty-five.

"During the days that followed," she wrote, "we could not endure being apart for more than an hour or two . . . there was a combustion of two forces, with some doubt as to which one was to be annihilated." [11]

William Woodward noticed the effects of this combustion. Formerly punctual and alert, his secretary now appeared at the office late and sleepy-eyed.[12] Indeed, shorthand was not her idea of the good life. She had saved some money. She wanted to go to Hollywood, to become an actress, and Dreiser thought her chances good. Sick of New York, he saw a possibility of selling material to the films, which he had long regarded as the greatest potential art medium—greater than the novel if handled with courage and skill.[13] Early in October they boarded a vessel for New Orleans, probably pooling their resources for the adventure. There was more to the Masters poem about Dreiser, as Helen would eventually learn:

> . . . *Or else a gargoyle of bronze*
> *Turning suddenly to life*
> *And slipping suddenly down corners of stone*
> *To eat you.* . . .

II. INTERSTATE TRAVEL

Dreiser left town quietly, like an escaping criminal, telling almost no one—not even Mencken, who was puzzled about it weeks later. Adding to his natural secretiveness was the fact that several women might think they had claims on him, and Jug might want money. Some of his friends did not know where he had gone for a month or more.

He and Helen spent an incandescent interlude in New Orleans, then went by train to Los Angeles, renting modest quarters in a private home on Alvarado Street. For three years they would live in the Los Angeles area, moving at least six times, with Dreiser keeping his address secret even from his closest friends, collecting his mail at a post-office box, quarreling endlessly with his publishers and getting less than his usual quota of good work done.

Like him, Helen was an emotionalist. Added to her beauty were other attractive qualities: a pleasant contralto singing voice; a naturally sweet nature; a real depth of feeling; an ingenuous reverence for skill in any field, particularly writing; an ambition to succeed as an actress; a practical knowledge gained from knocking around from coast to coast; a native shrewdness in money affairs; and remarkable courage. On the debit side, she was repetitive in conversation and her naïveté sometimes deserved a harsher name. From the start she deferred to Dreiser as a genius.

Regarding himself as a sort of principality of letters, Dreiser had a group of literary ambassadors on whom he would depend to run his errands in the East—Lengel, Mencken and Ed Smith among them. In New York, Gloom had an appendectomy and he paid the bill, poor as he was.

Liveright was still conferring with Jones in an effort to take over the Dreiser books under the Lane imprint. Jones argued that Dreiser owed Lane $2,143.06 and that the *"Genius"* contract stipulated that Lane should get Dreiser's next novel, *The Bulwark*. Dreiser's stand was that Lane had broken the contract in withdrawing *The "Genius."* "Jones—the snake—claims a contract when none exists. . . ." he wrote Mencken in understandable anger. "At the same time he has 500 copies of The 'Genius' which I can sell out here for $10.00 each which would yield him $5000 and pay of [*sic*] my indebtedness three times over & he won't release & won't do a damn thing." [14] Joseph Auerbach talked with Jones in Dreiser's behalf, but *The "Genius"* was still under lock and key and Dreiser wrote, "The 'Genius' case so far has cost me personally over $2,000." [15]

Liveright was certain Lane had forfeited all rights to *The Bulwark*. He was panting for it himself, urging Dreiser to finish it, confident it would be a huge success. Knowing the novelist's money worries, he made a gesture of sweeping confidence and generosity for the time. He arranged to pay Dreiser a $4,000 advance—$333.33 a month for 12 months—to keep him going while he wrote.[16]

For Dreiser it was the first feeling of security he had known for years. Yet he was angry over Liveright's alleged failure to push *Free, Twelve Men* (which had sold less than 4,000 copies) and *Potter* (989 copies). He was trying to land one or more of his works in the films. He was finishing the second volume of his autobiography, *A Book About Myself*. He was starting a dramatization of *The "Genius"* for Leo Ditrichstein. And he was outlining a batch of stories about women in his life—Edith De Long Smith ("Olive Brand") and Mary Pyne ("Esther Norn") among them—which would appear much later as *A Gallery of Women*. "God, what a work! if I could do it truly," he had written Mencken, "[the] ghosts of Puritans would rise and gibber in the streets." [17] He did little with *The Bulwark*, and he replied peevishly to Liveright's entreaties that he get at it.

"If you would have just a little more confidence in me," Liveright wrote, "you would save your soul a lot of bitterness and make it much more fun for me to continue to put my best efforts (poor as I know they are) into your books." [18]

Like an old refrain came news of further Sumner activities in New York. He had seized *Madeleine*, a dreary story of a prostitute, and arrested Clinton C. Brainard, president of Harper's, who had published it. He had seized James Branch Cabell's *Jurgen*, which had been widely praised, saying, "If the language of the book is lewd, or if it is suggestive of lewdness, it is a violation of the law, regardless of the literary or artistic character of the published matter." [19]

To Barrett H. Clark in New York Dreiser sent a signed protest, blasted the Authors' League for taking no action and offered $50 toward a defense fund for Cabell. "Every little 10th rate squeak of a minister or white slaver can now pass on France, Freud, Andreyolff [*sic*], Chestov [*sic*] and who not else," he wrote Clark. ". . . These cattle must be debarred from indicting the characters & morals of their betters." [20]

To add to his gloom, *Hey Rub-a-Dub-Dub* was disparaged when it was published in March. "It is receiving the rottenest sort of reviews," Liveright wrote. ". . . The cheap brainless critics simply won't see you as a philosopher." [21] The critics were not alone, for dialectics was not Dreiser's forte. "This book is not Dreiser at his happiest. . . ." [22] Edward Smith wrote him candidly. "I could have done the book much better myself," Mencken wrote, "whereas I couldn't have done a single chapter of 'Twelve Men' or 'Sister Carrie.' " [23]

Dreiser refused to give anyone his address, even Mencken. "P. O. Box 181 is all you get," he wrote Mencken. To Boyd, Mencken wrote, "Dreiser is in Los Angeles. What he is doing there I don't know. . . . I have heard that he is being kept by some rich wench." [24] To Burton Rascoe he wrote: "[Dreiser and I] remained on good terms so long as I was palpably his inferior—a mere beater of drums for him. But when I began to work out notions of my own it quickly appeared that we were much unlike. Dreiser is a great artist, but a very ignorant and credulous man. He believes, for example, in the Ouija board. My skepticism, and, above all, my contempt for the peasant, eventually offended him. We are still, of course, very friendly, but his heavy sentimentality and his naïve yearning to be a martyr make it impossible for me to take him seriously—that is, as man. As artist, I believe that he has gone backward— but he is still a great man. Think of 'Twelve Men.' " [25]

And Dreiser knew who the sender was when he received a letter from "Garfunkel, Fishbein, Spritzwasser & Garfunkel," a strictly mythical firm of lawyers:

> Dear sir: We are advised by a mutual friend who asks that his name be withheld that you would be interested in the pamphlet "How to circumvent the Mann Law" prepared by our Mr. Spritzwasser. . . . We can recommend it most highly to those who have affectionate natures and whose occupation requires them to do traveling of an interstate nature. . . .[26]

Indeed, Dreiser was a violator of the Mann Act as he had often been. He and Helen enjoyed a romantic idyll as Helen sought roles at the studios. She noticed his inordinate interest in a 15-year-old neighbor girl and reflected, "I began to realize how very susceptible he was to a certain mood in the opposite sex, and for the first time felt a slight foreboding. . . ." [27] Yet as he and Helen stood on a hill and watched Japanese farm laborers sing as they worked, he was so moved by the beauty of the scene that tears came and he suddenly cried, "I shall never leave you, Helen! Never!" [28]

Such emotional avowals had to be taken with reservations. Women he met casually at restaurants or gatherings were surprised to get notes from him with comments on their charms accompanying a request for an early interview. Various manuscript libraries contain proof that Dreiser, even while facing writing deadlines, could write dozens of letters totaling many thousands of words in an effort to win over one woman. He was always entangled in intrigue and deceit. While he sometimes admitted that his libido was a burden, he more often felt that sex was the most rewarding of experiences, "the quintessense [sic] of beauty," and linked it with courage and adventure. "The coward sips little of life," he wrote; "the strong man drinks deep." [29]

"I doubt that I have ever been in love with anyone, or with anything save life as a whole," he observed, probably without realizing his self-revelation. "Twice or thrice I have developed stirring passions but always there was a voice or thought within which seemed to say over and over, like a bell at sea: 'What does it matter? Beauty is eternal. . . . Beauty will come again!' But this thing, *life* . . . that did matter!" [30] Thus the woman in his arms was a passing symbol of beauty who did not matter, since it was not she he loved but life—i. e., his own temporary enjoyment of her, his freedom to cast her off and enjoy the next.

Meanwhile he was writing Bettina Morris, the yellow-haired girl he had met but once in New York:

> That night I saw you in your home I felt a chemic flare which was delicious. . . . I had the feeling that you were a big, forceful, dynamic girl—one who would fit in to much of my work & my efforts in general,— that you really needed to join in with someone like myself—maybe not. We might have quarreled & disagreed horribly at every turn, but a conversation or two then might have cleared up much. Now you seem much more tentative & dubious. Great occasions are neither made nor taken that way. . . . It may win the approval of the M. E. Conference & the D. A. R.—but what more. . . .[31]

Liveright pleaded that he hurry with *The Bulwark*, planned for fall publication. "I do wish that you could get it out of your mind that we have been asleep at the switch on FREE, TWELVE MEN, HEY RUB-A-DUB-DUB," he wrote, maintaining that Dreiser was known as a novelist and anything else by him was not well received.[32] Fall publication proving impossible, he later wrote,

"Hurrah! You have put new life into me. When you say that you will do your very best to give me The Bulwark before Christmas, I feel that the trick is turned. . . ." [33]

At Dreiser's urging Liveright was doing what he could with Maxwell's enormous manuscript about Shakespeare. A Columbia expert found it interesting but unconvincing, and Liveright saw no possibility of publishing a five-volume tome that would sell only some 300 copies. Women occasionally came into the Liveright office—Jug among them—to inquire about Dreiser. When he learned of this he sent a hot letter insisting that *no* information be given about him or his whereabouts. "From now on," Liveright assured him, "I shall refuse to mention Dreiser except to Chinamen, truckdrivers and zoo-attendants." Dreiser sent another warning, to which Liveright replied, "There seems nothing further for me to say. I once more assure you that I'm through discussing you with anybody except in so far as it will result in publicity for your work." [34]

Dreiser, who had suffered at the hands of several publishers, seemed to take revenge on the one who was genuinely interested in him and was giving him a $4,000 advance. So wary was he now that he had refused to give Liveright the usual publisher's contract and had given him merely a five-year lease to publish *Free, Potter, Twelve Men* and *Hey Rub*. He felt that Liveright was more interested in money than art, that he had failed to promote those four books, and had failed to take over the titles owned by Lane. "Quietly and under cover," he wrote Mencken, "I am negotiating a return to Harper & Brothers." [35]

III. BRILLIANT MEN AND WOMEN

"The other day a dog peed on me," Mencken wrote. "A bad sign." [36] Possibly Dreiser recognized this as a subtle reference to his own weakness for omens. He recalled Mencken's custom, after a beerfest, of taking friends to Poe's grave and urinating on it as a mark of respect. "A spirit message informs me," he replied, "that the dog who so offended you now houses the migrated soul of Edgar Allan Poe, who thus retaliates." [37]

Mencken alternately angered and charmed him. In July the Baltimorean had gone to San Francisco for the Democratic National Convention and they had talked of getting together either there or in Los Angeles, but had failed. Yet in mid-October, on the invitation of Paul Elder, a San Francisco bookseller who proposed a reception in his honor, Dreiser and Helen made the trip north. He was glad to get away from a Los Angeles woman who had been pestering him. And he wanted to see George Sterling, whom he had met briefly in New York and whose *Lilith* he admired. Sterling, as impressed by him, had probably suggested the Elder reception. Sterling was a Western pioneer in the fight against puritanism, living in poverty because he wrote honestly. For such a man Dreiser would do anything—anything but make a speech. To George Douglas, literary editor of the *San Francisco Bulletin* who asked Dreiser to speak at the reception, he wrote: "I . . . would be delighted to hear you speak against the Puritans anywhere . . ." but insisted, "I am no speaker . . ." and "I am chronically reticent and hesitant about such affairs. . . ."[38]

"The lion refused to be lionized," Douglas later wrote about the reception, "for the truth is that he is the most modest lion that was ever dragged out of his literary cage. The man of boldest writing is the most diffident of speech."[39]

Shy at first, Dreiser relaxed after the Elder formalities were over and mingled pleasantly with the guests. "Yes, women seem to like Dreiser," Douglas noted, "and, needless to say, he likes them." In San Francisco he had more fun than he had had in years. To Bettina Morris he had written that although he seldom mixed with society, "When I do I want only brilliant men—or women—or both & they are not so terribly numerous."[40] He found them here. The classic-featured Sterling was gay and charming. For curly-haired, Australian-born George Douglas, Dreiser took an instant liking. With Helen he visited the studio of Douglas' friend Henry von Sabern, the German-born sculptor, whose wife fondled an eight-foot pet snake named Alice. In Los Angeles Dreiser had been abstemious, but one did not travel dry with Sterling and he later admitted, "Nightly I was led to my room full to the ears."[41]

Lecturing in San Francisco at the time was his friend John Cowper Powys, the gentle mystic, and with him his younger brother Llewelyn. Both of these members of the gifted Powys family were rebels against their strait-laced clergyman father. The beautiful, indomitable Llewelyn, for years a consumptive, was having trouble subsisting by writing. Dreiser, generous to the point of self-sacrifice in helping fellow realists, was urging Liveright to publish Llewelyn.

When Helen came down with a stomach ailment, George Sterling insisted that she must see his friend Dr. Albert Abrams, who was actually one of the most ingenious quacks of the century. Abrams diagnosed all ills by taking a blood sample and examining it. He had recently invented his "oscilloclast," a mysterious-looking wired box replete with dials which could be set to emit different electrical waves to treat and cure any ailment. Llewelyn, suffering from paroxysms of coughing, had gone to Abrams on Sterling's advice, got no relief and suspected the doctor. Dreiser, always boyishly fascinated by new discoveries, went with Helen to Abrams and underwent examinations. The suave doctor told Dreiser he had tuberculosis, while Helen suffered from sarcoma—nothing to worry about, Abrams assured them, thanks to the oscilloclast. Each sat in front of the machine, absorbing its vibrations, and felt better. Dr. Abrams, not one to keep such a curative from the world, had manufactured oscilloclasts in quantity and was leasing them out to other physicians in the West. When Dreiser and Helen returned to Los Angeles they took a course of treatment from the oscilloclast man there and noticed continued improvement.

They had moved from Alvarado Street to Highland Park, then to Larchmont Boulevard in Hollywood. Although Helen's mystery was wearing thin, she had one most endearing quality: reverence for his genius. Starting as an extra at $7.50 a day, Helen now found minor film roles at $20 a day and was studying dancing and voice on the side, eager for stardom. To Bettina Morris, Dreiser wrote:

> If I could I would blow out of your mind every trace of religious & moralic cant & faith. . . . I would have you give yourself to happiness in your youth—so that in the latter days you could not complain. Those who have been happy do not. Look up sometimes the true meaning of the old biblical quotation "Remember thy creator in the days of thy youth." That word *creator* does not refer to God. That is a horrible, slavish Christian perversion. It refers to the male organ—once worshipped as a symbol of the creator. And it is certainly is [*sic*] as good as any other symbol. If you ever came to me it would have to be because you very much wanted to. . . . I could neither love nor live with anyone who was not a happy pagan. The days of social lies for me is dead. . . . When love is dead it is dead. . . . Each one must save himself whole as best he can. . . . Moralic cant & religious theory kill life. They are cancers, horrible growths that should be cut out before they kill life itself. . . .
> You are beautiful & full of a fine physical & mental strength & lust. Don't waste the next ten years. If ever we meet & you are very much drawn to me don't temporize. The years slip by so quickly. . . .[42]

From Paul de Kruif, a young bacteriologist at Rockefeller Institute, came a request for advice. He wanted to become a writer—so badly that sometimes "I have a violent desire to assassinate all of my monkeys, guinea pigs and other inferior fauna. . . ." [43] Could Dreiser, one of the few writers whose works he respected, talk to him?

Dreiser replied encouragingly. Sometime later De Kruif quit science, visited California and talked with him—not at his home, for Dreiser would never disclose his address. De Kruif had an idea for a novel about science based in part on the character of his former colleague, Dr. Jacques Loeb, and evidently wanted Dreiser to collaborate with him on it. Dreiser, already too busy, turned down the idea [44]—a decision he later regretted, for Sinclair Lewis, with De Kruif's help, would turn it into *Arrowsmith*.

"We simply must not let Sinclair Lewis, Floyd Dell, Sherwood Anderson, etc. do all the writing of 'the great American novel,'" Liveright wrote.[45]

With his books still scattered among four American publishers and several in England, and The *"Genius"* still dead in the Lane vault, Dreiser was working hard to straighten out the confusion he felt that Liveright had only compounded. He was dickering with Harper's and Century, as he soon would with Scribners, hoping to find a publisher who would take him over in toto and *sell* his books. In this he was not fair to Liveright, who was paying him $4,000 on his promise to send *The Bulwark*. He wrote Mencken, "I am and have been conducting an individual struggle to live and write and I will continue to do so as my best wits help me and not otherwise." [46] He had long since finished *A Book About Myself*, keeping it secret from Liveright, sending one script to Gloom and another to Lengel, who was trying to sell portions of it for magazine publication.

In New York these secrets did not keep. Liveright discovered that Dreiser was (1) looking for another publisher and (2) having Lengel show *A Book About Myself* to the magazines without letting Liveright see it. He wrote Dreiser in protest, pointing out, "I have published everything you brought to me without any sort of qualifications; even 'The Hand of the Potter' " and saying, "Your last few letters to me show me that you have no feeling of regard or loyalty for me, personally so our affairs must be regarded in the strict light of business proceedings." [47]

Who had told Liveright? Dreiser thought Tom Smith of *Century* may have leaked the news of his dickerings with that company—a suggestion Liveright denied. Dreiser wrote Lengel accusing him of telling Liveright about *A Book About Myself*—a charge that made the loyal Lengel explode in indignation:

> What a jolly lot of friends you must have, if you think they are waiting for a nice, sweet opportunity to stick you in the back! You ought to know very well that I haven't shown Liveright "A Novel About Myself," nor have I talked with him about it . . . and here you openly accuse me of doing that very thing. That is just about as rotten and insulting as anything that has ever come my way, and I was both hurt and surprised that it should have come from you. [48]

Dreiser apologized. Meanwhile Helen had bought a used Overland and was made so distraught by Dreiser's nervous shouts of warning as he rode beside her that she let him know firmly that he must keep quiet. Later they had their first real quarrel, his mien reminding her of "a flash of lightning and a peal of thunder" before he "rushed out of the house, slamming the door so hard I thought it would break." [49] He came back. No one could say she was a puritan, anyway, and he was proud of her beauty. Llewelyn Powys wrote ungrammatically:

> I have hardly yet recovered from the shock of seeing your lady how ir-resistable [*sic*], how perfectly charming, how divine, how lovely, God! what a rascal you are to have discovered anybody so wonderful. . . . [50]

When Fort's *Book of the Damned* came out, Dreiser and Mencken had an epistolary quarrel about it. "Is it that Fort seriously maintains that there is an Upper Saragossa Sea somewhere in the air," Mencken inquired, "and that all of the meteors, blood, frogs and other things he lists dropped out of it? . . . He seems to be enormously ignorant of elementary science, particularly biology." [51] Dreiser replied:

I consider Fort one of the most fascinating personalities I have ever known. He is a great thinker and a man of a deep and cynical humor. To dub him enormously ignorant of anything is to use an easy phrase without correct information[.] Fort is not enormously ignorant of anything. He is so far above any literary craftsman now working in this country—your own excellent self excluded—that measurements are futile. . . . to me no one else in the world—so far—has suggested the underlying depths & mysteries and possibilities as has Fort. To me he is simply stupendous & some day I really believe he will get full credit. . . .[52]

IV. SHRINERS AND ELKS

Dreiser's war against the puritans and his defense of the brave non-comformist was constant. He continued his efforts to get Ben Huebsch, Mencken and others interested in Maxwell's overweight assault on Shakespeare. He praised Dell's *Moon-Calf*. He was cautious in criticizing Sherwood Anderson's new *Poor White*, which he thought unsuccessful.

"There is much of repetition & what I consider weak deduction," he wrote Huebsch, who published it. "But for heaven sake dont show Anderson this letter—for after all he is a realist—and working in the right direction and I don't want to discourage any realist anywhere or at any time. . . ." [53]

Although he saw no chink in the solid wall of American philistinism, he took every opportunity to chisel at it. He sacrificed his own time to propagandize revolt. To Charles Boni, Jr. of the *New York Globe*, who wrote to ask if he did not see postwar signs of intellectual freedom, he sent a loud Bronx cheer, hoping that it would be published. Yes, there were a few free souls but they were rare birds.

The vast majority—and this goes for the female as well as the male—are interested in but one or two things & chiefly one, for the second follows upon the first,—getting into business where he will be able to make money quick, ("sting" the other fellow) and, having made a little, lording it over the people in his vicinity. He yearns to build a stuffy home wherein, soon, he can intellectually lie down and take the count, spending his days thereafter in riding around in a Ford . . . and joining, if they will have him, the Rotarians, the Shriners, the Elks or the Odd-fellows, and then wandering off by the trainload to conventions, picnics, re-unions and what not else and there parading in standardized uniforms. . . .

He still forms, daily, outside some fourth rate moving picture palace block-long queues wherein he waits patiently, for hours, if need be, in order to be permitted to see Blossom Springtime or Cerise Fudge illustrate, or so he thinks, the honor, virtue, heroism, self-sacrifice, charity, etc., of American manhood and womanhood. His real, yet self denied purpose, is to view Cerise and as many of her ilk as may be, in a state of smirking nudity, dreaming the while of some happier realm in which a closer contact may be possible. Yet he is only happy when, for the billionth time, at the end, he has seen that no one has had the courage to do the thing that he would like to do or, at worst, see done. Yea, all the good people, which same includes Cerise, must come off pure and uninjured, if a little naked. . . .

In sum, in the eyes of the American old or young, the salvation of the world lies in more business and more dogmatic religion, the twain mingling so ideally. He can believe that, too. All he has to do, after robbing his neighbor, is to trust in God and avoid exact knowledge of the facts about life. The less he knows about life and the more he knows about God and the hereafter, the better. God is on His throne. In God we trust,—after having put aside a stiff bank account and closed the libraries.[54]

M. Charles Cestre, professor of American literature at the Sorbonne, drew a Dreiser shaft when he compiled a representative list of American authors. Dreiser was on the list, all right, as were James, Twain, Norris and Edith Wharton. But to Ernest Boyd, now back in the United States as an editorialist with the *New York Post*, he wrote urging that he pour scorn not so much on the list as on the culture it represented. For along with the great names were listed Zane Grey, Harold Bell Wright and Eleanor H. Porter.

This was fine, said Dreiser. It was so true. But why had Laura Jean Libbey and Bertha M. Clay been forgotten? They were what America stood for. "Let America be properly represented," he wrote Boyd, "by that which is honestly democratic. . . . The French and every other nation should certainly know us as we are,—at our best, as it were." [55]

For the much-arrested Margaret Sanger—another victim of philistinism—he wrote, gratis, a piece that appeared in her *Birth Control Review*. He wondered at the need to champion a movement so obviously beneficial. Pointing out that fish lay thousands of eggs that were gobbled up by other fish, he noted that nature's creatures had fewer and fewer offspring as they rose in intelligence. He attacked the moral and religious enmity toward birth control, writing, "It is exact knowledge that [man] needs. And as I see it contraceptal means are not only exact but most beneficial economically and so socially of course. The individual should be better cared for at every turn if he is to do better, and where better to begin with him and his proper care than at the source—by regulating the number of him to as many as can be intelligently cared for." [56]

And to a group in Newark which was unveiling a bronze plaque to Stephen Crane, he expressed the hope that it would inspire others to be fearless in their interpretation of life: "If so, our American vice societies and their associate dullards can be safely trusted to do the rest, i. e. make his life a burden and his name anathema." [57]

V. SEDUCTION AND MURDER

Largely because of Helen's earnings and shrewdness, she and Dreiser were not really poor. She secured supporting roles in such pictures as *The Flame of Youth* and—most exciting—Valentino's first film, *The Four Horse-*

men of the Apocalypse. She speculated, buying several lots in the Montrose section and selling them at a profit of $1,000 each—a coup that staggered Dreiser. After living for a time in a rented bungalow on Sunset Boulevard in Hollywood, they bought a corset-tight cottage in Glendale for $4,500, paying $1,000 down. They turned in their old Overland for a new Maxwell. It was a year before they could afford to buy furniture for their barren living room, where they had no guests anyway.

"I noticed in Dreiser a definite poverty complex . . ." Helen wrote, "he believed that money would never come to him in a big way." [58]

Early in 1921 Liveright offered him a $1,000 advance on *A Book About Myself* despite his earlier $4,000 advance on the still unfinished *Bulwark.* Although he wired Dreiser that *Myself* was "COMPARABLE ONLY WITH THE GREATEST WORK OF THE GREATEST MASTERS," [59] he was really disappointed. The public wanted a Dreiser novel, and he was biting his nails as he played his temperamental author along in the hope of getting it. Dreiser, however, was not yet ready to give *Myself* to Liveright. Ambassador Lengel, who praised the substance of the book but found the writing "not only careless, but extremely slovenly" and full of errors, was trying to sell excerpts from it for magazine publication, getting rejections from *Metropolitan, Century, The Saturday Evening Post* and *The Atlantic.* Dreiser was stymied on *The Bulwark* and needed whatever financial help he could get.

Liveright must have torn his hair when he learned that Dreiser was putting aside *The Bulwark* after eight years of sporadic work on it. He would have been less exercised had he known that Dreiser's new novel would eventually emerge as *An American Tragedy,* a book which would bring fame and profit to them both.

For years Dreiser had been fascinated by a kind of murder that regularly made headlines in American newspapers. It was a crime in which the killer was motivated less by hatred than by the passion to rise in society and thus, as Dreiser saw it, was a recurrent and bloody indictment of the nation's false standards. Illicit sex was always involved. In 1914 he had considered and rejected the Molineux case. Since then he had looked into a dozen others, among them the following:

In 1891 in New York, a young medical student named Carlyle Harris became involved with Helen Potts, then realized that she was a threat to his dream of attaining the social status of a prosperous physician. His rich grandfather, who was sending him through medical school, would cut him off if he learned about Helen Potts. Harris, trying to safeguard his dream, murdered her with poison.

In 1906, Chester Gillette, a poor-relation straw boss in his wealthy uncle's skirt factory in Cortland, N. Y., seduced a pretty millhand, Grace Brown. He then became enamored of the daughter of a wealthy Cortlandian, who encouraged his suit and his dream of rising through marriage to the town's upper set. The pregnant Grace now represented a menace to his social ascent. So Chester escorted Grace to Big Moose Lake in the Adirondacks, pretending that he would marry her. Instead, he took her boating, stunned her with a tennis racket, overturned the boat and swam to shore while she drowned.

In 1911, handsome Rev. Clarence Richeson of the struggling Baptist church in Hyannis, Massachusetts, seduced a young parishioner, Avis Linnell. His love for the country girl waned when he was called to a fashionable church in Cambridge, where he was soon involved with a local woman of impressive family and financial standing. Richeson, born poor and hungering for wealth and position, had to do something about the pregnant Avis Linnell. He eliminated her with potassium cyanide.

All three killers were executed. Yet to Dreiser, none was murderous by nature and was driven to homicide only by ignorance and an inability to withstand the pressures of the shallow American yearning for money, success, fashion—dreams about which Dreiser himself was indeed an authority. The fault lay less with the murderers than with a society that worshiped such preposterous values, refused admittance to all but a few and had such a morbid fear of sex.

At first leaning toward the Richeson-Linnell case, he wrote six chapters based on it before he switched to the Gillette-Brown case.[60] This scandalous affair had so convulsed the nation that the New York newspapers had sent correspondents to cover it in 1906 and 1907 and the wire services had spread it all over the country. Dreiser had read about it while he was editing *Broadway*, had cut clippings of the exhaustive court testimony and had discussed it with Richard Duffy as a possible basis for a novel. Probably he had saved the clippings as he saved everything. He must have begun writing it in California by the summer or fall of 1920, for in December, with excessive optimism, he wrote Liveright about the new novel "which I hope to have done by spring." [61] He kept quiet about its theme, working daily at a breakfast-nook table and characteristically interlacing it with other projects—poems, the *"Genius"* play adaptation, sketches of New York, efforts to sell *Jennie Gerhardt* as a play, and his intimate portraits of women.

He was growing bored with Los Angeles, which he called "the city of folded hands." Much as he needed Helen's income, he was jealous of her mingling with lordly directors and suave actors. From the New York law firm of Garfunkel, Fishbein, Spritzwasser & Garfunkel came a reminder of his own vulnerability:

> Dear Sir:—We have been instructed by our client, Miss Adelaide Lewin, at present of 172 west 13th street, New York, to enter suit against you in the sum of ten thousand dollars ($10,000) for assault and personal injuries. In view of your public position and the unpleasant scandal that might accompany a public trial of this issue, it occurs to us that you may desire to settle the case privately. . . .
>
> Miss Lewin complains that her letters to you regarding her hospital bill and the care of her child . . . have gone unanswered. . . . She contends that your access to her person was gained by force and fraud. . . .[62]

10. Going to Seed

I. A CONFUSION OF PUBLISHERS

Early in 1921, Dreiser urged Mencken to advance him for the "Noble" prize, calling it "a nice piece of change" and offering a bribe. "Start the ball," he wrote, "and if I snake the forty thousand—isn't that what the lucky mutt is supposed to draw?—you get five thousand. . . . One thousand on the side for George [Nathan], if he will privily aid and abet the idea." [1]

Though his tone was jocular, he was evidently serious. Mencken gave him the correct spelling of Nobel, pointed out that a candidate should be of unsullied character, but said he would try. [2] He seems to have made no effort at all, although Dreiser reminded him on February first, "Please forward the Nobel prize at your earliest convenience," and returned to the subject again on February 28.

Mencken thought he was slipping. Was there a tinge of disapproval in the Baltimorean's fun? "Every tourist coming back from the Coast," he wrote, "has some tale about your Roman levities. Yesterday I heard that you have gone over to the Theosophists, and are living at Point Loma in a yellow robe, with hasheesh blossoms in your hair and two fat cuties to fan you. My congratulations." [3]

Dreiser *was* slipping in a sense, thanks to the Comstocks, his own money and publishing problems and the joys of touring in a Maxwell. For the first time in years he was anxious to sell money-making magazine articles. William Lengel had recently become managing editor of *Hearst's International*, and Dreiser fairly peppered him with article ideas. He made a $400 sale of an article, "Hollywood Now," to Burton Rascoe, now with *McCall's*, Rascoe wiring that it was "much too long" and he would cut it. For the unprestigious film magazine *Shadowland* he wrote a disorganized four-part piece based largely on Helen's accounts, "Hollywood, Its Morals and Manners," assailing the commercialism of the industry. [4] At last, after much effort, Lengel sold five episodes from *A Book About Myself* to *Bookman* for a helpful $500. Ambassadors Lengel and Mencken were still trying to sell other portions of the book elsewhere.

Although on March 31 Dreiser wired Liveright, "DEVOTING ENTIRE TIME TO NOVEL NOT THE BULWARK WHICH SHOULD BE DONE BEFORE AUGUST FIRST," certainly referring to *An American Tragedy*, he seems actually to have been engaged in scattergun work on diverse projects including several movie scenarios.

Helen contended with the problem of living with him. Like him, she gave

no one her address, avoiding studio social life. Yet she was hurt by his
infidelities, ambitious for more important roles, not immune to flattery. In
Hollywood, where an aspiring actress was expected to mingle socially with
film people, she caused puzzlement by her withdrawal. At length she did
attend a party given by a director, a gay affair with music and dancing from
which she returned at 5 A.M. to find Dreiser waiting in a rage.

"He was beside himself," she wrote, "and threatened to teach me a lesson,
which he did by leaving the house and remaining away for two days. That,
for me, was the end of any such experiment in social life. . . ." [5]

With Helen driving, they went on a series of motor trips—to Santa Barbara,
Yosemite, Mexico and, in the spring of 1921, to Portland to visit with Helen's
family. Helen, inordinately proud of him, showed him off to her mother and
sister Myrtle, who found him charming. Then Helen and Dreiser drove on to
Seattle and Vancouver before returning home, Dreiser fascinated as always
by scenery, towns, people. That summer, his building at 165 West Tenth in
New York was sold, requiring him to move his belongings into storage. He
always found helpers for such tiresome chores. One enthusiastic Dreiser
reader in New York, James Ettinge, had corresponded with him, often
inquiring if there was anything he could do for him.

"Ah, ha!" Dreiser wrote him. "Sometimes a man will put his head directly
in the trap. Excellent." [6] Ettinge became a Dreiser ambassador, supervising the
removal of the piano-desk, phonograph, dozens of letter-files and scrapbooks
(there were three files on *The "Genius"* alone), a photograph of Kirah
Markham, 17 paintings framed and unframed, and such oddments as a bronze
statuette of a condor on a peak, a silver mazuza and "1 small porcelain
Hoti—Chinese god of Pleasure."

Dreiser's sinister reputation made news in Milwaukee, where another of his
admirers was beefy, jovial Robert L. Moody, the wealthy president of a
large foundry concern. Moody, a married man with a small son, had taken
enough interest in a seventeen-year-old girl named Hildegarde Wells to subsidize her musical education. When her uncle and guardian found her in a
Chicago apartment paid for by Moody, he scented motives other than
educational and brought charges against the industrialist.

He complained that Moody had presented the girl with copies of *Sister
Carrie* and *Jennie Gerhardt*—prima facie evidence, as he saw it, of evil
intentions. In a Milwaukee courtroom *Carrie* and *Jennie* were produced as
proof of Moody's depravity. [7] To Dreiser Moody wrote, "It is a wholesale
attempt at blackmail. . . ." [8] He was so enraged at this libel on his favorite
author (and so eager for evidence in his own favor) that he wrote to Mencken
and many other editors and critics in America and Europe asking their
opinion of Dreiser's literary standing. In odd contrast with his sponsorship
of a professional baseball team and his interest in prizefighting and bowling,
Moody was Milwaukee's foremost Dreiserian, even subscribing to a clipping

bureau to keep abreast of the news about Dreiser. The case against him was dismissed, but he would remain a colorful Dreiser friend for years.

Liveright, with an air of desperation, was still trying to get a book out of Dreiser. "If I can't sell twenty-thousand copies of your next novel," he wrote, "I am willing to quit the publishing game." [9] There was no next novel. *An American Tragedy,* which Dreiser had expected to finish first by spring and then by August, was hardly more than begun. Not only that: he still refused to sign a contract allowing Liveright to publish the completed *Book About Myself.* He was dickering with several houses in an effort to unsnarl his publishing muddle and to achieve the end that had become an obsession—a collected edition of Dreiser books, uniformly bound, published and promoted by one publisher.

Against this lay an almost insuperable obstacle that must have kept him awake nights.

The rights to various Dreiser books were still owned by four publishers. Any one of them publishing a complete set would have to pay royalties to three others, a prospect none of them would consider. Dreiser saw only one solution: He must buy back the rights and plates for all his books—as he had long since done with *Carrie*—and then settle on one publisher on a lease basis, as he had done with his books under the Liveright imprint. On this basis he would have something close to personal control of his own works.

"Then they can all kiss my royal standard. . . ." he wrote Mencken.[10]

But where would he find the time and money for such an enterprise? His books were distributed as follows:

Harper's	Century	John Lane	B & L
Jennie Gerhardt	*A Traveler at*	*The Titan*	*Free*
The Financier	*Forty*	*A Hoosier Holiday*	*Twelve Men*
		The Plays	*The Hand of the*
		The "Genius"	*Potter*
			Hey Rub-a-Dub-
			Dub

In addition, Dreiser owned *Carrie* free and clear and had the two completed but unpublished autobiographical books, *Dawn* and *A Book About Myself*— fourteen books all told.

He was so irate against the John Lane Company that through Arthur Carter Hume, his New York attorney, he had brought suit against Lane for $20,000, alleging breach of contract. If he settled on Liveright he had seven books to buy out from three different publishers. But he was far from happy with Liveright either, and in addition Liveright owned only five-year publishing rights to his four books, all of them growing closer to expiration. So the field was wide open. Dreiser began by trying to shake loose *Jennie* and

The Financier from Harper, writing William H. Briggs of that firm that "Harper's owe me a decent turn" in view of their abandonment of *The Titan* in 1914.[11] Briggs did not see it that way. Meanwhile, Mencken feared that Dreiser was going to seed, devoting too much time to play.

"How long are you going to stay out there among those swamis, actors, tourists, and whores?" he demanded. He wrote indelicately of the possible effect of senility on Dreiser's penchant for affairs. He added, however, that while in San Francisco for the convention he had heard much gossip about Dreiser's amatory prowess, and warned him against such excesses at his age.[12]

Dreiser's reply to the Hollins Street sage was addressed to Henry Hollins Baltimore, Esq:

> Dear Mr. Baltimore: Your kindly, if excessive, interest in my private parts moves me greatly. Let me explain. At the age of thirty a prediction, almost identical with yours, i.e. that unless I controlled my then excessive veneries I would find myself impotent at forty, carried me most safely and comfortingly to that prescribed age. At forty another well-wisher volunteered that unless I controlled my then excessive veneries I would most certainly find myself impotent at fifty. At fifty, God bless you, dear Mr. Baltimore, you arrived—a most comforting omen. I feel sure now, dear Mr. Baltimore, that I shall come safely through to sixty, anyhow. . . .[13]

And in reply to a reader, Robert James Ullman, who asked why his books were so filled with grammatical lapses, Dreiser in part blamed his editors, who he thought should have corrected them. But he made an admission few other writers would have made:

> In regard to grammer [*sic*] and syntax I write as some people play—by ear. Grammer was ever a mystery to me and I never mastered its rules. . . .[14]

II. THE GORILLA AND THE LAMB

In New York, Ambassador Edward H. Smith had long tried to get *The Hand of the Potter* produced, simply out of loyalty. On December 5, 1921, George Cram Cook's rebellious amateurs finally mounted it with a cast of 27 at the Provincetown Theater on MacDougal Street. It was a flop. Abraham Cahan and Dorothy Dudley Harvey (she had married) were among the few who praised it, the *World* finding it "conspicuously offensive," the *Herald* calling it a "repulsive play" and even Smith himself feeling it badly done and writing Dreiser, "Give thanks, oh brother, that you were three thousand miles away." [15] The Players lost $1,500 in the effort.

Dreiser, unable to conceive of it as a poor play, blamed a faulty production and the puritanical attitude of the critics.

His friendship with Lengel was proving more than ever helpful, for

Lengel's boss, Ray Long, now the editor-in-chief of the Hearst magazines, opened a new cornucopia. Long visited Los Angeles in February, 1922, and Dreiser came out of hiding to visit him at the Ambassador and sell him the idea of publishing a series of six of his sketches of women in *Cosmopolitan* at $1,000 apiece. Dreiser also got word of a publishing change in New York that affected him.

Early in 1922, John Lane's unprofitable New York branch closed and was taken over by Dodd, Mead & Company. As a result, Dodd, Mead now owned the rights to *The Titan, A Hoosier Holiday, Plays of the Natural and Supernatural,* and *The "Genius"*—possibly also the unfinished *Bulwark,* although Liveright felt he had the strongest claim here. Dodd, Mead also inherited Dreiser's $20,000 suit against Lane and would be the defendant when it came to court.

Thus Dreiser's publishing patchwork became further confused. His attorney, Arthur Hume, conferred with Dodd, Mead to see if some agreement could be reached. He now owed Dodd, Mead (formerly Lane) $1,597.92 and owed Liveright $1,338.13. As he saw it, if Dodd, Mead would pay him a $3,000 advance on his next book, the sum would wipe out the two debts and he could start with a clean slate. Ambassador Mencken joined in these conferences in New York, giving generously of his time in an effort to get Dreiser out of the wilderness. Dreiser was not sure he wanted Dodd, Mead. Did they have guts? Would they publish the long-suppressed *"Genius?"* He had an even better test of the Dodd, Mead courage: He would give them a book containing his most daring story, "Olive Brand"—the one based on the headlong career of Ed Smith's late wife Edith. If they would publish *that,* then he could embrace Dodd, Mead. "If they stall around with a few select ifs, ands etc.," he wrote Hume, "you may know that they are not for me. I want none of them." [16]

Apparently it never struck him that the publication of "Olive Brand" might wound his benefactor, Ed Smith.

Although publishers respected Dreiser's work, he had had several weak sellers and was known as a Tartar to deal with. Dodd greeted him with caution rather than ardor.

"The Dodd people are not publishers of liberal books," he wrote Mencken testily. "They approach me about [as] a Baptist snouts a pervert. I am to alter my books. I am to let them pick and choose. They will see whether I can do anything worthy of them. They do not want the Genius unless it is properly pruned around the vitals. . . ." [17]

Nevertheless, Hume continued negotiations that would go on for months. And Mencken, much as he disliked *The "Genius,"* was willing when Dreiser asked him to meet with John Sumner in an effort to compromise on the number of cuts Sumner had first demanded so that it could be published in something like its original form. "But," Mencken warned, ". . . I want to be sure in advance that after the work is done you will not buck." [18]

On May 31 Mencken went to New York and spent the whole afternoon with the little vice crusader—a literary gorilla nuzzling a puritan lamb. One can be sure that Mencken, the diplomat, entered the sanctum sober and never once swore. He found Sumner polite and even fairly flexible for a bigot. The conversation must have been droll. *Mr. Sumner, now that we have had six years to think this over, surely there cannot be serious objection to that good-humored little quip of the art instructor—the one where he says a woman's breast is round, never square? . . . Or the description of Bouguereau's nudes—a painter famous everywhere? . . . Or to that tender scene between Witla and Suzanne? . . . We must remember, Mr. Sumner, that we are dealing with the work of a serious artist, not a sensationalist. . . .*

Sumner could not stomach the Bouguereau, and insisted on eliminating frank passages of physical desire. Yet he agreed to the restoration of two whole chapters previously barred and he gave ground in other significant respects. "He receded from probably four-fifths of his demands," Mencken wrote,[19] sending a list of the new stipulations and feeling that the book could now be published without outraging Dreiser's sense of truth.

Dreiser agreed except for one preposterous Sumner specification—the removal of four paragraphs in which Witla's wife contemplated having a child in order to regain his love. Again Mencken talked with Sumner, who receded on that too. The book was ready for republication, if anyone wanted to publish it.

Meanwhile Dreiser was afflicted by odd symptoms: "I don't know what it is, lassitude, a cough, no appetite for anything and so much weakness that I prefer to lie flat all day long. . . . My scalp and the skin of my forehead, the lids of my eyes and the bones below my temples are all sore to the touch. . . . My wrists and hands ache too, a little." [20]

He had finished the dramatization of The *"Genius"* for Leo Ditrichstein. Ditrichstein had conferred with him and the two had immediately quarreled: "We have fallen afoul each other over the contract. I swear I'm always in hot water with everything I do. It may get into the courts now. . . . I can't imagine a man being so small and so perverse. He wants the play but he is so swollen with vanity that he wants it at my expense. . . ." [21]

Some recompense was the arrival in California of Bettina Morris, the girl with whom he still corresponded and who was now frankly leading him on. She had read *Hey Rub-a-Dub-Dub* and the *Bookman's* excerpts from Dreiser's autobiography and had written, "What a tremendous mind you have, Theodore Dreiser! You write circles around anyone else in this country." [22] Dreiser could love anyone who said that. "My telephone number is Glendale 2562-M," he wrote, "and your [sic] the only person that I know of in all the while I have been here that I have given it to, so how is that. . . . Will meet you anywhere you say. . . ." [23]

She came down from Palo Alto and they met for the first time in three years. "If ever we meet . . . don't temporize," he had written her. Yet she held aloof and evidently was enough annoyed at the Dreiser ego to grow a trifle sarcastic.

"Sorry our contact came out so badly," he wrote her afterward. "I still think you are a fine person. . . ." [24] And she repented, writing him later, "You're the only man I do want to see. . . . Don't forget me. I'm much wiser since I got rid of the inhibitions. You would like me now. (My goodness, the girl doesn't care what she says, does she?). . ." [25]

In August Dreiser and Helen drove—Helen always was chauffeur, the awkward Dreiser feeling unequal to handling a car—to the "cool grey city of love," as George Sterling called his beloved San Francisco. More than ever Sterling and Dreiser were brother rebels, poets, rakes, pessimistic philosophers. In San Francisco Sterling was a seedy civic institution, charming drunk or sober, given a free room at the Bohemian Club, known and liked by policemen and headwaiters, a strange mixture of angel and wastrel. Once more Helen and Dreiser—sometimes Dreiser alone—were off with Sterling on visits to the Douglases, the Von Saberns, the quack Dr. Abrams. Again, Sterling took Helen and Dreiser on a round of bistros, winding up at Tait's on the beach, where Sterling was still able to dance with Helen. To him, she outshone Beatrice and the Dark Lady. En route back to the St. Francis, where Dreiser and Helen were staying, they passed Stow Lake in Golden Gate Park at 4 A.M.

Sterling asked Helen to stop the car. He got out, disrobed and plunged into the lake. "And it was a lovely sight to see him, too," Helen admitted, "as his slender body gracefully moved through the misty, foggy atmosphere. . . ." He came back with a dripping bouquet of water lilies for Helen as a policeman arrived and seized him. Sterling identified himself and the bluecoat let him go. The story made the morning *Examiner* and *Chronicle*, with pictures of Sterling and Dreiser, but Helen was not named.

"The reporters tried desperately hard to get your name. . . ." Sterling wrote Helen later.[26]

III. FINISHED AT FIFTY?

For three years Dreiser had promised Liveright books and had failed to deliver, had written biting accusations that Liveright was gossiping about him, divulging his address, selling Dreiser's books at a discount, lacking in real appreciation of his work, interested only in money. Liveright accepted this steady derogation, hoping that his belief in Dreiser's genius would be gratified by a best seller. He had learned to frame his letters with caution and liberal portions of the praise he knew Dreiser expected. He was still hoping for a novel.

"What," he inquired, "is the big novel that is going to rub Sumner the wrong way?" [27]

This, of course, was *An American Tragedy*. There were several reasons why Dreiser did not get on with it.

One was money. With Helen's winnings and his own profitable deal with Ray Long, there was no difficulty in meeting bills. But to carry through his project of buying back all his books and plates he would need real capital. He could scarcely gamble a year on a novel.

Another was his own lack of discipline. He did not like to grind away at one chore. He preferred to carry along several projects, switching from one to another as his mood suggested.

A third must have been doubt. Was there any real use in slaving over a novel that would rub Sumner the wrong way, if Sumner and the rest of the nation's censors banned it?

In 1922 appeared *Civilization in America*, in which Harold Stearns and a battery of intellectuals (including Mencken) dissected a national culture which Dreiser had been fighting for 22 years—its preoccupation with money and respectability, its paucity of ideals and thought. The failure of American literature, Van Wyck Brooks wrote, was merely a reflection of the failure of American life itself, adding, "There is no denying that for half a century the American writer as a type has gone down in defeat." [28]

Dreiser did not conform to type. He was one of the few undefeated. Not once had he lowered his standards in the things that mattered. Out of his own experience he could have given Stearns and his colleagues chapter and verse for many of their arguments.

But in a crucial way he *was* defeated. He had not published a novel for seven years.

Was there any hope for American art, any relaxing in the fearful philistine grip? He did not think so. Were not *Carrie* and *Jennie* used as evidence of sin in Milwaukee? Had not the University of Michigan reserved Dreiser's works for the faculty only? Had not *Potter* been attacked by the puritans? Had not the Kentucky legislature defeated by a bare 42–41 margin an act to prohibit the teaching of Darwinism and agnosticism?

He was wrong, if only in small degree. "Even Doubleday would print Sister Carrie today," Mencken wrote. [29] The Stearns book itself was a hopeful sign of self-examination and widening revolt. In New York that year Judge Charles Nott freed *Jurgen* from its ban, declaring it not lewd but a book "of unusual literary merit" [30]—a decision, it was said, that sent Sumner reeling from the courtroom in shock. There were other heartening omens: honest books by Floyd Dell, Scott Fitzgerald and Sherwood Anderson—the willingness of Sumner to compromise on *The "Genius."* While E. Phillips Oppenheim and Zane Grey had been the best sellers of 1920, *Main Street* had eclipsed them in 1921 and by the end of 1922 had sold 390,000 copies. All America was talking about Sinclair Lewis and his assault on national complacency.

If the philistines were retreating, it was largely because Dreiser had raised the issue, waved it like a flag, brought it to clarity before writers, critics, publishers and the public, and had taken painful wounds in the battle. The younger ones coming up—Anderson, Dell, Lewis, Fitzgerald, Waldo Frank and others—knew that the freedom they were collecting had been bought and paid for by Dreiser in odd literary transactions dating back to 1900.

Indeed, Dreiser was in danger of being forgotten by the public. "I believe it would be a good idea for you to show up in New York again," Mencken had written him; "you are so damned securely buried that thousands of boobs are growing up who have never heard of you."[31] The spirited Kirah Markham wrote him sharply from New York:

> I never met a writer or painter or anything else while I was in California that had not gone soft as mush . . . [in] that ever sunny climate, and I'd be ready to bet that you're doing the same and don't even know it. . . . People are saying you are done, finished, but I know that you are only finished at fifty if you choose to be. . . . These latter years you are inclined to take the attitude that the poor old world is a little unworthy of you and therefore why should you struggle?[32]

To Bettina Morris he wrote defensively, "I think you think that I am beginning to fade. Well, wait and see. . . . I haven't even struck my big themes. I'm trying certain things on the piano."[33]

He had to get back to New York to solve his publishing dilemma. He was sick of Los Angeles anyway. The films were a triumph of stupid commercialism. To a reporter he snapped that Los Angeles was no place for an artist, nobody gave a hang about him, film moguls and actors were uniformly ignorant, and he was returning to New York where at any rate there was toil, struggle, people of interest.

"The United States today is a continuation of old Rome," he said. "The Romans knew two things—money-getting and war."[34]

What to do about Helen? Now legally free, she wanted him to divorce Jug and marry her. But he was tiring of her, and as for marriage—heaven forbid!

"As for my picture career," Helen wrote, "I knew I should stay in California and Teddie agreed on the wisdom of this."[35]

Helen herself did not agree. "I longed to develop spiritually. . . ." she added ingenuously. "Where, I thought, could I do this better than at the side of so great a man as Dreiser?"[36]

She threw away a promising film career and tagged along with him. They sold the house, stored the Maxwell and early in October they boarded a train for New York.

Book Four

AN AMERICAN TRAGEDY

1. Kite Against the Wind

I. ORDER OUT OF CHAOS

While Helen always denied any regret for her choice, she was not a strict realist in matters of the heart. After three years of her, Dreiser recoiled from her matrimonial designs. Fond though he was of her, he regarded love as essentially a selfish passion and was determined to be free. In mid-October he took a two-room apartment at 16 St. Luke's Place, one of the Village's most pleasant byways, and wrote Mencken, "I hear that Theodore Dreiser is at large in New York & that he has already pulled several crooked deals." [1] Helen rented a flat on West Fiftieth Street, took voice lessons and suffered.

"However, he kept in close touch with me," she wrote bravely. "We dined together often, and sometimes I could not resist following him to what we then called 'home.' Possibly the next day the other woman would be there with him, and it seemed almost more than I could bear." [2]

After three years' absence, Dreiser found New York preoccupied with Mah Jong, Coué, the Red scare, jazz and bathtub gin, but the thing that impressed him was its hard commercialism and its Jews. "Don't care for it," he wrote Ettinge. "Too many Jews. Too smoky. Too dirty." And to Bettina Morris: "To [sic] many unidealistic Jews. Hence the old vivid, searching idealism has gone." And to Mencken: "N. Y. to me is a scream—a Kyke's dream of a Ghetto. The lost tribe has taken the island." [3] He did not approve of Jews in the mass, much as he liked some individuals.

Immediately he quarreled with his landlady, Josephine Brokaw, over the window shades in his apartment. "You showed a great deal of unnecessary temper," Mrs. Brokaw wrote him. ". . . I am very sorry you rented my apartment and if you can find another to suit you, I will *gladly release* you from your agreement." [4]

He replied furiously, but stayed. Casting about for money, he played a cheap-Jack trick on Robert Moody, the Milwaukee industrialist-Dreiserian. Moody, who had been moved to tears by *Jennie Gerhardt*, wanted to collect Dreiser first editions and manuscripts. "I would like these just for my own personal library. . . ." he wrote. "One thousand dollars does seem a little high for *Jennie Gerhardt*, but the fact that I am purchasing them directly from you will offset my hesitation." [5]

Dreiser, evidently reasoning that Moody was a millionaire and could afford to pay dearly, rigged the prices. To his friend Ettinge, now in Los Angeles, he wrote:

The man who bought Jennie Gerhardt [Moody] has now, in conjunction with some one else whom I do not know, a new scheme for assembling all of my mss under one roof. . . . I do not care to part with them for less than they have already brought in certain instances. For instance Free sold for $300. The Blue Sphere went for $150. . . . One of these two men is interested in The Lost Phoebe. If either of them write you—or anyone does I want you to say that you own the ms & want $300 for it. That will fix the price for this short stuff. . . .[6]

He persuaded David Karsner to pose as the owner of the original ms. for "Laughing Gas," which was still in Dreiser's hands. Moody, unaware of these machinations, wrote Karsner, who replied that he could have "Laughing Gas" for $300. But in Dreiser's mind the big prize was the original ms. for *Sister Carrie*, a gem for any collector.

There was a drawback. In 1914 he had presented the ms. to Mencken in return for services literally too valuable to compute.

Nothing daunted, he wrote Mencken obliquely:

You will receive shortly, I am fairly sure, an inquiry in regard to the Sister Carrie ms. The gentleman will want to know your selling price. . . . I have nothing to say—no desire to interfere—as to any use or disposition you choose to make of the ms. But if you do decide to sell will you be good enough not to ask *less* than $2,000. The ms. will be cheap to him at that price and unless you do ask it you will be underselling me & some others—cutting the price. . . .[7]

"I received a letter from [Moody]," Mencken replied, "but answered, of course, that the MS. of 'Sister Carrie' was not for sale. However, if you think it would be a good thing to let him assemble all your MS., I might be induced, by suitable arts, to hand the MS. back to you. Let us be frank. If you are short of money, it is yours, now or at any time. But no other scoundrel ever gets it. I hate to think of it going to Milwaukee. When I die my kidneys go to the municipal museum of Altoona, Pa., and my liver to Oberlin College, but it would take much eloquence to make me leave even my thyroid gland to Milwaukee."[8]

Dreiser now disclosed that with proper wire-pulling the script might bring more than $4,000 and that he hoped to profit in the deal. "I do not ask you to sell the [manuscript]," he wrote cryptically. "As a matter of fact if approached again—even with an offer of $2,000 I wish you would rest until you hear from me. Certain things have developed here which make a high priced sale entirely possible[.] If I should arrange a deal such as you personally could not effect and it meant a round sum & you wanted to take over some ready cash, would you split the returns. Your share would be over $2,000. Same to me & something to a third mysterious grafter."[9]

Always irked by Dreiser's weakness for the furtive, Mencken was further annoyed by his huckstering of Mencken's private treasure. The deal fell through, for although Dreiser got $1,000 from Moody for *Jennie*, *Carrie* remained in Mencken's hands. Mencken was then perturbed by a rumor that Dreiser was planning to bring out a new edition of The "Genius," *unexpurgated*.

"Is this true?" he wrote. "If it is, I'd like to know it in advance, so that it may not appear to Sumner that I was fooling him about the cuts." [10]

It was, although not yet a certainty. Dreiser had been conferring separately with Horace Liveright (Albert Boni had left the firm), William Briggs of Harper's and Edward Dodd of Dodd, Mead, trying to reach some publishing solution. Liveright, Briggs and Dodd agreed that a new edition would sell much better if it could be advertised as unexpurgated. Indeed, Liveright was so anxious to get his hands on the undraped *"Genius"* that although he still did not have the rights to it he had two New York assistant district attorneys read the script and was delighted to find that they thought it within the law. Liveright was all but kneeling before Dreiser in his pleas that he settle on Boni & Liveright as his publisher, and was preparing a financial plan that would offer strong inducements. Dreiser held him off but accepted a $1,000 advance for *A Book About Myself*. Liveright cut 200 pages from it and hurried to get it into print.

Dreiser invited Charles Fort to call. He visited with Llewelyn Powys, who lived nearby on Patchin Place and defied his tuberculosis by sleeping on the roof in all weather. Dreiser had written a preface for his *Ebony and Ivory*, and the grateful but hard-pressed Llewelyn handed him a check for $50 just paid him for a lecture. "He at once concluded that I was handing him a cheque written out by myself," Llewelyn wrote, "and seizing it between his enormous finger and thumb, tore it into a hundred fragments." [11]

Dreiser avoided Ed Smith, still hurt by Smith's criticism of *Hey Rub*. Sherwood Anderson lived in a cellar apartment only three doors from Dreiser, but was awed by the great realist. Ernest Boyd, living with his French wife Madeleine on East Nineteenth Street, was awed by no one, and he and Dreiser often lunched together at the Pig and Whistle off Sheridan Square. Boyd's Nineteenth Street neighbor, Carl Van Vechten, had a Prohibition party one night at which Dreiser passed from gayety to such semistupor that Van Vechten and Boyd had to struggle to get him down the elevator and outside.

"He was unable to stand," Van Vechten recalled, "so we propped him against a tree." [12]

He looked so unlettered in that posture that they laughed and left him there, clinging to the tree. Evidently he managed to get a taxi home, for sometime later Helen was aroused by her telephone.

"Come right down," Dreiser said over the wire. "I need you." [13]

Frightened, she hurried to St. Luke's Place to find him inert on a couch. Although he spoke rationally, he was otherwise paralyzed. With great effort she undressed him and got him into pajamas.

"The next morning he awakened perfectly normal," she wrote. "He was extremely surprised to see me there, for he did not remember one thing about calling me the night before. . . ." [14]

He was at a standstill with *An American Tragedy*, for one reason because he had to see the scene of the murder and trial in upstate New York. He was dividing his efforts capriciously on about a dozen ideas, among them another novel, *Mea Culpa*, plus *The Stoic* (the final volume of the Cowperwood trilogy), two new plays, several movie scenarios, short stories, more woman sketches and a poem whenever the mood struck. "Don't give my address to a soul," he wrote Mencken, and gave the same warning to Liveright, Karsner and other friends. To Karsner he wrote that critical blasts no longer bothered him:

> Like a kite I have risen against the wind—not with it.[15]

To Ettinge in Los Angeles he wrote, "Thanks for the letter to [Moody] in Milwaukee. If he writes you for the manuscript wire me, collect and I'll send it to you registered. . . . I think he will take it at $300 or $250 anyhow." And he urged Mencken, who was feeling unwell, to send a blood sample to Dr. Abrams, writing, "I *saw* several remarkable things done by this wave machine. . . ."[16]

But if he scattered his energies, he did achieve one goal. At long, long last he settled on a publisher. On December 18 he issued an ultimatum to Dodd, Mead: Either they would publish *The "Genius"* unexpurgated within two months or he was through with them. They hedged, and he signed up with the waiting Horace Liveright.

Indeed, Liveright arranged such an attractive proposition that one might think the writer involved was Gene Stratton Porter. Working largely on credit, he did the following:

> From Harper's he bought the rights, plates and stock of *Jennie* and *The Financier* for a total of $5,100.
>
> From Dodd, Mead he bought *The Titan, A Hoosier Holiday, The Plays* and *The "Genius,"* also paying off Dreiser's remaining indebtedness to them, for a total of $4,531.38. A Dodd, Mead condition was that Dreiser drop his $20,000 suit against them, which he did.
>
> Liveright took five-year leases on all these books.
>
> He agreed to publish the unexpurgated "*Genius*" in the spring.
>
> He agreed to pay Dreiser $4,000 a year as a drawing account for four years.
>
> He agreed to publish a book of Dreiser poems.
>
> He agreed to publish a collected edition of Dreiser's works starting in January, 1927, and that on completion of the sale of 1,000 sets Dreiser's royalties would be no less than $10,000.

But Liveright knew his man—knew he had to be cudgeled into systematic production. He insisted that Dreiser deliver no less than two new novels within three years, and suggested the following order of publication:

> Winter, 1922: Volume II of the autobiography (already published).
> Spring, 1923: *The "Genius."*
> Fall, 1923:   A novel or *Twelve Women.*

Spring, 1924:   *The Color of a Great City* (Dreiser's New York sketches)
                or a novel.
Fall, 1924:   Volume I of the autobiography.
Spring, 1925:   A volume of short stories or a novel.
Fall, 1925:   A volume of short stories or a novel.
Spring, 1926:   Volume III of the autobiography.[17]

The schedule was far less grueling than it appeared. *The "Genius"* and two
of the autobiographical volumes were completed, *Twelve Women* (later
called *A Gallery of Women*) and *Color of a Great City* nearly so. At last
Dreiser's affairs were in order. All of his books were now in his own hands (or
B & L's) with the lone exception of *A Traveler at Forty*, still owned by
Century. He had a program, an enthusiastic publisher, a guaranteed base
income. He could thank Horace Liveright, who was gambling some $25,000
on him and was buying a lot of trouble as well as lasting fame as a publisher.

II. THE PURIFIERS

In the winter of 1922-23 Dreiser made occasional visits to the West
Seventy-first Street apartment of the sociable psychiatrist, Dr. A. A. Brill,
with whom he discussed the psychology of murder with *An American
Tragedy* in mind. Another Brill caller was Van Vechten, who chatted with
Dreiser about the effects of narcotics with which they had both experi-
mented.[18] Dreiser also met at last with Dr. Jacques Loeb, who invited him to
Rockefeller Institute. The tough-minded Loeb looked on psychiatrists as
amateurs playing games with the most inexact of methods. Like Dreiser—and
for scientific rather than philosophical reasons—he saw the human being as a
chemical mechanism, the victim of blind forces. If one asked how then
humanity could harbor ethical impulses, Loeb would reply that ethics arose
from instinct just as surely as sex or maternal love, that the urge for justice
was merely an instinctive need to see fellow beings happy.[19] If one argued that
each man had his own will, Loeb felt that Pavlov's dogs and the heliotropism
of certain organisms indicated that for "will" one should substitute "instinct,"
and that instinct was at bottom chemical. The man who thought he was
making constant decisions might merely be the helpless instrument of a series
of tropisms over which he had no more control than the young caterpillar
that climbs upward toward the light to get at the tender green leaves. Life
seemed to be only a complex and endless series of tropisms.[20] While Dreiser
was not equipped to follow the great physiologist's scientific methods, his
interpretation of their import would be seen in *An American Tragedy* and in
later undertakings.

Other tropisms were evident when bluenosed New York Supreme Court
Justice John Ford found his daughter reading D. H. Lawrence's *Women in
Love*. Ford hurriedly alerted religious and civic organizations, the Clean
Books League was formed, and Ford got a Clean Books Bill before the state

assembly aimed at giving Sumner precisely the narrow definition of obscenity he wanted.[21] Horace Liveright, always a staunch fighter against censorship, tried to rally New York publishers against the bill. As the crisis approached, Dreiser threw one of his rare parties.

To this stag gathering in St. Luke's Place came Mencken, Sherwood Anderson, Van Vechten, Llewelyn Powys, Boyd, Burton Rascoe and others. Powys did not know some of the guests, and others were also meeting for the first time. Dreiser did not trouble to introduce them. He stood in the center of the room, Powys recalled, "entirely ignorant of the fact that the guests he had brought together were not mixing well, and ready . . . to forget all of us as he followed the flounderings of his own wayward imagination. . . ." [22] Rascoe asked Dreiser if he really meant that stuff about always meeting a "kindly little Jew" before some pronounced change in his life. Of course he had meant it, Dreiser replied. It had happened again and again.[23]

He served only beer to this hundred-proof group. They sat around the bare, rugless room in disconsolate, desultory conversation until the door opened and a handsome young man staggered in, bearing a bottle of champagne. He was Scott Fitzgerald, already famous for *This Side of Paradise* and *The Beautiful and Damned*. An admirer of Dreiser, whom he had never met, he teetered from one guest to another, then located Dreiser and gave him the bottle.

"Mr. Dreiser," he said, "I get a great kick out of your books."

As Boyd recalled it, "After a gallant effort to engage Dreiser in literary discussion, [Fitzgerald] retreated to a seat near his overcoat and proceeded to extract from the pocket of this garment a substitute for the intoxication of the mind which he had anticipated." [24] The other guests, hoping at least for some champagne, saw Dreiser put the bottle in the icebox. The party was long remembered as fascinating for its very dullness.

Liveright's efforts to enlist other publishers and the Authors' League against the Clean Books Bill elicited little response. Concerned though Dreiser was, he felt that his position as an author of "controversial" books made his own participation in the fight inadvisable. But there were rumors that Sumner planned to ban *The "Genius"* when it appeared, and Dreiser could not forbear from erupting to newsmen in a manner unlikely to soothe the censors. He assailed Sumner as a publicity-seeker and said, "If it comes to action I am going to fight for a jury trial this time and get it. . . ." Blasting the American mentality, he said, "You can slam its young people into universities with their classrooms and laboratories and when they come out all they can talk about is Babe Ruth. . . . It is a hopeless country for intellectuals and thinking people. . . . The majority of its people have the mentality of a European or Asiatic peasant." [25]

In April the book bill passed the assembly and seemed certain to pass the senate. The Authors' League contented itself with sending a few telegrams and a letter from George Creel opposing the bill. Liveright got an attorney and with four writers traveling at their own expense went to Albany, where hey joined New York newspapermen in energetic lobbying. Liveright lost every cent he had in an all-night poker session with newsmen and legislators, and had to wire home for money, but he got the support of urbane young Senator James J. Walker. Walker's influence and his quip in the senate, "I do not know of any young woman who has been ruined by a book," was instrumental in the defeat of the bill on May 2.[26]

When Rex Beach of the Authors' League asked his cooperation in a plan to improve the artistic quality of moving pictures, Dreiser let him have it. Where had the League been when the Catholic and Episcopal churches, the Salvation Army, the Y.M.C.A. and other groups had fought to pass the book bill? Calling the League indifferent to this greatest of all threats to honest art and interested chiefly in money-making, he wrote in part, "And you have the effrontery to ask me to give of my time and my suggestions to this soul-shaking [film] cause. . . . Pardon me for not availing myself of the invitation." [27]

Never shunning publicity for his cause—or for himself and his books—he gave this letter to the newspapers. Gelett Burgess, vice-president of the League, replied publicly that the organization had indeed taken action and said of Dreiser, "If he should devote as much time to furthering the cause of literature as he does to seeking personal publicity, he wouldn't need to ask an association he doesn't belong to to help protect his dubious sex-fiction." [28]

Here Dreiser had Burgess on the hip. In a long reply, again given to the press, he described the feeble opposition of the League and then answered the personal charge:

> You have referred to me in various newspapers as the author of "dubious sex fiction." Very good. Granted, we will say, for the purpose of argument, that this is true. What then, however, would you think of a writer and an executive of the Authors' League, who holding this opinion of the work of a fellow writer and broadcasting it to the world over his signature, would nevertheless find it artistically and morally possible to importune that same shameless writer on behalf of the fiction of his wife, to wit; that he read the same, and give him and his wife, his honest critical opinion. . . . I am not pointing definitely to anyone. I am merely posing to you an odd question.[29]

It *was* an odd question. On March 14 Burgess had written him:

> My dear Dreiser: Estelle [Mrs. Burgess] has a story in the March Mc-Clure['s] that she is very desirous of having you read and give her your most brutal criticism. . . .
> Will you get it and let her know?

In his reply, however, Dreiser himself was not free from error. Outlining the grudging gesture the League had made for him in the "*Genius*" case, he added, "I fought the 'Genius' issue single handed for five years. And I am still fighting it—single handed."

This was news to Mencken, who demurred: "With all due respect, you lie like an archbishop. Young Hersey sweated for you like a bull, and there was a critic in Baltimore who, as I recall it, laid out $300 cash to round up the authors of the United States on your side." [30]

Dreiser, who had a tendency to think himself more alone than he was, apologized for his "archepiscopal failing."

III. THE MURDER SCENE

In May 1923, Claude Bowers, the Indiana-born journalist and historian, moved to New York to join the editorial staff of the *World*. As a reporter in Terre Haute twenty years earlier he had heard gossip about the scandalous Dreiser family and had noted how popular Paul Dresser was while the far greater brother was generally disliked as a pessimist and pornographer. Bowers had written glowing reviews of Dreiser novels and had received one grateful note from him. When Bowers reached New York, he wrote him from the McAlpin Hotel.

This was an occasion when Helen happened to be with Dreiser. The couple had beer at the hotel with Bowers who, keenly interested, observed Dreiser's tall clumsiness, his handkerchief-fiddling, and noted, "he impressed me instantly as coming from peasant stock." [31] Sensitive, a trifle bitter, he was unlike most authors in that he did not care to talk about his work to strangers, but Bowers drew him out.

He did not think highly of *Jennie Gerhardt*, Dreiser said. "I wrote it in an emotional mood and liked it immensely in the process of composition, but almost immediately afterward I concluded that I had overdrawn Jennie. I think so still."

Which novel did he like best?

"Some people think *Sister Carrie* the best. I like *The Genius* best of all. There's more of myself in it." He added, grinning, "Liveright likes *The Titan* best, maybe because he too is a bandit." [32]

He much preferred to talk politics. Here Bowers, a seasoned Democratic politician who had served six years in Washington as a senatorial secretary and had run for Congress himself, found him surprisingly uninformed, with views that were "mostly fantastic."

"Do you think that democracy has worked out in this country?" he demanded—one of those belligerent questions to which one had better give the right answer or face a quarrel. "Do you think this form of government is the best?" [33]

Bowers replied diplomatically that he knew no better form. Dreiser, once the spectator of man's futility, the scoffer at politics, had lost the detachment that his own mechanistic philosophy logically required. To a large extent he identified the American political heirarchy with the philistinism he despised. He needed only leisure for a later exploration of politics. Now he was too busy writing and wrangling with Horace Liveright.

"Dear Dreiser:" Liveright wrote him, "I cross my heart and swear to our Lord that your note of yesterday absolutely mystifies me. . . .

"You say . . . that you would like to stick and work with me, etc. but upon the condition only 'that I absolutely get a square deal.'

"Your letter leaves no interpretation open other than that you question whether you have always gotten a square deal from me. . . .

"Let me reiterate what I have frequently said to you: That I am heart and soul for your work; that we now have a very big investment in it, and that from now on you will see a very much greater concerted campaign for the sale of all your work. . . .

"In spite of your letter, which it is possible I have misinterpreted, my admiration and affection for you remains the same." [34]

Liveright had flooded the country with publicity about his new sponsorship of Dreiser. Indeed the *Boston Transcript* complained, "Every few days there reaches us from Boni & Liveright, or possibly from Mr. Dreiser himself, a black-bordered sheet of information that 'We announce with pleasure and pardonable pride that we have acquired the publication rights for all of Theodore Dreiser's works.' " [35] Liveright was also laying out a $2,000 advertising splurge on Dreiser, most of it to run in *The New York Times*. The ballyhoo and the critical discussions of *A Book About Myself*, published in December, 1922, reached Dreiser's old friend Alice Phillips, now living in Ohio. She wrote him:

> Dear me! Mr. Dreiser. What a lot of blurbing is going on! When you write a book it's exactly like throwing a cake of soap in a geyser—the whole country starts erupting.[36]

Yet *A Book About Myself* had sold less than 3,000 copies, and he felt that Liveright must be falsifying the records.

This book was symbolic of the long confusion in Dreiser's works—the second volume of his autobiography, but published first. He was withholding the completed Volume I because it would infuriate his sisters Mame, Emma and Sylvia. He was angry at Liveright for titling Volume II *A Book About Myself*, claiming that he had never authorized such a title, although it must be admitted that Dreiser himself had long called it that. The title was indeed a bad one, since the autobiography was planned to run to three or four volumes, each of which would be "a book about myself." But the main complaint was the poor sale, which seems not to have been Liveright's fault. He had taken it and praised it only in order to wheedle a Dreiser novel. He was right. The public was not particularly interested in the autobiography.

In many respects Liveright was Dreiser's ideal publisher. He was liberal, anti-philistine, had some knowledge of good literature, and had shown his courage by publishing authors feared or disapproved by the conservative houses—O'Neill, Latzko, T. S. Eliot, Evelyn Scott, David Karsner's biography of Debs, and Dreiser himself. Above all he *believed* in Dreiser and gave him a generous drawing account. But his incompatibilities with Dreiser were as pronounced. He was flamboyant, reckless, prone to plunge on hunches that at times could be terribly wrong, a grandstander determined to be spectacular. One had the feeling that, to him, books were a stage backdrop with Horace Liveright spotlighted in front of them. In May of 1923 he moved his firm from West Fortieth Street to a converted brownstone mansion at 61 West Forty-eighth and surrounded himself with a luxury that Dreiser eyed scornfully, even though Liveright placed a head of Dreiser sculptured by Onorio Ruotolo in the reception room. While Dreiser considered all publishers as parasites battening on artists, and would have been happy with none of them, he could not shake his conviction that Liveright was dishonest. For years their relations would amount to a perpetual quarrel, Dreiser always the accuser and attacker, Liveright the defender and explainer.

The publication of The *"Genius"* had been set back to August 15, evidently because Lengel, after long effort, had sold his own 100,000-word condensation of the book for serial publication in *Metropolitan*, which insisted on preceding the book. For this Dreiser got a $900 first instalment, with one or two similar instalments to come, and for the first time Lengel accepted a commission after years of labors for friendship's sake. Suddenly Dreiser was flush, for he sold "St. Columba and the River" (which *The Saturday Evening Post* had bought for $750 in 1917 and finally returned, preferring not to use it) to *Pictorial Review* for $800. To *Century* he sold two of his woman sketches, "Reina" and "Ida Hauchawout," for $400 each. All three of these sales were negotiated for him by David Karsner, another admiring unofficial agent who evidently accepted no commission.

While Helen was a good typist, he had no faith in her editorial faculties. That spring an intelligent young woman recently from Illinois, Sally Kusell, learned through a friend that Dreiser sought a secretary-editor. She called at St. Luke's Place. He eyed her suspiciously and said, "Well, come in." She thought she had never seen such an austere, forbidding man, his face distinguished above the nose but collapsing into the loose, almost evil mouth. He gave her a couple of his short stories to criticize by way of try-out. Not visibly offended when she called one of them "maudlin," he hired her and set her to typing *An American Tragedy* from the start, asking her to edit it where she felt it overlong or repetitive. She lived nearby on West Ninth Street, and almost every morning he would breakfast with her at a Childs restaurant on Sixth Avenue near Twelfth Street, bringing with him more pages of script to discuss before giving them to her. "Are you Jewish?" he asked her once. She replied, "Yes. Why?" He said it made no difference and uttered that old bromide, "Some of my best friends are Jews." Miss Kusell noticed that his lip curled at the mention of the best-selling Sinclair Lewis.[37]

Helen, still on Fiftieth Street, had had the Maxwell shipped to New York, so in June Dreiser asked her if she wanted to tour the *American Tragedy* country with him. They drove to Cortland, where he examined the homes of the wealthy, the poorer sections, the factories. One can picture him taking notes on fanlights, gables, shrubbery, fences. Then east to South Otselic to see the ramshackle home where Grace Brown had lived; northeast to Herkimer where the trial was held; and north over primitive roads into the Adirondack fastnesses to remote Big Moose Lake, where the murder occurred.

There they stayed at the Glenmore Hotel while Dreiser soaked up the atmosphere of this place where frightened Chester Gillette had brought the unsuspecting Grace seventeen years earlier. He found a boat attendant who had been there in 1906, remembered Gillette and pointed out the spot in the lake where Grace's body had been found. Dreiser rowed out there with Helen, obsessed by thoughts of the tangle of dreams and fears that had brought the young couple here—the despairing screams of Grace Brown in that awful moment when she realized that Chester had come here not to marry her but to kill her. Dreiser was so affected by the mood of tragedy and violence that Helen worried a trifle about her own safety, thinking:

> Maybe Teddie will become completely hypnotized by this idea and even repeat it, here and now.[38]

After they returned to New York, they went their separate ways during the week but invariably took weekend jaunts into the country. Late in July they drove to the Catskills and took a cabin near Monticello for a month while he worked on the novel, complaining of constant nausea and headache. Helen typed his handwritten copy, read *Wuthering Heights* aloud to him and at times returned to the old refrain: When was he going to divorce Jug and marry her?

Marriage was the last thing he wanted. Jug as his estranged wife was a protection for his freedom. She was supporting herself, no trouble to him at all, whereas a divorce would mean alimony. He was fond enough of Helen—at times—to call her "Babu" and other pet names, but he wanted her only when he wanted her.

To Sally Kusell he wrote almost daily, addressing her variously as "My Little Yankee Zulu" and "My bobbed haired pirate": "It's odd how people grow on one. . . . I found your talk & your moods so dynamic. . . . Haven't seen hide nor hair of any lady since I've been here. I'm as pure as driven snow—for once—actually." "[But I have] the damnedest qualms & struggles in connection with the book." "I can't get you out of my mind for as much as an hour steady. . . ."[39]

From Monticello he wrote at least two angry letters to Liveright, who had adopted a policy of answering all charges, however insulting, with soothing restraint.

"I have yours of August 4th," Liveright wrote, "and will make no comment on it until you come back to New York, when I can show you just what advertising we did on A Book About Myself. I would not be at all ashamed to have every author in the country know just what we spent on this book and how we spent it." [40]

He hedged a bit on the soon-to-be-published "*Genius*," writing, "I hope to show you real results on THE GENIUS, although it's only a *republication* and we may have some real trouble from Sumner who is more active than ever. We have been told . . . that he is going to try to get a grand jury indictment on the book. . . ." And he wrote one line characteristic of him:

"Stick to me, kid, and you'll wear diamonds." [41]

From Henry Van Dyke, alias Mencken, came a black-bordered card announcing Dreiser's appointment along with Nicholas Murray Butler, Bugs Baer and others to a committee designated to lament the sudden death of President Harding, to which "Van Dyke" added, "The tears shed here have raised the Patapsco River 4 feet and spoiled the crabbing." [42]

While Dreiser was out of the cabin, a bundle of letters to him drew Helen irresistibly.

"Ordinarily I would not have touched them," she wrote artlessly, "but at that moment I could not overcome the feeling that they concerned me in some way and I should read them. After reading two or three . . . I had seen enough to know that this was a more serious triangle than I had supposed. I was jealous, fiercely so.

"When he returned, I told him that I was . . . leaving . . . for good. . . ." [43]

They drove back to New York, a trip she described as a "nightmare." She went to his apartment the next day to get a few things she had left there, "fully intending to break off our relationship," as she insisted. His eyes hollow, he said, "I walked the streets all night long." Her resolution crumbled. She stayed on at Fiftieth Street. [44]

IV. DREISER ON REALISM

The "Genius," published during Dreiser's absence, got off to a good sale at three dollars a copy. He had already handed in the script for *The Color of a Great City*, to be published October first. Late in September he moved to 118 West Eleventh Street, a two-room apartment in the old grillwork-fronted Rhinelander Gardens where his sister Mame and Austin Brennan, who lived next door, served as rental agents. Brennan, for whom Dreiser in the nineties had predicted an early death from overindulgence, was still hale at seventy-seven, a genial patriarch with white hair and flowing mustaches. Mame was sixty-two, big and hearty, a creature of great sympathies, enthusiasms and rages, much like her novelist brother, who had often helped the Brennans financially.

Dreiser was contemplating a trip, as he often did when his *affaires amoureuses* grew harassing. "Am thinking of New Mexico—either Santa Fe or

Taos," he wrote Bettina Morris in California. ". . . How about coming over there." [45]

Edgar Lee Masters lived nearby at the Chelsea Hotel, but he was angry at Masters, not explaining why. After avoiding Ed Smith for months, he finally had Thanksgiving dinner with him and talked of going to New Mexico. He was moody, unhappy, probably in part because he feared that his sexual powers were waning. There is ample evidence that he had reached a point where he needed constant change to gain erotic stimulation—a time-consuming business in a conventional world—and that Helen, for all her beauty, no longer excited him. Certainly this fear had an effect on his already scratchy temper.

Without consulting the Dreiser family, Selwyn's Vitagraph Company was bringing out a picture based on Paul's "On the Banks of the Wabash." When Vitagraph asked a favor, Dreiser loosed a bolt:

> You have the insolence to address to me a request . . . for permission to use my personal tribute to my brother as bait to catch audiences for your porch-climber's capitalization of my brother's property. . . . I will thank you to ignore me and my comments on my brother entirely. Failure to do so will entail some interesting publicity . . . which neither the Vitagraph nor Mr. Selwyn will relish. [46]

Robert L. Moody arrived from Milwaukee that fall for the World Series, put up at the Plaza, had several meetings with Dreiser and later wrote, "I . . . want to say that it will be a week that will be always refreshing in my memory." [47] He would have been less refreshed had he known that Dreiser was still using Ettinge in Los Angeles as an aide in selling manuscripts to Moody.

"Thanks for your letter in regard to the [Moody] offer," Dreiser wrote Ettinge. "As I wired you I think it is all right to close at $275. . . . I have offers now for quite a few of my ms—The Girl in the Coffin for one, but want to bull the prices a little." [48]

In December, Rose Feld was assigned by *The New York Times* to interview Dreiser for the Sunday book review. Very young and pretty, Miss Feld had recently interviewed Robert Frost, whom she found charming, and Masters, who upset her with the announcement that he had slept with two different women the previous night and was in poor shape. She was wary about Dreiser, with his reputation for eccentricity, but he met her cordially. She eyed his Spartan diggings.

"In the corner was a washstand with the intimacies of toilet frankly displayed," she noted. "There was a huge lump of coal in the grate. On the mantelpiece above it sat a fat Buddha. A couch, a table, a couple of chairs and a few books completed the furnishings. It was quite evident that this author was not being pampered." [49]

No sooner was she seated than he began what she soon realized was a clumsy effort at a fast proposition. "He was terribly nervous," she said later. "Folding his handkerchief interminably, he asked me very personal questions. Was I married? Did I have a fiancé? Was I interested in men? Did I like to go out to theaters and entertainments? There was an air of tension about him. I could see that if I gave him the slightest encouragement the situation could grow embarrassing. I adopted an attitude of severest reserve." [50]

He gave up on Miss Feld and answered her questions about American realism.

"Realism," he said, "is not literature; it is life. That is where most of our present-day writers are making their big mistake. They set out to write a novel of realism and then proceed to ignore life entirely. They choose one dark, dank, ugly corner of life and spend themselves lavishly upon it, forgetting that life consists of many corners and many open spaces."

This happened to be one of those days when he thought life in America not quite hopeless at that, for he went on:

"The realistic novel of America is not the torpid, sick, neurasthenic novel. Life in America is not like that. . . . A foreign writer once said to me that people can't be poor in America. They can't stay poor. There is always a push upward. He was right. In the same manner the life, or the soul if you will, of an individual needn't stay poor. . . .

"Yet if a stranger in this country decided to get the spirit of the people—the life of the people—through our present-day novels . . . what would he think? This is a people that spends its hours in miserable suffering and useless agonizing." Evelyn Scott and Ben Hecht, he said, had fallen into this error even though their distortions had some of the attraction of Van Gogh or Gauguin. He had no praise for any current American novelist. Not a word did he say about Sherwood Anderson or Sinclair Lewis, who had followed *Main Street* with the best-selling *Babbitt*. He mentioned his friends Homer Croy and Ethel M. Kelley as employing the "short-story technique" and he defended the full-blown Dreiserian novel:

> Life is larger than they paint it. If you want a great scene you can't get it in a miniature. The great realistic novels of the past, "The Idiot," "Anna Karenina," "Madame Bovary," "The Brothers Karamazov," could they have been written in the so-called present style of realism? Their authors needed breadth and length. They took the trouble to make their picture complete. The little canvases of today will never displace the larger ones of yesterday.

He deplored the influence of Gertrude Stein and of shallow critics who encouraged young writers to a concern with style at the expense of fullness. He assailed the slavish admiration for English novelists: "We follow blindly because we have such a stupid, unreasonable respect for everything English. . . . [W]ho are the reigning American novelists of today? H. G. Wells, Arnold Bennett, D. H. Lawrence, Hugh Walpole, Joseph Conrad, Gilbert Cannan. Yes, American."

And in discussing the burgeoning sex novel, which he felt was a reaction against the old evasion of sex, he gave a measured view of that touchy subject:

> I, too, am sick of the exaggeration of sex in the novels of today. But the person who ignores sex is as much of a fool as the person who over-emphasizes it. You can't write a novel of realism and let sex out of the picture even as you can't write a novel full of sex and call it realism.[51]

Meanwhile he was alternately quarreling with Helen and moving in with her for fond reconciliations. Mencken and Nathan were planning to dynamite all Babbitts with the *American Mercury*, to be published by Knopf. There was growing medical criticism of the methods of Dr. Abrams, now a millionaire. A foxy Michigan physician sent Abrams a blood specimen on blotting paper, from which Abrams diagnosed his ailments as malaria, cancer and two social diseases, all amenable to treatment by the electric oscilloclast. The Michigander announced that the blood specimen had come from a healthy Plymouth Rock rooster. Dr. Abrams himself contracted pneumonia—always easily cured by the oscilloclast. In his case it failed and he died before the law closed in.[52]

"*How* in hell did he perform so big a percentage of remarkable cures?" George Sterling wrote Dreiser.[53]

The Color of a Great City sold only 2,274 copies by the year's end. *The "Genius,"* however, sold 12,301 copies by the same date—the biggest first sale of any Dreiser book—and was still going strong, with not a word from Sumner. Yet Dreiser, whose hopes had been high, felt that Liveright was doctoring the figures. "I have a feeling that the statement I have is off. . . ." he wrote Mencken, asking him to check sales in Baltimore stores.[54]

Mencken, friendly with Liveright and impatient at Dreiser's endless suspicions, replied, "I fear that if I inquired about the sales . . . here it would cause gabble, and that the gabble would get to Liveright instantly." [55]

But at Dreiser's request, Claude Bowers, Robert Moody, James Ettinge, Bettina Morris, F. W. Skiff and others were repeating the futile chore of checking bookstores in various parts of the country.

By March, 1924, Helen had tired of her humiliating role. She told Dreiser she was quitting him, going back West. He agreed until he discovered that she really meant it, when he protested. How could he work on the novel without her? She was firm, and he saw her off on the train March 23. Helen spent much of the four-day trip to Portland weeping.[56]

2. Chipping at Rock

No sooner had Helen gone than Dreiser missed her terribly. He had black fits of morning depression and other symptoms. He was unable to play sentimental phonograph records. He wrote Helen daily for nine days—handwritten letters often 2,000 words long, addressing her as Babu Mio, My Golden Girl and Dearest Deario. He even broached (grudgingly) that subject he despised, marriage, but his letters contained the inevitable evasions and falsehoods. Tender, flattering, he admitted failings and sought to heal the breach:

> Sad thoughts are sadder than tears I think. And yet I have been trying to think of only the better side of it all—the future that is wrapped up in so genuine a feeling. Bad as I have been there is only one Babu for me & always will be. . . . You are my April girl and my December girl,—too. You play all seasons.
>
> You think bad of me I know. And I have done bad things I suppose but I really love you—my Babu. . . . And I promise to tell you quite all that I do & to do much better than I have.
>
> There's a mysterious chord that stretches from here to you. . . . I try all sorts of things[,] poems, books—my work, but I can't shut out the past. . . . I begin to see now that I need my Babu more than anyone & when I come to her again, I won't worry about anything else except my work.[1]
>
> I may have said harsh things and seemingly meant them—even to myself at moments. I may have seemed cruel and to you have been cruel but I have tortured myself more in so doing because within me you have always been —safe and centered in my very heart—and when I have hurt you I have felt so sad afterwards—ah—so very sad.[2]

He described the mental torture her absence caused him:

> I had a bad night last night. Dreamed of you on the train. And once I thought I heard you cry. It was awfully sad & made me feel dreadful.
>
> Last night & this morning—just before going to sleep & on waking I had the heaviest & saddest depressions.
>
> Every so often these days I suffer through half hours and hours thinking of you. . . . I put on "Somewhere a Voice is Calling" this morning & had to take it off.

He felt that at times electric thought-waves coursed between them:

> In the mornings for as much as a half hour just after I wake I feel as though I were entirely bathed in a ray of some kind—emanating from some-

where which rather strengthens me than not. . . . Does that emanate from
you by any chance?

I've been sending helpful [thought] messages your way all day because
I've been thinking that maybe you needed them.[3]

Helen had no doubt that the messages spanned the 3,000-mile gap, commenting later, "There were nights when I lay awake with a gnawing torment
in every nerve, yearning to be in his arms again, and almost invariably . . . a
letter would arrive telling me of similar longings on his part. Attuned
chemisms, one highly responsive to the other, is the only explanation I
know of this thought transference, which happened over and over again between us."[4]

Dreiser suggested that her very beauty sometimes rendered him impotent,
hinting at his peculiar sexual difficulty:

No one in the world that I have ever seen has had a body as really classic in its lines as yours. I once told you that you had a body so beautiful that
it rather quieted passion because of its perfection & I meant that. It has that
effect at times. At other times your own imagination transforms the beauty
or rather infuses it with a lust that is terrible & beautiful too.

He became practical, recalling Helen's profitable land speculations and
feeling also that similar joint ventures would help restore him in her favor.
"But so long as your out there Babu," he wrote, "you might just as well
. . . see what can be done to make a little money for us[,] a few investments."[5]

After three weeks with her mother in Portland, Helen went to Hollywood,
put up at Christie's Hotel, got a voice teacher and looked around for property
likely to swell in value. She took no job, relying on her shrewdness. She and
Dreiser still owned several lots in Montrose and Manhattan Beach, some of
which she now sold at a great profit to gain capital for reinvestment. Dreiser
got $450 for their jointly owned Maxwell, which he was unable to drive
anyway, and sent her the money, later sending her $2,000 more he scraped up.
Now it was his turn to feel jealous doubt:

Your last several letters have been so high spirited I'm thinking that
Hollywood must look good to you. Who else is stopping at the Christie?
And whose car are you using. . . . Next I'll be hearing your on [your]
way to Honolulu or China with some heavy director whose soul is mush.

Later:

I suppose the heavy German and the Shakespearian actor who used to
write you—to say nothing of some others—Allan Dwan & Rex Ingram possibly are all on hand.

Again:

But I gather from your letters that you have plenty of temporary consolation. I know you too well to know that you wouldn't. . . . If you must

you must. And if I don't like it my satisfaction is in dropping you entirely.
. . . But since I am moved to do something different I will not. The love tie
is not entirely sexual. It is also mental. I think it is identified with beauty &
the worship of it—mental & physical. It comprises mood & longings & which
seem to take their rise from some need of the mind as well as the body.

He joked about going to Hollywood and spying on her:

> I think I might get news of the blonde German that way—to say nothing
> of Dwan, Noah or Wallace Beery & a few others. Your mind runs to gross
> rhinocerii these days and no doubt they are about like pachyderms from the
> zoo.[6]

Three times he mentioned the idea of divorcing Jug and marrying Helen,
obviously as a painful concession. "When this job [the *Tragedy*] is over,—
and I can't leave here until it is—I'll go out there or anywhere—Paris if you
wish, establish a residence, get a divorce & tie up as per your dream. I don't
care for anyone else in life but you—really. I suppose after I've done so I'll
have to walk the chalk but still, if it's going to make you really happy I can
do all that you wish."

He poked fun: "One line in this last letter kills me. It reads, 'Perhaps you
like a coarser type' (sexually you mean.) Yes? And since when have you
become delicatessen in that field. I have been drifting along under the impression that when it came to that you were the queen bee—about as energetic &
riotous as they come. But I now learn different. There are those who have
more punch. Well it's something to know. I may as well be on the look
out. . . . You have not only the fire but the imagination and without that, as
you know, there is no sex at all." [7]

In reply to Helen's pointed query, he insisted that he had no typist. He had
at least two, Miss Kusell aiding him in New York, Mrs. Campbell in Philadelphia. Secretively he kept each unaware that the other was working for
him. A few days earlier he had written Mrs. Campbell about one of his shorter
pieces:

> Dear Loweez—The mss. goes same time as this. 2 copies please. So you're
> showing up Tuesday. If you're going to deign to grace this cell I'll save din-
> ner time for you. We can eat in a Greenwich Village Hell Hole.[8]

"You ask so many questions," he wrote Helen. "And I know you think I
have a girl hanging on my arm every night. I'm like a poor man who gets
credit for being enormously wealthy. (Now don't throw anything). Just the
same I'm presenting an honest picture." "I've done nothing since you went
away that you would object to, I know." "I'm not sleeping with anyone. I
have these two big rooms—as bare as small barns & nightly I'm in my high,
small four poster bed between 11:30 and 1—rarely later than 12." When he
wrote of attending a Writers' Club dinner with Art Young, the cartoonist, he
added, "And at once you'll say what ladies? And though I say no ladies you'll

never believe it. And if you could see Art Young—62 years of age . . . you might believe it." [9]

Tom Smith, of Liveright's, meanwhile was writing him, "I enjoyed the evening with you so much and also with Miss Kussell [sic]. Don't make her too literary. This characteristic has a tendency to spoil all women." [10]

Helen, knowing from experience that he was lying, could not be sure of the extent of it. By this time a knowledge of Dreiser's novels had become a hallmark of sophistication among the more daring and advanced college students. He received admiring letters from Esther McCoy, a student at Washington University in St. Louis, and from Amy Parsons at Ohio State University. On Dreiser an intelligent, applauding letter from an unknown young woman reacted as a powerful aphrodisiac. Behind in his work though he was, he exchanged photographs and many letters with Miss McCoy and Miss Parsons, urging both to come to New York.

"Your delicious—you really are," he wrote Miss McCoy. "Your mind I mean. . . . I think you have a *hard* mind—very. And a most searching & stoic & pagan point of view. You . . . would most likely lead an ordinary male a sweet dance . . . . I wouldn't care a damn really whether you were honest with me or not so long as you were interesting and intriguing. If you weren't those the honesty wouldn't help much." [11]

To Miss Parsons he wrote, "I judge from [your] picture that you can be hurt. People who are without emotion or do not understand it—do not understand me and do not trouble to write me. A primary letter is a primary confession." [12]

Miss McCoy remained aloof, but Miss Parsons showed interest.

"So that you can come when the whim seizes you," Dreiser wrote her, "I am enclosing a check for a [sic] $100 that should get you here & back. If you have no hotel picked . . . I suggest the Empire at 69th [actually Sixty-third] & Broadway." [13]

Miss Parsons visited him. Charmed, he later took a train to Columbus and spent a weekend with her, posing as her "Uncle Magnus." "What a delightful day and-a-half," he wrote her. "But you must not publish anything about my being there. *No* I do not want that." [14]

To Helen he wrote, "The book isn't done yet. . . . There's no one I want to live with but you. . . ." [15]

Miss Kusell, working with him regularly, noted his megalomaniac sense of greatness. Usually unhappy, he had few sentiments of gratitude, feeling that whatever came his way was more than due him. He read little and was often ungenerous in his opinion of other novelists, Dostoyevsky being an exception. He lied as persistently in personal matters as he clung to integrity in his writing. He was apt to steal ideas without realizing it, or indeed caring very much. Miss Kusell had written a short story about a poor dressmaker who fell in love with a struggling artist, which she showed him. He shrugged, saying it was not bad. Later, he wrote a story on that identical theme, giving it to her to edit. He was surprised when she pointed out that it was her idea, having forgotten that entirely.[16]

He had read Sherwood Anderson's *Winesburg, Ohio*, published five years earlier, and had been impressed by emotional sentiments in the story "Tandy." By this time he had obviously forgotten the origin of the story. Now he took Anderson's lines, modified and chopped them into a free-verse poem he called "The Beautiful," inscribed it to Helen and sent it to her—a forgetfulness that would embarrass him later.

II. RUSTY WIRES AND IRONS

Always troubled, Dreiser in 1924 was more deeply disturbed than usual. Helen's departure was a blow at his ego as well as his happiness. If as a mechanist and the propounder of Dreiser's Law he could justify intellectually his deceit with women, emotionally he had occasional pangs of conscience. He had fearful dreams. He was bothered by Mame, who was starting a restaurant called the Green Witch with another woman, quarreling with her partner and visiting her difficulties on him.

"Mame is a nuicance [*sic*]," he wrote. ". . . I am warning [her] today though that this has got to be cut out or I move. . . . I am in no mood to be annoyed now."

He faced a deadline on *An American Tragedy*, which Liveright had announced for fall, 1924, and he was not meeting it. This novel was big in theme, a supreme challenge. "For some reason," he admitted, "this book is harder than any I ever wrote. I might as well be chipping it out of solid rock. . . . Either my brain or my method must have changed a lot." [17]

At times he drank heavily enough to worry Mame—even took to smoking cigarettes for a while. Once he went to Mame, weeping bitterly because of his troubles with the novel. Liveright did not like the title *An American Tragedy* and was in favor of calling it simply by the name of the protagonist; but Dreiser had named his protagonist Griffiths, which Liveright thought fatal because of the difficulty in pronouncing it. "I feel that I must once more implore you to call the book Ewing or Warner or some other good representative name. . . ." he wrote. "Commercial, I may appear, but in the end it is you who will keep after me and after me if the book doesn't sell. . . ." [18]

Now and then Dreiser dropped in at the splendid Liveright offices, constantly trying—and failing—to date the pretty Irish receptionist. He chatted with Tom Smith and with Manuel Komroff, editor of Liveright's Modern Library. Modern Library should publish *Crime and Punishment*, he said. Komroff agreed, except that Everyman Library already had it for sixty cents, and he later felt that Dreiser's admiration for Dostoyevsky showed its influence in the *Tragedy*.[19]

Always seeking documentation, Dreiser arranged a visit to Cluett & Peabody's factory in Troy so that he could watch the manufacture of men's collars, the better to picture Clyde Griffiths at work. "I may as well confess that I will never be able to write this book fast," he wrote Helen. "It is too intricate in its thought & somehow my method if not my style has changed. I work with more care—and hence difficulty. My style isn't as fluid. . . . Two & three chapters a week is the best I can do."

To still his nerves he took morning walks in Washington Square. He was shooting for October first as completion date, but soon knew he would not make it. "Sometimes I get so low I have to drop everything and do a turn around the block." He ate irregularly, once boiling three eggs and having them with a glass of ginger ale for dinner. Insomnia sometimes followed his nightmares. "My body appears to be made of heavy, wet leather & my nerves & joints of rusty wires & irons." When he worked, he worked with utter dedication:

> I'm to where the factory girl & the rich girl in Clyde's life are enlarging & by degrees destroying him. . . . It seems simple. I know the story. The right procession & selection of incidents should be as nothing but it just chances to be everything. And so I write & rewrite. Sometimes I write enough to make two chapters or three in a day & get ⅓ of a chapter that is eventually ok. . . . But just the same & failure or no failure I feel it an honor to be permitted to even attempt to tell such a tale & on that basis I am working on.[20]

He was still trying to market Maxwell's Shakespeare script, getting another publisher to look at it and seeking Van Vechten's and Mencken's cooperation.

"Who gives a damn who wrote the Shakespeare plays?" Mencken demanded. "The evidence is massive that Shakespeare lived, and that all his friends thought he wrote them. Personally, I believe that they were written by Beethoven." [21]

Despite his troubles, Dreiser's social life was active. With William Lengel he went to the Dutch Treat Club at the Waldorf ("It's a men's club only," he assured Helen), meeting there with Ray Long, Heywood Broun, George Jean Nathan, Irvin Cobb and others. He dropped in at Patchin Place to visit with the Powys brothers, John complaining that he could hardly hold body and soul together with his lectures. With Mencken, Nathan and Van Vechten he attended a party at Zoë Akins' on lower Fifth Avenue. With Ernest and Madeleine Boyd he saw an O'Neill dramatization of *The Ancient Mariner* at the Provincetown. He dined at his old friend Arthur Henry's apartment (Henry had divorced Anna and married another old Dreiser friend, Clare Kummer), where he argued with Alexander Woollcott about New York critics and had "plenty to drink but I didn't get drunk." He talked with the psychiatrist Brill, who thought privately that some sexual symbolism must underlie Dreiser's constant handkerchief-folding. He attended the opening of

Mame's new restaurant, finding the Powyses there and also his brother Ed Dreiser, who had quit the stage after a serious accident and become a textile appraiser. "I haven't seen him . . . in 6 or 7 years," Dreiser wrote Helen, "and he came over—said hello—stayed about ten seconds & left. . . . His hair was dyed a youthful chestnut & he looked about 35."

Through Nathan he met W. C. Fields, who celebrated his triumph in *Poppy* by leasing a Larchmont shorefront mansion and giving a large party, which Dreiser attended along with Robert Benchley and many actors and chorus girls. "Of all the dumb-bells & bone heads," he observed, "give me the average actor & actress. Nothing got the least applause or interest unless it was smutty or smart-aleck—not a thing. . . . And, of course, some one asked me if I was related to Dreicer the jeweler." [22]

Ridgeley Torrence, who had moved into Patchin Place, was having group discussions there at which Dreiser must have heard much about the revolutionary experiment in Russia. From his radical friend Art Young, who introduced him to the Russian Bear restaurant on Second Avenue, he doubtless heard more. To the Russian Bear he escorted Claude Bowers, who found the place patronized by radicals praising the Soviet and applauding balalaika-playing entertainers.

"That night," Bowers wrote, "Dreiser again amazed me by his interest in politics and his abysmal ignorance of it." [23]

Politics was in the air, for late in June the Democratic National Convention opened at Madison Square Garden, Fifth Avenue was hung with bunting and photos of Al Smith, and Mayor Hylan had an open-air floor built in Washington Square where delegates could dance to Paul Whiteman's orchestra. Bowers, politicking actively behind the scenes, gave two tickets to Dreiser, who attended one session with Lengel—or so he wrote Helen. Years later Lengel insisted he did not attend the convention, so the chances are that Dreiser had a girl with him. He did not see his fading hero, William Jennings Bryan, whom he had applauded in this same arena in 1896. Sourly he watched what he regarded as Catholic machinations to foist Smith on the Democrats—Smith, whose song was the old Howley-Haviland hit, "The Sidewalks of New York." "They were staging an obviously manufactured Al Smith ovation," he wrote, "& I couldn't stand it. The Catholics were about as thick as flies—priests & Tammany politicians—I left early & shall not go again." [24]

"My God . . . " he said later to Bowers. "And is that the way we're governed in a democracy?" He also said passionately to Bowers, "You enjoy life, don't you? Do you never get morbid, depressed and disgusted?" [25]

He was fascinated by the Leopold-Loeb case in Chicago, writing, "Just a desire to kill doesn't seem to explain it. There must be something more it seems to me, a great novel there somewhere." [26] His sister Mame fascinated him in a different way. Although her new restaurant was an immediate success, she quarreled so bitterly with her partner that she withdrew after only five weeks.

Dreiser relied heavily on Louise Campbell, sending her chapters of the *Tragedy* piecemeal and writing her in mock German:

Dear Lucy—Da mit ein chapter. Ess iss to go mit der odders.
Read.
Entwader gifs schlagen und knocken kraachen.
Hürst du?
Mach mir kine spass.
Soust, in ein augenblick kann alles zu sammen kommen.
                                    —Freidrich Neitche [*sic*] [27]

Writing in longhand by his open back-window in stifling summer heat, he could hear the Elevated roar by, could see old Austin Brennan reading the paper in the yard—could see cloistered Patchin Place and the Jefferson Market clock beyond. He was fifty-three in August. The writing was painfully slow—nothing like the *Sister Carrie* days in 1900 when he could rip off 5,000 or more words a day. Claude Bowers mentioned to him that the book was announced for fall.

"It will not be ready until spring," Dreiser said.

"But the publisher—" Bowers began.

"I can't help that," Dreiser snapped. "You can't write any faster than you can." [28]

III. THE NASTY, MEAN THINGS

Dreiser, who considered Helen an adorable doll, occasionally used baby-talk with her. He was putting baby-talk into the mouth of Sondra in the *Tragedy*, and he tried it on Helen, who had moved to a private house and then had been forced to move again because of family changes:

Did they treat the Babu so bad. The nasty, mean things. Well, we'll dis fix them. Wait an' see. Making her move. We'll do something terrible— punch um in the eye or, diss knock teeth out. An' pinch toes sompin awful.

For *Cosmopolitan* he dropped the baby-talk and made a quick trip to Detroit to interview the great, profane Ty Cobb—a strange assignment for one who knew no baseball, and yet the two men probably understood each other, both being ferocious competitors. Soon after his return he went to Rose Hill, near Philadelphia, to see the premiere of a new play, *Art*, at the Hedgerow Theater recently opened by Jasper Deeter, an old Provincetown hand. In his letter to Helen about this he said his companion was Tom Smith.[29] Actually she was Kirah Markham, long a member of the Provincetown group, who had a leading role in the Hedgerow play. Other letters in which he mentioned solitary excursions were probably similarly artful.

Miss Markham's friend, the artist Wharton Esherick, went backstage before curtain time to greet her. To Esherick she mentioned that there would be a reception after the performance that would not end until late, and she asked if he could put her and Dreiser up at his country place near Paoli. He assented gladly. Never having met Dreiser, the tall, genial Esherick got Miss Markham's description of him, spied him in a forward row in the still-lighted house, slipped into the row behind him and said, "Mr. Dreiser?"

"Yes," Dreiser replied coldly, without turning.

Esherick, taken aback, introduced himself and said, "Kirah tells me you'll be staying at my place for the night."

"Yes, I believe we are," Dreiser said, still not looking around and appearing to feel that the conversation was closed.

Esherick, his hand extended for a handshake, retired in indignation. "Not once did he turn to see whether I was Hottentot or Chinese," he said afterward. He had encountered a Dreiser mood. Later that night at the Esherick place Dreiser thawed and in fact took a great fancy to the artist—a man of force, a doer after his own heart who painted and worked beautifully in clay or wood—and to his wife, Letty Esherick.

To Esherick he said that although Miss Markham no longer had any romantic interest in him, he would always have the highest regard for her and for her talents. "You know, Kirah has been a very important person in my life." [30]

"I thought of you all the time," he wrote Helen, "& how much you would have enjoyed being there." [31]

Helen was dying to rejoin him, half hoping that he had reformed although she knew better. "[He expected] his complete freedom," she later wrote, "in which he could indulge to the fullest, at the same time expecting my undivided devotion to him." [32] Dreiser, scorning the Republicans and Democrats, was supporting La Follette without real fervor. In October he suffered a four-day siege of grippe, wrote Helen pathetically about his problems with the novel and still made ambiguous mention of marriage, wiring her, "What I said about Paris goes if we can be happy together." [33] She persuaded herself that it was her duty to go back, to comfort and inspire him. "I would picture him ill or depressed so that he could not work, and this disturbed and troubled me. . . . Perhaps I should be with him—good or bad. . . ." [34]

Her mind made up, she returned for a final visit to Portland, where her mother—now convinced that any woman dealing with Dreiser came off second best—tried vainly to dissuade her. Late in October, after an absence of seven months, she boarded an eastbound train.

Dreiser met her at Pennsylvania Station, kissed her, said "It's Babu, all right," and took her to dinner at Mouquin's. He was in a predicament, for although he had begged her to come back he did not want her to live with him, both because it would hamper other affairs and because her constant presence would slow his work on the *Tragedy*. Helen therefore put up at the Albert Hotel on Tenth Street, a few blocks from his apartment, on the promise that they would soon find housekeeping quarters.

To Amy Parsons, who was paying him another visit in New York, he wrote, "I suggest the Empire at 65th [actually Sixty-third] & Broadway.

(. . . I can arrange if you wire or write.) . . . Wire train & I'll meet you & place you nicely somewhere." [35]

After his meeting with Miss Parsons, he took Helen to Washington, showed her the sights and returned with her to face one of those contretemps which the best-laid plans could not always eliminate. "We were getting out of a taxicab in front of Dreiser's studio," Helen recalled, "when a woman dashed toward him, making a sharp and accusing statement. Taking my arm, he pushed past her to the door . . . and told me to wait inside; he would be back shortly. I heard them talking outside, his voice low and firm, hers troubled and insistent. Shortly afterward he entered the room and locked the door behind him without comment." [36]

To Mencken, who still deprecated his habit of demanding large advances, he directed a reply addressed to "John Wesley, Esq.":

> I know your Methodist soul resents the immorality of it but all my literary life I have worked on *advance* royalties. If I hadn't been able to trick the moral publishers out of the immoral money—and to the prejudice of such writers . . . whose books sell—I wouldn't have been able to work at all. . . . Major Leigh would testify that he died—my owing him $3,000. The Century will testify that I stung them for an advance of $2,000. John Lane closed his house here with $2,000 due from me. I am ahead of B & L to the extent of $3,000 & I would to God it were more.
>
> But dear John, you will never get it. Neither will you ever get certain other devices by which I have lived and moved.[37]

And to Miss Parsons, who offered to send him a local opinion of his work:

> No, honey, I am not interested in arguments & estimates from all and sundry. I've been pushed and slapped too long. It cuts no ice—so long as I make a living.
>
> All my nicest thoughts. You know I still have those smartly tinted cigarettes you left. I think I'll smoke them.[38]

He wrote Upton Sinclair, whom he had met in California, to thank him for sending a book and to disagree with his philosophy:

> But don't forget that the brotherhood of man—(this entirely apart from some of the co-operative phases of Socialism) is mere moonshine to me. I see the individual large or small—weak or strong as predatory & nothing less.[39]

The *Tragedy* had been announced for fall and had missed. Liveright's brochures then trumpeted it for spring, 1925, but by the time Helen rejoined him Dreiser must have known that he would not make that either. Although he was missing deadlines scandalously, it was not for want of trying. True, he could not resist ready money, and he had sacrificed time to do two stories for the Hearst magazines and two for the new Mencken-Nathan *Mercury*. But he had dropped his chaotic habit of working on a half-dozen projects at once. For Dreiser, considering his usual disorder, this was a period of almost total concentration.

3. Propinquity

In January, 1925, Dreiser and Helen took a $60-a-month apartment at 1799 Bedford Avenue in Brooklyn. For privacy Dreiser rented an office in the Guardian Life Building on Union Square, where the attorney Arthur Carter Hume also had offices. He needed Hume's advice in narrating the legal maneuvers after Clyde Griffiths' arrest, and the separate office made it easy for him to meet with other women. Since Helen also was typing for him, he had at least three women involved in the *Tragedy*, but it was Louise Campbell and Sally Kusell to whom he entrusted the important chores of cutting and editing.

Again he warned his friends not to divulge his two addresses, and demurred when Mencken gave one of them to a colleague. "I have been very careful in the past," Mencken replied. "At least once a week someone asks for your address. Sometimes they are of the female sex, and beautiful. But I'll be discreet." [1]

There was another effort to jam through a Clean Books Bill which Dreiser denounced as "a subtle two-edged menace to liberty." It was defeated in the assembly with Liveright again influential in the opposition. By now Liveright was regarded as the boy wonder and/or the prize screwball of the publishing business. He had promoted books with a genuine flair. He was generous with money to writers he believed in. He made money fast and spent it faster, drove a speedy Fiat and was out to corral the world's best authors, among them Sherwood Anderson, although Anderson had never had a best-selling book.

Anderson was then published by B. W. Huebsch. In January Huebsch gave a luncheon party for Anderson at the Brevoort. Dreiser failed to attend, but about 80 literary figures were there, including Mencken and Stuart Sherman, the Illinois professor who was now critic for the *New York Tribune*. Sherman had flayed both Mencken and Dreiser periodically for ten years. Now, with the trend against him, he was deserting the old guard in favor of the moderns. He crossed the room, eager to meet his old arch-enemy, Mencken. Mencken, who could be unforgiving, wheeled and turned his back on the man who had assailed the realists. But perhaps the most embarrassed man there was Sherwood Anderson himself. After the brilliant gathering Huebsch had assembled in his honor, he had to tell Huebsch sheepishly that he was going over to Liveright, who had offered him a fat drawing account. [2]

Liveright had surrounded himself with talented people. Julian Messner was vice-president and sales manager, supervising salesmen who included Bennett Cerf, Richard Simon and Edward Weeks. Tom Smith, as head of the editorial department, had the advice of Komroff and the assistance of Louis Kronenberger, Lillian Hellman and Beatrice Kaufman. When Liveright badly needed money in 1925, he took on another vice-president, multilingual Donald Friede, just twenty-four, who had been fired not only from Harvard but also from Yale and Princeton and had spent a year in Komroff's department. Friede's ticket to the vice-presidency, as he well knew, was his heavy investment of money in the firm. Liveright, madly ambitious, was spreading into the theater as a producer. He gave occasional jazz-age parties at the Forty-eighth Street brownstone where writers and critics could be sure to meet beauties from the stage as they quaffed whiskey off the boat and danced to a Negro band. "You met everybody there," recalled Madeleine Boyd, who sometimes helped revive comatose guests and put them in cabs.[3]

Dreiser left one of these celebrations with Mencken and lurched into the Gotham Book Mart next door. Before salespeople could stop them, Mencken scribbled on the flyleaf of a valuable antique Bible on display, "If it wasn't for me, Dreiser would be raising chickens in Kansas," and Dreiser penned a suitable retort. These inscriptions enhanced rather than diminished the value of the Bible, which later became a part of the Lewisohn collection.

Meanwhile Helen Richardson essayed to answer a letter from Josephine Piercy of the English department at the University of Illinois asking Dreiser to describe his writing methods. Helen wrote in part:

> All I have been able to obtain from [Dreiser] thus far is this: "Can it be that the Department of English of the University of Illinois is approaching so humble a source for advice on the composition of the English Language? Has not Dr. Sherman sufficiently convinced the student body . . . of the fact that I cannot write and know nothing concerning the composition of the English Language?"
> And he also added: "The fact is that technically this is true. I never took a course in English composition and I never consciously mastered the rules of grammar and do not to this day know what they are. . . ."
> This is not what I personally hoped to have him write but it is the best that his present mood will furnish.[4]

An American Tragedy—Dreiser had definitely decided on this title—was now announced for fall, 1925, with Liveright aiming for October publication. Dreiser was delayed by a heavy bronchial cold, but chiefly by his own dissatisfaction with his treatment. Moving a large cast of characters through intricacies of love and law took organization, for which he had little knack. He pondered, revised—rewrote one chapter seven or eight times, then threw it out. Convention, always a compelling force in his novels, was here vicious and triumphant, the villain of the piece. Frank Cowperwood had fought convention with some degree of success, but Clyde Griffiths, lacking the character and intelligence to fight it, was utterly defeated by it—just as

Dreiser himself, for all his courage, felt that he had been "pushed & slapped" and cheated of his dearest dreams by convention.

The murder—how should it be committed? In the 1906 case, Chester Gillette had a tennis racket with which he stunned Grace Brown as he overturned the boat. Dreiser could not have his killer so brutal, the issue so clear. He solved the problem with a device—a trick of fate—akin to the accidental closing of the safe door that turned Hurstwood into a criminal. His Clyde took not a racket with him but an innocent camera. Although Clyde had murder in his heart at the outset, his courage failed him at the supreme moment, he could not go through with it, the overturning of the boat was accidental, and as he swam away he was torn between a desire to save the sinking Roberta and a fear that she would pull him down. He was half crazed by terror, not really a murderer at all—or was he?

As he wrote the murder scene, Dreiser admitted to Miss Kusell, he wept unrestrainedly. Even as he told her about it, tears were in his eyes.[5]

In depicting Clyde's trial, he clung to fact when he could, lifting some 30 pages verbatim from old New York newspaper accounts of the court proceedings and the letters between the ill-fated lovers. In other instances he altered the news reports to heighten the drama and the sympathy for Clyde. Probably with Sumner in mind, he (or was it one of his editors?) eliminated mention of the introduction of the victim's uterus and the foetus as courtroom exhibits.[6] Like his admired Dostoyevsky and Tolstoy, he took trouble to make his picture complete, working on an immense canvas and spilling off on all sides. Miss Kusell in New York and Mrs. Campbell in Philadelphia quailed at the excess wordage and cut drastically.

He was inundated by manuscript. At his invitation, Wharton Esherick on a trip to New York called at the Brooklyn apartment. Dreiser opened the door a crack, peering out suspiciously.

"Oh, it's you, Esherick," he said without real warmth.

The artist saw slabs of manuscript on Dreiser's desk, on chairs, on the floor. "You're in the thick of it," he said. "I'll go."

Dreiser grabbed his collar and pulled him in. "I am busy, but you're here and you're not going to go. Lie down in the bedroom while I finish."[7]

Late though he was, he had to relax regularly. He met Mencken and Burton Rascoe at the Algonquin. Several times he joined Mencken, Boyd, Ed Smith and the painter Kenneth Hayes Miller, who had a studio on Fourteenth Street, for drinks in New York before taxiing to a scofflaw Hoboken rathskeller. With Helen he spent a summer weekend at Esherick's in Pennsylvania, then going off to sail with Esherick on Barnegat Bay, Dreiser with typical impulsiveness removing his shirt and suffering sunburn that put him under a doctor's care for ten days—another delay on the book.

Jug Dreiser meanwhile had an office job at the printing establishment of Dreiser's old colleague Fremont Rider. Ed Dreiser's daughter Vera found her so charming that Vera looked forward to her visits with delight. She took a cocktail now, she had gone to Europe again, she enjoyed sporting events and had beaux, but she had determined never to marry again. She was the ideal cast-off wife, never troubling Dreiser for money. That summer she visited the Fire Island cottage of the newsman, Gene Fowler, who noted, "It was apparent that she still loved [Dreiser]." She spoke of her sacrifices 25 years earlier when he was writing *Sister Carrie*. And she said something that stuck in Fowler's mind:

"Theo hasn't written anything worth while since our separation—and he never will." [8]

II. THE DEATH HOUSE

Dreiser, feeling that the conflicts of sex heightened his awareness and creativity, used his affairs deliberately to make the *Tragedy* a better book. As Helen put it, "He tried to place himself between opposing forces in order to gather reactions of a stimulating quality. . . ." On rare occasions he sensed a debasement in his deceit and yearned for some religious solace. Surprisingly, he was corresponding with a bookish Chicago Catholic priest, Father Paul Lacosky, who (equally surprisingly) had praised *Sister Carrie* and The *"Genius."* To Father Lacosky he wrote in evident remorse, "If some day a weary author heavily laden with sin arrives at your confessional—absolve him if for no more than the reality he sought—in vain, I fear, to portray." [9]

It appears that the original manuscript of *An American Tragedy* must have been at least a million words long. Miss Kusell feels that she cut Dreiser's original copy about in half. Mrs. Campbell, who then worked on successive batches of the script in her turn, feels certain that she cut it more than in half, and that Dreiser let the cuts stand although at times he wailed at her cruelty.[10]

When he handed in the last chapters to Tom Smith in mid-July, it was about 400,000 words long. Smith felt it still wordy. With the help of Manuel Komroff he pared away about 50,000 words more, both men feeling that as much more again could be cut but realizing that they could push the sensitive author only so far. "I have not cut out anything," Smith wrote him, "that I did not honestly believe for your sake should not [*sic*] be left out." [11]

Dreiser insisted on restoring more than half of what they had cut, and the completed book ran to some 385,000 words. Komroff, though impressed, feared it was too long-winded to have a good sale. Smith, while worried about the tediousness of the first half, was elated about the rest, writing Dreiser, "The slow, fatal working-up to the death of Roberta is one of the grimmest and most gripping tragedies that I have read in years." [12]

The book was planned for two volumes to sell at four dollars. Final copy went to the printer late in July. Proof began to stream in ten days later, and Smith and Liveright found to their dismay that they would never make the October publication date. Dreiser, who always looked on proof as something to be changed, was still dissatisfied. He called Louise Campbell over from Philadelphia to help him with extensive revisions. Meanwhile Smith sent a set of proofs to Sinclair Lewis, asking him to review the book. Lewis, who had a deep respect for Dreiser, thought the novel decidedly inferior and preferred to skip reviewing it.[13]

Smith's enthusiasm held—but when would Dreiser finish? Although he was only one of many authors on the Liveright list, his book was their biggest fall production and he was missing the best selling months before Christmas. He would not be hurried. He made changes requiring heavy resetting and evidently was not finished until late October. Meanwhile Mencken sent him an appraisal he had received from Sarah Gertrude Millin in South Africa that should have pleased him:

> I think Dreiser is the greatest of American novelists. He comes along—step, step—inexorably, irresistibly, over everything—like a war-tank. Not shiny, not elegant: and he mustn't be.[14]

While he still worked over corrections, he and Helen had Claude and Sybil Bowers to the Brooklyn flat for a duck dinner. Characteristically he gave the Bowerses the wrong address and was "thoroughly annoyed and resentful" when they were late, though the fault was his own. He warmed up over cocktails and duck as they discussed a fellow Hoosier, Booth Tarkington. "He does not know reality, does not know life, work, the average human being, or sex," Dreiser said. He commented on *The Turmoil*, a big subject which he felt Tarkington had falsified by having a poet with no business training solve problems that had stumped an industrialist. "It's not real life. If he had dealt only with the raw realities, what a marvel he would be with his exquisite style."[15]

Liveright must have been horrified late in October when Dreiser decided that he was not satisfied with his depiction of Clyde's life in the death house. Earlier he had visited Sing Sing prison to get the feel of it, and had told Komroff how, when the electric chair was turned on the lights in the whole institution dimmed. But he had not been permitted to see the cells of prisoners awaiting execution, this being against regulations. Not having seen condemned row, he felt he had not written of it with real authority. He tried vainly to wangle admission through an attorney, then fell back on Mencken, writing him:

> I hear Al Smith or Jimmy Walker can fix it. I hear that Herbert Swope [of the *New York World*] can fix it with either. I hear that you can fix it with Swope. Can you hear me.[16]

Mencken immediately wrote James M. Cain of the *World*, who queried city editor James W. Barrett. Barrett wanted to get a scoop death-house interview with a condemned Brooklyn murderer, Anthony Pantano, and the idea of having him interviewed by the realistic novelist intrigued him. He went to the trouble of getting a court order permitting Dreiser to enter the death house as a "representative of the *World*."

Here arose a misunderstanding. Barrett understood that Dreiser, in return for the favor, would write an account of the interview for the *World*. Dreiser, his thoughts elsewhere (and with a genius for misinterpreting details) had the impression that he was merely to report verbally. He went to Sing Sing on or about November 26, inspected the death house and talked at some length with Pantano. Returning to New York, he telephoned the *World* and learned that they expected a 5,000-word article. Angrily he said he had no time, that such an article would take him a week, and if he did it, his price would be $500.

The *World* sent word to Mencken, who wired Dreiser:

WORLD COMPLAINS THAT AFTER GETTING YOU PERMIT WITH GREAT DIFFI-
CULTY BY SAYING YOU REPRESENTED IT YOU NOW DEMAND MONEY THIS PUTS
ME INTO A NICE HOLE INDEED.[17]

Dreiser replied immediately, "THE WORLD LIES YOUR TELEGRAM IS AN INSULT." [18]

The disgruntled *World* settled by sending Dudley Nichols, then a young reporter, to Brooklyn to interview Dreiser about his interview. Dreiser, dropping from the exhaustion he always felt when finishing a book, wanted only to get a change of scene and a rest. He made his final corrections, which were rushed to the printer. He quit his Union Square office and with Helen cleared out of the Flatbush apartment, storing his furniture. They moved temporarily into the Hotel Empire—the place he recommended to girl friends from out of town. He wrote Mencken explaining the *World* quarrel, but still ending irascibly:

A telegram from you *charging me* with extorting money from the *World*. Upon my word. And when I asked this as a favor. Have I ever exacted anything from you for a favor. . . . The editors of the World give me a large pain. . . .[19]

Publication of *An American Tragedy* was now announced for December 10, a date that would be missed by a few days. Liveright was taking a long gamble, boosting the price of the two-volume book to five dollars. He was doing Dreiser a signal honor—publishing a limited, signed edition in fine laid paper at $12.50—and he gave him a party. Floyd Dell wandered into a café that night—he does not remember which café—and saw a group of celebrants including Dreiser, Liveright and Tom Smith. Dreiser was hunched over the table with his head in his arms. Someone remarked facetiously that he had had one glass of beer and collapsed. He raised his head.

"You know, Dell," he said, "I took a girl away from you once." [20]

III. COCKTAILS WITH MENCKEN

Dreiser and Helen bought another Maxwell and headed for Florida on December 8, stopping at Mame's on the way out of town to give her $20. (She had asked for $75.) Among other things Dreiser was fleeing the reviews, which he thought would be disparaging, and he talked more pessimistically than he really felt about the book's sale. The trip did not begin auspiciously. He had a bronchial cold and was tired and cranky. Helen also had a cold, actually fearing that she would die of pneumonia, and was emotionally upset after her year-long spiritual struggle with several unseen female rivals. Dreiser, a compulsive writer, kept a chaotic diary on this odd journey.

Stopping at Philadelphia, he got Helen out of the way by sending her on to Esherick's in Paoli while he talked over his writing plans with Louise Campbell. So far he had contrived to keep the pair from meeting, just as Mrs. Campbell and Miss Kusell had never met. The practical Mrs. Campbell had seen him in all his moods, seen his copy at its loosest, and had few illusions about him. She enjoyed his simplicity and appreciated his generous encouragement of her own writing, but was familiar enough with his uneven temper and his intellectual confusion to know that the only reason they got along well was because their association was intermittent. Helen saw him simply as a genius. In all but her most despairing moments she was not without some pride in being the mistress of so gifted a man.

Dreiser and Helen drove on next day to Baltimore, where they stopped at 1524 Hollins Street while Dreiser went in to see if Mencken was home. Mencken was, and Dreiser, seldom the gallant with a woman he was sure of, let Helen sit outside in the cold while they chatted.

Mencken was still irked about the *World* incident. His relations with Dreiser had deteriorated gradually for several years as he grew more and more contemptuous of Dreiser's gaucherie, ignorance, sex vagaries, superstition and defects of style. He had come to regard him with the intellectual curiosity of the scientist who studies a fascinating but unruly specimen under the microscope. Mencken himself was changing. His *American Language* had been applauded by scholars, and with Nathan's help he had made a sensational success of the iconoclastic *Mercury*. The former bad boy of letters was famous at forty-five, revered across the nation by rebels who hailed him as their prophet.

His mother, to whom he was deeply attached, was seriously ill when Dreiser called, and in fact she died next day, December 13.

Nevertheless he was a cordial host, giving Dreiser a chair before the hearth. He was aghast when he learned sometime later that Helen was waiting outside in an open car. He rushed out, brought her in and served cocktails. When Dreiser asked for a bottle of whiskey to take with him, he produced one from his ample private stock but was annoyed when Dreiser made a fuss about paying for it, remarking that he had not yet become a bootlegger. But what hurt him profoundly was Dreiser's apparent unconcern about the grave illness of Anna Mencken, his failure to utter the expected words of sympathy and hope. Mencken himself described his feelings briefly in a letter to Helen twenty years later:

> I remember how I resented his leaving you to sit in a cold car up the street, and how I resented likewise his aloof indifference to my mother's illness.[21]

Dreiser's own diary entry was scanty: "Call on Mencken. He furnishes me a bottle of booze. . . . His mother is very ill. [They drive on to Washington.] Arrive at about 8. Helen & I quarrel. I threaten to blow the trip & frighten her. . . . I eat alone in the Union Station at about 11. Still a bad cold." [22]

En route southward they bought Christmas cards and sent them. B & L had worked fast, for on December 16 in Winston-Salem Dreiser was able to buy a copy of *An American Tragedy*, the first he had seen. Sally Kusell, to whom he had given his itinerary, wrote him:

> The book has come, its gay yellow jacket belieing the awful tragedy of its contents. I have just finished it, and, oh, the emotional stratas of those last ten chapters. . . . God, its [*sic*] thrilling!! . . .[23]

"Rear left break goes on the bum," Dreiser told his diary. "Also speedometer. Get break taken off at Aiken by negro. . . . Fierce roads. . . . 12.50 for car repairs. . . . Helen & I quarrel over S. K. A bad night. . . . Hard feelings. How they spoil everything." But he was sympathetic with trees: "The bleeding pine trees (turpentine) I bleed with them." In Georgia he received a letter from a lady he identified only as Veronica: "She wants me to come to France & live with her."

He was touched by the human yearning for communication: "In every city one is affected by the living relationship—the exquisite, frail moment of pure conjunctive contact. One senses the life around one—so multiplex & inarticulate—but so moving or devastating. So here. A thousand [*sic*] thoughts, moods, dreams spring up. One wishes this & that. Understands this & that; suspects this & that. But does not know." [24]

They entered Florida on Christmas Day at the height of its historic real estate boom—a place of mass madness swarming with tourists and promoters. Good hotel rooms cost $40 a night, whiskey $12 a quart and land salesmen all but assaulted visitors to offer beach lots at $5,000 a front foot. They stayed in miserable rooms to save money. Dreiser's diary mentions no gift to Helen—possibly the trip itself constituted the gift—and their relations seemed mostly on a basis of guarded truce that alternately rose to mutual enjoyment and sank to hostility. He would have agreed whole-heartedly with Thomas Hardy's wry comment: "Love lives on propinquity, but dies of contact." He had squeezed out of his promise of marriage and had scarcely "walked the chalk." Taking pills and smearing his chest with Vapo Rub, he tried to keep in touch with the other women furtively, but Helen was watching.

"I sent S. K. a telegram," he confided in his diary. "Trouble with Helen at once." And next morning: "Helen still sore. We don't speak. Dress & go to wretched restaurant. . . ." In Palm Beach they had to pay $12 for a dingy room next to the busy bus depot, kept sleepless by roaring exhausts and chattering travelers, but in the morning, "Helen picks gray hairs out of my eyebrows." [25]

Dreiser retained his enormous interest in sightseeing, social theorizing and sex, but was close with his money and apt to quarrel about bills. Random excerpts from his diary give a picture of varying moods and impressions:

> Florida better than Calif. . . . Greater hotels. I never saw such hotels anywhere.
> We go & get the car. Quarrel over charges.
> The young girls of Glenville. . . . Painted cheeks. Rolled stockings, a bursting sense of sex sex mad—beauty mad.
> On a sign outside was "Washing & Polishing 1.50. Washing 1.00." The car was only washed & he charged me—or tried to—1.50. I called him.
> No sewers—no toilets inside. . . . A cold bed in a cold room.
> A California morning. Sunlight like gold. Warm. We go to a good restaurant. Then walk on the beach.
> Convicts on road. Meaninglessness of stripes & chains in these days. Too many crooks on the outside.
> I bawl the [garage] man out. . . . He tells me not to get "hard boiled."
> The hot, vain, sensuous strutty girls. Where is the farm girl of twenty years ago.
> A wretched restaurant with high prices & no menu worth a damn.

To Lengel he wrote, "But I am sold on Florida. It's a great state . . . absolute jungles dotted with the smartest towns imaginable. The Riviera has nothing on this." [26]

To Louise Campbell a few days later he expressed a revised opinion: "I liked California oh, ever so much better. . . . A swarm of [Florida] realtors shouting about their subdivisions . . . mere plans on paper. The bunk." [27]

On January 4 they settled at Las Olas Inn at Fort Lauderdale as their base of operations, but Dreiser suddenly yearned for home and Helen was in despair. "A row because I suggest returning to N. Y.," he noted. Next morning this capricious child of moods played the lute, but alone: "Up at dawn for a dip. Spend over an hour in sea. The warmth of sand & water. Sunrise! Gulls." By evening the lyric had soured. "Helen grouchy," he wrote, so he left her and strolled the beach: "The stars over the sea. Music & dancing in the small pavilion. Return & find Helen sitting outside alone. At midnight Helen decides to make up." [28]

On January 9 Tom Smith wired:

THE REVIEWS ARE AMAZING ENTHUSIASTIC AND DIGNIFIED YOUR POSITION IS RECOGNIZED THE SALES ARE EXCELLENT. . . . LOVE TO YOURSELF AND HELEN. [29]

Dreiser, apparently skeptical, did not even mention the telegram in his diary, although he wrote briefly three days later, "A telegram from S. K. saying book has sold 17000." If this was true—17,000 copies at five dollars a set in less than a month—it was terrific, but he held his counsel. He deliberately read no reviews, but took notes for some magazine articles about Florida. He and Helen, remembering their real estate winnings in California, were touring the towns, looking for a piece of land. Although in his diary he never wrote with warmth or praise of Helen, and once noted bleakly about his former "Babu Mio" and "Dearie Deario," "Wretched days with someone I really don't care to be with," they shopped around for property with Helen as chauffeur. Land promotion in Florida had assumed the hysteria of mass revivals, with realtors setting up stands and luring crowds with bands and speakers. Dreiser sank $4,000 in a Fort Lauderdale lot that later washed into the sea in a hurricane. [30]

He thought belatedly of Mencken and wrote him to ask about his mother. He wrote a fond letter to his coed friend, Amy Parsons, and later recorded, "Big bunch of mail. Many fine letters about book. A love note from Fermos. Decide to write her and K. Helen returns. Comments on my writing. A quarrel. Bad night." [31]

On January 24, Dreiser and Helen put the Maxwell aboard ship at Miami and sailed next day for New York. Their vessel turned out to be the *Kroonland*—the same on which Dreiser had sailed from Europe in 1912, escaping the *Titanic*.

4. Success

I. A COLOSSAL BOTCH

Dreiser reached New York to find himself a literary sensation. Most of the reviews that counted were glowing. Joseph Wood Krutch in *The Nation* praised even his style and called the *Tragedy* "the greatest American novel of our generation."¹ *The New York Sunday Times* front-paged it with a toothy photo of the author. Sherwood Anderson in the *Saturday Review* admitted that some of Dreiser's words and sentences made him cringe but acclaimed the book and urged Americans to read it: "Find out, once and for all, the difference between a human flesh and blood, male man, full of real tenderness for life, and the smarties, the word slingers, the clever fellows, the nasty cock-sure half men of the writing world."²

Stuart Sherman, who could be expected to bound snarling out of his lair, trotted out purring in the *Herald Tribune* with a laudation, writing in part, "I do not know where else in American fiction one can find the situation here presented dealt with so fearlessly, so intelligently, so exhaustively, so veraciously, and *therefore* with such unexceptionable moral effect."³

As time went on, experts would wrestle with the problem of how Dreiser could write such faulty prose and still produce a masterpiece. H. G. Wells ascribed it to the fact that "Dreiser is, in the extreme sense of the word, a genius."⁴ Arnold Bennett alternately tore his hair and genuflected:

> [The book] is written abominably by a man who evidently despises style, elegance, clarity, even grammar. Dreiser simply does not know how to write, never did know, never wanted to know. . . .
>
> Indeed, to read Dreiser with profit you must take your coat off to it, you must go down on your knees to it, you must up hands and say, "I surrender." And Dreiser will spit on you for a start.
>
> But once you have fairly yielded to him he will reward you—yes, though his unrelenting grip should squeeze the life out of you. "An American Tragedy" is prodigious.⁵

Some saw his stylistic crudities as an aid to a book whose sincerity would have been impaired by glossy writing, and mistakenly thought them intentional, the artist's cunning device. "Dreiser is so anxious to make the reader receive the story as true," wrote Joyce Cary later, "that he pretends to have no art at all, not even grammar. And this itself is high art."⁶ Dreiser, who wrote as he wrote because it was the only way he could write, would have been interested to hear that.

Waiting for him at the Liveright office was a check for $11,872.02 representing royalties on 13,914 copies sold in the last two weeks of 1925. The sale was nothing like that for *Main Street* or *Babbitt*—or for Liveright's own publication, *Gentlemen Prefer Blondes*—but at its price, and for Dreiser, it was enormous. He and Helen settled modestly at the Hotel Empire again. Letters of congratulation streamed in from Lengel, George Sterling, Bowers, Ficke, Karsner, many others. R. L. Moody, the Milwaukee Dreiserian, wrote that he had opened the novel aboard a California-bound train and was so moved that he read the last 50 pages aloud to his eight-year-old son.

What did John Sumner have to say? Not a squeak of protest came from him. With the overwhelming acceptance of his book, Dreiser had virtually won his 25-year battle for freedom of expression. In 1920 Sumner had arrested 184 "immoralists" and convicted 150 of them. In 1925 he had arrested 41 and convicted a measly 21. He was still hard at work, and would be heard from again, but his day was waning.

Another big question: What did Mencken have to say?

Dreiser had sent him a copy of the limited edition. On February 5 Mencken wrote in part, "I am performing upon you without anaesthetics in the March *Merkur*, but *with* reservations." Although his review was late, when it came it showed that, unlike Bennett, he would not permit any writer to spit on him. Headed "Dreiser in 840 Pages," it began:

> Whatever else this vasty double-header may reveal about its author, it at least shows brilliantly that he is wholly devoid of what may be called literary tact. . . . It was ten years since he had published his last novel, and so all his old customers . . . were hungry for another. . . . The time was thus plainly at hand to make a ten strike. What was needed was a book full of all the sound and solid Dreiser merits, and agreeably free from the familiar Dreiser defects. . . . Well, how did Dreiser meet the challenge? He met it, characteristically, by throwing out the present shapeless and forbidding monster—a heaping cartload of raw materials for a novel, with rubbish of all sorts intermixed—a vast, sloppy, chaotic thing of 385,000 words—at least 250,000 of them unnecessary! . . .

The plot, Mencken said, was simple: "Hardly more, in fact, than the plot in a three page story in *True Confessions*. But Dreiser rolls it out to such lengths that it becomes, in the end, a sort of sequence of serials." He complained that the 431-page first volume got only to Roberta's pregnancy.

> Obviously, there is something dreadfully wrong here. Somewhere or other, there must be whole chapters that could be spared. I find, in fact, many such chapters—literally dozens of them. They incommode the action, they swamp and conceal the principal personages, and they lead the author steadily into his weakness for banal moralizing and trite, meaningless words. In "The 'Genius'" it was *trig* that rode him; in "An American Tragedy" it is *chic*.

Mencken assailed his "stale Freudianism," his old "chemic" theory of sex, and was appalled that his style had deteriorated rather than improved over the years. One wonders what he would have said had he seen the original manuscript before Sally Kusell and Louise Campbell cut it in half and Tom Smith and Komroff polished it off. He picked out a few horrible examples of Dreiser sentences, one of them indeed ruinous:

> The death house of this particular prison was one of those crass erections and maintenances of human insensibility and stupidity for which no one primarily was really responsible.

Wrote Mencken: "What is one to say of such dreadful bilge? What is one to say of a novelist who, after a quarter of a century at his trade, still writes it?"

He had a few good words: " 'An American Tragedy,' as a work of art, is a colossal botch, but as a human document it is searching and full of a solemn dignity, and at times it rises to the level of genuine tragedy. . . . Once Roberta is killed and Clyde faces his fate, the thing begins to move, and thereafter it roars on, with ever increasing impetus, to the final terrific smash." Of Dreiser's characters he said, "Their thoughts are muddled and trivial—but they can feel. And Dreiser feels with them, and can make the reader feel with them. It takes skill of a kind that is surely not common. Good writing is far easier."

Mencken might have put more stress on that last sentence. He ended: "Hire your pastor to read the first volume for you. But don't miss the second!" [7]

Taken as a whole, the review was murderous. Certainly Mencken was not consciously venting spite because of Dreiser's gaucheries in Baltimore. Mencken was reacting normally. He had read the laudatory reviews and he was more than ever the iconoclast, hating to run with the crowd—especially if the crowd included Sherman. He had defended Dreiser when he needed a defender. Now everybody seemed to defend him. For years he had coached Dreiser on style and found it time wasted. Allowing for these unconscious influences, his review was undoubtedly the honest appraisal of a martinet who revered style.

Later, Charles Angoff, Mencken's subaltern on the *Mercury*, met Dreiser strolling in Central Park. As Angoff recalled it, Dreiser told of stomach trouble, headaches and other pains, then said, "That boss of yours ought to stay in Baltimore on the *Sun* and keep out of writing about books." [8]

After eighteen years, the Dreiser-Mencken friendship was over. Dreiser had also found fault with Miss Kusell, writing her:

> Dearie: The trouble between us springs in my mind at least from the firm conviction that your interest in me is somehow based more on a desire for mental & artistic recognition through me than it is on any innate, personal and ineffective as well as effective qualities which may characterize me. In other words as a searching, blundering faulty male—however constructive my unrecognized aspirations might be you would not see me. . . .

Meaningful & moving affections are not like that. . . . I have missed this note I have described & for want of which I have always been dubious & resentful. . . .[9]

II. COFFEE AT THE RITZ

"Have you my letter?" another young woman wrote Dreiser. "And aren't you going to call me? You *must* you *must*. I simply cannot go on like this. I must see you. Words on paper cannot tell you the things I have to say. . . . I *must* see you. You cannot leave me like this, deluded about my love for you. . . ."[10]

But he could and he did as he had before. He wrote a savage letter to the Pennsylvania Railroad for bringing him home 32 minutes late in a snowstorm after a Philadelphia conference with Mrs. Campbell. The corporations enraged him. He could explode over a nickel overtime charge for a telephone call. But he was impartial, for as often he vented his anger on the masses with whom he sympathized in the abstract—cab drivers, waiters, delivery men.

Now Liveright was eager to adapt the *Tragedy* into a play and produce it himself on Broadway. He got hold of Patrick Kearney, an actor-turned-playwright best known for his play *A Man's Man*, who started work on a script late in February. Liveright saw Glenn Hunter as perfect in the role of Clyde Griffiths, while June Walker would make an ideal Roberta. As producer, Liveright at first asked 50 per cent of the motion picture rights, although because of the theme's violation of the Hays code he wrote, "It's extremely doubtful that AN AMERICAN TRAGEDY can ever be done on the screen."[11]

Here he was wrong, although he was friendly with Jesse Lasky and Walter Wanger of Famous Players and knew much of the "inside" of screenland. It was true that a group of Lasky's readers had explored the book for screen possibilities and rejected it. However, Quinn Martin in the *New York World* had written that the novel, if courageously treated, would make "the greatest film yet produced"[12]—an observation not lost on the moguls. The producer Jed Harris soon afterward visited the Lasky office to speak glowingly of the novel's drama and to outline a scenario on the spot. Then letters came in from Hollywood directors urging the *Tragedy*'s picture potentialities. By this time the cold Lasky had turned hot. He and Wanger had some talk with Liveright about the screen rights, and they arranged a luncheon meeting with him in mid-March at the Ritz-Carlton Hotel to discuss it further.

The events that followed can only be approximated, for none of the participants agreed about them afterward.

Just before the luncheon, Dreiser met with Liveright at the latter's office to complete the contract for the Kearney play. As always in the presence of the publisher, Dreiser was suspicious. As he recalled it later, Liveright said that Lasky was skeptical and had no interest in the book at all until he learned that

Liveright was producing the play. Lasky then said he would be interested if the play was successful in the fall. Liveright told Dreiser he might get a top price of $35,000 for the film rights.

Dreiser suspected that Liveright, to enhance his own cut, was suggesting that without his services as play producer there would have been no film interest at all. Dreiser felt strongly that he could sell to the films before the play was produced, in which case, as he saw it, Liveright would deserve no cut of the film rights whatever.

In this atmosphere, Liveright did a strange thing. He at length agreed to waive any percentage of the film rights if Dreiser sold them for $30,000 or more *before* the play was produced. In the light of what followed, this seemed senseless. One can only speculate that Liveright, always the gambler, was backed into this corner by his insistence that there would be no screen sale until the play appeared.

The two had "several drinks" as they parleyed. Only then, as Dreiser recalled it, did Liveright admit that Lasky did not want to wait until the play was produced. He was anxious to close the deal immediately. Indeed, Liveright was lunching with Lasky and Wanger that very noon, and if Dreiser came along the matter might be settled at once. For the first time, he asked Dreiser what his price was. Dreiser named an astonishing $100,000. Here, according to Dreiser's later recollection, Liveright completely changed his ground. He did not blanch at the $100,000 figure. Although he suggested $60,000 as a more likely price, he seemed to feel that Lasky might go higher than that. And, having thrown himself entirely on Dreiser's mercy, he asked Dreiser if he would "take care" of him.

Dreiser felt his mistrust confirmed. Why had Liveright first been so pessimistic, naming $35,000 as the top price? Could it be that Liveright had whispered with his friend Lasky and offered, for a commission, to get Dreiser to settle for that modest figure? Now that this stratagem had failed, was he whooping up the price in the hope of getting a large gratuity from Dreiser?

Neither of the two men was known for precision of recollection. Despite the contract just signed, the hard-drinking, money-ridden Liveright felt entitled to a large commission because of his sponsorship of the play and his initiation of negotiations with his friend Lasky. As he recalled it, Dreiser told him he could have everything over $60,000.

Dreiser remembered no such thing. He later said Liveright asked a 70-30 split on whatever was paid—a proposal that made him smile but to which he made no rejoinder. He intended to play his own hand at the luncheon. Liveright, whom he felt he had caught in trickery, would get only ten per cent. As the two men walked over to the Ritz on Madison Avenue, Liveright again asked if he would "take care" of him. To this Dreiser replied enigmatically that he would, leaving Liveright with the mistaken impression that his cut would be generous.

Liveright evidently expected the luncheon to be decisive, for he had asked the manager of his theatrical productions, Louis Cline, to take luncheon also at the Ritz in case he was needed to complete business details of the deal. At about one o'clock Dreiser and Liveright sat down in the luxurious dining room with Lasky and Wanger for one of the more noted collations in publishing annals. Cline was nearby, seated so that he had a view of the four and could easily be hailed. Lunching with him were June Walker and Glenn Hunter, who were eager for the roles of Roberta and Clyde.

Wanger recalled that both Dreiser and Liveright seemed sober and unruffled when they arrived. However, Lester Cohen, a Liveright author who later made an investigation of the affair, was convinced that both were intoxicated, and indeed the confusion of events and recollection argues against strict sobriety. Over the luncheon, Liveright asked $100,000 for the rights—$30,000 for himself and $70,000 for Dreiser. In his later recollection he said he thought Dreiser was pleased at this, that he made no remonstrance. Dreiser later said that he did remonstrate, telling Lasky and Wanger, "It [is] all news to me." Liveright left the table for a few minutes so that Dreiser and the two Famous Players men could parley. They did so, settling verbally on $90,000. When Liveright returned, one account says he claimed $30,000 of this as his.

"You will get your ten per cent," Dreiser said.

Liveright protested that he had promised to "take care" of him. Dreiser snapped that he had made no explicit promise at all.

"You're a liar," Liveright shouted.[13]

Dreiser leaped to his feet, ready to swing. He ordered Liveright to stand. He was over six feet and weighed more than 200 pounds. Liveright, equally tall but a pellucid 130, wisely remained seated. Dreiser dashed his coffee at him and stalked out in a rage.

"The coffee wasn't cold," Wanger recalled. "It scored a direct hit on Horace's face, shirt and suit. It was most embarrassing, with other diners staring at us."[14]

A waiter helped to dry him off. The luncheon ended and it was not until a few days later that Dreiser closed the deal at $80,000 for himself and $10,000 for Liveright. There was an exchange of letters between them, Liveright denying any guile and insisting that he had no previous agreement with Lasky. "Please again believe that there was no price mentioned between me and Lasky," he wrote in part, "and that there was no staging of this affair."[15]

"I consider that I have been most outrageously insulted and sharply dealt with into the bargain," Dreiser wrote him. "Neither commercially or socially have I ever lied to you. On the contrary I have been of immense commercial and literary aid to you and you know that."[16] He demanded a written apology, which Liveright finally tendered, observing:

It's a darn shame that now that fortune is, after so many years, spilling gold into your lap . . . that what has happened between us should have arisen These are the days when we should be riding around together in band-wagons with champagne flowing and beautiful slave girls fanning us with peacock feathers.[17]

From one of his lady friends, who did not know where he was staying and addressed him at Boni & Liveright, Dreiser received a telegram next day:

I NEVER KNEW SUFFERING COULD BE SO TERRIBLE AM NUMB WITH ANGUISH AND DESPAIR I SIMPLY CAN'T GO ON WITHOUT SOME WORD FROM YOU. . . .[18]

III. THE BURDENS OF WEALTH

"I'm likely to be rich," Dreiser wrote Lengel, who was in England for the Hearst magazines. "I just sold the moving picture rights for $100,000 [a slight exaggeration]—so judge for yourself. My immediate cash worries are over." [19]

He strode into John Cowper Powys' Village apartment saying, "I am opulent, opulent! What can I give you?" Powys mentioned a rare and expensive book he had long wanted. Dreiser got it for him.[20] In general, however, his habitual parsimony persisted. He had driven a close bargain with Liveright, whatever the publisher's weaknesses. He had done the same with Patrick Kearney, who was so anxious to adapt the *Tragedy* that he took 45 per cent of the play royalties instead of the usual 50 per cent and agreed to waive stock royalties entirely. Having paid Louise Campbell a nominal sum for her work on the book, Dreiser might have sent her an extra check as her share of its success, but he did not.

As news of his sale to Famous Players hit the papers, he heard from several indigent friends, one writing, "I need two hundred dollars in the worst possible sort of way."

And he heard from Jug, with whom he had carried on a sparse correspondence and whom he had paid nothing since 1915. Still living at 160 Waverly Place, she wrote:

My Dear Theo: I have just heard of your wonderful good fortune, and I congratulate you. It's been a long time coming but was due you in the end, and bound to come. Yours, Jug.[21]

Nearing fifty-seven and not in robust health, she was fearful of losing her job. She had long wanted to act as "mother" to Rosemary Carr, the daughter of her late sister Rose—the sister Dreiser had so admired those long years past. He did not reply at once. She wrote him again a week later:

When I wrote you the other day congratulating you on your good fortune I hadn't an idea that such an enormous sum had been paid you. . . .

I am wondering if you wouldn't be willing to give me something, now that you are able to do so, and let me go back home and have little Rosemary. You know how I wanted her and still long for her, and you wanted me to have her, only you weren't able then to help me.

She is adorable. . . . While she doesn't look so much like Rose . . . she
is so like her in her ways and is very pretty.

I wish I could have her. Yours, Jug.[22]

Dreiser's reply, written just before he received the second letter, was
unfeeling:

My Dear Jug: Your congratulations on the *financial* outcome of my labors in connection with An American Tragedy are appreciated. What interests me about this prompt notice of your pleasure in connection with the
sale of the moving picture rights of the book is that, in the last twelve years
or so I have written eight or nine books—all of which seemed to me, at least,
to be worthy of some form of congratulation, however little the financial
return. They represented the best I could do. It remains for you, however, to
congratulate me only on the financial outcome of the only book that has
achieved a financial outcome worthy of the name. To me there is something
rueful in the thought of your very special and purely financial interest in my
career. T. D.[23]

After eleven years of supporting herself, she hardly deserved this. In reply
she pointed out that while she had been unable to follow his literary career,
she had congratulated him on *Hey Rub*, and added, "You have always written
that you would be only too willing to do something for me if you could. I
have worried you as little as possible because you had but little. . . .

"How can you be so unfair when you can't have forgotten how every
word of Jennie Gerhardt was so precious to me. . . .

"I suppose though it is useless to try to defend myself. I can only throw
myself on your mercy and ask you to please make life a little easier for me
now that you can do so without limiting yourself." [24]

Getting no reply, a fortnight later she consulted Attorney Frederick
Hemley, who wrote Dreiser's attorney, Dudley Field Malone, "For a great
many years Mrs. Dreiser has eked out a miserable existence through her own
efforts, but surely Mr. Theodore Dreiser would not want his wife to continue
to work in a weakened and sickly condition. . . ." [25]

Dreiser was willing to aid her, though he hoped to keep the payments
modest. He wrote Attorney Malone about his financial condition, explaining
his inability to pay her anything since 1915 and outlining characteristic plans
he had made for his sudden film riches:

I desire to invest [this money]—along with what my book—as a book
earns me, in order that the income . . . will keep me independent of publishers, permit me to do my own work in my own way—guarentee [*sic*] me
against a rainy day in the future and possibly permit me to do at least a few
of the many things I have always wanted to do.[26]

Apparently there was no talk of divorce. Dreiser evidently did not want
one, for a divorce would give him no advantage he did not already have and
would deprive him of a handy defense against other women—particularly

Helen, who was yearning for marriage. The attorneys worked out a separation agreement whereby he contracted to pay Jug $200 monthly starting July 1, 1926, and continuing so long as he lived and she remained unmarried.[27] The payments were made through his attorneys so that Jug would not discover where he banked.

Dreiser meanwhile gave $50 to a girl friend on her uppers, planned a trip to Europe with Helen, and a party to celebrate his new affluence. Prosperity, however, did not incline him to loaf. He had sold a series of three articles to *Vanity Fair* on "This Florida Scene," [28] and to the same magazine sold his poem "The Beautiful," having forgotten that he cribbed the material from Sherwood Anderson. He was preparing a batch of earlier short stories to be published under the title *Chains*. He planned to revise *The Financier* with Louise Campbell's help and to publish a new edition that would whoop up interest in Cowperwood; then to finish *The Stoic*, the third volume of the Cowperwood trilogy, and also the long, long-awaited *Bulwark*.

Having no idea how to give a party, he wheedled the help of the sophisticated Dwight Taylor as arranger, telling Taylor he wanted it at the most fashionable night club in town, with "plenty of champagne." About twenty guests were invited, including Ernest and Madeleine Boyd, Edward H. Smith, Carl Van Vechten and his wife Fania Marinoff (whom Dreiser usually called Sonia), young Miguel Covarrubias, the caricaturist Hans Stengel, and Taylor. They arrived to find Helen and Dreiser waiting in the foyer "as a sort of receiving line of two." As Taylor recalled it, "Helen wore an evening gown, bought especially for the occasion, shimmering with red spangles like a circus rider's. Dreiser, big as he was, had managed somehow to find evening clothes that were even bigger," and he "clutched an enormous pair of white cotton gloves. . . ." There were roses on the table and a champagne bucket at every place. When the floor show started, Dreiser turned his chair—and his back— squarely to his guests, the better to see it. Although he obscured the view for the others, and Helen and Madeleine demurred, he stayed there "impervious as a monolith." [29]

IV. THE RED CARPET

Like a rolling snowball, *An American Tragedy* accumulated success. Reporters interviewed Dreiser. Magazine editors begged him for copy. In London, Constable & Company, formerly not interested in him, hurriedly contracted to publish the *Tragedy* in England and to take over his other works. After years under a cloud as a banned author, a sensationalist and vulgarian, he was now sanctified by success and admitted to respectability. Liveright dotted the papers with two-column advertisements showing Dreiser's profile and containing the statement, "We are proud to be the publishers of the works of Theodore Dreiser," cannily listing the previous books. People who read *An American Tragedy*—and people who had never heard of Dreiser before—now wanted to read his other books. The twenty-six-year-old *Sister Carrie* doubled its 1925 volume, selling 3,412 copies in 1926. The fourteen-year-old *Jennie Gerhardt* sold 1,393 and the eleven-year-old *"Genius"* swelled to 8,087. Having heard about the coffee incident, Harper and Doubleday were trying to lure him away, Harper laying out an elaborate presentation to show Dreiser how they would promote his works and Harper's president, Douglas Parmenter, writing him, "I thought you were going to telephone me for lunch some day this week." [30]

In that one plaintive sentence, and the identity of the sender, Dreiser could measure his own new importance.

Whether or not he actually intended to switch, he used these offers as a club over Liveright. Evidently he enjoyed browbeating Liveright, relishing an ascendancy over him that he would be unlikely to have over any other publisher. When he told Claude Bowers about the coffee episode, he laughed and said that Liveright had been writing him "love letters ever since." Mr. Parmenter of Harper's would not be likely to take Dreiser's coffee in his face, hear Dreiser call him a trickster, and come back for more. Liveright did. "Of course, your propositions from Harper and Doubleday are extraordinary ones," [31] he wrote, and went on to make one even more extraordinary. It contained the following inducements in addition to others already granted:

> Liveright would pay Dreiser a 20 per cent royalty on the retail price of all subsequent books.
>
> He would pay Dreiser $500 a month as a drawing account against royalties.
>
> He would spend $10,000 in advertising the *Tragedy* in the remaining seven months of 1926, and a proportionate amount on Dreiser's next new novel. In 1927 there would be a Dreiser advertisement every week in *The New York Times* book supplement.
>
> In the fall of 1927 Liveright would issue a one-volume edition of the *Tragedy* at three dollars and advertise it heavily.
>
> Also in the fall of 1927 Liveright would give him the ultimate honor by issuing a *limited edition* of the collected works of Theodore Dreiser.
>
> In the spring of 1929 he would issue a regular library edition of the collected works, with a big mail-order campaign.
>
> And finally, Dreiser was invited to become a member of the board of directors of Boni & Liveright. [32]

No redder or thicker carpet was ever laid out for an author. Dreiser knew that Liveright, a master of publicity, had advertised him and the *Tragedy* with a prodigality that amazed other publishers. He stayed with B & L.

V. THE POOR BASTARD!

On June 22 Dreiser and Helen sailed for Oslo on the *Frederick VIII* as "Mr. and Mrs.," not as a concession to convention but simply to avoid needless explaining. His purpose was to sightsee, collect material about Yerkes for *The Stoic*, talk with his European publishers and if possible to visit with personages including Freud. Freud's theories of sex and dreams so fascinated him that he had asked Dr. Brill, America's leading Freudian, for an introduction.

Although this, if ever, would have seemed the time for him to divorce Jug, Helen was too fearful of Dreiser to press her claim to marriage resolutely. In public his attitude toward her was sometimes indifferent—as if she were not there—and sometimes contemptuous. Some friends were so startled by this open brutality that they had no doubt that he occasionally beat her. She never recorded a beating although she admitted that once, as she and Dreiser walked down Fifth Avenue, he became so angry that he slapped her face, causing passersby to stare. Helen had temporarily settled for reflected fame and this trip to Europe.

They toured Norway, Sweden and Denmark, Dreiser insisting on an exhausting dawn-to-dusk regimen of sightseeing—fjords, glaciers, museums, churches, the graves of Ibsen and Björnson. Copenhagen and its women delighted him ("Here there is room to breathe!"). He visited the eighty-four-year-old Georg Brandes. Reporters frequently interviewed him, finding him ready to deliver blunt judgments. Asked who would be the next President, he replied, "The man whom the financiers on Wall Street select as their tool," adding that it would be that way "this time and for all times to come." [33] In a warmer mood he said, "Just as it is a mistake to believe that all Germans are militarists, it is also wrong to believe that all Americans are fools. Their worship of the concept of 'success,' which to my countrymen is half their religion, may not merely be pardonable in itself, but necessary in a business man's existence, and does not become a mortal sin until it infringes upon art. And be it granted that art is in a sorry state within American literature." [34]

In Berlin, where he visited his German publisher, he felt that "The Germans are so dynamic they remind me of a race of giants. I don't know but what they could run the world and run it well." [35] He and Helen moved on to Prague, where he was the palace guest of President Masaryk, a Dreiser admirer; then to Vienna, where he failed to see Freud, and to Salzburg, Budapest and Munich, reaching Paris early in September.

Here he lamented the flood of tourists, the commercialization of the quiet city he had known in 1912, and the fate of the once romantic Seine: "What does one see now? Boats being loaded with cement." [36] But Victor Llona, translator of some of his books, took him to the old homes of Hugo and Balzac, and he was touched by the tiny rooms hung with mementos of Balzac—even the coffee pot from which he poured the black brew that kept him awake nights.

In Paris at the time was the anarchist Emma Goldman, who had come upon hard times since the Village days. Deported from the United States with her lover Berkman in 1919, she had gone to Russia, quarreled with the Bolsheviks and taken refuge in France. Reading that Dreiser was in town, she arranged a meeting with him and Helen. Poverty-stricken and lonely, persona non grata almost everywhere, she was attracted to Helen and delighted by Dreiser's warm friendliness.

"You must write the story of your life, E. G.," he said; "it is the richest of any woman's in our country." [37]

Any publisher, he said, should give her a $5,000 advance. Although he later sent her money, it was his belief in her that moved the hard-shelled revolutionist almost to tears. "The very people who posed as my friends are now among my bitterest enemies," she wrote him before he left. "Imagine then my joy to find you so eager and so intensely interested in my struggle and the things I want to do. Really it was a revelation, a bright ray from a dark horizon. . . . Thanks old man. . . ." [38]

In New York a literary squall blew up when Franklin P. Adams of the *World* read Dreiser's poem "The Beautiful" in the October *Vanity Fair*. FPA promptly put it side by side in his column with part of Anderson's "Tandy":

"Tandy"	"The Beautiful"
He grew angry and scolded. "They think it's easy to be a woman, to be loved, but I know better," he declared. . . . "I understand," he cried, "perhaps of all men I alone understand."	They think that it is easy to be a woman— To love and be loved, But I know better. Perhaps, of all men, I alone understand. I know about her because She has crossed my path. I know her struggles And her defeats.
His glance wandered away in the darkened street. "I know about her, although she has never crossed my path," he said softly. "I know about her struggles and her defeats. It is because of her defeats that she is to me the lovely one. Out of her defeats has been born a new	It is because of her defeats That she is to me The lovely one. For out of her defeats Has been born A new quality in woman. I have no name for that But I have a name for her. I call her Beautiful. I have made up the name Because before it And before the thing in her That it represents My own vile body And my weary soul Bow, and bow reverently. She is to me

quality in woman. I
have a name for it,
Tandy. I made up the
name when I was a true
dreamer and before my
body became vile. It
is the quality of be-
ing strong to be loved.
It is something that
men need from women
and that they do not
get." [39]

The quality of being strong to be loved,
Of needing and being capable of
Complete and ceaseless
And insatiable and yet generous
Love.
Of loving fatefully,
And yet not destroying
But healing—building.
It is the one thing men need
From women—so many men—
And that
They do not find.[39]

"DREISER 'CRIB' FROM ANDERSON SHOCKS FRIENDS," head-
lined the *Herald Tribune*. Dreiser was beyond reach, but Tom Smith at B &
L believed it was either "unconscious plagiarism" or that Anderson had given
Dreiser permission to put the thoughts into verse. Anderson himself settled
that by telephone from Virginia.

"Mr. Dreiser is not the kind of man who needs to take lines from me or
anyone else," he said. "It is one of those accidents that occur. The thought
expressed has come, I am sure, to a great many men." [40]

The idea that two men's brains could be so attuned aroused guffaws. It was
recalled that in *Sister Carrie* Dreiser had lifted descriptive matter from
George Ade's "Fable of the Two Mandolin Players and the Willing Per-
former." Interviewed in Indiana, Ade agreed that this was true but laughed
about it, saying, "We Hoosiers are proud of him, for he erects literary
skyscrapers while we're busy pounding out chicken coops or bungalows." [41]
The Times laughed too, wondering if Dreiser had instilled poetic immortality
into Anderson's line, "It is because of her defeats that she is to me the lovely
one," by rendering it:

> It is because of her defeats
> That she is to me
> The lovely one.[42]

Privately much annoyed, Anderson wrote a friend, "Another idol
smashed." [43] The plagiarism actually harmed no one but Dreiser, who could
have purged his sin and endeared himself to the public by a frank admission
of his unconscious theft—something he did not do. One hopes at least that he
explained later to Anderson.

After a reception at the Paris P.E.N. Club, Dreiser and Helen left on
October 3 for London, where he established one of the warmest friendships
of his life with Otto Kyllmann, a director of the Constable firm. He had
hoped to go to Dorset to visit with old Thomas Hardy and also with
Llewelyn Powys, who was there with his wife, Alys Gregory. He was so
smitten by Kyllmann that apparently he saw neither. He seems also to have

missed Arnold Bennett, his truest British champion, though Bennett had invited him to call. He did gather data on Yerkes' London operations for *The Stoic*, and he did call on Shaw. When Dreiser mentioned Shaw's vegetarianism, Shaw jumped up, took two chairs, put his chin on one and his toes on the other and stretched himself horizontally between these two bearing points to show the efficacy of his diet. "[Shaw is] witty, delightful, flashing with ideas," Dreiser later commented. "He reminds me of H. L. Mencken." [44]

After a trip to Somerset with the Kyllmanns, Dreiser and Helen sailed from Southampton on the *Columbus* October 15, reaching New York on the 22nd to be surrounded by reporters. Possibly sensitive about the Tandy incident, he snapped, "I refuse even to pass the time of day." He and Helen settled at the Hotel Pasadena on Broadway and Sixty-first, where he relented and talked to a *Tribune* man who printed not a word about Tandy.

"America is curiously indifferent to its fate," Dreiser said. "Our leaders are merely cheer leaders. None of our politicians has the courage to deal with, none of our newspapers has the courage to discuss, really fundamental issues such as the Catholic question, the Negro question, the money-power question or even the liquor question. We are too cowardly or too stupid to face them." [45]

An American Tragedy was playing to packed houses at the Longacre Theater, spurring the sale of the book. Liveright's manager, Louis Cline, had been dubious about the play when it opened October 11, for the Theater Guild's heavily publicized *Juarez and Maximilian* opened the same night and offered stiff competition. He had solved the problem by hiring a 75-man claque on opening night who applauded lustily and shouted, "Bravo, Dreiser!" [46] The critics, generally reserved about the play's artistic merits, were taken in by the ruse, the *Graphic* saying, "They went mad. They yelled! The applause was deafening," while the *Herald Tribune* remarked on "an ovation the like of which is seldom seen in a theater."

Donald Friede, co-owner of the Liveright firm, took Dreiser to see it a few nights later. Glenn Hunter and June Walker having had other engagements, Morgan Farley appeared as Clyde, Miriam Hopkins as Sondra and Katherine Wilson as Roberta. Although Kearney's adaptation—a most difficult task—was spotty, Dreiser folded his handkerchief, enthralled. "He would not get up in the intermission," Friede noted. "He would not talk. He just sat there. And when the curtain went down on the death-cell scene he turned to me, and I could see that there were tears in his eyes. 'The poor boy!' he said. 'The poor bastard! What a shame!' " [47]

5. The Studio Dream

I. IS THIS THEODORE DREISER?

In San Francisco, George Sterling went on a dreadful drunk and on November 17 committed suicide with poison. Dreiser, who had sent him a five-spot a year earlier, dispatched flowers and almost wept because he had not been more generous to the poet who had died in poverty.

"What a damn fool I was!" he said to Esherick. "If I had only known, I could have helped him." [1]

Money rolled in. The play was grossing around $30,000 a week, a big take in the twenties. The Metropolitan News Service coaxed Dreiser to do three easy articles for newspaper syndication at $400 apiece. The Hearst press offered $5,000 to syndicate *An American Tragedy. Cosmopolitan* paid a stiff price for his story "Typhoon." *Collier's* asked him for a series of articles about Mack Sennett. Publishing rights to various Dreiser novels had been sold in eight European countries. Abraham Cahan offered him $1,000 for a story to feature in the 30th anniversary edition of the *Jewish Daily Forward.*

Was Dreiser going to continue to live in cheap hotel rooms or Village dives?

Not if Helen could help it.

"It soon became apparent," as she put it, "that a larger and more suitable place in which to live was absolutely necessary to cope with our increasing social and professional obligations." [2]

She set her heart on the splendid apartment building known as the Rodin Studios at 200 West Fifty-seventh Street where Willy Pogany lived. "Too expensive," Dreiser said. He made a great fuss, finally saying he would take it to please her if the management would cut $500 a year off the rent. The knockdown was granted, the lease signed at some $3,500 a year, Helen consulted with decorators, and late in December they moved into a duplex apartment on the thirteenth and fourteenth floors that included an impressive foyer and a vast double-height living room with indirect lighting and enormous stained-glass windows facing north on Fifty-seventh.

Helen bought gowns, startling ones. She acquired a Russian wolfhound, Nick, and a Steinway concert grand.

Dreiser bought Oriental rugs and flamboyant haberdashery including pastel shirts, bright bow ties and a new cane.

They hired a colored maid.

In January he started sending out letters (on thick gray paper with his name engraved in blue) to many friends:

In order to provide an informal meeting place for the seven arts and the nine or more professions Helen Richardson and I have fixed on every Thursday evening, from 9:30 on, at 200 West 57th (Studio 13B) where you are likely to find a wide range of personalities in conversation. If at any time you find yourself without anything better to do at that hour—on that day of each week,—you might wend your way here. And any personality you choose to sponsor and bring with you will be as welcome as yourself. My compliments.[3]

He sent these letters out by the dozen. At his first gathering he appeared in a blue artist's smock in need of washing. Thereafter, perhaps intimidated because some of his guests arrived in dress from the opera or theater, he donned a dinner coat, and two Negro servants passed around the drinks.

It was wonderful to be able to entertain in the grand manner—to realize at last the studio dream of his youth—but his motives were not wholly frivolous or exhibitionist. While he was well aware of the publicity and literary value of these gatherings, and he was as vulgar an admirer of show as anyone who ever lived, he had an endless yearning to grow, to learn, to rub elbows with intellectuals in all fields and soak up what he could. Helen remained in the background, charming and entirely likable, somewhat awed by her great handkerchief-folding consort and his famous friends. One of the guests, a Hungarian pianist named Kovacs, fell promptly and unwisely in love with her.

Although the apartment's decor struck Manuel Komroff as "a cross between Gimbel's and Roxy's," and the walls were disfigured by some of Dreiser's lurid nudes, his "Thursdays" became famous if not precisely fashionable. One never knew whom one would meet among the hundred or more callers but was sure to find someone interesting. Guests remembered a montage not likely to be seen elsewhere: Ford Madox Ford chewing his words into unintelligibility; Burton Rascoe talking like a phonograph; Ernest Boyd laughing so that his copper beard fluttered; Miriam Hopkins flashing her wicked eyes; Dr. Brill commenting humorously on human folly; Joseph Wood Krutch expounding on literature; John Cowper Powys discussing his ulcers; Jacob Wassermann, so shy that he scarcely spoke; the borzoi Nick stretched before the hearth, bringing the inevitable sallies that Dreiser must have gone over to Knopf; Elinor Wylie, preening herself and arousing jealousy in every other female heart; Otto Kahn, distinguished and ingratiating, more interested in pretty women than anyone save the host himself; Arthur Ficke and his artist wife Gladys; Deems Taylor, Alexander Woollcott, Van Vechten, Claude Bowers, Donald Friede, Walter Wanger, Grant Overton, Konrad Bercovici, William E. Woodward and many others. Sometimes there was music—a pianist, accordionist or soprano. Always there was a great punch bowl banked by hundreds of pretty sandwiches and petits fours.

It was saved from utter absurdity by Dreiser's lumbering honesty, his insistence on inviting old friends still scratching for a living, and by Helen's sincere delight. Although there was plenty of Prohibition liquor, and he was drinking more than of yore, drunks were frowned upon and were few. Dreiser was a trifle sheepish over the grandeur of it all and liked to construe it as Helen's idea, not his.

"You know," he said aside to Komroff, "I was sort of inveigled into this." [4]

Claude Bowers thought it ridiculous, out of character for him. Van Vechten found him unchanged amid the glitter, as earnest and unhousebroken as ever. Many guests had the same reaction as Fannie Hurst.

"Is it possible," she demanded of George Jean Nathan as they left the place, "that that host of ours was Dreiser, *Theodore Dreiser?* Say what you will, I won't believe it!" [5]

II. CLAIR DE LUNE

By the end of 1926 the *Tragedy* had sold more than 50,000 sets and Dreiser's royalties on that book alone totalled $47,647.53. The play went on the road after 216 Broadway performances. In 1921 he had paid $10.96 in income taxes, in 1924 $40.17, but now the Internal Revenue Bureau was a menace. To minimize it he divided himself in two and formed his own corporation, the Author's Royalties Company, a holding company which listed a part of the income and expenses of the Dreiser enterprises. In 1926 Helen, as president of the company, was reported as receiving a salary of $1,000, Dreiser himself as vice-president getting the same, both sums deductible.

He paid one tax as Dreiser, another as a corporation. In the total of these two payments for 1926 he deducted (if his records are correct) an eye-popping $16,577.19 for salaries he had paid, $3,343.11 for rent and $2,807.95 for legal expenses. The total of the two reports showed a stated gross income of $91,225.65 on which he appears to have paid a total tax of $5,473.46. [6]

For all his hatred of Wall Street he was studying Anaconda, General Motors and other stocks including A.T.&T. (the despised telephone trust) and investing his money. For country use he bought a 37-acre tract with a comfortable cabin overlooking Croton Lake near Mt. Kisco. So many literary propositions were now hurled at him that he retained the high-powered George Bye as agent. His mail was a burden requiring a full-time secretary. He received scores of letters requesting his autograph or photograph, asking him to make speeches or support worthy causes. He had an affinity for convicts, several of whom wrote him gratefully that his delineation of prison life in *An American Tragedy* was real and understanding. College students solicited his counsel about courses to take. People entangled in sex difficulties appealed for advice. Others frankly asked for money, Dreiser regretfully writing one of them:

I have a waiting list now that overwhelms me—from close relatives in large numbers to perfect strangers in still larger numbers who appear with requests of all descriptions. . . .[7]

Astonishingly, he heard from his wild older brother Rome, whom he had long thought dead. The indigent Rome was living in a fleabag Chicago hotel, and Dreiser, already aiding Mame and Austin Brennan, sent money to Rome. For his old friend Arthur Henry he tried vainly to interest Liveright in a group of stories Henry had written. He urged B & L and five other publishers to give Emma Goldman an advance on her autobiography, and had to write as he sent her money, "The thought of an honest radical seems to chill them to the marrow." [8]

On April 13, Boston's District Attorney William J. Foley suppressed *Elmer Gantry* at the instigation of the Watch & Ward Society, then followed by banning *An American Tragedy* and others. Donald Friede of B & L, outraged by the tyrannical Boston censorship, saw a chance to make an issue of it as Mencken had a year earlier with his *Mercury*, and (perhaps not quite incidentally) to stir up a second wave of publicity for the book. With Attorney Arthur Garfield Hays he went to Boston, sold a copy of the *Tragedy* to Police Lieutenant Daniel J. Hines and was promptly pinched. To his surprise, however—and unlike Mencken—he was not acquitted. On April 22 he was convicted of selling literature "manifestly tending to corrupt the morals of youth" and fined $100.[9] He appealed the case and had a long wait coming. Meanwhile Liveright dreamed up new ballyhoo—a nationwide contest with a $500 prize for the best answer to the question, "Was Clyde Griffiths guilty of murder in the first degree?" gravely appointing Attorney Hays, Heywood Broun and Bishop William Montgomery Brown as judges.

From Sergei Dinamov, a Moscow critic specializing in American and English literature, Dreiser received a letter praising his *Tragedy* and other works, adding:

I think you are the greatest writer in the world. . . . You don't like capital and capitalism. But what do you want to have instead of them? Socialism or communism? . . . . What do you think about Soviet Russia?" [10]

The incorporated Dreiser had to reply that however he might deplore capitalism, he had no better plan and saw no hope in theories for social improvement because of the built-in failings of man:

Nothing can alter his emotions, his primitive and animal reactions to life. Greed, selfishness, vanity, hate, passion, love, are all inherent in the least of us, and until such are eradicated, there can be no Utopia. . . . And until that intelligence which runs this show sees fit to remould the nature of man, I think it will always be the survival of the fittest, whether in the monarchies of England, the democracies of America, or the Soviets of Russia.[11]

He would meet Dinamov in Moscow before the year was out. Meanwhile, much taken by the new idea of companionate marriage, he found a dissenter in Dr. Brill. The psychiatrist, a firm believer in conventional marriage and the family, told him it was poppycock.

When Louise Campbell came to New York, Dreiser showed her his Fifty-seventh Street aerie and for the first time introduced to Helen the woman who had helped him editorially for ten years.

"He obviously couldn't resist pretending he was 'on the spot,'" Mrs. Campbell wrote, "... a helpless male facing two female rivals. Assuming the stance of a referee for a prize fight, he ordered us to go to our corners and come out fighting. Helen, I was glad to notice, shared my embarrassment, because she gave me an understanding smile."[12]

Proud to show off Helen's beauty in this splendid setting, he felt that he had made great concessions to her in supplying it and in displaying her to the world as his mistress. In return he expected his own sexual freedom. Usually, to keep the peace, he conducted his other affairs with some degree of secrecy, but when it came to a showdown he was full of the "primitive and animal reactions" he mentioned to Dinamov. When Helen objected to one of his affairs in particular, he reacted with explosive brutality.

He brought the girl home, telling Helen that as a lesson to her he would spend the night with the newcomer and wanted not a word of complaint. He did this and in the morning Helen, utterly cowed, served the pair breakfast without reproach.[13]

How she could endure such treatment is a mystery one might explain by her insecurity, her worship of genius and perhaps a strain of masochism. "[Dreiser] was my religion," as she explained it.[14] She took a forlorn pride in the fact that at any rate she was the woman he *came back to*. But he had little physical interest in her, needing always new women to stimulate him, and in the circumstances it is not surprising that she was attracted by the attentive Hungarian pianist.

Kovacs had received permission to practice on the Dreiser Steinway, his own piano being inferior. With Dreiser absent, and Helen listening to his rendition of "Clair de Lune," her heart melted. She even wrote a poem to him, one not found in the anthologies but representing sincere effort, reading in part:

> *Your hands run over the keyboard,*
> *And with your touch,*
> *The heavens open,*
> *And*
> *Showers of filtered stardust*
> *Rain upon the keys. . . .*[15]

Around March 22 Dreiser left on a walking-and-diet health jaunt. He took the train to Elizabeth, New Jersey, and hiked to Somerville without a morsel to eat for 24 hours. Here he suddenly decided that the homicidal Ruth Snyder might make a story or novel, for he wired Miss Kusell:

COLLECT ALL ITEMS FROM ALL PAPERS ON SYNDER CASE FROM FIRST. . . . MAY NEED.[16]

He also wrote Helen, inviting her to join him for a few miles, "& you could bring me a clean shirt and a few handkerchiefs." [17] Helen, troubled about the pianist and seeking honest understanding, joined him before he reached Bethlehem. As she recalled it, in his hotel room she asked him if, "in view of the way you live, you would understand my forming a constructive emotional attachment to help me live through the time you leave me so much alone."

He was incensed. "Do as you please," he growled. "But when you do, I'm out!"

His anger rose as she tried to reason. "You've always talked about freedom," she pleaded, "written about it, preached about it. What does freedom amount to if it cannot stand one test?"

"I don't want to discuss this," he shouted at last, so furious that she admitted, "his tense expression frightened me." [18]

Helen, now thirty-one, was unable to meet this challenge to her self-respect. Next day she walked a few miles with him—two tormented persons side by side in western Jersey. Then she returned to New York and broke off with the pianist while Dreiser hiked on to Bethlehem and wrote her forgivingly, "Was sorry to see you go & hope you got home safe."

He pressed westward, suffering from sore feet, taking refuge in barns when it rained. From Reading he addressed her as "Dearest Babe," complaining that "This hotel soaks me four bones for a single room with a bath." [19] He followed the Schuylkill to Philadelphia, there coaxing Louise Campbell to ride by train with him to Lancaster, where he left her and shuffled on to York. After examining the Gettysburg battlefield, he crossed Maryland's rugged panhandle. From Martinsburg, Virginia, he wrote Arthur Pell, treasurer of B & L, to protest about the commission taken by Brandt & Brandt, his agents for foreign rights: "Really I do not know why Brand & Brand should have 15%." [20] As he walked he was thinking that the Nobel Prize would be a pleasant honor as well as a "nice bit of change." He was in Winchester April 11 and went little farther, for by the 14th he was back on Fifty-seventh Street writing Mrs. Campbell, "Do this. Write to F.P.A. of N.Y. World—or Broun —and suggest me for the Noble Prize this year. I might get it." [21]

Mencken's instruction about the spelling of Nobel was wasted.

Dreiser also learned the identity of the other half of Helen's former "constructive emotional attachment."

"For days," she wrote, "he came in and went out without speaking a word. . . . If I thought I had been neglected and lonely in times past, I was to learn what spiritual isolation meant . . . he seemed to be trying to kill me by degrees with neglect and indifference. Day after day he spent most of his time away from the apartment. . . .

"And yet I never gave up in my attempt to draw close to him again. While he was shaving or dressing, I would try to talk with him. This usually led to abusively cruel words on his part, with a final sarcastic remark as he went out slamming the door behind him." [22]

Jug had turned to Christian Science for succor. Helen, after weeks of this, bought a book by Swami Vivikenanda and took up yoga. Daily she climbed to the roof of the Rodin building and practiced controlled breathing, remarking that soon "I had the distinct sensation of an expanding consciousness." [23]

Book Five

RUSSIA

1. An Innocent Abroad

I. THE GOD OF BEAUTY

Dreiser had cooled toward his old friend Ed Smith, who had left the *World* and was writing for the magazines. Possibly Smith had heard either of Dreiser's acquaintance with Edith De Long before she married Smith, or of Dreiser's frank account based on Edith's life, the yet unpublished "Olive Brand." At one of the Thursday gatherings Smith had said something that displeased Dreiser. Smith tried to heal the breach, writing, "I repeated to you, in the wrong way and at the wrong time, something that had been told me that filled me with incredulity and with dismay. Surely, I could not eventually conceal from you this absurd talk, the circumstances and relationships being what they were. But do let us forget it. . . ."[1]

Their correspondence ended. Six months later Smith died of pneumonia at forty-two, calling for Edith in his last delirium.

On October 11 Dreiser had a caller, F. G. Biedenkapp, secretary of the International Workers' Aid, an organization he described as a sort of "Russian Red Cross" devoted to the interest of workers all over the world. Russia was soon to celebrate the tenth anniversary of the revolution. Would Dreiser go as the guest of the Soviet government—all expenses paid?

Dreiser questioned Biedenkapp warily. "But I am not interested in any celebration or convention," he said, adding that he *would* be interested in seeing the famine districts on the Volga, the collective farms, the engineering and mechanical feats. "But supposing my opinion should prove unfavorable?"

"We will risk that," Biedenkapp said. The Russian government, seeking U. S. recognition, was inviting some 1,500 Americans to witness the great strides made there. Dreiser was one of the few whose expenses would be paid entirely. Most of the guests would be reimbursed only for expenses in Russia itself. "The Soviet believes you to be the outstanding literary intelligence of America. . . ." Biedenkapp went on.[2]

This was persuasive. Dreiser was so intrigued that he began a diary after Biedenkapp left. He broached the subject to Helen, with whom he was again on pleasant terms. She felt that his presence would be a stroke of prestige for the Russians, but she had an inevitable objection as he recorded it:

> You gonto [*sic*] fall in love with one of those Russian girls and get yourself all tangled up again. . . .[3]

325

He did not decide to go until he had been assured that he could stay in Russia a month or two if he wished and could travel wherever he wanted, all expenses paid. His entanglements already were formidable, for in his diary he mentioned his sorrow at leaving women listed as B——, Ch——, Ella, Ruth and Maud, noting, "Am conscience stricken about Maud," and later, "I have a meeting with B—— at the office. She is upset by the change and more passionate than ever." He promised to look for a Russian bracelet for B—— and a pair of Russian boots for Helen, apparently not committing himself on gifts for Ella, Ruth, Maud and Ch——.

"In spite of all my varietism," he wrote, "I realize that I really care for Helen. It is spiritual, not material. I feel sad at leaving her." [4]

From Joseph Freeman, who had visited Russia earlier, he got letters of introduction to artists and officials including Sergei Eisenstein, Olga Davidovna Kameneva (Trotsky's sister), Constantin Stanislavsky and Bill Haywood. Before sailing on October 19 he was given a dinner at Schwartz's MacDougal Street restaurant where he and William Woodward, Tom Smith, Konrad Bercovici, Diego Rivera, Joseph Wood Krutch and others listened to farewell speeches by Freeman, Ernest Boyd, Floyd Dell and Mrs. Woodward. Dreiser had to make a brief reply—a terrible ordeal. "He actually suffered physically," Helen noted, "and this night I suffered with him. . . ." [5] He boarded the *Mauretania*, was interviewed by reporters and found gifts from several girl friends in his stateroom as the vessel pulled away at midnight.

He had friends aboard—Ben Huebsch, Mr. and Mrs. Morris Ernst and the fat, swarthy Rivera, the latter also bound for the Russian decennial. Dreiser sailed an individualist, an evolutionist, scoffing at socialism and communism but eager to see Russia and judge for himself. His sparse reading led him to regard Trotsky as "a zealot, a sort of Christ of the economists," and Lenin "a genius of government." [6] He admired Dostoyevsky, Gogol and Chekhov and was sympathetic with the Russian efforts to form a model society even though skeptical about it. He noted that he had "queer dreams." Through a shipboard interpreter, one Judge Muller of Amsterdam, the individualist Dreiser had a long discussion over whiskey with the communist Rivera, who spoke little English but enough bad French for Muller to understand.

Individualism, said Rivera in essence, was wrong. Was it not the masses that gave the creative artist his hearing, thus creating the creator? The artist became greater the more he identified himself with the masses. Russia, he suggested, had carried this great truth into government itself—the rulers sensitive to and responding to mass needs. What could be more artistic, humane and inspiring? [7]

To Ernest Boyd, Dreiser wrote, "A pontifical kiss on the southeastern exposure of your whiskered piazza." [8] Landing at Cherbourg, he carefully listed his tips—generous ones for him—so that the Russians could later reimburse him: "Tips—Boots $1.00 Bath Steward 2.00 Room Steward $7.00 Dining Room Waiter 5.00 Hat check man 1.00 Doorman 1.00 Elevator man 50cts

Total 17.50." A dockside beggar girl so fascinated him that he wrote a squib revealing his susceptibility: "This [girl]—age, say, 14—was obviously compelled, either by her mother or a padrone to beg. But she had a natural beauty and the smile is the point. I find myself a chronic victim of nature's creative formula, as expressed in women even at this age—knowing the girl to be a beggar and merely using her smile for what she could get by it—still this smile . . . this artful use of her mouth and eyes with a purely practical intent was still sufficient on the beauty or art side to sway me to throw her money. I might almost say I could not help it. It was like electric energy or force conveyed from her to me." [9]

In Paris October 25 with Huebsch and Muller, he delighted in the crepes suzettes, the "gayety of the French temperament" and resented the constant tipping—"to change even so much as our minds or use a public urinal." To a *Paris Herald* reporter he admitted scant knowledge of Russia, which he would view with an open mind. Criticizing American materialism, capitalism and fake religiosity, he said, "Russia has a dream. . . . I am interested in it, its change, its ideals, its dreams." [10]

After a quick look at lovely Sainte-Chapelle, he pulled out all the stops of emotion in his diary:

> I sacrifice to the God of Beauty—the impulse to beauty in nature. Here are flowers. Here is wine spilled on the floor. I will burn incense & mirrh [*sic*]. I will kneel & strike my breast & touch the dust with my forehead. I will! I will! Only do not forsake me, oh God of beauty. Touch my eyes! Incline my heart & my mind. Give me ever—sensitivity—pain—at beauty. Let my heart ache! The tears flow. Bring me—oh, bring me again to Sainte Chapelle to pray as I do now. [11]

He joined Huebsch again at a sidewalk café on the Rue des Fous, about which he wrote: "And meeting of all people—& whom I have been hoping to see, Llona (Victor Llona) in Paris for the day . . . and with him Ernest Hemingway ("The Sun Also Rises") and someone else. Talk, talk, talk. . . ." [12] What was the talk about? Dreiser, who seemed more interested in Llona than in Hemingway, mentioned offhandedly that they discussed James Joyce and the French economy. Huebsch remembers the event, and the handsome young man saying, "I'm Ernest Hemingway," but recalls nothing else, for he and Dreiser soon had to catch their train. [13] The only meeting ever to take place between Dreiser and Hemingway passed quickly, without great impression on either side.

Aboard the train Dreiser and Huebsch discussed society and government. In Berlin they separated, Huebsch going to the sedate Kaiserhof and Dreiser to the grander Adlon. On October 28 he wrote, "I am sick this morning—not able to rise. Sore throat. Bronchitis worse than ever." Forty representatives of the International Workers' Aid crowded into his room with greetings and flowers. Next Dr. Felix Bernheim arrived to look him over, shake his head and write two prescriptions. Next came a Hearst representative to offer him $3,600 for two 3,000-word articles on Russia, a proposition he accepted tentatively. Next a telephone call from Huebsch, Dreiser noting:

"He has connected with Sinclair Lewis, a Miss Thompson who represents the Public Ledger of Philadelphia in Germany and Fran——*, the wife of the man who wrote *Power*. . . ."

Mrs. Feuchtwanger and several companions called on him at 10. "Fran—— proves very charming. I suspect an affair here if I could but stay. The smiles, giggles. And she explains that I need someone to *mother* me. I heartily agree. And at 11:20 Sinclair Lewis & his friends—a to me noisy, ostentatious and shallow company. I never could like the man. He proceeds—and at once to explain why he did not review An American Tragedy—as though the matter was of the greatest importance. . . . They [have] beer & sandwiches & silly talk until midnight when all decide to leave."

He could not forget Lewis' disparaging comments on the *Tragedy* before it was published. Lewis telephoned him next day to see how he was. "The man is seething with an ill concealed dislike but somehow feels it his duty to pay attention to me." Dr. Bernheim returned, now with stern warnings: Dreiser had an enlarged aorta as well as bronchitis. He must not go to primitive Russia—certainly not without a doctor as a companion. "I see it all," Dreiser wrote, "—they think I am a millionaire—am I not an American!" He announced that he was going to Russia, and no doctor. Later he had qualms:

> I am seized with homesickness. Here I am—nearly 4000 miles from N. Y. —9 or ten days at the shortest, and I am ill—maybe seriously. Supposing I were seriously ill—to die. And Helen so far away. And I have been so bad to her. I grow wretched and send a twenty word cable. If only she were here.[14]

The physician later told Miss Thompson he believed Dreiser had the beginnings of lung cancer. Lewis had been proposing hourly to Miss Thompson, who tore herself away from him and left for Moscow to report the celebration for her papers, the *New York Evening Post* as well as the *Public Ledger*. Dreiser lingered, feeling enough improved to visit Lewis at the Hercules Hotel on the Wilhelmstrasse. Lewis was most attentive and considerate, telephoning him daily and suggesting another doctor, whom Dreiser visited. He was relieved to be told that there was nothing wrong with his heart but that in his condition he would be mad to risk the Russian climate. He was mad. On November 3 he left for Moscow.

II. LEAD ME TO STALIN AND TROTSKY

"Warsaw I don't like, nor Poles either." Dreiser, aboard a train packed with pilgrims, rode with an almond-eyed delegate from Chicago, Mr.

---

* He left a blank here, the name Feuchtwanger escaping him.

Gee, and saw snow and troikas beyond Bialystok. He grew boyishly excited when they reached the border and were serenaded by a Russian band as they changed cars: "One senses a change at once. Something softer more emotional, less iron." Reaching Moscow November 4, he was let down: "But the wretched collection of autos. . . . The shabbiness. Georgia or Wyoming both would outclass them. And the people! The mixture of Europeans and Asiatics!" [15]

He was given Room 112 at the Grand Hotel ("shabby grand," he observed) near Red Square. An immediate caller was his correspondent Sergei Dinamov, a former professor now connected with Gosizdat, the state publishing house. Dinamov was enormously interested in Teodor Draizer and his *Amerikanskaya Tragediya* as well as in Sinkler Lyuis and his several assaults on the capitalistic bourgeoisie. Gosizdat and the few remaining private publishers were putting literature to the service of the revolution by translating and pirating foreign works critical of capitalism, manipulating the translation a trifle to make them more critical that the original.[16] Gosizdat had already published three stories from *Twelve Men* as well as *The Color of a Great City*, whose descriptions of poverty and of men crushed by capitalism the Russians compared to Dante's *Inferno* in its picture of hell. They were preparing to publish the *Tragedy*, which they saw as an even greater indictment of the bourgeois nightmare.

Dinamov might have recoiled had he known that Dreiser was a corporation personified, the embodiment of the Author's Royalties Company, and was dirtying his hands in Wall Street. What did Dreiser wish to do? he asked. Whom did he want to see? He must have been startled when the American named Stalin and Trotsky first among those he expected to interview. Probably Dreiser did not yet know that Trotsky was on the verge of expulsion and it was already growing a bit dangerous to mention his name. "I frame questions which might be asked of Stalin," he told his diary.

His whole attitude in Russia was characterized by intense curiosity, an excited realization that he was witnessing something never seen before, a desire to interview and cross-examine every available Russian, high and low, and underneath it all a belligerent conviction that he was competent to weigh and judge.

Since the first Five-Year Plan had not yet begun, remnants of private enterprise still functioned. Moscow was packed with foreigners, newspaper people, Americans. He met Scott Nearing, Junius Wood of the *Chicago Daily News*, William Reswick of Associated Press, Anna Louise Strong, Louis Fischer, Walter Duranty and many others. He met pretty Ruth Kennell, a socially dedicated American woman who had come to Russia five years earlier, and now, as an attache of VOKS, the cultural relations office, was assigned to aid him. Though still weakened by bronchitis, he followed a routine that would have wearied a younger man.

On November 5 he was escorted with a group through a "model" Moscow prison: "The smell. The cells. Yet all a great improvement on what was in the days of the Czar." Returning, he visited Bill Haywood at the Hotel Lux—Haywood, whom he had known slightly in the Village: "[His room] is crowded with dubious radicals. He himself has aged dreadfully. I would not have believed that one so forceful could have sagged and become so flaccid and buttery. But life has beaten him as it beats us all. . . . [His Russian wife] came in later—a kind of Slav slave."

With a Russian woman underling he walked in Red Square, viewed Lenin's tomb and the grave of John Reed, then back to his hotel: "I complain of loneliness & she comes up. We finally reach an understanding and she stays until two." [17]

On November 7, the anniversary, he saw a parade like none other. All day long, through gaily decorated streets, thousands and more thousands of men, women, children—Ukrainians, Georgians, Kurds, Kazaks, Cossacks, Siberians—marched with banners and floats into Red Square, saluting reverently as they passed the embalmed Lenin. Although the decorations reminded him of "a 14th St. Fire Sale," he was moved by the seeming national unity and hope, writing, "But, mayhap, this program is to [*sic*] beautiful to succeed;—an ideal of existence to which frail & selfish humanity can never rise. Yet I earnestly hope that this is not true—that this is truly the beginning of a better or brighter day for all."

That evening, with Dorothy Thompson, Scott Nearing and others, he visited the Cathedral of Our Savior and preened himself: "I gather en route that D. T—— is making overtures to me." Later they went to Nearing's room. "D T—— & I continue our flirtation. After a supper with the American delegation she comes to my room with me to discuss communism & we find we agree on many of its present lacks as well as its hopeful possibilities. I ask her to stay but she will not—tonight." [18]

One feels that he was swayed by vanity. He later suggested that he and Miss Thompson had had an affair, though his diary mentions no more than flirtation. Later he also said that at Miss Thompson's insistence he was moved to a better room upstairs near hers, whereas the diary says plainly that the move was made through the intervention of his IWA friend Biedenkapp. Miss Thompson, believing Dreiser a victim of lung cancer, would naturally have been solicitous. To Lewis she wrote, "I am getting tired of being educated by Scott [Nearing] . . . and being facetiously nudged by old Dreiser, who has turned quite a gay dog in Moscow, constantly making rather lumbering jokes. Still, I find him sympathetic, because he has a sort of healing common sense about life. And, curiously enough, he has a genuine—if rather elephantine—sense of humor. . . ." [19]

His new room overlooked Red Square and a huge sign characterizing religion as "the opiate of the people." He was repelled by Russian shabbiness, bad food and propaganda. He liked Russian vodka, the easy marriage-and-divorce laws, the free doctors and clinics. A sunny view of the Kremlin

1. John Paul Dreiser

2. Sarah Schänäb Dreiser

4. Emma Dreiser

3. Paul Dresser

5. Theodore Dreiser (seated second from right in rear) with cave-exploring group at Indiana University, 1889-90

6. Theodore Dreiser, aged 22—a St. Louis newspaperman with roseate dreams of financial and romantic triumphs

 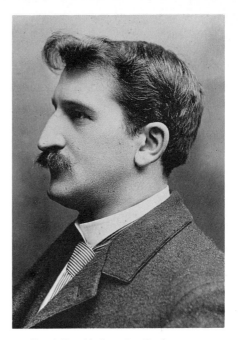

7. Arthur Henry, the inspirer   8. Frank Doubleday, the discourager

9. Thelma Cudlipp, Dreiser's dream of beauty

10. Jug Dreiser, the puritan, wedded to a rake

11. Dreiser as Butterick's stern editor-in-chief

12. Lillian Rosenthal found a flaw in *Jennie*

13. Kirah Marksham helped revise *The "Genius"*

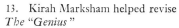

14. Vice-hunter John Sumner, Dreiser's nemesis

15. Horace Liveright, Dreiser's life-saver

16. William C. Lengel, for 35 years Dreiser's counselor, "ambassador," agent and friend

17. Dreiser in his St. Luke's Place studio, 1923. Note desk made from Paul's piano at rear

18. Louise Campbell, perennial Dreiser editor

19. George Sterling, poet and bohemian reveler

20. Sally Kusell helped create *An American Tragedy*

21. Earl Browder tactfully rejected Dreiser's application for Communist Party membership

22. Dreiser (with Aunt Molly Jackson) during his 1931 investigative tour of the Harlan coal area

23. Sinclair Lewis and Dorothy Thompson accused Dreiser of plagiarism

24. Esther McCoy, often a Dreiser writing aide

25. Floyd Dell deplored Dreiser's determinism

GEORGIA O'KEEFFE, FOR THE ESTATE OF
ALFRED STIEGLITZ

26. Sherwood Anderson—to him Dreiser
was the trail blazer against philistinism

27. John Cowper Powys, another
comrade in the battle for a liberated
literature

28. H. L. Mencken, beer and all—by far the most important single literary influence
in Dreiser's life

29. Speakeasy meeting of *Spectator* chieftains (l. to r.) Richard R. Smith, Boyd, Nathan and Dreiser

CARL VAN VECHTEN

30. The frequently gloomy titan caught in outright laughter

31. With Helen, who proved in the end to be the one woman without whom he could not get along

32. Iroki, a creature of Dreiser's whims, changed repeatedly during the course of construction

33. Mame and Rome at Iroki

34. Rosa Vermonte, Helen, Olin Downes and the white-clad host (l. to r.) at one of the Iroki gatherings

35. Ralph Fabri (by Iroki tent) was an observer of the stormiest period in Dreiser's and Helen's lives

36. The sporty Dreiser in Paris, 19[

38. Marguerite Tjader Harris

37. With Edgar Lee Masters at Iroki—a reunion of rebels

39. S. S. McClure, Willa Cather, Dreiser and Paul Robeson at 1944 American Academy ceremony in New York

40. The beetle-eyed brooder (1944) —only one of many swiftly changing moods

LOTTE JACOBI, N. H.

41. The last photograph of the living Dreiser, with Helen at the 1945 wedding of Lieutenant George Smith

42. The far greater brother is forgotten in Terre Haute

enchanted him: "The towers! The spires!—The pinapple [*sic*] domes. And so gloriously colored—red, gold, blue, green, brown, white. . . . Baghdad! Aladdin['s] world! And yet real! Here before my eyes." Two days later he noted, "At midnight some one taps on door. I fear it is some girl & since I do not feel up to more excitement do not open it. But I guess who." He had a dream that would have interested Dr. Brill. He was dancing in the nude, swinging a barbell "the while I threw myself joyously here & there. . . ."

But mostly it was work, research. Stalin and Trotsky not being immediately available, he interviewed Kogan, director of the State Academy of Artistic Science, assuring him that "science has nothing to do with art"; talked with two Tass men, Madame Litvinova, Madame Kollontaya and an *Izvestia* editor who told of the perfect freedom of the press in Russia. He was impressed by English-born Madame Litvinova, wife of the assistant foreign commissar, who blithely admitted her poverty, said, "You see how I dress," but gave her word that she was happy only in Russia. He met Lina Goldschmidt, a German writer who worshiped his novels and would later figure in his life. Characteristically, he quarreled so violently with a taxicab driver over 50 kopecks that a crowd gathered and a policeman settled the argument in Dreiser's favor.

III. COCKROACHES IN THE SOUP

On November 14 he flew into a Dreiserian rage. The Russians—and particularly Madame Kameneva of VOKS—were giving him the run-around. So far he had been unable to see the top Soviet officials and there was no action on his request for a tour of Russia and Siberia. He had spent $550 of his own so far and no one seemed in a hurry to give it back.

"I was invited by the Soviet Government," he told a frightened girl attaché. ". . . Yet I have been treated vilely. Now Madame Kameneva and the Soviet Government can go to hell. . . . What I desire is the cash return of my expenditures and that is all. Then I shall go."

Madame Kameneva herself came running to assure him it was a mistake. Officials gathered to help him plan his tour, though advising him not to go to bleak Siberia because of his bronchitis. Whom did he want to interview before leaving? Dreiser noted, "I gave him a list [including] Stalin. Done."

Things improved immediately. He was allowed to see the director of Gosizdat, Commissar of Trade Mikoyan, old Stanislavsky of the Art Theater, and others including brilliant young Sergei Eisenstein of *Potemkin* fame, questioning all of them closely. His opinions depended much on his fickle mood. To Eisenstein he said that "the Russian temperament is such that in 30 yrs. Russia will lead the world." Later, seeing jackdaws wheeling over the Kremlin, he philosophized, "It is a sad, drastic, tyrannical world that is below . . . misery, dogma, mysticism—a pathetic slavery to an age old fallacy. . . ." [20] With Miss Kennell as interpreter he visited the gigantic young poet Vladimir Mayakovsky who, though rich from his verse, lived in the usual Moscow squalor. He was paid a ruble a line, which local wits said accounted for his habit of breaking his lines into one or two words, somewhat as in Dreiser's "The Beautiful." There was fish, caviar, vodka and merriment, Dreiser astonishing his host by adding vodka to a dessert of prunes and whipped cream. "We shall call it 'Dreiser's cream,' " Mayakovsky roared.[21]

The old Bolshevik Karl Radek sneaked a visit to Dreiser at his hotel late one night, admitting that as a friend of Trotsky he was under surveillance and had to exercise caution.

Capitalistically Dreiser cabled his agent, George Bye, a series of thirteen suggested articles about Russia, ending, "Length fifteen hundred words price fifteen hundred each," [22] a proposition that would bring him $19,500 if accepted.

Still no interview with Stalin. No tour of Russia.

With Miss Kennell he went to Tolstoy's home and museum at Yasnaya Polyana, where it was ten below zero, and came back to be delighted at the Bolshoi Theater by the Russian Ballet interpreting Hugo's *Notre Dame*. In the audience was William Reswick, the AP man, with whom he had a conversation about the ballet that would later cause him trouble. Reswick said that when Otto Kahn was in Moscow a year earlier he had urged Kahn to help bring the ballet to America. Kahn had declined, and Reswick asked Dreiser if, on his return, he would renew the plea. Reswick would later charge that Dreiser entered into a business agreement with him about the ballet.

Although Dreiser found a horseshoe, and saw jackdaws light on the ledge outside his window—both of which he considered good omens—still no action from Soviet officialdom. Disgruntled, he saw communism bleakly again. He argued with Dinamov about it, criticizing the leveling of the "little brain & the big brain" and even noting, "As opposed to communism and its enforced equality I offered international, benevolent capitalism as very likely to achieve the same results." [23] The phrase "benevolent capitalism" gives one pause, for he saw capitalism as strictly rapacious and he would never have used the phrase in America. But Dinamov was a confirmed, cocksure Marxist, and Dreiser's argument here showed his liking for disputation and his tendency to contradict anyone with set opinions. He also declared that society might best be governed by a "narrow group of intellectuals," [24] which was more in line with his distrust of the masses and his growing belief in a power élite—a belief that would underlie much of his later thinking.

On November 26, with Miss Kennell and a Russian official he was sure was a spy, he went for a week's visit to Leningrad, hoping that on his return the Red tape would be unsnarled.

He toured Leningrad, saw the Winter Palace, a circus, the library, the opera, the museums, fired endless questions at an official of the local Soviet ("What is the Soviet Government going to do with the loafer?"), interviewed a prelate of the Sovietized church, drove out fifteen versts to see the summer palace. He interviewed the director of a rubber factory and informed him of the achievements of American capitalists. Though vodka was a help, he was bored by Russian insistence on Russian perfection and noted, "I wish I were out of Russia and at home in 57th Street. . . ." To Helen he wrote, "I return [to Moscow] Tuesday to interview Stalin & Trotzky."

Back in Moscow December 3—still no Stalin, no Trotsky, no tour, no reimbursement of funds. He did see Sinclair Lewis, who was in town for a ten-day visit with Miss Thompson, but did not bother to mention it in his diary. Lewis found him impatient at the Russian inefficiency, writing, "But I've never liked him so much—he was really charming." Vincent Sheean, also meeting Dreiser in Moscow, thought him a "pompous old bore." [25]

An impression grew on Dreiser that the Russians really did not *want* him to go on a tour. He lamented the likelihood that in this dirty country "there may be bed-bugs or a cockroach in the soup." The food was uniformly bad. "I find myself turning to Vodka—vodka plain, vodka in tea, vodka over a dessert in order that I make a go of things."

He complained again to VOKS, threatening to go home, and got quick promises. He was admitted to the Kremlin (absent-mindedly forgetting to wear his necktie) to see the charming Politburo member Nikolai Bukharin. He so needled Bukharin about Soviet failings that he reddened and swore that in ten years Russia would be a heaven on earth. He talked with Foreign Minister Georgi Tchicherin and the potent Alexei Rykov, always challenging: How could an altruistic political economy succeed when the human animal was incorrigibly selfish? What did the officials get out of it personally? [26]

Now a VOKS factotum gave him a sad story, saying they had only 2,000 rubles left in their fund, that they could not afford to pay his expenses on a tour or even his expenses home—this after the official Russian promise. He blew up.

"I said," he noted, "that I didn't want to talk with them any more. That VOKS could go to hell, he could go to hell, and when he begged me to see Kameneva, who was waiting for me, I said she could go to hell also." He was taken to Madame Kameneva again, and his bluster at last got results. Next day, December 8, he started his tour.

IV. A LOUSY COUNTRY

The Russian-speaking Miss Kennell was Dreiser's traveling secretary, a third and unwelcome member of the party being a bespectacled woman physician, Dr. Devodovsky. Although ostensibly assigned to protect his health, he regarded her as a government spy and stupid to boot. He had been sending endearing letters and cables to Helen, in one of them declaring that he would go as far east as Novosibirsk, but the Soviet officials dissuaded him on the ground that Siberia would be dangerous for his health. His first trip was

east to Nizhni Novgorod, where a routine was followed identical with that
wherever he went.

His party was met by obsequious officials of the local Soviet. They bundled
him around in a freezing open car, proudly showing him model apartments,
factories, collective farms, hospitals and schools, avoiding the slums. Dreiser,
suspecting this surveillance, frequently tried to escape it by questioning
citizens he met. In a village near Nizhni he insisted on interrogating the local
priest—and Dr. Devodovsky and the officials insisted on accompanying him.

"Do you think," he inquired, "the condition of the village is better or worse
social[ly] and economically since the revolution[?]"

"I cannot give my opinion," the priest replied nervously. "You must ask the
local representatives of the government."

They left him; then Miss Kennell returned alone to get her forgotten
gloves. The priest said to her, as Dreiser noted in his diary: " 'Please explain to
the gentleman that I would gladly have answered his questions, if we had been
alone, but before . . . the government representatives and a newspaper correspondent! If I had given my opinions—' He drew a finger across his
throat."

Dreiser said only half jocularly to Miss Kennell, "If I ever get out of this
country alive, I'll run as fast as I can across the border, and looking back as I
run, I'll yell, 'You're nothing but a damned Bolshevik.' " [27]

The trio returned to Moscow and on December 12 left on a long trek
south. In contrast with the comfortable, if dingy, Grand Hotel, they found
hotels in the provinces chill and dirty, dispensing vile food. The depots
stank. The air in the crowded trains also made one reel, and any train less
than three hours late was admirably prompt. Dreiser began to take a more
forgiving view of the capitalistic Pennsylvania Railroad and the Pullman
Company. "I was filled with rage," he wrote, "at everything Russian, such a
lack of system, such inexcusable negligence. . . ." He admired Kiev, then
went on to Kharkov, going on the usual conducted tours, praising a Ukrain-
ian performance of *Rigoletto*. At a Kharkov electrochemical plant he noted,
"One worker stepped up and said to my secretary, we should not believe that
the conditions of the workers are good, that they live very poorly, that they
have not freedom at all, they can't open their mouths to criticize and so on."
Other workers, much annoyed, assured the visitors that the man was mentally
defective.

At Stalino in the Donetz, Dreiser was taken 140 meters down the shaft of a
mechanized mine, where he questioned miners as to their impressions of life
under communism. He quarreled with Dr. Devodovsky and even had differences with the efficient Miss Kennell. "I had another fit of doubts about this
Soviet thing. . . ." he wrote. "I said when I saw that most of these industries
were not even new but had been running years before under the czar, that
some were not even up to pre-war production . . . that those tractors they
were turning out in such great numbers in Leningrad were admitted by this

agronom to be far inferior to the American and to cost more. . . . I said this thing couldn't work at that rate." Miss Kennell snapped that the industries had been destroyed during the war and revolution and had to be rebuilt—that he was a typical American, expecting to find everything as it was at home.

He veered from blame to praise, writing the same day, "One sees [here] a country with no abandoned—if as yet wretched poor; no foolish & meaningless rich." They moved on to Rostov, where he questioned the manager of a state tobacco factory about salaries, working hours, housing and exports. In Kislovodsk he visited a sanitarium whose name had hurriedly been changed from "Trotsky" to "October," then quarreled with a government clerk over the rate for a telegram and growled, "What a lousy country anyway." [28]

They arose at four on Christmas morning to catch the "fast train" to Baku, then waited in the smelly station because the train was five hours late. Dreiser understandably was weary, experiencing symptoms of illness although Helen in New York was protecting him with thought waves. "I could help him by giving him psychic support," she wrote, "and to that end I concentrated my every thought on his well being. This telepathic current between us was as real as any tangible means of communication, and through it I was able to follow his 'spiritual temperature.' " [29] Although their relations were often sweeter by telepathy or mail than in person, Helen sailed late in December to meet him in Constantinople.

V. STRONG LANGUAGE

Dreiser's spiritual temperature sank further when they reached Tiflis. He was struck by the beauty of the city of Stalin, but he brawled with a taxi man over a seven-ruble fare, suffered chest pains and went without dinner on New Year's Day, all restaurants being closed. The next stop was Batum (train four hours late), where they boarded the Black Sea steamer *Pestel*, bound for Odessa. The ship's food was abominable, there was no bathtub, and the sea was so rough for a time on the five-day voyage that it was safest to stay in bed (no sheets).

"We noted the second and third class passengers," he wrote, "as Asiatic and dreadful as ever. The huddled masses of them gave me a sense of nausea. Russia is permanently spoiled for me by the cold and dirt. Bukharin talked of building a paradise. But when? In fifty or a hundred years. I will seek mine while I am still alive."

A constant itch made him fear he had lice. He was barely on speaking terms with Dr. Devodovsky. After stops at Novorossisk, Yalta and Sebastopol, the vessel reached Odessa January 8, where he made the horrifying discovery that there was no boat to Constantinople for ten days. Near the end of his rope, he could not stomach the thought of waiting—just waiting—in Odessa for ten days. He decided to flee Russia by land via Poland, and wired Helen (already in Constantinople) to meet him in Paris. A new snag developed. At the passport office he learned that he had no visa for Poland, that he would have to pay 21 rubles, make application and wait; also that he would have to apply to take money and written material out of the country. He—a guest of the Russian government! He flew into a rage at Dr. Devodovsky, who seemed unsympathetic, noting:

> I then used some strong language about the lousy organization and about her, and about the whole God damned business.

An English-speaking Odessa reporter interviewed him at this inopportune time, hearing things he surely could not print. "I made him a long speech about what I thought of conditions, that it was an interesting experiment, but—they had a long way to go before they could try to put the system in other countries." He cooled off that evening when he took Miss Kennell (*not* Dr. Devodovsky) to the opera, enjoying Rimsky-Korsakov's *Sadko* so much that he hummed the "Song of India" occasionally for the rest of his life. He urged Miss Kennell to return to America, and said something which he later forgot:

"I'd rather die in the United States than live here." [30]

Next day, in his cold hotel room, bundled in fur coat, fur cap and mittens, he dictated to Miss Kennell a 1,500-word statement of his impressions, heading it "To the Russian People."

"Personally, I am an individualist and shall die one," he said. "In all this communistic welter, I have seen nothing that dissuades me in the least from my earliest perceptions of the necessities of man. One of these is the individual dream of self-advancement, and I cannot feel that even here communism has altered that in the least."

Having thereby repudiated the basic communistic philosophy, he went on to praise the gains made since czarism, the restraint of "brain-stultifying religion," the advances in industry, schooling, science. Then more heresy: He doubted that the Russian masses really understood the program that was supposedly enriching their lives, and even if they did he doubted that they could be sure their leaders would always be idealistic and selfless. "In Russia as elsewhere I am sure you will find the sly and the self-interested slipping into the positions of authority. . . ." He assailed the failure to care for the thousands of "wild" orphan children roaming the land, then loosed a broadside against Russian filth:

> The Russian house, the Russian yard, the Russian street, the Russian toilet, the Russian hotel, the individual Russian's attitude toward his own personal appearance, are . . . neither creditable or [sic] wholesome and . . . cannot possibly be excused on the ground of poverty. There are as poor people in Holland, Germany, France, and England, as there are in Russia, but you would never find them tolerating the conditions which in Russia seem to be accepted as a matter of course. . . .
> You live too many in one room and are even lunatic enough to identify it with a communistic spirit. I rise to complain. And I suggest in this connection

that more individualism and less communism would be to the great advantage of this mighty country. . . .[31]

Dreiser innocently believed that this bourgeois obstructionism would be printed in the Russian newspapers. He gave it to Miss Kennell for dissemination in Moscow. Dr. Devodovsky left for Moscow unmourned. Two days later Dreiser's visa and other troubles were cleared. On January 13 he and Miss Kennell boarded a train, separating at a junction point in the Ukraine where he made an affectionate farewell, then rolled westward toward blessed sanitation. Miss Kennell wrote him humorously that she would inform Madame Kameneva "that you crawled across the border on your hands and knees, stopping now and then to put your thumb to your nose and shout feebly: 'What a lousy country. . . . When I get back home I'm going to stay there for the rest of my life. And may the Lord punish me if I ever complain again.' " [32]

The free Soviet press decided that Dreiser's statement to the Russian people was not newsworthy. It appeared, somewhat cut, in two newspapers in the whole world, the *Chicago Daily News* and the *Oakland Tribune,* through their correspondent and Dreiser's friend, Junius Wood.

VI. RETROSPECT

Paris! Bathtubs—even bidets! Crepes suzettes, Sainte-Chapelle, and Helen! She saw that her Dody was exhausted when they met at the Terminus Hotel in mid-January. He did not tell her that he had stopped to visit with Lina Goldschmidt in Berlin. With Helen he went to rest at Mentone, where he met a charming young American woman, and his mind began undergoing a change as he digested his experiences in Russia.

He had worked hard and intelligently there, seeing more than correspondents who had remained comfortably in Moscow for years. As a materialist, he had seen Mayakovsky, the greatest poet of the revolution, well paid but living in a tenement so different from the Rodin Studios in New York. As an artist dedicated to freedom of expression, he had had a taste of the Soviet perversion of the arts into an organ of government. He had witnessed Russia's cruelty and fraud. The implications of the horror of the dictatorship were not lost on him—the brutal struggle for power between those idealists, Stalin and Trotsky; the Trotskyist Karl Radek, under surveillance and fearful; the village priest, his lips sealed by terror. His statement to the Russian people, severe though it was, had soft-pedaled the maledictions of his diary. He had left the country disillusioned and disgusted, an individualist confirmed in his individualism.

For everyone, time tempers impressions. For Dreiser, whose keen mind was subjugated by his helpless emotionalism and deep prejudices, retrospect and reality were two different things. He began to remember the beauties of

Russia—the Kremlin's colorful towers in the sunlight, the Rimsky-Korsakov opera, the ballet at the Bolshoi, of which he later said, "I tell you it was like getting to Heaven, to sit there and witness that magnificent moving mass spectacle." People in actuality often annoyed him, as Helen could testify. As Sally Kusell said, "He could weep for the downtrodden and let his own brother die on the doorstep." He fought personally with proletarians and later sympathized abstractly with their difficulties. It was in retrospect and reflection that he discovered his deepest strains of pity. The Asiatic countenances in Moscow had displeased him. The "huddled masses" aboard the Black Sea boat had given him a "sense of nausea." Now, safely removed from them, he was filled with sympathy for these millions of ragged Slavs who had often repelled him.

He had been frantic to escape Russia, to enjoy cleanliness, order and luxury again. Now that he had it, with supreme contrariety he disapproved of it, scowling at the gay, crapulous Riviera crowd. "He was thinking of how little the Russians had in comparison . . ." Helen noted, "and yet, how happy and grateful they were to have it." The light-hearted French temperament, so delightful to him in October, now "bored and irritated him." [33]

During strolls along the beach he described the sterling Russian virtues to Helen, who observed, "he truly loved this people." [34]

On January 27 they went to London where, through the intercession of Ray Long and the local Hearst representative, he had an interview with Winston Churchill, then Chancellor of the Exchequer. Dreiser, already regarding himself quite seriously as competent in international economics and politics, was again ready to take a belligerent negative when confronted by cocksure opinions. When Churchill shrugged off the Russian experiment as a certain failure, he disagreed sharply and went on to criticize the poverty of English millworkers.[35] He conceived a dislike for Churchill that would grow.

With the Kyllmanns he and Helen visited Glastonbury and Bath. He talked with his English agent Curtis Brown, with Michael Sadleir, and visited 76-year-old George Moore, later saying, "I . . . hoped to have a long chat on literature with the old fellow. And what do you imagine he spent the whole three hours talking about? About his prostate gland!" [36] He went on a tailoring binge at Flight's, Ltd., buying a dress suit, four business suits, an overcoat, a spring coat and assorted haberdashery. He and Helen sailed from Southampton, reaching New York February 21 after a stormy crossing. To ship news reporters he said the Soviet was "splendid."

"Nowhere in Russia . . . will you find men without overcoats standing in bread lines," he said. He conceded that it was a dictatorship that tolerated no opposition and that there were some economic troubles, but he was enthusiastic nevertheless. Communism, he declared, insisted that everyone be fed and clothed. There was no private property. Stalin did not even own his home but paid the government $125 a month for his flat. He described his tour of Russia with "two secretaries," saying, "I wasn't a communist when I went abroad and I don't return as one," but demanding, "Why should there be bread lines in a nation as rich as America?" [37]

Dreiser, in his search for ultimate truths, was often shaky on mere facts and statistics. In the *New York World* a Russian specialist caught him up in errors: There *was* private property in Russia, and Stalin lived rent free. An American Legion official scoffed that he had been taken on the usual guided tour and had swallowed the typical Bolshevik malarkey. In *The New York Times* Simeon Strunsky purred:

"Now, it was Stalin who declared at the recent Communist Party Congress that unemployment was one of Russia's unsolved problems. Trotsky's case against Stalin, as printed in the Pravda, speaks of 2,000,000 unemployed. All the cables from Moscow speak of long queues before the food stores, soaring prices, and conditions suggesting famine. From all this it would appear that Mr. Dreiser in Russia did not employ the extraordinary gift for minute observation revealed in 'An American Tragedy.'" Strunsky allowed himself a quip about Dreiser's interest in women, adding, "Yet it may be that if Joseph Stalin had detailed only one secretary to accompany Mr. Dreiser wherever he went, Mr. Dreiser might have seen more than he did." [38]

This kind of treatment was inclined to make Dreiser love Russia the more. Certainly there were unemployed in Russia, he wrote Strunsky with heavy sarcasm, but they were all fed. Certainly there were queues, not for bread but for scarce items. He had seen no famine. "You are so cruelly sarcastic, Mr. Strunsky, and so devilishly insinuating. . . ." [39]

His diary showed that his easternmost point on the tour had been Baku. Boy-like, he could not refrain from telling Helen and Louise Campbell (and perhaps others) that he had gone as far as Samarkand, "600 miles east of the Caspian sea—about 400 from Afghanistan." [40]

2. Thursdays and Other Days

The *Tragedy*, after holding up remarkably for two years, dwindled to a sale of 2,601 copies in 1928. The new edition of *The Financier* sold only 4,077 in its first year, *Chains* doing better at almost 12,000, but Dreiser's income from other sources was high. His foreign sales now were very profitable. He picked up constant fees for reprints of "The Lost Phoebe" and others of his short pieces, usually charging $50. To *Cosmopolitan* he sold three more of his woman sketches, "Rella," "Regina C——" and "Olive Brand," probably at $5,000 apiece. A *San Francisco Examiner* columnist unloaded a quip about this kind of writing:

> "Mr. Dreiser, who was that lady I seen you walking down the street with yesterday?"
> "That wasn't a lady. That was material." [1]

He capitalized on his Russian tour in several directions. The *New York World* was among the newspapers carrying his syndicated articles,[2] while other Dreiser pieces on Russia appeared in *The Saturday Evening Post* and *Vanity Fair*. With the help of Louise Campbell and others he was padding out these articles into a book on Russia to appear in the fall. Dorothy Thompson, whose Russian observations were appearing in the *New York Evening Post* and elsewhere, was also preparing to enlarge them for book publication.

The non-smoking Dreiser won a new accolade—an invitation to take the Old Gold cigarette blindfold test, to be used in nationwide advertising *if* he selected Old Golds. He was playing the market, often with the advice of Arthur Pell of Liveright.

"I really don't need or want money," he told George Jean Nathan, "though under the existing order of things you may be sure I want and get every dollar that is coming to me." [3]

To newspaperwoman Zoë Beckley he said his money had come too late for real enjoyment. "Who wants money after the fires of youth have died?" [4]

His income tax notes for the previous year, 1927, suggested that he did rather like money despite the flickering fires. He listed a gross income on the Author's Royalties half of his divided self of $97,611.66. However, he jumped his own salary as an officer of Author's Royalties Company from $1,000 to $19,900, taking this as a deduction along with many others including $21,685.17 for "selling commissions," $7,200.92 for travel expenses and $7,-847.04 for "Advances on plays failed during year." His deductions totaled

$68,504.28, leaving him a net income (as a corporation) of $29,107.38, on which he appears to have paid only $3,929.50 in taxes. Since the Russian government paid his expenses on that trip, and he made no other sizable journey in 1927 except for his walking tour, one views his $7,200.92 travel deduction, as well as some of the others, with surprise.

His "Thursdays" resumed, assuming an ever more international flavor. Helen was taking voice lessons from Maria Samson, the pretty Hungarian-born soprano, who was often a guest with her physician husband. Other Hungarians were the painter Ralph Fabri and Margaret Szekely, who had come to this country as a representative of a Budapest newspaper but had switched to dress designing. Dreiser now made it a point to invite Russians from Amtorg and the consulate in New York, while at Helen's invitation swamis often drifted up from the Vedanta Society, located in the Rodin building. Lina Goldschmidt, the Berlin critic now visiting New York, was a favored guest, determined that Dreiser would get the Nobel Prize. A new visitor was Dr. Boris Sokoloff, a Russian-born endocrinologist with the Rockefeller Institute who persuaded Dreiser to write a preface for a book of short stories he had written. Another was the beautiful Marguerite Tjader Harris, the wife of a New York attorney, whose life would interweave with Dreiser's until his death. Donald Friede brought along young Philip Wylie, whose new novel *Heavy Laden* Dreiser praised for its skill but criticized on grounds of morality and taste, an odd reaction from the "vulgarian" who had fought morality so long:

> Why do you insist you are an atheist, nobody cares. . . . Why do you insist so strenuously upon a certain frankness about life: even the cat covers up after herself. . . .[5]

While he could not make up his own mind about Russia (Margaret Szekely noted that "his philosophy changed every week"[6]), he was apt to be sharp with anyone who criticized the Soviet. "Before he had talked more than five minutes," William Woodward wrote, "I realized that his trip to Russia had converted him to Communism. He declared that Russia was not what we imagined it to be, and that it was one of the most democratic countries."[7] Claude Bowers observed, "From Dreiser I heard nothing to indicate that his Russian sojourn had not been a veritable delight."[8] Yet in his Preface to Sokoloff's book, *The Crime of Dr. Garine*, Dreiser called the Russians a fascinating people "when not badly crippled by a wholly lunatic theory in regard to altering the very nature of man. . . ."[9]

Lina Goldschmidt, now on a cruise to South America, wrote him romantically: "I have seen you in many incarnations. There is one I will never forget. You seemed to be one of the ancient Gods. . . . Women knelt before you, men of name and fame arose when they were addressed by you. . . . For me your friendship is a marvel every day nearer and dearer to my heart. . . ."[10]

In June old Austin Brennan died, leaving Mame alone and largely dependent on Dreiser. Early in July, at Sokoloff's invitation, Dreiser and Helen drove in their sporty open Chrysler Imperial to Woods Hole, where he spent three weeks observing the work of some 180 scientists at the Marine Biological Laboratory. This was the beginning of a massive Dreiser project that would occupy him at intervals for the rest of his life—an effort to formulate a philosophy, in part through science, that would suggest answers to the ultimate riddles.

He loved every minute at Woods Hole, forming lasting friendships with scientists including Dr. L. V. Heilbrunn of the University of Michigan, Dr. Calvin Bridges of Caltech and Dr. Robert Chambers of Cornell. He watched experiments in progress, peered through microscopes and interviewed researchers as to what they were doing, what they hoped to achieve. At evening bull sessions over lab alcohol and water, he demanded answers to the unanswerable. Was there a God? He believed there was some directing force over the universe, and was dissatisfied to learn that these men who were delving into biological mysteries had no pipeline to the infinite. And why did they not conduct open war on that enemy of knowledge, the Catholic Church?

He was staggered to discover that one of the scientists there was a *Catholic priest*. He questioned the priest endlessly, and also the others. How could a Catholic priest—an apostle of benighted reaction—possibly be interested in pure science?

With Helen and Bridges he visited Marguerite Tjader Harris, who had a cottage on Nantucket. On leaving Woods Hole he wrote a tribute to the scientists that was published in their small newspaper, then returned to New York to meet Suzanne of *The "Genius."* [11]

Thelma Cudlipp meanwhile had married the wealthy attorney Edwin Grosvenor and had read *The "Genius"* for the first time. Angry at his use of the events of 1910, she relented because of the suffering it obviously had caused him and wrote him a note. Dreiser and Helen dined with the Grosvenors. Thelma told him of her mother's suicide several years earlier, to which he replied with typical forthrightness, "I am glad." [12] She was amazed at his treatment of Helen.

"He humiliated Helen before us," she recalled. "He simply ignored her. She didn't seem to resent it. I could not understand how Dreiser, kindly as he was, could treat her this way, nor could I understand how she could put up with it." [13]

II. D. T. *vs.* T. D.

The project-juggling Dreiser was now in the position of an executive directing a heterogeneous staff in a multiplicity of enterprises.

With the help of Louise Campbell and others he was piecing together his book on Russia.

Also relying on Mrs. Campbell, he was preparing *A Gallery of Women* for book publication and another account of women, "This Madness," for *Cosmopolitan*.

He was gathering his poems for a volume called *Moods*.

He had met H. S. Kraft, a New York theatrical man, who proposed dramatizing *Sister Carrie*, with Paul Muni to play Hurstwood. He was willing. John Howard Lawson, well-known for his *Processional*, was engaged to do the adaptation—a project that missed fire but nevertheless took time.

Dreiser was having a researcher gather material for an assault on the Catholic Church.

He was outlining articles for proposed newspaper syndication.

He was writing a story based on the life of Ruth Kennell.

He was trying to supervise the construction of a large new house at his Mt. Kisco property.

He sat for his portrait by Wayman Adams, an Indiana-born painter who lived in the Rodin building and who polished off a flattering likeness in a day and a half of fast work.

On top of all this he was quarreling with Helen, involved with other women, thinking of quitting Liveright for Harper's or Simon & Schuster, boning up on science, devoting time to his investments, looking for a new secretary, and upset by minor annoyances such as a dispute with Flight's in London because the two overcoats did not fit. He was nervous, taking an occasional morning nip to relax.

Under these conditions, he did not give his new book, loftily called *Dreiser Looks at Russia*, the attention he should have. He instructed Louise Campbell to collect Dorothy Thompson's newspaper pieces to aid in the padding.[14] Mrs. Campbell did so, but knew better than to incorporate them verbatim. As she recalls it, the script she sent to New York underwent further revision there. After Dreiser's return from Woods Hole, he mentioned that he was driven "almost mad" because he did not have a "competent detail secretary." It is possible that Helen was helping him, but he also had a disorderly habit of involving casual women friends in his writing problems. If this was done, with several women aiding in the job, it is easy to see how the accident happened. Or was it an accident?

Miss Thompson's book *The New Russia* was published by Holt September 7. Liveright, though unenthusiastic about Dreiser's book, brought out *Dreiser Looks at Russia* November 11. Miss Thompson meanwhile had married Lewis and they were living at the Grosvenor Hotel on lower Fifth Avenue. They called over Albert Boni, who lived across the street at the Fifth Avenue Hotel. Boni found Miss Thompson upset and Lewis furious over passages in Dreiser's book identical or similar to those in Miss Thompson's:

Dreiser's book, page 36:

But there is of course the primitive society of the Communist workers, who put on their own festivals. . . .

There was (or is) the rather arid and pitiful society of the diplomatic group, which has only the limited foreign colony on which to draw and the members of which, living in huge and sumptuous houses, with silver, porcelain, and space for entertaining hundreds, give each other little luncheons and talk about how long it will be until they can "get out" again to Paris or London.

Miss Thompson's book, page 41:

There is the primitive society of the Communists who put on their own festivals. . . .

There is the very limited society of diplomatic circles, who have only the limited foreign colony on which to draw, and who, living in vast and sumptuous houses with silver, porcelain and space for entertaining hundreds, give each other little luncheons, and talk about how long it will be until they can go "out" again to Paris or London.

Page 37:

The Artists' Club I found to be one of the most amusing and comfortable places in Moscow. It is one of the few places where one can dine, dance or play billiards. The food and wines are not bad and not, relatively, expensive. Here, amid over-ornate Empire mahogany and bronze taken from private houses of pre-revolutionary days. . .

Page 66:

The Artists' Club is one of the most amusing and comfortable places in Moscow. It is one of the few places where one can dance, play billiards and dine, and the food and wines are excellent and not, relatively, expensive. . . . The club is furnished with valuable over-ornate Empire mahogany and bronze taken from some private house.

Page 38:

They [the businessmen] sit moodily in the restaurant of the Grand Hotel, drink Russian wines, watch the dancing and think themselves lucky if a ballerina from the opera dances with them. . . .[15]

Page 43:

The business men sit moodily in the restaurant of the Grand Hotel watching the dancing and thinking themselves lucky if they have a ballerina from the opera to dance with.[15]

There were other passages equally similar. Miss Thompson gave the scoop to her own paper, the *Post,* which reported, "Mr. Dreiser denied emphatically . . . that he had 'lifted' any material from Miss Thompson's book and, on the other hand, asserted that she, in the course of talks with him in Russia, had obtained from him material later incorporated in her articles and book." [16]

This was a churlish evasion. The issue was not one of facts or material, but of wording. No one would have complained had he commented on the same facts, but for him to appropriate phraseology from Miss Thompson's news-paper articles was plagiarism. He was angry because he had been in Russia eleven weeks to Miss Thompson's four, had traveled extensively while she had remained mostly in Moscow, and felt himself far more qualified than she. This was still beside the point. Miss Thompson rightly said:

> Mr. Dreiser's explanation does not explain the parallel passages which occur in our books, and which were in my original articles. Mr. Dreiser says he traveled around Russia and saw lots more than I did and gave me some of his material which he couldn't or didn't want to use.
>
> I wonder when he gave me that material. As I recall it we only met two or three times and then had merely casual conversations about what we'd seen and been doing. But the point about these passages is that Mr. Dreiser did use them—and so did I, first. And none of the passages in question has anything to do with what might have been seen on Mr. Dreiser's tour out-side of Moscow. . . .
>
> But here are two books in which actual verbal passages or purely de-scriptive matter, literary passages, let us say, are identical. I protest against this and have asked an explanation of it, because I feel, even if Mr. Dreiser doesn't, that it puts one of us in a bad light.[17]

The newspapers again mentioned Dreiser's crib from Anderson's "Tandy" and his lifting of newspaper material in the *Tragedy*. In *The New Yorker* Corey Ford satirized the case with a piece called "Corey Ford Looks at Russia." Miss Thompson's attorney wrote Liveright that the Dreiser book was "an infringement of her literary property" and demanded that "you forthwith recall from circulation all copies of the book 'Dreiser Looks at Russia,' that you surrender for destruction all copies bound and unbound, sheets, plates, etc., and that you account to our client for all profits. . . ."[18]

Arthur Garfield Hays was Liveright's attorney, while Dreiser retained Arthur Carter Hume to defend him. Hays, after a discussion with Dreiser, said, "His attitude seemed to be that the whole thing was of no importance and that we should do nothing about it." Hays agreed it was as well that Liveright and Dreiser each had his own attorney, writing Liveright that otherwise "Dreiser will always suspect that any advice I give him is in your interest."[19]

In a statement to the press, and also in a mimeographed explanation of the similarities which he sent to friends, Dreiser had another story. He attributed them to the fact that he and Miss Thompson had used the same Soviet handouts, including a weekly news bulletin published for foreign visitors. Even if true, it would hardly do him credit to accept Russian propaganda verbatim. But his memory, or his word, seemed shaky here. It is evident that most of the similar passages, being reflective and even critical, are outsiders' comments rather than Soviet propaganda. Later, in a conversation with Robert Elias, Dreiser reverted to his first story—that Miss Thompson in her newspaper articles had used his material, that it was originally his own so he went ahead and used it.[20] But there is also the fact that none of Dreiser's sentences was quite identical with Miss Thompson's. Clauses had been transposed or a word changed as if in a hasty effort to avoid outright copying. The incident hardly redounded to his credit.

Miss Thompson eventually dropped her case against him. Meanwhile no sense of taste forbade him from hinting privately that he had had an affair with her in Moscow—a report that must have got around.[21]

A better title for his book would have been *Dreiser Between Two Stools*. What he said on one page he often qualified or contradicted on another. His difficulty lay in his long-held belief in individualism and the inevitability of the law of the jungle in human effort—a belief he was not ready to discard but which now was entangled with his hatred of capitalism, of American poverty and wealth, and his delighted hope that in Russia altruism was replacing selfishness, eliminating the capitalist and giving the lowest peasant security. One could not logically hold the belief that man was at once a ravening tiger and a sweet altruist. Dreiser tried, struggling between fact, emotion and intuition.

"I am an incorrigible individualist," he began his book, "—therefore opposed to Communism."[22] Yet he found "wonderful features" in the Soviet system and on page 21 he said, "I am not inclined to complain, but applaud. . . . And out of Russia, as out of no other country to-day, I feel, are destined to come great things, mentally as well as practically." He spoke of the "honesty" and "selflessness" of Russian leaders. Stalin, he wrote gravely, was paid a mere $112.50 a month.

He persisted in stretching his yarn, claiming to have been in Samarkand, Tashkent and Novosibirsk, places he had never seen. He was typically careless about facts, saying on page 101 that there were "less than a million Communists" in Russia and on page 123 placing the number at 1,200,000. On page 49 he wrote admiringly, "This dictatorship is a weapon for a particular end—the bringing of that classless, brother-loving society in which no dictatorship will be needed." On page 79 he remembered that as an individualist he did not believe in such balderdash, writing, "I am dubious of the result because I cannot even conceive of a classless society any more than I can conceive of life without variations and distinctions. It is these same which give us our sense or illusion of reality, and without these there is no reality." He affirmed this on page 80: "Communism or no Communism, it is brain, or cunning, or both . . . that makes all the difference between who is respected and who is not, in Russia as elsewhere." Despite his earlier statement that he was "opposed to Communism," on page 74 he wrote, "Is Communism all wrong? Far from being all wrong, I consider . . . many of its aspects and developments to be very much right and progressive. . . ."

But he had strong criticism. He detested the "inescapable atmosphere of espionage and mental as well as social regulation which now pervades every part of this great land. The prying. The watching." He deplored the "air of suspicion, and in places even terror," the armed GPU men at every railroad station, the fact that for political offenders "hope of a fair and impartial trial is slight." "One feels [the terror] as one feels a fog. . . . And along with it, rumors of secret trials and executions. . . ." [23] On page 128 he said the secret terror "chills the heart of man." After thus describing the crushing of all freedom and civilized values, he could, two pages later, take phrases from his diary and call the Soviet program "beautiful":

. And it is possible, if not entirely probable at this writing, and if only human nature can rise to the opportunity, that here at last is a genuine betterment for the race. Yet again, mayhap not—the program being possibly too beautiful to succeed, an ideal of existence to which frail and selfish humanity can never rise.

Helen's favorite new outfit was a white homespun dress "fashioned after the Russian Cossack coat," and a "striking white Russian hat." Mrs. William Woodward thought it all rather ridiculous, with Dreiser himself sometimes appearing in a Russian robe or other "silly Russian clothes." The chief impression Dreiser made on Mrs. Woodward was one of suppressed violence—so strong that one could feel it all over.[24]

III. QUARRELS

Wharton Esherick alternated between admiration for Dreiser's understanding and aversion for his lack of taste and his shabby "private" life. Sherwood Anderson told racy stories with gusto, whereas Dreiser not only refused to tell them but glowered when anyone else did—an attitude Esherick felt indicated some inner disfigurement. His nearest approach to a ribaldry was a bitter one. He said of the swank studios on Fifty-seventh Street, "No artists can afford them because wealthy business men rent them all. They like to fornicate by north light." [25]

Esherick, staying overnight at the Dreiser studio, had dressed and was about to go downstairs when he heard Dreiser screaming in fury. Pearl, the colored maid, rushed upstairs in tears. Helen followed her, weeping. Esherick, who never did know what the quarrel was about, went down to find Dreiser cooling off.

"Maybe I did the wrong thing," he said, "but a good thunderstorm now and then clears the air." [26]

Esther McCoy, the former Missouri coed who had corresponded with him in 1924, was now working in New York and doing research for him on the side. Arriving at the studio to help Helen prepare for a party, she was about to go upstairs when a frightened servant called her back. Then she heard Dreiser bellowing at Helen, who replied in angry shrieks. Miss McCoy also noticed that Dreiser at times would be cruel to the wolfhound Nick, which she felt was motivated by his knowledge of Helen's fondness for Nick.[27]

He had no false modesty. A woman guest, bathing in the Dreiser tub, neglected to lock the door. Dreiser entered the bathroom, let down his pants, squatted on the toilet and began discussing literature with the lady in the tub.[28]

Needing a confidante, he leaned on Margaret Szekely, who lived on Ninety-first Street. On several occasions he telephoned Mrs. Szekely frantically in the middle of the night to ask if she had an extra bed for him. "He would come and weep because Helen didn't understand him," she recalled. "He needed a mother and I supplied the need. One of the things he said repeatedly was, 'Life is so difficult, so complex that I have to knock my head against the wall to regain my equilibrium.' " [29]

In the fall of 1928 he employed Esther Van Dresser, a vivacious young lady from St. Louis, as his secretary. She had read his books with an admiration that remained despite her tribulations. One of her duties was publicity. If Dreiser was mentioned in the papers, she ordered extra copies and sent clippings to his friends. She found him grouchy in the morning when she arrived to go over his mail, sometimes greeting her, sometimes not. He invariably had a half-dozen kinds of pills on his desk for assorted ailments. As the day went on he usually mellowed and could be wonderfully amiable. "He had a great animal magnetism," she recalled. "You almost felt it." [30]

She discovered that he regarded a hat on a bed as a sure sign of death. Friday was an unlucky day for starting any sizable project. He kidded her about her Episcopalianism, called her "Aimee Semple McPherson," and sometimes was biting on this subject, saying that anyone who believed in the conventional God was "a boob from Boobsville." She learned to be ready for sudden wrath that might be caused by an interrupting telephone call or an annoying letter. Sometimes he merely scowled and muttered, but he could fly into paroxysms of rage quite out of proportion to the cause. He would stamp and shriek, his face purpling, his off eye swinging farther askew, then grow hoarse and begin to sputter from bronchial congestion. "It was not becoming," Miss Van Dresser said. Yet the fact remains that she found him so charming in his better moods that she stayed on.

His capacity for error was stupendous. His ancient enemy Stuart Sherman had died of heart failure in 1926 while swimming with his wife and some friends near Manistee, Michigan. Dreiser in a later account placed the tragedy vaguely in "New Jersey or Pennsylvania," said "his wife [was] on the coast at the time, I believe," suggested that Sherman was enjoying a rendezvous with his girl swimming companion, and to top it off said that the girl had drowned.[31] He was as confused about the shooting of Henry Clay Frick by Alexander Berkman, although he had arrived in Pittsburgh only two years after Berkman wounded Frick and the story was a bromide among newspapermen he knew. Now he was writing a sketch of Emma Goldman, Berkman's paramour, and he alarmed Emma when he wrote her in Paris for more information.

"I was amazed," she replied, "to read in your letter that I personally slew Henry Frick. You state that I told you this. You must have mixed up something else with this. . . . But the facts are that even Berkman did not slay Frick—he recovered from the bullet wounds soon after. I hope you are not as mixed up about the other facts in my life as you seem to be on this. . . ." [32]

Dreiser now exchanged so many cables with foreign publishers that he obtained the code address THEODREIS NEW YORK. He was quarreling as bitterly as ever with Liveright, saying to Nathan:

"What I am still looking for in the midst of all this success . . . is some little, greasy, one-horse publisher who wouldn't know a mahogany desk if he saw one but who has a high and very real love for literature. . . . I am sick of these business-men publishers with their offices that look like the *Ile de France* and with their minds that look on books as if they were so many boxes of merchandise." [33]

One of his complaints seems to have been Liveright's failure to publish the collected edition of Dreiser's works as promised. Friede had done preliminary work on this before leaving Liveright to form Covici-Friede, but the cost of such an edition and the small probable sale had caused Liveright to give it up, doubtless reflecting that Dreiser also had failed to produce his promised novel. The day of collected editions, once a publishing staple, was about over. Dreiser was disgruntled also by the weak sale of the Russian book—a bare 4,000 copies. It was true that Liveright now was more interested in his stage productions than his publishing, and was sometimes helplessly drunk. Yet he still tried to hold Dreiser, feeling that losing him would be a blow to his prestige. Dreiser pushed his advantage relentlessly, reminding Liveright that other publishers were after him and threatening to switch. Although his great days were over, neither he nor Liveright knew this and he was convinced that his writings and his fame had been a major factor in the firm's success. Liveright even consented to an auditing of the company's books by an accountant employed by the suspicious Dreiser. Although he had never formally accepted Liveright's invitation that he become a director of the company, on February 11 he sent Miss Van Dresser to represent him at a board meeting attended by Liveright, Julian Messner, Arthur Pell and Tom Smith. Miss Van Dresser took the following notes:

> Mr. Arthur Pell advised the Board that the books of the company had that day been reviewed by an auditor employed and commissioned by Mr. Theodore Dreiser. Mr. Liveright sanctioned this, saying that as a director, Mr. Dreiser was at all times at liberty to examine the condition of the books. Mr. Liveright further explained to the Board that Mr. Dreiser had a short while ago asked him to call at his studio for the purpose of going over a proposal he wished to make him. This proposal was . . . : That in consideration of the prestige and position [Dreiser] occupies and because of his foreign contacts and connections, as well as influence among various au-

thors here, he believed that he could be of considerable service to the publishing firm of Horace Liveright, Inc., by securing various authors for them, and that by joining hands with the publishing house and coming in with them as a stockholder, the firm could be developed into one of the largest of its kind in the world. Mr. Liveright mentioned here that he believed that if an author really did wish to work for the growth and success of his publishing house, he would naturally endeavor to use his influence in the securing of as many authors as possible and that he did not consider it advisable, because of professional jealousy rampant among writers, to have too prominent and close a tie between an author and the publisher. . . .

[He stated] that he believed that Mr. Dreiser should diversify and not invest too heavily in one thing—such as a majority holding would entail. It was brought out that Mr. Dreiser had requested a substantial increase in his advance, from $6000.00 to $15,000.00, which has been approved and a contract continuing six years on this basis, drawn, which contract has not as yet been signed. Mr. Dreiser, it was pointed out, wished the contract to run for ten years, instead of six. This contract also provides for a book every other year. . . .[34]

Almost the whole meeting was devoted to Dreiser. The notes hint that he had suggested buying a large—perhaps a controlling—share of the company. On reading them, he reacted violently with two letters to Liveright, one saying in part:

I will thank you to advise me immediately . . . whether my name is being carried along as a director or officer of your corporation, and if so, since when, and the specific authority therefor. . . .[35]

His other letter enclosed a copy of Miss Van Dresser's notes and showed that he felt Liveright had falsified his report of the discussion the two men had:

As you will see, it is stated here that I asked you to call at my studio for the purpose of going over a proposal which I wished to make to you. Then follows a very fine bit of imagining on your part which relates an author's duty to his publisher. What, if he had wholeheartedly the interest of his very worthy publisher at heart, he would do.

You now have the privilege of writing me a letter in which you will state what did happen from first to last. . . .

I am not willing to wait longer than Monday afternoon next for your reply.[36]

At the same time he wrote his friend Kyllmann in London:

Cape has opened a publishing house over here and is picking up quite a few American writers. Why don't you join up with some big American house and let me move bag and baggage over into your American organization. I own all my books. My contract expires in two and [a] half years & I am thinking of breaking it by suit & for a very good reason. . . . I have been offered a $50,000 cash advance against a ten year contract as it is. . . .[37]

Kyllmann replied suggesting a hookup with Harcourt, Brace. Dreiser vetoed this idea, cabling, "DO NOT CARE FOR HARCOURT BRACE," [38] probably because that company published the despised Sinclair Lewis.

In the end, Dreiser again stayed with Liveright.

IV. I LIKE AMERICA

When pretty Sulamith Ish-Kishor interviewed Dreiser about Russia for the *Jewish Day*, he was in a cheerful mood. Although he refused to autograph a copy of *An American Tragedy* she brought along, saying he had a rule against it, he added, "But if I like your interview I will." He went on to say:

> America is the ideal country for the individualist who is capable of getting ahead. I like America and best of all, New York. Look what it's given me—what it gives everybody. You know, Communism isn't independence. It's just the opposite. It's the cutting off of every kind of independence! . . . I have the greatest interest in the Communist experiment; even if it doesn't—as the Comintern is so sure it will—bring heaven on earth in fifty years. . . .[39]

One of his "Thursdays" that winter is still remembered. Otto Kahn, George Luks, Rosamond Pinchot, Samuel Hoffenstein, Wallace Irwin, Ernest Boyd and about a hundred others heard Maria Samson sing. Dreiser then asked another guest, the fat but pretty-faced Russian-born diva Nina Koshetz, to sing. Jealous of the applause accorded Miss Samson, Mme. Koshetz first refused outright, then complained that there was too much smoke in the room. Guests doused cigarettes, windows were opened and she finally delighted the group with a splendid performance.

"The best is yet to come," Dreiser said aside to Claude Bowers. He had arranged a surprise with Caroline Dudley, the dancer sister of Dorothy Dudley. Miss Dudley led in a troupe of a dozen Negro "dancers from the Congo" (said actually to have come from Harlem) who startled the crowd by entering with shrieks and yells and a deafening din of tomtoms. Some were all but naked, some clad in costumes representing animals and birds. For two hours they executed dance routines, in one of them beating swords on the floor so that neighboring tenants later complained. "It was a warm evening," Bowers noted, "the room was close, the air was anything but pleasant. Dreiser watched the performance with sparkling eyes. To him this was the best. Here was something primitive. Another side of Dreiser was revealed."[40]

Dreiser cultivated Kahn because by February he was acting on Reswick's suggestion in Moscow and was launching a campaign for funds to bring the Russian Ballet to America. "It's wonderful!" he said to Nathan. "There's nothing in the whole world like it." [41] He formed a fund-raising group headed by Hy Kraft, the theatrical producer, for whom he had taken a great liking.

He opened an office in the French Building on Fifth Avenue and detailed Esther Van Dresser, Dorothy Dudley and Marguerite Tjader Harris to canvass. He enlisted the aid of the wealthy Alma Clayburgh, persuaded Louise Campbell to sound the tocsin in Philadelphia, and wrote to Fremont Older in San Francisco and George Douglas, now in Los Angeles, soliciting their cooperation in raising money in California. Among others he asked for help were Roy Howard, Frank Crowninshield, Deems Taylor and Olin Downes. Crowninshield warned him that he was moving into difficult terrain and would do better to put the drive in the hands of professionals. But Kahn contributed $25,000, Conde Nast $10,000, smaller sums came from others, and Dreiser was enthusiastic.

In the midst of it he was off to Boston on April 15 with Friede, whose appeal on the *Tragedy* conviction was finally coming to court. Friede, now co-owner of Covici-Friede, was simultaneously in Sumner trouble in New York for his publication of Radclyffe Hall's *Well of Loneliness*. In Boston, Clarence Darrow and Arthur Garfield Hays appeared for the defense, but were confronted by flinty minds in a community that recently had confiscated thirteen copies of *Candide* and forbidden Margaret Sanger to speak on birth control.

Mrs. Sanger was an honored guest at a Ford Hall dinner ridiculing the local censorship. Dreiser, Darrow and Friede were among the guests who saw Mrs. Sanger ostentatiously rise and seal her lips with adhesive tape as policemen eyed her narrowly. Other satirical skits were presented, and Darrow gave a jocular speech.

This made headlines which did not sit well with the jury that heard the case against Friede next day. The jurors had not read *An American Tragedy*, and there was a feeling that the book advocated birth control. Indeed it was the successful intent of Prosecutor Frederick Doyle and Judge Hayes, backed by aged statutes, to prevent the jurors from knowing the import of the whole book. Doyle read "immoral" passages to the jury, and the defense was forbidden to introduce the rest of the book in evidence or even to give a summation of it. The fact that the *Tragedy* was assigned for reading in Harvard literature courses made no difference. Attorney Hays complained that the case should not rightly be called "Commonwealth against Donald Friede," saying, "It is Commonwealth against American Literature."

Prosecutor Doyle extolled "those good Puritans who left England [and] brought with them the innate feelings and instincts of decency. . . ." He said, "Well, perhaps where the gentleman published this book it is considered not obscene, indecent and impure for a woman to start disrobing before a man, but it happens to be out in Roxbury where I come from." In *An American Tragedy*, "we find . . . the most disgusting, the most filthy, the most vicious, the most devilish language that a human being could think of." Dreiser was put on the stand but was muzzled, forbidden to answer questions relating to the general theme of his book. Although Friede remembers him as laughing at the absurdity of it, the fact that the judge and prosecutor were Catholic and the jury predominantly so was not lost on him.

Friede, of course, lost his appeal and paid a $300 fine.[42]

The losers returned to New York, where Friede had some satisfaction the very next day in defeating the Protestant Sumner, being acquitted in the *Well of Loneliness* case. To Dreiser, however, the Catholics were the most fanatical of book-banners. When Rabelais shortly afterward was tabooed in Philadelphia, he wrote Bowers, a Protestant Democrat strong for Al Smith:

> Personally I am convinced that this is a direct attempt on the part of the officials of the Catholic Church, with possibly the cooperation of . . . other denominations. I have stated over and over that the chief menace to the world today is the Catholic Church because it is a world wide organization and because chiefly it attacks intelligence—the development of the human mind in every country in the world—since for its own prosperity's sake it believes in mass stupidity.[43]

Fear of the Catholic Church, he felt, was one of the reasons why Famous Players had failed after three years to make a picture of *An American Tragedy*. Hearing that the company was producing another film to be called *The Genius*, he retained Hays as his attorney and sent Famous Players a telegram:

> I OBJECT DEFINITELY AND FINALLY TO YOUR USE OF THE TITLE THE GENIUS UPON ANY FILM MANUSCRIPT WHICH YOU MAY DEVISE OR PRODUCE SUCH USE IS NOTHING LESS THAN A BAREFACED ATTEMPT TO CAPITALIZE FINANCIALLY AND WITHOUT EXPENSE A VALUE WHICH MY BOOK HAS CREATED. . . .[44]

Famous Players changed the title. Meanwhile, the drive for the Russian Ballet had languished. Miss Van Dresser went to Chicago to petition Samuel Insull, who reddened at the idea of giving aid to the godless Bolsheviks. "Young lady," he growled, "I should throw you out the window."

"The Russian Ballet, I am sorry to say, is a dream of the past," Dreiser wrote Alma Clayburgh. "We found it impossible to interest a sufficient number of the monied people, most of whom had already left to be gone all summer. . . ."[45]

3. Mr. Bang

Although his attitude toward Russia was still ambivalent, Dreiser moved toward a more persistent, if undisciplined, social protest. He wrote sympathetically to Tom Mooney in San Quentin, then to Governor C. C. Young of California demanding to know why he did not free Mooney. He contributed ten dollars to the American Civil Liberties Union, five dollars to the *New Masses*, donated to a strikers' fund, signed a protest against high taxes, and smote the Catholics hip and thigh. He was friendly with the fiery, Russia-loving Mike Gold, who was appalled by the hopelessness of a recent Dreiser statement. Dreiser had said:

> I can make no comment on my work or my life that holds either interest or import for me. Nor can I imagine any explanation or interpretation of any life, my own included, that would be either true—or important, if true. Life is to me too much a welter and play of inscrutable forces to permit, in my case at least, any significant comment. . . . As I see him the utterly infinitesimal individual weaves among the mysteries a floss-like and wholly meaningless course—if course it be. In short I catch no meaning from all I have seen, and pass quite as I came, confused and dismayed.[1]

Gold tried to lead him into more constructive (communistic) social thinking, writing him, "I have always been worried about your philosophy because it makes a revolutionary philosophy seem trivial. But the more I think about you and your writings the more I feel your confusion and pessimism comes from a very profound and honest *social pity* & without letting this emotion work fully & consciously—that is, working for it, finding social forms to express it—one must feel as bad as if one consistently repressed sex or other desires. . . ."[2]

Dreiser also was ambivalent about the Jews. Among his many Jewish friends were Dr. Brill, Hy Kraft, Dr. Heilbrunn, Milton Goldberg and the painter Jerome Blum, now living in Westchester. He regarded the Jews as marvelously gifted. "Just think of what they have achieved!" he cried to Ralph Fabri. "Just think!"[3] In private he heaped maledictions on them, swore they could not be trusted. His quarrels with Liveright often set him off in violent diatribes against Jews in general. He was irked because his name was sometimes thought Jewish, writing the Jewish Biographical Bureau in response to their query, "I have not the honor to be a member of your distinguished race. The loss is mine."[4]

Indeed, "ambivalent" was a good one-word description of him except in areas where his prejudices had become fixed, as against the English and the Catholic Church. Close friends had to become reconciled to his mental fluctuations. Claude Bowers understood that logic was not to be expected from him. Louise Campbell, candidly regarding his thinking as a "mishmash," twitted him about his involvement in Wall Street while he scored the capitalists. Fabri was so fascinated by his contradictions that he noted many of them in a diary he kept.

Kirah Markham had been aware of them for years. Dreiser invited her to the Fifty-seventh Street studio, where Helen showed her the handsome Wayman Adams portrait and asked what she thought of it.

"Just as he always wanted to think of himself, a success," Miss Markham said bluntly, noting that it could have been the portrait of a wealthy financier or stockbroker.[5]

Dreiser and Helen so admired Ralph Fabri's portrait of Maria Samson that he was commissioned to paint Helen. Sitting for him almost daily at Fifty-seventh Street with Nick at her side, she admitted in turn her need for a confidant and poured out her troubles, always repeating herself several times.

Fabri, a man of warm sympathies who thought Helen one of the most beautiful (though not the most intelligent) women he had ever seen, got an earful.

A believer in numerology, tea leaves, the power of the will and other doctrines, she said, "All you have to do is *believe* in something and it will happen." [6] Apparently her own beliefs were of insufficient strength, for the things she wanted to happen did not, particularly in relation to Dreiser. She had no regular allowance, she said. He gave her money when he thought of it and was in a good mood, but often he forgot entirely. She felt humiliated to be forced to ask him for cash. Sometimes she essayed a hint by wearing an old and ragged dress—a failure because he never noticed what she wore. Now she was urging him to deposit $60,000 in the bank for her so that she could have a regular income of $300 a month.

She worried because he drank bromide constantly, as some youngsters drank coke. His doctor had warned him against this. Once, when Dreiser was leaving on a trip, she found seventeen bottles of bromide in his bag.

But her real complaint was about his endless affairs. More than ever he seemed attracted to younger women—even mere girls. On one occasion she knew about he took three different women to bed in one day. He described sex as "the real business of life" and acted accordingly. Helen listened in on the telephone extension, trying to get wind of his plans. Sometimes he would leave without a word, to be gone with some woman for a day or two, or a week or more. She never knew where he was, how long he would be gone, or whether he would come back at all. Women imposed upon him, she felt, costing him time and money. When entering the apartment, she always looked to see if his bag was in its usual place in the foyer. If it was gone, did it mean he was gone for good? She had had no sexual relations with him for two years, she said.[7]

Fabri, a painstaking painter, had virtually a full-time job as he tried to capture her on canvas while she drenched him with her troubles. He recognized her limitations but saw that her emotions were entirely sincere. While she had a few temporary affairs with other men, she was deeply devoted to Dreiser. She would call Fabri in the middle of the night, weeping, to say that Dreiser was gone, and what should she do? Sometimes when abandoned she would taxi to Fabri's studio at 45 Washington Square South, where the bachelor painter would listen to her repetitive accounts of her woes, then put her up in his spare room for the night—just as Dreiser occasionally fled in desperation to Mrs. Szekely. Once Helen telephoned Fabri past midnight to say frantically, "If he won't settle everything with me, I'll shoot a bullet through his head. I'll shoot a bullet through his head." [8]

That crisis passed, but others were sure to come. "I just had a fight with Teddy," she sobbed to Fabri over the telephone. "It's all over now. We're breaking this time." [9]

The break did not come. Three days later she returned to the studio to find Dreiser and his bag gone, empty cocktail glasses on a table—bad signs. "He must be fixing up a place for himself," she told Fabri. "He probably wants to leave me on the street. He took writing materials with him." The very next day she informed Fabri happily that Dreiser had returned and was in a good mood.[10]

Once, when Dreiser felt guilty after an absence, he gave her a white fur cape. Delighted as a child at Christmas, she went to Fabri's studio to show it to him, then insisted that he walk up Fifth Avenue with her so that passersby could admire her. When Dreiser was in good spirits and the household calm, she would take voice lessons from Maria Samson and practice religiously, certain that she was almost ready for professional engagements. At times he enjoyed her singing, particularly liking her rendition of the sentimental "Among My Souvenirs." Then a Dreiser thunderstorm or absence would throw her into panic, making her drop her singing and concentrate on the crisis.

The Butterick firm, which Dreiser had left eighteen years earlier, forwarded him a recent note signed "Josephine" which read, "Is it foolish to think I will ever see you again?" [11] He now had Daphne Walters—the woman who in Rome in 1912 had regaled him with the story of the Borgias—working on a dramatization of *The Financier*.[12] That same fall he coaxed Louise Campbell to come to New York so that her literary help would be instantly available. She became friendly with Helen, sometimes commiserating with her over Dreiser's latest infatuation. "Once," she recalled, "I had to restrain her from tossing out of the window a plaster head of Dreiser which had been sculptured by a girl he had admired." [13] Mrs. Campbell was less worried about the sculpture than she was about passersby thirteen stories below.

Soon after she arrived, Wall Street crashed. Miss Van Dresser, working closely with Dreiser in his speculations, had been one of those who warned him of a threatening market outlook. He had made cautious moves into sounder investments, apparently putting some of his money in gold. He had made killings in Electric Bond & Share and other stocks during the palmy days, accumulating an estimated $200,000, perhaps more, at his peak. When the crash came, Miss Van Dresser judged that he had lost considerably less than half his savings. Horace Liveright lost every penny he owned.

II. IROKI

The fact that Dreiser took his losses without loud complaint indicates that they were relatively small in that time of disaster—perhaps $75,000. His own later recollections were unreliable, for he once said he had been "lucky" and lost little, and again that he had been shorn of $300,000. He stayed on at Fifty-seventh Street although he growled to Fabri that this was Helen's fool idea, as was the big Chrysler and her own Buick roadster. He kept his servants. He continued building his place near Mt. Kisco, which he called Iroki—Japanese for "beauty."

Iroki was a product of his changing whims. The new house had been started as a large garage, built of the fieldstone that abounded there. As it took shape, Dreiser admired the handsome fieldstone, saying, "It's ridiculous to waste this on a garage. We'll make it into a studio for me." [14] Plans were revised, a great stone studio with an immense fireplace was completed and the roof was almost finished when he changed his mind again. The original cabin at the top of the hill was too small, he decided. It could be used as a guest house. Now he wanted the new building enlarged into a complete country house, with a living room, music room, kitchen, bath and two bedrooms above the studio.

The roof was torn off and a frame second story added. It was at this point that he persuaded Fabri, a practiced man at construction, to take a hand in the work. He now decided he wanted an open porch at the end of the studio floor, which Fabri built of natural stone. It was necessary to cut through the 18-inch fieldstone studio wall to make a door between the studio and the porch.

Dreiser belatedly hit on the idea of having a handy bath and shower in the cellar underneath his studio. There *was* no cellar. At great expense a portion of the floor and the shale under it was blasted out to make room for the subterranean bath. The kaleidoscopic Dreiser house became the talk of the neighborhood.

"Most houses are built from the foundation up," Fabri told him. "This is the first I have seen built from the roof down." [15]

Dreiser sought the suggestions of all his friends. At least five artists—Fabri, Esherick, Jerome Blum, Henry Varnum Poor and Hubert Davis—had a hand large or small in the construction or design. Esherick, himself a builder, supervised the construction of two small cabins with thatched roofs, set apart from the others. Devoid of refinement in taste, Dreiser loved a picturesque and extraordinary quality in the things around him, as he did in people, and a sentimental attachment for Iroki grew on him because of the contributions of his friends. Easy, cordial, he could veer from warm, human insight to dark superstition. He attended spiritistic seances and remarked on their astonishing revelations. To John Cowper Powys, always a welcome guest at Iroki, he told how a "vast, mysterious hand" had once appeared over his shoulder, pointing at what he was writing.[16]

He had a Norwegian immigrant named Sorensen as caretaker at the estate. He was fond of Sorensen until that winter, when he let a fire get out of hand and the original frame cabin burned to the ground. Furious, Dreiser fired him and refused to pay his wages. Sorensen sued for his pay. Dreiser sat tight, saying he had a better lawyer, that he could get the case continued again and again and the Norwegian would ultimately give up. It was not until many months later that he was seized by remorse and he paid Sorensen in full. "I am ashamed of myself," he told Esherick. "I shouldn't have pushed that man so far." [17]

The Catholic Church, however, he would push forever. When Paul Palmer, Sunday editor of the *World*, asked him to contribute to a symposium about existing marital laws and customs, Dreiser sent him an article assailing them. In it he mentioned the difficulties of unhappily married couples forced to flout foolish laws, writing, "Not only that, but that world's largest real estate organization, the Catholic Church, condemns them to hell besides." [18]

Palmer asked permission to delete the phrase "that world's largest real estate organization," saying it would be "offensive" to Catholic readers. Dreiser countered with a proposition: His price for the article would be $200 *with* the phrase, but $500 without it—possibly the only time a writer ever charged $50 a word in reverse. When Palmer demurred, he called off the deal, writing, "It is gratifying to find the New York World so careful of the feelings of the Catholic Church." [19]

He was still quarreling with Flight's about the two coats bought two years earlier. He had become an eccentric people talked about and wanted to meet. A few of his many callers were Martha Ostenso, O. O. McIntyre, Sarah Gertrude Millin on a visit from South Africa, and Evelyn Scott. He charmed them all but Miss Scott, later writing her:

"Your saying that I am the rudest man you ever saw reduces me to the point where I have lost my power of composition," and asking for "a bill of particulars." [20]

When Count Michael Karolyi visited New York in January, there was a reception for him at the Dreiser studio. The place was jammed, and Dreiser, as was his wont when warmed by a drink or two, took a succession of willing girls into his lap and fondled them rather freely. Helen, for whom a third cocktail was usually disastrous, downed it and took tipsy revenge. "Helen sat in Karolyi's lap, kissing and petting him," the non-drinking Fabri noted.[21] Margaret Szekely was upset because Dreiser was planning to write an introduction to Boris Sokoloff's book on cancer. Long disturbed by his capacity for assuming all knowledge as his province, as well as by his sometimes maudlin worship of "beauty," she argued with him a few days later while riding with him and Helen to Iroki. He knew nothing about medicine, she said, and would merely expose his ignorance by writing such an introduction. Dreiser disagreed.

"Stop the car," she said, out of patience. "I am getting out!"

At her insistence Helen finally stopped. Mrs. Szekely alighted on the Saw Mill River road, aiming to take a taxi home. Dreiser got out and pleaded with her, at last saying, "All right. I won't write the introduction." So they drove on to Iroki.[22]

He was continuing his correspondence with Sergei Dinamov, who bemoaned his "low standart [sic] of living" in the Soviet state: "It is dreadful, dear Dreiser. Why we must have family, lovers, stomach?" [23] A confirmed Stalinist, he regarded Dreiser as a bourgeois radical who could not shake off the capitalistic shackles, yet wonderful for all that. He wrote later:

> It is very strange—you are for me like the best friend. Only some days we were together . . . but it is quite enough for me to think about you as my good big friend.
> I don't like to write you in this style of passion—I am wonder what happened with me.[24]

III. POTATO MINDS

On November 30, Liveright published Dreiser's *A Gallery of Women*, 15 of his kiss-and-tell stories, some of them written seven years earlier. The book was published in two volumes at $5 because the firm felt that anything less would injure his prestige. Now at last, in "fictional" form, appeared his appraisals of Ed and Edith Smith, Hutchins Hapgood, Mary Pyne and Harry Kemp, a niece of Jug's, a tea-leaf reader Dreiser had patronized, and many others. In "Rona Murtha" he treated of Arthur Henry and Anna Mallon so that Henry, when he read it, knew precisely how Dreiser had loved him and then given up on him as a charming but shallow fellow. It was a devastating portrait of futility, one that evened the score for Henry's description of Dreiser's waspishness in *An Island Cabin* in 1904.

On the very day of publication, Dreiser complained about the advertising. Liveright, who was preparing a $20 limited edition to appear later, invited him to come in and see the promotion plans for himself. Although Dreiser in 1919 had contemplated the book as one that would make the "ghosts of the Puritans rise and gibber in the streets," he found that in ten years puritanism had subsided considerably. The critics received the book without shock and with limited praise, feeling generally that this was not the Dreiser of the *Tragedy* or even of *Twelve Men*.

Meanwhile Kathryn D. Sayre, a graduate student at Columbia, took Dreiser as her subject and called on him by way of research. He was so impressed by Miss Sayre and her choice of subject that he persuaded her to become his part-time assistant. This was necessary because he was sending Miss Van Dresser to Europe to spread publicity which he hoped would fetch him the 1930 Nobel Prize. Lina Goldschmidt, a gifted pianist and painter as well as drama critic, had been beating the drum assiduously in Europe, writing, "For—my dear Mr. Dreiser—you must know, that I did not forget my purpose, of which I spoke you [*sic*] in New York. To make you even more known, more popular, so that your name will be on the lips of everybody and that will be the moment when you will get the *Nobel-Prize*. You must. . . . Thomas Mann—whom is he compared with you?" [25]

Madame Goldschmidt had given talks about Dreiser over the Berlin radio, had produced a "Dreiser evening" over the Hamburg radio and had succeeded in getting *The Hand of the Potter* presented on several German stages. Her enthusiasm had spurred a new and revolutionary stage adaptation of *An American Tragedy* by the avant-garde Erwin Piscator, not yet produced. She had written Dreiser fondly, "I know, that a Genius can not be measured by human measure. And that a Genius has every right to ask his friends to smooth his path by any means, even with the blood of their hearts." [26] Taking her at her word, Dreiser replied that these European productions were gratifying but "have resulted very unsatisfactorily to me from the standpoint of any kind of royalty returns." [27]

It would be Miss Van Dresser's job to meet with Frau Goldschmidt and with Dreiser's various European publishers and to work incessantly for newspaper and radio mention of him from London to Prague. She was also to question the publishers—particularly those in Berlin and Vienna—about royalties he suspected they were holding out on him.[28]

Dreiser himself was plagued by bronchitis and nervousness. He had a new lady friend, he was anxious to shake off another, and he was curious about the effects over the country of the strange economic depression that had followed the Wall Street crash. On March 20, with the girl, he left by train for the Grand Canyon and Tucson. From Tucson he sent Fabri a postcard picturing a spiny pincushion cactus and writing:

> Here's what I call the friendly spirit—the right hand of fellowship. Made into a door mat it would automatically yell "Welcome." Standing as is—its other name is *Love*. Dreiser.[29]

As he toured, he told the country off in a series of newspaper interviews.

"I think that the Mann act is absurd," he said to a Tucson reporter, doubtless reflecting that he was violating it himself. "So is the statute against adultery. Why, the trains are full of Mann actors—and where would we get enough penitentiaries to put everybody who had committed adultery?"

He assailed Prohibition, said the American people were "ethically brow-
beaten," "the slaves of an asinine code of ethics," always cracking down on
the "little offender" and letting the "big fellow" get away with murder. "But
some day America, the big Gulliver, will tear off the Lilliputian strings that
now bind him." [30] After two front-page columns of what the reporter referred to as the "Dreiser vinegar works," he took the bus with his lady on
April 5 to Albuquerque, where he continued his strictures at the Franciscan
Hotel.

"The trouble with America is too many potato minds," he said. He in-
veighed against Y.M.C.A. secretaries, reformers in general, and called the Ten
Commandments "a bunch of bugaboos." Birth control, he insisted, was an
economic necessity. Prohibition was "bunk," and he was looking forward to a
visit to El Paso where he could cross the border and get a decent drink. "The
hypocrisy in American life today is nauseating," he said, adding that "even
the clergy take off their collars and go to Chicago or some other big town for
a holiday." Newspapers were too craven to print the truth. The reporter,
noting his handkerchief-folding, wrote:

> Dreiser claimed to be the only man in the country who has the courage
> to put down on paper what he really thinks.

Occasionally using profanity—a sign of real anger—he attacked a recent
Will Hays pronouncement on what would be allowed in the films: "He gave
me my biggest laugh in the year with his list. I suppose he thinks he'll get to
be president with that stuff." [31] The rich were in the saddle, he said. "Money
is the hall mark of all that is best in America. Because he has millions, Henry
Ford is an authority on any sort of intellectual matter." [32]

In a few days he was off with his companion to Santa Fe, then south to El
Paso, where they put up at the Paso del Norte. When the *Herald* there
telephoned to ask an interview, he snapped that he would see a reporter
provided he "found one worth talking to." Two reporters arrived, waited an
hour, then were told he was "too busy." Possibly he had already crossed the
border to 100-proof freedom, for "with an attractive young woman" he visited police headquarters to report the loss of his wallet containing $210. A few
minutes later he telephoned from his hotel to say that he had found the
wallet.[33] Next day, April 26, he relented and talked to a *Post* man:

> Religion in America is just a total loss. . . . Boot out your El Paso minis-
> ters along with all other religionists and your city and America will be
> much better off. At least you will have cleared this country of just so much
> pure dogmatic bunk. That is all this religion is—just fool dogmatic bunk.

He had shifted somewhat in his view of the press, saying, "Thank God there
is the newspaper and it is not dogmatic. This country has gone forward in
spite of the churches and the newspaper has helped. . . .

"And these anti-vice crusaders! You know who they are? Some crack-brained religionist needs a job. He pours out the publicity so that he can continue to draw a salary."

Love, he said, was simply an electro-physical and chemical reaction of short tenure:

"The duration runs from three months to three years. The spark is dead at the end of three years. If two persons remain together after that, it is because of some other reason. . . ." The death of love, he added, could be determined by an "examination of the body cells." [34]

His remarks aroused a storm of protest in the *Post*'s subscribers' column, Mrs. P. E. Gardner writing that Dreiser must have been loaded with "white mule" and adding, "In my opinion, Mr. Dreiser is just a lot of bunk, himself." [35] By this time, however, Dreiser was on his way to Tucson again, where he told the *Citizen* that religion was "a total loss" and advised:

> Close the churches, and open scientific laboratories that seek to know the secrets, if not the meaning of life and its creative forces—and see how much more quickly we shall come by wisdom and beauty. . . .[36]

All of these interviews were given front-page display, were of considerable length and contained his criticisms on other subjects such as prison management, the commercialization of literature and the sending of Christian missionaries abroad. Dreiser was referred to respectfully as "America's leading novelist," but some astonishment was evident at his vehemence. On May 5 he arrived in Dallas and put up at the Baker Hotel. Possibly by now he had given his companion her return fare, for there was no further mention of her and Helen was soon to join him. He warned a *Morning News* reporter that unless something was done about unemployment a revolution was quite possible. Democracy, he said, was a "farce," America was "rapidly approaching Communism," and women would play a vital role in the change. Americans were suckers, always buying things they did not need:

> You buy a new car. You do not want a new car, you do not need one. You buy a country place: When I was young I wanted a country place. At 30 perhaps I would have enjoyed it. When I got it 30 years later, it cost me $150,000 [It had cost him less than $50,000 so far.] and I didn't want to live in it anyhow.[37]

In New York, Martha Ostenso, Ralph Fabri and others saw Helen off as she put the Chrysler (and Nick) aboard a boat at Pier 36. She also had stateroom 36 and was numerologically delighted, certain that this would bring her good luck.

IV. DREISER, INC.

Meanwhile Dreiser had a friend of Willy Pogany's, the agent I. M. Sackin, working to sell his wares in Hollywood. He had wired Sackin that should a film company buy one of his books he would be willing to work with them in California for six months, selling his services separately. He would take no less than $75,000 for any of his books—more for *An American Tragedy* and *The "Genius."* Although he had already sold the *Tragedy* to Famous Players, they had not produced it and he felt he might swing a sale from them to some other studio. He stressed that he must have a free hand in any production so that film companies could not debase his works.

Sackin wired that Warner Brothers was actively interested, so Dreiser, meeting Helen's boat at Galveston, got into the nine-passenger Chrysler with her and Nick and drove to Hollywood. The "active interest" fizzled. On May 29 they went on to San Francisco, where he arranged a meeting with Tom Mooney at San Quentin. "If Tom Mooney is not freed," he told newsmen at the Mark Hopkins, "he should, by rights, be taken out of prison by force." [38]

At the prison, he and Helen found Mooney to be healthy and neatly dressed. He told Dreiser the history of his case, of his anxiety to be released so he could work for the cause of labor. Dreiser pointed out that in prison he was a figure of international prominence and influence—a position he would probably lose when freed. Mooney nodded, then suddenly broke down and wept, causing the emotional Dreiser to come near tears himself. He called on Governor Young, who insisted that the wheels of justice were turning in Mooney's case. He picked up his sculptor friend Henry von Sabern, who was with him and Helen when they visited the home of Fremont Older, the influential editor of Hearst's *Call-Bulletin*, to discuss Mooney. "[Dreiser] seemed the most unattractive man that I had ever met," Mrs. Older noted in her diary. "I wondered how his pretty wife ever married him. He had cold grey eyes always looking for copy. In the evening, however, I liked him better." [39]

Back at his hotel, he castigated Governor Young and American justice before a circle of reporters.

"We call this country a democracy," he said. "It's really an oligarchy. The seat of government is Wall Street, not Washington. . . . Why, democracy is a joke. Everything about it is a joke. Voting? Here's what it amounts to: That people who go to the polls are merely going through the motions of voting. . . . For a long while the country has been moving unconsciously toward communism. Whether or not it will come to that I don't know. But some change must come." [40]

Seeking to exert political and newspaper influence for Mooney, he requested an audience with William Randolph Hearst at San Simeon, who telegraphed, ". . . GLAD TO HAVE YOU COME HERE IF YOU CAN." [41] With Helen he rode 200 miles down the coast to the castle, where they drove up the hill through gazelles and other imported fauna, to be met sweetly by Marion Davies. Lunching with Hearst, they were as impressed by the donkeys that hauled in huge logs for the fireplace as by the pleasant demeanor of the master, who spoke confidently of getting Mooney's release. Returning to San Francisco, Dreiser told the *Jewish Journal*, "The Jews are one of the greatest races which ever stood on earth!" but complained, "You Jews . . . want to be a race which envelops the earth. You'd like to have your fingers in every pie." [42]

They swept north to Portland, where they visited Helen's mother and sister Myrtle. Perhaps forgetting that he was a corporation, Dreiser told newsmen, "The government has ceased to function. Government is a corporate function—the corporations are the government," and they might as well get together and move to Washington. He had tried and failed to get Mooney out, he said, adding, "William Randolph Hearst promised me he would do it and now we'll see." Informed that some New York publishers were reducing the price of novels due to the depression, he snapped, "They won't sell any of my novels for $1.50. . . . I don't have to give any of these publishers my books." [43]

Increasingly alert to what he regarded as injustice of any kind, he was angered by legal action taken against a Portlandian, Robert G. Duncan, who he claimed was being persecuted for radical utterances. The local *Oregonian* replied that Dreiser had his facts entirely confused, that Duncan was being prosecuted "for spouting poison against individuals," not for his economic views.[44] When New York's left-wing John Reed Club sent him an appeal for a statement against the suppression of free speech and assembly, he gave them more than they asked for. He composed a long attack on "industrial absolutism," declaring that Russia was trying to eliminate economic injustice while here there was not even any comprehension that such an effort was vital, advocating public ownership of utilities and banking and the abolition of inheritance. He had his statement printed as a leaflet, which he later distributed by the hundreds.[45]

When a wire from Sackin in Hollywood informed him that Carl Laemmle, Jr. of Universal wanted to talk business with him about one of his books, he replied that he would come if Laemmle would send $500 for expenses. The money was sent and he returned alone by plane to Hollywood, where he had an inconclusive talk with Laemmle. Again he joined Helen in Portland. They boarded the enormous Chrysler with Nick and headed homeward, enjoying Yellowstone Park but encountering such bad roads in Montana that Dreiser blew up.

"To hell with the trip," he shouted; "we are shipping the car and taking the train back to New York in the morning." [46]

Helen soothed him and they drove on. In Minnesota he noted that a radical Minneapolis paper had been suppressed by "big business" on the ground that it was a public nuisance. At Rochester they tarried at the Mayo Clinic while Dreiser underwent an examination by a physician, who reported:

> There are two conditions present, the most important being an old fibroid pulmonary tuberculosis affecting the upper portion of the left lung which is so densely scarred that multiple small cavities are present. I feel sure that these are mere enlargements of the bronchi and produce what is

equivalent to a chronic bronchitis. Such a condition of course explains the persistent cough, the repeated respiratory infections and the production of rather large amounts of sputum which may have a foul odor and at times contain blood. The second finding was that of an enlarged prostate gland which, however, seems to be causing very little trouble at present and the kidney functioning itself is quite normal.[47]

In Chicago they picked up Rome Dreiser at his men-only hotel, bought him a health belt and new clothing, then put him in the back seat with the dog for the trip to New York, where he would take up his abode with Mame. Rome's powerful physique was eroded, his memory somewhat cloudy, and for a time he insisted on calling Dreiser "Paul."

Reaching New York early in July, Dreiser had seen a large part of the country in his 10,000-mile tour and had expended prodigal energy for a man nearing fifty-nine. The Mooney case, the widespread unemployment he saw—and possibly his own market losses—had outraged him. These things had become real to him because he had witnessed them personally. George Jean Nathan remarked, "One always finds Dreiser surprised and amazed at what has long been familiar to most persons," noting that he had discovered the Grand Canyon on this trip and was indignant that it was not known to all. "People should be told about it," he said.[48]

Many of his choleric utterances had been picked up by the news services and published in papers all over the country, giving him a reputation as a collector of complaints, a Terrible-Tempered Mr. Bang in the flesh. He was not finished. He went over the same ground with James Flexner of the *Herald Tribune*. Constitutional government had abdicated . . . the country was controlled by trusts . . . the little man was crushed . . . the situation was much like that in Russia before the revolution.

"All newspaper interviews are stupid," he told Flexner. "I will bet you $10 that you cannot get into your paper the things that I . . . say." [49]

He lost the bet. To Forrest Davis of the *Telegram* he commented on the beauty and riches of the country, and its failure to use it equitably. He urged that Wall Street move into Pennsylvania Avenue, since the moguls were in charge anyway. "Make Mr. Rockefeller Secretary of Oil and Gas. Send Mr. Atterbury to Washington to be Director of Railroads. Keep Mr. Mellon where he is. . . ." [50]

The *Herald Tribune* thought all this strange coming from a man sitting in a baronial apartment "with his blooded wolfhound lying at his feet," and concluded that "a man may be a great novelist and still be something of a fool." [51]

The *Evening Post* said, "The trouble with that fellow is that he has been reading too much Theodore Dreiser." [52]

4. Rising Indignation

The Dreiser cross-country explosions suggested a mind that could not conceive that it might ever be in error. They also reflected a hypothetical sympathy for humanity that had no logical connection with his own ruthless employment of capitalistic devices and his frequent browbeating of underdogs he theoretically loved. Living under capitalism, he was entitled to its fruits. Yet one feels that his hatred of such tycoons as Ford and Rockefeller contained an element of envy and that if he could have amassed millions he would have done so. The Dreiser ego, one of the largest extant, was easily able to accommodate a furious collection of contradictions.

His stay in the Southwest had inspired a new enthusiasm. The dry climate of New Mexico had so soothed his bronchitis that he planned to move there permanently, writing a dozen letters to town officials and realtors in the area north of El Paso to inquire about available ranch homes. To Horace Liveright, now in Hollywood as a producer for Paramount (formerly called Famous Players), he suggested a Dreiser film based on the activities of the Jesuits in opening up the country.

He decided to build a secular monastery on his future New Mexico property—a large, simple structure devoted to the ascetic encouragement of the arts. It would contain a bare cell for Dreiser and each other resident, with common kitchen and dining facilities. At his urging, Fabri, knowing it to be a dream, laid out a floor plan and exterior design which Dreiser studied intently, suggesting changes. He wrote the Catholic church in Santa Fe to ask if they had carved beams for sale. Carried away, he bought a brown Franciscan cloak with rope belt and hood which he wore at times at Iroki. "He looked like a monk in an Albrecht Dürer etching," Fabri recalled.[1]

When the John Reed Club urged him to join a group of writers and artists in supporting the communist candidates that fall, he was cautious. He asked that they send someone to brief him on "the entire policy of the Communist Party in America and its proposed program, if any."[2] In the end he gave his endorsement on the ground that the communists were the only party constructively working against unemployment, but he did not give blanket endorsement of communism. He had called on Roy Howard about the Mooney case, with the result that the Scripps-Howard newspapers had come out with a campaign for Mooney. He was as exercised about Paramount's failure to produce *An American Tragedy*, which he blamed (a) on the Hays code and (b) on the fine Italian hand of Horace Liveright.

At the time he sold the rights to Lasky, all films were silent. Now that the talkies had arrived, he joined the Dramatists' Guild and got an opinion from them that the contract included only the silent rights, thus letting him in for additional payment for the sound rights. He had an attorney threaten suit against Paramount for failing to produce the silent picture, on the ground that the studio thereby deprived him of returns for the sound version. He was soon reassured that Paramount planned to produce the *Tragedy* in sound. Having already maneuvered Patrick Kearney out of any royalties from the stock production of the play, he now coaxed Kearney to renounce any interest in the talkie rights, all of which would go to Dreiser.[3] Then a hitch developed over the additional price to be paid Dreiser, and over a commission Liveright (though now working for Paramount) felt due him as producer of the stage version. Dreiser, certainly mistakenly, was convinced that Liveright had got his Paramount job as a reward for steering the *Tragedy* to them. He wrote Liveright bitterly:

> Are you still going to demand five thousand of me or anyone for something which you do not own and are not entitled to? (Have you not had sufficient benefits at my hand already?) Do you intend, at whatever gate I apply, to seek to block the realization of this fine screen picture? If so, say so!
> I want to know finally—and from you personally—not from any lawyer or moving picture intermediary.[4]

Liveright replied in part:

> My lawyers advise me, in no uncertain terms, that I have a decided interest in the valuable talkie rights. It was only because I was associated with this concern [Paramount] that I made my price so ridiculously low.[5]

Dreiser at times was seized by paranoiac suspicion and rage. He suspected that M-G-M, in a picture called *Wonder of Women*, had stolen the plot from his "*Genius.*" He wrote Warner Brothers that their picture *The Second Choice* was remarkably like his story of the same name and demanding to know their sources. He seemed to have forgotten his borrowings from Sherwood Anderson and Dorothy Thompson. He wrote CBS, which had produced his "Blue Sphere":

> Kindly inform me by what authority you announced . . . that I wrote THE BLUE SPHERE for you or especially for radio.
> Since the contract which I signed with [you] was an agreement for one performance, I would like to ask what you mean by the announcement that it is to be given again.[6]

He hatched another quarrel with Liveright over the stock rights for the *American Tragedy* play. The contract stipulated that if the play was presented in stock fewer than 75 times in one year, all royalties reverted to Dreiser. He contended that it had come under the 75 mark, Liveright disagreed, and the argument went into arbitration. Dreiser's claim was ultimately rejected.

Miss Van Dresser had returned from Europe, where she had organized a publicity campaign with Frau Goldschmidt, got *The Hand of the Potter* produced in Hamburg and done other promotional work such as giving talks about Dreiser to club groups in Vienna, Prague and other cities.[7] Dreiser, who had yearned off and on for the Nobel Prize since Grant Richards first mentioned it in 1911, expected to get it this time. The newspapers in October were full of rumors that he would be the choice. It would not only be a great honor—the first American to win—but the honorarium of $46,350 would be pleasing and the sale of his books would be spurred.

In Stockholm, the Swedish Academy met, heard the nominations and appointed a three-man committee to take the vote. The winner—two votes to one for Dreiser—was Sinclair Lewis.

When the news reached America November 5, the choice was generally disparaged. Dreiser was bitterly disappointed, not only in missing the prize but because of his special dislike for Lewis. One friend said he was "almost suicidal" about it.[8] To Madeleine Boyd, who wrote to express her regret, he replied:

> I appreciate the feeling that lies behind your letter, but I believe you will understand me when I say that I cannot welcome sympathy, because I do not need it. In fact, I would be happy, and even delighted, if I could elimi- nate the thought of the necessity for any such feelings. . . . I cannot imag- ine the prize lessening or improving the mental standing of any serious writer. . . .[9]

His hurt was not assuaged by Lewis' generous speech to the Swedish Academy in which he praised O'Neill, Willa Cather, Cabell, Hemingway and others but gave a special laudation to Dreiser, saying in part:

> Now to me, as to many other American writers, Dreiser, more than any other man, is marching alone. Usually unappreciated, often hounded, he has cleared the trail from Victorian, Howellsian timidity and gentility in Amer- ican fiction to honesty, boldness and passion of life. Without his pioneering I doubt if any of us could, unless we liked to be sent to jail, express life, beauty and terror.[10]

After having maneuvered with all his might, Dreiser told Fabri that Lewis had won the prize because of his "clever maneuvering." [11] Komroff was one of those who received from Dreiser a letter containing mimeographed copies of the remarks of various critics protesting the choice of Lewis. The Nobel wound was deep and lasting in this man who claimed to be indifferent to such honors. A few weeks later he called on Sir Rabindrinath Tagore, visiting in New York, and was in a fury because he had to wait in an anteroom for a few minutes. But when Tagore entered, gazed at him and exclaimed, "Ah! A Brahmin!" all was well. "Instantly," Helen wrote, "Dreiser was transformed;

the best note in him was sounded and his irritation disappeared into nothingness." [12]

II. HOLLYWOOD SWILL AND BUNK

The $46,000 Dreiser had lost to Lewis came back to him, with a dividend, from unpredictable Paramount. When his friend Sergei Eisenstein visited Hollywood in 1930, Paramount, after putting *An American Tragedy* on ice for four years, proposed that he and Ivor Montagu prepare a script and produce the film. At first, according to Montagu, he and Eisenstein feared that the Hays code would make any truthful production impossible. Assured by Lasky and others that the Hays office had approved an honest treatment, they went ahead on a big 12-reeler slated to cost $1,000,000.

Eisenstein, an admirer of Dreiser's book, correctly conceived it as an indictment of American society and it was in this spirit that he and Montagu prepared the script. He visited Iroki to talk with Dreiser, who was delighted by his interpretation. When it was completed, Lasky and B. P. Schulberg first praised their script, then began to find fault with it. Schulberg asked Eisenstein whether Clyde Griffiths was guilty or not guilty in his treatment. Eisenstein replied, "Not guilty," whereupon Schulberg said, "But in that case your scenario is a monstrous challenge to American society. . . ." [13]

Eisenstein and Montagu got the impression that the film magnates had not read the book and that what they expected was a simple detective story about a boy, a girl and a murder. Montagu also felt that Paramount began to fear criticism if they produced a socially critical picture adapted by two radicals from a book by the radical Dreiser, who even then was spouting strong talk on the West Coast. In the end, Paramount rejected their script on the ground that the worsening depression made a million-dollar picture impossible.

In December, 1930, Paramount decided on a shorter sound version with a script by Samuel Hoffenstein and the direction by Josef von Sternberg. On January 2 Dreiser signed a contract which paid him $55,000 for the sound rights. In it he agreed to defend Paramount against any possible claim by Liveright, while Paramount said in Clause Ten, "the Purchaser agrees it will use its best endeavors to accept such advice, suggestions and criticisms that the Seller may make in so far as it may, in the judgment of the Purchaser, consistently do so." [14]

Although this clause gave lip service to Dreiser's demands, the ultimate authority to accept or reject his advice rested with Paramount.

The Liveright Publishing Company was functioning under Messner and Pell while Liveright, technically head of the firm, was in Hollywood. Dreiser, in lieu of his promised novel, took *Dawn*, the first volume of his autobiography, out of the bin and selected it for his next book. There was still the problem of the personal revelations about his sisters Mame, Emma and Sylvia. All three, however, were now widows dependent on him for financial help, and in any case his sense of privacy was never strong. After a hasty review of the script with Louise Campbell, he handed it in to his publisher early in January, having partly concealed his sisters by giving them fictitious first names.

To save money, he had Mame and Rome living in one of the Iroki cabins that winter. Politically he was moving, with some reservations (and depending on his mood), toward the left. He was able to write a friend "quite flatly" that "my solution for the difficulties of the world, and particularly those in America, is Communism." [15] He had allowed the communist-sponsored National Committee for the Defense of Political Prisoners to make him its chairman.

On February 1, Dreiser (with a new Dulcinea) left Helen and boarded a Ward liner for Havana. His mail was now formidable, and Miss Van Dresser had left to get married. However, Mrs. Campbell and Miss Sayre were on hand in New York, plus a new full-time secretary, tall, brunette Evelyn Light, a former assistant editor of *Plain Talk*.

Meanwhile the pen of Samuel Hoffenstein was borne on wings. Only five weeks after the contract was signed he had finished the shooting script. On February 9 he wired Dreiser from Hollywood that he was bringing it to New York at once to let him see it.

Dreiser was somewhere in Cuba, or possibly on his way to Miami. Helen and Mrs. Campbell did not know, for he had been purposely vague about his itinerary in his wish to keep business worries from interrupting his romantic holiday. Mrs. Campbell wired Hoffenstein that he was out of town. Hoffenstein telegraphed her February 10 that he was planning to fly to New York to show Dreiser the script. Time was short. When would he be back?

Louis E. Swarts, a Paramount executive in New York, got in touch with Helen in an effort to locate Dreiser. He found that she did not know where he was and that he might not return until March first. On February 13 Swarts sent Dreiser a letter at Fifty-seventh Street—obviously for the record —saying that he and Hoffenstein had tried vainly to trace him. He added a warning: If Dreiser was not heard from by February 20, Paramount would assume that he did not wish to avail himself of Clause Ten and would proceed with production without conferring with him.[16]

Dreiser of course received none of this. His exact whereabouts were unknown until he reached Fort Myers, Florida, February 16, where he wired Hoffenstein. Hoffenstein replied by telegraph, expressing regret that he had been lost to communication. He added that he had been ready to meet Dreiser anywhere in the country, but now it was too late, for production was about to begin. He felt sure that Dreiser would like the script, since it reflected the text faithfully.[17]

Dreiser felt that Paramount was in unseemly haste after long delay and was maneuvering to eliminate his advice. He wired Hoffenstein from Tampa:

YOUR TELEGRAM . . . IS THE USUAL HOLLYWOOD SWILL AND BUNK SORRY
TO SEE YOUR NAME ATTACHED. . . . PARAMOUNT PUBLIX DISTINCTLY AGREED
TO SHOW ME SCRIPT AND CONSIDER MY ADVISE ((SIC)) STOP IF THEY ARE HON-
EST AND SINCERELY WISH TO WORK WITH ME IN THIS YOU CAN CONSULT WITH ME
YET HERE OR ANYWHERE ELSE SINCE I AM GOING WEST SUGGEST YOU MEET ME
NEWORLEANS FEBRUARY TWENTYTHIRD. . . . WIRE ME GENERAL DELIVERY NEW-
ORLEANS OTHERWISE MAIL SCRIPT TO SAME PLACE NOW.[18]

Hoffenstein replied with a resentful protest at his attitude, saying that despite these unkind implications he was ready to go to New Orleans.[19]

"IF YOU CAN DISCUSS THIS AMICABLY YES OTHERWISE NOT," Dreiser replied. "WILL BE IN NEWORLEANS WEDNESDAY FEBRUARY TWENTYFIFTH." [20]

Meanwhile a copy of the script had been sent Dreiser. He read it before Hoffenstein flew to New Orleans and put up at the Hotel Jung, where Dreiser had agreed to meet him. Dreiser could not have read it in a friendly mood. His novel was a difficult one to adapt to a film of normal length, and the Hoffenstein-Von Sternberg job had failed. The script dealt mainly with Part Two of the book, eliminating most of the social message and concentrating heavily on the trial scenes.

Hoffenstein's flight was in vain. At his hotel he received a note from Dreiser:

On my arrival here I found the proposed scenario for *An American Tragedy* . . . and have just read it. To me, it is nothing less than an insult to the book—its scope, actions, emotions and psychology. Under the circumstances, and to avoid saying personally how deeply I feel this, I am leaving New Orleans now without seeing you. You will understand, I am sure.

If, at any time, the studio should permit the construction of a script representative of the book and will seriously agree to work along the lines I know to be most valuable for this purpose, I will be glad to cooperate, and at once, but not before.[21]

Hoffenstein, fuming, returned to Hollywood. When Dreiser reached New York he was further ruffled by a newspaper account of Josef von Sternberg's reaction to criticism of American films by George Bernard Shaw. "[Shaw] emptied himself twenty years ago," Von Sternberg was quoted, "and that applies to many of the so-called literary giants—in particular, Theodore Dreiser." [22]

Dreiser was therefore glad to read a *Times* review of Marlene Dietrich's picture *Dishonored*, which Von Sternberg had written and directed, calling the writing "clumsy" and "emphatically amateurish." He had Miss Light send a clipping of the review to Von Sternberg, whom she addressed as "Joseph Sternberg." In retaliation, the director, who insisted on the "von," had *his* secretary write Dreiser asking an explanation of the "mystic significance" of the clipping, misspelling Dreiser's name in two different ways and inquiring if she might call him "just plain Teddy." [23]

Childishness could hardly have gone farther on either side. It was in this spirit that Von Sternberg began the picturization of one of America's great novels.

On March 10 Dreiser wrote Lasky, now in New York, rejecting the script because "Sternberg and Hoffenstein have 'botched' my novel." They had instilled no sympathy into the characters, he said, depicting Clyde as a sex-starved drug-store cowboy. He blamed the botch on "Sternberg's lack of sympathy for my writing." He suggested that he and Hy Kraft go to Hollywood to work on a revision and that Von Sternberg be removed as director, warning that "unless radical and advantageous changes are made, [I] will most certainly protest against the use of my name." [24] Lasky replied by outlining Dreiser's failure to cooperate and saying that shooting had already begun. Dreiser countered by questioning Paramount's sincerity, saying that the present script would result in "a cheap, tawdry, tabloid confession story," and threatening legal action. [25]

Paramount backed down, agreeing to see him in Hollywood and to do what could, in their judgment, be done.

III. THE SLAP

Meanwhile Ray Long, back from a trip to Russia, planned a dinner at the Metropolitan Club for Boris Pilnyak, the visiting Russian novelist. Pondering his guest list, he said to his aide, William Lengel, "We'll have to have our Nobel Prize winner." Lengel agreed, saying, "We should also have the man who deserved it." Long feared that there might be bad blood between the two, but Lengel felt sure that there would be no trouble.

Some two dozen guests gathered on the night of March 19, including Heywood Broun, Arthur Brisbane, J. Donald Adams, Irvin S. Cobb, Burton Rascoe and Laurence Stallings. Dreiser, in typical confusion thinking the dinner was at the Plaza, searched that hotel vainly before telephoning Helen to discover it was at the Metropolitan Club. He arrived at the club late.

Lewis, Lengel noticed, had been "eating little sausages, drinking, drinking and drinking." Had a rumor reached him that Dreiser gossiped of an affair with Dorothy Thompson in Moscow? Dreiser stopped beside him to say, "Congratulations, Lewis." Lewis replied by puckering his face and emitting a Bronx cheer. Dreiser moved on. Dinner was served, after which Long arose to introduce the speakers. He first called on Lewis, who got to his feet deliberately.

"I am very happy to meet Mr. Pilnyak," he said. "But I do not care to speak in the presence of one man who has plagiarized 3,000 words from my wife's book on Russia. Nor do I care to talk before two sage critics who objected to the Nobel committee's selection of me as America's representative writer." [26]

He sat down. The critics probably were Broun and Brisbane, whose disapproval of the award had been outspoken. No one had any doubt as to the word-stealer. Dreiser reddened. Long hurriedly called on Irvin Cobb, who saved the situation with Paducah humor. Other speakers followed, including Pilnyak himself—a friend of Dinamov's—who gave Lewis short shrift while heaping praise on Dreiser. The crisis seemed forgotten, but Lengel, eying Dreiser, had misgivings.

As the party broke up, Dreiser walked over to Lewis and asked him to step into an anteroom. There he said, "You made a statement about my taking stuff from your wife's book."

Lengel entered the room in time to see Dreiser slap Lewis' face resoundingly.

The skinny Lewis made no effort at self-defense or retaliation. "Theodore," he said, "I repeat that you're a liar and a thief."

Smack! Dreiser slapped him again. Still Lewis raised no hand, seeming bemused rather than enraged. Lengel got between them and propelled Dreiser toward the elevator. "I'll meet you anywhere you say!" Dreiser shouted as the elevator arrived.[27]

Despite attempts to hush up the affair, the newspapers learned of it a day later and publicized it from Moscow to Sydney. There were the inevitable comments about "Battling" Dreiser and "Kid" Lewis. Dreiser was referred to as the "heavyweight champ of American letters." Fight Promoter Jimmy Johnston wired the rivals an offer to match them in a 15-rounder at Ebbets Field, while Westbrook Pegler suggested that angry writers should use "ghost-fighters." Although both had written unflatteringly of America, Dreiser received a batch of fan mail mostly favorable to him, some regretful that he had not floored Lewis for the count. Notwithstanding his explosions while touring the country, he seemed less in disfavor than Lewis, whose books had outsold his by hundreds of thousands. Dreiser's 1911 friend Alice Phillips, now in Los Angeles, read of the affray and wrote him with customary candor:

> Not that [Lewis'] face didn't thoroughly need slapping but why you? Especially when you've got such a beautifully vitriolish pointed tongue. And when too no one in the universe could ever believe you took words from any Tompkins or Thompson . . . you're too well satisfied with your own. . . .[28]

Three days later, Dreiser and Kraft boarded a Ford tri-motor plane, bound for a different kind of bout with Hollywood. The "slap heard 'round the world" was still making news. Lewis, on a lecture tour, praised Dreiser in Toledo, calling *Sister Carrie* "a book written from American soil." Dreiser, stopping over in Kansas City, was surrounded by reporters. "I admire some of his [Lewis'] writings," he said. ". . . 'Arrowsmith' is a good story. . . . Paul de Kruif, who gave Lewis the material, first asked me to write the book, but I didn't have time." [29] While it seems likely that they had at least discussed the idea during De Kruif's visit with him in 1920, he would have been generous had he forgotten that and avoided a note of disparagement. Reporters immediately queried De Kruif, who denied it obliquely, saying there had "never been any negotiations" between him and Dreiser.

Dreiser and Kraft flew on, Kraft miserably airsick and made all the more so by Dreiser's joyous eating of bananas as he admired the scenery. "He was like a big golem come to life," Kraft said.[30] For all Dreiser's shrewd publicity sense, Kraft felt him utterly sincere in his desire for an honest filming of his book. He had thrown a scare into Paramount. Schulberg and other bigwigs met them at Burbank airport but thereafter tried to keep them at a safe distance, certain that Dreiser was a mere publicity-seeker. They seemed unaware that a genuine artistic principle was involved.[31]

He and Kraft got to work on scenes dramatizing the social influence on Clyde's earlier life, and on others aimed at strengthening the picture's finale. Kraft stayed at the Ambassador, but Dreiser soon rented a bungalow in the Hollywood hills and attended to his primary need, securing a blonde young woman to live in. "I went up there every morning," Kraft recalled, "to find him in his bathrobe, eating a steak breakfast, homely, clumsy, and this beautiful girl with him." [32]

In New York, the National Committee for the Defense of Political Prisoners (NCDPP) planned an April 9 get-rolling meeting at his studio. Evelyn Light sent out invitations to 47 persons including Lincoln Steffens, Malcolm Cowley, Edmund Wilson, Louis Adamic, Alma Gluck, Langston Hughes and John Howard Lawson. Sinclair Lewis was not invited. When Dreiser's parleys with Paramount, and perhaps with the blonde, took longer than expected, it became apparent that he would miss his own party. The meeting was postponed until the 16th, Miss Light sending out 47 letters warning people *not* to come on the 9th, and 47 more a few days later asking them to come on the 16th. When Dreiser returned on the 11th, he belabored Hollywood in a newspaper interview, calling it "Hooeyland" and saying the studio had not produced his picture but "traduced" it, made "a Mexican comedy" out of *An American Tragedy*.

"When we get a Volstead," he cried, "who will put through Congress a bill prohibiting free thought, it will be a great boon to Hollywood. I don't recall contacting any producing brains that assayed more than one-half of one per cent."

He planned to view the finished picture, and if it did not satisfy him, one reporter noted, "Dreiser almost surged out of his armchair with rage," saying, "I'll get a lawyer and take them to court." [33]

Despite his excesses and follies, his reputation was still high. When Malcolm Cowley arrived at the studio for the meeting and was given a drink of Scotch by the butler, he and others felt they were answering "almost a royal summons." [34] They also felt that he was illogical, groping in confusion among principles veering from Marxism to fascism to sentimental reform. It was his demeanor of bumbling sincerity that won them. Some 40 persons were there, including young Joseph Pass, who had arranged the meeting.

Dreiser, terribly nervous, rapped on a table and folded his handkerchief as he read from a prepared statement, dwelling on the breadlines, the unemployed, the ghastly conditions in mining areas, the breakdown of government. "The time has come," he said, "for American intellectuals to render some service to the American worker." [35] He threw the meeting open for discussion. Lincoln Steffens spoke of newspaper suppression of facts, a few others contributed remarks, and the group disbanded.

Although Dreiser was friendly with Maria Samson's physician husband, he made a herculean effort to bring the exotic Miss Samson to bed and was puzzled by her determined resistance. Another woman told Waldo Frank of a "dreadful experience" she had had, chancing to meet Dreiser alone in a room and being forced literally to fight her way out.[36] That summer he had trysts at Iroki with a seventeen-year-old schoolgirl, paying her way out and back. To Esther McCoy he told how he had ridden alone in an elevator with a pretty girl he had never seen before, how it took every atom of his will power to keep from seizing her. Why, he demanded, should he be tormented this way? He was fascinated by the case of Starr Faithful, the lovely nymphomaniac found murdered at Long Beach, sympathizing with her, feeling her driven as he was. At Iroki, Hy Kraft was embarrassed when Dreiser appeared with a woman, had lunch with Helen, Kraft and the lady, then promptly disappeared with her into one of the remote cabins.

"It's not my fault," Dreiser told Kraft. "You walk into a room, see a woman and something happens. It's chemical. What are you going to do about it?" [37]

Helen described his actions as "a new pattern of behavior that I found difficult to accept." [38] Deciding on a partial separation, she moved to Iroki, where her mother and sister Myrtle arrived to keep her company along with Mame and Rome.

On May 8, *Dawn* was published after long storage, representing the Dreiser of 1917 rather than 1931. Although there were complaints about the careless writing, the reception was generally favorable. Critics were amazed at his frank revelations of his childhood poverty, the family tensions, his libido, his masturbation, his abstraction of funds to buy an overcoat, the sexual adventures of his sisters. His sisters were also amazed, especially Mame. Fabri, working at Iroki, recorded in his diary:

> Mame was howling when I arrived Monday morning. She hadn't read the book of course and never would, but according to the papers Teddy calls all the women in his family prostitutes and he is a liar and a madman. . . . How can they survive such horror? . . . Teddy just invented all these fantastic stories.[39]

When Dreiser arrived at Iroki, Mame leaned from the window to shriek vituperation, threatening violence to him.

"Well, relatives," he shrugged. "What can you do about it? Now I can't go into my own house." [40]

Emma and Sylvia also were outraged, while Rome had a different reason for complaint. At the time *Dawn* was written Dreiser had believed Rome dead. Now, on page 11, it told of Rome dying an alcoholic death in a Clark Street dive—an error Dreiser had neglected to correct.

IV. THE JURY

Dreiser's case against Paramount involved a comparatively new principle in the conception of moving pictures. Were they to be regarded as an art or as mere entertainment? No novelist had ever raised such a howl about the adaptation of his book. The film industry was yet a young one, so accustomed to playing fast and loose with story material that even many novelists and critics had come to accept the pictures as the half-baked crowd-pleasers they often were. Dreiser shocked Hollywood with the idea that the studios had an obligation to interpret serious work with integrity and intelligence.

Dreiser, never troubled with doubt that his own cause was the cause of true art, appointed an 18-man committee to sit with him in judgment on the picture. He loaded Miss Light with the job of writing 1,200-word letters explaining the whole issue to the 18: Ernest Boyd, Harry Elmer Barnes, Dr. Brill, Barrett Clark, John S. Cohen, Jr., Harry Hansen, Patrick Kearney, Fannie Hurst, James D. Mooney, George Jean Nathan, Hermann Oelrichs, Harrison Smith, Carl Van Doren, Floyd Dell, Ray Long, Chester Erskin, Burton Rascoe and Kenneth Hayes Miller.

Then he decided on a sub-jury of some 20 more who would view the film and give him their opinions, though with less juridical authority than the original 18. Miss Light perspired over her typewriter to address similar letters to Herbert Bayard Swope, William C. Lengel, Alexander Woollcott, Otto Kahn and others. Paramount had agreed to give them all an advance showing. A fair-sized audience crowded into the New York projection room on June 15 to see Phillips Holmes, Sylvia Sidney and Frances Dee portray Clyde, Roberta and Sondra.

Barrett Clark did not condemn what he saw, pointing out that "Any novel that is as long as yours requires a proportionately long medium." [41] Ray Long wrote, "Frankly, Theodore . . . I do feel [it] certainly is a picture of which you need not be ashamed." [42] But Dr. Brill thought the dead-pan Phillips Holmes interpreted Clyde as a "shut-in, unemotional, catatonic type" who seemed cold-blooded rather than the weak, socially driven boy of the book.[43] Most of the rest agreed that the picture was an inferior representation of the novel. Although Paramount was adding almost 1,000 feet of film embodying some of Dreiser's suggestions, he rejected it. Through his attorney, Arthur Garfield Hays, he obtained an injunction directing Paramount to show cause why it should not be restrained from distributing the picture.

The case was heard in White Plains July 22. Paramount's attorney, Humphrey J. Lynch, disparaged the novel and its author with such effect that Dreiser twice exploded and was reprimanded by Justice Graham Witchief. Lynch described the *Tragedy* as a "cold-blooded plagiarism" of the Gillette case and a poor one at that. Dreiser, he said, was a "temperamental artist" who wanted the film to indict Christianity and to bristle with erotic indecencies—a publicity-seeker who had boasted that his slapping of Lewis won him front-page notice.

"It's a lie!" Dreiser shouted, leaping to his feet.

"Tell your client, Mr. Hays," the judge warned, "that if he cannot control himself he'll have to leave the room." [44]

In the end, Witchief denied Dreiser's claim. He pointed out the difficulty in transmitting psychological subtleties to the films, then uttered a thought that might have come from John Sumner:

> In the preparation of the picture the producer must give consideration to the fact that the great majority of people composing the audience . . . will be more interested that justice prevail than that the inevitability of Clyde's end clearly appear. [45]

Dreiser won a partial moral victory nevertheless. He had forced Paramount to make some concessions, made novelists more aware of the need for honest filming and shaken Hollywood's complacency a trifle. Yet his whole involvement in the adaptations of the *Tragedy*, though it won him $135,000 from Paramount and an unknown but tidy sum from the stage version, had been bitter. It had begun with coffee in Liveright's face, caused a lawsuit against Liveright, and ended with a lawsuit against Paramount.

At Iroki Dreiser had his men put up a large tent, painted with colorful caricatures. From Washington State he obtained a totem pole which was erected nearby. Under Fabri's supervision the main house had been finished, its high roof sheathed with heavy bark-covered oak shingles Dreiser insisted on, having seen something like it in Sweden. He had Fabri build a garage next to the house, then had him start his workmen on a small structure intended for servants, next to the garage. He changed his mind, deciding to make it a guest house with two small rooms for servants.

"Dreiser doesn't know what he wants," Fabri told his diary. "Everybody out there is making fun of him." Indeed, people even drove out from Mt. Kisco to see what would happen next, and the local *Times* mentioned that the house "attracted much attention." [46]

Fabri pleaded that he have one large room in the guest house taking advantage of the view of the lake. He refused, saying he must economize. The foundation for the small house he ordered was finished and the walls were going up when he came out to see it with his own eyes and agree it was too small. Fabri's men tore out one wall and enlarged the foundation. They encountered a huge projecting rock that had to be blasted away carefully, at great expense, to prevent damage to the half-finished superstructure. Later, Dreiser decided on a changed layout of the rooms, requiring the dismantling of inner walls and the erection of new ones.

While he trusted Fabri implicitly, admiring his talents at design and construction, he felt that the workmen were loafing. At times he would picture communism as an ideal existence, again as a threat. "If those fellows lived under communism," he grumbled, "they'd have to work, and work hard." [47] Hy Kraft felt that Dreiser's trouble was that he had no real loves to balance his hatreds, that he had sympathy for the mass but not for individuals.

Dreiser's bark-covered shingles proved to be a constant fire hazard. His huge studio room, below ground level, sometimes seeped water and was so damp that he seldom used it. Helen found it so difficult to get into a narrow third-floor bedroom intended for her that she gave up and converted the dining room into a bedroom. The heating, an afterthought, was uncertain. To dispose of kitchen garbage it was necessary to carry it through the living room and out the front entrance. Thelma Cudlipp Grosvenor, an occasional visitor, thought the place fantastic. Homer Croy, after a call at Iroki, said, "It looked to me like a warm-up for the World's Fair." [48]

5. *The Reformer*

The time of Dreiser's greatest fame as a public figure marked his decline as an artist and as a capitalist. Grievance was essential to him. He had to *fight* something. For a quarter-century he had assailed censorship and prudery. For him that battle was virtually over—in fact, he complained that some works that got by the censors were unnecessarily raw. Now and for the rest of his life the enemy was entrenched wealth, the Cowperwoods, "the corporations." Doubtless his own trimming in the market and his waning fortunes were a factor in his anger, but another factor was a national distress so shocking that thousands of intellectuals were moving to the left or embracing communism.

Although he was still prosperous, the money was not coming in as of yore. The magazines were not paying so well. Not in six years had he published a book that made real money as he reckoned it now. His book of poems, *Moods*, sold a humiliating 922 copies. *A Gallery of Women*, for which he had had high hopes, had a mediocre first-year sale of 13,653, and *Dawn* totaled only 5,992. He turned hopefully to the film studios he despised, urging Sackin in Hollywood to exert every effort to sell *Jennie Gerhardt*. His writing slackened as his energies turned to reform. The old anti-reformer who regarded life as an inevitable chaos of injustice had turned full circle and come out for justice. The Spencerian-Darwinian who believed in the survival of the fittest now felt that the lobster should succor the squid. The mechanist who saw man as a helpless pawn devoid of free will nevertheless shouted that helpless man should exert his will and become helpful.

His crusading zeal impaired his art. When Dorothy Van Doren of *The Nation* asked him to look at New York's unemployed and write a graphic story, she hoped for something human and moving after the manner of the jobless Hurstwood. When Dreiser turned in a polemic twice too long, she wrote regretfully:

> Instead of a picture of how the men in New York City who are out of work think and look and feel, you have told us how many there are. You have included, also, various economic theories—why we have unemployment and what we might do to prevent it. . . .[1]

The communists were vamping him. They had Mike Gold, Joseph Freeman, Scott Nearing and a host of others on their side, but they wanted the big name of Dreiser. Although he loved their anti-capitalism, he was not in full agreement with them, feeling that America needed a communism different from the Soviet brand. He was against revolution, against the stark appeal to the workers, favoring rather a reform movement that would also win the conservative middle classes. He tended to be suspicious of any movement not originated by Dreiser. Yet, when plagued by left-wing appeals for statements and protests, he wrote accommodatingly to the editor of *Solidarity:*

> It seems to me that when you, or Mr. Engdahl, or Mr. Pass, or the John Reed Club, or The Masses, approach me for an article, they, being closer to the movement than I am, would have some particular suggestions, or perhaps a definite collection of data on a given topic which could be either selected from or re-cast by me so that I would not be outside the facts most interesting to the Party. . . .[2]

In the *Daily Worker* he assailed the arrest of communist organizers, writing, "It is the Communists, and the Communists alone, who realize that American labor—principally non-unionized—is made the goat of corporation aspirations and the billionaires' dreams of more billions."[3] In the *New Freeman* he castigated America's "intellectually bankrupt" failure to deal with unemployment in an article that was reprinted in the English-language *Moscow News.* In a letter he released for publication, he attacked the power trust which, he said, could influence news reporting by its ownership, for example, of 250,000 shares of the *Chicago Daily News.* Once again his carelessness was evident, the *Daily News* writing him angrily that this charge was untrue and Dreiser admitting a "typist's error."[4] He wrote President Hoover and Labor Secretary Doak protesting the deportation of aliens considered undesirable, and three days later his statement demanding justice for the Scottsboro boys was read at a Town Hall mass meeting sponsored by the N.C.D.P.P.

He seized on the idea of social justice with characteristic pugnacity, printing many of his statements in handbill form and mailing them out wholesale. He set Miss Light up in an office on Columbus Circle where she kept in close touch with communist HQ at 50 East Thirteenth Street and devoted fully half her time to social issues. She was aided by Miss Sayre, who was also doing research for a Dreiser book assailing the American political system. Esther McCoy occasionally helped him, and at times he had four secretaries busy at reform. The communists enthusiastically made use of these facilities, which complemented their own. Dreiser sought Earl Browder's advice in preparing the book, Browder writing him, "It is entirely understood by us that you are taking only those opinions which express your own profound convictions, and that our contribution is merely in the nature of assistance to help get the sharpest formulation of them."[5]

For *Liberty* he wrote an article he grandiosely titled, "I Can Run Any Railroad in America With a Personnel Drawn Over Night From Among College Boys." In it he described himself as a former railroad worker (he had put in two days as a boy for the C. B. & Q. and a few months as laborer for the New York Central), described the railroads as beholden to a few bloated corporations instead of to the people, and blasted them in sweepingly irresponsible statements. He advocated government ownership as in Russia, forgetting his anguished complaints about the stinking, chaotic Soviet trains.[6]

Daniel Willard, who had risen from trackworker to president of the Baltimore & Ohio, replied in an article barely concealing his contempt for such noisy ignorance. "If I tried to correct all the misstatements in Mr. Dreiser's article I would have to write a book," he observed, pointing out among other things that a dozen Soviet commissions had visited this country to learn railroading, one of their leaders writing, "The achievements of the United States in railway transportation . . . are far above those we have seen in other countries." [7]

At the request of Emma Goldman, Dreiser wrote Pierre Laval, France's Interior Minister, asking that Alexander Berkman be given the right of peaceful asylum there. In his letter were errors as well as a vagueness suggesting that Berkman had wounded Frick seriously, which he had not. When Emma received a copy, she wrote:

> You will forgive my saying that your letter to Laval while not doing good may even do some harm. . . . I am certain you meant for the best and since your letter . . . can not be recalled there is nothing more to be said about it.[8]

On June 24, at the urging of William Z. Foster and Joseph Pass, Dreiser went to Pittsburgh to investigate conditions in the nearby mining area where violence had erupted. The communists recently had organized their own National Miners' Union in opposition to the American Federation of Labor-affiliated United Mine Workers and had launched a strike which the U.M.W. did not support. The operators had secured injunctions, deputies had slain several striking miners and Governor Pinchot had sent the state police to restore order. In Pittsburgh Dreiser questioned some twenty miners, mostly N.M.U. men, hearing evidence of starvation wages. The bleak houses and ragged children in mining towns were evidence enough of poverty, and he had words with a constable whom he believed to be on the side of the operators and who finally growled, "Watch out or I'll take you in too." [9]

Dreiser had long detested the A.F.L., which he believed selfishly exclusive in its membership and dictated by the corporations. On June 26 he released a statement praising the N.M.U., urging the "disestablishment" of the A.F.L. and saying, "Further, I know for a positive fact there was proposed, and now is being put into effect, a close union between the chief corporations . . . and the A.F.L. to put a quietus, in so far as possible, on strike and labor troubles, and bring about the general poverty of the rest of the people." [10]

William L. Green, the Federation president, replied, picking up Dreiser in one obvious error, defending its mine union's record of collective bargaining, calling the communist N.M.U. destructive and revolutionary, challenging Dreiser's accusation of an A.F.L. entente with capital and saying, "It is difficult to understand how a man with such a reputation as you have gained would engage in making such reckless statements." [11]

Dreiser consulted with Foster and Browder on his reply to Green, which covered 28 typewritten pages and totaled some 6,000 words. He was unable to give proof of the alleged A.F.L.-capitalist hookup. He refused, however, to follow the Browder-Foster line on injunctions, Browder later chiding him, "I notice you retain the argument that the A. F. of L. should have attempted to use the injunction weapon against the employers, although I suppose Comrade Foster expressed to you our opinion that this is a mistake. Such an argument presupposes that the government which issues the injunction stands above classes. This, of course, is not true. It is impossible for the workers to make use of the government which is the class instrument of the capitalists for its own benefit." [12]

Green replied again to Dreiser, whereupon Dreiser answered *his* answer, then published his controversy with Green in pamphlet form. "Conditions here grow worse and worse," he wrote Sarah Millin. "The misery & poverty of these poor people [in Pennsylvania] is simply indescribable." [13]

On August 27 Dreiser was sixty years old. He told Henry Varnum Poor that now he must face the possibility that he might die any time. He received greetings from many of the friends and associates who had enjoyed the studio Thursdays. The Thursdays were over now—too expensive. So was the studio, which he would soon vacate. From the International Union of Revolutionary Writers in Moscow came a birthday cable:

> LIKE ALL HONEST AND CONSISTENT OPPONENTS OF IMPERIALIST WAR, THE OPPRESSION OF THE PEOPLES AND THE EXPLOITATION OF THE WORKING CLASSES, YOU HAVE THROWN IN YOUR LOT WITH THE REVOLUTIONARY PROLETARIAT. WE KNOW THE VALUE OF YOUR COOPERATION. WE KNOW THAT THROUGH ALL THE CHANGES AND EVENTUALITIES IN THE TREND OF WORLD EVENTS YOU WILL FIGHT ON OUR SIDE. WE ARE VERY GLAD TO BE ABLE TO CALL YOU COMRADE. . . .

The *New Masses*, heeding this word from Moscow, reprinted the cable along with a flattering article about him and its own birthday message:

> On your sixtieth birthday we bring you the homage of many thousands of workers, farmers and intellectuals in America, and of the world. One of its few great living writers has repudiated the pessimism, sophistication, shallow liberalism and other vices of the intellectual world here and has come forward boldly and grandly as the champion of the working class revolution. . . .

Dreiser had not quite done this. The *New Masses* went on to admit that he was still gripped by a few bourgeois deviations:

Let us not split hairs. It is, at this moment, not important that Dreiser is not a Marxist, that he does not believe many things which Communists believe, and believes in many things which they do not. It is more important that at the height of his career he has the vision and the courage—like Bernard Shaw and Romain Rolland in Europe—to take sides openly with the world revolutionary movement of the working class.[14]

Dreiser, who had longed all his life for praise, soaked up the encomiums which the communists regularly fed him. Preparing to move out of the Rodin studio, he told a reporter wistfully, "It was a beautiful place. I'm glad I was able to have it. But a writer doesn't strive for material things."[15]

He gave up temporarily on Sackin in Hollywood, who had lately been unsuccessful in getting him the material things, and empowered another cinema agent, Leo Morrison, to represent him exclusively for 30 days. He wired Morrison:

ONE HUNDRED THOUSAND DOLLARS FOR TALKING PICTURE RIGHTS SISTER CARRIE.[16]

II. KENTUCKY TOOTHPICKS

On September 24 Dreiser moved to a two-room suite—bedroom and study—on the fourteenth floor of the Hotel Ansonia, Broadway and Seventy-third Street. Here, at a mere $110 a month, he had a view of the same Hudson that flowed by twenty years earlier when he worked on *Jennie Gerhardt* in the Rosenthal apartment. Only occasionally did he see Helen, who, when she came to New York, took another room at the Ansonia. Having said that three years was the utmost duration of love, and that any couple remaining together longer did so for "other reasons," he evidently found one other reason in her steadfast devotion. "Don't worry," he told Louise Campbell. "Helen will be there at the end to close my eyes."[17] Being involved in one of his more stormy infatuations, he wrote Helen (at 60), "I am trying to find myself. If I can solve my own problem I can solve yours."[18]

He still maintained Miss Light and her occasional assistants in the Columbus Circle office. In October, the communist-sponsored International Labor Defense gave him a 32-page indictment of conditions in Harlan and Bell Counties, Kentucky, asking him as chairman of N.C.D.P.P. to form a committee, visit the area and center national attention on the injustices prevalent there.

This feuding coal district of southeastern Kentucky normally was gunshot country. The shooting had risen sharply since June, when the communists moved in to continue their union-splitting program, assailing the U.M.W. and enrolling miners in the new N.M.U. The operators, who had resisted unionization of any kind, replied with ruthless suppression, firing miners who joined the union. Rifles were oiled. In one pitched battle between deputies and miners, three officers and one miner were killed. National guardsmen were sent to the scene. The communists set up soup kitchens which in some cases were dynamited. The whole coal industry was sick, but in the Harlan area it was in a desperate condition, with many miners on strike or unemployed, others working part time at eight to twelve dollars a week, and with life imperiled by bullets as well as actual starvation.

Dreiser objected that a lay committee would meet with indifference. By telegraph he urged eighteen prominent liberals to join him in Kentucky, among them Senators Norris, La Follette, Shipstead and Couzens; Felix Frankfurter, Roy Howard, and William Allen White. Not surprisingly, all declined, probably feeling it impolitic to link themselves with the violent Dreiser and his communist sponsorship, and doubting that he was the right man to bring sweet reason into the shambles. Dreiser then called a meeting of the N.C.D.P.P. and asked for volunteers. John Dos Passos, Lester Cohen, Samuel Ornitz, Bruce Crawford, Melvin P. Levy, and Charles Rumford Walker and his wife Adelaide agreed to go with him.[19]

It took courage to enter that chauvinistic, strife-torn area. Helen begged Dreiser not to go. He brushed aside her pleas, but he did wire Governor Flem D. Sampson of Kentucky, who agreed to give the committee military protection. He left New York by train November 4, while others of the group left separately by train or car, to meet in Lexington November 5. John Dos Passos recalls meeting Dreiser in a train, possibly between Lexington and Pineville, seat of Bell County. Dreiser had a "very attractive" woman with him, evidently one he had brought from New York.[20]

At Pineville Dreiser was greeted without warmth by the mayor, who assured him pointedly that the trouble had been caused by "outside agitators" and was now over. He and his companions were given a welcome similar to that accorded General Sherman and his men in Georgia. A group of Pineville citizens said conditions were not perfect in New York and talked of sending a deputation to intercede with Mayor Walker. Dreiser told newsmen that the committee's purpose was "to let the American people know just what conditions are." He added, not quite truthfully:

"Our committee has no affiliations with any other group. Personally I am affiliated with nothing but my own ideas."[21]

He and his committee registered at the weatherbeaten Continental Hotel, where they immediately felt themselves under surveillance. They were among enemies watching them for a misstep, eager to seize any opportunity to discredit them. The committee members were upset that Dreiser had chosen to bring a woman. "We all thought it was a foolish thing," Lester Cohen recalled. "We almost knew there would be trouble about it."[22] John Dos Passos later wrote, "Why Dreiser didn't have better sense . . . I never could imagine."[23] But Dreiser was the head man, older than the rest, weighted with prestige and prickliness. No one remonstrated with him.

The committee had arrived with no set plan of operation. At the hotel, Ornitz and Cohen talked it over and felt that it would be effective to hold public hearings, with Dreiser as moderator, questioning miners, townspeople and officials, with newsmen present to report the proceedings.

Cohen, who admired Dreiser tremendously, went upstairs to present this idea to him. Dreiser, perhaps feeling that his authority was being undercut, flew into a towering rage. If they did anything like that, he shouted, he would return to New York at once. Cohen, whose whole purpose was to place Dreiser in the central role, was at a loss to understand his anger. It took some two hours, plus a conference with Dos Passos, before Dreiser cooled off and agreed that the idea was sound.[24]

The hearings began in the morning in a room off the hotel lobby, and continued in the afternoon at the Lewallen Hotel in nearby Harlan. The newcomers, accompanied by several national guardsmen, were not molested. A number of miners and their wives, some refusing to give their names out of fear that they would be persecuted for cooperating with the outlanders, came in to be questioned. It appeared that most were members of the communist N.M.U. gathered by union representatives aiding Dreiser's committee, so that their testimony may not have been precisely unbiased. Yet these people in their soft hill tongue described conditions that cried for correction. Dreiser evidently had been briefed about his witnesses in advance, as when he questioned Lloyd Moore, a Harlan miner who was helping at a soup kitchen where two miners were killed by sheriff's men:

Q. Have you ever been warned?
A. Not personally but a rope was hung on my door about three weeks ago.
Q. Was it just a straight rope?
A. It had a noose tied in it.

And when he questioned another miner, J. W. Freeman:

Q. Is there any particular reason why you are out of work?
A. I guess the reason now is that they have me victimized.
Q. How does that work?
A. It don't work. You don't work at all. They just let you rest.
Q. You mean you are on a black list?
A. I suppose I must be black listed. . . .

Others told of a reign of terror conducted by sheriff's thugs, of union members beaten and warned to leave the county, of members jailed for possessing copies of the *Daily Worker*. There were tales of miners' families subsisting on pinto beans and "bulldog gravy," of babies dying of malnutrition. Aunt Molly Jackson, a militantly radical midwife, testified, "There is a lot of little children in destitution."

Q. How many children die a month or a year under these conditions?
A. Now in the summer, it would be three to seven each week up and down this creek. . . .
Q. Is your husband a member of the N.M.U.?

A. My husband is a member of the National Miners' Union, and I am too, and I have never stopped, brother, since I know of this work of the N.M.U. I think it is one of the greatest things that has ever come into this world.[25]

Dreiser warned his committee members to act circumspectly and to do no drinking. He took his woman friend to lunch and dinner, introducing her to his colleagues as Marie Pergain—possibly a fictitious name. "He seemed to want to dramatize himself as one who was beyond what other people would think sensible," Lester Cohen said. "It was obvious that the whole circle of officials wished to make trouble for us." [26] Dos Passos, while he admired Dreiser's senatorial manner of conducting the hearings, felt that he took a lordly satisfaction in flaunting his unconventionality. Spies were busy. Samuel Ornitz, in his hotel room, was kept awake much of the night by a drunken sentinel posted in the next room who occasionally shouted through the keyhole of a connecting door, "I can see *you*, but you can't see *me*." [27]

The local press, strong for the coal operators, depicted Dreiser as a radical blessed by Moscow on his recent birthday. Yet a few local officials consented to be questioned, the sheriff and district attorney insisting that Dreiser unfairly presented only one side of the picture. He caught a tartar when he questioned Herndon Evans, editor of the *Pineville Sun*, who said he made about $60 a week.

"That is $240 per month," Dreiser observed, "against $40 per [for the miners]. . . . And do you expect them to take things just as they are and not try to better themselves any?"

Evans asked Dreiser if he minded answering a few questions.

Evans: You are a very famous novelist, and have written several books. Would you kindly tell me what your royalties amount to?
Dreiser: I do not mind. $200,000, approximately. Probably more.
Evans: What do you get a year, if you do not mind telling?
Dreiser: Last year, I think I made $35,000.
Evans: Do you contribute anything to charity?
Dreiser: No, I do not.
Evans: That is all.

Dreiser, trapped, hurriedly sought to explain that he did not believe in charity, that the government should handle public welfare. He told of his support of members of his family, of his low-income years. "I am a writer, and I am mostly interested in the theory of equity. I employ four secretaries and I do not pay them any small matter for salary. They work continuously on facts and so do I. I am not dancing around at the Waldorf, but work most of the time. I am conducting this investigation at my own expense, as I do most of my investigations, and when it comes to the spending of money I think I will average among the rest of them."

"What I was trying to say," Evans replied, "was that me, with my $60 per week, give more to charity, and believe more in the standard of equity than you do with your $35,000 per year." [28]

Dreiser's cause was hurt when his wealth and his non-charity was published, although this had nothing to do with human rights in Harlan. He and his committee were seeing one of the sorriest spots in the country, a place where capital indeed had seized control of the law and abrogated all freedom, and where the condition of the people was ghastly. One could scarcely view these things and feel that the American dream of justice and opportunity was being realized.

"I find the same line-up of petty officials and business interests on the side of the coal operators as I have discovered in almost every other controversy," Dreiser said later. "The small town bankers, grocers, editors and lawyers, the police, sheriffs, governor—all are subservient to the money barons and corporation masters." [29]

From New York Helen wired him:

BEST OF LUCK TO YOU PROUD OF YOUR COURAGE AND SPIRIT LOVE. [30]

When Dreiser returned to his hotel at Pineville on November 7, local observers were present. They saw a woman enter his room at 11 P.M. They leaned a few toothpicks against the door. When the toothpicks stood undisturbed a few hours later, they drew an obvious inference. On November 9, after he had left for New York, Dreiser and Marie Pergain were indicted by the Bell County grand jury on charges of adultery.

III. IN THE HEADLINES

The Dreiser-Pergain indictment hit the nation's front pages, getting far more space than the appalling conditions he sought to publicize. The Senators must have been glad that they stayed home. Reporters crowded into his Ansonia suite. He gave them a press release about conditions in Harlan prefaced by a statement about the condition of his virility—doubtless the first public utterance the newsmen had ever heard on such an intimate subject. He said ambiguously that "at this writing" he was "completely and finally impotent," adding:

> In fact, today, you may lock me in the most luxurious boudoir with the most attractive woman in the world, and be convinced that we are discussing nothing more than books or art or some aesthetic problem of one kind or another. [31]

Claude Bowers, calling on him at the Ansonia, found him seething. "The telephone was ringing constantly," Bowers wrote, "and he answered with barks . . . he paced the room like a caged lion, bitterly describing the treatment of the miners, and indulging in profanity that amazed me, since ordinarily he never swore. On the table was a pitcher of wine, and time and again he stopped to fill a glass and drain it with a swallow."

"I told them I was impotent," he said, as Bowers recalled it. "They can't prove I'm not." [32]

Some felt—though Bowers did not—that his statement about his impotence was a Dreiserian joke. While it was true that for years he had needed a succession of new women to excite his flagging senses, and he often feared impotence, he would never be truly impotent as long as he lived. Even women he had known for some time complained that, given any sort of semi-privacy, he was an amatory wrestler.

"I'M WITH YOU TO THE LAST TOOTHPICK," Lengel wired him.[33]

"It is both funny and sublime—an event in the cultural history of man," Max Eastman wrote.[34]

"Like most peasants," H. L. Mencken wrote a friend, "[Dreiser] is bearing money very badly." And later: "True enough, he can't write, but nevertheless he is a great writer, just as Whitman was. But now, instead of doing another 'Jennie Gerhardt' . . . he wastes his time clowning. . . . I have no animosity to him, but he has become too tragic to be borne. Seeing him would be like visiting an old friend who had gone insane. . . ."[35]

Bruce Crawford wrote Dreiser: "It is a terrible commentary on newspapers and public that a sex scandal can obscure such inhumane and tragic conditions as exist in Harlan."[36]

From the agent George Bye, who had received little Dreiser copy of late, came another slant: "Since the toothpicks have made you a national figure, I bet you the magazines crave your presence, more than ever."[37]

And another from John Plummer of Florida, a reader worried about Dreiser's impotence: "Well that is easy to cure. I cured myself of it when I was past sixty, by the proper food water and exercise."[38]

And out of the past, the peppery words of Alice Phillips:

> How did you ever come to do anything so wild as to get tangled up in an affair when you were on a Crusade? . . . It's bad policy & worse—it's execrable taste. . . . I've always been sure you needed a guardian—I was never more sure than I am this minute.[39]

Dreiser was evidently annoyed enough not to reply, and a 20-year correspondence ended.

A week later Dreiser and his committee were indicted in Kentucky on charges of criminal syndicalism, an offense carrying a possible penalty of 21 years in prison or $10,000 fine, or both. Adultery being a misdemeanor, there was small chance of extradition on that charge but there was talk of extradition on the other—a move which, if successful, would expose him to prosecution on both. He was worried enough to send a lawyer, William D. Cameron, to Kentucky to make inquiries costing $492.77. Cameron, advised that the Kentucky authorities would forget the matter if Dreiser would stop his publicity, wired:

> . . . I AM OF OPINION THAT NOTHING MORE WILL BE DONE IF THERE IS NO MORE AGITATION.[40]

Dreiser, busy collecting relief funds for the miners, courageously refused to buy immunity at the expense of his crusade. ". . . FINDINGS OF COMMITTEE WILL CONTINUE TO BE PUBLISHED AND SENATORIAL AND OTHER ACTION SOUGHT THEREON," he replied to Cameron.[41]

While some observers deplored his failure to walk the moral line while probing another kind of illegality, others admired his courage and understood that his own morality was quite beside the point of the massive injustices in Harlan. Indeed, the toothpick episode secured the miners publicity they otherwise would have missed. Reporters pressed Dreiser for interviews and got them. Clubs begged him to speak and were refused only on the score of his shyness. He did appear in a newsreel and speak over the radio about the miners' plight. The eminent lawyer John W. Davis agreed to defend the committee against the Kentucky charges, and Governor Roosevelt was sympathetic enough to promise Dreiser an open hearing if extradition should be requested. To the communists he was a hero. Best of all, Senator Norris called for a Senate investigation of the Harlan situation that promised action.

On Dreiser himself the Pittsburgh and Kentucky expeditions reacted with an emotional violence that for years virtually destroyed him as an artist and transformed him into a pamphleteer and reformer. He had grown up with injustice, and now again had seen it—as he had seen the Grand Canyon—with his own eyes. His direction of the hearings in Kentucky had given him a sense of power and leadership that would soon break down that frustrating barrier, his lifelong fear of public speaking. Julian Messner at Liveright wrote him anxiously that he was expecting *The Stoic* for spring publication. But how could he write sympathetically now of Cowperwood, whom he had once so admired, when Cowperwood was a glorified image of the coal barons who ground down the proletariat?

His new fame added to his already heavy mail a flood of letters from utter strangers who regarded him as a sort of national problem-solver. While a few came from mental patients, most were from reasonably sane persons seeking counsel on personal, financial or employment difficulties, or sending solutions to the depression, or asking aid in marketing manuscripts. Sympathizing with them as victims of capitalism, he became a tribune of the people and answered all he could. On heavy days he sent out around 75 letters, easily averaging 250 a week.

He answered such queries as one seeking aid in marketing a patented circuit-closer; one suggesting a method which would enable Russia to improve its manufacture of iron castings; and another concerning an alien arrested while trying to enter the United States from Canada. When a correspondent asked his support in an anti-vivisection campaign, he wrote two scientists for opinions before giving his answer. His Negro butler had written a play, which Dreiser pressed on Cheryl Crawford for consideration. He wrote Governor James Rolph of California protesting Mooney's continued imprisonment. He replied to requests for information about Russia. In the midst of these were such Dreiser letters as one declining an invitation to a dinner for the Maharajah of Burdwan and others quarreling with a moving man over a bill for $40 and with a garage over a $2.04 charge for 12 gallons of gasoline.

And—one to Dr. Brill containing an excerpt from Sisley Huddleston's criticism of the selection of Lewis instead of Dreiser for the Nobel Prize.

Jug, visiting in Missouri, wrote him from a St. Louis hospital where she recuperated from pneumonia, asking help with the bill: "When the Assoc. Press got hold of the news that I was here it looked better for your sake that I was not in a ward. . . . I know you have lots of money. . . ." [42]

From H. G. Wells in London, to whom he had sent copies of Fort's books, he got a spirited reply:

> I'm having Fort's *Book of the Damned* sent back to you. Fort seems to be one of the most damnable bores who ever cut scraps from out-of-the-way newspapers & thought they were facts. And he writes like a drunkard. *Lo!* has been sent to me & it has gone into my wastepaper basket. . . . [43]

Dreiser replied that Fort's theories might yet be substantiated. When Christmas came, he went to Fort's grubby Bronx apartment and gave him $100.

6. Tightening the Belt

I. TRAGIC AMERICA

Just as he felt qualified to question science, serve as ballet impresario, design a country house and lecture on marriage and morality, so Dreiser now moved in on economics, sociology and politics. He worked at it with a sort of fury, sacrificing time and energy in a period when his income slipped badly. Actually he was the most non-political of men, thinking in vague philosophical terms and unaware of political realities. Always the victim of grandiose dreams, his dream now was of national leadership in reform. His efforts in one respect were less misguided than those of the party-serving fellow travelers, for he usually retained an independence of thought, however blurred, that kept him from skidding outright into the communist fold. But he was unrivaled in his violence, his misinformation and his blind hatred for capitalists.

Capitalists, whom he had so admired as ruthless but essential doers, were now consigned to his private hell along with the Catholic Church and the English. He wanted "equity," John Dos Passos noted. He was always talking about equity but seemed vague as to its definition. Dos Passos thought a fundamental part of his meaning was to take from the rich and give to the poor. After years of firm belief in individualism, in the inevitability of the law of the jungle as proved in nature, he now insisted that nature proved the opposite:

> Society is not and cannot be a jungle. It should be and is . . . an escape from this drastic individualism which, for some, means all, and for the many, little or nothing. And consciously or unconsciously, it is by Nature and evolution intended as such. For certainly the thousands-of-years-old growth of organized society augurs desire on the part of Nature to avoid the extreme and bloody individualism of the jungle. . . .[1]

On January 15 Liveright published his outline for reform, *Tragic America*. Tom Smith, unenthusiastic about it, had urged him to hold it to 50,000 words. He must have groaned when Dreiser loaded him down with some 250,000 repetitive words. Even more than with the Russian book, Dreiser, with his fingers in too many pies, tossed this one together from scraps of material supplied by female assistants. As Emma Goldman could have testified, he was literally incompetent in the hard field of facts. *Tragic America* was a shambles. Written at an unvarying fortissimo of shrill anger, disorganized, replete with sweeping generalizations and gross inaccuracies, it was so bad that surely no publisher would have accepted it but for the name behind it.

Dreiser assailed corporations, banks, the administration, the Supreme Court, the judiciary, the railways, the school system, the rich, the A.F.L., the church, the police. He was as furious about excessive telephone charges on page 244 as he was on page 214 about the case of a state trooper raping a worker's wife. He was mistaken enough to charge that capital opposed any solution to the depression because the depression was in its interest.

True, he was drinking more, though he was seldom drunk. He leaned on liquor to pacify nerves jangled by sexual difficulties, money worries and that most haunting fear of all, failure and poverty. But *Tragic America* was the work of a bitter and uninformed man rather than a drunken one. Although he had had Browder's advice, he followed it only when he believed it. In the book he praised the Russian system but stressed that he would not transport it bodily to the United States. His recipe for reform, though unclear, included the removal of competition from business, government ownership of utilities and the strict secularization of education.

Norman Thomas rightly said the book was jumbled, inaccurate and unimportant.[2] Sergei Dinamov in Moscow, delighted by the attack though appalled by the dialectics, hailed Dreiser as "the great master" who at any rate had exposed bourgeois America for what it was.[3] Fellow travelers cheered his leftist sympathies even though the line-following *New Masses* said he did not understand communism and was guilty of many of the fallacies of rotten liberalism. He was wounded by a *Herald Tribune* review by the liberal Stuart Chase suggesting that he had ignorantly excerpted data piled on his desk by radicals. Chase, though he agreed with Dreiser's general thesis, wrote, "I would not dare on my life to use a single figure from [the book] without checking back to the original source," and added that he had found "eighteen errors of fact in one chapter."[4] The Liveright publishing house, which had feared possibly libelous statements, was busy answering protests from groups or individuals who found errors or felt themselves maligned.

Most galling to Dreiser was a review by his old enemy, Father James M. Gillis, in the *Catholic News*. Gillis, offended as were other religionists by his roundhouse swipes at the church, called him "the most unpleasant kind of fanatic, the man with a fixed idea," and advised him, "Snap out of it, Theodore. Look up at the sky. Take a squint at the sun. Go out on the hillside and inhale deeply. Get out of the gutters. Come up from those sewers. Be decent, be clean, and America will not seem so tragic."[5]

Dreiser sent copies of the book to Senators Norris, Borah, and other dignitaries. He had high hopes for it, telling L. V. Heilbrunn that it was not his intention to make money on it and he would take no royalties until after the first 100,000 had been sold. His publisher, more realistic, issued a first printing of 5,000 copies and sold only 4,562 of them. While a few libraries rejected *Tragic America* because of its sulphurous anti-religion, he was unable to grasp the thought that its failure was primarily due to its unreliability and unreadability. He was certain he was being suppressed in a plot engineered by the trusts, the Catholics and the reactionary press. When he received an anonymous letter from a Catholic critical of Father Gillis' review, he sought to balloon this letter into newspaper and magazine advertisements he would pay for himself; and when all leading publications refused to accept such anonymous Catholic-baiting, his suspicions of a suppression plot were confirmed.

II. THE KEARNEY OUTRAGE

Dreiser was fond of the ex-Wobbly William Z. Foster, taking him occasionally to New York night clubs where they could discuss social reform amid capitalistic tinsel. He dropped in at the Thirteenth Street headquarters and chatted with the communist head man, Browder. Feeling that only the communists, despite some misconceptions, were fighting for true equality, Dreiser early in 1932 told Browder he wanted to join the party.

"He wanted to make a publicity splash of it," Browder recalled, "but there was no question about his sincerity. He sought publicity for his ideas as well as for himself. He did not seem quite adult, which was a part of his charm."

Browder felt that Dreiser, far from being a Marxist, was gripped by a jumble of outworn political concepts dating back to populism. The rigid party discipline demanded of communists was alien to him. As a friend he was highly useful, since the party took no responsibility for his often heretical utterances, but as a member he would be as dangerous as Casanova in a convent. There was friction between Browder and Foster, who had been replaced by Browder as party head, and Browder felt that Foster was in favor of Dreiser's admission. Browder turned him down with gentle diplomacy, asking him to remain a friend. "He was surprised and hurt," Browder said. "He had expected to be welcomed with open arms." [6]

Thereafter he was never really warm toward Browder. Probably the refusal was a factor in his new disillusionment with the American communists even as he cooperated on those of their programs he approved. Indeed his theories seemed more in line with socialism than communism, but the socialists had not wooed him and they lacked the mystic tie with Russia. He had given up on them and the progressives as well, writing a friend, "any attempt at reform through legislation has shown only dismal failure so far." [7] He seemed unable to decide whether he wanted revolution or not, adding, "the American temperament will not accept Communism as technically stated by the Russians. But I believe that Communism as practiced by the Russians, or, at least, some part if not most of it, can certainly be made palatable to the average American if it is properly explained to him and if the title Communism is removed." He would substitute "Equity." Deeply confused as to an actual program, he was yet ready to start a new political organization he named redundantly the American League for National Equity, writing the same friend, "If we get enough followers, I would be glad to take the leadership." [8] He sent exploratory letters to radical friends on this point, and talked with neighbors around Mt. Kisco about the forming of an Equity party.

His willingness to assume political leadership was spurred by one of the surprising events of his life—his first public speech, an informal talk on *Tragic America* before The Group in New York March 20. His determination to conquer his terrible stage fright was proof of his longing for leadership. He was delighted at the result, his secretary writing that the experience had "entirely dispelled his anxiety as to his ability to address a gathering." [9] Promptly deciding to spread his Equity leadership via the stump, he conferred with the lecture agent James B. Pond and wrote, "In September, I am going on the lecture platform, making a national tour, and my one subject will be . . . the need of drastic change with all the reasons which I can bring to bear to substantiate it." [10] But with Dreiser plans were subject to sudden revision (he had confidently told Sarah Millin that he expected to visit her in Africa) and the "national tour" would dwindle.

Too diversely entangled, he was unable to do anything well. Dorothy Dudley Harvey, finishing a book, *Forgotten Frontiers*—a biography of Dreiser—was furious at his frequent refusals to see her. Earlier he had been helpful in supplying material. Mrs. Harvey had even asked him the ultimate question: Wasn't it unfair and unreasonable for him to expect absolute fidelity from a woman when he insisted on his own freedom? His reply mirrored the great, shattering solipsist:

"I suppose so. I know it's illogical, but it's a rule with me. Without it I should have been destroyed long ago by this or that woman." To save himself, he said, he could not allow any woman to gain ascendancy over him. "I made it a rule . . . to break at once before I was done for! A clean break! How could I have done any work otherwise?" [11]

Now he was unavailable to Mrs. Harvey. To the lion-hunting Alma Clayburgh, inviting him to a party, he snapped, "Oh, a crowd—I don't care for such damn things." When Mrs. Harvey finished her book, Dreiser did not read his own biography but had three female assistants check it for him. He was upset by the plight of strangers who wrote him for help, harassed by communist demands on his time—more help for the Scottsboro boys, more articles for *The Masses*, and would he be a sponsor for the anti-war conference in Europe? On top of this was a threatened lawsuit by a firm claiming to have been libeled in *Tragic America*, and a real lawsuit by William Reswick, late of Moscow.

Reswick claimed to have been a partner of Dreiser and Otto Kahn in the Russian Ballet enterprise, to have secured Soviet permission for the tour, to have gone to great effort and expense on this and other items in Moscow. He was suing for $365,000—suing Kahn also, who settled with him out of court. Although Dreiser called Reswick's claims "entirely unjust," Kahn's settlement suggested that Reswick had some case, and Dreiser's own irresponsibility in factual and business matters was growing notorious.[12] At the same time he employed capitalistic pressure in his efforts to sell something to the films. He switched from one Hollywood agent to another, giving each a 30-day authorization to represent him exclusively on the theory that the time limit would make them stir. He was dealing again with Sackin, who had nibbles from Universal for *Jennie Gerhardt* and Dreiser's story "Fine Furniture." He was irked that Sackin asked him his price, insisting that it was up to Universal to make an offer, and he suspected that Sackin was playing both ends.

"If you are representing both Universal and myself," he wrote, ". . . then I should think it would be fair for you to split the commission and take half from them and half from me." He urged Sackin not to forget that "Universal is . . . approaching me at the top of my publicity value," and that the price should reflect this.[13]

Universal's interest waned. To save money Dreiser dismissed his butler, Frank Womack. Hy Kraft noticed that Dreiser was despondent, once standing in front of the Wayman Adams portrait (now at Iroki) and saying abjectly, "I am not that man any more." He seemed so distraught that Kraft suggested that he see a psychiatrist—an idea he angrily vetoed.[14] Helen, saying something that displeased him while he was shaving, fled in terror when he emerged roaring from the bathroom, brandishing his straight-edged razor. At times she feared that he might kill her.[15] Yet he recognized her loyalty, writing Louise Campbell, "Somehow I admire Helen as much as anyone," [16] and instructing his attorney, Arthur Hume, "In redrawing my will do as you suggest [,] give Helen two thirds of all my property." [17]

In April he wrote Mrs. Campbell:

> I am sick of running a bureau & of being a clearing house for nothing. My dream is to get out—this month if possible. . . . Me for a simple hut in [the] West where I can write and save expenses. Everything seems to be going under.[18]

His clearing-house activities resulted from his own helpless addiction to causes. Patrick Kearney, now a writer for Universal in California, telegraphed him a challenge that made the adrenalin flow:

> A great pal of mine named Martin Mooney under contract to Universal as I was, spoke at the local John Reed Club Friday night at my instigation about the horrible conditions at Boulder Dam. Next morning, Mooney was fired and yesterday I was dismissed; this in spite of the fact that Mooney's work for Universal has been at all times highly acclaimed and my first picture, The Doomed Battalion . . . is acknowledged to be the biggest thing Universal ever did. . . . I am consequently depending on your fairness in things regarding social conditions to help us both bring this matter before press. . . .[19]

Although Dreiser was busy trying to get Bernard Shaw to speak by transatlantic telephone, and Roland Hayes to sing in person, for a huge New York rally for the Scottsboro boys, he leaped to the screen writers' aid. To *The New York Times* he sent a copy of Kearney's telegram and commented:

"If this, like so many others, is not an attempt to silence, by a method as irrelevant as it is cowardly, the free expression of opinion on a matter of vital national importance, what is it? . . ." [20] He sent similar letters of protest to the *World-Telegram*, Harry Elmer Barnes, Arthur Garfield Hays, Walter Winchell, Bruce Crawford, the secretary of the N.C.D.P.P., the Dramatists' Guild, and to Forrest Bailey, director of the American Civil Liberties Union. He wrote George Douglas in Los Angeles, asking him to investigate.

When *The Times* published Dreiser's letter April 11, R. H. Cochrane, a Universal vice-president in New York, wired California for details, then wrote Dreiser tartly.

Kearney's charges were entirely erroneous, he said. For one thing, Kearney had not been fired but merely suspended while he was hospitalized for alcoholism. Cochrane quoted part of a telegram he had received from the Coast: "Nurse today stated Kearney getting worse in tantrums and has suicidal mania. Apparently his telegraphic dispatches sent during period his present condition." As for Mooney, his dismissal had been part of a studio cutback. Dreiser, said Cochrane, took the word of a temporarily unbalanced man and flew into the papers with it. [21]

From Bailey of the A.C.L.U., Dreiser got later word:

> I have just received from the secretary of our Los Angeles branch a report on the Kearney matter. . . . I dislike to tell you what she reports, but that seems to be necessary.
>
> In the first place Kearney is back on the payroll. The apparent reason for his dismissal was drunkenness. At least his membership in the John Reed Club had nothing to do with it. According to Variety both his and Mooney's options ran out about the time of the dismissal. Mooney's speech is reported to have been quite innocuous. . . . Our secretary's informant believes that the speech had nothing to do with the dismissal. . . . Kearney, it is stated, was stretching the point a long way when he spoke of The Doomed Battalion as *his* picture. Universal merely touched up a German film and added a love interest to it. If Kearney had anything to do with it, he probably wrote the dialogue.
>
> By the way, Kearney also cabled Joseph Stalin about the affair. . . . [22]

III. JERSEY LIGHTNING

For almost three decades Charles Fort had been to Dreiser an unheralded genius who steered his thoughts boldly into mystic, uncharted realms feared by orthodox scientists. Almost a hermit, Fort visited occasionally at Iroki when assured that no other guests would be there. "You—the most fascinating literary figure since Poe," Dreiser had written him. "You—who for all I know may be the progenitor of an entirely new world viewpoint: you whose books thrill and astound me as almost no other books have thrilled and astounded me. . . ." [23]

Early in 1932 Fort jotted down signs of his own decline: "Without being definitely ill, I can't take walks, can't smoke half as much, have cut down meals one half, am sleeping poorly, have cut down beer." He noted that packages of sugar jumped off the shelves, seeming to feel this an omen of death.[24] Suspecting science, he refused to consult a physician. He succeeded in finishing *Wild Talents,* another cosmic excursion, before he died at fifty-eight on May 3.

Saddened, plagued by bronchitis, his nerves in shreds, Dreiser a few days later put the Chrysler on a boat and sailed for Galveston. En route he had strange dreams, he noted, "all of them seeming to mean something." Apparently he was alone on this trip—unprecedented if so, though he was not averse to patronizing prostitutes when the need arose. He drove to San Antonio, put up at a motel under the name T. H. Dryer to avoid publicity, and worked at *The Stoic,* still less than half done. "I had to get out of N. Y.," he wrote Louise Campbell, who was helping him with the novel. "Couldn't get a thing done. Besides expenses were eating me alive." [25]

He had strong recuperative powers when he gave them a chance. To Helen he wrote fondly, lamenting "my present women troubles" and adding, "you are never out of my mind and I wish so much that we might be together in freedom & peace. But whether that can ever be I wonder. We are so individual & both of us were born free." [26]

To Esther McCoy on June 9 he wrote that he was moving to El Paso:

> I am going there because for six cents I can cross over into Juarez, Mexico & buy all I want to drink. And some how I need to drink to work—but not to work to drink.[27]

After almost a decade a letter was forwarded him from Bettina Morris, visiting in New York from California and thus missing him. "My dear," he wrote, "I am here in Texas writing a novel. . . ." [28] He turned down an RKO proposal relayed by Sackin offering a miserable $2,500 each for *Sister Carrie* and *Jennie Gerhardt* plus a percentage of the receipts, noting that the receipts might be negligible in the present doldrums: "Here in Texas eleven of the largest moving picture houses in its principle [*sic*] cities are closed for want of patronage." [29] Even in Texas the communists sought him out for a statement supporting William Z. Foster and James Ford, their running mates for 1932.

Early in July he drove homeward. One of the worst of drivers, he got by until he reached Somerville, New Jersey. Here on July 8 he swerved to avoid another car and crashed through an iron fence into the beautifully tended shrubbery of Dr. W. H. Long, ending up against a tree. Dr. Long, whose yard was to be an exhibit in a garden club show and now was ruined, came out shouting. Dreiser, unhurt, growled, "What of it?" Long called a policeman, who took Dreiser to the borough physician for a drunk test that established his sobriety.[30] He had damaged the landscaping to an extent that later cost him $147.50. Leaving his battered car for repairs, he was driven to Mt. Kisco by a friendly Somerville newspaperman, young C. Stewart Hoagland, for whom he took an immediate liking and urged him to send him some "Jersey lightning" applejack.

Dreiser came home to bad news. The Liveright firm was in financial distress. Horace Liveright himself, fired by Paramount, had returned to New York but had lost financial control of his own firm and was rapidly drinking himself to death. The company was being reorganized under Arthur Pell, with drastic economies. One of the economies was the fat allowance paid to Dreiser, which indeed he had not earned for several years. "I'm suddenly cut out of a guarantee of 1200 a month to nothing," he wrote Mrs. Campbell.

The income from his investments, he said, had sagged from about $6,000 a year to $210. He had been paying $200 monthly to Jug, $100 to his sisters Emma and Sylvia and $80 to Mame and Rome. The payment to Jug was a legal obligation, but he reduced the stipends to the brother and sisters with the result that "Personally I am being assailed with bitter letters from my relatives. . . ."[31] He cut Evelyn Light's salary and trimmed his sails in other ways. Although he talked of eating at Horn & Hardart's and applying for a janitor's job, he was probably talking poorer than he was in actuality, for not long thereafter he sought advice in investing money.

Nevertheless, the gay days were over with a vengeance. He knew his weakness for wasting his energies and tried—without success—to close off the world and finish *The Stoic*. The communists, with their propensity for committees and big-name sponsors, made incessant demands on him. Although he had resigned as chairman of N.C.D.P.P., they ignored it and clamored for more help, among other things asking him to head a delegation to Washington protesting the repulse of the bonus marchers. While he loved their dependence on him, he found that membership in any communist committee automatically included him in other committees and that his name was being used in campaigns of which he had no knowledge. He was involved on his own in correspondence with the Intellectual Workers' League, the League of Professional Groups for Foster and Ford, the American Committee for the World Congress Against War, the Communist Party National Campaign Committee, Proletcult of Seattle and others, even including a letter to the "Provisional Secretary, Provisional Committee for the Anti-Injunction Conference." He was asked for articles or statements on Soviet triumphs or anniversaries by such Russian publications as *Pravda, International Literature, Smena, Izvestia* and *Vechernyaya Moskva*. He received letters and cables in Russian he had to send out for translation. To Joseph Pass he protested:

I cannot understand why you want another statement [supporting Foster and Ford]. I wrote one for you which you used and must still have, and then I joined with Edmund Wilson and Malcolm Cowley in a second statement.[32]

His secretary, Miss Light, wrote the N.C.D.P.P.:

Mr. Dreiser feels that his name, used as it is, in publicizing all activities, large and small, of the Committee, will soon lose the weight that it would carry if it were used only in connection with the major cases and protests in which the Committee acts.[33]

After discovering that the League of Professional Groups for Foster and Ford was using his name on its stationery and publicity without his authorization, and demanding that they cease, he relented a trifle, having his secretary write Pass:

He [Dreiser] is content to remain a member of the League . . . on the basis of your . . . written assurance that the League will automatically dissolve after election, and that he will not then be informed that it was a nucleus of some larger group which will then come into existence and of which he will be, without his knowledge a part or member.[34]

Yet when George Jean Nathan and Ernest Boyd proposed starting a literary newspaper, the *American Spectator,* he could not resist becoming one of its editors (once he had made sure that Sinclair Lewis was not connected with it), though this would demand even more of his time than the communists. Simultaneously he began a series of twelve conversations with Dr. Brill at his apartment on Central Park West on the subject of life and happiness.

Brill liked Dreiser. Dreiser admired Brill, whom he likened to Socrates, though he was sharply resentful at times when the psychiatrist bluntly punctured his irrationalities. These meetings were not doctor-and-patient consultations, although Dreiser perhaps hoped to gain knowledge that might still his anxieties. It was agreed between them that their conversations, taken down by a stenographer, would form the basis of a book or series of articles to be published jointly under both their names.

Brill always served cocktails, noting that Dreiser liked to have the shaker near him and that he could pour himself drink after drink without appearing intoxicated. The talks were extended at night beer-drinking sessions at Lüchow's during which no stenographer was present. That part of them which was transcribed did not prove vastly revealing. Dreiser assailed religion, described love as utterly selfish, and conceived life (a subjective deduction) as nothing more than chaos. Although at one point he insisted that there were times of happiness, he later repudiated this by saying that life had no value. Some of his statements mirrored familiar attitudes:

[There is] nothing to hope for, nothing to live for, nothing to be honorable for, nothing to be dishonest for.

Accidentally, I have enough to get along on, you have, a few other people have, but the percentage is so very small. And then look at those people who come and scheme out their own personal welfare, and really break down so many other people by their grinding and scheming. . . .

I think it [life] is a lousy deal, and if there is any motivating consciousness or intelligence or whatever it is, that understands the meaning of the word lousy, I hope he hears me.

Brill, who thought life challenging and felt that society was somewhat better than chaos, finished the colloquy with a sage comment:

You have never detached yourself from your early Christian training—you expect rewards. . . .[35]

IV. TECHNOCRACY

Nor could Dreiser resist when he was urged to address a San Francisco rally for Tom Mooney. Arriving by plane November 5, he was met by Lincoln Steffens, Ella Winter, Samuel Ornitz and Orrick Johns, who took him to San Quentin for another meeting with Mooney. Returning to the Mark Hopkins, he was surrounded by reporters who found him good copy not only because of his literary fame but because of his great shambling bulk, his explosiveness and the well-remembered Kentucky toothpicks. Edgar Gleeson, managing editor of the *Call-Bulletin*, later recalled that long before Captain Queeg of *The Caine Mutiny* manipulated two ball-bearings, Dreiser seemed to get the same solace out of his handkerchief. A woman reporter said, "Don't you think, Mr. Dreiser, that even if Mooney is innocent, he is a dangerous anarchist and should not be at large?"

"If you mean that," Dreiser snapped, "then you are an idiot, and ought not to be at large." [36]

He called on District Attorney Matthew I. Brady, pressing him so hard about Mooney that Brady finally growled, "Don't tell me what I should do in pursuit of my duties." [37] He called on Judge Louis H. Ward, who would hear the Mooney appeal and therefore declined to discuss it with him. Dreiser, indignant about the Mooney injustice, had no similar feeling about the thousands of suspected Trotskyites imprisoned or shot in Russia. The Russians, he felt, were trying to build an ideal state and were justified in eliminating obstacles.

Five thousand union members paraded around the Civic Auditorium before the Sunday mass meeting, chanting, "Free Tom Mooney." Some 15,000 jammed the auditorium, where Steffens and others spoke but Dreiser was the real drawing card, Johns observing, "without him the newspapers would hardly have given us a line." He recounted his visit to Kentucky and said the Mooney case was an instance of "the same class warfare that has troubled Kentucky." Later, to Johns, he said the spilling of wine was lucky rather than otherwise, for Mencken had spilled a glass of wine the day before the first issue of the *American Mercury* had appeared.[38]

Perhaps Dreiser himself had spilled a bit of wine, for luck was with him this trip. He went on to Hollywood—not to see Bettina Morris but to sound out the studios in person. Interviewed there, he made headlines when he paid his respects to Captain W. F. Hynes, head of the Los Angeles police "Red" squad, who devoted himself to breaking up communist meetings. He did not know that he would lecture, Dreiser said, but if he did, Hynes would get a "punch in the nose if he tries to drag me from a platform." [39] B. P. Schulberg read the papers, discovered that Dreiser was in town and called him up. Dreiser soon came to terms on *Jennie Gerhardt* with Schulberg and the Paramount studio he had sued only the previous year. Prices were down, and he was perhaps outwitted, but he received a needed $25,000 for the screen rights plus a seven per cent interest in Schulberg's own one-third interest in the profits. And no agent's commission! Schulberg promised a faithful production and introduced him to Sylvia Sidney and Marion Gering, who would be the star and director. Certainly he called on George Douglas, the Los Angeles newspaperman for whom he had conceived a great fondness. But he neglected Miss Morris, who also read the papers and later wrote, "I hear that you were actually in Hollywood a short time ago, and that you are coming back again in a couple of months. Is that true? If it is will you come to see me, or call me up—or something?" [40]

Cheered by the sale, he pondered other screen possibilities. After his return, he wrote Stewart Hoagland, the Somerville newspaperman:

> This is the Christmas season, everybody is wishing everybody else a Merry Christmas. I am wishing myself three gallons of Jersey lightning, for which I am wishing myself twenty-five dollars to pay for it, and I wish that you would wish to procure it for me. I wish you a merry Christmas.[41]

But meanwhile his social thinking had collided against a new concept. The engineer Howard Scott, whom he had known in the Village, had warmed over some Thorstein Veblen ideas and founded the Technocracy group, who calculated the immense productivity possible if the economy were given over to technicians utilizing the full efficiency of automation. Magazines featured articles about Technocracy. Men in the street felt it the solution to the depression. Dreiser was so impressed that he had a long talk with Scott and even entertained the notion that his previous measures for reform had not embraced full economic and technical understanding. To Sergei Dinamov in Moscow he wrote:

> I see some things which I did not see anywhere near as clearly when I was in the midst of it last year, and one is the enormous significance of the machine in any equitable form of society, and the need of the technician as a part of the newer kind of state. The technician, the chemist, the physicist, the mathematician, the inventor and the economic student and expert are not quite the same as the factory hand or the farmer, but the introduction of the working formula with which to remedy their troubles is not quite clear. I am thinking about it. . . .[42]

7. American Spectator

The *American Spectator* was a four-page sheet of intellectual comment, devoted to the unlikely proposition that it could exist without advertising at ten cents a copy in the depths of the depression. It was published by the new book house of Ray Long & Richard R. Smith at their offices, 12 East Forty-first Street, with Nathan and Boyd as the active editors. Dreiser, Eugene O'Neill and James Branch Cabell were unsalaried contributing editors, but O'Neill and Cabell did little. Dreiser worked hardest of all. Miss Light was given desk space at the Long-Smith office—a financial saving for him—and he pitched in on the *Spectator* as he once had at Butterick.

Although his attention span usually was short, he played with ideas as a child plays with blocks. Concerned with problems all over the world, he saw the *Spectator* as a forum for his ideas and those of others. He and his colleagues were unabashed by their payment of one cent a word (on publication) and their length limit of 1,500 or 2,000 words, which meant a maximum payment of $20. It was an honor to appear in the *Spectator*, for one had to satisfy not one editor but five, all with impressive reputations.

"If possible," Dreiser wrote Dinamov, "I would like a five- or six- or seven-hundred-word signed statement from Stalin on anything that he chooses to talk about. For instance, if he would like to deny that he lives richly and is guarded by machine guns, and explain that the truth is that he lives very simply and is not guarded . . . it would be really priceless for this paper." If Dinamov could do this, and get other Russian articles "without Communist dogma being lugged in," Dreiser promised, "I will send you a couple of white shirts, or a bunch of American magazines or some book of your choice."[1]

"I have no direct personal contact with . . . comrade Stalin . . ." Dinamov replied a bit nervously.[2]

Dreiser tried again for Stalin via an Amtorg official, Peter Bogdanov, reminding him:

> I am constantly being asked by the editors of Russian publications for statements on various matters. . . . I have responded and responded; my books are translated and printed in the U.S.S.R., sold to the profit of the Russian Government, but not to me; I am constantly doing this and that to assist Communist issues here in America . . . and yet when I ask for connections of the sort mentioned above, I get nowhere. . . .[3]

Stalin remained unavailable. Dreiser asked Howard Scott to write on Technocracy, Diego Rivera on the Mayans, Sarah Millin on South African literature, Leopold Stokowski on modern music, Plutarco Elias Calles on Mexico's suppression of the Catholic Church, Einstein on any subject he chose, Baroness Keichi Ishimoto on the feminist movement in Japan, Angna Enters on the dance. He sent out a perfect gale of letters requesting material from Sherwood Anderson, Ford Madox Ford, John Dos Passos, Lion Feuchtwanger, Evelyn Scott, George Douglas, John Cowper Powys and his brother Llewelyn, Claude Bowers, Lincoln Steffens, Carl Van Vechten and scores of others, many of them unknown. Fascinated by the reforms of Kemal Ataturk in Turkey, he tried a dozen methods of getting an article about them out of Turkey, writing among others the State Department, the American Friends of Turkey, the Chase National Bank and the Turkish foreign minister.

The first issue of the *Spectator*, dated November, 1932, was successful enough so that an extra print order of 20,000 copies was necessary. The paper was refreshing, if uneven, but was impossibly handicapped by its length limitations and disputes among its temperamental editors. Dreiser, Nathan and Boyd had frequent editorial conferences at Mike's, a Sixty-first Street speakeasy. Dreiser, working at it as if it meant salvation, urged the others to do likewise, writing Nathan, "I do not think it is fair that . . . I should do all the pushing." [4] He complained about a Thomas Beer piece that was accepted: "It is so worthless that it would really be ideal in the *Bookman*. Why not make a present of it to them?" [5] He was embarrassed when articles which he had solicited were rejected by Nathan or Boyd over his protest, and he had to write explanatory letters to his contributors.

Meanwhile he saw the makings of a socially critical moving picture in the 1906–7 revolt of Kentucky and Tennessee tobacco farmers against the starvation prices paid them by the Duke trust. Characteristically he involved others in the project, forming a corporation to promote it and driving to Nashville with Hy Kraft and Milton Goldberg on January 29 for field work. They drove north to Hopkinsville, Kentucky, where skirmishes had been fought and tobacco warehouses burned. Although no longer under indictment in Kentucky, Dreiser registered at the hotel as T. Dresser and in freezing weather drove with Kraft in a search for the cabin of one of the leaders of the revolt. Dreiser took careful measurements of it while Kraft, shivering, kept notes, when a passing farmer informed them they had the wrong cabin.

"One cabin is as good as another," Kraft protested. But Dreiser, reproving him for his laxity toward realism, insisted on finding the right cabin and repeating the process. Kraft noted that Dreiser ate like a horse and drank any liquor available. He had a sure cure for hangover—a drop or two of ammonia in Bromo-Seltzer.[6]

They interviewed a survivor of the tobacco war, examined skirmish scenes, consulted yellowed issues of the local newspapers telling of the struggle. Dreiser was so enthusiastic that he wired Helen to come down with Clara

Clark, a secretary who was helping him with *The Stoic*, and also to bring the artist Hubert Davis to make sketches. They visited tobacco auctions and cigarette factories, returning to New York in mid-February to hear a disturbing rumor. The incoming President Roosevelt, it was whispered, would declare a bank moratorium. Terror-stricken, Dreiser feared he would lose his savings. Consulting with Kraft and Goldberg, he hurriedly transferred what he could into Postal Savings and gold notes while Helen rushed to Mt. Kisco to stock up on canned goods.

"When do we open a soup kitchen," Dreiser wrote Louise Campbell. "I want the job of chief ladler." [7] Hearing from Anna Tatum again after many years, he set her to working on the new script he called *Tobacco*. Soon he was quarreling with her because she laughed at the social theories he wanted to embody in the script. He reminded her that it was his script: "The trouble with this relationship . . . is your fierce insistence on your individualism for the world, as opposed to my personal theories [of] individualism plus compromise, which I believe to be fundamentally enforced in nature." [8] He hired another writer, Martha Aldrich, to do research on the telephone trust, telling her of his rage when the operator demanded another nickel and adding, "I suffer personally every time I go to the telephone in New York City to make a call." [9] (Did "personally," a word he worked to death, have an egoistic significance?) Writers protested to him about the low rates paid by the *Spectator*, some even suggesting that the editors were getting rich on it. When he submitted an idea for an article to correct stereotyped arguments against socialism, Boyd wrote on it, "Bernard Shaw—in addition to a few thousand other Socialists—did this job in 1887. . . ." [10] He wrote Boyd:

> To Nathan, any topic that has been once done in the entire fifty years of his daily criticism is done forever. With you it is exactly the same. Anything that you saw done, as in this instance, in 1887, is old in 1933. The assumption is dumb. So dumb that it makes me laugh even though I am sore at finding it in this office. [11]

He traveled to Maine to lecture on realism at Bowdoin College April 4. Burroughs Mitchell, one of the audience, noted that Dreiser's voice did not carry, few could hear him and that everybody simply watched in fascination as he hulked over the lectern, nervously kneading a handkerchief in each hand. On his return a Schulberg telegram informed him that Paramount was shooting *Jennie*. Dreiser had read a news account saying that Schulberg had made sure that Paramount's contract for *Jennie*, unlike the one for the *Tragedy*, granted the author no authority over the script. Schulberg was quoted as saying that if Dreiser did not like this picture, "that is going to be just too bad." [12] He wired Schulberg:

. . . PARAMOUNT RELEASE QUOTING YOU IN REGARD TO MYSELF AND GERHARDT PRODUCTION CHEAP DISHONEST DISGRACEFUL STOP YOU KNOW THAT YOU

YOUR DIRECTOR GERING SYLVIA SYDNEY [*sic*] WHO IS TO PLAY JENNIE SAT DOWN
WITH ME AND AGREED THAT THIS PICTURE WAS TO BE MADE SO THAT IT WOULD
NOT ONLY PLEASE BUT DELIGHT ME. . . .[13]

Schulberg replied that he saw nothing wrong about the Paramount release,
expressing his confidence that the picture would indeed delight Dreiser.[14]
Dreiser wired him:

YOUR ACKNOWLEDGMENT OF YOUR RESPONSIBILITY FOR PARAMOUNT GER-
HARDT RELEASE . . . LEAVES YOU AS DESCRIBED IN MY TELEGRAM.[15]

"DREISER AGAIN BURSTS OUT IN WRATH," *Variety* headlined,
summarizing the quarrel, and adding, "This latest Dreiser outburst brought
only yawns from Par execs as studio took the precaution before buying
'Gerhardt' to insure legally against the author's having a finger in the film." [16]
Evidently in saving an agent's fee Dreiser had failed to safeguard his own
interests.

"Mr. Dreiser wishes to take legal action against [*Variety*] to force a
retraction," Miss Light wrote Attorney Hume. Hume replied, "There is
nothing libellous in what they state. Their language is, of course, undignified
and slangy, but . . . it is nothing but a statement that Mr. Dreiser has
expressed his indignation. . . ." [17]

To Sherwood Anderson Dreiser listed several steps he should take in any
dealings with the films, including, "have an American lawyer, not a Jewish
one," and adding, "If you do not do these things, you will probably find that
you have let yourself in for complete defeat in whatever it is you wish to
do." [18]

From Llewelyn Powys in Dorset he received a complaint about a Boyd
rejection of an essay he had sent: "God! I would like to pluck Ernest Boyd
by his combed golden beard, and use my arse as a trumpet before their
office!" [19]

II. DREISER ON THE JEWS

Dreiser was no longer sure that revolution could or should be avoided
in America. "[If] this present economic pressure continues and increases," he
wrote, "the time will certainly come when [Americans] will begin to think
how to compel their government to give them work, and that would certainly
constitute revolution." [20]

Some intellectual leftists were growing restive over signs that benevolence
was not universal in Russia, news that suspected Trotskyites were being
arrested in droves, to disappear much as if they had been sent to Siberia or
murdered. When Trotsky's daughter committed suicide in exile, Charles Yale
Harrison blamed it on Stalin and resigned from *The Masses* staff, saying it had
"ceased to be an organ of free expression and has degenerated steadily until
today it is nothing more than the servile mouthpiece of the Stalin apparatus in

this country." He gave this statement to the press, adding, "I appeal to men like Sherwood Anderson, John Dos Passos, and Theodore Dreiser and a few others to openly take a stand and declare themselves on this latest bloody act of Stalin." [21]

Joseph Freeman of *The Masses* wrote Dreiser anxiously, hoping he would denounce such heresy. The John Reed Club wired him in part:

> WE REQUEST YOU AS FRIEND USSR REPUDIATE THIS ATTACK CLEARLY PLAYING INTO HANDS WORST ENEMIES USSR.[22]

There seems no record that Dreiser responded either way. He considered the problem, however, when Max Eastman wrote him in concern over "Stalin's substitution of bureaucratic doctrinairism for intelligent revolutionary thinking" and his ruthless suppression of the Trotskyite opposition. Would Dreiser join in an appeal for funds to help the Trotskyites? [23]

Dreiser replied that he must think it over. "I am so much interested in the present difficulties in Russia and in Russia's general fate, that I am not prepared, without very serious consideration, to throw a monkey-wrench such as this could prove to be, into their machinery.

"It seems to me, whether badly managed or well managed, that it is at least a set-up which should be preserved and fought for. If that means serious and, in some cases, seemingly cruel sacrifices, it is, as we say, just too bad." [24]

But he "meditated almost prayerfully" over Eastman's appeal before he later declined, writing, "Whatever the nature of the present dictatorship in Russia—unjust, or what you will—the victory of Russia is all-important. I hold with Lincoln: Never swap horses while crossing a stream." [25] When a reader, addressing him as "Comrade Dreiser," suggested forming "Dreiser Clubs" across the nation using *Tragic America* as required reading, he liked the idea. Twice he wrote Esther McCoy, now in Los Angeles, to see if she might spread the gospel on the Coast, adding, "I do not see, really, why organizations of this sort could not use TRAGIC AMERICA as a kind of Bible. . . ." [26]

In June he invited the 300-pound Diego Rivera to Iroki along with the Woodwards, the Henry Varnum Poors and others. Rivera startled them all by seizing big black ants running across the outdoor table and crunching them between his teeth, saying they had a "pungent taste." Dreiser scoffed at Rivera's insistence that all men were born equally endowed but with unequal opportunity and environment. "Look at a litter of pups," he said. "Some are bright, some dull. It's the same with people." [27]

When he saw Paramount's sentimental picturization of *Jennie*, he was delighted, wiring Schulberg:

> JENNIE MOVING IMPROVISATION UPON MY THEME EXCELLENTLY CAST BEAUTIFULLY INTERPRETED CONSIDER UNDERSTANDING BETWEEN YOU MISS SIDNEY AND MR. GERING FULFILLED THANKS.[28]

He also wired his praise to Miss Sidney and Gering. As nervous as ever, he admitted to Burton Rascoe, "The content of my most typical dream is extreme danger to myself. I am always just one lap ahead of death or disaster in some horrible form, and escape by waking up." [29] His restlessness called for movement, travel, change. That summer with Helen he made at least five trips—to visit the Fickes and John Cowper Powys upstate at Hillsdale, to Vermont, to the Eshericks at Paoli, to the World's Fair in Chicago, and to Halifax by boat. Esherick was annoyed because Dreiser arrived not only with Helen but with two other women with whom he was on intimate terms. Esherick disliked this parade of bohemianism before his young daughters, whom he had long since warned to keep at a safe distance from Dreiser.

In July the Fickes visited Iroki, noting that he ate an enormous meal, then lapsed into gloom. Later he walked the hills with Ficke, confessing a sense of deep unworthiness.

"But Theodore," Ficke said, "a man must learn to forgive himself."

Dreiser walked on for a moment, then turned with tears in his eyes, his face radiant. "Arthur—that's the most wonderful thing I've ever heard! A man must learn to forgive himself!" He kept repeating it, as one in need of self-forgiveness. [30]

In August he was one of those writers asked to fill in for the vacationing Walter Winchell. Like a philosopher entering a cabaret, he replaced Winchell's gossip with a piece, "Flies and Locusts," assailing the profit-makers as thieves. [31] Manuel Komroff, now in Hollywood, wrote to praise the piece but added, "What I did not like was to see it appended to Walter Winchell. Was this really necessary? . . . Excuse me for throwing a fit but I hate like hell to see your name in places where it don't belong." [32]

On the letter, Dreiser scrawled, "One Jew speaking of another!" His opinion of American mentality was implicit in a squib he proposed for the *Spectator:* "The editors of The American Spectator distressfully contemplate the possible shortage of obituary mourning resources of the American press in the event of the sudden demise of Mickey Mouse." [33] Bertha M. Clay and Laura Jean Libbey, who once represented the nation's culture, had been displaced by a mouse. But as he watched Roosevelt's radical moves for recovery, he was half inclined to approve, to spare Roosevelt his opposition. "Drop the idea of the Dreiser Clubs for the present," he wrote Esther McCoy, "because I am interested to see how this Roosevelt experiment works out." [34] He was continually annoyed by the unauthorized use various communist-front organizations made of his name, apologizing for it and then using it again. He had Miss Light write the N.C.D.P.P.:

[Mr. Dreiser] requests that in the future, and so that the routine may not continue monotonous, the N.C.D.P.P. apologize in advance for any intended unauthorized use of his name. . . . [35]

That summer, the *Spectator* editors—Dreiser, Boyd, Nathan, Cabell and O'Neill—gathered in a mythical "Editorial Conference (With Wine)" on the subject of the Jews and the rising question of a Jewish homeland, published in September. Except for Dreiser, who firmly believed in a Jewish national home, the remarks were largely flippant. Nathan belittled Jewish poetry and music. O'Neill proposed a homeland in Africa, while Boyd suggested giving the Jews the state of Kansas. Dreiser insisted that "the world's quarrel with the Jew is not that he is inferior, but that he is superior," and said, "The Jew, to me, particularly in the realm of commerce and some practical professions, wherein shrewdness rather than any creative labor is the chief issue, might well be compelled to accept a handicap—limitation as to his numbers in given lines. Thus 100,000 Jewish lawyers might be reduced to ten and the remainder made to do farming." [36]

Hitler had recently become chancellor in Germany. Anti-Semitic riots had burst out in Berlin. Jews had begun to flee the country, among them Lina Goldschmidt and her husband. It was not surprising that some of Dreiser's friends—Jerome Blum, Hy Kraft and Hutchins Hapgood among them—saw no humor in the *Spectator* whimsy. Hapgood protested in a letter to the *Spectator*. Dreiser's reply was more blunt than the published symposium.

The Jews, he insisted, were internationalist rather than nationalist, refused to intermarry with gentiles and thus formed an unassimilated racial group that threatened to overrun America. They avoided muscular labor. They entered the dominating professions, winning wealth and eminence at the expense of ethical standards. "If you listen to Jews discuss Jews, you will find that they are money-minded, very pagan, very sharp in practice. . . ." They would, he said, if unimpeded, undermine American culture (which he had identified with Mickey Mouse), and the logical solution was for the Jews to found their own nation. [37]

Hapgood replied in anger, starting a correspondence that would later explode in the press. Meanwhile, the individualist Henry Ford refused to sign the certificate of compliance with Roosevelt's N.R.A. automotive code, which among other things guaranteed employees the right of collective bargaining. Dreiser sent the President a telegram:

YOU ARE FACING THE OUTWORN EXPONENTS OF A DEFUNCT AUTOCRATIC INDUSTRIAL SYSTEM OF WHOM HENRY FORD IS ONE. OWING MORE TO THE LAND THAT HAS PROSPERED THEM THAN THE LAND OWES THEM THEY STILL SEEK TO DICTATE NOT THE DETAILS OF THEIR BUSINESS BUT THE POLICY OF THE NATION THAT MAKES THEM POSSIBLE [.] SOME PUBLIC ADULATION OF BUSINESS SUCCESS HAS CAUSED THEM TO LOOK ON THEMSELVES AS NOT MERELY TRADESMEN BUT STATESMEN. DISPEL THAT ILLUSION [.] ORDER THIS SWOLLEN FORD TO APPEAR BEFORE YOU IN WASHINGTON. USE YOUR OFFICIAL POWERS IN FULL AND DICTATORIALLY FOR ITS EFFECT ON THE AMERICAN PEOPLE. THE LEGAL TECHNICALITIES CAN BE BRUSHED AWAY AFTERWARDS. YOU ARE THE PRESIDENT OF ALL THE PEOPLE OF

THE UNITED STATES, ALMOST UNANIMOUSLY THEY RESTED IN YOU AUTHORITY
TO EXPRESS THEIR WILL. . . . REALLY GENEROUSLY YOU HAVE SNATCHED FROM
DISHONOR, REPRISAL AND OBLOQUY THESE SO-CALLED CAPTAINS OF INDUSTRY WHO
HAVE NOT ONLY SWEATED WEALTH OUT OF AMERICA, BUT LIKE PRODIGALS AND
INGRATES HAVE WASTED IT OVER THE WORLD [.] TOLERATE DEFIANCE FROM NOT
ONE. WITH THE AUTHORITY OF ALL THE PEOPLE OF THE UNITED STATES WHICH
IS YOURS SAY TO HIM WHAT HE IS TO DO IT [*sic*]. IF HE DEFIES YOU TAKE FROM
HIM THE SANCTIONS WHICH THE AMERICAN PEOPLE THROUGH ITS OFFICIAL SERV-
ANTS HAVE GRANTED HIM. CLOSE HIS FACTORIES AND SALES ROOM [S] AND DE-
MAND BEFORE PERMISSION FOR THEIR REOPENING IS GRANTED THAT HE APOLOGIZE
THROUGH YOU TO THE AMERICAN PEOPLE [.] YOU CANNOT DO LESS [.] HE DARE
NOT. THEODORE DREISER, MT. KISCO, NEW YORK.[38]

In October, Floyd and Mrs. Dell, Sherwood Anderson, George Jean Nathan and Lillian Gish were guests at an Iroki gathering. Dell frankly thought
Dreiser stupid. He was not surprised to hear him praise Russia, but was
staggered when he went on to find good in Germany under National Socialism. Dell, who had quit the *New Masses*, had deep suspicions of both Stalin
and Hitler. There was an argument between them in which bitter things were
said. Yet, when the Dells left, Dreiser went out to the car with them and bade
them an affectionate farewell. He could be kindly, and no one could say that
his interests were not far-reaching. A few days later, his secretary wrote the
Boeing Aircraft Company:

> Mr. Dreiser asks me to inquire of you whether the use of dry ice for cool-
> ing airplane engines in flight would in any way serve to obviate the crashes
> periodically reported in the press.[39]

III. TALKING THINGS OVER

When Isobel Sperry, a seventeen-year-old freshman at Bryn Mawr
College, wrote him to praise *An American Tragedy*, the sixty-two-year-
old Dreiser laid careful plans to seduce her. He coaxed her to send her picture,
was delighted by it, and commented on the books she had read:

> I might say never mind the books of the ages—or at least not too much.
> Live a little. Live a lot. Youth is a short span. At best ten years. And after
> that. Well, after that there still are the books of the ages. And if they're for
> the ages it won't hurt them to wait a little. . . .
> Do you ever come to New York? Does [Bryn Mawr] permit week-end
> visits? If so you might let me know. I'd gladly visit with you here over a
> Saturday and Sunday. . . .[40]

While Miss Sperry hung in the balance, Horace Liveright, the wonder boy
of the twenties, died of pneumonia at forty-nine. The obituarists remembered
his astonishing generosity, his support of good literature and his long fight
against censorship. Dreiser, who owed much to Liveright but had treated him
as a lackey, attended the funeral. So did Upton Sinclair, then visiting in New

York. The water-drinking Sinclair, blaming Liveright's untimely death on liquor, felt with some exaggeration that Dreiser was headed in the same direction. "I remember walking downtown with Theodore Dreiser after the funeral," he wrote. "We discussed the tragedy of drinking, and I knew the anguish that Theodore's wife [that is, Helen] was suffering. But he learned nothing from the funeral or from my arguments." [41]

Liveright's old firm finally had gone bankrupt, the receiver acquiring possession of 13,000 unsold Dreiser volumes as well as the plates for all 22 of his books.[42] Dreiser offered to buy back the unsold copies at 25 cents each and the plates for $2,000, but the receiver asked one dollar a volume and $12,000. The dispute went into arbitration, which would drag on for a year while Dreiser was in effect without a publisher, without advertising or promotion and therefore selling practically no books. He was particularly upset because the *Jennie Gerhardt* film would surely have spurred the sale of that book had it been advertised and available. At the same time he was having trouble with at least three of his foreign publishers. He had signed a contract giving the publisher Paul Zsolnay in Vienna the German-language rights to his books for the duration of the copyright. Not until later did he learn that in Vienna this meant a period lasting 30 years after the author's death. European finances were in chaos, some countries forbidding payments outside their borders. Zsolnay had published ten of his books, but of late had sent neither reports of sales nor remittances.[43] Dreiser had also failed to get reports or payments from his publisher Nepszava in Budapest. He had two attorneys working on these matters in Europe—money going out instead of coming in. In Madrid, Ediciones Hoy had published *The Financier* in 1930 and *Jennie* in 1931, and thereafter Dreiser had received neither reports, royalties nor answers to his letters.

At the *Spectator* he toiled to get serious sociological articles, only to have Nathan and Boyd, both of whom he liked but considered fluffy, blackball them in favor of lighter material. Martha Aldrich's exposé of the telephone trust was rejected. He paid her out of his own pocket. He had her gather material against the Catholic Church—also rejected, indicating cowardice. Articles he had secured with great difficulty from Russia were turned down, as were pieces he had solicited from the Powys brothers and others. He had induced Sherwood Anderson to become a part-time *Spectator* editor in the vain hope that he would bolster Dreiser against the Nathan-Boyd combine. When an essay he persuaded Benjamin De Casseres to write on the dancer Shan-kar was rejected with the comment, "junk," he blew up. He wrote Nathan that he would resign unless changes were made, saying, "I refuse further to be a figurehead for something which misrepresents me entirely." [44]

Nathan and Boyd urged him to stay on. He did, but he induced Marguerite Tjader Harris, recently back from Europe, to watch rejections at the *Spectator* office for him. He now had Miss Light, Mrs. Harris, Miss Aldrich, Mrs.

Campbell, Miss Tatum, Miss Clark and Miss McCoy doing chores for him. Possibly he reasoned that this was enough. When Lina Goldschmidt arrived in New York after fleeing Germany, she wired him:

. . . WOULD BE DELIGHTED TO SEE YOU MY ADDRESS HOTEL BREVOORT.[45]

Did he also hold the Nobel failure against her? He had his secretary write her that "he is evidently out of the city." Although he dictated other letters that day and immediately thereafter, not until twelve days later did he write the woman who had befriended him, and then with icy repulse. To Isobel Sperry he wrote:

"Your probably not unaware that your something of a puzzle to me & quite a little something of a problem. For you are 17. And I am—well, no matter." He commented on her earlier letter saying she was close to her mother. "It troubled me not a little. . . . I am still wondering as to whether the same dual arrangement still holds. For the law says that girls under 21 do not know their own minds. . . . Which raises the question of what sort of girl you are personally—all by your lone. Of what are you thinking. How personally dreaming. And are you really & truly your own master or mistress rather. . . . A single bit [of] personal conversation might help to clarify that but would you be indulging in it of your own free will or with permission or what. It sounds very severe doesn't it. But it's less than that—a lot —and very honest. . . ."[46]

George Douglas visited him in December. For the thoughtful Douglas he had conceived a passionate fondness similar to that he held for John Cowper Powys and Kyllmann and which lasted only with people he saw infrequently. He had rashly urged Douglas to quit his Los Angeles job and come east to be an editor of the *Spectator*—a proposal Douglas wisely declined, for the *Spectator*'s days were numbered. But Dreiser was such a devoted host that Douglas wrote, "What might have been simply a trip to New York turned out to be the turning point in a life of many minor turns. I awoke to find myself appreciated beyond anything I had dared to dream. . . ."[47]

Early in January Dreiser himself resigned from the *Spectator*. He had stayed almost a year and a half—a long span for him—lavishing time and energy on it when money was becoming important. He was also expending efforts to finding publishers for books by perfect strangers, trying to secure a Guggenheim fellowship for the artist Hubert Davis, composing angry letters about the Terre Haute committee that had raised $35,000 for a Paul Dresser memorial and had done nothing with it for years, and many social-protest causes such as that of a man imprisoned in the West, he believed for political reasons. He was dickering with three Hollywood agents, Robert Thornby, Vivian Gaye and Leo Morrison, in an effort to sell something to the films. He was writing elaborate letters aimed at getting arbitrators to settle his dispute with the Liveright firm, and more letters to Europe trying to solve his publishing problems there. The words Miss Light sent out for him ran into the millions. He had an idea for a picture starring Lillian Gish, wiring her to telephone him at the Ansonia and unconscionably charging the telegram to the *Spectator*. When Samuel Goldwyn visited New York, Miss Light wired him:

MR. DREISER SUGGESTS THAT HE WRITE AN ORIGINAL SCRIPT FOR ANNA STEN.[48]

Goldwyn eluded the bait. Dreiser turned to Isobel Sperry:

"Have you money enough to come to New York as and when you wish or would you like an invitation. . . . Are you honest or the reverse, or indifferent. Truthful or merely a mental wrestler. You talk so wisely about man and woman, struggling, playing and living together after man and man have first contested to gain the woman. . . . I wonder truly what you expect to find in me. Is there a practical or romantic motive in all this or both. And practical or romantic do you envision youthful enthusiasm without much subtlety and so a quick surrender to the youthful woman of you? It seems heavily realistic to ask but after all you are boldly realistic. . . . But supposing—this being sight unseen—supposing you did not find me as interesting as you imagined? And I—well the reverse of this? Be sure of one thing. I would offer you a seat and conduct a cross examination. Or most decidedly I think I would. As opposed to that I read: 'Would we act as a great writer & his admirer or as man & woman,—two individuals?' " In a postscript he said he might have to leave town, adding, "If you are planning a contact you had better plan it on paper and soon. . . . All forces down." [49]

And to one of the many strangers who wrote Dreiser for financial help, Miss Light sent a routine reply:

> [Mr. Dreiser] feels that one of the most unfortunate things which has happened to him is the creation of a general impression that he is a person of wealth, since this is not true, and since it has led to requests of all kinds the necessary refusal of which has been responsible, in some cases, for ill-feeling.[50]

He dined with Fabri, who noted in his diary: "We went to the 77th Street Chinese place. . . . He likes Chinese food. . . . After dinner he started knocking the Jews, out of a clear sky. Hitler was right, he said. Something had to be done about this question. The Jews were all right but shouldn't live with the others. Let them have their own country. Not Palestine, he admitted—that was a difficult place, not the right place for a highly civilized race like the Jews. But England would be glad to create a large Jewish country in South Africa. Let the Jews all go there and be happy.

" 'The Jews are peculiar,' [Dreiser said]. 'I suggested this to a Jewess the other day. She's a very fine woman. She started to cry hysterically. She said I was just like the others—I hated the Jews too. Yet I don't hate them.'

"[Fabri asked him,] 'Do you think it is easy to give up one's home, one's native country and move to a new unknown place?'

" 'Why,' he said, 'the Jews are supposed to be very clever. They can create their own home anywhere in no time at all.' " [51]

To Isobel Sperry he wrote:

> If you come now it will have to be either Friday or Saturday Feb. 9 or 10, or Feb. 16–17. . . . Anyhow if you will come would you mind checking into this hotel [the Ansonia], that is taxing [*sic*] here & taking a room. I am in Room 1454 and once you were settled you could call me up and we could do our visiting comfortably. By the way, do you drive a car? And do you have a driver's license? . . .

> Your last letter makes me welcome the thought of talking things over. There are things to be presented by me which you would want to know I am sure. [52]

IV. THE CONTACT

In January Dreiser learned that the Indiana superintendent of public instruction had picked a list of fourteen famous Hoosier authors including Charles Major, Gene Stratton Porter, George Ade, Kin Hubbard, Claude Bowers and one Louis Ludlow, an Indiana Congressman. Dreiser went unmentioned—an asininity that inspired a story in the *Evansville Press* headed "Theodore Dreiser is Indiana's Forgotten Man." [53] He had Miss Light send for 25 copies to distribute among his friends, then soon left for a three-week motor trip with Helen to Florida, where he used the name Dresser. He had come to deplore the existence of many splinter left-wing groups ridiculing each other over Marxian interpretations "when the world situation and particularly the American situation requires a united front against the very obvious problem." [54] On his return he joined with Max Eastman in an effort to unify dissident radical organizations, starting with groups led by Alfred Bingham and A. J. Muste. It was his hope to weld them into a united front, with a vigorous publication representing them all. He had an innocent faith that if quarreling men could only be brought together, they could find agreement.

But Dreiser, too inflexible and impatient to be a conciliator, soon bowed out because of the very dissidence he was trying to heal. He was forever starting things he did not finish, plunging in with enthusiasm and retiring in disgust. Similarly, he had persuaded Sherwood Anderson, John Dos Passos and Carl Van Vechten to join him in writing a series of radical film scenarios, then cooled when they did not produce scripts quickly. To Dos Passos, who did prepare one and naturally wanted him to see it, he acted as if this would be doing him a favor, writing, "I do not object to looking at your script if you want me to do so," but pointed out the failure of the others. [55]

He was chagrined to discover that Isobel Sperry had visited New York during his absence, with a companion. He asked her to come again:

> But you should stick to your original suggestion and come alone. No harm is coming to you. . . . Anyhow give me preliminary notice. . . .

Three days later he wrote her in part, "Must you wait until Easter[?] I would like to know for I have various engagements. . . ." And five days after that:

> This last letter is charming—quite. . . . I wonder if you are as sweet as this little picture of you? If so your plenty sweet. . . . But I wish your possible dates weren't so few in number. Isn't there a train that leaves Saturday afternoon and gets here by six or seven? Then I could take you to a theatre or the opera. I say all this because this last letter is more girlish & yet wise and amusing and I think you must be good company. . . .[56]

Having seen *Tobacco Road*, he wrote the critics Brooks Atkinson, Percy Hammond, Robert Garland, John Mason Brown and Richard Watts, plus the Pulitzer Prize committee, urging that the play deserved the prize. He had added another agent, I. E. Chadwick, to the list of those representing him in Hollywood. He now gave each agent an exclusive option on one or more of his works for a month or two, then took it away if there were no results within that time. He was hoping to get $30,000 for *Tobacco*, $50,000 for *Sister Carrie* and proportionate prices for other works. But he was suspicious of all agents, angry when they asked him his price instead of relaying offers from the studios, convinced that they represented the studios more than he. Having so many agents, each of whom requested free copies of his books, ran into money. To Leo Morrison he wrote, "They are all available in book stores. . . ."[57]

His February royalty check from the reorganized Liveright firm was a shocking $31.55. Although he was selling occasional articles and stories, there were some rejections and he got modest payments for those he sold. His income by now must have been lower than his expenses, requiring him to draw on capital. His arbitration case with Liveright dragged on, one of the difficulties being in getting a trio of suitable arbitrators in addition to expert witnesses to bolster his case. To Isobel Sperry, who had written that she would make an Easter visit to New York, he replied eagerly, "I shall be here Friday, Saturday, Sunday & Monday—so—if you are coming any one of those days you will find me," and reminded her again, "I will be in the Ansonia Hotel. Suite 1454."[58]

His old friend William Lengel had left *Cosmopolitan* to become an editor of *Liberty*, which had rejected two of his stories, "Mathewson" and "A Start in Life." Arnold Gingrich of *Esquire* had then bought "Mathewson," but "A Start in Life" was still going the rounds unsold on April 3 when he sent Lengel a third story. He was not above pressuring Lengel and fibbing to him about the success of the other two:

> Here is something which I highly esteem but which Liberty may dislike. . . . At any rate the price is $500—check on acceptance. At the moment I know where I can sell it, hence the take it or leave it sound of this although I'm not writing in that spirit. *Mathewson* went to Esquire for $600—and the story I sent you, A Start in Life, to Collier's for the same sum.[59]

Esquire had paid him $400, not $600, and not until three months later was "A Start in Life" sold to *Scribner's* for $275.

When Isobel Sperry knocked at his door over the Easter weekend, one can be sure that the aging satyr was in transports. Although he wrote her later that she had a "clear, charming, vari-coloured mind" and was "an armful of sweet girlieness," it was evident that the contact (to use Dreiser's delicate term) was not entirely successful. Miss Sperry was on her guard. She stayed only briefly. She did indeed have a practical motive. Wanting badly to become an actress, she sought his aid in getting a start. In his letter he invited her to come again, suggesting that he might introduce her to Cheryl Crawford in New York and Jasper Deeter of Hedgerow, but holding these out as inducements for her return rather than flat promises.

Her reply wounded him because she pressed him about the theater connections without dwelling on his own charm. He did not answer until she appealed to him again, when he wrote:

> [My letter] expressed the warm liking that your personality evoked. Yours was a most reserved and formal request for some service in connection with Jasper Deeter. Naturally I drew the obvious conclusion. You were interested to the service point—on my side. But no more. But you see I am not looking for that sort of a relationship. I can be useful to all sorts of people if I choose so to be. But I do not achieve my friendships—or my affections through usefulness. If you harbor such a thought dismiss it. . . .
>
> I fancied from what you said (certainly not by the length of time you staid [*sic*]) that you were a little interested in me personally. But that illusion being dispelled I saw no reason for writing or further seeking to interest you. Likings are fairly instant. If they are not—well—in my case I am not moved to a long pursuit. . . . You do not look to me to be anyone who could be taken by pleas. You certainly neither act nor talk so. Hence—with me—or perhaps I had best say us—it is a matter of quick understanding or nothing. Besides I recall that in several of your earlier letters you laid special stress on your wonder as to whether our contact would provoke an instant man-woman fever. I can't quote you but it's in several letters. When that— judging by your first letter appeared to have failed—I decided as I say that you were not interested. Hence as they say—that's that.
>
> Please don't feel that this letter is an effort to provoke or persuade to [*sic*] you toward a friendlier reaction . . . the one contact passes for me automatically into the limbo of the forgotten. My life is not limited. It's full. If yours is full of vivid and amusing as well as comforting contacts and you do not like me, you do not need me. So—. But I compliment you on youth, charm, gaiety, mentality.[60]

This was the Dreiser whose sympathy for Carrie, Jennie and Roberta was so sublime. When Miss Sperry wrote in puzzlement at his anger and his refusal to perform the service, he replied:

> Yours is the letter that leaves me puzzled. I can clear up everything for both of us, I think, by saying that I want nothing of you. Now you tell me

what it is you want of me. A letter to Mr. Deeter? I will write it. What else? Such courtesies attended to I think we can let the contact rest there can't we.[61]

V. THE DRY-ICE POLITICIAN

Perhaps unknown to himself, Dreiser had evolved a new and eclectic political ideology. Although it was laden with contradictions and subject to sudden change, there were certain constants in it reflecting his own sentimentalities and violences. It was metaphysical rather than practical, emotional rather than logical, subjective rather than objective. It contained the following peculiar elements:

A burning hatred for the rich, for capitalists.

A tender sympathy for the masses in the abstract.

A simultaneous suspicion of the masses in actuality.

A Nietzschean belief in the superman, complicated by the conviction that he was one of them.

A fear that his supermanship was unrecognized, that he was sinking into financial, artistic and social failure.

A resulting compulsion to leap before the public in articles, lectures and statements often ill-advised, bellicose and misinformed.

His hatred for the rich contained an element of admiration and envy. The hatred had waned noticeably in the period of his own affluence, and had exploded anew as his corporate worth diminished. He had played the capitalist game to the hilt while he was part of it. One feels that his sympathy for the masses was enhanced when he had to leave the Rodin studio and dismiss two of his servants.

Nevertheless, his abstract tenderness for humanity was sincere and sometimes proven. The poverty of the Kentucky miners had shaken him. He took time to send kindly letters of encouragement to strangers who wrote him in despair. He gave money to Emma Goldman and a few others. As often, however, he was stingy, suspicious and contemptuous of "the people," whom he identified with Mickey Mouse, and his direct relations with them at times were unpleasant. Convinced that they were out to swindle him, he was hard on servants, laborers, auto mechanics and tradesmen. He was alternately generous and churlish toward his own relatives. He was so wary of the Mt. Kisco grocer that he would thrust his nose into the scales to see that the weight of beans was not one bean short.

Over the years he had seen superman qualities in such disparate characters as William Jennings Bryan, Cowperwood-Yerkes, Witla-Dreiser, Jacques Loeb and Charles Fort. Now he saw evidences of the superman in Stalin—even a trifle in Hitler and Roosevelt. In his attitude toward Russia was a strong flavor of religious ecstasy, a vision of a state struggling for equity under the leadership of a titan. Dictatorship did not trouble him so long as the dictator was holy, for did not the mob have to be led? Typically, he remembered once having seen Stalin in a Moscow cinema, his eyes filled with tears over a film depicting Russian sacrifices in the war.[62] Stalin was a humanitarian, making human errors but moving toward perfection—and he eliminated the capitalist as he laid down the law for the masses to follow for their own good. The Russians praised Dreiser, comparing him with Dostoyevsky. In capitalist America praise was conspicuously lacking.

In *Tragic America* his complaint was that the nation had abandoned the Constitution and its promise of freedom and democracy. But Dreiser, with his disdain for the proletarian mind, did not really believe in democracy or the Constitution. What could one expect of the Mickey Mouse addicts and their misuse of the vote?

The suffering of the thirties caused millions to seek solutions, to look for leaders. In Dreiser one sees a man driven by primal passions he could neither govern nor analyze—impulses he tried vainly (though he thought successfully) to clothe in logic. His bumbling sincerity could also hide an underlying ruthlessness. The qualities he admired in Roosevelt were those of the superman destroying ancient fallacies and smiting the topdog. The despot in him spoke when he telegraphed the President to close Ford's factories and salesrooms, urging, "Use your official powers in full and dictatorially for its effect on the American people. The legal technicalities can be brushed away afterwards."

It spoke also in his guarded admiration for Hitler, who at any rate hated the English and faced the "Jewish problem" squarely.

In these years Dreiser was a frustrated ex-artist and ex-capitalist, an angry, confused man, dwindling in wealth and prestige. He yearned for attention, even political power, fumbling for it in lectures, the *Spectator*, the abortive Dreiser Clubs, and by mailing out broadsides of his political writings. He was unaware that he was motivated as much by resentment as by benevolence, convinced that he was working for the good and the beautiful. He had never forgotten nor forgiven the humiliation of picking coal from the tracks in Indiana. His knowledge of politics was in the airplane-and-dry-ice category. That such a psychopathic potpourri of prejudice and zeal could have been considered seriously as wisdom came about because of his deserved fame as a compassionate novelist, his stentorian volume and the confusion of the times. Given any sort of following, he could have been a dangerous man—the emotional visionary. Luckily, a conviction was growing that there was something wrong with him. Yet he would remain for the rest of his life the loudest and strangest literary voice in America.

8. The Inner Sanctum

I. MAE WEST AND SOCIAL REFORM

For five years John Cowper Powys had quit the lecture trail, lived with a woman friend and an ancient cocker spaniel in a remote cottage near Hillsdale, and written *Wolf Solent* and *A Glastonbury Romance*. Having a horror of linen, he would blanch if confronted at dinner with a linen napkin. Kindly, indomitable, he took a daily enema, prayed for Llewelyn's health and for the trout in a nearby pool, worshiped trees and stones and shunned God. He lay flat on his back to ease ulcer pains as he worked on his autobiography. He had selected gravesites on the property for himself and his companion. Now, however, he planned to return to England with her.

Dreiser, who felt that his fondness for Powys and Kyllmann proved that he was not anti-English, just as his liking for Dr. Brill and Jerome Blum exploded the idea that he was anti-Semitic, wrote Powys:

> What about your graves in front of the house? If you really are not coming back and will have no use for them, I have a couple of people I'd like to bury there.[1]

To Sulamith Ish-Kishor, writing a biography of Hadrian, he gave warm encouragement. He had a habit of touching her arms or shoulders in a way suggesting romantic inquiry, which she politely discouraged though she was overwhelmed by his kindness. He told her matter-of-factly that he was impotent. At lunch they discussed reincarnation and mental telepathy. Referring to Hadrian's deification of Antinous, Dreiser said, "I do think it possible for human beings to be gods."

"I think you are," Miss Ish-Kishor said.

He modestly disclaimed godhood, though he thought Paul Robeson might qualify.[2] Early in April he traveled by bus to lecture at Bennington College and Haverhill, Massachusetts, taking with him Matthew Josephson's *The Robber Barons*, another assault on capitalism. He was dickering with several publishers and asking Leo Morrison what Hollywood might offer for a picture idea starring Mae West. When Morrison replied with great interest, Dreiser said he would not send an outline without first getting an offer, then later admitted, "There is really nothing I can say about the Mae West story, since it isn't ready now—not yet on paper, even."[3] Later he wrote Louise Campbell, "Give me an idea for a movie for Anna Sten and another for Mae West. If I put them over I'll pay you [a] commission. I understand that

$25,000 is now *top* for almost any picture." [4] To another Hollywood agent, Al Kingston, from whom he received a $35,000 offer for *Sister Carrie*, he suggested otherwise. "Fifty thousend [*sic*] less your ten percent," he wired Kingston firmly. "No Hollywood book-keeping for me." [5]

The strange birth of that novel 34 years earlier, with Arthur Henry spurring him on, must have come vividly to mind when Henry died June 2 at Narragansett Pier. A brilliant conversationalist, he had been far less successful as a writer than his clever third wife, Clare Kummer, who would later cross Dreiser's path again.

He had occasional dinner meetings at Lüchow's with Sherwood Anderson. Sometimes Helen and Mrs. Anderson were with them, though Helen might as well have been absent, since Dreiser ignored her. "Everybody was sorry for her," Mrs. Anderson recalled.[6] Late in June Dreiser traveled to Pennsylvania to see the premiere of Anderson's dramatization of *Winesburg* at the Hedgerow, now the nation's best-known repertory theater. He thought the play "interesting, but somehow I question popularity for it unless it is pulled together more." He found a young woman there more intriguing, taking her back with him to Esherick's, where Anderson, his wife, his mother-in-law, Mrs. B. E. Copenhaver, and members of the cast were staying for the weekend. The place being crowded, Dreiser slept outside with his new friend. In the morning, a group including the Anderson party and the Eshericks were breakfasting at an outdoor table when Dreiser appeared. He shambled across the lawn, clad only in his bathrobe, which was wide open, exposing him from chin to ankles. "Disgusting," Mrs. Copenhaver murmured, and fled. Dreiser, apparently unconscious of the display, wandered into the house.[7] Anderson, always one to improve on a story, would later write that Dreiser took off his bathrobe before the group while a youngster present gave him a bath with the garden hose.

The Russians by now had published all of Dreiser's important books, selling them by the tens of thousands without so much as a by-your-leave. Since there was no publishers' convention between the two countries, they had paid him no royalties except for a $1,000 payment for *A Gallery of Women* and a few small token payments after he had complained strenuously to Dinamov and others. Now they expressed interest in his *Tobacco* scenario, as yet unpublished and unsold. Dreiser replied to L. Cherniavsky, an official of the Soviet Society for Cultural Relations, that it was time they showed a spirit of mutual assistance:

> I have been called upon by the militant communists of this country to perform every known service from writing and speaking to entering dangerous areas in order to bring about favorable results for mistreated and injured American workers, and always at my expense. . . . I am constantly being called upon by Russian newspapers and various organizations to submit opinions, articles, and what-not to their publications and causes without any return to me whatsoever.[8]

Indeed his replies to Russian requests had cost him heavily in cable charges, an expense he now eliminated by arranging through the Soviet consul in New York for Russian payment of his cables. Continuing hitches in the Liveright arbitration kept him hamstrung, preventing his association with a new publisher who would advertise and distribute his books. "Further delays can do me more harm than anything else at present," he wrote his attorney, Hume.[9] Another upset was the departure in June of Evelyn Light, his highly efficient secretary for three years, to be replaced by Henrietta Helston. Deciding to augment his slumping income by more lecturing, he quit the Pond bureau and signed up with Ernest Briggs, insisting on a $500 fee and on dignified promotion cards rather than the usual handbills.

He tried to get Howard Scott to help him with an article on Technocracy. He wrote the secretary of the Committee for Unified Action for A Man of Plenty [sic], advocating the union of dissident groups and adding, "Personally I believe that the key organization in the whole business should be Technocracy, although it might be surrounded and aided by many other organizations. . . ." [10] Still intrigued by the thought of leadership and power, he sent a trial balloon to a man who urged that he stand for office: "I might be willing to run for Governor of the State of New York, but I see no evidence of any following that will put me on the ticket. . . ." [11] To Izvestia, which asked him for a 150-word statement and got 550 words, he paraded his familiar grudges. He called the American social system "rotten to the core," assailed organized religion, the "[l]oafers, wasters, sybarites, enthroned as Lords and Kings," and said America made democracy safe only for "the Standard Oil Company, Telephone Trust, the Power Trust, the Railroad Trust, the Steel Trust, the Aluminum Trust, the Food and Textile Trusts . . . exacting, as might any tyrant in any part of the world, all that the traffic will bear. . . ." [12]

Speaking to a meeting of the A.C.L.U., he said that Roosevelt's program needed more teeth: "No man should be allowed millions—not even one million—while other people starve. There should be a readjustment of this Government . . . in favor of the mass, and this particular capitalistic crowd now entrenched in wealth and power and in control of the principal functions and forces of this government, should be swept away." [13]

One listened in vain for the specific, down-to-earth, workable political program. But if audiences heard nothing constructive, they were perhaps struck by Dreiser's arresting personality—his bulk, his obvious sincerity, his attitude of the child discovering evil, his bohemian reputation—which made him a spectacle apart from what he said.

"When I get to the point where I don't find [life] interesting," he told reporters at his sixty-third birthday, "I'll get out of it." "Remember, I wrote the 'American Tragedy' when I was fifty-seven *. . . . I believe that my best

* He started An American Tragedy at fifty and was fifty-four when it was published.

work is ahead of me. . . . A few people, a few hundred, own all the real wealth in America. . . . The small stockholders are wiped out—I lost $300,-000 in a few days. . . ." "Millionaires? They're petty, pathetically dumb, hams of the purest ray." [14]

II. RENEWED HOMAGE

Although the Reswick lawsuit was ultimately dropped, Dreiser was surrounded by troubles real and imaginary. He had found a satisfactory new publisher in Hungary, but matters with the important German-language publisher, Zsolnay in Vienna (a Jew, he noted), were more snarled than ever. He had employed a German attorney, Dr. L. Mohrenwitz, to investigate the problem on the spot, then had quarreled with Mohrenwitz, who threatened to sue him for his fee. Dreiser then retained a Viennese attorney, Maurice Deutsch, who informed him that Zsolnay owed him between 50,000 and 70,000 schillings. But Dreiser balked at Deutsch's proposed settlement, suspecting that Deutsch was in league with Zsolnay. There was the further difficulty of getting any money out of Austria, which had placed a moratorium on foreign payments. [15]

Other troubles arose from his suspicions, which at times reached alarming proportions. He had turned against H. S. Kraft, of whom he had been so fond. "Kraft was out in Hollywood," he wrote Goldberg, ". . . trying to put over a love version of TOBACCO and incidentally a stage dramatization of SISTER CARRIE for which he has no authority. . . . I have a feeling that one of these days we may have to deal with him in the matter of infringement." [16] When he learned that Anna Sten's new picture concerned tobacco farming, he wrote the *World-Telegram:*

> Will you be so good as to advise the title of Anna Sten's new picture and also by whom it was written? . . .
> This is the story of a tobacco farmer, but would it be possible for you to advise as to the nature of the story, that is, what phase of tobacco is employed?
> Has H. S. Kraft anything to do with the story? [17]

He was informed that the picture had no similarity to his own scenario. No payment had been received from Schulberg for Dreiser's percentage of the profits from *Jennie Gerhardt,* though Schulberg had sent statements showing that there were no profits to distribute. Dreiser contemplated a suit against Paramount for an accounting of the earnings. Hearing that Universal's picturization of Fannie Hurst's *Back Street,* which had a kept-woman theme, was much like *Jennie Gerhardt,* he proposed another lawsuit even before seeing *Back Street.* He wrote Hume, "If it is as much of a swipe as I am told we will bring an action against Paramount [he meant Universal] and Fannie

Hurst." [18] When he saw *Back Street* he was so convinced of the theft that he had Hume write Universal, charging infringement. Universal's attorney pointed out that *Back Street* was published in 1930, that the film followed it closely, and added, "Circumstances such as these naturally give rise to serious question as to the good faith of your client's claim. We wish to state definitely and finally that we have no intention of even discussing any adjustment with Mr. Dreiser." [19]

At a lake near Wilkes-Barre, Pennsylvania, young Robert Edwards had murdered his pregnant ex-sweetheart, Freda McKechnie, when he became enamored of another girl. The case was promptly called another "American Tragedy." Dreiser, as an authority, contracted to do a series of articles about it for the *New York Post* syndicate and also a piece for *Mystery Magazine*. He left for Wilkes-Barre on September 7 with his secretary, Miss Helston, soon to be followed by Helen in another car. Since *Mystery Magazine* was paying his expenses, he listed expenditures for himself and both women, including tire repairs and "5.25 for drinks." Still a third woman became involved—Louise Campbell, who polished his copy for him. Immensely interested in the case, he thought Edwards less a callous killer than a victim of baleful American social pressures as Clyde Griffiths was—trapped by "the very chemical and physical influences which betray all of us" [20]—and wrote 40,000 words which *Mystery Magazine* would later have to cut drastically even though it ran the piece in five instalments. He forwarded copies of his sympathetic analysis to Pennsylvania's governor and pardon board in a vain effort to save Edwards, who later was electrocuted. He then composed a piece about actual "American Tragedy" murder cases in general, one so replete with factual errors about the various cases—even his own Gillette case—that Lengel, to whom he sent it, returned it with candid comments about his carelessness. [21]

Indeed Dreiser was now so irresponsible about fact as to be an editorial risk. His one-man-against-the-world complex also allowed him occasional latitude with truth. After lying habitually to scores of women for forty years, it is not surprising that his equivocations at times extended into one other field, that of money, where he was the prey of his own insecurity. Yet in most other respects he was painfully honest. When he died, one feels that he was less an intentional liar than he was gripped by that self-protective disposition common among extreme egocentrics. In sex, the same egocentricity allowed him full license while denying it to others. To a girl who was pursuing him, he wrote:

> The trouble with you is not that you are a bad girl but rather an unthinking and indiscreet one. Granting that you are a pagan and that you feel that you can do as you please, sexually and in every other way, it might occur to you that you cannot just plunge madly into every man's life and assume that because of your physical and mental charm you can have your way. . . . [22]

In September, after more than a year, the Liveright arbitration case was settled in a fashion that distressed Dreiser. He had to pay $6,500 instead of $2,000 for his plates, and also what he felt an exorbitant price for the 13,000 copies of his books. He was not yet out of the legal woods with the Liveright firm, which claimed he owed them for advances paid on the promised novel which was never delivered, but he was now free to find another publisher. He had complained of Liveright's extravagance, insisting he wanted a one-horse publisher interested only in art. He had complained of his dealings with Jews. Now, surely, he would affiliate with a small, earnest, gentile firm—for example, Coward-McCann, one of those who sought him.

Instead, he signed a contract with Simon & Schuster, the most flamboyant publisher of the Thirties, just as Liveright was of the Twenties.

There were contributing factors. Simon & Schuster made a great fuss over him. They satisfied that old Dreiser *idée fixe*, promising a uniform edition of his works. He was susceptible to flattery and also to their $5,000 advance. But fundamentally Dreiser loved showy self-advertisement as strongly as he claimed to detest it. He signed up with Erich Posselt of the International Literary Bureau, who handled the new contract and who Dreiser hoped could unsnarl his European publishing birdsnest. Simon & Schuster burst out with prideful advertisements saying, "The works of THEODORE DREISER, past, present, and future, will henceforth be published by SIMON AND SCHUSTER," listing his 21 books, describing him as a "[t]rue genius" whose fame was "an unshakable bulwark" and declaring, "No higher privilege has ever been granted the INNER SANCTUM, [who] undertake the responsibility in a spirit of homage and affection." [23] M. Lincoln Schuster wrote Dreiser, "I took 'Moods' out to the country and want to tell you at once how deeply I was affected by many of the poems. . . . It is an outpouring selfhood. . . ." and ended, "With renewed homage, I am, yours as ever." [24]

Dreiser replied delightedly, "Your reaction to MOODS was to me a revealing document in itself. At long last I am happy to know that I have a publisher who speaks my own language. . . ." [25]

Nor is there any record that he protested when Simon & Schuster proposed a huge blowout at Iroki celebrating the marriage, though he would have been within his rights to refuse the use of his estate for such capitalistic extravagance while people were starving. He sweated over a guest list of some 200: film bigwigs such as Jacob Wilk and J. Robert Rubin; columnists including Arthur Brisbane, O. O. McIntyre, F. P. A. and Harry Hansen; theater personages of whom a few were the Gish sisters, Libby Holman, Jasper Deeter, Elmer Rice, Maxwell Anderson and Miriam Hopkins; the dancers Ruth St. Denis and Angna Enters; artists including Ralph Fabri, Hubert Davis, Wayman Adams and Wharton Esherick; shoals of critics including John Chamberlain, Robert van Gelder, Heywood Broun, Joseph Wood Krutch, Lewis Gannett, J. Donald Adams and Alexander Woollcott; dozens of book people, among them Ben Huebsch, Alfred Knopf, Bennett Cerf, Donald Friede,

William Soskin and Harold Guinzburg; magazine editors including Henry Hazlitt, Arnold Gingrich, Henry Seidel Canby, Herschel Brickell and Frank Crowninshield; and the writers Erskine Caldwell, Sean O'Casey, Sherwood Anderson, Max Eastman, Floyd Dell, John Dos Passos, W. E. Woodward and many others. Psychiatry was represented by Dr. Brill; the law by Arthur Carter Hume and Arthur Garfield Hays; music by Maria Samson, Olin Downes and Lillian Rosedale Goodman (who as the young Lillian Rosenthal had criticized *Jennie Gerhardt*); and Technocracy by Howard Scott. Although there was a strong deputation of leftists, Dreiser appears not to have invited Earl Browder or William Z. Foster.[26]

Simon & Schuster sent out the invitations on rich gray double-fold paper with the name "Iroki" engraved in blue, reading:

> Simon and Schuster, on the occasion of becoming the publishers of Theodore Dreiser, request the pleasure of your attendance at Mr. Dreiser's home, Iroki, The Old Road, Mt. Kisco, on Sunday afternoon, after three o'clock.

The Inner Sanctum's Clifton Fadiman (who had noted that "The fear of poverty is the central drive behind [Dreiser's] entire career as an artist" [27]) ordered Hearn's to deliver a truckload of spirits, Prohibition now being ended. Helen dealt with the caterer, hired three butlers and bought 300 pounds of ice, which was stored in Dreiser's six-foot bathtub.

"There were at least 50 cars parked," Fabri noted when he arrived, and more were streaming in. "Helen looked stunning in her Russian dress. Teddy was on the verge of being cockeyed already. He cried when Maria [Samson] sang." Since many of those invited were twosomes, the guests numbered almost 300. Dreiser, who regarded Hubert Davis as an unsung genius and had written Earl Browder and others in an effort to get him a trip to Russia, took Davis around, introducing him as "one of the greatest artists in America." [28] Later in the afternoon a couple of drunks were loaded into taxis, but in general the party was pleasant if noisy, the houses jammed and the overflow guests gathering outside in nippy autumn weather.

III. THE GUN IS LOADED

Dreiser had let *The Stoic* slide as he worked on magazine pieces and contemplated novels about Madalynne Obenchain, a California lady accused of murder, and Harry New, another alleged slayer, sending for newsclippings on both cases. Now he was busy finishing the five-parter for *Mystery Magazine*, after which he was due to resume the half-finished *Stoic* for his new publisher.

In November, Burton Rascoe mistakenly wrote in his introduction to the *Smart Set Anthology*, "Mencken broke with Dreiser, because Dreiser would not contribute to a fund to defend *The American Mercury*" (when it was banned in Boston). He went on to make other erroneous statements about Knopf and the other two, ending, "That's Dreiser's side of the break with Mencken as Dreiser related it to me." Knopf sent a copy of this to Dreiser without comment.[29] Dreiser immediately wrote Rascoe, "What the devil do you mean by imagining things and putting them in my mouth?"[30] He went on in kindly vein, asking Rascoe to correct the errors, which he did. Dreiser got an appreciative note from Knopf. And he received his first letter in almost nine years from Henry Louis Mencken in Baltimore, thanking him and adding:

> I am seriously thinking of doing my literary and pathological reminiscences, probably in ten volumes folio. This is my solemn promise to depict you as a swell dresser, a tender father, and one of the heroes of the Argonne.[31]

This was a note that had been missed. Dreiser replied with stiffness and uncertainty but with longing:

> Dear Mencken:
> Thanks.
> It pleases me that my rating is no worse, and I doubt that I need reassure you of my unchanging respect and good will.
> I assume that you are not often in New York, but if and when you are—we might meet, white flag in hand. A genial, if visibly armed neutrality. . . .
> Helen and I still hold together. Mt. Kisco is a very lovely place—guest rooms and all conveniences. Three days a week—sometimes four, I am here at the Ansonia—sometimes alone, sometimes with Helen. Whether alone or with your wife you are welcome. And to assemble a congenial half dozen is no trouble whatsoever.[32]

At fifty in 1930, Mencken had astonished the world by marrying the fragile Sara Haardt. His *American Mercury*, the sensation of the Twenties, had skidded badly and passed out of his editorship in 1933 because of the depression and his refusal to take it seriously. He had broken with his two oldest friends, Dreiser and Nathan, and missed them both. He seconded Dreiser's suggestion that they dine together, writing, "I enclose a recent portrait, so that you may recognize me."[33] The picture was that of a tottering, white-bearded octogenarian.

Early in December, Arnold Gingrich, who made monthly story-hunting trips to New York from his *Esquire* post in Chicago, arranged to take Dreiser to dinner. When he arrived at the Ansonia suite, Dreiser met him in the hall in some trepidation. "Mencken is here," he said. "We haven't spoken in years. Come and help us break the ice."

He and Mencken were drinking vodka, and Gingrich was given a third glass. "I was only 30," Gingrich recalled. "I sat there tongue-tied between these two contentious giants."

Mencken said they should dine at Luchow's. Dreiser was in favor of Suesskind's—much closer. Mencken said the beer and sausages were infinitely superior at Luchow's. Disputing amiably about this, Chicago's status as the Athens of the West and other subjects, they attacked another bottle of vodka. After two hours, Gingrich had to forego dinner and catch a plane to Chicago.[34]

The friendship between these two, both of whom had known great vogue and had seen it dwindle, was resumed, but it would never be the same. The battle for art that once had united them was over, Dreiser had become a world-saver, and they disagreed about almost everything. Mencken, amused by Dreiser's habit of reading sociological messages into sensational crimes, could not see that Robert Edwards was a victim of peculiarly American social forces. "The truth is," he wrote, "that society is probably fundamentally wise in putting its Edwardses to death. After all, they are decidedly abnormal, and when they live their careers are commonly very costly to the rest of us." [35]

But sentiment there was on both sides. Dreiser at once leaned on Mencken for advice, sensing in him a practical wisdom lacking in himself. When Henry Seidel Canby (who had been invited to the Simon & Schuster party) wrote Dreiser that as a "leading American novelist" he had been proposed for membership in the National Institute of Arts and Letters and would certainly be elected if willing,[36] he was tempted even though Nathan had always scoffed at the Institute as the "Young Men's Canby Association." He was even then contemplating having a new head of himself done by the sculptor Onorio Ruotolo. His yearning for recognition was shadowed by a natural resentment that it had been withheld so long. He wrote Mencken:

> You are more familiar with this Association than I am. I wish you would tell me what you think of this request and whether my rejection of it will do more harm than good. I ask that because in some instances where I have felt fully justified in ignoring a request of this kind I have aroused a fairly lasting bitterness that shows itself in the public as well as the personal reactions of some when I encounter them.[37]

Mencken replied:

> [Canby's] letter offers you a great honor, and if you were a man properly appreciative you'd bust into tears. The National Institute of Arts and Letters includes all of the greatest authors of the country. Prominent among its members are: Louis Bromfield, Stephen Vincent Benét, Struthers Bart [sic], Owen Davis, Edna Ferber, Herman Hagedorn, Don Marquis, Ernest Poole and Agnes Repplier. One of the most eminent members is Hamlin Garland, whose efforts to put down "The 'Genius'" you will recall. These great men and women now propose to lift you up to their own level, and I think you should be full of gratitude.[38]

Dreiser sent Canby a polite rejection, sticking by it despite a second Canby solicitation. A week later a report that the Hitler government had banned his works convinced him that the reason was the belief that he was Jewish. He was more interested in continuing a potentially profitable German sale than in withdrawing his books on principle from a country where savagery toward the Jews had become notorious. "What procedure could I apply," he asked Mencken, "to disabuse the authorities over there of the notion that I am Jewish?" [39] He sent a similar query to George Douglas the same day.

His attitude came out in the open when Hutchins Hapgood at last published his correspondence with Dreiser in *The Nation* under the title, "Is Dreiser Anti-Semitic?" [40] He did so with the permission of Dreiser, who was quite willing to stand behind his opinions. His communist brethren had closed their eyes to his earlier *Spectator* statements, Dreiser being so useful to them, but this new and sharper blast could not be ignored. One can envision tense conferences at the communist Thirteenth Street headquarters under Alexander Trachtenberg, the powerful Yale-educated party member known as Moscow's "Cultural Commissar" to the United States. How to coax the temperamental novelist to retract without antagonizing him? Dreiser was invited to call at the *New Masses* office and clarify his position.

Trachtenberg, Joshua Kunitz, Mike Gold and a few others were present when he arrived. "Dreiser was drunk," Kunitz recalled. "He came lunging in, his face flushed, wearing a rakishly flamboyant suit and hat. He had a challenging bravado under which I sensed a feeling of guilt. He behaved like a child."

He lurched up to Trachtenberg, a little round man who looked like a Turk, and tried to pull his mustache.

"Where is the stiletto?" he demanded. "Where is the stiletto?" [41]

It was evident that constructive talk was impossible. Later, a deputation including John Howard Lawson, Henry Hart, James W. Ford and Orrick Johns went to see him at Iroki. "Dreiser was absolutely infuriated," Lawson recalled, "when someone suggested that he might be getting old." [42] As the *New Masses* later put it, "It was only with the greatest hesitation, with continual shifting of his position, with the use of analogies which have their roots in hoary fable and race-hatred, with repeated confusion of the interests of the Jewish masses with those of the Jewish masters, that Mr. Dreiser came around to see a few of the contradictions involved in his stand, and eventually acknowledged that, with fascist gangsters on every hand encouraging the same ideas, his words had a widespread and dangerous effect." The *Masses* ended forgivingly, "We decline to believe that it will be impossible for Theodore Dreiser to regain his traditional place as a fighter for human liberty." [43]

Dreiser wrote a short statement appearing in the same issue that fell far short of the recantation expected. In fact, he retracted nothing, though he repudiated the use of his views by Nazi propagandists and wrote, "I have no hatred for the Jews and nothing to do with Hitler or fascism."

Mike Gold was so angry that, speaking for himself, he wrote a piece titled

"The Gun is Loaded, Dreiser," accusing him of nationalistic, fascist leanings and writing, "It is now my belief he can undo this damage only by years of devoted battle against anti-Semitism and Fascism." [44] But the party contented itself with slapping Dreiser's wrist, needing his voice even if his ideology was shaky.

It was shakier than they knew. "Personally, I despair of communistic efforts in this country," he had written Bruce Crawford. "There are too many groups, too much quarreling, and the mass sentiment of America seems to be more anti than pro." He saw hope in another direction. "Recently I have become interested in Technocracy as a way out; really a better way for American purposes I think than the various isms we have been following. The logic of it is so plain. . . ." [45]

IV. MOODS OVER *Moods*

The Dreiser-Simon & Schuster honeymoon suffered a rift when they planned publication of his revised *Moods*. During Fadiman's illness, his secretary, Margaret Halsey, wrote Dreiser that the book would run at least 535 pages. She suggested that it might be cut: "As you know, the normal maximum length for a book of verse is about half of this." [46] Dreiser replied:

> The maximum length of a book of verses or Moods may be, as you say, 217 pages [his arithmetic was in error]. Never-the-less, the original Moods as published by Liveright for me was 385 pages, which somehow conflicts with your maximum theory. . . .
>
> Perhaps Simon & Schuster have a maximum poetry book length, but if they have, they did not inform me of this when arranging my present contract with them. . . . [47]

Richard Simon wrote him a long, diplomatically worded letter pointing out that the book would sell better if shorter but assuring him that if he wanted it full length, "then we will certainly publish it just as it is." [48]

Dreiser replied that Simon & Schuster evidently did not understand or approve of his *Moods*. He suggested that the contract be revised so that some other publisher who did understand and like them could publish them, saying, "Decidedly . . . I am not interested in either a forced or half-hearted or anything less than a wholehearted endorsement of any volume that I propose to publish; nor am I to be turned over to minor secretaries with instructions as to what the Simon & Schuster book length for poetry is." [49]

Simon wrote to assure him that he had the firm's full sympathy, that they were launching a Dreiser "five-year plan" and could not agree to releasing *Moods* to another house. Dreiser's new novel, he added, would be a "red-letter day for American literature." There was another austere Dreiser letter and another careful Simon & Schuster reply before the matter was healed. *Moods* was eventually cut a trifle by Dreiser and Miss Ish-Kishor, but was still published at a hefty 424 pages. Among its contents was Dreiser's lift from Anderson's "Tandy."

Simon & Schuster's troubles were only beginning. In February Dreiser was stricken by grippe, then by bronchitis and mental depression. He lost 18 pounds. He was subject, he wrote George Douglas, to "the most amazing morbid fears. These began to descend in periods of from three to seven seconds, at most a minute in duration, but they were really startling and productive of a reflective depression, not an integral part of the seven seconds but the consequence of it. . . . I have been mentally startled and illuminated by something for which I have no words. Perhaps I might call it a sense of psychic earthquake as though something abysmal and final were first opening under or splitting once and for all the so-called conscious something which is me." [50]

He thought of entering a sanitarium. Instead, he left the Ansonia for good at the end of February and moved to Iroki for a rest. He was convinced that he was being systematically suppressed, writing, "For years I have had ample evidence that the Catholics were doing their best to stop not only the reading but the distribution of my books and I also know that in a given list of corporation [news]papers the use of even my name is out except for the purposes of attack. The *New York Times* for instance will use the name if it happens to be prominently identified with some public affair but no more. . . ." [51]

Although his illness suggested that he should narrow his activities and concentrate on his commitment to his publisher, he proposed to Mencken that they start a new magazine. Simon & Schuster were eager to get *The Stoic*, which he had contracted to deliver by the end of 1935. The trouble was, he was not interested in *The Stoic*. He was excited about his complex philosophical-scientific work, *The Formula Called Man*, for which he had been gathering material for years. He had sold occasional magazine articles based on his studies, one of them, "The Myth of the Creative Power of Man," being rejected by Charles Angoff of the *American Mercury* with the comment, "The plain fact is that I do not understand it. The chances are that many other people will not understand it either." [52]

He needed an admirer to work with him in completing *The Formula*. His specifications for such a collaborator had always been clear: he should be somewhat younger, enthusiastic, intelligent, less well known than himself, and imbued with a sense of Dreiser's genius and ready to put aside personal considerations to serve him. Through the years literally dozens of persons had filled these requirements, among them Arthur Henry, Mary Fanton Roberts, Mencken, Kirah Markham, Lengel, Sally Kusell and Louise Campbell. Now he selected George Douglas, with whom he felt on a basis of "psychic osmosis," even suggesting that Douglas quit his job and come east to aid in the work. Although he admitted that his finances were "not so hot as they were," he expected a film sale and would pay Douglas for his time, adding, "you would be the most stimulating, illuminating and corrective force that I could have." [53] Douglas, probably aware of his enthusiasms, politely declined such a step, and Mahomet thereupon decided that he would go to the mountain as soon as he could.

While recuperating at Iroki, he went on a science-philosophy regimen. He ordered Loeb's monographs on experimental biology, and *Forced Movements, Tropisms and Animal Conduct; The Organism as a Whole*, and *The Dynamics of Living Matter*, by the same author; Arthur Avalon's *The Principles of Tantra;* and popularized scientific pamphlets from General Motors. He visited the Rockefeller Institute for consultations with scientists. He wrote the Hearst science editor Gobind Behari Lal for information about the effect of gases "on the emotions or mental states of individuals," Robert Andrews Millikan for "evidence of disorder or chaos anywhere" in the universe, and the geneticist Calvin Bridges asking about microscopic processes and other things, urging Bridges, "Will you answer these questions for me quickly. . . ." [54]

After signing up with Ernest Briggs the previous summer and demanding fancy cards, he had delivered no lectures. Now, feeling better, he agreed to lecture at Northwestern University and the University of Chicago on consecutive April evenings, in part because he was eager to confer with scientists there. He warned that the auditorium must be acoustically good: "I cannot and will not strain at making myself heard." Before boarding a plane April 15, he had arranged to meet Dr. Arthur Compton, Dr. Harvey Lemon and at least one other physicist there, as well as to have cocktails with Arnold Gingrich.

At Gingrich's home on North State Parkway, the modernized mansion of a tycoon of the Yerkes era, Dreiser smiled and said, "You know, Gingrich, this house is much too good for you." He downed whiskey in such quantities that Gingrich ranked him near Sinclair Lewis as a tosspot and even became alarmed. How could he possibly deliver his scheduled lecture at Chicago University that evening? But Dreiser, with his great bulk, held his liquor well. As Gingrich drove him to the Midway campus, Dreiser noticed his 1934 Ford and said, "At least the car fits." [55]

When he finished his talk on realism and romanticism, a note from Bettina Morris, now living in Chicago, was handed him by a messenger. She invited him to call, writing, "Come now—you always were a good guy, so don't disappoint me and be up stage." [56] Dreiser, having a date with science, was forced once again to miss her. He was back at Iroki April 18. About a week later he left in the Chrysler for Los Angeles with Helen's sister Myrtle Patges, who wanted to go West, helping him with the driving.

9. Off in Betelgeuse

I. WITH GEORGE DOUGLAS

Dreiser stayed at Douglas' home on Westmoreland Avenue, west of the business district, shared expenses and thoroughly disrupted Douglas' life in a manner that the newspaperman fortunately enjoyed. He assumed that Douglas' chief interest in life was to aid the philosophy work, which luckily was true. The poetic, philosophic Douglas, a lover of San Francisco, was bored stiff in Los Angeles and welcomed the intrusion of a spirit so consonant and compelling. His two daughters were grown and his wife was visiting in San Francisco. Dreiser hired a secretary and a housekeeper and appropriated Douglas for philosophical discussion during his off-hours from the *Examiner* editorial job he hated.

Dreiser's aim was a philosophy of life based on mechanistic science but extended at unknown length by his own interpretations. Science alone did not satisfy him, since it ruled out the field of speculation in which he reveled and which he believed had validity if anything had validity. The world of reverie and intuition, the abstractions of good and evil, the mysteries of creation were at least as important to him as the life cycle of a crustacean, and if stuffy scientists feared to enter these arenas, he did not. He would bridge the gap between limited science and limitless speculation, giving due weight to the esoteric and the unperceived.

"There is a great deal to be said for non-science or non-truth," he had observed.[1]

In his inquiries he would employ biology, psychology, physics, astronomy and other sciences, along with speculations he much admired—Mark Twain's *What Is Man?* and *The Mysterious Stranger* among them—plus other commentaries including the writings of Charles Fort, Einstein, the *Bhagavad-Gita* and *Hey Rub-a-Dub-Dub*. No human being—least of all Dreiser—was competent for such a task, and academicians would throw up their hands at his methods. If he had doubts, they did not stop him. He so enjoyed this cosmic inquiry that he came near forgetting that he had contracted to finish *The Stoic* by the year's end. Apparently he did forget his agreement with Dr. Brill that they would publish jointly their conclusions about life. He had already published several magazine pieces embodying material discussed with Brill—"The Myth of Individuality" and "You, the Phantom" [2] among them—and was embodying or enlarging them in his projected book.

Had he been a trifle drunk when he made the agreement with Brill? Had it become lost in his enormous forgetfulness, or had he concluded that these

431

thoughts were, after all, his own? Brill, though puzzled and hurt, made no complaint. From Los Angeles Dreiser wrote to ask him about the functioning of the brain.[3] He denied any animus toward the Jews, writing Goldberg, "In spite of my alleged anti-semitism, I still pick and choose, as you know, and I would not trade one of my selection, for some ten thousand of another kind."[4]

He was concerned about the condition of the highly excitable Jerome Blum. Blum, wounded by his published remarks about Jews, had suggested that people born as German Catholics such as Dreiser might be exiled to Arkansas, and had added Gauguin's admonition: "Giant, you are mortal; that is enough to humble any man."[5] He had later gone violently insane and was now in an institution—a fate doubtless reserved for him in any case but which could nevertheless provoke sober thought on Dreiser's part. There were other disasters—the death on May 31 of Mencken's thirty-seven-year-old wife, the suicide in Hollywood six weeks later of Ray Long. This time, with Mencken, Dreiser observed the amenities he had neglected nine years earlier, sending a telegram followed by a sympathetic letter.

He ordered medicines from New York. He visited in Pasadena with Dr. Donald McCord, younger brother of the lamented Peter, and with Drs. Millikan, Bridges and other scientists at Caltech. Dreiser gazed at the stars from Mt. Wilson Observatory and saw General Electric's Magic Kitchen display at San Diego. He read Carrel's *Man the Uknown* and Dr. Lemon's *From Galileo to Cosmic Rays*, wrote Dr. Simon Flexner for information about the autonomic nervous system and the solar plexus and added, "Something creatively astounding seems to be waiting for proper biological, chemical and physical attention."[6] Pleading illness, he refused an Henri Barbusse plea that he attend a communist-sponsored Congress of International Writers in Paris.

Helen arrived in the Buick with Nick and discreetly rented a room near the Douglas home so she would not interfere with the project. Dreiser revived his plan for an intellectual monastery in New Mexico, enlisted the adored Douglas as a lay brother and half jokingly invited Mencken's membership. Responding to a dinner invitation, he wrote, "I am not very much interested in writers as table mates. I would much prefer a physicist, even a doctor, lawyer or prizefighter."[7] From M. Lincoln Schuster came the voice of contracts and obligations:

> In the world of letters there is . . . one ray of hope, and that is the prospect that you will soon be finished with the novel! Can we await any further news at this stage?[8]

"In regard to the book," Dreiser replied, "there is nothing that I care to say at this time, except that I am putting in full time every day. . . ."[9] He admitted that some of this time was expended not on the novel but on *The Formula Called Man*. Schuster, aware of the sales failure of *Hey Rub*, was faced by the worries that years earlier had plagued Liveright. He tried to show courteous interest in the philosophy at the same time that he delicately urged the importance of the novel. Dreiser promptly unloaded on him the job of unsnarling his publishing difficulties in Europe.

He had hoped that his agent, the International Literary Bureau, would free him from such worries. However, Thomas White of the bureau's Vienna office had looked into the Zsolnay situation and decided that Dreiser's previous emissary, Maurice Deutsch (whom Dreiser had distrusted), had made the best settlement possible with Zsolnay. White had managed to get a few payments through to Dreiser, but was recently unheard from. Dreiser had received a financial statement from the bureau which he could not understand. "A great deal of my time is being wasted," he wrote Schuster, "over a series of letters out of which I get nothing except further complications." [10]

The Simon & Schuster office took over the correspondence on these matters for study. Schuster seized the opportunity to write:

> I know you will not misinterpret the spirit that prompts this inquiry . . . we must look ahead and do the necessary advance planning, and as we are now shaping up our 1936 publication schedule, we are inquiring whether you care to report to us any further news on the novel. [11]

He must have been appalled by Dreiser's reply, which ignored *The Stoic* and indicated complete preoccupation with the philosophy book:

> There are some 30 topics or chapters that have to be dealt with. . . . Some 8 or 9 of the chapters are written. Once the data under each chapter-head is thoroughly digested the writing is nothing. I really hope to finish this book late this fall; but I do not believe it is advisable for you to publicize the subject. . . . [12]

From Dinamov in Moscow came another exhortation: "It has been several years already that the world has not tottered under the sledgehammer of your books. Strike, Theodore, give the world such a blow that it fails [*sic*] to its feet at the count of ten." [13]

Dreiser worked with a religious ardor. "Awe and reverence . . . walk with deep understanding," [14] he wrote after gazing through the Mt. Wilson telescope. "Every great man is fitted for one job," he told a reporter. "It's amazing how surely a great man's genius leads him to that work and no other. It's as if he had a powder keg inside him and the job is the only match that will set him off." [15] On the mundane side, he was now convinced that Universal had bought Fannie Hurst's *Back Street* chiefly with the intention of using it as a framework on which to hang artistry stolen from *Jennie Gerhardt*. To Carl Laemmle, Jr. of Universal he wrote in fury:

> Because of this theft I had to take less for a novel (Jennie Gerhardt) that would otherwise have brought much more. And though you knew of Jennie Gerhardt, you preferred to pay Miss Hurst $35,000 and steal my book rather than pay me the price of my book and give me proper credit. . . .

Mr. Laemmle, either you are a common thief, or Universal is, or both are, operating as so called distinguished picture producers.

The reason that I am writing you now is because I am here in Los Angeles where you are, and where I can be reached—by suit for slander, if you choose, in which case I can publicly and legally air my grievance. Or, if you have a satisfactory explanation—one which would naturally and honorably extract an apology from me, I am here to receive it, and, if necessary make such apology.

Or, perhaps, you will sufficiently resent this imputation to personally seek me out with a demand that I retract it. In which case, you will find me here and at your service at any time.[16]

Laemmle replied semi-jocularly through a vice-president, accusing Dreiser of shallow envy of Miss Hurst. In mid-August, by which time Helen had probably tired of her furnished-room existence, Dreiser left the Douglas home and moved with her to a rented bungalow a mile away on Rosewood Avenue. In Russia another edition had been published of the immensely popular *An American Tragedy*, appreciated for its literary quality as well as for propaganda purposes. Dreiser wrote Dinamov asking him to see if some royalties could not be sent, saying, "just now I need the money." He wrote Kyllmann in London, saying he had been paid $168,000 for the film rights to the *Tragedy* (actually $135,000) and $50,000 for *Jennie* ($25,000), and urging Kyllmann to spread propaganda for possible British film production of his works. He wrote the director John Ford to praise his brilliant screen portrayal of O'Flaherty's *The Informer*, and, when Ford replied, invited him over to discuss possible screenplays in *A Gallery of Women*.

In mid-October he tore himself away from his *fidus Achates*, Douglas. Douglas, deeply moved, composed a sonnet to him ending:

> *Oh what a little thing is man! Still less*
> *His power to reason when compelled to feel*
> *The pangs of parting from his dearest friend:*
> *His ego shrinking into nothingness*
> *As o'er his senses sadly, swiftly steal*
> *The taste and terror of all things the end.*[17]

Helen and Dreiser headed east in caravan fashion, Helen driving the Chrysler and Dreiser (at peril to himself and others) the Buick. In Arkansas they encountered torrential rains that leaked into the trunk and dampened hundreds of pages of notes for *The Formula Called Man*. At Little Rock they rented a cabin and laid out pages to dry on beds, chairs and the floor.[18] They reached Iroki October 26.

II. OF ALL THINGS THE END

"After L. A. [,] N. Y. looks cluttered, grimy and Jewish," Dreiser wrote Louise Campbell.[19] He promptly protested Chicago's Mayor Edward

Kelly's ban on *Tobacco Road* as a "mental outrage" ("What I suspect is that it is the Catholic Church," he wrote Gingrich).[20] In November, to raise money, he lectured on realism in Detroit and Toledo ("Absolutely I will not autograph any books. I do not care to be annoyed with attentions of any kind.").[21] His absorption in the philosophy study had all but eliminated any income from current writing. Far from finishing it that fall, he was only getting into it. He stayed at Iroki, had no New York suite, and his personal stationery was no longer engraved. Helen served as his secretary until late in November, when he hired a pretty Smith College graduate, Harriet Bissell. On December 19 he went to Schenectady to see the General Electric laboratories and talk with Drs. Irving Langmuir and W. D. Coolidge, later plying Langmuir with questions:

> (1) Is there any evidence to the effect that anywhere in space there is a region of absolute zero as to temperature? If so, by what is that area surrounded? Evidently by non-zero—but how near and how remote?
> (2) At absolute zero what happens to the interior content of the atom? to electrons, protons and their movements? Or is this unknown? [22]

Surely no man so untrained in science had such curiosity and such ambitious intentions. But more than curiosity and ambition was involved. A large factor was his own peace of mind. Deeply disturbed, challenged by doubts and contradictions in his own nature, he felt that in perfecting his own approach to the unknowable he might ascend a peak of spiritual understanding and calm. "What I am really doing," he wrote Sherwood Anderson, "is seeking to interpret this business of life to myself. My thought is, if I ever get it reasonably straight for myself I will feel more comfortable." [23]

Anderson wrote disparagingly of "[t]his goddam science and mechanical development you talk of" [24] and urged him to return to the story-telling he had abandoned so long. Dreiser disagreed:

> Science is certainly not dull, lifeless, nor even mechanical in a narrow way. I think the reason people reject it is because they haven't got the capacity to see how enormously rich, mysterious, varied, and in fact, entirely satisfactory in an emotional way, science as such can be, while at the same time they are taking advantage of it in practical life.[25]

He was interested chiefly in those authorities who would corroborate his own determinism. He disliked to read—probably was too nervous for concentration—and even those books he skimmed himself he often had reviewed for him by a researcher. He resorted to the *Reader's Digest* for its condensations of "scientific" lore. Esther McCoy, now back in New York, was scanning scientific works and digesting them for him, as was Marjorie Stengel. To Miss McCoy he wrote, "Santayana wrote a book called *Beauty*. See if he interprets beauty mechanistically & give me some exact quotations—if any." [26]

To *Pravda*, in response to a request for New Year's greetings, he wrote in part:

To me the Soviet Union today is like a light, glittering afar in an irrationally dark and savage profit-seeking world. . . . To the Soviet Union, the light glittering above this darkness! Hail! [27]

Schuster sent him a letter from a Minnesota librarian asking when the next Dreiser novel would appear. "I repeat again our frequently expressed desire not to rush you. . . ." he wrote, and a fortnight later tried again:

Again our attitude is not one of unseemly impatience, but genuinely profound interest and an effort to plan our important publications intelligently, with the necessary advance work. We rise, therefore, to inquire whether you wish to tell us anything new about the progress of the novel. [28]

Dreiser seemed unaware that he had contracted to deliver the manuscript by the end of 1935, a date now passed.

"As to your letter about the STOIC," he replied, "I cannot give it to you for Spring publication. Will it make so much difference if presently I give you a really important book and follow it later with the STOIC?" [29]

After a Howard Scott visit to Iroki, Dreiser urged Upton Sinclair in California to incorporate Technocracy into his EPIC movement: "The more I talked with him, the more I am satisfied that Technocracy is the method." [30] He lunched with Dr. Langmuir at the Chemists' Club in New York. He arranged a visit to the Westinghouse laboratories in Bloomfield, New Jersey, to see the "wonderful device which gives off a lethal ray which will kill germs." Ralph Fabri was astonished by his childlike wonder at scientific marvels, but thought he would be as impressed by an alchemist. Yet Dreiser had a remarkable ability to converse with scientists who recognized his limitations but were charmed by his yearning—"lust" would be a better word—to know, to understand. He needed someone at his elbow with the same yearning, someone critical and stimulating, a true friend of the mind and spirit. In short he needed George Douglas, who was 3,000 miles away. It was his intention to move permanently to Los Angeles to escape bronchitis and be near Douglas, as soon as he could sell Iroki and settle his legal quarrel with the Liveright firm. His longing poured out in a letter to "George dear":

We were happiest alone, but I dislike thinking of you alone again. . . . Most naturally and affectionately my mind runs to the evenings—walking under the still trees, and saying over and over that life is what it is. To return as we did and open Swinburne or Shakespeare, or Keats, or Sterling, or Shelley! The tall bamboos are outside the window! a mocking bird begins at midnight! I can see the green electric words Gaylord over the roof-tops! And you read or present in your own words what is or was—the mutton birds of Australia, the one-time Bohemia of San Francisco.
Hail, George! Oh, ho! I am grateful. And I could cry. [31]

In his preoccupation with science he neglected his friends, some of whom were drifting away. Anderson, noticing his withdrawal, wrote him urging a "return to the old habit of letter writing between man and man. . . ." [32] The magazines, except for *Esquire,* had mostly forgotten him now. Even the New York Red front bothered him little. The communists had executed an amazing reversal. Stalin, after failing to make a pact with Hitler, had sought safety by wooing the democracies, signing a pact with France and inaugurating the "popular front." Earl Browder had left for Moscow an assailant of the New Deal and had returned an admirer of Roosevelt and American democracy. The *New Masses* and the *Daily Worker* suddenly saw virtue in an administration they had despised. Even before this, some of the more discerning of the radicals had resented and protested the meek submission to Moscow. Dreiser, engrossed in his work, was more divorced from politics than he had been for years. He made few belligerent public statements, and was capable of wry humility when he had Miss Bissell answer a reader's letter:

> Mr. Dreiser . . . finds it impossible to accede to your request for an account of some particularly embarrassing moment which he has experienced. He finds . . . his life has been nothing but one long, progressively embarrassing moment. . . .[33]

At long last he had received an accounting from Paul Zsolnay in Vienna admitting he owed Dreiser some $2,000. Through the cooperation of Ben Huebsch, now with Viking Press, the problem of getting at least some of the money out of Austria was solved. Viking had published in America *The Forty Days of Musa Dagh* by Franz Werfel, a Zsolnay author. On Zsolnay's authorization, Huebsch agreed to pay Dreiser Zsolnay's share of Werfel's royalty earnings as they accrued. From Viking Dreiser received $500 in December and $393.88 in February, though his letters indicate that he did not understand the arrangement. He was having further trouble getting reports and payments from his publishers Nova in Budapest and Cin in Prague, and emissaries there were looking into it. His American book sales now were almost nil. His royalties from the poor-selling *Moods* were less than $200. As he sent his autographed portrait to his old Ohio friend Charles Yost, he wrote, "If you want a fine collection of wolves at your front door, hang my picture outside. They never fail to respond."[34]

From Jerome Blum at Rockland State Hospital came a pathetic plea:

> For God's sake help me all you can and please come and *visit* me. . . . I do not seem to have a chance in the world of getting out of here unless?!! I get help. at this sitting I am absolutely OK and have been but the surroundings and misunderstanding of the Artist blocks *all* chance that I have *perhaps* if you came, and I could have a half hour with you to tell you of the rotten Raw deal life has handed my darling girl and yours truly I could get get [*sic*] out—the lack of sympathy for the complex individuality of the artist is beyond all belief—please come as quick as you can . . . but Oh I do need a friend and a person that is not *afraid* to stand up for me and our rights as Americans and as intelligent capable & contributing factors to life —come please[.][35]

And from Los Angeles came a telegram from George Douglas' daughter Halley:

FATHER DIED SUDDENLY THIS AFTERNOON FROM HEART ATTACK STOP HIS DEATH WAS PEACEFUL AND WITHOUT WARNING.[36]

"He missed you dreadfully," Douglas' widow Margaret wrote in part, "but I am so glad that he had such a happy three months with you." [37]

To Dr. McCord in Pasadena Dreiser wired:

GEORGES DEATH HURTS ME BEYOND BELIEF   WILL YOU PERSONALLY SELECT FOUR DOZEN ROSES   SEND WITH CARD SAYING FROM DREISER TO GEORGE. . . .[38]

III. FORTY-EIGHT HAIL MARYS

From May Calvert Baker, now ill and retired in Indianapolis, Dreiser got word that the Paul Dresser Memorial Committee had at last gone into action, with the aid of a federal grant, and was preparing to landscape a park in Paul's memory on the west bank of the Wabash in Terre Haute. "I had an inspiration," she added. "Theodore will come to Indiana. Will you and if you do will you come and be my guest . . . ?" [39]

"I have never been invited to participate in any way," he replied to "Dear Teacher," but said that if he was invited to the dedication he would certainly visit her. "You will always be May Calvert to me—the teacher that made the public school a sort of Paradise." [40]

Meanwhile Erwin Piscator's German adaptation of *An American Tragedy* had been translated by Louise Campbell and produced with enough success by Deeter's Hedgerow troupe in 1935 so that Milton Shubert paid Dreiser $1,000 and prepared to produce it with the Group Theater in New York. An expressionist like his friend Bertolt Brecht, the radical Piscator had created a highly stylized drama stressing the social implications of the book which Paramount had ignored—indeed going much farther than Dreiser had. At the end, Clyde's mother says, "He dies as a sacrifice to his rebellious, yearning heart, and he will be forgiven." But an accusing answer comes just before the curtain, "He dies as a sacrifice to society, and *it* will not be forgiven!" [41]

Dreiser liked the Piscator version better than Kearney's. "Light two candles and say forty-eight Hail Marys at once," he urged the Catholic Mrs. Campbell.[42] Now titled *The Case of Clyde Griffiths*, the play opened at the Ethel Barrymore Theater March 13, with Morris Carnovsky as Speaker, Alexander Kirkland as Clyde, Phoebe Brand as Roberta, and Elia Kazan and John Garfield in minor roles. A few radical critics praised it, but others condemned its partisan didacticism. "The first night was marvelous," Helen wrote Eleanor and Sherwood Anderson. "The smoothest performance and such excellent acting on the part of the Group! And *then* the critics walked out and wrote *trash* dull and unappreciative of all the real quality of a really **new** art form. It made me sick." [43]

The play closed in three weeks. Soon Dreiser was in another legal tangle, this one not his own fault. Lina Goldschmidt had apparently prepared a preliminary scenario from which Piscator wrote the finished play, and they had been billed as co-authors. Piscator's agent threatened suit, insisting that he was sole author and entitled to the full percentage. Madame Goldschmidt had died in 1935, but her husband declared that she had indeed collaborated and was entitled to equal billing and percentage. Dreiser, after consulting with Attorney Hume, finally washed his hands of it by sending Piscator $300 and Dr. Goldschmidt $75—a settlement that apparently satisfied the disputants. That left him $625 of the $1,000 payment, out of which he paid Mrs. Campbell for the translation.

To his old friend Lillian Rosedale Goodman he gave a three-month authorization to sell *Sister Carrie* to the films for "not less than $50,000." [44] Seeking more lectures, he signed up with the agent Clark Getts in addition to his current agent, Ernest Briggs. Though neither was happy about this double-teaming arrangement, each agreed to it. Dreiser was interested in dignified radio engagements, but refused to speak regularly on programs advertising big corporations. Receding noticeably in his fee, he wrote Getts:

> I would want from $300 to $500 depending on the size and wealth of the group involved. However, in the case of a small but distinguished group I would take $250. [45]

From Lincoln Schuster: "We would like to see you soon to discuss the whole publishing program. . . ." [46]

Dreiser consulted Dr. Robert W. Chambers of New York University on chemical problems and invited him to Iroki: "I will fix you up a chemical drink which will be the equivalent of ordinary unscientific whiskey." [47] He instructed Esther McCoy to look into the relation of color and emotion:

> What colors seem to be consistently with what emotions—for example, love and hate, sorrow and joy? Is there anything inherent in color and unconnected with color values by association that seems to be able to arouse emotions, or, on the other hand, is it purely because of the connection in experience of certain colors with certain emotions that colors have the power to arouse emotion? For example, has color the power of arousing emotion in the same way that a bell can cause evidences of hunger to appear in a dog who has been trained to associate the bell with its feeding time, or could color rouse emotion without any previous association? Also, does the intensity of color have any connection with the emotional stress, irrespective of the particular color or emotion? [48]

Agreeing to lecture at Purdue University May 18, he arranged to meet with scientists there. To *Izvestia*, asking his opinion on the fostering of personal liberty in Russia, he made plain his conviction that the repression there was purely a temporary safeguard, writing, "I hear, as I have from Russians themselves, that there is as yet no individual liberty in Russia. I think this must be true, but still necessary. The communist ideal may not yet be safe. . . . When communism is achieved freedom of opinion should be assured." [49]

Helen grew unhappier as Dreiser suffered a new infatuation. Finding some fulfillment through his work, she could stand up to several passing rivals better than to a single serious one. She had veered from yoga to Buddhism, then Christian Science in her search for peace of mind, and had sought some expression of her identity by resuming the writing of poetry. In the spring, nervous and ill, she resolved to return to her mother in Portland. "I am going away for a couple of months," she wrote Eleanor and Sherwood Anderson. "Hate to leave Teddie but am very tired." [50]

It was decided that Helen would take the Buick and that Dreiser would ride with her as far as Lafayette, for the Purdue lecture. They would stop over in Cleveland, where he had arranged a meeting with the eminent Dr. George W. Crile, whose book, *The Phenomena of Life,* fascinated him. Esther McCoy, who was returning west, would be a passenger, as would the well-traveled wolfhound Nick.

They left by May 14. Miss McCoy recalls that Dreiser and Helen were friendly and solicitous to each other. At the time they had great faith in home-made celery juice as a health drink. Helen had brought some along (as well as a Colt automatic for self-protection), and they all quaffed celery juice in a Cleveland motel before dining with the Criles. The two women dropped Dreiser off at Purdue and drove on westward with Nick. [51] At Purdue Dreiser visited the physics laboratory and had a discussion with the director, Dr. K. Lark-Horovitz, from whom he later requested a written explanation of his theories, writing:

> You told me about a very interesting idea in connection with the close similarity of the crystalline forms of snow, diatoms, and vitamin B2. . . . [52]

To Miss McCoy he wrote:

> Thanks for your nice letter although the part about Helen makes me very sad. I care for her truly although often enough we don't get along. But the drift of her temperament is truly lovely and she suffers keenly through her reactions to the beautiful and the dreams and ideals evoked in her by the elusive phantoms of beauty in life. So often I wish I wish [sic] I could make her wholly happy. . . . I know she is sick. Have written her to rest & take medical aid. I will always look after her to the best of my ability as she knows. . . . I want her to get well & I want to pull myself together & then maybe we can make a go of it out there. [53]

That summer he cut expenses by leasing the main and guest houses at Iroki and occupying one of the small cabins, sans plumbing or telephone. Here he did his writing on a flimsy card table and battled mice. He had put the estate on the market, saying with scandalous exaggeration that "I have put at least $100,000.00 into the thing," but admitting willingness to take $50,000 for it. [54] Among his visitors were Burton Rascoe and his wife, though

Rascoe said he was the most niggardly of hosts—you got one drink and one cracker. Mary Fanton Roberts, who had helped edit *Sister Carrie* 36 years earlier, called with her husband. Mencken, who had never seen the Rodin studio, was unable to get to Iroki, but he did send Dreiser (as well as Masters, Upton Sinclair and others) a genuine two-pound Maryland madstone which he described as efficaceous against all manner of unmentionable diseases. He warned that it had radioactive properties and had to be handled with care.[55]

Dreiser went along with the jest: "A small dog went mad here last Monday and I applied it [the madstone] at fifteen feet, seven amperes strength, Eastern Southern time. Result a complete cure. Am having the hide stuffed by a taxidermist." [56]

He had a pleasant enough meeting with Schuster at Iroki, but Simon & Schuster were worried. After their loud hosannas two years earlier, their advance on royalties and expensive advertising program had been largely wasted. He had produced only a poor-selling book of poems, mostly reprints at that, and now he was somewhere in Betelgeuse.

He thought of raising money by selling some of his literary treasures—the original notes for *A Hoosier Holiday*, the galley proofs and a first edition of the same, the penwritten sheets of *Free*, the original notes for *A Traveler at Forty*, and others. But Dreiser manuscripts were in little demand now, and he gave up the idea. He was having trouble with the income-tax people over alleged lapses of memory. The country was awash with odd political movements, both the Coughlinites and Townsendites holding national conventions and the Republicans putting up Landon against Roosevelt. The communists had nominated Earl Browder. Dreiser was *not* for Browder, writing, "[The radical parties] are so mismanaged that I cannot support them." [57]

He was sixty-five on August 27. A few years earlier all the New York papers had sought birthday interviews, but this time only the Republican *Herald Tribune* seemed interested. Dreiser stopped writing at his card table to talk, telling the reporter he was for Roosevelt. Possibly the newsman merely assumed, as he reported, that Dreiser was finishing "a new novel." Schuster wrote hopefully, "In addition to our birthday greetings, Dick Simon and I want to tell you that we were immensely interested to learn from your *Herald Tribune* interview that the new novel is making such notable progress." [58]

10. Scattered Talents

I. FLOWERS AND TEARS

Publishers occasionally sent Dreiser new fiction, hoping for a blurb, but he seldom responded. Starting *Anthony Adverse*, he soon threw it down in disgust. He did praise William Saroyan's pessimistic *Inhale and Exhale*, which Saroyan had sent him, but he seemed utterly unaware of Thomas Wolfe, a writer as emotional, undisciplined and egocentric as Dreiser himself. "I have a feeling that the novel is dying. . . ." he wrote Mencken,[1] without really knowing much about the current novel.

On October 1, when his tenants left, he moved back into the big house, where Helen soon rejoined him to face the same problem she had faced before. On October 13 he journeyed to Yale to see Professor Clark Hull's psychic mechanisms or thinking machines, and was enormously impressed. "I'm so busy getting an education," he observed, "that I never have an hour any more for idling just to be idling." [2] He did idle enough to dine with Mencken and Ernest Boyd at Lüchow's, where several of the waiters had known both him and Mencken for years. The Nobel Prize for 1937 went to Eugene O'Neill, who replied to Dreiser's congratulations, "I have a sneaking feeling of guilt—as if I had pinched something which I knew damned well should, in justice, be yours." [3]

Late in December Dreiser and Helen moved for the winter to the Park Plaza Hotel on West Seventy-seventh Street. At the end of January he picked up $650 by lecturing again at Northwestern and the University of Chicago. Feeling low, worried about money, he had his tonsils removed in March and at long last, after many delays, the Liveright suit against him came to court in April.

The publishing house, now headed by Arthur Pell, sued for $14,000 in advances paid him between 1929 and 1932, allegedly unearned because he had not produced the promised novel. An additional $2,480 was asked for copies of Dreiser's own books which he had bought from the firm. Dreiser, in an astonishing counterclaim, asked $67,500 he said Liveright owed him for advances due on his contract since 1932. Justice Salvatore Cotillo heard the evidence and lowered the boom, saying, "The defendant is clearly in default of his agreement [to deliver *The Stoic*]." [4] Dreiser was ordered to pay Liveright $12,789—and he was now also in default of his agreement to supply Simon & Schuster with the same manuscript.

In Moscow the "traitors" were being decimated in a purge that staggered the world. Alleged plotters took the stand and confessed treason in an orgy of self-abasement. Firing squads cut down leaders including Zinoviev and Kamenev, and unknown thousands of lesser suspects. Dreiser's friend Karl Radek was lucky to get off with ten years in prison. While convinced of Trotsky's guilt, Dreiser admitted puzzlement at the bloodletting in a gem of ambivalence:

> To me, they [the Moscow trials] are very confusing. But somehow they seem characteristic of what might be called the Russian temperament. If it is true that all these confessions were made without undue pressure . . . then I think that the trials represent a real triumph of the spirit of self-abnegation. . . . On the other hand, there are so many strange and curious factors, and so much more factual explanation that needs to be made before I can really believe this myself, that I do not know what to say. It is hard to believe that . . . any man would willingly and knowingly sacrifice his life. . . . And still, I believe that it is possible. . . . Under the pressure of a donouement, and of the imagined or real pressure of mass feeling, public disgrace, and personal moral confusion, a man is likely to defy all ordinary rules of psychology, and elevate himself to a martyr's place.[5]

Exploring St. Francis at the public library, he met Fannie Hurst and drew her into a discussion of philosophy and religion. She explained that she was catching the 4 o'clock plane for St. Louis. "I'll go along," he said, not wanting to end the conversation. He took her to LaGuardia Field, then talked urgently all the way to St. Louis on many subjects, often turning to religion. Not once did he mention his indignation over *Back Street*, and in St. Louis he said good-by and took the next plane back to New York.[6]

That summer, he left Helen to spend three months with another woman at the Carnegie Biological Laboratory at Cold Spring Harbor, Long Island, joining there his good friend Calvin Bridges and scores of other researchers. His aim was quite different from that of the rest. He used a term which he knew was anathema to most of his scientific colleagues, saying he was interested in "speculative biology." He was impressed by the pure beauty of science and the dedication of the workers. "They are interested in knowledge for itself. They want to know, and they are willing to make sacrifices of money and time and work to know. The most beautiful spirits I have ever encountered I have encountered in science, not religion, or statecraft or business or even art."[7]

He found beauty in what he saw while peering at slides through the microscope in search of the fundamental units of protoplasm. Going outside, he saw tiny yellow wildflowers by the path and stooped to examine them. The flowers had an intricately detailed design similar to what he had viewed through the microscope. Growing there by chance among the weeds, they were so lovely that tears came to his eyes and he suddenly felt that the creative force, which he had so often described as blind and heedless, might after all be intelligent—possibly even loving—in its bestowal of beauty on all objects in nature.[8]

Helen, whom he felt unable to follow such flights, was closed off from him even had it not been for the other women in his life. Ralph Fabri, still her father confessor and deeply sympathetic, assured her that Dreiser would never abandon her because she gave him an unselfish devotion no one else could match. Yet he had abandoned her for many weeks now. That summer she took the familiar escape, driving the Buick back to her mother and sister in Portland.

Schuster wrote Dreiser: "Dick Simon and I would like ever so much to see you and arrange a session at your convenience." [9]

Early in October, after a trip to Woods Hole, Dreiser saved money by taking a second-floor apartment at 116 West Eleventh Street in the same old Rhinelander Gardens row where he had lived with Mame in 1924. A $1,000 payment from Zsolnay was a help. Through Lengel, now an agent, he sought to exploit *Sister Carrie* in two ways—as a series of twelve radio dramas and as a motion picture. Lengel interested Warner Brothers at a tentative $40,000 figure, then ran into the old, heartbreaking obstacle, the Hays office, in the person of Joseph Breen. "It is again the 'kept woman' theme," Breen wrote him "without any compensating moral values whatever. The heroine is an immoral woman. . . . At no time throughout the story does she pay the penalty for her sins. . . ." Breen also cited Hurstwood's suicide as morally objectionable. Lengel telephoned Breen about it and was surprised to hear the moral arbiter of the films using profanity as vivid as any heard on the docks.

Meanwhile, twenty-five-year-old Robert H. Elias, a graduate student in literature at Columbia, had taken Dreiser as the subject of his thesis. Dreiser interested him as the forgotten man of modern letters—the pioneer who had made *Main Street* and *The Sun Also Rises* possible but was no longer much read—and also as the determinist who said individuals were helpless, yet who shouted for reform. Dreiser cooperated in supplying information for the thesis, and when he read it was admiring and grateful. "The research! And your careful deductions!" he wrote.[10]

Elias was his guest one October evening on Eleventh Street, where Dreiser served highballs as they discussed T. S. Stribling, Oscar Wilde and the Hemingway-Eastman fracas at the Scribner office. Dreiser found James Thurber delightful but had never heard of Vernon Parrington. He spoke scornfully of Sinclair Lewis. About determinism and human helplessness, he said of course he was helpless personally and the efforts he made for social equity were not of his own volition but things that he had to do because the forces that moved him required him to. Elias noted: "He said he could go into the laboratory and prove there was no free will, that we were really con- trolled by glands, chemism, hormones, and compulsions; e.g., castrate a bull and he becomes an ox with no bullish characteristics. He asked . . . what I'd be like if I were born in the Congo—thus we are controlled by environment." Socrates, Spinoza, Spencer, Schopenhauer and Watson, he said, all tore the will to shreds. Elias took careful notes:

I came back to the idea that his doctrine of futility made even asking Why worthless. I said why ask? He said no reason to if you don't mind being ignorant. I asked what kind of knowledge you'd get and what its use would be or its good. He never answered that but said we were all at the mercy of glandular reactions and sense perceptions and that since one's physical state controlled one's activity . . . one's will was set at naught.

Elias found him likeable but illogical. If man was a will-less machine, what was the point in Dreiser's sociological activities and his insistence on the freedom of the individual? "When you see him close up," Elias noted, "hot, in his shirt, standing above you pouring whisky, you realize he's not young. In a sense, I felt sorry for him. There seemed to be something so lonely." [11]

Dreiser, who had been hoping for years that someone would write his biography, urged Lengel to find a publisher for Elias' thesis. He had turned against Simon & Schuster, feeling that they were pressuring him unbearably and also that they had failed to keep his old works in print. When he asked Attorney Hume about a possible suit to force the publishers to do this, Hume reminded him of his own unfulfilled contractual obligation.

He was now almost two years late with *The Stoic*. Ill and depressed, he wrote Helen, who had inquired as to whether their relationship was ended:

Dear Helen: I have been really sick in bed for the last three days or I would have written you before, particularly since this last letter of yours is the only one in heaven knows how long that has not confirmed me in my desire to close the account between us. This letter doesn't tell me much of anything that I didn't know but it acknowledges a lot that I do. And the absence of that acknowledgment, coupled with the constant assertion of worthlessness, and intense cruelty and what I owe you for what you have done for me, has about broken up the alliance. For as this letter of yours shows you were getting something—(a quite considerable thing) even though you were not getting all of what you wanted or needed.

But at that it all comes down to what human beings are entitled to ask of each other *in return for what*. The quick answer is 50–50 and it sounds fine. But who is to say that the 50 that one person sees as his contribution is the exact duplicate of the 50 that the other person sees as his as [*sic*] contribution. . . .

You have your needs, I have mine. You want your needs fulfilled, I want mine. You charge me with cruelty in refusing or failing to supply what you need or needed. I sit back & consider my needs & then place opposite them the things I haven't, that I might have or might have had. No one can go with us into our deepest selves. To make things come out at all large sacrifices have to be made, I suppose, but who makes them—or makes them understandingly.

You ask am I going to leave you. What springs in my mind immediately is could we ever live happily & profitably together. My thought without alteration is on my work. Mentally I never leave it. Mostly, as at Cold Spring Harbor, I find myself happiest talking to those who can throw a light on it. It is true, on the other hand, that you do and always have represented a certain untutored and uncontaminated emotional response to beauty which is very moving. Except for your singing and some of your worded comments on nature it is voiceless. You rarely read a book. Your poetry does not take form on paper—only in song.* Yet I read your silent moods. Most of my deepest and tenderest reactions to you have been at these times.

Despite all this you are not an easy person to live with—any more so than am I. . . . You insist you supply an atmosphere—an artistic and poetic one. It is true [except] for such times as your brooding over and interests in things which do not coincide with my interests or moods. But those times were very numerous. And mostly I have found that I could not go to you with my intellectual or emotional interests. . . . Largely I have gone abroad for intellectual and emotional reactions which I felt necessary for me at the time. Add to all this the natural resentments and quarrels on both sides and you can see to what we would come.

So when you say am I going to leave you I scarcely know what to say. If I only knew or could believe that we could go on in some helpful constructive way. But I can't help feeling that it is likely to come to nothing. At the same time just now I am in the midst of so many financial ills that I scarcely see how I can go on. If any thing comes through I would be the last person to throw you on your own. Even though I feel that if you had some task of some kind, it would be good for you, and would, in your case, lead to some development favorable to you. The idea of uncreatively dreaming, whether in marriage or out of it, seems self-destructive and dangerous to me. Everybody ought to be made to work at something. . . .[12]

II. CLING TO YOUR RAFT

After working three years on his philosophy book, Dreiser was far from finished. He wanted badly to move to California but could not do so until he had sold Iroki (which he had actually deeded to Helen) or made some profitable deal. Although he wrote Thelma Cudlipp Grosvenor and other friends that Iroki was for sale, even offering a commission, there were no takers. He had not heard from Mencken in months. Lonely, seeking a friend who would take Douglas' place, he exchanged visits with the novelist Edward Dahlberg, who lived nearby on West Sixteenth Street. He wrote McCord in Pasadena: "I comfort myself with the reflection that I don't have to stand anything much longer. . . . I have reason to be [in low spirits] as my affairs have taken every possible turn for the worse. And I know I am old because I don't care a hell of a lot. In fact, I am almost cheerful." [13]

For the first time since the separation agreement with Jug, he was unable to scrape up the $200 monthly due her. To Sergei Eisenstein, now back in Hollywood, he wrote hoping that Eisenstein might produce his own version of An American Tragedy "or in fact, any one of my other novels." [14] He thought of selling a parcel of Iroki land. He put the original manuscripts of The "Genius" and the Tragedy on the market, asking $3,000 and $3,500

---

* She evidently had been afraid to show him her poems.

respectively—no takers. Seeking a new publisher who would bail him out of Simon & Schuster by paying his debt to them and taking over his books, he vainly approached Scribners and Viking. His rather cavalier treatment of Simon & Schuster was no recommendation; there was little interest in a Dreiser philosophy and a suspicion that as a novelist he was through. He was aided by a couple of windfalls: $500 from the Limited Editions Club for a special issue of *Sister Carrie*, and a $200 payment from his Czech publisher. To Helen he sent a check along with Christmas greetings and a long account of his difficulties, adding:

> I read all you say about the past. It was lovely, unforgettable. But today —the way things are—I don't seem to care whether Life keeps or not.[15]

When John Dos Passos called on him December 17, the pair had a confused and disillusioned conversation about the Soviet program and the mass exterminations. Dreiser, though still insisting that many of Roosevelt's social reforms had been spurred by the Russian example, actually said, "Well, I was strong for Russia and for Stalin and the whole program, but in the last year, I have begun to think that maybe it won't be any better than anything else." [16] A few months later, after another series of Moscow trials, Alexei Rykov, Boris Pilnyak and Nikolai Bukharin were among those shot as traitors. Dreiser, who had talked with them all, was particularly shaken by the execution of the charming Bukharin, who had promised a "heaven on earth" in Russia.

For years he had avoided Edgar Lee Masters, long a resident of the Chelsea Hotel on Twenty-third Street, but when he received a Christmas card from him he went to the Chelsea for drinks and talk. The two anti-Victorians were having similar troubles now. Masters, separated from his second wife, had published his autobiography in 1936 but could find no publisher interested in his current poems. Delighted at the reconciliation, he urged Dreiser to finish *The Bulwark*, which they had discussed in Chicago in 1912. He wrote a 16-stanza poem, "To Dreiser," likening him to "a lofty pine . . . tossed by storms" and paying the price for "standing high and true." He ended with an admission that the storm was not over:

> Cling to your raft, my friend, and may some isle
> Of palm and coral save you at the last.
> There by the rollers cast
> Look at the setting sun and smile.[17]

Masters, with a friend from St. Louis, Alice Davis, visited Dreiser on Eleventh Street. Miss Davis, who recently had joined the Marble Collegiate Church, found him amiable until he got on the subject of formal worship. "The big event was his denouncement of religion," she noted in her diary, "particularly the Catholic religion." He told bitterly how his father had forced him to go to parochial school, saying, "Years afterward, if I passed a couple of nuns on the street I almost felt ill." [18]

By the time he moved out to Iroki in April, his affairs were in disorder. He had three major works all unfinished: *The Stoic, The Bulwark* and the philosophy. He was fed up with his publisher and in his usual confusion with agents. Lengel, who handled some of his magazine work in New York (as did George Bye and the International Literary Bureau), sought to make a film sale for him in collaboration with Leland Hayward. Hearing that Claude Bostock was also representing Dreiser in Hollywood, Lengel tried to get the matter straight, then wrote Dreiser resignedly, "I expect that wherever possible you will name me as agent but that in case there is any argument with regard to the question as to whether or not I am to be considered as partly agent or not [sic], I will leave the decision to your discretion." [19] Claude Bostock in Hollywood was upset to learn that Lengel-Hayward were also representing Dreiser. Dreiser's secretary, Miss Bissell, wrote him, "At this time it is essential for Mr. Dreiser to make some sort of arrangement whereby he can put a movie sale over. . . . Leland Hayward's representatives here made it clear that they would be very glad to cooperate with you. . . . I suppose that the split in the fee would be fifty-fifty. . . ." [20] Dreiser's two lecture agents, Briggs and Getts, were disagreeing over bookings. Dreiser himself, with his feeling that all agents were parasites, even cracked the whip over his old friend Lengel, who had done him countless favors. To raise money he was quitting his big projects to write occasional short pieces, accepting as little as $150 for an article for *Your Life* magazine.

He was excited over a nibble from the producer John Golden, who saw a revised and expanded version of his old play *The Girl in the Coffin* as a possible vehicle for Gertrude Lawrence. Golden asked for less emphasis on the capital-labor theme and more attention to the romantic story. Dreiser attended a performance of *Susan and God*, met Miss Lawrence, worked on the revision and invited Golden to Iroki. On a lone stroll at the estate, he encountered a puff adder which he killed, thinking it poisonous, then was remorseful when he learned that these snakes were harmless. Seeing another puff adder a few days later, he tried out a theory he had—that one could communicate with wild animals and birds. He stood still as he spoke to the snake reassuringly, saying, "I'm not going to hurt you, so you can just stop puffing." The snake uncoiled and slithered fearlessly by his feet into tall grass, confirming his feeling that it had understood him. [21]

Although involved with several New York women, he arranged a lecture tour that would help pay his way to California. Still unable to sell Iroki, he again leased out the main buildings for occupancy June 1. On May 13—a Friday—the roof of the big house caught fire from a chimney spark, apparatus roared out from Mt. Kisco and firemen quelled the blaze with streams of water that leaked into the rooms. Neighbors helped carry out furniture, carted out the liquor and later offered Dreiser a drink from his own depleted stock. Seeking to nick the insurance company, he hurriedly wrote Fabri asking him for a complete list of the work that had been done, adding, "Leave the charge (or cost) blank to be filled in by me."

"The reason I say this is that I saved them from paying $55,000 insurance on both houses by insisting that they take a standard water pumping engine down to the pool and so supplying enough water to save both houses."[22]

He was irked rather than upset because the highly personal letters he had written Isobel Sperry were now for sale by a New York dealer. Literally thousands of his letters to various women were abroad, some of them inevitably finding their way to the market place. Badly as he needed money, his principles held admirably. He would not compromise his serious work to make a sale. When Golden, for whom he vainly expended much time and labor, suggested a glamorized dramatization of The "Genius," he replied, "The plan of the play as you suggested would probably be successful but it is not anything to which I would sign my name."[23] Although he was still accommodating in furnishing Russian publications with propagandist statements, he refused to follow the "artists in uniform" ideal and drew a firm line against propaganda in art. "Only the other day," he wrote Evelyn Scott, "some young writer was telling me that a man could write a better book if he had read and understood the Marxian dialectic! Imagine!"[24]

Yet his principles succumbed to his prejudices when it came to the Nazis, for whom he still had respect. "You probably know that [Dreiser's] books were banned by the Nazis in Germany," Miss Bissell wrote his Vienna agent. "Mr. Dreiser has always thought that this was because they thought he was Jewish. . . . Another factor which he feels might affect the present situation in Austria is the fact that Zsolnay is Jewish. In this country the report has it that the Nazis are pushing all the Jews out of cultural life, especially the publishing business, and Mr. Dreiser is afraid that something may be done to Zsolnay or that his business may be ruined.

"In view of all this, Mr. Dreiser asks you to inform him of the situation and whether or not you think it advisable to look for another German language publisher."[25]

He hired still another Hollywood agent, William Watters. On June 1, at the invitation of Marguerite Tjader Harris, he moved out to her beach cabin at Noroton, Connecticut, where she was editor of the little magazine *Direction*. Helen, in Portland, wrote to Fabri:

> I am undecided what to do. If I go back to Calif. and T. does not come out then there I am alone and I am not happy that way any more . . . he tells me that he is coming out and keeps on telling me that, and he does not come. He is in some kind of rut that I think will finish him if he does not snap out of it. He and I could do fine things together in Calif. I think he knows it but there he sits. If I come back to New York, and, as he says he is going to go to Calif. then there is another wasted trip. . . . If I knew how things *really* were perhaps I would know exactly what to do. . . .
>
> I am in better voice than I have ever been. I could handle a radio job easily. . . . I could do so many things in the way of placing things for him and myself. Maybe when you see him soon you will be able to tell me some-

thing that may throw some light on the way I should go. I certainly need some honest advice just now. I have hung on and hung on and stayed away because I thought it best. But soon I *have* to make a move. Can you tell me anything? [26]

III. UNCHAIN WATCHDOG

Dreiser's financial condition was the worst it had been since 1926. True, Iroki should fetch close to $50,000 if anyone would buy it. Though Helen technically was the owner, as she was of the house and property in Los Angeles, he expected a communal sharing of the proceeds from the sale of Iroki. Thus she had a financial hold on him which she did not exercise in the least. He still owned an unknown value in stocks and bonds, but for several years he had been living above income, drawing on his reserve, and though always inclined to exaggerate either his poverty or his wealth, he was entitled to worry.

"Nothing—*nothing* exists," he said with great finality to his hostess, Mrs. Harris.[27]

At Noroton he swam daily in the Sound. Aided both by Miss Bissell and Mrs. Harris, he worked on the philosophy, swamped by science notes which he kept in triplicate and filed under different headings. Masters, growing visibly shaky, came out for a weekend. Robert Elias, now working on a biographical analysis of Dreiser's thinking for his doctorate, drove out from his home at Armonk to join a Sunday gathering. Mrs. Jerome Blum, her husband still at Rockland, was there, as were Dorothy Dudley Harvey, Olin Downes, Kenneth Hayes Miller and the venerable Art Young. The towering Howard Scott and two underlings arrived in a car labeled "Technocracy G.H.Q." Drinks were served, and although by nightfall the party grew gay, Dreiser remained imperturbable as he discussed criticism with Downes.[28] He had little contact with his family. Emma had died the previous year, but Mame, Sylvia, Rome and Ed were still in New York, all but Ed partially dependent on him.

For quick money, Dreiser agreed to edit *The Living Thoughts of Thoreau* for Longmans, Green. Yet in July, when the League of American Writers asked him to attend a writers' conference and an international peace conference in Paris, he put aside Thoreau and his three other uncompleted works, also forcing Ernest Briggs to cancel lectures arranged for him in Portland and San Francisco. He dropped everything and hurried to New York. He could not resist a humanitarian cause, a free adventure and an experience that should give him material for articles and lectures. It was assumed that he would join the League as one of its official representatives. But although he approved of the League's aims, he stubbornly refused to join. Franklin Folsom, the League secretary, and Malcolm Cowley reasoned with him, but he was adamant. They wanted him so badly that they let him go anyway.[29]

He sailed July 13 on the *Normandie*, leaving Miss Bissell to work on Thoreau for him. He dashed off letters to John Golden and a half-dozen women including Helen. To his six-week hostess, Mrs. Harris, he sent a fond thank-you letter, adding, "I think of you plenty and wish you every good thing—most truly—most of all to be happy because you honestly try to make other people happy.

"So there, beloved. And send me a few kind thoughts. I don't intend to stay any longer than I need to. Its hard work. . . . But if you were here we'd make out because I'd unload all this social stuff on you and I don't mean maybe. So love and good wishes. I'll put you in my prayers." [30]

He found friends on board—Alma Clayburgh, Marian Powys, John O'Hara Cosgrave of Butterick memory—but was annoyed by the luxury of the ship: "It is built almost exclusively for the 1st class world and the rays that emanate from these same irritate like mosquito bites[.]" He reached Paris on the 18th to find it decorated for a state visit of the king and queen of England, and was scornful when he glimpsed the king in the procession: "He looks like a poor, confused luny. . . ." [31]

Putting up at the Hotel Lutétia on the Boulevard Raspail, he sent one of his hosts, the writer René Blech, on a merry chase for American gin, hard to find in Paris. He participated in meetings of the International Association of Writers as well as the larger peace conference, the latter led by Lord Robert Cecil and Pierre Cot and attended by delegates from 42 countries. The delegates, representing all political shades from right to left, were variously concerned about Hitler, the wars in Spain and in China, and the bombing of open cities. Dreiser felt that the British, as well as some of the French, were committed to a hands-off policy of talk without action. It angered him that Hitler's treatment of Catholics was protested whereas he sensed an indifference to the plight of the anti-clerical Loyalists in Spain. Countless pacific speeches were made—the hopeful utterances that seem so futile in retrospect. Dreiser's own speech, delivered to a thousand delegates at the Palais de la Mutualité, bristled with idealistic generalities. He said in part:

> Until men of good will and good sense the world over sit down together and think out ways and means of making their governments deal fairly between the strong and the weak, the intelligent and the unintelligent, the cunning and the innocent, man will struggle to take care of himself in any way he can.
>
> More fair play must come into life. We are all co-heirs of all that is. We should find ways and means of sharing peacefully what has been given us by nature. . . . [32]

To Miss Bissell he exulted, "Whereas the many speeches that preceded me were given paragraphs—mine got space (See the Paris *Herald Tribune* [)]." But he admitted, "My morning depressions are stupendous," and added, "When I get enough whisky in me I'm all right for a little while, but then come the blues again—the blue devils. I feel alone." [33] Probably his blue-devil mornings were aggravated by his tendency to keep an alcoholic edge on in the afternoons and evenings, nervous as he was in such gatherings. He had a luncheon quarrel with Lord Cecil and Georges Bonnet. He wrote a piece for *Pravda* on the promise of a $100 payment. He became involved with at least one French woman with whom he later corresponded. He worried about the deadline on the Thoreau book. He had written his old friend Claude Bowers, still ambassador to Spain, who had moved because of the war from Madrid across the border to St. Jean de Luz, and got a cordial reply. At the end of the peace conference, invited by a group of Loyalists to visit Barcelona, he again wrote Bowers asking aid in entering Spain. This letter never reached Bowers, and Dreiser unjustly turned bitterly against him because of his failure to reply. On July 29 he took the train to Perpignan and was driven by Loyalists in an old car to Barcelona.

He was appalled by the destruction in this fading fortress of the severed Spanish republic, where an air raid the day before had killed 30. His hotel, the Ritz, had been damaged by a bomb. The elevators did not work. There was no sugar, butter or milk and little meat, and some citizens were reduced to eating weeds. From the start the anti-Catholic Dreiser's sympathies had been with the government forces. Now he was moved by the spirit of the people despite awful privations—pleased by audiences with President Manuel Azaña, Premier Juan Negrin and Minister of State Julio Alvarez del Vayo, who asked him to intercede with President Roosevelt in a plan to get food to Spain. "I am here in a dangerous atmosphere," he wrote Miss Bissell, adding about the Spaniards, "The courage of them[.] The pride. They won't beg!" [34] He was interviewed by newspaper correspondents, he visited a hospital, an army camp, interviewed a half-dozen prisoners, and after three days in Barcelona was off to London.

He was in such a hurry to get to London that he rode straight through despite a promise to meet his colleagues in Paris, causing great worry to Langston Hughes and other delegates. "His hotel here in Paris claims he has never returned to claim his baggage there," Hughes wrote anxiously to Franklin Folsom. "But a wire to Barcelona brought the answer that he left Spain August 2nd. And Perpingan [*sic*] reports that he departed for Paris August 5th [actually the 3rd]. But so far, we have been able to find no one who has seen him in Paris . . . so today it developed into a major mystery as to his whereabouts, with the Spanish Embassy, the Writers Association, and [Louis] Aragon's associates on CE SOIR all trying to trace him. . . ." [35]

In London Dreiser neglected to send word to Paris. He was relieved to learn that his publisher was giving him an extension on Thoreau. He saw his old friend Kyllmann and also tried to get help for the Loyalists from English officialdom. "England is an autocracy," he wrote Miss Bissell. "The masses are underpaid; stupid, silent. The gang at the top wants not only to rule England but the world. They want beggars & stupid slogan-fed workers and they have them—while they loaf and entertain and shoot deer in great preserves!" [36] He had no time to visit Llewelyn Powys in Dorset (and possibly feared contracting tuberculosis), but Corwen, Wales, where John Cowper Powys lived, was only fifty miles from Liverpool where he would catch his boat. He wired the older brother:

UNCHAIN WATCHDOG SET BURGLAR ALARM NOTIFY POLICE ADJUST LIFE BELT I ARRIVE SOME TIME WEDNESDAY.[37]

He spent two days with Powys and his consort at their cottage in the lee of a heather-covered mountain, envying them a peace his own nature denied him. "The felicity of a true mental companionship!" he later wrote them. "To how many, in any century, does that come?" [38] He sailed on the *Laconia* August 13 (while efforts were still being made in Paris to locate him), writing McCord en route that he would move to California soon and adding, "I do not know about Helen." [39]

To Fabri, Helen wrote from Portland, "I do wish that [Dreiser's trip to Europe] would put an end to that other phase of it. That will never bring him anything but ill luck. . . . He wrote me that he would positively come out when he got back. Of course she will do all possible crookedness to keep him there but I don't think she can do it." She had been sending Fabri her poems, numbered consecutively. With this letter she sent "Poem No. 12," a sonnet beginning:

> *I stand before you, World, as one apart,*
> *With wonder in my eyes, and open heart,*
> *Seeking liberty, and understanding too. . . .*[40]

IV. LUNCH WITH ROOSEVELT

In New York Dreiser stayed with a woman friend at the George Washington Hotel at Lexington and Twenty-third Street, the residence also of his friend of the Nineties, Richard Duffy, now widowed and a Funk & Wagnalls editor. Though he had had little commerce with Duffy in the interim, he gladly renewed the friendship. He was faced by immediate obligations: to finish four quick articles on Spain for the North American Newspaper Alliance at $300 apiece, to finish (or help Miss Bissell finish) the Thoreau book, and to see President Roosevelt about food for Spain. Shipments would have to be sent impartially to both sides to satisfy partisan American opinion—an idea Dreiser accepted since the Loyalists were worse off and would benefit most. On August 23 he wrote the President, telling of his meeting with the Loyalist leaders, mentioning "a problem associated with both sides," and ending, "Since they requested me personally to present this to you I am writing to ask if you will be willing to receive me." [41]

Roosevelt, first reserving ten minutes for him, reconsidered and handed the matter to Assistant Secretary of State A. A. Berle, Jr., who replied. Dreiser again wrote the President, saying, "It is not that I personally hesitate to discuss this plan with whomever you see fit, but that I promised Mr. Azaña and Mr. del Vayo to talk with you, if possible, about this, and if it not be possible, with no one." He added, "The plan which they suggested has really no military or political implications, and is not liable to any interpretation except on grounds of plain humanity which all of us must feel to some extent." [42]

On this letter Roosevelt scribbled to his secretary, Marvin H. McIntyre, "Mac—tell him to come to HP & give him 15 minutes on Wed. morning—"

Meanwhile Dreiser spoke of his European experiences to the League of American Writers at the City Club ("It was a terrible shame that they made a hash of that beautiful city [Barcelona]."). Interviewed by *The Times* on his sixty-seventh birthday, he lauded T. S. Stribling's trilogy, *The Store*, *The Forge* and *The Cathedral* and gave equivocal praise to William Faulkner and Erskine Caldwell: "The couple of spoonfuls of genuine realism you will find in their books makes them two really important writers." [43]

On September 7 he journeyed to Hyde Park, where Roosevelt, instead of giving him fifteen minutes, ushered him aboard the yacht *Potomac* and lunched with him on the Hudson as they discussed aid for Spain. It was Dreiser's first meeting with a President since the one thirty years earlier with Theodore Roosevelt, and one wonders whether FDR remembered that violent Dreiser telegram about Henry Ford. He did show interest in Dreiser's message from the Loyalists. He made it plain that despite his sympathies the administration could not initiate even non-partisan shipments of food. The sum of his advice was that Dreiser should organize a committee of no more than three or four eminent citizens to devise plans for raising money and arranging shipments. Dreiser evidently fell under the spell of the Roosevelt personality, and probably the reverse was true as well.

So the inveterate partisan of causes (who believed that man was helpless, that "nothing exists") had another. For committee members he considered such people as John D. Rockefeller, Jr., Nelson Rockefeller, Roy Howard, Monsignor John A. Ryan, Edsel Ford and Captain Joseph Patterson. The Spanish issue, however, aroused such passions that he found no one who wished to identify himself with either the communists or the fascists or both. He had long been an admirer of the Quaker faith, and recently had praised the work of the American Friends Service Committee headed by the distinguished Quaker Rufus M. Jones. In September Miss Bissell drove him to Jones' home on the Haverford College campus, where the two men had a long discussion of the Spanish relief problem. The aged but vital Jones agreed to help. Although their combined efforts would fail, Dreiser was so impressed by this staunch Friend that he was tempted to resume his Quaker novel, *The Bulwark*, when he could get to it. [44]

Dreiser called personally on eleven well-known New Yorkers without getting a single committee member. Meanwhile Lengel was trying to land a 26-week Dreiser radio program for which the material would be written by Irwin Shaw but would be announced as "by Mr. Theodore Dreiser," and on which Dreiser would speak briefly. Lengel was also promoting *Sister Carrie* as well as a film based on Dreiser's "My Brother Paul" through his current Hollywood representative, Edna Schley. But Lengel was impatient at Dreiser's habit of dealing indiscriminately with several agents at once so that none knew where he stood. "Mr. Dreiser is ready to jump to anyone who rushes him off his feet with the promise of a sale," he wrote Miss Schley, sending a copy to Dreiser. "And right now, due to circumstances which I need not recount here, Mr. Dreiser is desperate to see a sale made." [45]

Dreiser dunned *Pravda* for his $100, still unseen. Reading a *Times* story about the Nazi appropriation of Catholic property, he wrote McCord, "It cheers me no little—even stopped an aching bunion," sending the clipping to McCord and adding, "Dr. Hitler seems to know how to proceed." [46] He was urging his lecture agents to get speaking dates for Masters and Richard Duffy, but Briggs and Getts were having their troubles too, with Dreiser playing one against the other. He was seized by a money-making idea to exploit oversize human beings, writing Briggs a long letter about it:

> My proposition is to erect at the coming New York World's Fair or if not there at the coming San Francisco Fair and later to transport the same wherever it might prove profitable, a house or hotel to be known either as the Giants' Hotel, or the Giants' Castle, or the Ogres' Home. It would be constructed in every detail to accommodate and make comfortable men and women of this unusual height. . . . Accordingly there would have to be made for them . . . things that would naturally arrest and astound the average spectator—books and newspapers suitable to the size of the hands of Giants. For instance, the *New York Times* would be double its ordinary size. Books would be about the size of the old family Bibles. . . .

The giants, he suggested, could enact a play. "For instance, a man giant might fall in love with an ordinary sized girl and finally be accepted. In the case of a villain giant, he might be arrested by a midget policeman, and be sentenced by a very small judge. In connection with this there would be obviously an opportunity for moving pictures, radio, and photographic rights. Also I imagine that furniture manufacturers, automobile manufacturers, and many manufacturers of things which ordinary people use, would be delighted to manufacture their products on a giant scale for the giants' use. . . ." [47]

To safeguard his idea, he had the letter witnessed and notarized.

He gave thought to the disposition of his vast store of letters and papers—particularly now that Robert Elias, anxious to get at them, suggested that he put them in the library at Columbia. After looking at the room available there, he found it inadequate. He also had reservations about letting Elias read his personal papers, writing him:

Opening one's private files to even special inspection is a matter to be most carefully weighed beforehand. First, before oneself, come others—their right, feelings[,] privileges. The person who should first reinspect them is myself, torch in hand. After that one duly certified to the public as well as myself.[48]

After a long hiatus, Mencken wrote him about the visible advance of senility, brought up the question of the disposal of Dreiser's ashes, and made a prediction not really jocular: that Dreiser, as death approached, would embrace the church. "I propose," he added, "that you and I and Masters have a sitting at Lüchow's. When Eddie Fink [the band leader] sees us he'll undoubtedly order his band to play 'Nearer My God to Thee.' "[49]

"As to my ashes, alas," Dreiser replied, "I have already contracted with the N.Y. Ash and Garbage Corporation for their removal."[50] The "sitting" never took place because of his frantic activity. On November 2 he finally finished his 32-page preface to the Thoreau book, working from selections made by Miss Bissell and a summary of biographical criticism done by Miss Bissell, who should have had equal billing. Indeed, she was astonished at his whole attitude of haste, his failure to digest all of Thoreau for himself and his anxiety to find in Thoreau echoes of his own thinking. She thought the book haphazardly done.[51]

On the 11th he was off to Indianapolis, where he addressed 2,000 high school members of the National Scholastic Press Association. He spent the night as the guest of May Calvert Baker, who was now failing and losing her eyesight but still hoping that he would see the true light of religion. Next day he was in Detroit for another lecture—a tour that prevented his requested presence at the cornerstone-laying of the Soviet pavilion at the World's Fair. Returning to New York, he found time to write waggishly to George Bye, who had suggested a Dreiser piece on sex in the *Nutmeg Magazine:*

I feel that I personally, would do the subject far more harm than good. As a matter of fact if it were known that I was in favor of it people might desert the cause. But I will give a faint cheer as you pass by, what you know as the greetings of a lay brother.[52]

After a final lecture in Boston November 20, he packed for the longer journey. Iroki was still unsold, but he was rejoining Helen. The woman with whom he lived at the hotel protested, and they had such quarrels that the management complained. "Helen will be with me a part of the time anyhow," he wrote Mencken. "She spends a good deal of time with her mother in Portland. Sorry to miss you."[53]

There was a farewell party at the Sherwood Andersons in Washington Mews—Anderson, who had written of his sadness at seeing him go and added, "Anyway Teddy you are my Nobel Prize man."[54] There was a farewell Thanksgiving dinner at Luchow's with Masters and Miss Davis. Next day, November 25, he took the train for Portland.

Book Six

THE WHITE CHRIST

1. *The Simple Life*

1. GOD IS SLICKER THAN WE ARE

To Helen, Dreiser's return was a triumph and vindication—utter defeat for the other woman, for he had traveled 3,000 miles to rejoin her. "He came out here after me," she wrote Fabri. "Came up north to get me. I should think that would be enough for her to realize that he did leave her. Not her. She is too vain." [1]

They tarried only briefly in Portland, then headed south in the Buick, which was now nine years old. As Helen put it, Dreiser "had the desire to change his entire mode of living, that is, to simplify everything to the bare necessities." [2] By December 8 they had moved into a tiny, bare-necessity court apartment at 253-A West Loraine Street in Glendale. Dreiser had warned McCord to keep his arrival secret—that he would be too busy for a while for visiting. He even kept his publisher in the dark as to his whereabouts. Lincoln Schuster had to address him through Lengel to ask how he liked California and to add, "Are you getting a chance to do any more work on the long awaited novel." [3]

He saved money in another way, for Helen was now his secretary. Although several of his friends felt that he had funds hidden away, he acted downright poor, now owing Jug at least $2,000. But seemingly unable to resume either *The Bulwark* or *The Stoic*, he returned to his philosophy work, arranging more discussions with scientists at nearby Caltech. He wrote Mrs. Upton Sinclair for information about the solar plexus, saying, "I have had peculiar experiences with mine." [4] With *The Bulwark* in mind he did read three of Rufus Jones' works, *The Later Periods of Quakerism, Finding the Trail of Life* and *The Trail of Life in the Middle Years*, also dipping deeply into John Woolman's *Journal*. Despising religion by rote, he respected sincere reverence and independent inquiry. For "God" and "religion," which he associated with slavish dogma, he would substitute "the creative force" and "understanding." He had long been drawn to the Quakers because of the simplicity with which they expressed their mysticism, their elimination of priests and ceremonies and their insistence that each individual could establish communion with the creator—a liking increased by his admiration for Rufus Jones.

He was not merely stubborn in refusing to finish a novel. Dreiser, in his great unhappiness, in his consciousness of advancing years and waning powers, needed more than ever to strike some balance with the universe, to attain some comprehension of his place in it. He was on a religious quest,

59

though he called it a quest for understanding and peace. Science was the road he took, even if it went only part of the way, stopping at the mysteries he sought so eagerly to pierce that he seemed to be beating his fists at a closed door. "Edgar, God is slicker than we are," he wrote Masters. "He's always one lap ahead. . . ."[5]

Though a formal philosopher would have found his thinking confused, it was never shallow. He believed that man was a myth, not living independently but being lived by the creative force, as was every ant, elephant and orchid. Among his departures from conventional religion had been his rejection of an after-life and his long-held conviction that the creative force was at least as evil as it was good—responsible for hate, inequity, capitalists and war. "Up until I was forty years of age," he said, "I believed fully that the world belonged to the Devil."[6] Now, moved as often by emotion as by intellect—the yellow flowers at Cold Spring Harbor, the conversation with the snake—he was inclined to give the creator the benefit of the doubt. To the finite mind it appeared impossible that there could be good without evil, perhaps the creator was not intentionally cruel, and life on the whole seemed "more good than evil. . . ."[7]

Mencken had long felt that he would end up repentant. "I laid [Masters] a bet that you will enter Holy Orders before you leave this earth," he wrote, not entirely in jest.[8]

The astonishing thing about Dreiser's philosophy was not its profundity but the vast hunger it revealed. In January he and Helen attended a seance at the Pasadena home of Upton and May Craig Sinclair, both believers in psychic phenomena. In a darkened room, a blindfolded medium named Arthur Ford summoned spirits. Dreiser, who had partaken of liquid spirits (*not* at Sinclair's), fell sound asleep in his chair until the party ended. On the way home, Helen told him what had transpired, among them the statement of one spirit that a man named Yost sought to get a message through to his son. Dreiser, remembering his old friend Charles E. Yost in Fayette, Ohio, wrote him immediately to find if he was deceased. He was glad to learn that Yost was alive, but still half convinced of the authenticity of the message even though this disputed his denial of any after-life.[9]

With his inclination to shoulder the whole world's woes, Dreiser was upset not only by the mental conflict between himself and Helen but by defeats suffered by the Spanish Loyalists and graft in the Los Angeles fire department. Mrs. Lorna Smith, a Glendale housewife who contributed to the local paper, called to interview him one day and found him intoxicated. "You seem like a good sort," he said drunkenly, and she beat a hasty retreat.[10]

"Strangely enough," Helen wrote Fabri, "now that T & I are together again I feel that things will break for us again. . . . I do hope we'll be left alone a while if you know what I mean."[11] Fabri knew what she meant.

To President Roosevelt, who at last had initiated a plan for sending food to Spain, Dreiser wrote gratefully, "You did what I so much would have liked to

do for you." [12] But after Barcelona fell and the Loyalist collapse was imminent, he was no longer interested when the Friends asked his continued support for Spanish relief. "The Loyalist cause was what I was most intensely
sympathetic with. . . ." he replied. "I now feel that the Fascists should now
[sic] take care of their own. . . . I feel that any aid to a Fascist Government is a marked disloyalty to American Democracy." [13]

Still high on the money-making possibilities of his Giants' Hotel, he wrote
Briggs, "It seems to me that you are neglecting The Fair idea. You seemed
greatly interested at first but not since." Through still another Hollywood
agent, A. Dorian Otvos, he got an encouraging nibble from Universal on
Sister Carrie. Through George Bye he sold the Rotarian (for $125) an article,
"Life at Sixty-seven," in which he commented on the achievements of men
long past youth. Masters wrote to praise it but pointed out, "Some of your
statistics are wrong. . . . Grant was 39 when the war broke out. He was 46
when elected president. Du Maurier was just 60 when he published Trilby,
and 62 when he died. Samuel Butler died at 77, and was 47 when he published
Erewhon, and he was dead when The Way of All Flesh was published. . . .
Dante lived to be 56 years old. . . ." [14]

II. HITLER IS CORRECT

Jettisoning Clark Getts, who expected a 25 per cent commission,
Dreiser settled on Ernest Briggs (who took 20 per cent) and in February went
on a grueling lecture tour—Oakland, San Francisco, Portland, Salt Lake City,
Logan, Ogden and Provo. His subject in most of these lectures was "Life," a
topic large enough to include politics. Politically he was guided almost
absolutely by his blind prejudices, which in such areas as Russia, England and
capitalism had become obsessions. He had stilled his doubts about Russia,
reasoning that the elimination of traitors was justified in so holy a cause. He
had exulted over Hitler's humiliation of the British, and he was convinced
that the lying, British-slanted American press greatly exaggerated the German outrages as they had in 1914.

On the platform he repeated his concern about the shameful gap between
the haves and have-nots. In Portland he leveled such a blistering tirade against
the British that there was some hissing, newspapers panned him and complaints were made to his lecture agent. In Utah he castigated Americans for
reading comic strips and dancing "swing stuff" instead of preparing for the
war that surely would come. Although he said of Roosevelt, "He's the only
president who has done anything for the country since I was born," he was
fretting about signs of Rooseveltian sympathy for England. He returned
home exhausted late in February, $1,570 richer for the six lectures (minus
commissions and expenses), to write Briggs that thereafter "I am not taking
less than three hundred dollars for an appearance." [15] To Franklin Folsom he
wired:

HAVE WRITERS LEAGUE CABLE POPE AS REPRESENTATIVE OF CHRIST ON EARTH
URGING FRANCO TO SPARE LIVES OF FALLEN SPANISH FOE SAY CHURCH NOW DOM-
INANT IN SPAIN SHOULD BE FIRST AND QUICK TO EXERCISE CHRISTIAN CHARITY.[16]

He devoted time to money-making efforts, as if really pinched. The evidence suggests that Dreiser, with his terror of poverty, kept a few little sums
hidden away—perhaps unknown even to Helen—and that he was never quite
as poor as he appeared. The terror was there nevertheless. In addition to
continuous dickering with several film agents, he tried vainly to land himself
on a "personality" radio program. He sought to promote a series of motion
pictures about the wonders of science, writing the would-be producers that if
they used his name widely in the series "you have the equivalent of what
would be in the field of finance an important investment." He continued his
efforts to free himself from Simon & Schuster, whose statement showed that
he owed them $10,114.39, representing their advance plus legal and other
charges—a figure he felt far too high.

Though he was now more than three years late with the novel promised to
Simon & Schuster, he saw himself as the victim of a Jewish plot to suppress all
his works in retaliation for his writings about the Jews. He suspected that
Arthur Pell, head of the Liveright firm, and Simon & Schuster were parties to
the plot. He wrote Lengel:

"As you know, [Simon & Schuster's] present attitude toward me, and their
attitude, really, ever since I went in their [sic], has been amazingly antagonistic. It may be nothing more than a suspicion but I have had the feeling all
along that the dreadful deal I got on my left over Liveright books . . . was
arranged between Pell and themselves through Mr. Shimkin [Leon Shimkin
of Simon & Schuster], and that all along he has been a cause as well as a
party to their attitude toward me." He went on, "This constant under-cover
talk about my anti-Judaism . . . has caused all sorts of people who are
inimical to me . . . to not only play this up but exaggerate it in every
quarter, so that I feel that Simon and Schuster may themselves be joined in
this issue to the end of taking me off the market entirely. It may be that they
identify me with Germany and have decided to include me in their campaign against Teutonic Culture." He saw sinister significance in the fact
that a Miss Kransbaum, formerly Pell's private secretary, now worked for
Simon & Schuster: "I am convinced that Pell has been identified with this
house [Simon & Schuster] since I was mistakenly led into dealing with
them." [17]

To another New York friend, Dayton Stoddart, he wrote, "Get me the
names of a number of fairly recently organized non-Jewish publishers,"
adding, "Can you tell me whether W. W. Norton or anyone connected with
his organization in a financial control sense is Jewish? All this is strictly
private. . . ." [18]

Confident that he would sell Sister Carrie to Universal, who had taken an
option, he wrote to John Barrymore, recently in the headlines because of his

collapse in Chicago while appearing in *My Dear Children,* "Get well. Decide to. Don't die. Live to present Hurstwood for me. I have, for so long, thought of *you* treading—in art—his sorrowful way—his via dolorosa. Will you not? I so completely admire and respect you." [19]

But hitches developed in the sale, again because of the everlasting objections of the Hays office. Dreiser was making frequent motor trips to the Hollywood studios, trying to close the deal that would free him from immediate worry. His defeat by the film censors 39 years after *Carrie* was published—long after it had become a classic—was maddening. Certainly no American author had suffered so long and so grievously at the hands of petty moralists.

He wrote Mencken, "This region is stuffed with hard boiled savage climbers, stuffed and mounted shirts, the lowest grade of political grafters, quacks not calculable as to number or variety, all grades of God-shouters (now welcoming Heywood Broun) and loafers, prostitutes, murderers and perverts. In the bland sunshine here they multiply like germs in the canal zone. What saves it is the wisdom, taste, honor and virtue of the moving picture industry[.]" [20] To Dayton Stoddart he amplified the description: "This is a selfish, self-concentrated, mean, loafing town. The business and political world is hard boiled & cruel. The movies are solidly Jewish[.] They've dug in, employ only Jews with American names and buy only what they cannot abstract and disguise. And the dollar sign is the guide—mentally & physically. That America should be led—the mass—by their direction is beyond all believing. In addition they are arrogant, insolent, and contemptuous." [21]

Now Jug's attorneys were dunning him for back payments. He replied that her demands were unjust, that his moral obligation was not to her but to Helen: "Now I am in a low period, financially, in my life. I am 68 years old. I have to devote considerable attention to my health." He would pay Jug when he could, he said, ending:

> You can do what you will about this but as I see it you cannot get blood out of a turnip. If I sell anything you will probably be the first one to know it. And I might add that I am trying everything to bring that about. [22]

Esther McCoy, now living in Santa Monica, one day drove him to Torrance, where he consulted a fortune teller while she waited outside. Visiting the home of Lorna Smith, who was doing research for him (as was Miss McCoy), he spied a set of an Englishman's books on a table and said with supreme contempt, "Galsworthy." But he wrote Mrs. Smith kindly to discount her tendency to epilepsy: "For heaven sake quit worrying about this epilepsy business. Look at the company your in. *Julius Caesar, Napoleon, Mohammed, Peter the Hermit, Ignatious* [sic] *Loyola* (Founder of the Jesuits), *Dostoievsky,* probably Shakespeare, if the truth were known. . . . Your too big mentally to let a thing like this annoy you. I've had consumption three times—three big fibrous patches are a part of my lungs. I've had appendicitis, neuritis, high blood pressure, chilblains, bunions, corns, only one good eye, falling hair, falling of the womb, scarlet fever, Anglophobia and a lot of things and here I am." [23]

He could be wonderfully comforting to those he liked.

In May he and Helen moved to another cheap apartment at 1426 North Hayworth Avenue, just off Sunset Boulevard in Hollywood, so that he could be closer to the film people he was dickering with constantly. "I did it to save 10.00 a month in gasoline," he wrote Mencken.[24] Feeling forgotten by the world, he was pleased when Boris Chaliapin arrived in July to paint his portrait, commissioned by the Indiana drug magnate, Josiah K. Lilly, who was having portraits executed of many Hoosier authors.

Chaliapin, warned of Dreiser's touchiness, was cautious as he began the sittings. But the painter was a man of warm temperament, a *doer* after Dreiser's heart. They got on famously. Chaliapin thought his face fascinating—not handsome but strong and dour. Avoiding talk about politics, the painter finished the portrait after about ten sittings, getting in the dourness. Dreiser hesitantly suggested that perhaps it was a trifle harsh. "I'll change it," Chaliapin said. He raised the corners of the mouth into the suggestion of a smile, though he disliked the effect. Dreiser did too. "My God," he said, much upset, "why did I tell you to change it? Of course you were right the first time." Chaliapin happily changed it back and remained a friend for the rest of Dreiser's life, finding him always straightforward and companionable and wondering how anyone could think him quarrelsome.[25]

To Lengel, who was trying to sell the manuscript of *An American Tragedy* for $4,500, Dreiser suggested an approach to the Hoosier Lilly:

> As you know he is very wealthy. . . . I feel, though, that in this situation the price should be around $10,000 for the manuscript. . . .[26]

So anxious was he to sell *Carrie* that for the first time in his life he was willing to retreat a trifle to settle the two chief Hays-office objections—the unpunished sinfulness of Carrie and the suicide of Hurstwood. To his agent Otvos he wrote, "I think the two main suggestions can be adjusted," [27] while to another film man he pointed out that Hurstwood could be shown dying in a breadline and added, "I personally suggested that a different ending could be used—a somewhat more optimistic ending—several of which I have in mind." [28] A few years earlier Dreiser would have cut his throat before writing such words.

In August, the astonishing Nazi-Soviet pact that so stunned Earl Browder and most American communists brought only relief to Dreiser. It represented safety for Russia and a threat to England. It showed Hitler's basic goodness. For *Common Sense* he wrote an article, "The Dawn Is in the East," which, like so many of his political observations, he had printed in broadside form and sent to a large mailing list of friends, newspapers and public officials, including the President. In the pact he saw no threat to civilization—only to capitalist oppressors. Russia, he wrote, represented a world hope for equity, while Germany was merely seeking legitimate expansion and, when this was gained, would be tolerant toward the Jews.[29]

Roosevelt soon betrayed him. He recognized Franco Spain, gave England's king and queen a rousing welcome during their American visit, and after Germany's September first invasion of Poland made no secret of his hostility toward the Nazis. Dreiser wrote Mencken:

> I begin to suspect that Hitler is correct. The president may be part Jewish. His personal animosity toward Hitler has already resulted in placing America in the Allied camp—strengthening Britain's attitude and injuring Germany in the eyes of the world. The brass! [30]

Helen, who had long believed that women were a necessary stimulus to his writing, wrote Fabri, "He is trying now to do better. . . . This is no time to play too soft a hand with him. Women can't help him. . . . Not any more. From here on they can only help to break him down. . . . He is not so terribly strong. And yet he is very domineering. . . . He will never give me up altogether. . . . Knowing that he really cares for me down deep, and very deep, made me fight on and come back and fight on some more." [31]

One of Dreiser's New York women friends had come to California to visit him. But Helen was now fighting on chiefly against Estelle Manning, a young Hollywood widow he had met during the summer and to whom he had addressed a poem, fragments of which read:

> *I think of your Boticelli [sic] face and body!*
> *Your wistful, understanding, observing Eyes!*
> *Out of the renaissence [sic]—you! . . .*
>
> *Its Saturday.*
> *I'm lonely.*
> *For the room misses you.*
> *And the streets—*
> *And so do I—so much—*
> *And love you, too.*[32]

Mrs. Manning, believing him unencumbered (as he was in a sense), sometimes picked him up in her car while Helen gazed angrily from the window. He could not help himself since there was no free will and it was, as he wrote Mrs. Manning, "a chemic and psychic fact." Soon he was encouraging her in her writing, recommending her work to three agents—Lengel, Bye and Jacques Chambrun—and collaborating with her on several film scenarios.

For years Sherwood Anderson had been a Dreiser admirer, lamenting his desertion of fiction and also his increasing isolation. When the Andersons visited Los Angeles that fall, Dreiser clung to his privacy. He and Helen did not invite them to the skimpy Hollywood apartment (was its cheapness a factor after the New York splendor?) but met them downtown and dined with them at a Mexican restaurant near the Figueroa Hotel. This was the last Dreiser-Anderson meeting, and their correspondence ended thereafter.

Dreiser's social retrenchment was that of a man worried about money and preoccupied with women and causes. Enthusiastic about *The Grapes of Wrath*, he reproved Lorna Smith for finding fault with it, saying sternly, "That book has done too much good for you to *ever* say a word against it." His moods, usually low, could swing high. "It is refreshing," he wrote, "to live in a time when there are so many truly humane and important things to do. How wonderful to be useful—to something or somebody—most of all to the truly needy." [33] Clad in a green suit and green shirt as he addressed a bevy of Bel Air Junior Leaguers who were not truly needy, he said, "Women's clubs are a lot of baloney," and added, "You are not so hot. What do you do or accomplish? Go out and attack the politicians and concern yourselves with local conditions." But he was so charming that the women were not really angry, even when he expressed disgruntlement that they served tea—not a drop of liquor—at the end of his talk.[34]

Llewelyn Powys, to whom he had sent a touching letter of encouragement, died in England December 2, a loss of one of the old friends who now seemed almost his only friends. Later that month, at a Hollywood cocktail place with Helen, Dreiser was handed a note by a waiter. A patron at a nearby table—the name appeared to be John Stemtuck—had recognized him and invited him to have a drink with him. Dreiser joined the stranger, had the drink, traded a few generalities and left. Six weeks later he found the note in his pocket and was mortified to learn that Stemtuck was really Steinbeck. He wrote Steinbeck a remorseful note of explanation, adding:

> Christ, what a dunce! The one man I've been truly wanting to meet since I read *Of Mice and Men*, not to mention your beautiful and powerful *Grapes of Wrath*. And there I sat and then walked away without saying anything!—trashy formalities. My God! [35]

III. I AM NOT A DEAD AUTHOR

Fighting off old age, rejecting the rules of caution usually observed by men in their late sixties, Dreiser was occasionally ill, spending about a month in bed in the spring of 1940. Helen always cared for him tenderly. Since she was also his secretary and they had no servants, her work was strenuous and she could hardly be blamed for resentment when, after she nursed him back to health, he would run off with another woman.

Unlike Sinclair Lewis, who kept batting out a best-selling novel of dubious merit every year or so, Dreiser had published no new novel in fourteen years and no original full-length work since the sorry *Tragic America* in 1931. Although his works still sold substantially in Europe, he was almost forgotten as an author in the United States. Indeed, many of the younger American generation thought him dead. It hurt him terribly that no American publisher seemed to *want* him, Scribners, Viking and Longmans Green having parried his overtures. He blamed his plight on Simon & Schuster for failing to promote his old books, convinced that they were deliberately keeping him poor and unpublicized in order to force him to produce *The Stoic.* When Leon Shimkin of Simon & Schuster wrote to ask him about his plans, he replied:

"It is quite true that I have been looking for another publisher—and failing that, to pay the entire sum due you from me, in order that thereafter I may subsidize a publisher to represent me in the matter of publicity and sale. For it so happens that I am not a dead author." He added, "Since Horace Liveright died I have never had a publisher," accused Simon & Schuster of dumping his books on second-hand dealers so that there were no royalties, and of doing nothing for him.[36]

He retained a New York attorney, Stanley M. Moffat, to take action against Simon & Schuster, but Moffat could give him no help since he was still in default himself. At times Dreiser likened his own eclipse to that of Herman Melville, thinking with sympathy of Melville's nineteen-year service in the New York custom house and half convinced that this was the sort of neglect great authors had to expect.[37] Saved that spring by a $3,000 payment from RKO for an option on *Sister Carrie,* Dreiser was again too inflamed by social causes to concentrate on his own work. When requested by the Hoover-sponsored Finnish Relief Fund for a statement in behalf of the Finns, then bravely standing off the Russian assault, he replied, "I am not just another American propaganda 'sucker.' " Where, he demanded, was Hoover when the Spanish Loyalists needed help—the Abyssinians and the Chinese?[38] He circulated his letter and followed it later with a longer circulated broadside describing Finland as the tool of English designs on Russia. He leaped to the defense of the *New Masses,* now being harassed by the F.B.I., writing in part, "Our profiteers have already tortured the people to a point where they are about ready to recapture what rightly belongs to all."[39] He wrote Governor Culbert Olson urging him not to return a captured chain gang fugitive back to the "obsessed sadists" of Florida. He wrote the chairman of the state pardon board asking mercy for an artist imprisoned for a homosexual offense, pointing out the artistic loss to the world because of Oscar Wilde's imprisonment.

When the Nazis imprisoned Lion Feuchtwanger, his tenderness vanished, possibly because of Feuchtwanger's race and because of Dreiser's lingering hope that his own books would be cleared of the Nazi ban. On a letter from Franklin Folsom of the League of American Writers, urging that he protest, he scribbled to Helen, "Write Folsom I am on vacation in Old Mexico & can't be reached."[40] To a similar request from Ben Huebsch, he replied that he did not see what he could do: "As far as Hitler is concerned I am taboo. My books are banned—so."[41]

He was anything but distressed by the German breakthrough into France and the British retreat across the Channel, writing, "But according to England it is not going to surrender until all of its colonies & the U. S. have been exhausted. Really the gall of that gang makes me laugh." [42] To Lorna Smith he gave a new research job, telling her, "I want you to find everything anti-British that you can find." [43]

Helen, as would become her habit when Dreiser became too heavily involved with other women, went to Portland in June. He thereupon joined Mrs. Manning, visited the new Mt. Palomar observatory and wrote Helen affectionately, suggesting that he was hard at work. A week later he flew to Portland to join her, thereby offending Mrs. Manning, whom he wrote from Portland:

"I did not expect that you would begin looking on Helen as the other girl or another girl, since she was with me from the first & if I had preferred her I certainly would not have begun devoting myself to you. But now it begins to look as though you had decided that I must drop H—— entirely and have only to do with you. . . ." Bearing in mind that Mrs. Manning had a small child, he went on, "But for two writers trying to work in separate fields and yet at one & the same time to jointly manage a family in the same household. I did not and cannot see that. I felt—and I still feel that you would be better & more happily placed at the head of your own family group writing—and with me (if you truly wanted me) as not only your friend and companion, but as one who could advise & help in the matter of your development; while privately pursuing my own literary ways as best I could. And I really thought that was what we were doing most happily until the matter of this trip came up & I went off with you first. . . . As for all this bitterness on your part I do not get it. I have assured you I have no passion, love or sexual relations with H—— & that is true. At the same time it appears she is also undergoing a change of life & is suffering in various ways due to it." [44]

In June, when Lengel relayed him an offer of a flat $5,000 to write a short book urging America to stay out of the war, for Oskar Piest of the new and small Veritas Press, he jumped at the chance. He needed the money. It also gave him an opportunity to show that America was controlled by "Mr. Morgan and the Sixty Families" [45] who were hand in glove with the foxhunting aristocracy of England, and that any aid to England was the negation of democracy. Since his recent reading of Ferdinand Lundberg's *America's 60 Families*, that phrase had become a standby.

IV. FORTY YEARS AFTER *Sister Carrie*

In July, just forty years after the young Theodore Dreiser in Missouri received disturbing news from New York about his first novel, the old Dreiser began a book for which he was temperamentally unsuited. It was a crash three-month job, aimed at hitting the bookstores before America could move farther toward intervention in the war. For $1,000 Dreiser engaged Cedric Belfrage, the young British novelist who was then in Hollywood and whom he had met through Lorna Smith, to aid him in the writing. He assured Lengel that the book would be pro-American rather than pro-Communist, although he had difficulty in distinguishing between the two and he added, "My study of it [communism] leads me to feel that it is *developing* (and for the first time) ambition in the millions. . . . (It is true they have a few dogmatic non-liberal laws covering free speech, etc., but these will pass, I know.)" [46]

Belfrage worked with Dreiser at the Hayworth Avenue apartment about three mornings a week, continuing at his own home the rest of the time. An anti-capitalist, a sharp critic of his own native land and an admirer of Dreiser's novels, he felt that this book could be an important influence against the enlargement of the war. Tremendously struck by Dreiser, he came to see both his greatness and his failings.

"I soon discovered," Belfrage recalled, "that Dreiser's feelings about England and the economic royal families of the United States amounted to phobias. Indeed he managed . . . to connect the two in a kind of international plot in which 'the Jews' were also involved." Belfrage was troubled by Dreiser's bias and choler as well as by his admiration for Hitler. He found himself counseling the older man against anti-Semitic outbursts in the book and trying to hold his spleen against the English within reason. Yet he observed, "[Dreiser's] basic motivations were transparently good. The overwhelming impression he gave was love of people, especially his own people, and hatred of oppression and all violence."

He was amazed at the apparent straits of the world-famous writer—the cramped apartment, the cheap furniture: "I believe he was absolutely broke, with debts on top of that. . . ." And he was distressed by the disintegration of Dreiser himself: "I would judge that Dreiser had only some two or three hours per day in which he could work coherently. What happened on the days I worked at his 'home' was invariably the same: along about noon he would begin to sag with weariness and he and I would stroll along to the drugstore . . . to get a pint of whisky. With this in a paper bag we returned . . . and within a few minutes Dreiser was out of action. He could not take liquor any more (though he could not do without it) and after two drinks, sometimes just one, I saw that the working day was over, for Dreiser began to ramble and could not organize any thoughts. My practice was to leave as soon as possible after this, although he wanted me to stay and chat, for he was one of the loneliest men I ever knew." [47]

The anti-British material which Dreiser had ordered from Mrs. Smith now proved useful. Belfrage, though he saw that the book would not be what he had hoped, managed to restrain Dreiser from some extravagances. To Mencken, Dreiser wrote, "Can you tell me where I am likely to pick up data explaining the financial hook up between big American finance and big

British finance,—Threadneedle Street and Wall Street?" [48] He sent the same query the same day to Corliss Lamont at *Soviet Russia Today*. He wrote both the President and John L. Lewis seeking data on the maritime enterprises that would show corporation graft.

Belfrage knew that he was witnessing a tragedy of unappreciated genius—that Dreiser was declining not only because of his brooding over social injustices but because of the oblivion into which he had sunk: "Somehow his position took on a particularly ghastly hue against the backdrop of Hollywood, where callousness was part of the air one breathed. . . . I can recall introducing him to movie people whom I knew . . . who obviously had never heard of him." Yet the old mastodon could laugh until tears came at a "peace" recording of the Almanac Singers which Belfrage played for him and whose words went something like:

> *Franklin Roosevelt told the people how he felt*
> *And we darned near believed what he said.*
> *He said I hate war, and so does Eleanor*
> *But we won't be safe till everybody's dead.* [49]

Belfrage felt that Dreiser had virtually no close friends. The glitter of Fifty-seventh Street was gone, and the circle had indeed narrowed. The leftist John Howard Lawson, formerly a *Daily Worker* correspondent and now a top film scenarist, was an admiring caller. Lillian Rosedale Goodman, a friend since she was a girl in New York, lived nearby with her lawyer husband Mark. Clare Kummer, Arthur Henry's widow, was in Beverly Hills. The widowed Maria Samson was now in Hollywood. Dreiser was close to Dr. McCord in Pasadena and friendly with many scientists at Caltech and Mt. Wilson. Among other good companions were Esther McCoy, Lorna Smith and her husband Byron, and the A. Dorian Otvoses. Indeed, he let the agent Otvos, who was working hard to sell *Sister Carrie*, know that he could stand a little less friendship, writing him:

> Friendships—true friendships—are valued by me as by others and I seek, as others do, to make the most of them. Half friendships and half business relationships are another matter; very common and not to be taken too seriously. One senses, always, the practical interest at the bottom. . . .
>
> As you know our relationship began as a business one, and, at bottom, has remained so, involving, as it has, meeting people whom, in the main, I have not been interested in meeting, writing letters to people to whom, on my own account, I would never have written. . . .
>
> However, my feeling toward you is about as it has been all along. The strong point is that I am not a person who covets intimacy with anyone and I never have been. My work is the all absorbing thing; it takes the most of me. And so in saying what I did at first I feel that I am not discriminating against you personally in any way. Rather it is that I prefer to return to the author-agent or agent-author base, leaving the personal intimacy phase in the background. I know you will know that this involves no reflection on either your personal virtues or abilities. [50]

From Mencken came a letter including a query:

> The *New Masses* brethren sent me a circular in which you are made to speak of the *New Masses* as "our magazine." Is this authorized? If so, have you turned Communist? I certainly hope you haven't. It must be manifest to any one that Communism stands in contempt of the imperishable truths of our holy Christian religion.[51]

Dreiser was too preoccupied with the book, tentatively called *Is America Worth Saving?*, to answer. But Helen would not let his birthday pass without observance. There was a small party on August 27 which Lorna Smith thought the saddest thing she ever saw. Only about a dozen guests were there—the Smiths, the Goodmans and Esther McCoy among them. "Helen had on a gorgeous gown," Mrs. Smith recalled, "but it was years old. They still had their old Buick. They seemed almost down and out." But there was punch and some gayety, with Maria Samson singing "Happy Birthday" and kissing Dreiser on the cheek. Helen herself sang Negro spirituals, possibly with mixed feelings, for another of Dreiser's woman friends from New York was one of the guests.

When Lengel received the first part of the Dreiser-Belfrage script, he wrote, "Is it really necessary for you to be so hard on the English so as to injure your own publishing relations in Great Britain?"[52]

"Don't worry about my English publishers," Dreiser replied. "The war seems to have finished them. . . ."[53] Lengel was downright uneasy when he received the remainder of the script in September, writing, "Considering the fact that the book was designed to show the futility of America getting into the war and to show that our interests lie in developing our own national identity, you have wandered pretty much afield at times, and the book indicates that you believe our salvation rests in communism rather than in the development of democracy within the frame-work of the Constitution."[54]

Dreiser admitted that he *had* wandered, that he could not see how to do it otherwise but was willing to consider suggested modifications. Oskar Piest, the publisher, an alien who had taken out only his first papers, feared the book was so radical that it might cause che rejection of his application for citizenship. Fearing libel as well, he had lawyers examine the script and send Dreiser about 50 queries concerning questionable statements—items which Dreiser treated with some sarcasm. Opposite one of their observations, "The charge that Morgan and Rockefeller control politicians is libelous," Dreiser wrote, "This remark by a presumably intelligent firm of lawyers surely ought to be framed for posterity." Rage came quickly, as when *Editor & Publisher* innocently asked him to contribute to an issue celebrating National Newspaper Week and "the blessings of [America's] free press."

He replied, "What between sheer awe of the corporation gall which unquestionably prompts and no doubt finances this industrious labor of yours, and wonder as to how, at this late date, I still come to be on your

National Corporation sucker list I am fairly flattened—not flattered." He arraigned the American press as corrupt, corporation-owned and inimical to labor, and ended:

"Actually if this were a really liberty protected country—one not ruled and stifled by a heartless and greedy band of profiteers, you and your paper might well be charged with fraud, and, if you ventured to take a court oath in behalf of your innocence, convicted of perjury." He had the exchange printed in leaflet form and distributed to his extensive mailing list.[55]

He could support neither Roosevelt nor Willkie (both pro-war and pro-British) in the 1940 election. Swallowing his dislike for Browder, the communist candidate, he spoke on the radio for Browder, saying, "I'm not a Communist and I don't agree with the entire program of the Communist Party," but insisting that only a communist vote would protest "the determination of the rulers of our country to defend the British Empire in every quarter of the world." Browder, following him, declared, "The all-important question before our country is this: Shall America be plunged into the catastrophe of the imperialist war?" [56]

That fall, Dreiser was saved from real or imagined poverty. At long last he sold *Sister Carrie* to RKO for $40,000, the deal being made by A. Dorian Otvos.

2. Publisher No. 8

I. LET THERE BE PEACE

At a September convention in Chicago was founded American Peace Mobilization, a leftist organization dedicated to keeping America out of the war and branding any aid to non-democratic England as a threat to peace. The communists, having learned the advantages of clerical connections, set up an obscure Oklahoma parson, the Rev. John B. Thompson, as president. Among those elected vice-presidents were Dreiser, Richard Wright, Joseph Curran and Vito Marcantonio. Frederick Vanderbilt Field, a lawyer and scion of the Vanderbilt family, was national secretary.

Thoroughly approving, Dreiser was happy to fly (expenses paid) to Washington to make a radio speech and address a mass meeting there for A.P.M. on November 9. He had already written about his book to Field, who was checking it for libel. Oskar Piest being delighted to resign as publisher—especially after the F.B.I. began to investigate his citizenship qualifications—Lengel arranged for its publication by the almost equally little-known Modern Age Books. Since the book amounted to virtually a Bible of A.P.M. beliefs, Field planned to promote its sale through the organization.

From Washington Dreiser sent Estelle Manning a fond telegram. In front of the White House paraded the A.P.M. "perpetual peace vigil"—pickets bearing placards and chanting for peace. Because of a general suspicion of A.P.M.'s objectives—Dreiser was convinced the President was to blame—Field was unable to find a hall available for the mass meeting, so Dreiser addressed a crowd in a chilly public park. In his speech the same day over NBC, he repeated the mossy clichés—praise of Russia, scorn for "England's Lords and Ladies and rich loafers" and urging that America refuse to "fight and die for the one great power in the world that hates all democracies. . . ."[1] On his return west he stopped in Chicago to address a similar A.P.M. rally there, receiving an admiring telegram from Helen. Back home, he wrote Lengel to protest the delay in the publication of the book, wrote Field to put more stress on criminal British machinations, and looked for a house.

Although he had said that the Hayworth Avenue cheesebox was perfectly adequate, now he had a little money, though some of it had gone to pay off Jug and the Internal Revenue claims. Hardly a mile away, at 1015 North Kings Road near Santa Monica Boulevard, he and Helen found a six-room Spanish-type white stucco house with red tile roof and a spacious yard. Off the sizable living room was an ell containing a bedroom, study and connecting bath—ideal for Dreiser's work space. They bought it for about $20,000 and moved in December first. It would be Dreiser's last home on earth—not grand but quiet and pleasant. Furniture stored at Iroki was shipped west. The big desk made from Paul's rosewood piano, which Dreiser had not used for two years, was installed in the study. He was still trying to sell to the films the story based on Paul's career, called *My Gal Sal*, making use of "On the Banks of the Wabash" and others of his songs. These songs having become the property of the Dreiser family, Helen had secured the permission of the brothers and sisters for their use, and Donald Friede, now a Hollywood agent, was looking for a buyer.

Because of his publishing dilemma and his social involvement, Dreiser was doing little work on any of his three unfinished books. He wrote a script for Edward G. Robinson's "Big Town" radio program ("In this case, I will accept $500.00 which is a very small fee for me." [2]). He was furious at the Anglophile Roosevelt ("To me it is terrible to see how we are slipping along [toward war]—the runway greased by that political spieler in the White House. . . . This man has, I am sure, a bulging and even traitorous ego." [3]). It enraged him that two printing companies had refused to handle his antiwar book because of its alleged un-Americanism. Not until January was a printer found, the title being changed from *Is America Worth Saving?* to the safer *America Is Worth Saving*. He sent one of the first copies off the press to Constantine A. Oumansky, Russian ambassador in Washington, writing him:

> I am taking the liberty of sending you a copy of my latest book . . . autographed to Joseph Stalin.[4]

Oumansky responded by sending him a handsome volume about Stalin plus a steady stream of Soviet propaganda. Dreiser agreed when the American Council on Soviet Relations invited him to address them in New York, asking $400 for his expenses, then revising this upward: "Expenses figured too closely. I will really need five hundred." [5]

Putting up at the Commodore in New York February 28, he had the always helpful Marguerite Tjader Harris serving as his secretary. He wired Estelle Manning, "DEAREST THANKS FOR LOVELY LETTER . . ." but inconstantly devoted much attention to two of the women he had left behind in New York. His midday speech at the Commodore before 400 friends of the Soviet was disastrous. The luncheon was delayed and a waiter kept handing him drinks, so that when his time came to speak he was not strictly sober. Clifford Odets, Richard Wright, Dashiell Hammett and Muriel Draper were among the audience who heard him plead for the spread of truth instead of lies about Russia, then get lost in interminable tales of poverty in America: "Forty dollars for a family for a month—my God, you'd think the Government had never heard of $40. But when it comes to billions to get us into war . . . they've got that alright [*sic*]." Robert Elias, now working for his doctorate at the University of Pennsylvania, had come over to hear him. He saw Dreiser shed tears at one point, unable to stop his rambling account of

American injustice, with the audience growing painfully embarrassed. Would he never stop? After some 45 minutes the chairman, Dr. John A. Kingsbury, finally ended the agony by shoving back his chair, standing up and applauding, as did many others—a stratagem that caused the unfinished Dreiser to subside.[6]

Although Dreiser inconsistently thought of himself as a special and superior brand of communist with Moscow connections few others enjoyed, the New York communists made extensive use of him, knowing his susceptibility to praise and attention. When William Z. Foster, Alexander Trachtenberg and Louis Budenz called on him at the hotel, he spoke warmly of Foster as "the most magnificent of Americans," and Budenz noted that when Trachtenberg gave him a party statement to sign, "Dreiser used it word for word as given to him."[7] He also addressed a Russophile mass meeting at Manhattan Center, then read a pleasant story in *The Times*. *My Gal Sal* had been sold by Friede to Fox for "approximately $50,000,"[8] and the thin-ice days were over for a time. Interviewed by Robert van Gelder, he said, "Oh, you can't beat that [Russian] system, you know. A whole country belonging to the people and run by and for the people." And when Van Gelder put a question about Stalin's pact with Hitler:

"Why shouldn't he have that pact? Don't you know your current history, darling? Hasn't anyone ever bothered to tell you the facts of life? Don't you realize that France and England were all set to attack Russia?" And later, "But what's the matter with Americans? They're not the people I think they are if they keep on being suckers to this system. . . ."[9]

He even told Van Gelder how Mrs. Doubleday had suppressed *Carrie* in 1900. He went on to speak in Philadelphia, where Helen had prepared the way for him with a letter to the local head of A.P.M.: "Someone there should look after him after the reception and see that he has a quiet dinner. Otherwise he might forget all about it. . . . It would be advisable too, I think to see that he has an hour to rest before the meeting. . . ."[10] Everywhere he went he had rows with people who disagreed with him. In Philadelphia he was greeted by Wharton Esherick, Louise Campbell and the Heilbrunns, managing to quarrel about politics with Mrs. Heilbrunn and saying, "Well, I didn't come down here to be knifed by my friends." In his speech in the foyer of the Academy of Music he flayed Churchill and the British, said he was not a communist but declared, "The Communist system, if not destroyed by the capitalistic system . . . will actually prove itself the salvation of the world."[11] He returned home in mid-March to spend a day and a half resting in bed and to hear from Mencken: "I trust that your beauty is unimpaired. Every now and then I meet some woman here who speaks of it with her fists clenched and her eyes flashing."[12]

"What letters of condolence have I not written!" he had remarked. "What letters of real sorrow!" On March 19 he wrote a little eulogy for the suddenly deceased Sherwood Anderson: "Anderson, his life and his writings, epitomize for me the pilgrimage of a poet and dreamer across this limited stage called life. . . ." To Eleanor Roosevelt he pointed out that in her "My Day" column April 10 he had been astonished to read that "Mr. Theodore Dreiser" had shown slides to the Roosevelts. The error was important, he said, only because it might dismay his large following, "which has come to believe, and quite correctly, that I am strenuously opposed to the present views and policies of your husband, the President, in regard to England and our support of that Empire. . . ." He closed with a touch of crudity: "Among other things I may add I am deeply touched by, as well as respectful of, your sincere and so loving devotion to all of your children—come what may." [13] Since Mrs. Roosevelt was traveling and did not reply immediately to explain that the name should have read "Theodore Dreier," he had his letter printed and broadcast to his mailing list.

On June 22 occurred an event that all but unhinged him. The Germans invaded Russia.

II. LET THERE BE WAR

The Nazi eastward push so shocked Dreiser that he took briefly to bed. For years he had had little nationalistic American feeling, being unable to applaud a nation ruled (as he saw it) by the plutocratic 60 families. He thought loosely in global terms. His agony reflected his terrible sense of danger to Russia, the light of the world, the founder of a classless society which (unless crushed by capitalism) would eventually spread its benefits to all humanity, America included. Thus the cause of Russia was the cause of America and every other nation. He knew little about Russia now. His attitude toward the Soviet had long since embraced the utter acceptance of religious faith—a glowing, intuitive concept of the one nation on earth that elevated the multitude and obliterated the capitalist.

So eccentric was his political thinking that his passion for Russia had not quelled his admiration for Germany and his hope that Hitler, too, had world-saving potentialities. Now his hopes for an enlightened world had crashed against the hard fact that the Nazis were bombing Kiev and other cities and pouring into Byelorussia and the Ukraine. *England was Russia's ally*. He had no doubt that Britain would play traitor.

Yesterday the American communists had lauded the Nazi-Soviet pact and shouted for American non-intervention. Today they were faced by a situation that compelled them to admit that yesterday's arguments were in error. William Z. Foster denounced the Nazi invasion as "an attack upon the peoples of the United States" and called for full American support against Hitler. On June 21 the A.P.M. issued a call for National Peace Week. On June 22, the day of the invasion, all talk of National Peace Week ceased and the "perpetual peace vigil" at the White House stopped short of perpetuity, the pickets vanishing quietly. Dreiser's *America Is Worth Saving* was instantly obsolete. A.P.M. itself went into seclusion for a fortnight, after which it announced that its initials now stood for American People's Mobilization and that it favored "aid to Britain." [14] Dreiser's thinking also changed. He wired Field of A.P.M.:

> SUPPORT RUSSIA. URGE AMERICAN GOVERNMENT SO TO DO. DENOUNCE ALL FASCIST CORPORATION ATTEMPTS TO STIR UP AMERICA AGAINST RUSSIA, INCLUDING LINDBERGH AND HIS AMERICAN PEACE CROWD, HOOVER AND HURST [*sic*]. JAPAN WILL PROBABLY ATTACK RUSSIA NEXT. IN THAT CASE DENOUNCE JAPAN. [15]

To the *New Masses* he wrote, "It is my conviction that this attack on the Soviet Union was planned from the very beginning by the Money International. . . ." [16]

To Mencken he later wrote, "I ceased following Hitler when . . . he attacked Russia—my pet. At first I thought that he had a progressive program for a United States of Europe. . . . But when I saw Russia being attacked . . . my interest in Doctor Hitler, save as a crook and a high finance stool pigeon passed. And that goes for today, tomorrow & the end of time." [17]

III. TODAY IS A SAD DAY

That summer, at Dreiser's invitation, Robert Elias arrived to make an office of the guest room above the garage, where he began an examination of Dreiser's papers for the biography. In New York he had sought to interview Jug, now living at 92 Grove Street in the Village. She had replied:

> I am sorry, but I can not oblige you by talking about my life with Mr. Dreiser. Altho I've been asked by many others, I have talked to no one. [18]

In Hollywood Elias occasionally questioned Dreiser about aspects of his life and writings, finding him entirely frank and open except about women—a subject Elias was forced to avoid. Dreiser, having been warned of the danger of reinfection in fiddling with a linen handkerchief, now mutilated Kleenex as he talked. On August 27, his seventieth birthday, Elias noted, not a single reporter came to interview him. The "lying, capitalistic press" was taking its revenge on a man now considered a crank, a bore and a Red. But Helen, with the Dreiser fortunes considerably improved, threw a sizable garden party at which the Almanac Singers entertained. She had traded in her old Buick for a newer second-hand one, while Dreiser himself bought a new Plymouth. Helen resumed her singing, taking lessons from Lillian Goodman, dropping them whenever her domestic situation grew too trying. Dreiser was often quite frank about leaving her to join a woman waiting in a car in front to be gone for a few days or more. To Mrs. Goodman Helen admitted, "I'm always surprised when I see him coming in the door." [19]

Yet the Dreiser-Helen relationship was gradually changing. She took care of all household as well as secretarial chores for him, saw that both cars were greased and serviced and that the lawn was fertilized and mown. She sent occasional financial help to the aged Mame, prepared health foods for Dreiser and saw that his bristling array of medicines and pills was in order. When he was ill, she nursed him as no one else could, regarding him more as a crotchety father than as a mate. Donald Friede was impressed by her devotion to him, "as if she were always drawing an invisible shawl around his shoulders." Cedric Belfrage felt that without Helen, Dreiser might have gone to pieces altogether. Although he still threatened at times to leave her, Dreiser needed Helen for survival, Helen knew that he needed her, and he knew that she knew.

America Is Worth Saving had been either ignored by the critics or condemned as the kind of propaganda Hitler would love. "I hear that [the] F.B.I. has a blacklist of books. . . ." Dreiser wrote George Seldes. "I know positively now that AMERICA IS WORTH SAVING and JENNIE GERHARDT are on the list." [20] Obviously John Cowper Powys in Wales never saw the former book, for he remained a friend, but copies did reach the bomb-damaged London office of Otto Kyllmann. Shocked, he wrote Dreiser:

Today is a sad day for me. . . .

I have looked at [the book] for an hour or two, but have not read it through. I doubt if I shall ever be able to. From what I have seen it seems based on ignorance and malice, and after all these years I have not the heart to go on perusing it.

My first reaction is that it is a stab in the back, and that you of all people should kick us when you think we are down is a very bitter thought. . . .

I gather that you are gloating at the thought that we are finished, and you urge your country to keep out of the war. "Let brutal and undemocratic conniving and plotting end for once in our national history; let us refuse to be suckers; let's guard our own homeland, not England's decaying and criminal Empire."

So be it. Under the "New Order," I suppose you will be happy and prosperous, and either work under a Gauleiter or be one yourself; more power to your elbow.

For us here, there is only one watchword—Victory or Death.

I hope you and those who feel like you will wax and grow fat and be happy and prosperous. Here we shall go down fighting: "We shall fight on the seas and oceans. We shall fight on the beaches, we shall fight on the landing grounds; in the fields; in the streets and in the hills. We shall never surrender."

When I think of the happy hours and days we spent together; when I think of the time we stood under the broken archway at Glastonbury; when I remember how we drove over Exmoor; when I remember the happy hours we spent at Garlands Hotel, which is now in ruins and where seven or eight people were killed by the bombs dropped by German bombers which apparently you rate so highly, I can only regret your entire ignorance of what this country was, and is, and will be.

Here in this building that I am writing from we have suffered four times from enemy action, but the shell of our building still stands and we carry on. . . .

I realise from what I have seen of your book that you will cheer when the day comes that you can cheer for the downfall of the British Empire. But you are mistaken. It may be weeks; it may be months; it may be years, and if, as you fondly hope, we are beaten to our knees, still you will be mistaken. . . .

> Your old friend
> O. Kyllmann

He was so wounded that two days later he sent a shorter letter saying in part, "That you of all people my dear Dreiser could feel & write and publish at this time such heartless & callous words about us was just more than I could bear. . . . Do you really only see Evil in all of us?" [21]

Dreiser replied:

Dearest Kyllmann: I cannot tell you how much your two letters, which came yesterday together, touched me from the personal viewpoint,—the viewpoint that is compounded of my deep love as well as respect for your sensitive and poetic temperament, your wholly honest, kind and socially and individually well meaning and well wishing approach toward every living thing on this earth. . . . And that viewpoint of mine has never changed from the first hour I was with you. . . .

And it will not.

However poorly you may think of me as the author of *America Is Worth Saving*, the critic or enemy as I fear you imagine me to be, of the English people—which I am not—I shall still continue to hold you, as I always have, as my dearest and best friend in England and the equivalent of any best friend I have here.

But, Kyllmann, dear, how can you—even in your extreme distress over the ills of England and its Empire—forget that you are an Englishman, seeing things wholly through your wholly English eyes and responding, as you must, emotionally through all your days to things English . . . and forget so completely that I am an American-born, responding from childhood, as you did to your England, to all the new and energetic and humane, as well as inventive and creative and pioneering traditions of my own country. . . .

But, darling, apart from all that, both as England and our present day Corporation America would see it, I am not really a true-blue American, for I am at heart and by nature a sympathizer with the great mass or underdog phase of humanity everywhere, but particularly with Russia at the moment, for I do not believe in the wisdom let alone the domination of amassed wealth and have said so ever since I began to write. More, over here, at least, I am really a "Bolshevik" or "Fifth Columnist" or "Red," or what you will, for I believe heart and soul in the value and probable successful outcome of the great Soviet or Communistic system or experiment. I most fervently pray for its success just as I do for that of a wise and rejuvenated China—and I despise the Hitler program of mass and world domination as he has outlined, and wish most earnestly that he might be seized and shot or executed tonight. . . . *

But, darling Kyllmann, please don't imagine because I say this that I have anything against the English people as such—the English rank and file —as set over against the English Lords and Ladies and financiers, whom as I have always felt and known, have not only ignored and bled the five hundred million natives of the Empire outside of England—who, to this hour have no representative in the British Parliament, nor any of any worth in their local halls of legislation. And for what? Well, I can tell you. In order that they might swagger about the world, ruling one fifth of the earth's land as well as five-fifths of salty oceans, and usurping the profits of the labors of the peoples of those lands for their own private purses and none other.

You must not forget that apart from my delightful trips and walks with you in England, I took many others *alone,* and on foot—in London, Liverpool, Glasgow, Birmingham, Manchester, Leeds, Sheffield. . . . And for poverty and human degradation I have never seen anything worse. . . .

But, dear Kyllmann, please, whatever you do, don't mix up or confuse your personal feelings for me with your intense and emotionally justified feelings for your native land. . . . For all I have said about myself, Russia and America and England, I still care for you deeply and always will. In truth, I care so much, that your letter, instead of irritating me in any way, only, instead, evokes in me a deep depression which springs from the fact that this book should have hurt you so much. . . .

You need not publish any more of my books. I can see how difficult that would be, but most surely you could continue to like me who truly loves and respects and admires you so much.

Just think about this for a little while and then write me. This war will surely pass. And you and I may still be alive. If so, I should feel so truly down and reduced if ever I came to England and could not take your hand and hold it in deep affection as I always have and most certainly always will in my own heart and mind, come what will.

Write me.

And forgive.

And hold me to you as your old friend, Dreiser, and I will keep you in my mind and heart ever, as my Kyllmann.

With love and regrets and sorrow for your ills, I am, as I have always been.

Theodore Dreiser.[22]

In the fall, Dreiser used $8,500 of his film winnings to buy his way out of Simon & Schuster, and Lengel was dickering with Putnam's for him. It was probably with this in mind that he agreed to lecture in November before a left-wing group in Indianapolis for $250, which would pay his way to New

* Here Dreiser listed England's appeasement of Hitler and other sins.

York, saying, "You understand, of course, that my regular speaking fees are much more." [23]

Quarreling with Helen and leaving home in a rage, he arrived in Indianapolis to find that conservative circles were aroused over his forthcoming speech and the fact that proceeds were going to Russia. The American Legion, in an open letter in local papers, recalled that only recently he had been an officer of American Peace Mobilization and that now he seemed to have undergone a mysterious change in thinking. A Legion leader declared, "It is a masked attempt to glorify the Soviet Union behind the respectability of a native author." [24] But Dreiser was introduced to an audience of 500 by Prof. Fowler V. Harper of the Indiana University law school and the speech was given without incident—indeed, without Dreiser saying anything unusual. He roasted the British for their traitorous failure to aid Russia. Later he visited the grave of John Dillinger, the bank robber and killer of sixteen, feeling inevitably that Dillinger was a victim of American social inequities. Then, as Harper's house guest, he went down to Bloomington to look around and to see the Old Oaken Bucket football game.

In Bloomington he was astonished at the growth of the university from a few buildings and 600 students when he was there in 1889–90, to a score of buildings and 6,000 students. "The author seems to have an insatiable curiosity about almost everything," a reporter noted. Returning to Indianapolis, he had a last visit with May Calvert Baker, now feeble and totally blind. He wrote Estelle Manning of his loneliness for her, saying, "We'll take the trip as soon as I can get there if I'm not sick," and ending, "You're probably short of cash so I'm enclosing $25." [25]

Suffering arthritic pains, he went on to New York, where he and Lengel met Earle Balch, vice-president of Putnam's. Although Balch talked enthusiastically about taking him over and publishing *The Bulwark*, it involved Putnam's purchase of the many old Dreiser titles still in Simon & Schuster's stockrooms as well as some doubt about Dreiser himself. He had lost some of his old following, was known as unreliable and difficult to deal with and was seventy years old. Balch offered a $1,000 advance,[26] the smallest Dreiser had been tendered for decades but one he eventually accepted. Putnam became his eighth publisher in America. Before he left he conferred with his attorney, Stanley Moffat, about that old, old complaint, the alleged *Back Street-Jennie Gerhardt* plagiarism.

He returned home late in November, evidently joining forces with Mrs. Manning, Helen being in Portland. He wrote Helen affectionately and at length, describing his trip, saying he was "working as usual" and commenting, "I was sorry we parted so but somehow I can't stand ruling by others and so we clash—often so uselessly it seems to me since nothing is gained by it. We go on as before." [27]

For thirty years William C. Lengel had been his loyal friend, sacrificing time and effort in Dreiser's behalf. For four years he had been Dreiser's sometime agent, never knowing where he stood, often finding Dreiser pieces snatched out from under his nose, or handled simultaneously by other agents. He had worked hard to sell *Sister Carrie* to the films—but Otvos had sold it and got the commission. He had worked as hard to sell *My Gal Sal*, only to see Friede make the sale and commission. Now he used every exhortation to urge Dreiser that he must finish a novel, writing, "I wish I had the power of persuasion to prevail upon you to put aside the philosophy and get at *The Bulwark* at once—and complete it. A new novel from your pen would be a sensational public event and would have a tremendous effect on the subsequent sale of the Philosophy.

"Please give heed to the soundness of this plea! It means so much to you!" [28]

Dreiser gave heed. He signed a contract to deliver *The Bulwark* to Putnam by June 1, 1942.

3. Alarums and Excursions

When the Japanese attacked Pearl Harbor on December 7 and
America was in the war, Dreiser's first thought was of aid to Russia. He *knew*
that perfidious Albion (in league with world capitalism) was exulting over
the Russian retreat, secretly anticipating the destruction of the Soviet before
turning on an overextended Germany. As emotional as ever—he could weep
over a "Dr. Alexander" radio program or a sentimental movie—he was moved
to new social causes. The sight of a crippled Negro boy selling newspapers on
a Santa Monica street corner could impel him to plan a radio series aimed at
ameliorating slums and aiding underprivileged children, and seeking the help
of Mrs. Roosevelt in getting the government to sponsor it.[1]

What with such compulsions, plus his romantic involvements and continued arthritis in the shoulder, it was difficult to find the mood of calm he
needed to finish *The Bulwark*. He had quite forgotten that a huge, earlier
unfinished script of that book was still stored at Louise Campbell's in Philadelphia. In February he took off for an unidentified meeting in Chicago, then
went down to the Mudlavia Hotel in Indiana to take curative baths. "Twenty-
one baths are considered a cure for arthritis," he wrote Mrs. Manning, adding
a few days later:

> I've missed and worried over you because I know how difficult your
> state is but I'm hoping to turn something out there, just as I'm hoping for
> you to turn something. Your really so able. For one thing I've got a rubber
> shoe idea for you which the Goodyear or Goodrich Rubber Co. should
> grab. Its entirely new and different and should yield a lot of money to the
> Rubber Co. . . . But dearie I'll be seeing you and we'll have our customary
> talks & love . . . & maybe we'll think some way out for you & for me
> also.[2]

Home again, he ended a long lacuna with an exchange of letters with
Mencken. "In New York the other day," Mencken wrote, "I encountered, by
chance, your son Julius. He told me that he was still at odds with you over
money matters, but that he regarded you with filial reverence and wished you
well. I suppose you know that he is now one of the captains at Lüchow's. He
tells me that his takings amount to $50 a week. . . ."[3] Dreiser was unable to
match Mencken at epistolary moonshine, but the humor that seldom showed
in his novels was evident when he wrote Fabri, who had sent him a telegram
blank as a hint:

483

Fairest Fabri: This is Good Friday. And I am writing this on my knees, in church. It's not so easy. . . . What helps me out in doing what I always want to do but don't—that is, write you, is your inclusion in your note of the Western Union list of proposed telegrams. Perusing these carefully I find several which check with my feelings in regard to you exactly. They are, as you will see, Nos 324, 326, 333, 343, 355 and 358. If I tried for weeks I couldn't evoke out of my chemism, such as it is, thoughts and feelings more appropriate or heartfelt. So here, dear Fabri, on this Holy Friday—here you are. . . .[4]

To Balch on March 13 he sent the first four chapters of *The Bulwark* for use in making salesmen's dummies, since Putnam was aiming for fall publication. Putnam persuaded Pearl Buck to write a brief biography of Dreiser for use in a promotional pamphlet, and he was again nursing the hope that had gripped him for twenty years—that Putnam would publish a uniform collected edition of all his works. He seemed unaware that this idea was fantastic now in view of the wartime paper shortage. "Believe it or not I am working on *The Bulwark*," he wrote Mencken, "and doing quite well with it, I think. Also enjoying it[.] After 8 years I managed to get loose from those lice labeled Simon & Schuster and am now in the hands once more of An American publisher. . . ."[5]

But an intestinal ailment cost him ten days, he found that even when he was well his progress was slow, and he began to hedge on fall publication. "You understand," he wrote Balch a few weeks later, "it is a long book and not an easy one to write. . . ."[6] He was pleased to get a modest royalty payment from Russia, though he never knew specifically what such payments were for. He was sending occasional messages of praise to Russian publications as well as comments to the American press, but the latter usually threw them away. "Various statements that I have prepared and addressed to our traitor corporation press have been completely ignored," he complained. "As a matter of fact I have proof that my name is on various blacklists."[7]

"I observe," Mencken wrote him, "that the first letter from you in my file is dated August 23, 1907. It thus appears that the thirty-fifth anniversary of our correspondence is only a few weeks ahead. I shall celebrate it by hanging out the papal flag and inviting the policeman on the beat to join me in thirty or forty rounds of sound malt liquor."[8]

Mrs. Campbell discovered the old *Bulwark* script and sent it to Dreiser, but it was of little help because his concept of the novel had changed. The delight that he once took in creative work seemed to have gone. By July—already a month late with copy—he wrote Lengel, "The book is not ready yet and will not be for some time. Not that I am not working on it or getting along with it but it is a very intimate and touchy problem in connection with religious family life—and, like the American Tragedy I find it difficult."[9]

Part of the difficulty was his continuing "search for beauty." Esther McCoy recently had married another old Dreiser friend, Berkeley Tobey, who had been business manager of the old *Masses* in the Village days and had attended the memorable Dreiser-Markham party for Masters. On a few occasions Dreiser arrived at the Tobey home in Santa Monica with a woman he had picked up. Once or twice Esther Tobey had a strong impression that he was tired of his companion, was uncertain what to do about it and was hoping that the Tobeys could somehow send her packing, get her off his hands. On one occasion, in the Tobey living room with a woman not otherwise mentioned here, he indulged in public sexual groping that caused the Tobeys—deeply fond of him though they were—to wish that he would spare them such visits.[10]

Even as he wrote Lengel of his creative struggles he was planning a new romantic experience. For months he had corresponded with thirty-eight-year-old Sylvia Bradshaw of Detroit, a reader who had praised his works and bought every Dreiser book available. Having been put on his mailing list, she received all of his political broadsides and felt an intellectual kinship as well as a strong psychic attraction. When he invited her to visit him, she pondered the matter and finally made the trip, arriving in Los Angeles on July 4.

Her train was five hours late, pulling in at 1:30 A.M. "He greeted me as affectionately and naturally as if we had known each other forever," she recalled. "He was much taller than I and he bent down so affectionately to kiss me."[11]

They put up at a Los Angeles hotel during her eleven-day stay—a period during which neither Helen nor anyone else knew where he was. Miss Bradshaw found the author of *An American Tragedy* a fascinating and kindly man. He took her on sightseeing tours—to Santa Monica, to nearby orange groves, to Chinatown, to restaurants blacked out because of the war. Together they saw *My Gal Sal*, with Victor Mature in the role of Paul and Rita Hayworth as Sal, to a background of "On the Banks of the Wabash" and other Dresser tunes. He did not tell her about Helen. Since the whereabouts of both were unknown, they received no telephone calls or mail and, as Miss Bradshaw put it, it was like "being in another world."[12] They got on wonderfully. No sooner had she left on July 15 than he resumed with other women but made plans to see Miss Bradshaw again.

"As to THE BULWARK," he wrote the anxious Balch, "all I can say at the moment is that I am working every day on it."[13] He wrote the new Russian ambassador in Washington, Maxim Litvinov, for a complete list of the scientific discoveries made by Russia in the last 25 years. To the *New Masses* he wired:

ENGLAND IS THE ARSENAL OF DEMOCRACY. WE MAKE THE WAR IMPLEMENTS AND THEY SIT ON THEM—MEN AND MUNITIONS—TO SAVE THEIR COMFORTABLE ISLAND. . . . AS TO A WESTERN FRONT TO SAVE RUSSIA, THAT'S TRIPE. ENGLAND NOW HAS THE ARSENAL. SHE HAS THE MEN (FOUR AND ONE HALF MILLIONS OF OURS PLUS HER OWN) SO WHAT IS SHE WAITING FOR? THE ANSWER IS UNTIL RUSSIA IS IRREPARABLY CRIPPLED AND CAN NO LONGER BE A POWERFUL VOICE IN

THE PEACE CONFERENCE. THAT IS THE ENGLISH WAY OF PRESERVING ENGLISH
DOMINANCE. . . .[14]

When the Toronto Town Forum invited him to speak in September on the
need for a second front, he accepted for a $225 fee, thinking immediately of
Miss Bradshaw in Detroit. He wrote her, and she joined him in Toronto when
he arrived by train September 20, feeling ill with a cold. Next day, reporters
interviewed him at the Royal York Hotel and heard strong words against the
British, although the Town Forum had warned him against this. According to
the *Toronto Evening Telegram*, he said in part:

"Should Russia go down to defeat I hope the Germans invade England. I
would rather see the Germans in England than those damn, aristocratic, horse-
riding snobs there now." Mentioning the "unbelievable gall and brass of the
English," he went on, "Churchill has no intention of opening a second front.
He's afraid the Communists will rule the world. So he does nothing except
send thousands of Canadians to be slaughtered at Dieppe. He didn't send any
English. They stay at home and do nothing. Nothing." The English, he
added, were "lousy." [15]

When the paper hit the streets, the city council in emergency session
moved to forbid his speech and to notify the Canadian Minister of Justice at
Ottawa. One alderman said, "I'll be surprised if he [Dreiser] is not interned
this afternoon," another urged that he be deported immediately, a third
saying, "Theodore Dreiser should be thrown into the North Sea." [16] The
Royal Canadian Mounted Police were alerted. The intended chairman for the
Dreiser speech, to have taken place at Eaton Auditorium, withdrew and the
meeting was canceled. There was talk that Dreiser would be arrested. Dining
with Miss Bradshaw, who was nervous about the feeling against him, he
decided to decamp. On the theory that the police might be waiting at the
Union Station, they taxied to the suburban Sunnyside Station, where they
caught a train for Detroit. Dreiser later said that the conductor received a
telegram from Canadian officials asking that the train be stopped, but ignored
it because they were about to cross into Michigan. Miss Bradshaw left him in
Detroit, worried because he was ill and coughing. He took the next train to
Indianapolis, where, since Mrs. Baker had recently died, he probably stayed
with Mrs. D. M. Parry, sister of the late John Maxwell.

"ARCH TRAITOR FLEES CANADA," headlined John Blunt's *Weekly
and Flash* of Toronto, referring to Dreiser as a "Fifth Columnist" and adding
an upper-case suggestion: "HE IS ONE OF THE MOST DANGEROUS
MEN ON THIS CONTINENT—AND IF CORDELL HULL IS ALIVE
TO HIS DUTY DREISER WILL BE INTERNED AT ONCE. OR
SHOT." [17]

The affair made international headlines. In New York, Rex Stout, chairman
of the Writers' War Board, condemned the Dreiser statement and took steps
to lecture himself in Toronto to restore United States writers in Canadian

eyes—a talk in which he said, "Dreiser doesn't think. He just feels." The Writers' War Board itself denounced him as a helper of Hitler. In London, George Bernard Shaw said, "To say that Dreiser's comments regarding the war are furiously inaccurate is only to say that they are like everyone else's comments regarding the war." [18] The Nazis made quick propaganda use of Dreiser's blast against the British, calling it "a sincere declaration of an American." [19] In Indianapolis, Dreiser was stunned and hurt by the hubbub. Insisting that he had been speaking off the record in Toronto and misquoted to boot, he broadcast a printed statement saying in part, "I did not ally myself with Hitler and I did denounce the titled class of England which I held and still hold responsible for the allies' failure to aid Russia. What I said was that if, due to this titled and moneyed class, Russia was defeated I hoped Hitler would attack England and abolish that titled class." [20]

On October 1, while he was still in Indianapolis, Jug died at seventy-three in St. Louis. He returned home to Hollywood to receive from Ambassador Litvinov an invitation to the 25th anniversary celebration in Moscow of the October revolution. He was too old and exhausted to accept. To Miss Bradshaw he wrote:

> We are so far apart. . . .
> The problem of getting together is not easy. . . . One thing I do know is that if your not coming out here to stay you are coming out here to visit me. . . . It won't be the same hotel—unless you want that. But it can be a hotel or furnished apartment taken by the week, maybe. . . . If I can only sell a picture shortly I am sure that I can fix it up for you to stay here. . . . As for your visit, that should occur sometime after Xmas because just now I have this novel & several picture scripts to work on and I can't afford to leave them.[21]

II. YOU SEE HOW IT IS

In Hollywood, as for years previously, Dreiser and Helen passed as Mr. and Mrs. Dreiser and were believed married except by such intimates as Lillian Goodman, Esther Tobey and Clare Kummer, who kept the secret. Lorna Smith was astonished to read a news item about the death of Mrs. Dreiser, but she kept silent also. Indeed Helen now hoped that Dreiser would marry her, but he opposed the idea. One day at Lillian Goodman's she wept hysterically and said, "He'll never marry me!" [22]

She came to regard Mrs. Manning not only as a serious rival but as a threat to Dreiser's well-being and a distraction keeping him from *The Bulwark*. Mrs. Manning later wrote, possibly with some exaggeration, "She [Helen] . . . hated me violently . . . and many times has come to my house packing a loaded pistol. Dreiser would telephone me, wherever I happened to be, and tell me not to go home until he telephoned me again to tell me that it was safe. When I would arrive home . . . I would find telegrams or

special delivery letters denouncing me and saying that she had been there.
. . ." [23] To Fabri Helen wrote of her high blood pressure and her mental
stress:

> But I am under high tension all of the time. . . . Living with T. does not
> reduce it any although it should be routine by now. Still it is not. I am ever
> under that pressure. . . . He is a wonderful man but he is so self centered.
> Nothing exists for him but his own sensations and his own interests. That is
> rather hard to live with unless one is completely sublimated. . . . I crave
> peace of mind, first, and then that lovely something that comes from con-
> fidence and an exchange of considerations between people. It is so silly to
> wish for something that is not in a person . . . every ounce of my strength
> goes to him and in helping him in every way. . . .[24]

From Powys in Wales came a letter for Dreiser:

> Think of your saying such things as I read in the papers—(but [I am]
> certain you were mis-quoted so [I am] not *very* rattled!) but even at
> our venerable age, if you were here or I were where you are, Jesus Christ!
> but I'd challenge you to a savage bout. . . .[25]

Helen promptly wrote Powys to assure him that Dreiser had indeed been
misquoted.

From the Toronto Town Forum came a letter blaming the imbroglio on
him, since he had been cautioned specifically against airing his anti-British
feelings, and asking the return of the $225 fee. Dreiser refused, denying
responsibility and fibbing grandly, "Incidentally, remember that ordinarily
my lowest rate is $500.00 and expenses." [26]

His memory, always tricky, was visibly failing. Discouraged at his poor
progress with *The Bulwark*, he felt at times that his genius had left him and
saw no way out but to sell more material to the films. RKO, after buying
Sister Carrie, had commissioned two scripts, found them unsatisfactory and
failed to produce the film. His affluence was waning, due to the new house
and car and the $8,500 repayment to Simon & Schuster. That fall he called on
Alvin Manuel, an agent on Sunset Boulevard, leaving three original scenarios
with him—possibly material done in collaboration with Mrs. Manning.
Manuel read the scripts, felt them unsuccessful and later visited the Kings
Road home to explain why. Dreiser took it in good humor and they became
warm personal friends, the Manuels occasionally having Helen and Dreiser to
their Beverly Hills home. "I was careful whom I invited to dinner with him,"
Manuel recalled, "because he would get up in the middle of the floor and
make outrageous statements. Then he would look around to see if someone
would disagree with him. He was looking for an argument." [27]

The Kings Road neighbors occasionally were disturbed by loud nocturnal
quarrels between Helen and Dreiser. The Edgar Wards (Mrs. Ward is the
actress Jane Wyatt), who lived next door, were aware of these quarrels,
which sometimes ended with Helen leaving the house in anger, slamming the
door and driving away.[28] On one occasion when Helen was away, Dreiser, in

his nightshirt, giggled as he chased a woman guest around the yard in the wee hours. On December 31 he wired to Tass a panegyric on Russian valor that included dark words about the British, then vanished from Helen's view until January first, having celebrated the New Year with Mrs. Manning. To Sylvia Bradshaw he wrote a few days later:

> I meant to tell you in my letter yesterday that I am not married—I was up to 1907 [*sic*] when I broke with the girl I had married. . . . That one experience was so drastic that I have been opposed to marriage ever since. . . .
> As for myself—I feel that I am too old to get married—that I will not live long enough to make it important. And perhaps the chief reason I am really grateful to the person who is with me is that she has never thought it important to enter on the subject of marriage. She had an unhappy experience of her own to begin with and that seems to have taken the edge off marriage for her. If we separated she would, I am sure, return to her mother & sister who are both alive and live together. But just suddenly to compel that when she does not interfere with my life & has proved really useful—well—you know how one might feel under such circumstances. If there were any sex attraction or any form of sex relationship between us it would be harder still. . . . I have thought of it—only—well, you see how it is—I crave more of you—really all of you and yet I find it hard to adjust to suit all, seeing that she knows so much of my practical affairs—handles them as any capable secretary would and does not ask more than living in the same house with me. . . .
> So there you have it. And just how it is to be adjusted I don't know. But I do know one thing—you are the most fascinating temperament that I have encountered so far—strong and wise and sensual and magnetic and I feel the pull of you all the time. . . . But how to fix this is keeping me awake nights. . . . You've got something that thrills me to my toes & my hair. . . . What's the answer?

He added an ambivalent two-line postscript:

> Shall I send you the money for another visit here.
> Incidentally I must finish the novel.[29]

Mencken, long puzzled about Dreiser's politics (he was not on the mailing list), put a direct question:

> What, precisely, are your ideas about the current crusade to save humanity? I have seen many statements of them, chiefly in the Communist papers, but most of those statements seemed to me to be incredible. . . . I observe that the Communists have ceased of late to list you as one of them, and I assume that this has been done in response to your protests. I continue of the opinion, as always, that they are a gang of frauds.[30]

Dreiser answered in small part:

> You see, Mencken, unlike yourself, I am biased. I was born poor. For a time, in November and December, once, I went without shoes. I saw my be-

loved mother suffer from want—even worry and wring her hands in misery. And for that reason, perhaps—let it be what you will—I, regardless of whom or what, am for a social system that can and will do better than that for its members—those who try, however humbly,—and more, *wish to learn how* to help themselves, but are none-the-less defeated by the trickeries of a set of vainglorious dunces, who actually believe that money—*however come by*—the privilege of buying this and that—distinguishes them above all others. . . . Upon my word! To be more specific—for Christ's sake!

   As for the Communist System—as I saw it in Russia in 1927 and '28—I am for it—hide and hoof. . . . [And] show me a Chekhov, a Dostoyevsky, a Tolstoy, a Gogol, a Moussorgsky in all the history of American art. . . .

   Darling—don't forget that I remember how, almost fatalistically, you arrived in my life when, from a literary point of view, I was down and out, and you proceeded to fight for me. Night and day apparently. Swack! Smack! Crack! Until finally you succeeded in chasing an entire nation of literary flies to cover. It was lovely! It was classic. And whether you choose to slam me right or left, as is your wont, in the future, Darling, Professor, Doctor, I will love you until the hour of my death. *And don't pull any Edgar Allan Poe stuff in connection with my forgotten grave either.* . . .

He added a postscript:

   As for the American Communists—well there are—or were and still are, I assume,—many fakirs and flies and camp followers who hope to pick up a living out of the cause. They have never interested me. . . . I am—and have been—content to deal with the Russian Government direct—its foreign office, its American Ambassador, its consuls, etc. I have written for Pravda often and have answered many cables that have come to me direct.[31]

Thus he suggested that he was no plebeian communist but one of select rank. Mencken, in reply, discounted his own literary help, saying, "What you forget is how we both enjoyed the battle, even when it was going against us." He went on:

   I simply can't follow you in your belief in Comrade Stalin. To me he seems to be only a politico like the rest, and if anything worse than most. All the Russian genii you mention flourished under the czars. Since Marxism came in the race has produced nothing [of value]. . . .

   Moreover, there is the indelible fact that the comrade . . . was quite willing, for two years, to share Hitler's burglaries. I am no gipsy, but I presume to predict that before this cruel war is over he will be burgling and butchering again. When you were in Russia you saw the show-window, but not much else. . . .[32]

Dreiser, sensing a total lack of understanding, did not resume the argument.

III. SIXTEEN MONTHS LATE

   Dreiser had grown wary of his own temper on the public platform, replying to a request that he address a Los Angeles club: "All too often I find

I am inclined to become a little to [*sic*] emphatic and even savage, for I carry a package of convictions which not so very many agree with." [33]

In March, he quit on *The Bulwark*. Lengel had given up prodding him, as had Helen, finding him resentful. To Fabri, Helen wrote of the perpetual white elephant, Iroki:

> It is *quite* necessary for us to sell the place as soon as possible. . . . T. is not any younger. He needs money *badly*. . . . But that place with its taxes is a terrible thing even to think about. I hate to see him work so hard at something that is far beneath him, as this last job. He has his book here The Bulwark and that in itself is a terrific job but he needs money while writing it. And so I can only pray for Iroki to sell. . . . If I went out and took a job he would have no one to look after him and he is so helpless about so many things. [34]

She knew that time as well as money was running short. Simply from the standpoint of the time it took, his magnetic attraction for women was a problem. He was porous to them, understanding them, making himself a great warm receptacle for their troubles. He could listen, sympathize, advise, praise. It was no accident that women he had not seen for years continued to correspond with him. Thelma Cudlipp Grosvenor (who had been widowed and was now the wife of New York's former Governor Charles Seymour Whitman—and who distilled memories of Butterick and *The "Genius"*) still carried on an affectionate exchange. So did Louise Campbell and Dorothy Dudley Harvey, among others. Life was so bitter, as he saw it, that he went out of his way to lighten it even for women he did not know but who aroused his sympathies—for one, the harried waitress at a café he patronized. He liked to bolster a woman's impression of herself, regardless of whether he had any romantic interest in her. He encouraged Esther Tobey, Lorna Smith, Marguerite Tjader Harris, Estelle Manning and Sylvia Bradshaw in their writing. In different ways, and with different understanding, these five, along with Lillian Goodman, Clare Kummer and others, thought him the essence of kindliness, a person whose mere presence was comforting and whose talk was almost hypnotically inspiring. Mrs. Harris felt him a "doctor of souls," regretful only that he could not seem to save his own.

In May, Dreiser and Mrs. Manning drove to the Coldwater Canyon home of Ginger Rogers to explain a scenario they had written with her in mind— an idea that failed to come off. Soon thereafter Miss Bradshaw arrived from Detroit and Mrs. Manning was neglected for a time. Indeed Dreiser later wrote her untruthfully that he was going to New York to try to sell Iroki. Miss Bradshaw put up at a hotel, got a position in Los Angeles, and thereafter Helen saw Dreiser only intermittently. Miss Bradshaw, who heard only one side of the story, felt that Helen did not give him affection and care, that he was lonely and unloved and that she furnished a true companionship he badly needed. Meanwhile Earle Balch of Putnam was growing dubious about Theodore Dreiser, whose strength was failing under his worries and involvements.

One day when he called on the Berkeley Tobeys in Santa Monica he was literally pallid and staggering with exhaustion.[35]

When Helen left for Portland August first because her aged mother was ill, she gave her permission for Miss Bradshaw to move into the Kings Road place as hausfrau while she was gone—that is, so Dreiser told Miss Bradshaw. Miss Bradshaw moved in. He took her to Clare Kummer's in Beverly Hills, where they met the actor Henry Hull. He took her, along with Mr. and Mrs. Clifford Odets, to Chasen's, where they met Jimmy Durante and other celebrities. (Dreiser had a non-proletarian weakness for celebrities and for such places as Chasen's and the Brown Derby when with a special friend, though when with Helen he favored hot dog stands or the corner cocktail bar.) Miss Bradshaw cut his hair for him, saving a lock as a keepsake. She was charmed by his stories of the New York of the Nineties, and she worried about his health and his occasionally excessive drinking. They had a common interest in the occult, Dreiser saying he had recently seen a ghostly figure—a woman he did not know—sitting in his living room chair. He told Miss Bradshaw she reminded him of the girl in Chekhov's "The Darling," urged her to write, declared that she had talent. Once he became furiously jealous when a young man in a cocktail bar eyed her with an interest he felt she returned, and occasionally, when depressed, he talked of suicide. She felt that he was not serious about this, since he seemed vitally interested in life.[36] Miss Bradshaw, a thoroughly honest and sympathetic woman, was unaware of Dreiser's career of sensuality, admiring him wholly, convinced he would have been true to her alone had he been free. She returned to Detroit late in August, not because she wanted to but because she felt (rightly) that he needed more time to devote to his work.

Although he had promised to join Helen in Portland for his seventy-second birthday, he stayed to see Miss Bradshaw off and reached Portland by bus, exhausted, August 31. By the time they returned to Hollywood five days later, he was ill with a cold. Soon thereafter Stanley Moffat, who had conferred with Balch in New York, wrote Helen anxiously that Dreiser was now sixteen months late in fulfilling his contract for *The Bulwark*: "I am dreadfully afraid that if the book is not forthcoming before long, Putnam's will lose all interest, and possibly we will run into a suit for breach of contract." [37]

Helen replied, "You are telling me something that I have fully realized for the past two years. In fact, I have done everything humanly possible to get him to continue exclusively with this book. . . . Psychologically, his mood has to be right about it. . . . And it does not seem to be quite right. Anyway, he is not a well man. . . . And yet I do feel that he might get a fresh start on it. . . . When—that I cannot say. Under too much pressure he seems to get more irritated than ever.

"I think it would be wicked and cruel to bring any breach of contract suit against him. . . ." [38]

To Dreiser, who also heard from Moffat but in gentler terms, Putnam now sounded exactly like Simon & Schuster—interested only in a *new* novel. Still apparently not convinced of a paper shortage, he had an innocent faith that a huge public was waiting for reprints of his old books and that a collected edition of his works would sell handsomely.

IV. THE GNAT AND THE EAGLE

The dichotomous Dreiser—on one plane a selfish, bullying, unreasonable, capricious, deceitful, evil old man—was in his other incarnation more than ever the awe-stricken contemplator of the creative force that made him what he helplessly was, a part of all nature in its infinite glory and sorrow. That fall he wrote an essay, "My Creator," that seemed the work of a pietist rather than an old lecher. Testifying to his wonder at the achievements of the universal mind, it went on:

> And so . . . I am moved not only to awe but to reverence for the Creator . . . concerning whom—his or its presence in all things from worm to star to thought—I meditate constantly even though it be, as I see it, that my import to this, my Creator, can be but as nothing, or less, if that were possible.
>
> Yet awe I have. And, at long last, profound reverence for so amazing and esthetic and wondrous a process of which I might pray—and do—to remain the infinitesimal part of that same that I now am.[39]

After a six-month lapse, he resumed work on *The Bulwark* in September. He soon grew discouraged and by Thanksgiving addressed a familiar lament to Mencken:

> Do you know anything about the Viking Press, Knopf combination? I hear there is one such. . . . I need to find some house that would really be interested in a complete set of my books. As far as I can make out the idea is never to bother about any past work—that is, call attention to the works as a whole—but always to yowl about the next novel. . . .[40]

Mencken, disabusing him of the thought that there was a Knopf-Viking merger, offered to speak to Knopf in Dreiser's behalf but reminded him of the war and its banishment of the complete-set idea: "It is simply impossible to get enough paper for it. . . ."[41]

Dreiser and Helen frequently attended soirées at the Russian consulate in Los Angeles, where they became friendly with Charles and Oona Chaplin and many others of leftward trend. Donald Friede, an occasional guest at Kings Road gatherings, noted that Dreiser liked to invite folk singers who lamented in song the oppression of the poor. Another intermittent guest was young Harold J. Dies, a native of Seattle who was related to both Dreiser and Helen, his maternal grandmother having been a sister of Dreiser's mother and Helen's grandmother. An army transport officer based in Los Angeles, he always called at Kings Road on his return from long Pacific voyages. He was a cousin of Red-hunting Congressman Martin Dies—a fact that first inclined Dreiser to be suspicious of Harold, for the Congressman was investigating Dreiser's activities. But he soon became friendly. Lieutenant Dies found him charming except on one occasion when Dies ventured to suggest that the Russian communists were no longer quite democratic. Dreiser became so furious—purpling and choking—that Helen feared he would have a heart attack and Dies thereafter avoided any discussion of politics, just as Alvin Manuel and other friends did.[42]

Worried about money, Dreiser lost considerable weight that winter as he suffered from colds, intestinal upsets, shingles and a deterioration of his one good eye. To Arnold Gingrich he suggested a series on unworthy characters—a "black sheep" twist on the *Reader's Digest* standby about "unforgettable characters." When Gingrich showed interest, he wrote Louise Campbell, Sylvia Bradshaw and other women friends asking them to send him accounts filling the specifications, which he would rewrite where necessary and sell to *Esquire* under his own name, paying the women on a 50–50 basis.[43]

To Miss Bradshaw he wrote of his loneliness, wondering if he was not being too considerate of Helen: "At . . . times I think of myself as being much to [sic] sensitive to the possible suffering of others—exaggerating the same very possibly, far beyond what might be the case if I did act to please myself. For naturally I notice that, on the part of the person I am seeking to save from too much misery there appears to be no great consideration of how I may be feeling throughout all this—at least not that I can see. And so, at times I am puzzled by my own course. . . ."[44]

In December his partly imaginary financial pinch was eased when he sold the house in Montrose which he (or really Helen) had owned for years. And in January he received a letter that heartened him:

> Dear Mr. Dreiser: Once in each five years, the American Academy of Arts and Letters honors itself by presenting to an American novelist, not a member of the Academy or Institute, the Award of Merit Medal, together with a cash prize of $1,000, for extraordinary achievement in his art.
>
> This year, the directors of the Academy have chosen you, not only for the distinction of such books as "The [sic] American Tragedy", "Sister Carrie", "Twelve Men", and a long line of other volumes, but also for your courage and integrity in breaking trail as a pioneer in the presentation in fiction of real human beings and a real America.
>
> We would be grateful if you would reply expressing your willingness to accept this award.[45]

The letter was signed by Walter Damrosch, president of the Academy. What would have been Dreiser's thoughts had he known that Sinclair Lewis, a member of the awards committee of the Academy, had argued "passionately" that the prize must go to Dreiser and had drafted the letter signed by Damrosch?[46]

Nine years earlier Dreiser had rejected membership in the Academy's parent body, the National Institute, but the present award did not involve membership and in any case his temper was humbler now. There were men he admired in the Academy or Institute—John Steinbeck, James Farrell, Erskine Caldwell and Dos Passos among them. He could use that $1,000, he could stand a little recognition, he needed to find a new publisher in New York and perhaps the publicity connected with the award would help. He replied:

It is pleasing to me that the American Academy of Arts and Letters should single out my work, and, in consequence, myself. . . . And, whether wholly deserved or not, I appreciate your friendly reference to my assumed "courage and integrity in breaking trail as a Pioneer in the presentation in fiction of real human beings and a real America."

I am grateful for the esthetic understanding and impulse that prompted these words. However, I am too much of a fatalist to believe that any one out of himself alone creates that which he does. He is, as I see it, an instrument, and, if he but knew, an humble one, of the great Creative impulse which chooses to make Life—its endless creatures—the amazingly varied and hence interesting instruments they are—from the gnat to the eagle—the Bird of Paradise to the humble sparrow. . . .

Whether or not I can come East in May in order to share the occasion of this award depends entirely on my health and the general state of my affairs, which are quite complicated. . . .[47]

The award would be presented May 19, with the Academy paying travel expenses if he could make the trip. To Miss Bradshaw he wrote meanwhile:

In fact solitude—silence—want of companionship—is about the worst thing that can befall anyone—no one to exchange ideas or even comments with, let alone love. . . . I feel forsaken—and so for a period at least I truly am. My one refuge most of the time is imagining what we might be doing you and I if you were here or I there. . . .[48]

4. Gretna Green

Knowing Mencken's opinion of the Academy, Dreiser wrote him that he would be in New York in May without mentioning why. He should have known better than to cozen the sage, who replied, "It begins to seem like ten thousand years since we last sat down for Christian communion together," then went on ominously:

> I hear that you are going to New York to be crowned with a laurel wreath by the American Academy of Arts and Letters. If this is true, I can only deplore the fact that you are having any truck with that gang of quacks. Its members for many years were your principal defamers. If they have actually offered you a hand-out, I hope you invite them to stick it up their rainspouts.[1]

Dreiser replied, "I'm taking the thousand [*sic*] and $500 expenses because I need it for some work in N. Y." [2] Uncertain of his tenure on earth, he dearly wanted not only to meet Mencken as a friend but to have Mencken as his early literary lifeguard take some part in the ceremonies. Almost pleadingly he asked that Mencken join him at a dinner to be given by Damrosch for the award winners: "Nor will I feel otherwise than justly reproved if you refuse. . . . Only—seriously what a pleasure it would provide yours truly if you were to go with me." His letters were sometimes a trifle disconnected now, and he added an extraneous postscript: "Think of decent whiskey at $7.00 a fifth! And I love and need it so." [3]

Mencken was uncompromising:

> Unhappily, I can't join you in the orgies. Some of the chief members of that preposterous organization made brave efforts to stab you in the back in 1916, and I am not disposed to forget it. I'd be most uncomfortable at the Damrosch dinner. . . . I only hope the speeches include a categorical apology for the gross injuries sought to be done to you in the past.
>
> Whether or not I'll be able to get to New York while you are there remains to be seen. . . .[4]

To Felicia Geffen, assistant to Damrosch, Dreiser wrote that he would travel by plane (then considerably more expensive than rail fare) and that his expenses would be $400. Later he boosted the figure, asking a total of $500 to cover hotel bills.[5] Miss Geffen replied that the Academy would pay air passage but had no funds for hotel expenses and sent him $400.

With mortality in mind, he made a momentous decision. When Helen, her mother seriously ill, was in Portland again for three weeks in March, his dependence on her was brought sharply to his mind. While there, she talked with her sister Myrtle, who subsequently wrote him on her own that it would be a fitting gesture if he married Helen. Probably the letter stirred a half-formed impulse of his own, for he replied kindly that he would if it could be done quietly.[6] He was gentler to Helen now, and also in his mind was the matter of his estate when he died. He fulfilled her long-cherished dream—told her that they should be married when he returned from New York and that he hoped it could be done with a minimum of publicity.[7] It was first planned that Helen would make the trip with him, but when her mother took a turn for the worse she gave it up.

"It is . . . physically very difficult for me to have to run two households," she wrote Fabri. She told him of Dreiser's coming visit, warned him of his lapses of memory, asked him to look after Dreiser as much as he could and gave Fabri her Portland telephone number: "In case anything at all went wrong back there I would want a call immediately. . . . He is pretty well, but life is very uncertain."[8] She wrote Marguerite Tjader Harris to ask her to serve as Dreiser's secretary during his New York stay. She wrote the socially prominent Alma Clayburgh, telling her of Dreiser's strange block in writing *The Bulwark* and asking her to exert what social influence she could in helping Dreiser find another publisher.

On May 10 Dreiser left *by rail* on the Santa Fe Chief, thereby saving some of that $400. In New York he hoped to arrange meetings with friends old and not so old including Kirah Markham, Sylvia Bradshaw, Wharton Esherick, Louise Campbell, and of course Mencken.

Mrs. Harris met him at Grand Central Station and escorted him to the adjacent Commodore Hotel. Ralph Fabri arrived to greet him. He had lost thirty pounds, his hair was white and downy, his once puffy face had shrunk into long hound-dog striations, but his gaze seemed as searching as ever. It would be his last visit to the metropolis that had been so cruel and so kind to him. He told of his belief in a creative force, of the experience at Cold Spring Harbor that had so moved him—the beauties seen through the microscope and the flowers outside. "He remembered distant events," Fabri recalled, "but when he got a telephone call he had to make a note of it immediately or he would forget."[9]

Dreiser's three-week stay in New York was a formidable round of luncheons, cocktail parties, interviews, visits, telephone calls, appointments. His prime purpose was to find a publisher who would sponsor a set of his books, now obtainable (except for *Sister Carrie*) only at second-hand dealers. In this he was motivated less by the old Dreiser vainglory—the chest-expanding thought of a score of volumes identically bound, with his name on them—than by a natural wish to make his works available and by his feeling of financial need. Since he felt himself unable to finish *The Bulwark*, there seemed no other hope for income than through a revival of his earlier books.

For the first time he caught the real meaning of the paper restrictions. Publishers were tough, seeking the sure-thing sellers, refusing to risk their limited paper on books of dubious appeal, unmoved by sentiment for a tired old author and utterly unable to find paper for a collected edition of Theodore Dreiser.

To save money he ate budget breakfasts at Thompson's cafeteria on Forty-second Street. He saved the grandeur for such affairs as his luncheon at the Century Club with Earle Balch, who was cordial but insistent that Dreiser's next publication would have to be the new novel. He consulted others including Scribners and Harper's, getting no encouragement except from Charles Scribner, who thought that a set of Dreiser books would sell once the paper shortage was over. But who could say when that would be? [10]

Earlier he had been snappish with rich Alma Clayburgh, accusing her of an indifference toward social problems. Now he was the honored guest at a Clayburgh Park Avenue dinner for 40, meeting generals, artists and a few publishers Mrs. Clayburgh had purposely invited, and who were sociable but not particularly interested in old Dreiser books. "Really I feel let down by this trip," he wrote Helen, "and now I wish I were back in Kings Road with you. . . ." [11]

Brother Rome had died in 1940. Mame, now eighty-three and living with the widowed Sylvia in Astoria, had just undergone an operation for cancer. Sylvia, a Christian Scientist, was certain that she would recover if she willed it, but it was obvious that Mame's days were numbered. Visiting her, Dreiser found her almost without funds. The Paul Dresser songs were now often played on radio, Dreiser's own payment from ASCAP amounting to some $2,300 that year, as did that to the five other heirs. "I am drawing up a small paper," Dreiser wrote Helen, "in which—in case of Mame's death all agree to allow one sixth of their Paul Dresser Estate share to be deducted from this current year in order to meet the cost of the funeral." [12] Helen meanwhile had been working by mail on the sale of Iroki, and Dreiser's attorney Moffat had a buyer willing to pay $15,000 for the house and half the acreage. Fifteen thousand dollars! It seemed a give-away but with gasoline tightly rationed buyers for country property were few.

Dreiser kept hoping that Mencken would come, wiring him, "WILL BE AT COMMODORE ALL THIS WEEK PLEASE COME OVER LATER TO TALK ABOUT [sic] REGARDS." [13] Richard Duffy, whose friendship dated back almost a half-century, called and was distressed to hear of his financial worries. He set to work on a plan for reissuing the old books which showed a warm heart but found no takers. As part of the Academy's publicity program, Dreiser and Mrs. Harris were taken to the Stork Club by Earl Wilson, "saloon editor" of the New York Post. Dreiser, ordering straight bourbon, surveyed the gilded crowd and as Wilson recalled it growled, "Some of the hams in this country think having $100,000 makes them a marvelous person. Like hell!" Saying that when the soldiers returned they would probably get the same capitalistic "baloney," he added, "I hope they react by ballot or by revolution." He aired another prejudice: "Dear old democratic, mass-loving England—like hell! I've been with some of those red-coated snobs who chase foxes. . . . And close by, the poor live in cheap, lousy cottages. . . ."[14] As they left at 2 A.M., Bennett Cerf, catching a taxi, paused to greet him—an old Liveright man now a publisher in his own right.

That gave Dreiser ideas next day about Random House. "Ask [Cerf] to come around and have a drink with me," he said to Mrs. Harris. But the day was over when publishers came hat in hand, and Cerf, too, faced paper problems. He was not interested.[15]

Dreiser's gloom lifted a trifle when the Office of War Information asked him to make two recordings for later broadcast to Germany and the occupied countries—a cheering sign that he was not entirely shelved. He went to the O.W.I. offices on Fifty-seventh Street, just a few doors from the Rodin Studios, where he dropped his Stork Club bitterness, spoke warmly of American strength, urged the Germans to overthrow their Nazi leaders and said, "Just for a try-out, let's have a few hundred years of the Brotherhood of Man!"[16]

No Mencken. (Dreiser would have been startled could he have peered into the future and seen Henry Louis Mencken, in 1951, himself accepting the gold medal of the Academy.) On May 19 he took Masters, now living with his second wife Ellen, as his companion to the Academy auditorium on West 155th Street. Mrs. Harris, Mrs. Masters, Mrs. Clayburgh, Robert Elias and the artist Kenneth Hayes Miller were among the few Dreiser friends in the audience. Lewis was in Minnesota.

Dreiser had not been selected for one of the awards with enthusiastic unanimity. His name had been advanced by Lewis and a group of younger members including James T. Farrell and Paul Green, and carried over the objections of some of the more elderly and conservative who were repelled by his foolish and violent public utterances and possibly by his life of sin. Planning to make a short acceptance speech urging that a Secretary of the Arts be included in the Presidental cabinet, he had been told that it was too "controversial" and that there was no time for the Academy to pass on it. He saw Willa Cather receive an award for fiction, and eighty-seven-year-old S. S. McClure for services to American letters, both presented with zestful appreciation by Arthur Train. Then Professor Chauncey B. Tinker of Yale spoke for Dreiser.

Tinker's citation was itself a public avowal of the Academy's reservations as well as his own understanding that some members felt that the Dreiser award needed careful explaining. Speaking somewhat in the manner of a dowager called upon to eulogize a slut, he praised Dreiser's novels but made it plain that the Academy's approval went no farther: "As a body, the Academy is neither conservative nor radical; it is catholic. . . . It sponsors no school and has no programme. Its aim is to seek out and reward ability wherever it appears and in whatever guise. . . . Had it existed in the seventeenth century, it would have wished to extend its recognition to Pascal as well as, later, to Voltaire.

"It therefore asks Mr. Dreiser, as an acknowledged leader of the Naturalistic School in America, to accept this award. . . ."[17]

But there was warm applause as Dreiser lumbered to the stage. Unlike Miss Cather and McClure, who had responded with short acknowledgments, he merely bowed to Dr. Damrosch and the audience, expressed his thanks and retired, to be followed by the presentation of an award to Paul Robeson. At the reception on the terrace after the ceremonies, where other recipients were encircled by Academy officers and congratulants, he found himself almost neglected. James T. Farrell spoke to him warmly. Louis Untermeyer, one of the younger members, came up to shake his hand. "You had a feeling that he was quite alone and isolated there," Untermeyer recalled. "I think he felt that he was there somewhat by sufferance."[18]

That evening at the Masters apartment on East Sixty-third Street he pondered the thought of getting into a tuxedo for the Damrosch dinner. "Phone and see if you can get me out of it," he said to Mrs. Harris. She spoke to a maid, who relayed a Damrosch message that of course Dreiser was expected. But he noted the willingness to relegate this word to a maid, and felt he was not wanted. He stayed away.[19]

II. A PRIVILEGED WOMAN

Masters, Mrs. Harris, Robert Elias and many others had urged on Dreiser the importance of finishing *The Bulwark*. He explained that he was stuck, blocked, unable to go on—precisely like Kipling, he said, who one day discovered that his genius had left him. His spirits were somewhat revived by a dinner with the tottering Masters at wood-paneled Luchow's, a place that evoked a thousand tender memories. The head waiter recognized him. With Masters he had sausages and beer, trading nostalgic reminiscences of the troubles of *Spoon River* and *The "Genius,"* the two of them drinking a toast to their mutual friend Powys in Wales. Dreiser had done his best for Masters, getting Longmans to publish a Masters-edited book of Emerson selections and trying vainly to interest the films in some production of *Spoon River*. But now Masters was dependent on his vigorous wife Ellen, and Dreiser himself could feel the chill draft of literary oblivion and hard times.

With Mrs. Harris he went to Mt. Kisco to say farewell to the estate that soon would be sold. He took a last look at the place where Simon & Schuster had given that shockingly capitalistic party—where Charles Fort had called alone, where Dreiser had been engulfed by famous visitors—Sherwood Anderson, Ford Madox Ford, George Jean Nathan, Max Eastman, Powys, Sarah Millin, Claude Bowers, Floyd Dell, Diego Rivera, Burton Rascoe, Earl Browder, Lillian Gish—how many others? He had done no great writing there. *That* had all been done when he was poor. Mrs. Harris noted that he showed no emotion about the sale of the place so identified with his years of success. What touched him was his discovery of a sparrow that had become imprisoned and had died in a screened porch.[20]

He dined with Dorothy Dudley Harvey and her husband Harry at their Ninety-second Street apartment, where he argued with the French art critic George Duthuit, who disputed his remarks about the decline of France. Dreiser evidently still had not read the biography Mrs. Harvey had written of him. He was invited to Robert van Gelder's Washington Square lodgings, where the guests were divided among civilians and the military, including a British officer, and where he drank too much and became embroiled in a political quarrel. He had not informed his relatives of his trip to New York, and they became aware of it only because of the illness of Mame. Now he visited his brother Ed at Far Rockaway, meeting Ed's only daughter Vera for the first time in years and finding her now a striking young matron, a recent mother and a consulting psychologist with a Ph.D.—Dr. Vera Dreiser Scott.

Here Dreiser entered a joyous, affectionate family circle such as he had never known himself—indeed had rejected for himself. Dr. Vera and her husband, Alfred Scott, both of whom had done professional singing, sang several of her own compositions. Ed, who was only two years younger than Dreiser but looked fifteen years younger, reminisced with him about early family days in Indiana. He sang a German lullaby Father Dreiser had sung for the children, speaking warmly of the old man Dreiser had so long disparaged. There was talk of brother Al, who had written poetry and music himself—Al, now long unheard from, his whereabouts unknown. Dreiser even relaxed enough to sing a comic song, "The Bold Fisherman," which he admitted Jug had taught him. He was delighted when Vera gave him her tiny daughter Sheri to hold, and terrified when the infant began to cry. Noting that Ed and his wife Mai—whom he had always called "Ed's wild Irish Catholic"—still held hands while seated together, he said in utter amazement to Vera, "You know, I believe Ed is still in love with her." Such fidelity was incredible, seeming to disprove his theory that three years was the utmost limit of love's duration. And when Vera told a joke with a racy edge, she had the experience of seeing her rakish old uncle blush deeply and say, "What a memory for low stuff!"

If once he would have called the Ed Dreiser family bourgeois, perhaps now he saw something to envy. He was downright smitten by Vera, finding a security and freedom from tension in her company. In the morning Vera and Ed drove him to the Kew Gardens hospital, where one by one they visited the feeble Mame—the same Mame whose troubled career as a young woman had been in part immortalized in *Jennie Gerhardt*. Of all the Dreisers she was the most like Theodore—big, magnetic, impulsive, intuitive, undisciplined, unschooled. She asked him to pray, a request that shook him.

Outside again, Ed decided to take the subway to Manhattan for greater speed. He and Dreiser talked for a moment beside the car. "There was a little tension and sadness," Dr. Scott recalled. "I felt that as they looked at each other they both thought this might be the last time. Finally, with a quick gesture, T. D. leaned forward and kissed Ed, saying, 'Long life, Ed.' Dad turned and hurried away, overcome with emotion."

Driving Dreiser to the Commodore, she asked him if he believed in God, she herself having left the Catholic Church.

"I not only believe in God," he said, "but I can go into any scientific laboratory and prove His existence."

When Dr. Vera later took him to see Paul Robeson in *Othello*, his admiration for Robeson was if anything exceeded by that for his sparkling niece. He urged her to come west and help him with his writing—an invitation with many previous precedents—but it was impossible because of her family and her practice.

"He told me he often felt depressed," Dr. Scott recalled, "when he thought about how much more he could have done with his life. We talked about some of his love affairs, and I told him that I felt he had had so many that he probably had never been in love at all, and he agreed that that might be so. . . . I had to keep reminding myself that this was the man who wrote *Sister Carrie* and the *Tragedy*. He was so childlike in many ways, and seemed to me so humble a person." [21]

But there was no denying that his stay had been disillusioning and exhausting. He gave a farewell cocktail party for his friends at a Commodore suite on June 2. The teetotalling Fabri helped mix drinks for George Seldes, Richard Wright, Hubert Davis, Dorothy Dudley, Edwin Seaver, Kenneth Miller, Isidore Schneider and others. Robert Elias, still gathering material for the biography, listened to Dreiser discuss the 1943 "disbandment" of the Communist Party and its reformation into the Communist Political Association, saying it was high time the communists worked along American lines as he had urged them to do in the thirties. He fell to reminiscing about the time he had contemplated suicide in Brooklyn, and came near weeping. In the midst of the party he got a telephone call. Mame had died. "He was not much upset about it," Fabri noted in his diary. "He was not terribly interested in his family at all." [22]

To James Farrell, Mencken wrote, "Dreiser came to New York to accept a prize from the American Academy of Arts and Letters. I didn't come to see him, for I simply couldn't endure any such transaction." [23]

With Mrs. Harris' help he got out an encomium for *Soviet Russia Today*, "The Russian Advance." He sat uneasily for portraits by the camera artist Lotte Jacobi. At Mame's funeral in Astoria (she had long since abandoned Catholicism and become a member of Unity) he was impressed by the young clergyman who read the service, saying, "He reminded me of Alyosha Karamazov." He was too fatigued to carry through his planned visits with

Kirah Markham, Sylvia Bradshaw and with Esherick and Louise Campbell in Philadelphia. "This time, New York was almost too much for me," he admitted as he left next day, June 5—the day before D-Day.[24] Mrs. Harris was the lone friend who saw him to the train and gave him fruit, bread and cheese in a paper bag to save him from fighting the wartime dining car crush.

Helen had found that the lumber town of Stevenson, Washington, 53 miles east of Portland on the Columbia, was a Gretna Green where weddings could be performed with only a three-day wait—ideal, since Dreiser's train would pass through there. She wired him to get off at Stevenson. She was waiting at the station at dawn on June 9 when his train pulled in. Dreiser got off, coughing, and so weary that he staggered and fell. Picking himself up, he greeted her warmly and gave her the Academy gold medal—a gesture that brought tears to her eyes, for if she did not precisely believe that she deserved a gold medal for loyalty, she did feel that she had a part in his writings. "What a youthful mind he had," she wrote, "and what a privileged woman I was to have had such a companion!"[25]

To which she added, "I have found that all great people are like children."[26]

They put up at the Sampson Hotel overlooking the wildly beautiful Columbia gorge, where he went to bed, convinced that he had picked up germs in his berth. Helen drove to Portland to get whiskey for him. He bought her a plain gold ring, and they applied for a license as Helen Richardson and Herman Dreiser. On June 13, with Helen's sister Myrtle Patges and her fiancé Chester Butcher as witnesses, they were married by Justice of the Peace Gertrude Brown, who had no idea that the groom was a well-known American novelist.[27]

Across the top of her first letter to Fabri after the event, Helen typed proudly, "Mrs. Theodore Dreiser."

The New York trip had shown Dreiser that it was the novel or nothing. *The Bulwark* was his only chance for publication and income. But how to surmount his writing block? More than ever rose his need for an understanding woman assistant who would stimulate him creatively. He picked Marguerite Tjader Harris for the job—a writer, a woman of beauty, intelligence and independent means, sympathetic with the Quakers. In New York she had worked devotedly for him. She fulfilled another need, for she regarded Dreiser with affectionate admiration as the greatest of American novelists and she felt that *The Bulwark* would be his crowning achievement. Still ailing, he wrote her from Portland:

> I am still confronted by *The Bulwark* and the book of Philosophy. Also by the, to me, so desirable and enticing thought of working toward the completion of both with and through you. . . . For with you—and your sensitive response to the realities and unrealities to address[—]all would come to me clearly enough. . . .[28]

Back home in Hollywood a few days later, he wrote Sylvia Bradshaw in Detroit to explain about his sister's death and the round of appointments that had kept him from seeing her:

> Now that I am back here I have the time once more but you are so far away and I keep wishing that you were out here. For once you were here it would be with us as it was before—you know that—as intense and delirious for I have never forgotten all the phases of all the hours and cannot. The one pleasant thing about this letter to you is that I am able to enclose a check for $50 which is exactly ½ of the sum paid me by *Esquire* for your interesting and humorous study of the man *Bill Brown*. . . . Do you love me? Tell me.[29]

He made no mention of his marriage. Nor was he quite truthful about the *Esquire* check, which was for $250.[30] Probably he had done some rewriting on the story and felt that $200 was due him.

5. The Bulwark

I. THIS PRACTICAL RELATIONSHIP

Any advertisement of the nuptials would disclose that the Dreisers had lived together unsanctified for 25 years. Perhaps also Dreiser was a trifle ashamed at so bourgeois a step as well as feeling that knowledge of it might cramp his other affairs. To Lillian Goodman he passed a hint about the marriage, but such close friends as Esther and Berkeley Tobey, the Manuels, the Smiths and the Lawsons remained unaware of it, as did Dreiser's remaining relatives. Helen mentioned it joyously to Lieutenant Dies on his return from a voyage, but otherwise it remained a triumph locked in her heart.

She was now moved by two further ambitions, one being to win spiritual calm for the unhappy Dreiser by getting him to accept religion. Innately though capriciously religious, she gained comfort by turns from Christian Science, Rosicrucianism, Protestantism and yoga, and felt that he would as well. "She kept pushing him toward the church," John Howard Lawson recalled, "and he kept resisting." [1] But he had attended services with her and Otvos in the spring, and now he occasionally gave in to her urgings, attending a few Christian Science meetings. He was as likely to go in less pious directions. One day Helen telephoned Manuel, saying she needed his help. He arrived at Kings Road to find that Dreiser had been missing for two days and that Helen had received a call from the madam of a brothel on Western Avenue saying that Dreiser was there, drinking and troublesome, and would someone come for him? This had happened before, Helen said. Manuel offered to pick him up, but pointed out that this might embarrass Dreiser, so Helen, agreeing, went for him herself.[2]

Her other aim was to help him finish *The Bulwark*—a hope frustrated by his insistence that he needed Mrs. Harris' aid. To Helen, this amounted to saying that Mrs. Harris had intellectual and inspirational qualities which she lacked, but there it was. She wrote to ask Mrs. Harris if she could come—a carefully phrased letter warning of his poor health and susceptibilities:

> As to T's work, well that is something that he decides. He picks his own temperaments, as he knows whom he can work with. . . . I only help him all I can in every way I can. . . . At all times I try to watch his physical condition. . . .
> As for harmony . . . I understand [the] necessity for it. I . . . need harmony more than almost anything. (Not exactly peace at any price, however). But, I have always been able to get along with people with a very few exceptions. But, after all, harmony does have to be achieved by both

parties involved. Doesn't it? . . . I am sure, Marguerite, that there will be no discord between us. Surely we are beyond that. . . .[3]

Mrs. Harris, on her part, was in a difficult position. The thought that she could help him finish *The Bulwark*, which would at once save him financially and become his literary capstone, was decisive with her. She agreed to make the trip with her fourteen-year-old son Hilary. Meanwhile Dreiser, smitten by his niece Vera, wrote her a four-page letter:

> What a nice brisk, ambitious healthy attractive neice [*sic*] it is that I have fallen heir to,—mentally and physically so alive and comprehending. . . . Really you are not only charming mentally but physically and I keep wishing that I had such an industrious as well as attractive maiden beside me—at my elbow—for most assuredly you would have me up and doing in connection with the things I should be up and doing about instead of myself complaining of this & that. In fact *I think of you all the time,*—your thoughtful and energetic and considerate approach toward everything. . . . If I had you here I'd be having you write my next book for you have the mind & the will and the delight in life and energy to make you capable of almost quite anything. . . . I wish I had such a charming whirlwind attached to my humble little go cart. Would I go places? . . .[4]

Fond of him though she was, Dr. Vera was never quite positive that his interest was entirely platonic.

He also wrote Madame Chiang Kai-Shek, who had impressed him when he met her after she spoke at Hollywood Bowl, and who had told him that Generalissimo Chiang wished to form a new China on a pattern of American capitalism rather than communism. He advised her earnestly that the American system was anything but a model and that Chiang should unite China in a more equitable economy friendly to Russia: "For it is quite obvious, from his writings and his life and action, that Stalin has no desire other than to help people gain their own freedom in their own countries." Now that the second-front-to-aid-Russia was a resounding reality, and Roosevelt had met Stalin at Teheran and spoken well of him, Dreiser had forgiven the President, calling him "one of the greatest Americans this country has produced." [5]

Dreiser had several abscessed teeth extracted. To Louise Campbell he sent $50 (forgetting that he had promised $100) for a sketch she wrote for *Esquire* and which was published under his name, with few changes.[6] At July's end Helen drove him, along with Esther and Berkeley Tobey, to Ensenada, where they stayed at a beach cottage for two days, enjoying sunshine and lobster. Esther Tobey noted that Dreiser was so weary that "he slumped as he walked." He liked Mexicans visually but mistrusted them, just as he mistrusted the Niseis and thought their wartime internment proper. Helen, who felt that she was making progress in steering Dreiser to religion, sang Hungarian and Welsh ballads and even led the foursome in hymns.[7]

Marguerite Harris arrived by car August 18 with her son and a German police dog, finding a cottage on Cadet Court in the Hollywood hills. On the 20th, a week early because Dreiser preferred to forget his birthday, Helen gave a garden party stressing *The Bulwark* rather than his seventy-three years. Among the 57 guests, in addition to the regulars, were Will and Ariel Durant, the Odetses, the Guy Endores and the Russian and Chinese consuls. Esther Tobey and Alvin Manuel agreed that such Dreiser gatherings were usually humdrum, involving people who did not mix—quite unlike the spectacular parties in the Rodin days. Helen served her usual orange punch, of low proof, and Donald Friede was seen looking for something harder. Howard Ross, a student of Lillian Goodman's, sang Dreiser's favorite song, "Jeanie with the Light Brown Hair," after which Helen herself offered a few ballads. The birthday cake was topped with frosting representing a book, *The Bulwark*, and mounted on a music box playing "Happy Birthday." "[Lillian Goodman] said I could have been a *great* singer if I had concentrated on myself and singing," Helen wrote enthusiastically to Fabri. ". . . Imagine! She says I have that different individual quality that makes for a *different* kind of singer. I feel that it is true. . . . But my whole energy has gone in another direction." [8]

To Mrs. Manning Dreiser wrote, "And for so many days previous I have been grieving because of your refusal to meet me," ending, "I love you, Babe!" [9] And to Miss Bradshaw:

> Well I take it that you have found some[one] else who pleases you and who is close at hand. And you certainly deserve to have one. I know how you feel about sharing any male. And to add a long range correspondence to that!—well it's a little too much I know. And the circumstances being what they are I think it's best for each of us not to bother. . . . My feelings concerning our joyous experiment are exactly as they always were only you are there and I am here and since I cannot bring myself to break up this practical relationship here—completely that is—well. Only please don't be angry with me. Hold those delightful memories—some of them at least in your heart—or some part of your mind as I most surely will and do. . . ." [10]

And he wrote Earl Browder to compliment him on his book *Teheran and America*:

> It is such a clear illumination of our path in war and peace. The sanest and most honest and helpful that I have ever read. [11]

II. MONEY FROM STALIN

The Bulwark had been gestating for 32 years—since 1912, when Anna Tatum first told Dreiser the family story on which it was based. John Lane, Liveright and Putnam had all paid him advances on it, Liveright even announcing its forthcoming publication in 1920. Despite his enthusiasm for it he had been balked, first by the suppression of *The "Genius,"* then by his preoccupation with *An American Tragedy*, and later by his immersion in social causes. Always, however, a part of the trouble had been his own dissatisfaction with his treatment. He had to *feel right* about it or he could not proceed. Now, with Mrs. Harris' help, he began at least to feel better about it. He also felt better when he repaid Putnam's advance, severing his connection with that firm and removing an obligation that had grown oppressive. Now, for a time, he was without a publisher, but Alvin Manuel, Jacques Chambrun and others were working on this.

The Bulwark was the story of the spiritual evolution of Solon Barnes, a Quaker who rises from humble Maine boyhood to wealth as a Philadelphia banker and finds that although his own dealings are scrupulously honest he becomes unwittingly involved in the sharp capitalistic promotions of his partners. Along the way he is stricken by personal tragedy—a "wayward" daughter, a reckless son who commits suicide after becoming involved in the seduction and death of a girl, then the death of his own wife. Dreiser's original plan had been to tell ironically of the failure of religion to meet the facts of life. Now, with the tempering of his own philosophy, he envisioned Solon as a man so enlarged in spiritual resources that instead of being crushed by his tragedies he rises above them to a mood of universal love.

Starting in September, Mrs. Harris picked up Dreiser daily at about ten, drove him to her cottage two miles north on Cadet Court, installed him in a rocker at an unpainted table and took his slow dictation in longhand. The place being sparsely furnished due to wartime shortages, she brought in the rumble seat from her Ford as an additional chair. There were two old partially completed scripts, some in longhand and some in typescript, as well as Dreiser's latest version, which was about half finished but with which he was not entirely satisfied. The task of sifting the best elements from the three scripts and sharpening the main theme was formidable. Mrs. Harris served chiefly as amanuensis, offering no advice unless asked, though she did cut obvious repetitions. Dreiser expected her to be as dedicated as he, even resenting it when she had guests in the evening on her own, feeling that it would interfere with her concentration.

Rocking slowly as he thought, he would sometimes say, "Now wait—I'll write this out and see if it goes." While she copied it, he might wander out on the patio, bordered with African daisies and roses and commanding a fine view of the Santa Monica mountains, then return to read it. She would fix a light lunch, after which they continued until about four, when she drove him home.[12]

The work took so much out of him that his once mountainous correspondence dwindled to a trickle. Mencken, obviously angry, had not written since July. Masters, now an invalid, wistfully urged Dreiser to write. When Dreiser got home in the afternoon he was weary, ready for a drink, a rest, dinner and usually nothing more strenuous than a ride to the shore with Helen at the wheel. At the instance of Lillian Goodman he sat for a bust by the sculptor

Edgardo Simone. When Paul Robeson came to Los Angeles, he was a guest, telling Dreiser of the education of his son in Russia. There were occasional small gatherings at the Kings Road house, at one of which John Howard Lawson, Charlie Chaplin, Clifford Odets and Dreiser had a spirited discussion of life, politics and art—"a crazy conversation," as Lawson recalled it, "but delightful." He was struck by Dreiser's growing mysticism, his desperate search for cosmic answers, and was one of the few who gave Dreiser credit for great intelligence. "He was contradictory and somewhat confused," Lawson said, "but out of the confusion would come massive illuminations." He drank excessively at times, Lawson thought, because of tensions with Helen, worry over *The Bulwark* and a fear that life was slipping away.[13]

On the advice of his physician, Dr. Samuel Hirshfeld, Dreiser had an ounce of brandy before breakfast, then tried to stay dry until evening. He ate carbohydrates to gain weight, took assorted medications prescribed for him, and on his own swallowed vitamin pills wholesale on the theory that they might do him good. Nevertheless he had a maddening train of ailments—an itchy rash on his shoulders, visual impairment, occasional kidney trouble and a siege of prostatitis. "The dear genito-urinary specialist among other torture-some proceedings inserted a form of curved metal rod in to the urinary tract. . . ." he wrote Mrs. Manning. "He wanted me to enter Cedars of Lebanon hospital but I refused to go." [14]

Indeed the efforts of Helen and Mrs. Harris (though there were tensions between them) were united in an aim to establish for him a creative atmosphere, hold down his intake of alcohol, discourage his affairs with other women and to preserve the dubious health that at times he seemed determined to destroy.

As he got farther into *The Bulwark*, he felt increasing sympathy for Solon, identifying him in part with his own father and his great tribulations with the stormy Dreiser brood. In these gentle moods the bitter, cynical Dreiser was gone. When speaking of Solon his eyes would fill with tears, Helen noting, "I knew he was thinking not only of his father but of what he considered his own shortcomings." [15] Surely also he was thinking of Solon himself, pitying his anguish as he had pitied Clyde Griffiths in the *Tragedy*. His few personal letters now—to Powys or Louise Campbell—were marked by affection and tenderness. Feeling himself more than ever an instrument of the creative force, he often refused to plan his writing a day ahead, sure that the inspiration would or would not come regardless of any conscious effort on his part, veering from elation to deep depression. He often quoted the Bible, particularly the Sermon on the Mount. Working at Mrs. Harris' cottage, he was interested in young Hilary's guinea pigs—charmed also by a bluebird that often perched near him on the patio, saying, "He knows me." [16]

Although at times he feared he was making *The Bulwark* too "religious," in his transcendental mood he was not always averse to going to church, actually finding himself moved by the services—as he would have been moved by a fortune teller, a bird or a flower. On Good Friday he attended holy communion with Helen and Mrs. Harris at the Mount Hollywood Congregational Church of the Rev. Allan Hunter, seeming almost shaken by the experience.

The world also shook. President Roosevelt died, and by May Day the Russians entered Berlin, hoisted the Red flag over the Reichstag and announced the death of Hitler. By May 6 *The Bulwark* was finished. In a spirit of celebration, the Dreisers, with Mrs. Harris and Hilary, drove to Ensenada for a two-day rest at the beach.

Now Dreiser had time to devote to politics, wiring President Truman and Secretary of State Edward Stettinius protesting the continued recognition of Franco Spain. He worried about the Allied disagreement over the implementation of the Yalta decision to reconstitute the Polish provisional government. He cabled Stalin:

> URGE CLARIFICATION POLISH QUESTION AS AMERICAN CAPITALISTIC REACTION IS CREATING MOST UNFORTUNATE MISUNDERSTANDING. OUR TWO GREAT NATIONS SHOULD GROW IN FRIENDSHIP. PLEASE DEAL WITH OUR AMERICANS GENTLY. JUST NOW IT IS SO IMPORTANT.[17]

That Stalin was too busy to reply made no difference. On Dreiser's misty emotional Olympus the Russian butcher had taken a firm, fixed place at the peak. Dreiser had written, "Feodor Dostoievsky . . . once said that he had had a vision, and that was that the White Christ—meaning human equity, human decency—would come out of Russia. And, unbelievable as it may seem, that same White Christ has come out of Russia and is still leading this great people to its obvious destiny and service to the world." [18]

He also addressed to Stalin a letter on an entirely different matter. Hearing of the huge sales of his books in Russia, and that a few American writers were receiving payments from the Soviet, he wrote to explain the situation and ask an accounting for past-due royalties. Two months later the Soviet government deposited to Dreiser's credit in a Los Angeles bank $34,600—a sum that eliminated financial worry for the rest of his life, though he still "talked poor." [19]

Meanwhile Manuel found him a publisher—No. 9, and not precisely new. More than 44 years after the original publication of *Sister Carrie* and its chilly treatment by Doubleday, Page, Dreiser went full circle and signed up for his seventh novel with the successor of that firm, Doubleday & Company. But *The Bulwark* was having its troubles. He had written affectionately to Louise Campbell, his intermittent literary doctor since 1917:

> For you are, as you know,—a swell editor[,] the best I have ever known and I'll feel troubled if you find yourself unable to edit it. . . . You'd be surprised dear how constantly you are in my mind and how high & how deep my affection for you truly is[.] [20]

She received the manuscript by mid-May—a move that distressed Mrs. Harris, who venerated Dreiser's style and felt that the book should not be tampered with. The script was long—almost as long as the *Tragedy*—and Mrs. Campbell found it wandering and boresome. She felt it the work of a sick man, a sorry decline in his talents. A touching letter Helen wrote her privately added to her concern:

> When the Tragedy was in the making, I was absolutely sure about the outcome of it. I can't say that I feel that same absolute confidence in this book. . . . I would rather not see it published than see it fail for I feel that a failure at this time of his life would hurt him *terribly*. And yet, my anxiety may be unfounded. . . . A success would mean everything to him just now. . . . So, Louise, please think of this when you write him exactly what you think. . . .[21]

In a painful predicament, reluctant to condemn his thirty-year project out of hand, Mrs. Campbell wrote Dreiser, diplomatically listing her reservations. Her lack of enthusiasm was obvious—a sad disappointment to him. Thanking her nevertheless—a mark of the true courage that never seemed to fail him—he called on James T. Farrell for help. Farrell had not only been friendly. He had been understanding and admiring, seeing Dreiser's greatness as few others now saw it, and recently he had written a long appreciation of *An American Tragedy* for *The New York Times*. It is doubtful that Dreiser had read any of Farrell's novels, but he knew a friend when he saw one.

When Farrell agreed to read *The Bulwark*, Mrs. Campbell expressed it to him in New York. On reading it, he differed from her view, seeing the need for some revision but in general praising the theme and treatment. He telephoned Mrs. Campbell, suggesting that perhaps she was influenced by modern fiction and that *The Bulwark* was something that required slow reading. She felt that she, if anyone on earth, knew Dreiser's style and how to read it. When Farrell returned the script to her, she began editing it in a conscientious effort to make it good Dreiser even if it could not be Dreiser at his best.[22]

6. The Stoic

In a sense it could be said that Helen—once the fragmented, the uncertain, the vacillating—had triumphed over the formidable Dreiser. True, she had accomplished it at first by yielding, but as her skill in skirmishing grew over the years she had gained by inches, so gradually that her victories were unnoticed except in retrospect. The gains were in part physical, the result of middle-aged stamina against enfeebled years. Now she still yielded, but not so much, not so far. Her reverence for his genius had been joined by a hard-headed understanding of what was good for him. "Once I allowed myself to worship him," she wrote a friend. ". . . It is so characteristic of a woman to worship. But it's not the way."

To her he was a boy as well as an infirm old man, and to him she was so indispensable that the inroads she made on his freedom had to be cheated when possible and countenanced otherwise. Certainly he knew that without her he would be dead. The temptation to wreck what remained of his health was still strong, so that he clung to her as he would to a lifeline even as he often resented the necessity. It is a safe guess that if either he or she had let go, his last two novels would never have been written. Perhaps she would never have been a great singer or actress, but as consort of the world's most unreasonable man she had reached a unique stardom, filling a role no one else could fill.

Now fifty-one, she was plump, a little faded, but never forgetting that she had once been a beauty. Though more conservative in dress, she still had a weakness for things shiny—sequins, jet buttons, glittering purses—and she dyed her hair a dark peach shade. As thoroughly unsophisticated as her husband, she was seldom a victim of her old hysteria, having achieved through battle a poise of her own—practical, cheerful, but firm when necessary. The Dreisers frequently exchanged visits with the Tobeys, who remarked on Helen's instant and intuitive understanding of Dreiser's moods and needs, and his greater appreciation of her. He occasionally praised her singing or her poetry. She had reworked Poem No. 16, a sonnet she had written to Dreiser and sent to Fabri several years earlier, titling it "To a Poet":

> *If I did touch the margin of your soul*
> *In its swift moving earthly seeming plight,*
> *And but beheld its burnished aureole*
> *That shed a brilliance to the inner sight,*

512

And opened up the windows of the mind
To rarer beauties far than most men feel;
Then I have sung the lark's sweet song designed
To fuse our senses with celestial seal
As once on grassy sward we lay enthralled;
But moved as quickened spirits to the birth
Of other joys to which our hearts were called:
To ride melodic wings above the earth
Where you, the song and I are now afloat
In that one crystal clear immortal note.[1]

The Chaplins were guests once or twice, the comedian convulsing Dreiser with his portrayal of a child selling violets on a London street. To Clifford Odets, now writing for RKO, Dreiser addressed a query: Was that studio ever going to produce *Sister Carrie?* [2] And with John Howard Lawson that spring he began discussing the idea of joining the Communist Party.

He felt a great rapport with the genial, gifted Lawson, who in a dozen Hollywood years had written for several studios, recently having done *Sahara* and *Counter-Attack* for Columbia. Lawson in turn so admired him that he liked to drop in at Kings Road now and then just to chat for an hour or two. Dreiser foresaw serious social conflicts after the war, and Lawson felt that in part it was this presentiment that made him consider joining the party.[3] There were other reasons.

Dreiser, physically and mentally weary, was gripped by the spiritual mood of Solon Barnes—a mood of religious revelation barely contaminated by reality. Solon had made his own affirmation—had read a sharp lecture to his conniving capitalistic bank partners and resigned. Dreiser, who *was* Solon philosophically, was impelled toward a similar spiritual affirmation. The time when he could continue his protests against capital was growing short—all the more reason to invest his protest in a publicly acknowledged rite, to perpetuate it, bequeath it to the party that would hold it in trust.

He had been impressed by his talk with Robeson about the education of Paul Robeson, Jr. in Moscow with none of the race consciousness so strong in America. In America Dreiser was all but forgotten and unpublished, whereas in Russia his books were widely read and praised. American friendship with the Soviet was still at a high point. That spring the United Nations met in San Francisco, and some of the Russian delegates came down to see Los Angeles and took the trouble to call on Dreiser, a flattering gesture. Against that he could place the activities of Congressman Dies, which made him livid and which did not recall any echo of mass extermination in Russia.

And had not the Russians sent him $34,600?

Then there was the important matter of Earl Browder, whom he had never quite forgiven for turning him away in the thirties. Browder was now getting the Russian boot. Stalin had met with Jacques Duclos, who published his famous letter in the French magazine *Cahiers du Communisme* in April

accusing Browder of revisionism, belief in class peace. This word from on
high threw American communists into bewilderment and fear when it was
reprinted in the *Daily Worker* May 25, and a party brainwashing began.
William Z. Foster assailed Browder. In a small-beer parody of the Moscow
trials, many U. S. Reds humbled themselves in penance, recanting their faith
in the leader who had professed some confidence in American "imperialists."
Browder, so recently revered, was being purged, Browderism was a dirty
word, a special convention was called for July and Foster was the certain
successor. Browder's book *The Marxists and the War*, just coming off the
communists' International Press, was burned. Dreiser may have known little
of this background. What he did know was that Browder was out and Foster,
who had always wanted him in the party and whom he considered a
"spiritual" man on the order of Stalin and Solon Barnes, was in. One need not
dig for intellectual reasons for his impulsion, since it was largely emotional
and religious, the logical step for a believer in the White Christ that came out
of Russia.

Yet he had one practical reservation. He knew that party discipline was
severe and that some members were badly pushed around by the hierarchy.
The classless ideal of his theories gave way when his own person was involved
(so like his attitude toward a contract, which he often forgot obligated
himself) for he wanted no infringement of his liberty. He was interested
enough in this to get reassurances on the matter from a party man he knew.[4]

Lawson himself, as he recalled it, was not at all sure it was the right step for
Dreiser to take in terms of his usefulness and his role as an artist. But the party
had lost members who could not stomach the Browder purge, it needed the
prestige of a famous figure, and there were communists who called on Dreiser
to urge him to join. Susceptible though he was to flattery, he seems to have
been influenced chiefly by his own occult vision. He "took instruction." On
July 20 he addressed a long letter to National Chairman Foster in New York,
beginning:

> I am writing this letter to tell you of my desire to become a member of
> the Communist Political Association.
>
> This request is rooted in convictions that I have long held and that have
> been strengthened and deepened by the years. I have believed intensely that
> the common people, and first of all the workers,—of the United States and
> of the world—are the guardians of their own destiny and the creators of
> their own future. I have endeavored to live by this faith, to clothe it in
> words and symbols, to explore its full meaning in the lives of men and
> women. . . .[5]

The letter was not written by Dreiser, though Helen said he approved and
corrected it; nor by Lawson, though Lawson gave advice about the wording.
The communists, aiming to make extensive propaganda use of it, could
scarcely trust the mystic Dreiser to say the right things. The letter was the
work of a well-drilled Marxist, or group of them, aimed at maximum impact.

Indeed, there is a mystery here, for Dreiser and Helen left for Portland by car July 11 and did not return until August 2. Yet the letter to Foster was dated July 20 from Hollywood—a time when Dreiser had been gone nine days— giving one an impression of other anxious hands involved. Foster replied ungrammatically from New York:

> Dear Comrade Dreiser: Your letter of application for membership in the Communist Party was, as you know by now, unanimously and enthusiastically accepted by our recent National Convention in New York, I therefore, extend to you this official welcome into our organization.
>
> Our Party is indeed honored to have within its ranks a writer of your great literary stature and integrity. . . .
>
> We feel that your joining our Party at this time is particularly appropriate, now that our organization is purging itself of the opportunism that seeped into it during recent years. . . . Welcome to the ranks of the Communist Party.[6]

"DREISER JOINS THE VANGUARD," headlined the *New Masses* August 7.

It was the final logic of his anti-logic.

II. TOIL AND TROUBLE

A few days after the Dreisers' return from Oregon ("T. D. got awfully tired & cross. . . ." Helen noted. "Too long a drive."), atomic bombs fell on Japan and the war was soon over. Meanwhile he had decided to drop the Philosophy, too much for him to handle now, and complete *The Stoic*. Again he felt the need of Mrs. Harris' help, but here, as is evident from the letters, Helen raised objections. With Dreiser weak and sickly, she would feel safer with him at home under her own wing. She also questioned the wisdom of any formal affiliation with the communists, but on this score she knew that the decision must be his own. To Mrs. Harris in Connecticut Dreiser wrote, "Life needs such stirring temperaments as yours. As to working with you . . . I need an *action program*—something constructive that will stir me to labor. If I did not feel so sickish—so lethargic I could think something out. . . . What I need most I guess is you." [7]

Helen was helping him with *The Stoic*, now about three-quarters finished, taking his dictation as he rocked rhythmically. On the Paul Dresser piano-desk were a carved-wood Chinese fisherman in a blue coolie coat and a small blanketed American Indian with black braided human hair. He also liked to carry luck pieces such as Chinese coins in his pocket. Helen later wrote, "Never . . . had we ever been so close, mentally, spiritually and physically as we were this last year of his life." [8] To Sylvia Bradshaw he wrote, "Only please before you cease and disappear—write me one more letter. I would so much like to hear from you—coldly or warmly—just so I hear." [9] In the late afternoon he sometimes sneaked out, to be picked up by Mrs. Manning and

taken to her home, where he would stretch out with a drink and talk for
hours. He evidently felt that Helen was intercepting some of his letters, for he
headed one to Mrs. Harris, "If you answer register your letter to
me—personal delivery." He went on in a tone indicative of his distraction:

> Double, Double, Toil & Trouble—
> Fire burn and cauldren buble [*sic*]

I turn and fret and worry. I had your understanding letter days ago but
as for an agreeable Solution for you and for me?—*not so easy*. Worry, jealousy. Discord. The feeling of injustice—unfairness[.] A sense of unjustified
scheming and plotting. And eventually *for some one*—retribution[.] And
because of all this the difficulty of creative labor.

As for myself I have but four hundred dollars at the moment that I could
devote to your coming here. . . . The only trouble or problem—is that of
CONTACT—our being together enough without outside irritation and friction to make the matter of constructive work—constructive writing possible.

> Double, Double, Toil & trouble—
> Fire burn and cauldron bubble

And yet if you were here. . . . For mostly you carry the atmosphere of
creation with you. You evoke effort[,] the atmosphere of creative work
with you—and so. . . . You may be pondering all this as disturbedly as I
have been doing. Hence I write[.] It is perfectly clear I think. Only I hate
delay—the lack of sufficient means just now to arrange all. For above all I
need the aid of a practical mind that can look after and handle for me so
many practical details.[10]

He was not as poor as he made out. Esther Tobey noted that he once gave
his watch to a friend to take to the jeweler because the friend looked
unprosperous and the fee might be lower.

On August 27 Helen gave him his last birthday party, his seventy-fourth—a
small one attended by the Goodmans, the Tobeys, the Smiths, Clare Kummer
and a few others. It was darkened by the death two days earlier of A. Dorian
Otvos, who had sold *Sister Carrie* and had been a good friend despite Dreiser's
suggestion that he be less friendly. The next day he spoke warmly of Otvos at
the services at Forest Lawn in Glendale. He had done the same for Maria
Samson, who had committed suicide three years earlier, and for several other
deceased friends, feeling that a simple public statement of the departed one's
virtues was the best kind of farewell.

To Mencken he had variously written that he would leave his own body to
the ashman or to Rush Medical College. To Helen in 1940 he had given a
letter authorizing her to bury him in any way she saw fit. Long scornful of
fancy burials, he had once had Esther Tobey do research for him on the
gouging practices of morticians and the ridiculous vanity that required an
expensive coffin, facial cosmetics and dyed hair. But the capitalistic-
communistic Dreiser looked approvingly around the Forest Lawn layout

with its mountainous statuary, its Inspiration Slope, Vale of Memory and Babyland. One recalls his phrase in *Sister Carrie*—"a truly swell saloon." This was a truly swell graveyard. "Teddie remarked to me that he had never seen a more beautiful resting place," Helen noted, and bore it in mind.[11]

"If you can," Masters had written months earlier, "I'd be glad to have a letter from you. If you can't write, I'll understand." [12] Dreiser did not find the time, just as Mencken had failed to write Dreiser for more than a year. To Mencken he wrote wistfully:

> Dear Mencken—Just to let you know that I am on earth worthy or unworthy. Have just finished *The Bulwark*—(final revision) and like it very much. In another week or so [he was far off the mark here] expect to conclude *The Stoic*. . . .
>
> How are you? The end of this international fighting makes me feel better if it is really ended. I have often wondered how certain phases of it have affected you? There have been so many tragic angles. Regards, best wishes, affectionately, Dreiser.[13]

Mencken did not reply, and it was Dreiser's last effort. On September 4 Mrs. Harris returned to Hollywood to work on a book about Dreiser as well as to help him with *The Stoic* if the opportunity offered. It did not offer on a regular basis, for Helen was determined to do the helping herself. Indeed, to Estelle Manning he complained that he was a prisoner in his own home, though this seemed inconsistent with his occasional meetings with her. A few days later Elias arrived to clear up some matters with Dreiser, whom he found "obviously tired and in the home stretch. . . ." Elias had talked with Mencken and heard some typical pungencies: Imagine an American Academy that didn't include Dreiser among its members! They knew he was hard up—took indecent advantage of him. Dreiser's belief in crackpots and tea-leaf readers was almost as bad as Upton Sinclair's, and his mysticism was similarly absurd. Dreiser was really unread in philosophy except for Spencer, Mencken thought. If death came slowly, he predicted that a repentant Dreiser would embrace the church, as with Heywood Broun. "It always happens," said Mencken.[14]

Elias found Dreiser's mind keen on some occasions but so clouded on others that it was useless to question him. On one of the "good" meetings Elias noted, "TD feels Russian leaders are truly spiritual people. Recalls how moved Stalin was at Lenin's funeral. . . . Wm. Z. Foster [spiritual] too.

"TD joined party because he approved of their program in Russia and their program here . . . the details of the party line are irrelevant to the joining. . . . When asked about their discipline and whether he could still disagree and criticize them, he said he would and if they didn't like it they could throw him out." [15]

The remark underlined at once his conception of his membership as a religious gesture rather than an enlistment in discipline, and his insistence that he must occupy a special category in a world that should have no special categories.

"What the world needs," he told Elias, "is more spiritual character," adding, "The true religion is in Matthew." [16]

Yet it does not appear that he underwent the conventional religious "conversion" Mencken had expected. While the focus and intensity of his beliefs had changed, he had always been profoundly religious, his old attitude toward formal religion simply reflecting his religious rage at the formalists' heretical disagreement with his own mystic creed. Now he was gentler, more tolerant of formalists (excepting Catholics), willing to call the creative force "God" on occasion but still hewing to his own mysticism and refusing to subscribe to any formal doctrine.

At three on the morning of September 16, Dreiser got up, turned on the lights and called for Helen. She hurried from her own room to join him, but he did not recognize her. He kept prowling the house looking for her, though she trotted beside him assuring him that she *was* Helen. She made notes about it: "I said, 'I am Helen.' First he said, 'Everyone thinks she's Helen.' Then I told him quietly that I could prove it. T. D. then said, 'I'll believe you if you say so.'" His irrationality recurred at intervals for several days. On one occasion she drove to Mrs. Harris' place to ask her help in bringing him back to reality. Mrs. Harris returned with her to Kings Road to find Dreiser lying on a couch. "It's odd," he said to Mrs. Harris. "A strange woman has been here." But when Helen a moment later walked in casually and greeted him, he recognized her and seemed perfectly lucid. [17]

With Helen he continued working on *The Stoic*. His appetite poor, his concentration uncertain, he struggled to complete the final few short chapters, finding the ruthless Cowperwood a difficult subject after the spiritual Solon. In the earlier parts of the book, already written, Cowperwood, foiled in Chicago, goes to London with his last mistress, Berenice, to promote a unified London subway. He hires a smooth gigolo to devote himself to the jealous Mrs. Cowperwood and if possible take her off his hands. But Cowperwood dies in the midst of his London operations. Dreiser, who originally had intended to end the book and the trilogy on an ironical note stressing the vanity of human effort and the futility of success, was unable in his new spirituality to follow this design. Cowperwood had to be redeemed in some way. Helen, gratefully feeling herself a part of the book, was occasionally hearing Swami Praharananda at the Vedanta Society—actually contemplating a visit to India to study yoga. Possibly her influence had something to do with the bizarre conclusion, in which the reader is carried off to India with the grieving Berenice, who finds comfort and understanding in yoga and thereafter devotes herself to good works. Yet Dreiser himself was fascinated by Oriental philosophy, and in his mystic mood must have liked the idea. [18]

In mid-October, as he and Helen dined at a Chinese restaurant, he became quietly irrational again, worrying about the strange woman (Helen) at home.

She drove him home, where he began looking for her although she was there at his side. When the handsome Dr. Hirshfeld looked him over, he said the trouble was not deep-seated and prescribed hormone injections and pills.

Meanwhile *The Bulwark* had been buffeted among disagreeing critics. Mrs. Campbell had edited the entire script and sent it to Dreiser, who praised her work, paid her $500 and mailed the script to Doubleday's editor, Donald B. Elder. Elder, disagreeing with Dreiser himself, felt that Mrs. Campbell had cut too drastically and in some cases had "modernized" Dreiser's Victorian flow of clauses. After conferring with Farrell, Elder had re-edited the script, restoring some of the changes.[19] Mrs. Harris was vitally concerned about this as well, feeling a natural kinship with the book on which she had worked and regarding Dreiser (with some justice) as being helpless with his own writing after the creative stage. Thus *The Bulwark* reflected in varying degrees the work of Dreiser, Mrs. Harris, Mrs. Campbell, Farrell and Elder by the time proofs reached Dreiser in December.

Mrs. Harris arrived at Kings Road, as had been agreed, to help read the proofs. Helen now took a firm stand, saying that she would aid in the correction—an idea that seemed illogical to Mrs. Harris, who was closely identified with the book and felt Helen unacquainted with the creative work. The quiet story of the saintly Solon Barnes became the center of a quarrel as the two women disputed the point. Dreiser stood helpless, almost wordless, and Mrs. Harris, greatly disappointed, left. As a result, the proofs were checked by Dreiser and Helen and returned December 22 with scarcely a correction.[20]

7. The Road I Came

On December 21 the last picture of the living Dreiser was taken as with Helen he attended the marriage of Lieutenant George B. Smith, Navy pilot and son of their good friends the Byron Smiths, at the Wee Kirk o' the Heather at Forest Lawn. Dreiser, clad smartly in dark jacket, light pants and a gay silk scarf, looked tired and unhappy.

On December 24 he telephoned Mrs. Manning, who picked him up in her car. He spent much of the day at her house, bringing Christmas gifts for her child, admiring the tree. He had been kind and helpful, praising her writing talent, sometimes collaborating with her and always giving her those thoughtful attentions he knew so well how to bestow. Like so many others, she believed what he said.

"He complained so bitterly of the imprisoned life he was forced to live," she wrote, "that I suggested again that perhaps if he would marry her [Helen], he might find life simpler. But he raged, and said that he had done many things for her, but that was one thing that he would never do. He wanted her to leave, and, as soon as THE BULWARK was published, he would have more money to give her, and then, maybe, she would go." He grew cheerful as they turned to other subjects, and Mrs. Manning, at his request, played "Drink to Me Only with Thine Eyes" on the piano. She added, "He seemed gay and relaxed—until I let him out of the car in front of his house. Then he wept terribly and said 'I am the loneliest man in the world.' And he walked slowly in." [1]

"The loneliest man in the world"—there is deep pathos in the words even though the loneliness was that of the imprisoned ego, the man who found no one who truly understood him and who must have felt at times that the fault was his own, that he had little love to give, that he had created his own loneliness because he had failed in truth and loyalty. The loneliness had been supportable—even rather grand—in his earlier years when women came and went and his work was supreme. Now, as the hour grew late and the work flagged, did he realize that the sanctity he had come to revere had eluded him, that the time for finding it had passed?

"Teddie flooded me with his love," Helen wrote of her last months with him. "He praised me for things I had long forgotten, and expressed many little tendernesses I didn't know he was capable of." [2]

The Dreisers had Christmas breakfast at the impressive Pilgrimage Trail home of the Goodmans. In the afternoon they visited the birdlike Clare

520

Kummer in Beverly Hills, Dreiser sitting beside her at the piano and growing tearful as she played some of Paul's old tunes, including "On the Banks of the Wabash," that poignant reminder of the Nineties, the days when his strength and dreams were boundless. He had always been a connoisseur of dreams. What was there to dream of now? He had sent Mrs. Manning a Christmas card emblazoned with a Russian girl holding aloft a candelabrum, writing on it, "Dear [Estelle]—Here is your literary genius guiding you to fame and fortune," and sending her warm greetings. To Sylvia Bradshaw in Detroit he had written:

> Forgive my silence. I've been working so hard—two long books in the last two years. And believe it or not you've been on my mind so much and me wishing as constantly that you were out here. . . .[3]

Doubtless to a dozen or more other women he had sent similar greetings that may still be treasured across the land.

On the 26th, with Helen at the Bowery cocktail lounge on Santa Monica Boulevard, he talked nostalgically of Greenwich Village—how he could walk around there meeting friends everywhere. Mencken's silence must have been a cruel blow. The thought of friends—of love he had missed—was much on his mind now, and he felt they could be found if he searched. Helen noted, "I said we would go to N. Y. in May but was wondering how disappointed he would be in it then. We decide to go in May. I feel sad because I know he is not very strong."

On December 3 he had sent Farrell the almost completed script of *The Stoic.* Farrell returned it on the 19th with a careful, nine-page analysis suggesting changes, among other places, in the ending. "As I wrote Elder," Dreiser replied, "I simply stopped writing at the end because I was tired, after writing the two volumes. Your suggestions are sound and logical, and I will re-write the last two chapters." [4]

With Helen helping him, he rewrote the next-to-last chapter December 27 and was exhausted by five, when she took him for one of his almost daily drives. They went to the beach at Venice, strolling the boardwalk as they watched the sun sink into the Pacific—"the most beautiful sunset I had ever seen," Helen called it. They had coffee and hot dogs and were home by 7:30, Dreiser going immediately to bed, feeling kidney aches. Helen, sleeping in the twin bed next him, was aroused by his call around three A.M.: "*Helen*, I have an *intense* pain." He struggled from bed and collapsed to the floor. Helen flew to the telephone to call the first number she could think of—that of the Goodmans. Lillian and Mark Goodman arrived, as did the doctor. By morning Dreiser's face was covered by an oxygen mask and he was rallying. "He may even pull through," Dr. Hirshfeld said.[5] Mrs. Goodman found him a docile patient and could not guess whether he knew he was near death.

Time, which he had feared all his life, was at his throat now. One can be sure that he felt alone as he faced his ordeal. The friendships had dwindled, not only because of death. Arthur Henry, Richard Duffy, Ed Smith, Hapgood, Dr. Brill, Claude Bowers, Esherick, Nathan, Boyd, Mencken, Masters—they and others had been dear to him, but not dear enough to last. Causes had been more important than friendships, and he had been unable to offer the sustained reciprocity that friendship requires. The rootlessness of his Indiana boyhood had persisted. Now he lay in loneliness in a hard commercial corner of the world—Hollywood—where he was a stranger even though he had lived there seven years. Helen was the link with all that had been. That day, Friday, although he was attended by a male nurse, he insisted that Helen stay with him.

In the afternoon the Congregational clergyman Allan Hunter called by pure chance, not having seen him for months, unaware of his illness. He greeted Dreiser, took his hand, uttered a prayer and left. Esther Tobey, likewise unsuspecting, dropped in. Helen, now hopeful, took her in to see Dreiser. Esther asked him how he felt. He dropped his oxygen mask and said one word: "Bum."

"He looked gray and tired," Esther recalled. "Whenever he was sick he had a very helpless look (Helen always bustled around him cheerfully at such times, giving him, it seemed to me, a feeling of safety). His eyelashes, which were long and soft, lay separately when his lids were lowered, for some reason giving him a vulnerable look."

The Goodmans having spent the previous night with Helen, the Tobeys at her request planned to be with her this night. Esther drove to Santa Monica to get her husband. "During this time the bright unseasonably warm day had changed completely," she recalled. "There was a light fog and it was cold. Before I had gone more than a mile the fog was so thick that I had to drive by the white lines. . . . Dreiser had spoken or written of death as an enveloping fog—'a woolly fog that blocks one's course and quenches all'—and recalling this as I drove made his death seem imminent."

At Kings Road, Dreiser asked Helen to kiss him. His hands grew cold, his breathing shallow. Alarmed, the nurse telephoned Dr. Hirshfeld. Helen, anxiously holding Dreiser's hands—his beautiful, tapering hands—saw him die: "There was something magnificent in the dignity of his departure, as though every atom of his body was in complete repose." Dr. Hirshfeld arrived to pronounce him dead of a heart attack at 6:50 P.M. on December 28.[6]

II. OH, SPACE! CHANGE!

Helen called the Tobeys to give them the news and ask them to come at once. She delayed her call to the undertaker for two reasons: She wanted someone who loved Dreiser to be with her when she did this, and she also had a conviction that the spirit remained in the body for some hours after death—a time during which she did not want him disturbed. She had always shared him, both as a person and as a public figure. Now she thought of the public. She telephoned Mrs. Manning, who had newspaper friends, to ask that the story of Dreiser's death be given the press.

"She . . . telephoned me—5 minutes after he had died," Mrs. Manning recalled, "crying so terribly . . . I felt sorry for her. After all, she had been kicked around horribly for thirty odd [actually 26] years." [7]

The Tobeys arrived, to wait while Helen made the inevitable calls—the Goodmans, Clare Kummer, Marguerite Tjader Harris, John Howard Lawson, many others. The Tobeys, still unaware of the Dreiser marriage, were concerned that a bourgeois scandal might trouble Helen now that the newspapers would learn the "truth." Helen did not think to tell them of the marriage until later.

"*Oh, many kinds of death are necessary,*" Dreiser had written in *Moods.* Each of his friends would now have his own collection of impressions about this singular man, knowing a few facets, unaware of others. Helen had the most comprehensive collection of all. She probably would not have been surprised to know that four days earlier he had disowned her at Mrs. Manning's. At last, satisfied that his spirit had fled, she called the undertaker.

She did not call a local, around-the-corner mortuary. Knowing Dreiser as the frustrated capitalist he was, she telephoned the Forest Lawn people who embalmed and buried all the film stars and producers and corporation profiteers. The Tobeys, recalling Dreiser's expressed contempt for lavish funerals, were distressed by this, but Helen *knew.*

The newspapers, which had wearied of Dreiser's latter-day fulminations and had given him little space, headlined his death—some, like *The New York Times,* giving elaborate summations of his career that had a flavor of the antique in 1945. His native state of Indiana, which had always rejected him, took the news coolly. The *Indianapolis Star* commented, "His wails about the bitter cruelty and brutality of life failed to impress this literary sector, where life usually ran in conventional channels," and added, "The late Paul Dresser, a brother, probably will be remembered much longer in Hoosierdom." [8]

No newspaper could catch the prodigious drama of this strange life—the sensitive, shoeless Indiana boy with hurts that never healed, the anguish over the stillborn *Sister Carrie,* the interval of dress-pattern splendor, then the long, bitter struggle for freedom and acceptance that would be his greatest glory and that ended with *An American Tragedy* in 1925. That the work he had done in those years made a bridge between Howells and Hemingway that no one else could have built was achievement enough of itself. It was not the final achievement. Bridge or no bridge, the work was colossal in its own right. The freedom he had fought for was pretty well won, if not a culture that valued it, and in 1945 it was easy to forget that blood had been shed in the battle. Others were using the freedom now, taking it for granted, and the man who had felt most of the pain had been out of the mainstream for twenty years. One can picture readers—those who remembered him at all—saying, "Dreiser? I thought he was dead long ago."

In a sense they were right. The original creative artist had languished after 1925, if he had not quite died, and the personality that persisted was something different: the crusading zealot, the bullheaded, uninformed visionary. The great realist had lost his way, abandoned realism, when he turned his enormous compassion solely on the squid and began to hate all lobsters. The intuition and sympathy that had created Carrie, Jennie and Clyde were poor weapons when they grappled with the hard world of politics. Hatred could grow tiresome. The newspapers did not say that Dreiser would have won greater honor had he fallen dead after penning the last line of the *Tragedy*, but it was almost so. Max Lerner, praising Dreiser's novels, touched on the decline: "He tried to go at the problem of the American political and social dilemma in much the same way he wrote his novels—by sheer assault, without fear and without probing into what other men had tried to do in figuring out the age-old difficulties. And it didn't work." [9] Mencken put it differently: "He had an insatiable appetite for the obviously not true." [10]

No one wrote the ultimate irony—that the earlier Dreiser who had denounced formal religion as "a weak man's shield," who had preached cool reason, had at last built his own private church, knelt alone before his personal shrine and embraced his own Russian White Christ out of blind faith, not knowing the deity for what it was.

Nor could anyone assess Dreiser the liar who demanded truth in the world; the hater who called for love; the money-grubber who denounced capital; the glorifier of the proletariat who held the mass in contempt; the relentless promoter of sexual intrigues, the love cheat who asked for a high moral order and "more spiritual character"; the ego so vast that it exempted only himself from his own standards; the boy who never really reached maturity and yet who exuded at times a charm and sympathy that is warmly remembered to this day. Mencken had hoped to "account for" Dreiser, but the job was beyond him and indeed any accounting would have to be done in the misty suburbs of abnormal psychology.

Serio-comic aspects emerged that might have amused or depressed Dreiser. A gravediggers' strike (he was always sympathetic with strikers) made a funeral impossible for a few days. The New Year's holiday also intervened. On Sunday, Helen telephoned the manager of Nancy's, a shop on Hollywood Boulevard, who opened up so that she could buy a black fur jacket and a dress for the funeral. Later the Dreiser safe deposit box at the bank was opened and found so stuffed with $20 gold pieces (which the government had long since called in) that they had a hard time carrying it to a table to count. [11]

There was sharp disagreement over the form the funeral should take. Who should have jurisdiction over the burial of the man who had once urged that the steeples be torn down and later had written, "I am moved not only to awe but to reverence for the Creator"—the man who had plunged in Wall Street when he had it and joined the Communist Party when he lost? Marguerite Tjader Harris and other friends were in favor of Congregational services to be read by Dr. Hunter, whose church Dreiser had attended a couple of times and who by chance had called on him the last day. Dreiser's communist friends wished to make a party affair of it. The churchly faction preferred to have no truck with the communists. The communists wished to exclude the church.

Helen, who must have reflected that Dreiser could not find peace even in death, compromised. She would have them both, much as each disliked the association, though she ruled out an "official" and political communist participation. Dr. Vera Dreiser Scott arrived from New York—the only relative to come. She went with the sculptor Edgardo Simone to the Forest Lawn embalming room, where Simone made a death mask of Dreiser and a cast of his right hand. Helen wrote, "I . . . picked a beautiful dark rich red hardwood mahogany casket lined with a beautiful delicate shade of velvet." [12]

The services, held January 3 at Forest Lawn's Church of the Recessional, were a pale but symbolic representation of the struggle and dichotomy of Dreiser's life. Fewer than a hundred persons, some of them strangers, were on hand as the two factions, without visible hostility, conducted the divided ceremony. An organist played Handel's "Largo" and Bach's "Come, Kindly Death." Dr. Hunter led off, then left it to John Howard Lawson to deliver the last tribute that Dreiser had performed so kindly for many others. Deeply moved, Lawson spoke with eloquent understanding (and an inevitable shade of partisanship) of Dreiser's literary career and the social drives that ultimately led him to communism. Charlie Chaplin uttered perhaps the most fitting requiem when he read Dreiser's own desperately questioning "The Road I Came," written at least a dozen years earlier and ending:

> Oh, space!
> Change!
> Toward which we run
> So gladly,
> Or from which we retreat
> In terror—
> Yet that promises to bear us
> In itself
> Forever.
>
> Oh, what is this
> That knows the road I came? [13]

The hundred mourners filed past the coffin where Dreiser lay in his black lecture suit and black bow tie that accentuated the downy white hair. Some habit-bound mortuary cosmetician had added a final capitalistic touch by brushing the lips with rouge. Just before the coffin was closed, Helen put her sonnet, "To a Poet," beside the body.

Dreiser was buried very expensively in Lot 1132 of the Whispering Pines section of this necrolatric splendor, hard by the grave of Tom Mix. A week later Helen began sending out letters enclosing a copy of the services, and her poem, to Dreiser's friends including some of the women in his life for years past—Kirah Markham, Dorothy Dudley, Louise Campbell, Sylvia Bradshaw, Estelle Manning, many others. Indeed, in a telegram to Mrs. Campbell she had added, "He loved you." In all this she was not only demonstrating that in death she was at last sole owner in full charge, but was paying sincere tribute to those who she was sure had contributed to his genius.

"It is like a miracle to be loved by such a man," Helen wrote. "My life has really been a wonderful thing." [14]

Appendix

Dreiser left an estate listed only as "in excess of $10,000"—of course much more than that, evidently more than $100,000. Possibly Helen herself was surprised by the amount. While there was some embarrassment and official inquiry about his hoarded gold, it was not confiscated. In his will he left everything to Helen, requesting that she pay percentages of the estate's income to his remaining relatives; and that on her death she bequeath these percentages outright, leaving the balance (about half) to a Negro orphanage of her selection.

Mencken, who seems not to have written Dreiser since July 4, 1944, kindly acknowledged Helen's letter about the funeral, adding, "If I had another life to live I think I'd attempt a long study of him, trying to account for him. But it is now too late." He also sent a statement about Dreiser, evidently intended to be read at the funeral but not used, perhaps because of its objective tone:

> While Dreiser lived all the literary snobs and popinjays of the country, including your present abject servant, devoted themselves to reminding him of his defects. He had, to be sure, a number of them. For one thing, he came into the world with an incurable antipathy to the *mot juste;* for another thing, he had an insatiable appetite for the obviously not true. But the fact remains that he was a great artist, and that no other American of his generation left so wide and handsome a mark upon the national letters. American writing, before and after his time, differed almost as much as biology before and after Darwin. He was a man of large originality, of profound feeling, and of unshakeable courage. All of us who write are better off because he lived, worked and hoped.

Three months after Dreiser's death, Soviet representatives called on Helen, read the will to assure themselves that she was heir, and paid her an additional $7,000 in royalties.

When *The Bulwark* (1946) and *The Stoic* (1947) were published by Doubleday, most critics found them inferior to Dreiser's earlier novels. *The Bulwark* sold well, however, bringing in $15,039.16 in royalties at the first accounting in September, 1946, and enjoying an extra printing of 200,000 copies for the Book Find Club. Dreiser's notes for the unpublished philosophy work, comprising thousands of pages, are at the University of Pennsylvania with the bulk of his papers and have never been entirely assayed. One scholar made a start on it but died in the midst of his work.

Helen's 1946 Christmas card was illustrated with a photograph of Dreiser's grave with its bronze plate bearing a quotation from "The Road I Came." She remained at Kings Road, devoting herself to a book, *My Life With Dreiser*, which she had started at Iroki years earlier when he was intermittently estranged from her. When it was published (World Publishing Company, Cleveland, 1951), it bore the dedication:

> *To the unknown women in the life of Theodore Dreiser, who devoted themselves unselfishly to the beauty of his intellect and its artistic unfoldment.*

In 1951 Paramount made amends for its early picturization of *An American Tragedy* with a new production under a different title, *A Place in the Sun*, Montgomery Clift appearing as Clyde, Shelley Winters as Roberta and Elizabeth Taylor as Sondra. Later the same year the same studio produced *Sister Carrie*, with Jennifer Jones and Laurence Olivier in the lead roles. In 1964 negotiations were begun to make a film of Dreiser's long-shelved *Tobacco* script.

In 1951 Helen suffered a cerebral hemorrhage and thereafter was an invalid in the care of her sister Myrtle (Mrs. C. A. Butcher) in Gresham, Oregon. She died there September 22, 1955, aged sixty-one, leaving an estate of $184,380.86. She was buried beside Dreiser at Forest Lawn.

Dreiser's lifetime dream—a collected edition of his works—never became reality in America. However, the World Publishing Company secured the literary rights and republished his six greatest novels and his best short stories.

In the fifties he became the most widely published of American authors in Russia, his earlier popularity spurred immensely by his joining of the party. In 1951 the state publishing house in Moscow published a 900,000-copy, 12-volume edition of Dreiser and also an anthology of his essays and articles in 150,000 copies. In 1961 his *Jennie Gerhardt* was dramatized at the Bolshoi Theater.

In Russia he is pictured as an artist whose exposures of capitalistic decay were continually suppressed in America, who gradually purged himself of his own bourgeois errors and finally experienced the ultimate communistic revelation. The Russians ignore the pietistic *Bulwark*, which reflects his final philosophy. They pass over his confusions and contradictions. They resent any suggestion that he was senile or mentally fatigued when he joined the party. At least one Soviet critic denounced Robert Elias' fine biography for pointing out that Dreiser's decision to join had a religious rather than a political motivation.

Appendix

Author's Note and Acknowledgments

This book is intended solely as biography, not criticism. There have been many analyses of Dreiser's works, but no attempt to study the whole man. Not even during his busiest writing years was he exclusively a writer, being always a self-taught philosopher with strong views about society. He collided repeatedly with American culture, religion and politics. For a quarter-century he waged a violent battle against the censorship of art, and his works, if not his words, had a large share in the victory. Indeed, Dreiser was a fighter incarnate, always battling something, living a life of constant struggle often far removed from literature. In his later years his compulsion toward social criticism and mystic philosophy so overmastered him that he all but abandoned creative writing. If his prejudices and contradictions were awesome, the mature Dreiser represents in extreme enlargement the confusions of the era after 1929 when intellectuals everywhere sought a better society, and when thinkers more competent than he proved as mistaken as he.

But Dreiser was, in the extreme sense, an original. There has been no one like him. He deserves study simply as one of the most incredible of human beings, a man whose enormous gifts warred endlessly with grievous flaws.

In this book, in a scattering of instances, it has been necessary to use fictitious names for actual persons who might otherwise be embarrassed. These fictitious names are indicated clearly in the notes.

The reader is warned that Dreiser's grammar, spelling and punctuation were often as original as the man himself. Throughout his letters one finds *alright, dispise, gaurdian, goverment, opourtunity, pleasent, thousend, rediculous,* and many other errata. He generally used *your* for *you're,* and often transposed the *ei* or *ie* order. To avoid a tiresome use of [*sic*], I ask the reader to assume that errors in Dreiser's quoted letters are his own, not the result of careless proofreading.

Hundreds of personal letters are quoted herein. For permission to quote the two largest groups I am indebted to Mrs. C. A. Butcher and Harold J. Dies, executors of the Dreiser estate, who also told me their recollections of Dreiser; and to August Mencken and the Mercantile-Safe Deposit & Trust Company of Baltimore, executor of the H. L. Mencken estate. Those who granted permission to quote smaller groups or single letters are listed below.

The help given me has made this book almost a public project, though the responsibility is always mine. My first thanks, coupled with real admiration, go to Mrs. Neda M. Westlake, who as curator of the Rare Book Collection at the University of Pennsylvania Library presides over the library's vast Dreiser collection, one of the largest of its kind. My wife and I spent ten weeks there at the formidable task of reading many original manuscripts and many thousands of letters, papers

531

and clippings. Endlessly helpful, Mrs. Westlake—herself a Dreiser authority—guided us skillfully through what seemed impossible complications. Later, she helped to steer our course through an intricate maze of publication permissions. She and her staff, including Lyman W. Riley, Cecily D. Baker, Barbara Stokes-Rees and Christian Didinger, made our work pleasant as well as enlightening. We came away with lasting gratitude and friendship.

Our debt is especially great to six persons:

Dr. Robert H. Elias of Cornell University, our foremost Dreiserian, knew Dreiser personally and took voluminous notes while preparing his own fine study of Dreiser and later editing the three-volume *Letters of Theodore Dreiser* (Philadelphia, University of Pennsylvania Press, 1959). These notes include transcripts of significant Elias conversations with Dreiser and contemporaries now dead, among them H. L. Mencken, Charles Hanson Towne, Edward M. Dreiser, Flora Mai Holly, Fremont Rider and many others. To the notes are added letters Elias received from Helen Dreiser and others, giving factual information. Dr. Elias not only told me his own Dreiser recollections but gave me the use of his invaluable notes and letters, which appear frequently in my text—a generosity that still astonishes me.

William C. Lengel first met Dreiser at Butterick's in 1910 and remained thereafter a warm friend, adviser, agent and literary ally, privy to his struggles and to many personal matters. He is the closest Dreiser friend over so long a span. He shared his memories with me repeatedly—often far into the night—gave me every aid including the use of his letters, and again confirmed his reputation as the kindliest of men.

Mrs. Charles Seymour Whitman, the former Thelma Cudlipp, was hardly more than a girl when Dreiser sought vainly to make her his wife in 1910. Delightfully helpful, she told me of the romantic, agonized, importunate Dreiser, and of the people and circumstances surrounding him. Mrs. Whitman also permitted me to read and quote from her own manuscript account of these events, as well as to publish Dreiser's letters to her.

Ralph Fabri was long a cherished companion both of Dreiser's and of Helen's. Since Helen often confided in him, he knew intimate details about the stormiest period in Dreiser's life and recorded them in a diary. Generously he gave me his recollections, portions of his diary and personal letters and photographs in his possession, supplying facts no one else could have known.

Dr. Vera Dreiser Scott, Dreiser's niece, knew him and Jug from childhood. She cheerfully sacrificed time from a demanding professional career to give me her own reminiscences as well as the Dreiser family lore passed on to her by her father and mother, and a fine group of family pictures.

Esther McCoy Tobey knew Dreiser and Helen from the late Twenties on. In addition to being a close friend who often aided Dreiser in research and writing, she is an analytical and understanding observer. Her kind testimony was especially valuable in illuminating Dreiser's years in Hollywood.

Helpful beyond measure were Louise Campbell, Dreiser's trusted editor on many writings from 1917 until his death, valued always by him and by Helen, author of the engaging *Letters to Louise;* Sally Kusell, who along with Mrs. Campbell took part in the creation of *An American Tragedy* and told me of that climactic period as well as lending me her Dreiser letters; Kirah Markham, who wrote me brilliantly detailed letters from the West Indies and proved her sense of humor as well as her memory of Dreiserian events dating as far back as 1912; the cordial David A. Randall, librarian, the Lilly Library, Indiana University; Lillian Rosedale Goodman, a Dreiser friend from her girlhood in New York until his last Hollywood years and fated to see him in his final illness; Marguerite Tjader Harris, on whom Dreiser repeatedly depended for aid and who in the end helped him with *The Bulwark;* Dr. Henry Wexler, the kind New Haven psychiatrist whose keen powers of analysis helped to clarify my own thinking about Dreiser but who must not be held responsible for it; and Mrs. Byron B. Smith, a Dreiser friend and researcher in Hollywood who aided me endlessly in personal talks and by mail.

Among those named above (and many listed below) I have been fortunate in finding witnesses who knew Dreiser at different times, in different relationships and under different circumstances from 1906 (when Carl Van Vechten first met him) until his death. In addition, the following contributed information or research aid, in person or by mail, rolling up a great tide of recollection and essential detail for which this modest mention is only a token of gratitude:

Mrs. Sherwood Anderson, Wayne Andrews, Cedric Belfrage, Edmund R. Biddle, Albert Boni, Charles Boswell, Madeleine Boyd, Dr. Sculley Bradley, "Sylvia Bradshaw," Earl Browder, Dr. Edwin H. Cady, Erwin D. Canham, Boris Chaliapin, and Alexander P. Clark, curator of manuscripts, Princeton University Library; Mrs. Kenneth Clark, Louis Cline, Stanwood Cobb, the late Lester Cohen, Malcolm Cowley, Homer Croy, John Dos Passos, Wharton Esherick, James T. Farrell, Rose Feld, Raymond B. Fosdick, Waldo Frank, Dr. Donald C. Gallup of the Yale Library, Maxwell Geismar, Arthur Gelb, Arnold Gingrich, Dr. Eric F. Goldman, and Edgar Gleeson; Dr. George H. Healey, curator of rare books at the Cornell University Library, and his assistants, Michael Jasenas and John F. Guido; Robert W. Hill, Keeper of Manuscripts at the New York Public Library; Arthur Sullivant Hoffman, the late B. W. Huebsch, Fannie Hurst, Sulamith Ish-Kishor, Lois M. Jones of the Los Angeles Public Library, Mrs. Matthew Josephson of the American Academy of Arts and Letters, Alfred A. Knopf, Manuel Komroff, Esther D. Kralick, H. S. Kraft, Dale Kramer, Joshua Kunitz, and John Howard Lawson; Tom Mahoney, Alvin Manuel, Sarah Mitchell, George Nally of the Yale Library, Mrs. George Jean Nathan, Amy Nyholm of the Newberry Library, Mrs. Fremont Older, Henry Varnum Poor, Max Putzel, Mrs. Burton Rascoe, George M. Rascoe, Jacob Raskin, Moses Rischin, Belle Rosenbaum, D. Nelle Runyon, and Herbert C. Schulz, curator of manuscripts at the Huntington Library; Charles Scribner, Jr., Martin F. Shea, Elizabeth M. Sherrard of the Baker Library at Dartmouth College, Dr. Page Smith, Henry Schnakenberg, Upton Sinclair, Constance Smith, Dr. Robert E. Spiller, J. L. Swihart, William Targ, Stillman K. Taylor of the Fairbanks Memorial Library in Terre Haute, Alice Davis Tibbetts, and Sister Trinita Marie, S.P.; Andrew Turnbull, Louis Untermeyer, Carl Van Vechten, Walter Wanger, Mr. and Mrs. Edgar Ward, Ann Watkins, David R. Watkins of the Yale University Library, Dr. Gerald Willen, William E. Wilson, and Mrs. William E. Woodward.

Others who aided by granting permission to publish letters were: Mrs. Sherwood Anderson, William Abramson, the American Civil Liberties Union, Charles Angoff, C. Waller Barrett, James Benét, the Bodley Head, Ltd., Dr. Edmund R. Brill, Earl Browder, Katharine S. Burlingame, Melville H. Cane, Constable & Company, Ltd., Dr. Paul de Kruif, Floyd Dell, Constance Garland Doyle, Max Eastman, Alyse Gregory, Harper & Row, Inc., Jesse Hemley, Houghton Mifflin Company, George G. Kirstein, Manuel Komroff, Dr. Robert F. Loeb, Mrs. Edgar Lee Masters, Stanley M. Moffat, Harold Ober Associates, Mrs. Eugene O'Neill, Walter H. Page, Arthur Pell, Phyllis Playter, Frank C. Preston, Jr., Martin Secker, Simon & Schuster, Inc., and A. P. Watt & Son.

A few others declined permission to publish letters.

The World Publishing Company of Cleveland and New York generously permitted me to quote at will from the works of Theodore Dreiser—and Helen Dreiser's *My Life With Dreiser*—for which they hold copyright.

Eleanor Sullivan's copy-editing of the manuscript was admirably careful and intelligent.

Four persons previously undertook the chore of reading and appraising the manuscript: Patricia Schartle, my scholarly and perceptive agent, whose steady poise found deviations in my own; the understanding Burroughs Mitchell of Scribners, who has worked with me on other books and whose criticisms of this one were characteristically discriminating; and Alfred Kazin, who interrupted his own busy schedule to give me the benefit of his matchless literary discernment.

The fourth was Dorothy Green Swanberg, my companion in research and discussion over many long roads and in many distant libraries—even in dubious restaurants—who saw the project through from idea to finished book and contributed more than can be listed here or anywhere.

Notes

Theodore Dreiser was among the most prolific of letter-writers. Those letters he sent out which are preserved at the University of Pennsylvania alone must number at least 20,000. I consulted them as well as smaller collections at Cornell University, Indiana University, Yale University, the New York Public Library, the Huntington Library, U.C.L.A., the Los Angeles Public Library and elsewhere. These Dreiser letters—and letters written as voluminously to him—often give an almost continuous account of his thoughts, struggles and activities after he was twenty-nine years old. I have relied primarily on them and, as far as possible, have let Dreiser speak for himself. All letters to or from Dreiser cited below are at the University of Pennsylvania in original or copy form unless otherwise noted.

In Dreiser's own autobiographical writings he sometimes altered names and incidents before publication to prevent embarrassment to his family or others. A study of the original manuscripts of his *Dawn* and *Newspaper Days* has often given the presumably correct names and facts before they were "edited" for the printer.

Dreiser's immense collection of newspaper and magazine clippings, now at the University of Pennsylvania, is cited frequently, as are others found on my own. Robert H. Elias' *Theodore Dreiser: Apostle of Nature*, a brilliant interpretation of Dreiser's contradictions and their effect on his career, was constantly enlightening. Dorothy Dudley's *Forgotten Frontiers*, written by a woman who had a keen understanding of Dreiser, furnished valuable insights. *The Stature of Theodore Dreiser*, edited by Alfred Kazin and Charles Shapiro, supplied a vivid selection of critical and personal appraisal. Helen Dreiser's *My Life With Dreiser* was a prime source.

The following abbreviations are used throughout the notes to indicate the various collections consulted:

CU: Cornell University Library, Ithaca, N. Y.

CWB: C. Waller Barrett Collection, New York City.

DC: Dartmouth College Library, Hanover, N. H.

FDR: Franklin D. Roosevelt Library, Hyde Park, N. Y.

Huntington: The Huntington Library, San Marino, Cal.

Indiana: The Lilly Library, Indiana University, Bloomington.

LAPL: Los Angeles Public Library.

Newberry: The Newberry Library, Chicago.

NYPL: New York Public Library.

PC: Princeton Library, the H. L. Mencken correspondence in transcript and on microfilm.

PU: Princeton University Library, Princeton, N. J., the H. L. Mencken Collection.

RHE: Robert H. Elias Notes and Collection, Ithaca, N. Y.
UP: University of Pennsylvania Library, Philadelphia.
Yale: Yale University Library, New Haven, Conn.

BOOK ONE

CHAPTER 1

1. Theodore Dreiser: *Dawn* (New York, Horace Liveright, 1931), p. 7; also, Dreiser's *A Hoosier Holiday* (New York, John Lane, 1916), p. 402.

2. Dreiser: *Dawn*, p. 7.

3. Baptismal record, Church of St. Benedict, Sept. 10, 1871 (copy at CU).

4. Dreiser: *Dawn*, p. 8.

5. Dorothy Dudley: *Forgotten Frontiers: Dreiser and the Land of the Free* (New York, Smith & Haas, 1932), p. 25.

6. Theodore Dreiser biographical folder (UP), family Bible entry.

7. TD mistakenly said his father owned the mill. People in Sullivan told A. R. Markle that the factory did not burn but was wrecked by a storm (Markle to Robert H. Elias, Nov. 22, 1946, CU).

8. Dreiser: *Dawn*, pp. 5–6.

9. The same, p. 19.

10. Dreiser: *A Hoosier Holiday*, p. 397.

11. Dreiser: *Dawn* ms. (Indiana), ch. 2.

12. Dr. Vera Dreiser Scott to Swanberg, May 18, 1964.

13. Dreiser: *Dawn*, p. 27. A. R. Markle (in unpublished article, "Theodore Dreiser—Historian?" at the Fairbanks Memorial Library, Terre Haute) says Theodore at six was punished for lifting girls' petticoats in the schoolyard.

14. Dreiser: *A Hoosier Holiday*, pp. 389–90.

15. Dreiser: *Dawn*, p. 35. See also Robert H. Elias: *Theodore Dreiser: Apostle of Nature* (New York, Knopf, 1949), pp. 3–7; "Art Souvenir of Terre Haute" (*Terre Haute Gazette*, 1894), passim; Max Ehrmann: "Paul Dresser . . ." (pamphlet, Indianapolis, 1924); "The City of Opportunity" (mimeographed booklet, Terre Haute Chamber of Commerce, 1964); William E. Wilson: *The Wabash* (New York, Farrar & Rinehart, 1940); and *Indiana—a Guide to the Hoosier State* (New York, Oxford, 1941).

I have been aided by Dreiser family recollections given me by Dreiser's niece, Dr. Vera Dreiser Scott (tape recordings dated May 4, 5 and 18, 1964). Other information comes from a small collection of news clippings and "Dreiser-Dresser Notes" at the Emeline Fairbanks Memorial Library, Terre Haute. This latter includes some inquiry into TD's boyhood by A. R. Markle, a Terre Haute annalist who lived near the Dreisers, knew Theodore slightly as a boy and candidly disliked him.

Much of my account of TD's boyhood and youth is taken from his own autobiographical writings. Though he was indubitably correct about the household atmosphere, he was notoriously unreliable about details, which cannot always be guaranteed. Markle seems the only investigator of these years. He notes numerous errors in TD's own recollections, among them the statement that he was born at Ninth and Chestnut Streets. After some inquiry Markle decided he was born on South Ninth near Oak Street, a half-mile south of Chestnut, but even this is not certain.

Whatever small interest Terre Haute and Indiana had in TD dwindled after the publication of *A Hoosier Holiday*, which spoke critically of the state, and still more after his later involvement in radical causes. The Terre Haute Chamber of Commerce booklet applauds Paul Dresser but ignores TD. Although Indiana University has a portrait of TD and a fine collection of his manuscripts and letters, the state as a whole seems virtually to have forgotten him.

CHAPTER 2

1. Dreiser: *Dawn*, p. 49.
2. The same, p. 78.
3. Dreiser: *Dawn* ms., ch. 15. Dreiser later used some of these details in describing Roberta's search for an abortionist in *An American Tragedy*.
4. Dreiser: *Dawn*, p. 107.
5. The same, p. 113.
6. Dreiser: *Dawn* ms., chs. 26, 27.
7. Dreiser: *Dawn*, p. 144. See also *Evansville Press*, Jan. 21, 1934 (UP).
8. Dreiser: *Dawn*, p. 135.
9. The same, p. 167.
10. The same, p. 182; also, Dr. Vera Dreiser Scott to Swanberg, May 4 and 5, 1964.

CHAPTER 3

1. Dreiser: *Dawn*, p. 193; also, David Karsner: *Sixteen Authors to One* New York, Lewis Copeland, 1928), p. 6.
2. Dreiser: *A Hoosier Holiday*, p. 318.
3. Dreiser: *Dawn*, pp. 193, 208, 209, 213; also, Dudley: *Forgotten Frontiers*, p. 50.
4. *Dawn*, p. 203.
5. *Dawn*, p. 195.
6. The same, p. 222.
7. The same, p. 228.
8. The same, p. 229.
9. George Steinbrecher, Jr.: "Inaccurate Accounts of Sister Carrie," *American Literature*, XXIII, Jan., 1952, pp. 490–93.
10. *Dawn*, p. 268; also, *Dawn* ms., ch. 48.
11. *Dawn*, p. 248.
12. The same, pp. 275–76.
13. The same, p. 294.

CHAPTER 4

1. Dreiser: *Dawn*, p. 305.
2. The same, p. 314; also, Dudley: *Forgotten Frontiers*, p. 60.

3. *Dawn*, p. 320; also, Elias: *Theodore Dreiser* . . . , p. 24.

4. *Dawn*, p. 329.

5. The same, pp. 343–44; also, *Dawn* ms., ch. 60.

6. *Dawn*, p. 349; also, Christian Aaberg to TD, Oct. 19, 1921.

7. *Dawn*, p. 354.

8. F. O. Matthiessen: *Theodore Dreiser* (New York, William Sloane, 1951), p. 17.

9. Dreiser: *A Hoosier Holiday*, p. 483; also, TD to George Bye, Oct. 29, 1939.

CHAPTER 5

1. *Dawn*, pp. 381, 386; also, *A Hoosier Holiday*, pp. 492, 498.

2. *Dawn*, p. 419; also, Elias, *Theodore Dreiser* . . . , p. 27.

3. *Dawn*, p. 398.

4. The same, p. 426.

5. The same, pp. 429–31. Dreiser's *Dawn* ms. (ch. 74) differs, saying he was so terrified that he kept his distance.

6. *Dawn*, p. 465; also, *A Hoosier Holiday*, p. 495. See also James Albert Woodburn: *History of Indiana University, 1820–1902* (Bloomington, Indiana University, 1940), p. 360 ff.

7. *A Hoosier Holiday*, p. 488.

8. Elias: *Theodore Dreiser* . . . , p. 28.

9. *Dawn*, p. 509.

10. The same, pp. 512–13.

11. The same, pp. 519–20. In this later account, Dreiser may have exaggerated the priest's anger.

12. *Dawn*, p. 525; also, Elias: *Theodore Dreiser* . . . , pp. 31–32.

13. Dreiser: *Newspaper Days* (New York, Liveright, 1922), p. 31; also, R. V. Carpenter to TD, Dec. 27, 1928.

14. *Dawn*, p. 546; also, Elias, *op. cit.*, p. 34.

15. Dudley: *Forgotten Frontiers*, pp. 66–67.

16. Frank Harris: *Contemporary Portraits*, Second Series (New York, 1919), p. 86; also, *Dawn*, p. 581.

17. *Dawn*, p. 583; also, Dreiser: "Tempted, I Stole," *Cosmopolitan*, June, 1931.

CHAPTER 6

1. Dreiser: *Newspaper Days* (hereafter called *Days*), p. 3; also, R. L. Duffus: "Dreiser," *American Mercury*, Jan., 1926.

2. Dreiser: *Days*, p. 11.

3. The same, p. 33.

4. The same, pp. 38–39; also, David Karsner: *Sixteen Authors to One*, p. 10.

5. The Maxwell quotations are from Dreiser: *Days*, pp. 50, 52, 59; also, Harris: *Contemporary Portraits*, p. 88.

6. Dreiser: *Days*, p. 67.

7. The same, p. 75.

8. The same, p. 80.

9. The same, p. 85.

10. Dreiser: *Newspaper Days* ms. (UP—hereafter called *Days* ms.), ch. 13–A, p. 8.

11. *Chicago Globe*, Oct. 23, 1892 (UP).

12. Dreiser: *Days*, p. 82.

13. Dreiser: *Days* ms., ch. 4–A, p. 1.

14. Dreiser: *Days*, p. 98.

15. Max Putzel: *The Man in the Mirror: William Marion Reedy . . .* (Cambridge, Harvard, 1963), pp. 26–27; also, Orrick Johns: *Time of Our Lives* (New York, Stackpole, 1937), p. 111.

16. Dreiser: *Days*, pp. 90, 97.

17. "Peter," in Dreiser: *Twelve Men* (New York, Fawcett Premier Books, 1962), p. 16.

18. Dreiser: *Days*, p. 127. Note also Dreiser: *The "Genius"* (New York, Boni & Liveright, 1923), p. 104; Cyrille Arnavon, "Dreiser and Painting," *American Literature, XVII*, May, 1945.

19. Dreiser: *Days*, pp. 128–29.

20. The same, p. 151.

21. *St. Louis Globe-Democrat*, Jan. 20, 1893 (UP).

22. Dreiser: *Days*, pp. 160–61, 167–68; *Globe-Democrat*, Jan. 22, 1893; also, Jim Allee Hart: *A History of the St. Louis Globe-Democrat* (University of Missouri Press, Columbia, 1961), pp. 141–42.

23. Dreiser: *Days* ms., ch. 12, pp. 9–13; ch. 13, p. 2.

24. Clarence E. Miller: "William Marion Reedy," *Bulletin of the Missouri Historical Society*, Oct., 1960.

25. Elias, *op. cit.*, p. 55.

26. *St. Louis Globe-Democrat*, April 1, 1893 (UP).

27. Dreiser: *Days*, p. 203; also, Karsner: *Sixteen Authors to One*, p. 11.

28. *Days*, p. 204; also, *Editor & Publisher*, Dec. 28, 1907.

CHAPTER 7

1. Dreiser: *Days*, pp. 208, 211.

2. The same, p. 241.

3. Dreiser: *Days* ms., ch. 26, p. 13.

4. Dreiser: *Days*, p. 251.

5. The same, p. 261.

6. Dreiser: *Days* ms., ch. 37, p. 3.

7. Dreiser: *Days*, p. 311.

8. William C. Lengel: "The Genius Himself," *Esquire*, Sept., 1938.

9. Dreiser: *Days*, pp. 342–43.

10. Dudley: *Forgotten Frontiers*, pp. 98–99.

11. Dreiser: *Days*, p. 359.

12. C. W. Knapp, March 2, 1894.

13. Dreiser: *Days*, p. 361.

CHAPTER 8

1. Dreiser: *A Hoosier Holiday*, p. 248.

2. Dreiser: *Days*, pp. 366–67; also, Dudley, *op. cit.*, p. 101.

3. Dreiser: *A Hoosier Holiday*, p. 254.

4. Dreiser: *Days*, p. 373; also, *The New York Times*, June 5, 1934.

5. Dreiser: *Days*, p. 395.

6. The same, p. 408.

7. The same, p. 406.

8. The same, p. 397.

9. Honoré de Balzac: *The Wild Ass's Skin* (Boston, Little Brown, 1900), pp. 98, 101, 106; also, Elias, *op. cit.*, pp. 73–74.

10. Dreiser: *Days* ms., ch. 60, pp. 9–11.

11. The same, ch. 61, p. 1.

12. The same, ch. 63, pp. 5–6.

13. Dreiser: *Days*, pp. 427–28; also, Dreiser: *Twelve Men*, p. 165.

14. Dreiser: *Days*, pp. 434–35.

15. The same, p. 435.

16. Dreiser: *Days* ms., ch. 67, p. 6; ch. 68, pp. 1–4.

17. The same, ch. 69, pp. 1–4, 7.

18. Dudley, *op. cit.*, p. 112.

19. Harris: *Contemporary Portraits*, p. 91.

20. Dreiser: *Days*, p. 459; also, Elias, *op. cit.*, pp. 81–83.

BOOK TWO

CHAPTER 1

1. Dreiser: *Days*, p. 464.

2. The same, p. 466.

3. Harris, *op. cit.*, p. 90.

4. The same.

5. Dreiser: *Days*, p. 496.

6. Dreiser: *Days* ms., ch. 75, pp. 9–13.

7. Dreiser: *Days*, p. 501. See also Joseph J. Kwiat, "The Newspaper Experience," *19th Century Fiction*, Sept., 1953. Dreiser apparently was with the *World* only about two months.

8. Dreiser told Elias, June 3, 1944 (RHE).

9. Carmel O'Neill Haley: "The Dreisers," *Commonweal*, July 7, 1933; also, Dudley, *op. cit.*, p. 139.

10. John F. Huth, Jr.: "Theodore Dreiser: The Prophet," *American Literature*, IX, May, 1937, pp. 209–10.

11. *Ev'ry Month*, Feb., 1897.

12. *Indianapolis Sunday Star*, March 31, 1940 (Indiana).

13. Dreiser: *Twelve Men*, p. 92.

14. *New York Morning Telegraph*, Dec. 28, 1919 (UP).

15. Dreiser: *Twelve Men*, p. 81.

16. The same, p. 90.

17. *Ev'ry Month*, Sept., 1896.

18. *Ev'ry Month*, Jan., 1897.

19. The same, Oct., 1896.

20. The same, Jan., 1897.

21. Mary Frances Brennan to A. R. Markle, Jan. 13, 1941 (CU).

22. Ed Dreiser recollection (Vera Dreiser Scott to Swanberg, May 18, 1964).

23. Arthur Henry: *Lodgings in Town* (New York, A. S. Barnes, 1905), p. 83.

24. Dreiser: *Twelve Men*, p. 93.

25. *New York Call*, Dec. 5, 1920: "The Romance of Two Hoosier Brothers" (UP).

CHAPTER 2

1. Charles Rolo (ed.): *Psychiatry in American Life* (Boston, Little Brown, 1963), p. 70.

2. Marden to TD, Jan. 21 and March 24, 1898.

3. Sedgwick to TD, Oct. 29, 1900.

4. *Cosmopolitan* to TD, April 29, 1898.

5. Duffy to TD, Oct. 2, 1898.

6. *Munsey's* to TD, Oct. 12, 1899.

7. Marden to TD, Sept. 26, 1898.

8. *Ev'ry Month*, Sept., 1896, and Feb., 1897.

9. Mary Annabel Fanton to TD, undated, before 1899.

10. Dreiser: *Twelve Men*, p. 95.

11. Dreiser told Elias, Sept. 10, 1945 (RHE).

12. Claire Dreiser to TD, Jan. 24, 1898.

13. Dr. Vera Dreiser Scott told Swanberg, March 9, 1963.

14. See *Ainslee's*, Aug., 1898; *Demorest's*, July, 1898; *Metropolitan*, April, 1898; *Cosmopolitan*, April, 1898.

15. *Ainslee's* to TD, Aug. 29, 1899, Oct. 17, 1899, and Nov. 7, 1898.

16. H. J. Miller to *Cosmopolitan*, Aug. 3, 1898.

17. These articles are in *Success*, Oct., 1898, and Dec. 8, 1898; and *Ainslee's*, March, 1899; and Feb., 1899.

18. Dudley, *op. cit.*, p. 161. Dreiser: *The "Genius,"* p. 170.

19. Dreiser: *Days*, p. 502.

20. Dreiser: *The "Genius,"* p. 245.

21. Maude Wood Henry to Elias, March 23, 1945 (RHE).

22. TD to H. L. Mencken, May 13, 1916.

23. Mrs. Henry to Elias, June 5, 1945 (RHE).

24. Dudley, *op. cit.*, p. 152.

25. TD to H. L. Mencken, May 13, 1916; also, Dudley, *op. cit.*, p. 160.

26. TD to H. L. Mencken, May 13, 1916.

27. Richard Duffy: "When They Were 21," *Bookman*, Jan., 1914, p. 524.

28. Frank Harris, *op. cit.*, p. 91.

29. TD to Johnson, Jan. 9, 1900.

30. TD to Johnson, Feb. 8, 1900 (NYPL).

31. Woodward to TD, April 30, 1901.

32. Carmel O'Neill Haley: "The Dreisers," *Commonweal*, July 7, 1933.

33. *New York Herald*, July 7, 1907.
34. Dreiser: *Sister Carrie* (New York, Modern Library, 1917), p. 557.
35. Harper's to TD, May 2, 1900.
36. TD to H. L. Mencken, May 13, 1916.
37. Norris to TD, May 28, 1900.
38. Dreiser: *A Gallery of Women* (New York, Liveright, 1929), "Rella," p. 482.
39. The same, pp. 494, 500.
40. Henry to TD, July 9, 1900.
41. TD to Henry, July [23], 1900.
42. Thomas H. McKee to Elias, April 3, 1949 (RHE).
43. Quoted in Henry to TD, July 19, 1900.
44. The same.
45. Page to TD, July 19, 1900.
46. Henry to TD, July 26, 1900.
47. TD to Page, July 23, 1900.
48. Page to TD, Aug. 2, 1900.
49. TD to Page, Aug. 6, 1900.
50. TD to Henry, July 23, 1900.
51. Norris to Henry, July 18, 1900.
52. Thomas H. McKee to Elias, March 23, 1949 (RHE).
53. TD to Kathryn Sayre, Oct. 23, 1929.
54. TD to Page, July 23, 1900.
55. TD to Henry, July 23, 1900.
56. Dudley, *op. cit.*, p. 185.
57. Stephen Stepanchev: "Dreiser Among the Critics" (pamphlet, abridgment by Stepanchev of his Ph.D. dissertation, New York University, 1950), pp. 1, 5.
58. Two reviews quoted in Alfred Kazin and Charles Shapiro (eds.): *The Stature of Theodore Dreiser* (Bloomington, Indiana University, 1955), pp. 55, 62–64.
59. Jan. 20, 1901 (UP).
60. Dudley, *op. cit.*, p. 197.
61. McKee to Elias, March 23, 1949 (RHE).
62. Doubleday statements to TD, Feb. 1 and Aug. 1, 1901, and Feb. 1, 1902. *McTeague* had sold about 4,000 copies.
63. Dreiser: "The Early Adventures of *Sister Carrie*," Colophon, part 5, 1931.
64. TD to Fremont Older, Nov. 27, 1923.
65. Rutger Jewett to TD, Dec. 30, 1901.

CHAPTER 3

1. Duffy to TD, Dec. 30, 1900.
2. Amelia Barr to H. L. Mencken, Nov. 27, 1916 (UP).
3. Phillips to TD, Nov. 3, 1900.
4. Woodward to TD, June 28, 1901.

5. Edward D. McDonald: "Dreiser Before *Sister Carrie*," *Bookman*, June, 1928.

6. Arthur Henry: *An Island Cabin* (New York, Barnes, 1904), describes the outing, with quotations from pp. 193, 161, 192, 186, 194, 192, 193.

7. *Jennie Gerhardt* was then titled *The Transgressor. The Rake* may have developed into the later "*Genius*."

8. Dreiser: *An Amateur Laborer* (unpublished, uncompleted ms., UP), Preface.

9. Heinemann to Doubleday, Sept. 10, 1901 (UP).

10. Jewett to TD, Sept. 30, 1901.

11. The English edition sold 1,161 copies to Jan. 1, 1902, bringing TD $111.46 in royalties (Doubleday to TD, April 8, 1902).

12. Reedy to TD, Oct. 15, 1901.

13. Dreiser: *Days* ms., ch. 37, unpaged.

14. Quoted in Jewett to TD, March 17, 1902.

15. TD to Mrs. Roberts, Nov. 14, 1901.

16. Duffy to TD, Dec. 6, 1901.

17. Bowler to TD, Jan. 20, 1902.

18. MacDonald to TD, Dec. 14, 1901.

19. TD to Duffy, Dec. 23, 1901.

20. Dreiser: *A Gallery of Women*, "Rella," p. 503.

21. Quoted in Jewett to TD, March 17, 1902.

22. Duffy to TD, Feb. 10, 1902.

23. New York Zoological Society to TD, Feb. 8, 1902.

24. Jewett to TD, March 17, 1902.

25. Jug to TD, March 26, 1902.

26. Henry to TD, June 11, 1902.

27. Jewett to TD, May 2 and May 20, 1902.

28. Jewett to TD, June 12 and June 27, 1902.

29. Alden to TD, Aug. 1, 1902.

30. Jewett to TD, Aug. 20, 1902.

31. *Booklover's Magazine*, Feb., 1903 (CU).

32. Jewett to TD, Nov. 5, 1902.

33. Both quotations from Dreiser: *An Amateur Laborer* ms., chs. 2, 1.

34. Jewett to TD, Dec. 19, 1902.

35. Dreiser: *An Amateur Laborer*, I. This ms., hereafter called *Laborer*, is the source of much of my account of Dreiser's ordeal.

36. TD to Hitchcock, Feb. 27, 1903.

37. *Laborer*, III.

38. The same, IV.

39. The same.

40. The same.

41. The same, V.

42. Dreiser told Elias, Sept. 30, 1945 (RHE). But in TD to H. L. Mencken, March 27, 1943, Dreiser gave a somewhat different account of the incident.

43. But in TD to William C. Lengel, March 6, 1924, Dreiser said the pawnbroker gave him $10 on an I.O.U.

44. *Laborer*, X. In *Twelve Men*, pp. 95–97, Dreiser's account of the incident varies.

45. Muldoon's bill, May 30, 1903. But Dreiser in *Laborer*, XVI, says it was $50 a week, and in *Twelve Men*, p. 144, $100.

46. Brennan to Paul Dresser, April 25, 1903 (UP).

47. *Laborer*, XVII.

48. The same, XX.

49. R. R. Mills to F. A. Strang, June 13, 1903 (UP).

50. Paul's letters dated June 22 and 26, and Oct. 18, 1903.

51. Paul to TD, Sept. 2 and Oct. (?), 1903.

52. *Laborer*, XXV and Notes.

53. *Laborer*, Preface.

CHAPTER 4

1. Henry to TD, Feb. 17, 1904.

2. De Camp to TD, July 9, 1914.

3. Quentin Reynolds: *The Fiction Factory* (New York, Random House, 1955), p. 147.

4. Paul to TD, undated.

5. Frank Harris: *Contemporary Portraits*, pp. 91–92.

6. William C. Lengel told Swanberg, March 2, 1962.

7. Helen Dreiser to Elias, June 20, 1948 (RHE).

8. TD to Johnson, March 22, 1905.

9. *Smith's Magazine*, June, 1905.

10. *Smith's*, Oct., 1905.

11. Duffy letters dated May 5 and Oct. 5, 1905.

12. Dudley, *op. cit.*, p. 206.

13. May 6, 1905.

14. Dreiser: *Twelve Men*, p. 99; also, *The New York Times* and *New York Herald*, Jan. 31, 1906.

15. Dudley, *op. cit.*, p. 209.

16. *Broadway Magazine*, June, 1906.

17. Duffy to TD, April 11, 1906.

18. Lyon sketch in promotional brochure, "Theodore Dreiser, America's Foremost Novelist," John Lane Company, 1916 (CU).

19. *Broadway Magazine*, Aug., 1906.

20. McKee memos dated Feb. 4 and March 29, 1907.

21. McKee to Elias, March 23, 1949 (RHE).

22. The same.

23. McKee to Elias, March 1, 1950 (RHE).

24. Contract dated June 6, 1907; also, Miss Holly to TD, Jan. 26 and March 5, 1907.

25. Mrs. Doscher to Neda Westlake, Aug. 12, 1954.

26. Undated proof of advertisement (UP).

27. In order: *Paris Modes*, Sept., 1907; *Ohio Journal*, quoted in Dudley, *op. cit.*, p. 216; *New York World*, June 1, 1907; *San Francisco Call*, July 7;

New York Sun, June 1; *The New York Times,* June 15; *New York Sun,* June 18, 1907.

28. Bowler to TD, Nov. 1, 1907.

29. June 6, 1907.

CHAPTER 5

1. Sept., 1907 *Delineator,* p. 284.

2. TD to Mencken, Aug. 23, 1907. See also Charles Hanson Towne: *Adventures in Editing* (New York, Appleton, 1926), p. 122.

3. Miss Holly to TD, July 16, 1907.

4. Miss Prescott to TD, July 19, 1907.

5. Oct., 1907 *Delineator,* pp. 491–2.

6. Oct., 1907 *Delineator.*

7. In the Oct., 1907, and July, Oct. and Nov., 1908, issues respectively.

8. Oct., 1907 *Delineator,* p. 601.

9. Towne: *Adventures in Editing,* pp. 135, 123.

10. Miss Splint told Elias, Feb. 13, 1945 (RHE).

11. Towne: *Adventures in Editing,* p. 159.

12. Two Dodge statements, each dated Sept. 1, 1907.

13. TD to Fort, May 20, 1908.

14. Towne told Elias, Feb. 13, 1945; also, Sarah Splint and Fremont Rider conversations with Elias, Feb. 13, 1945, and Nov. 25, 1944, respectively (all RHE).

15. TD to Mencken, July 16, 1908.

16. Nov., 1908 *Delineator,* p. 812.

17. Nov., 1908 *Delineator,* p. 801.

18. Isaac Goldberg: *The Man Mencken* (New York, Simon & Schuster, 1925), p. 379.

19. Mencken told Elias, Nov. 2, 1944 (RHE).

20. Hoffman to Elias, Jan. 19, 1945 (CU).

21. TD to Ross, Aug. 16, 1909.

22. Richards to TD, Dec. 6, 1908, and to Jug, Jan. 7, 1909.

23. *Washington Evening Star,* Oct. 10, 1908 (UP).

24. Hoffman to Elias, Jan. 19, 1945 (CU).

25. Dreiser's salary remains in doubt. He told Dorothy Dudley (*Forgotten Frontiers,* p. 225) it reached $14,000. He told Mencken (Mencken's *Minority Report,* Knopf, 1956, p. 35) it was $10,000. He later told his attorney (TD to Dudley Field Malone, after April 12, 1926) it stayed at $5,000.

26. Homer Croy: *Country Cured* (New York, Harper, 1932), pp. 144–45; also, Croy told Swanberg, Oct. 30, 1962.

27. TD to Mencken, July 11, 1909.

28. Aug. 8, 1909.

29. The same.

30. TD to Mencken, Nov. 2, 1909.

31. Miss Watkins told Swanberg, Nov. 12, 1962.

32. Croy told Swanberg, Oct. 30, 1962.

33. July, 1910 *Delineator,* p. 4.

34. Thelma Cudlipp (Mrs. Charles Seymour Whitman) told Swanberg, Nov. 11, 1962.
35. Dreiser: *The "Genius,"* p. 522.
36. Mrs. Whitman told Swanberg, Nov. 11, 1962.
37. Lengel: "The Genius Himself," *Esquire*, Sept., 1938; also, Lengel told Swanberg, March 2, 1962.
38. Lengel told Swanberg, June 12, 1963.
39. Miss Watkins told Swanberg, Nov. 12, 1962.
40. Mrs. Whitman told Swanberg, Nov. 11, 1962.
41. Thelma's (Mrs. Whitman's) ms., pp. 57–58.
42. Undated photostat at UP.
43. Lengel: "The Genius Himself," *Esquire*, Sept., 1938.
44. Mrs. Whitman told Swanberg, Nov. 11, 1962.
45. Miss Watkins told Swanberg, Nov. 12, 1962.
46. Croy told Swanberg, Oct. 30, 1962.
47. Lengel told Swanberg, March 2 and Oct. 29, 1962.
48. Miss Holly to TD, Oct. 5, 1910.
49. TD to Thelma Cudlipp, Oct. 3, 1910.
50. TD to Thelma, Nov. 7, 1910.
51. McKee to Elias, March 23, 1949 (RHE).
52. The same.
53. McKee to Elias, March 1, 1950 (RHE).
54. TD to Thelma, Oct. 7, 1910.
55. William Rickey to TD, Oct. 15, 1910.
56. TD to Thelma, Nov. 7, 1910.

BOOK THREE

CHAPTER 1

1. TD to Fremont Rider, Jan. 24, 1911.
2. TD to Mencken, Oct. 11, 1910.
3. Mark Schorer: *Sinclair Lewis* (New York, McGraw-Hill, 1961), p. 179.
4. Fremont Rider told Elias, Oct. 25, 1944 (RHE).
5. Jug's criticism was removed from the files by TD. It is mentioned in Katherine V. Oehler to TD, March 21, 1911; also, B. W. Dodge to TD, March 23, 1911.
6. Lillian Rosenthal to TD, Jan. 25, 1911.
7. Lillian Rosenthal Goodman told Swanberg, March 5, 1963.
8. TD to Fremont Rider, Jan. 24, 1911.
9. Noted in Ripley Hitchcock to TD, May 2, 1911.
10. Noted in letters of those named. "Barbara Langford" and "Louise-Ann Miller" are fictitious names.
11. Jug's London notes, dated March 24, 1911.
12. Robert Amick to TD, March 23, 1911.
13. Alice Phillips to TD, undated, 1911.

14. Huneker to TD, June 4, 1911. Also see Josephine Huneker (ed.): *Letters of James Gibbons Huneker* (New York, Scribners, 1922), p. 210.

15. Mencken to TD, April 23, 1911.

16. Marsh to Miss Holly (UP), March 9, 1911.

17. Miss Holly told Elias, Feb. 15, 1945 (RHE).

18. TD to Mencken, April 28, 1911.

19. TD to Mencken, Aug. 8, 1911.

20. TD to Lengel, Oct. 15, 1911.

21. *Lexington Herald,* March 24, 1912; *Chicago Examiner,* Jan. 4, 1912 (both UP).

22. *Chicago Evening Post,* Nov. 3, 1911 (UP).

23. *Bookman,* Dec. 10, 1911.

24. *New York Herald,* Oct. 28, 1911 (UP).

25. Adams to TD, Oct. 29, 1911.

26. *Smart Set,* Nov., 1911.

27. *The New York Times,* Oct. 22, 1911.

28. Reginald Pound: *Arnold Bennett* (New York, Harcourt Brace, 1953), p. 204; also, Bennett: *Journal of Arnold Bennett* (New York, Viking, 1932), II, pp. 22–39.

29. F. T. Leigh to TD, Nov. 8, 1911.

30. Jewett to TD, Oct. 24, 1911.

31. Jewett to TD, Nov. 13, 1911.

32. Anna Tatum to TD, Nov. 7, 1911.

33. TD to Mencken, Aug. 5, 1911.

34. TD to Grant Richards, May 27, 1910 (Yale).

35. TD to Richards, printed in Grant Richards: *Author Hunting by an Old Literary Sportsman* (New York, Coward-McCann, 1934), pp. 175–76.

36. The same, p. 176.

37. The same, p. 178.

38. Frank Scott to TD, Nov. 17 and Nov. 18, 1911.

39. Quoted in F. A. Duneka to TD, Nov. 14, 1911.

40. The same.

41. To Mencken, Nov. 11, 1911.

42. Miss Holly to TD, Nov. 14, 1911.

43. Miss Watkins to Thelma, Nov. 22, 1911.

44. To Mencken, Nov. 22, 1911.

45. Thelma's (Mrs. Whitman's) ms., p. 82.

CHAPTER 2

1. Richards: *Author Hunting,* p. 205.

2. *Philadelphia Press,* Sept. 9, 1917 (UP).

3. Quoted in *Author Hunting,* p. 191.

4. Undated—received Baltimore, Jan. 2, 1912.

5. Richards: *Author Hunting,* pp. 194–96; also, Dreiser: *A Traveler at Forty* (New York, Century, 1913), ch. 21.

6. Duneka to TD, Jan. 4, 1912.

7. TD to Richards, Jan. 16, 1912 (DC).

8. Richards: *Author Hunting*, p. 198.
9. Jug to TD, Jan. 16, 1912.
10. Anna Tatum to TD, Jan. 20, 1912.
11. Richards to TD, Feb. 16, 1912.
12. TD to Richards, Feb. 10, 1912 (DC).
13. To Richards, Feb. 16, 1912 (DC).
14. The same.
15. To Richards, Feb. 20, 1912 (DC).
16. To Mencken, March 3, 1912.
17. To Richards, Feb. 25, 1912 (DC).
18. Richards to TD, March 14, 1912.
19. Daphne Walters (a fictitious name) to TD, March 10, 1912.
20. Jug to TD, March 14, 1912.
21. To Duneka, March 2, 1912.
22. TD to Dell, March 12, 1912 (Newberry).
23. Dreiser: *A Traveler at Forty*, p. 480.
24. TD to Richards, March 27, 1912 (DC).
25. TD to Richards, March 17, 1912 (DC).
26. To Richards, March 23, 1912 (DC).
27. To Richards, March 27, 1912 (DC).
28. Richards: *Author Hunting*, pp. 184–85.

CHAPTER 3
1. TD to Richards, May 4, 1912 (DC).
2. Undated, May, 1912.
3. Miss Miller to TD, May 1, 1912.
4. Daphne Walters to TD, undated, 1912.
5. To Richards, May 4, 1912 (DC).
6. To Richards, May 26, 1912 (DC).
7. Richards to TD, June 7, 1912.
8. TD to Richards, July 7, 1912 (DC).
9. To Mencken, June 7, 1912.
10. *The New York Times*, June 23, 1912.
11. Dreiser: *The Financier* (New York, Dell, 1961), p. 23.
12. Richards to TD, Aug. 8, 1912.
13. Harper statement, Dec. 31, 1912.
14. Mencken to TD, Oct. 6, 1912.
15. Dec. 10, 1912 (PC).
16. Nov. 12, 1913 (PC).
17. Mencken to TD, Aug. 1, 1913.
18. *Life* magazine, Feb. 13, 1913. See also Stepanchev, "Dreiser Among the Critics," p. 2.
19. Van Vechten to Swanberg, May 4, 1963.
20. William C. Lengel told Swanberg, March 2, 1962.
21. Richards to TD, Dec. 17, 1912.
22. Richards: *Author Hunting*, p. 205.
23. Dudley: *Forgotten Frontiers*, p. 284.

CHAPTER 4

1. Dell told Swanberg, May 19, 1963.

2. Masters: *Across Spoon River* (New York, Farrar & Rinehart, 1936), p. 330.

3. Lengel told Swanberg, March 2, 1962.

4. Harry Hansen: *Midwest Portraits* (New York, Harcourt Brace, 1923), pp. 97, 107, 209; also, Anderson: *Sherwood Anderson's Memoirs* (New York, Harcourt Brace, 1942), Book 3, pp. 5–6; Floyd Dell: *Homecoming* (New York, Farrar & Rinehart, 1933), pp. 218, 224; John Cowper Powys: *Autobiography* (London, John Lane, 1934), p. 648; Maurice Browne: *Too Late to Lament* (Bloomington, Indiana University, 1956), p. 134; Lengel told Swanberg, March 2, 1962; Dell told Swanberg, May 19, 1963.

5. Margaret Anderson: *My Thirty Years' War* (New York, Covici-Friede, 1930), p. 39.

6. Garland to TD, Jan. 16, 1913.

7. Dreiser in *American Spectator*, Dec., 1932.

8. Hamlin Garland: *Companions on the Trail* (New York, Macmillan, 1931), pp. 532–33.

9. Lengel told Swanberg, March 2, 1962.

10. To F. T. Leigh, Feb. 19, 1913.

11. Doty to TD, Nov. 13, 1912.

12. Hitchcock to TD, March 6, 1913.

13. Lengel told Swanberg, Oct. 29, 1962.

14. Dell to TD, undated, 1913.

15. Lengel to TD, March 31, 1913.

16. Long to TD, April 9, 1913.

17. Dodge to TD, March 20, 1913.

18. TD to Mencken, March 23, 1913.

19. Mencken to TD, July 18, 1913. The play appeared in *Smart Set*, Oct., 1913.

20. Doty to TD, Nov. 7, 1913.

21. TD to Mencken, Nov. 18, 1913.

22. Richards: *Author Hunting*, p. 186.

23. Mencken to TD, Nov. 16 (?), 1913.

24. TD to Wright, Dec. 10, 1913 (Yale).

25. Dell told Swanberg, May 19, 1963.

26. Miss Watkins told Swanberg, Nov. 12, 1963.

27. Undated, 1914.

28. To Judge Nott, Jan. 29, 1914.

29. To Mencken, Nov. 18, 1913.

30. Doty to TD, Dec. 6, 1913 and Jan. 9, 1914; also, Century statement, Aug. 3, 1915.

31. To Mencken, Jan. 8, 1914.

32. Mencken to TD, Jan. 11, 1914.

33. Alton to TD, Jan. 11, 1914.

34. Masters: *Across Spoon River*, pp. 330, 331; also, Masters: "Dreiser at Spoon River," *Esquire*, May, 1939.

35. *Chicago Journal,* March 18, 1914 (UP).

36. The same.

37. Kirah Markham to Swanberg, Aug. 23, 1964.

38. Miss Tatum to TD, March 18, 1914.

39. Knopf to TD, March 10 and 18, 1914; also, Douglas Doty to Miss Tatum, March 18, 1914; Knopf to Swanberg, Oct. 22, 1963.

40. Miss Tatum to TD, March 16, 1914.

41. Mencken to TD, March 18, 1914.

42. Jones to TD, undated, 1914.

43. Miss Tatum to TD, March 18, 1914.

44. To TD, March 23, 1914.

45. TD to Mencken, March 25 and Aug. 10, 1914.

46. Mencken to TD, Aug. 11, 1914. Mencken later gave the script to the New York Public Library.

47. To Mencken, March 25, 1914. See Edmund Wilson: *The Shock of Recognition* (New York, Farrar, Straus & Cudahy, 1955), p. 1158, for Mencken's understanding of Dreiser.

48. Lengel told Swanberg, Sept. 29, 1962.

49. TD to Dudley Field Malone, after April 12, 1926.

50. To Mencken, April 5, 1914.

51. To Mencken, June 22, 1914.

52. Kirah Markham to Swanberg, Dec. 12, 1963.

53. Miss Markham to Swanberg, April 15, 1964.

54. *New York Evening World,* June 18, 1914 (UP).

55. *The New York Times Book Review,* June 23, 1912, p. 378 (UP).

56. *Chicago Examiner,* Jan. 13, 1913 (UP).

57. *Life* magazine, June 18, 1914.

58. Richards to TD, Oct. 21, 1914.

59. TD to Mencken, Aug. 10, 1914.

60. To Mencken, Aug. 29, 1914.

61. To Mencken, July 29, 1914.

CHAPTER 5

1. Hutchins Hapgood: *A Victorian in the Modern World* (New York, Harcourt Brace, 1939), pp. 359–60.

2. Miss Markham to Swanberg, Feb. 8, 1964.

3. Miss Markham to Swanberg, Jan. 19, 1964.

4. Miss Markham to Swanberg, Feb. 29, 1964.

5. Orrick Johns: *Time of Our Lives,* p. 217.

6. Untermeyer told Swanberg, Dec. 11, 1962.

7. Miss Markham to Swanberg, Feb. 29, 1964.

8. Frank told Swanberg, Jan. 22, 1964.

9. To Mencken, Aug. 3 and Nov. 10, 1914.

10. To TD, Dec. 15, Dec. 2, Nov. 12 and Dec. 23, 1914.

11. To TD, Aug. 17, 1914.

12. TD to Mencken, Aug. 22, 1914.

13. De Camp to TD, Sept. 16, 1914.

14. TD to Mencken, Sept. 11, 1914.
15. To TD, Oct. 13, 1914.
16. TD to Mencken, Oct. 13, 1914.
17. To TD, Oct. 14, 1914.
18. TD to Mencken, Oct. 15, 1914.
19. Mencken to Sedgwick, Nov. 2, 1914 (PU).
20. Undated (UP).
21. *New Republic,* Dec. 25, 1915.
22. Vrest Orton: *Dreiserana* (New York, Chocorua, 1929), p. 35.
23. Chapman to TD, July 8, 1915.
24. Dell: *Homecoming,* p. 269.
25. TD to Harry Hansen, Dec. 19, 1929.
26. Lengel told Swanberg, June 12, 1963.
27. To TD, April 6, 1915.
28. TD to Mencken, April 20, 1915.
29. To TD, April 22, 1915.
30. TD to Mencken, April 26, 1915.
31. To TD, April 29, 1915.
32. Doty to TD, June 10, 1915. The next year "The Lost Phoebe" appeared in O'Brien's *Best Short Stories of 1916.*
33. Century statement, Aug. 3, 1915.
34. Dell told Swanberg, May 19, 1963.
35. Jewett to TD, Oct. 1, 1914, and Aug. 2, 1915.
36. Undated *World* clipping (UP).
37. Masters: *Across Spoon River,* p. 367.
38. Dreiser: *A Hoosier Holiday,* p. 348.
39. The same, p. 183.
40. Dell told Swanberg, May 19, 1963.
41. Dreiser: *A Hoosier Holiday,* p. 181.
42. The same, p. 428.
43. See Elisio Vivas: "Dreiser, an Inconsistent Mechanist," in *The Stature of Theodore Dreiser,* p. 237 ff.; also, Charles C. Walcutt: *American Literary Naturalism* (Minneapolis, University of Minnesota, 1956), pp. 180–82.

CHAPTER 6
1. TD to Mencken, Oct. 10, 1915.
2. *The New York Times,* Oct. 10, 1915.
3. *Harper's Weekly,* Jan. 1, 1916.
4. Oct. 9, 1915 (UP).
5. Nov. 20, 1915.
6. Oct. 9, 1915 (UP).
7. Oct. 12, 1915 (UP).
8. Nov., 1915 issue.
9. *Chicago Tribune,* Dec. 4, 1915 (UP).
10. Oct. 30, 1915 (UP).
11. *New York World,* Oct. 13, 1915 (UP).
12. Mencken to TD, Oct. 17, 1915.

13. *Chicago Evening Post*, Oct. 22, 1915 (UP).
14. Masters to TD, Oct. 26, 1915.
15. TD to Hersey, Oct. 9, 1915 (CU).
16. *The Nation*, Dec. 2, 1915.
17. TD to Hersey, Dec. 19, 1915 (CU).
18. Miss Markham to Swanberg, Feb. 29, 1964.
19. Miss Markham to Swanberg, Oct. 26, 1963.
20. Miss Markham to Swanberg, March 17, 1964.
21. TD to Hersey, Dec. 13, 1915 (CU).
22. Huebsch told Swanberg, Oct. 31, 1962.
23. Mencken to TD, Nov. 2, 1915.
24. Dreiser: *A Hoosier Holiday*, p. 348.
25. Ouija notes, Dec. 26, 1915, and Jan., 1916 (UP).
26. To Mencken, Feb. 14, 1916.
27. Masters to TD, Jan. 21, 1916.
28. Mencken to TD, Feb. 21, 1916.
29. TD to Mencken, Jan. 19, 1916.
30. To TD, Feb. 2, 1916.
31. Savannah diary (UP), entry for Jan. 26, 1916.
32. Charles Rolo (ed.): *Psychiatry in American Life*, pp. 212–13.
33. Diary, Jan. 27, 1916.
34. Telegram included with diary.
35. W. J. Hoggson to TD, Jan. 22, 1916.
36. To TD, Feb. 5, 1916.
37. To Mencken, Feb. 8, 1916.
38. All entries from diary kept from Jan. 26 to Feb. 18, 1916.
39. Miss Markham to Swanberg, Dec. 12, 1963.
40. Dated March 17, 1916.
41. Kaempffaert to TD, Oct. 27, 1915.
42. To Mencken: June 11; undated; and June 24, 1916.
43. To Mencken, June 24, 1916.
44. To TD, June 26, 1916.
45. To Mencken, July 27, 1916.
46. Dell: *Homecoming*, p. 278.
47. *Cincinnati Enquirer*, Sept. 14, 1916 (UP).
48. Masters to TD, Aug. 21, 1916.
49. Fort to TD, Aug. 13, 1916.
50. To Mencken, July 29 and Aug. 4, 1916.
51. Quoted in Dudley: *Forgotten Frontiers*, p. 357.
52. *Seven Arts*, Aug., 1917.
53. Mencken to TD, July 28, 1916.
54. *Literary Digest*, Oct. 21, 1916; also, Dudley: *Forgotten Frontiers*,
p. 353.
55. Butler to Mencken, Sept. 21, 1916 (UP).
56. *New York Tribune*, Aug. 20, 1916.
57. Mencken to TD, Aug. 22, 1916.
58. Sept. 13, 1916, to John Lane Company (UP).

59. Both quoted in *Literary Digest,* Oct. 21, 1916.
60. Quoted in *Chicago Record Herald,* Nov. 7, 1916 (UP).
61. Mencken to TD, Sept. 5, 1916.
62. Mencken to Boyd, Sept. 6, 1916 (PU).
63. Mencken to TD, Oct. 6, 1916.
64. TD to Mencken, Oct. 9, 1916.
65. Mencken to Boyd, Oct. 9, 1916 (PU).
66. Dudley: *Forgotten Frontiers,* p. 363.
67. Benét to Mencken, Nov. 22, 1916 (UP).
68. Quoted in *Forgotten Frontiers,* p. 366.
69. Sumner to Harvey, Sept. 19, 1916 (UP).
70. Sumner to Keating, Nov. 22, 1916 (UP).
71. *Chicago Examiner,* Jan. 8, 1917 (UP).
72. Dated Sept. 27, 1916.
73. Mrs. Whitman's ms., p. 95.
74. TD to Frank, Dec. 30, 1916.
75. Waldo Frank (pseud. "Searchlight"): *Time Exposures* (New York, Boni & Liveright, 1926), pp. 160–61.
76. Mencken to TD, Dec. 16, 1916.
77. To Mencken, Dec. 18, 1916.
78. Mencken to TD, Dec. 20, 1916.
79. To Mencken, Dec. 21, 1916.
80. Lengel to TD, Jan. 13, 1917.
81. Jones to TD, Sept. 4, 1917.
82. Hersey to TD, Jan. 19, 1917.
83. Mencken to TD, Dec. 23, 1916.

CHAPTER 7
1. Mrs. Campbell told Swanberg, June 21, 1962.
2. Dr. Grant to John Stanchfield, Nov. 17, 1916 (UP).
3. *The New York Times,* March 19 and 22, 1917.
4. Kathryn Sayre notes (UP).
5. Hapgood: *A Victorian in the Modern World,* p. 266.
6. The same, p. 269.
7. Van Wyck Brooks: *John Sloan—A Painter's Life* (New York, Dutton, 1955), p. 189.
8. G. H. Casamajor to TD, June 5, 1917.
9. Hapgood to TD, May 17, 1917.
10. Mencken to Boyd (April?), 1917 (PU).
11. Undated, evidently 1918.
12. TD to Mencken, June 29, 1917.
13. Two Mencken letters to Dreiser, both after June 29, 1917.
14. Mrs. Jefferson to TD, June 22, 1917.
15. Doty to Lengel, July 12, 1917.
16. John Cowper Powys: *Autobiography,* p. 554.
17. Pullman Company to TD, Jan. 31, Feb. 20 and April 4, 1918.
18. Albert Boni told Swanberg, June 12, 1963.

19. Undated card at UP.

20. Mencken: *A Book of Prefaces* (New York, Knopf, 1917), quotations from pp. 93, 87, 123, 124.

21. Mencken to Boyd, undated, fall, 1917, and winter, 1917–18 (PU).

22. TD to Edward H. Smith, Nov. 25, 1920.

23. Dudley: *Forgotten Frontiers,* p. 398.

24. Fort to TD, Jan. 21, 1918.

25. TD to Huebsch, March 10, 1918.

26. *Journal of Arnold Bennett, III,* p. 158.

27. Edward H. Smith to TD, Sept. 20, 1916, and March 2, 1918. Elsie Smith to Helen Dreiser, Aug. 10, 1946, with undated news clipping attached.

28. Mencken to Boyd, March 9 and April 20, 1918 (PU).

29. All these rejections are noted in letters at UP.

30. Mrs. Roberts to TD, undated, 1918.

31. Ray Long to TD, March 14, 1918.

32. Doty to TD, July 2 and Aug. 7, 1918.

33. Thomas R. Smith to TD, Aug. 9, 1918.

34. Vance to TD, Aug. 22, 1918.

35. Stanwood Cobb to Swanberg, Jan. 29, 1964.

36. The Coburns to TD, Aug. 29, 1918.

37. Dreiser told Elias, Aug. 18, 1941 (RHE).

38. *Chicago Tribune,* June 1, 1918 (UP).

39. Edward H. Smith to TD, Feb. 24, 1918.

40. Karsner to TD, March 4, 1918.

41. Mencken to Boyd, March 9, 1918 (PU).

42. Joseph S. Auerbach: *Essays and Miscellanies* (New York, Harper, 1922), p. 156.

43. *The New York Times,* July 12, 1918.

44. TD to Mencken, May 10, 1918.

45. Liveright to TD, June 24, 1918.

46. Mencken to TD, Aug. 21, 1918.

47. Mrs. Baker to TD, Feb. 6, 1917.

48. TD to Mrs. Baker, Feb. 15, 1917.

49. Mrs. Baker to TD, Sept. 4, 1918.

50. TD to Mrs. Baker, Nov. 23, 1918.

51. Dudley: *Forgotten Frontiers,* p. 385.

52. TD to Mencken, Jan. 6, 1919.

53. Hersey to TD, Dec. 7, 1918.

54. Mencken to Boyd, Jan. 18, 1919 (PU).

55. George Jean Nathan: *The Intimate Notebooks of George Jean Nathan* (New York, Knopf, 1932), pp. 38–39.

56. The same, p. 39.

57. Edward H. Smith to TD, Jan. 9 and 13, 1919; also, Ludwig Lewisohn to TD, Jan. 10; Harold Hersey to TD, March 15, 1919.

58. Quoted in Hersey to TD, March 15, 1919.

59. The same.

60. Yewdale to TD, April 8 and May 24, 1919.

CHAPTER 8

1. Boni told Swanberg, June 12, 1963.
2. James Oppenheim: *Behind Your Front* (New York, Harper, 1928), p. 59.
3. Dell told Swanberg, May 19, 1963.
4. Untermeyer told Swanberg, Dec. 11, 1962.
5. Powys: *Autobiography*, p. 551.
6. Ernest Boyd: *Portraits, Real and Imaginary* (New York, Doran, 1924), p. 170.
7. Ludwig Lewisohn: *Expression in America* (New York, Harper, 1932), p. 492.
8. Frank: *Time Exposures*, p. 161.
9. Yewdale to TD, undated.
10. Dr. Brill to TD, Jan. 25, 1919.
11. Long to TD, Jan. 13, 1919.
12. Rascoe to TD, April 5, 1919.
13. TD to Fort, April 27, 1919.
14. Liveright to Fort, attached to Liveright to TD, May 9, 1919.
15. Loeb to TD, June 3, 1919.
16. To Mencken, Feb. 2, 1919.
17. TD to Kline, April 7, 1919.
18. Kline to TD, June 10, 1919.
19. Nathan: *Intimate Notebooks*, pp. 43–44.
20. "Milton Goldberg" (a fictitious name) to TD, April 3, 1916.
21. Lengel told Swanberg, June 12, 1963; also, Carl Van Vechten told Swanberg, April 28, 1963.
22. TD to Bettina Morris, May 2, 1919. "Bettina Morris" is necessarily a fictitious name.
23. Mencken told Elias, Nov. 2, 1944 (RHE); also, *New York World*, May 17, 1919 (UP).
24. Mencken to TD, May 14, 1919.
25. Edward H. Smith to TD, June 22, 1919.
26. Mrs. Baker to TD, March 29, 1918.
27. *Huntington Press*, June 18, 1919 (UP).
28. Swihart to Swanberg, April 20, 1963.
29. TD diary (UP), June 19, 1919.
30. Maxwell to TD, Oct. 15, 1918.
31. Maxwell to TD, Sept. 8, 1919.
32. Diary entries, June 24, 26 and 27, 1919.
33. Diary entry, June 30, 1919.
34. Mrs. Baker to TD, June 26, 1919.
35. Yost to TD, April 28, 1919.
36. Diary entry, July 2, 1919.

CHAPTER 9

1. TD to Mencken, Sept. 4, 1919.
2. Mencken to Boyd, Aug. 9, 1919 (PU).

3. Helen Dreiser: *My Life With Dreiser* (Cleveland, World, 1951), p. 6.

4. W. E. Woodward: *The Gift of Life* (New York, Dutton, 1947), p. 232.

5. Mrs. W. E. Woodward told Swanberg, Jan. 23, 1964.

6. Helen Dreiser: *My Life With Dreiser*, p. 6.

7. The same, p. 4.

8. Lane brochure, "Theodore Dreiser, America's Foremost Novelist," 1916 (CU).

9. Helen Dreiser: *My Life . . .* , p. 10.

10. The same, p. 13.

11. The same, p. 26.

12. Woodward: *The Gift of Life*, p. 232.

13. Dreiser later said (in "Myself and the Movies," *Esquire*, July, 1943) that he was paid by Famous Players to go to Hollywood.

14. TD to Mencken, Nov. 23, 1919.

15. TD to Mencken, Feb. 20, 1920.

16. Liveright to TD, Feb. 9, 1920.

17. To Mencken, April 8, 1919.

18. Liveright to TD, Feb. 6, 1920.

19. Henry F. Pringle: "Comstock the Less," *American Mercury*, Jan., 1927.

20. TD to Barrett Clark, March 17, 1920.

21. Liveright to TD, March 22, 1920.

22. Edward Smith to TD, May 16, 1920.

23. Mencken to TD, Dec. 11, 1920.

24. Mencken to Boyd, Dec. 20, 1919 (PU).

25. Mencken to Rascoe (UP, summer, 1920?).

26. Jan. 7, 1920. There seems no proof that Mencken was the writer.

27. Helen Dreiser: *My Life . . .* , p. 37.

28. The same, p. 40.

29. Dreiser: *Newspaper Days*, p. 428.

30. The same, p. 21.

31. To Bettina Morris, May 10 and June 1, 1920.

32. Liveright to TD, June 4, 1920.

33. Liveright to TD, Aug. 10, 1920.

34. Liveright to TD, Sept. 18 and Oct. 4, 1920.

35. To Mencken, Aug. 27, 1920.

36. Mencken to TD, Aug. 7, 1920.

37. TD to Mencken, Aug. 13, 1920.

38. TD to George Douglas, Oct. 7, 1920.

39. *San Francisco Bulletin*, Oct. 30, 1920 (UP).

40. To Bettina, Aug. 27, 1920.

41. TD to Mencken, Oct. 25, 1920.

42. To Bettina, July 29, 1920.

43. De Kruif to TD, undated, Sept., 1920.

44. L. V. Heilbrunn told Elias, Jan. 9, 1945 (RHE).

45. Liveright to TD, Nov. 22, 1920.

46. TD to Mencken, Sept. 20, 1920.

47. Liveright to TD, Dec. 21, 1920.
48. Lengel to TD (about Dec. 30), 1920.
49. Helen Dreiser: *My Life* . . . , p. 47
50. Llewelyn Powys to TD, undated.
51. Mencken to TD, Jan. 11, 1921.
52. To Mencken, Jan. 26, 1921.
53. TD to Huebsch, Nov. 24, 1920.
54. TD to Charles Boni, Jr., Feb. 14, 1921.
55. TD to Boyd, Aug. 26, 1921.
56. *Birth Control Review*, April, 1921 (UP).
57. TD to Max Herzberg, Nov. 2, 1921.
58. Helen Dreiser: *My Life* . . . , p. 44.
59. Liveright to TD, Jan. 5, 1921.
60. Helen Dreiser: *My Life* . . . , p. 75.
61. To Liveright, Dec. 21, 1920.
62. Jan. 10, 1921. There seems no proof that Mencken was the hoaxer.

CHAPTER 10

1. To Mencken, Jan. 2, 1921.
2. Mencken to TD, Jan. 9, 1921.
3. To TD, Feb. 7, 1921.
4. *Shadowland*, Nov. and Dec., 1921, and Jan. and Feb., 1922, issues.
5. Helen Dreiser: *My Life* . . . , p. 62.
6. TD to Ettinge, June 12, 1921.
7. *Milwaukee Sentinel*, Oct. 4, 1921 (UP).
8. Moody to TD, Oct. 8, 1921. "Robert L. Moody" and "Hildegarde Wells" are fictitious names.
9. Liveright to TD, June 15, 1921.
10. TD to Mencken, April 12, 1922.
11. TD to Briggs, April 9, 1921.
12. Mencken letters of Nov. 15, April 14 and May 31, 1921.
13. TD to Mencken, June 7, 1921.
14. To Ullman, Oct. 6, 1921.
15. Edward H. Smith to TD, Dec. 6, 1921. Also, Helen Deutsch and Stella Hanau: *The Provincetown* (New York, Farrar & Rinehart, 1931), p. 86.
16. TD to Hume, March 30, 1922.
17. TD to Mencken, March 22, 1922.
18. Mencken to TD, April 25, 1922.
19. To TD, June 1, 1922.
20. TD to Bettina, May 16, 1922.
21. The same.
22. Bettina to TD, undated.
23. To Bettina, June 30, 1922.
24. To Bettina, Aug. 23, 1922.
25. Bettina to TD, Oct. 15, 1923.
26. Sterling to Helen, Sept. 23, 1922; also, *San Francisco Examiner*, Aug. 23, 1922.

27. Liveright to TD, Sept. 1, 1922.

28. Harold Stearns (ed.): *Civilization in America* (New York, Harcourt Brace, 1922), p. 183.

29. Mencken to TD, April 22, 1922.

30. Margaret Freeman Cabell and Padraic Colum (eds.): *Between Friends: Letters of James Branch Cabell and Others* (New York, Harcourt, Brace & World, 1962), p. 269.

31. Mencken to TD, Nov. 15, 1921.

32. Miss Markham to TD, July 6, 1922.

33. To Bettina, Aug. 23, 1922.

34. *Los Angeles Times,* Sept. 17, 1922 (UP).

35. Helen Dreiser: *My Life* . . . , p. 63.

36. The same, pp. 63–64.

BOOK FOUR

CHAPTER I

1. To Mencken, Oct. 23, 1922.

2. Helen Dreiser: *My Life* . . . , p. 68.

3. To Ettinge, Dec. 2, 1922; also, to Bettina, Jan. 8, 1923; to Mencken, Nov. 5, 1922.

4. Mrs. Brokaw to TD, Nov. 1, 1922.

5. Moody to TD, Sept. 18, 1922.

6. TD to Ettinge, Oct. 23, 1922.

7. TD to Mencken, Oct. 29, 1922.

8. Mencken to TD, Oct. 30, 1922.

9. To Mencken, Nov. 5, 1922.

10. Mencken to TD, Oct. 28, 1922.

11. Llewelyn Powys: *The Verdict of Bridlegoose* (New York, Harcourt Brace, 1926), p. 65.

12. Van Vechten told Swanberg, April 20, 1963.

13. Helen Dreiser: *My Life* . . . , p. 68.

14. The same, p. 69.

15. To Karsner, Feb. 12, 1923.

16. To Ettinge, Dec. 2; also, to Mencken, Nov. 14, 1922.

17. Jan. 9, 1923, memo of agreement.

18. Van Vechten told Swanberg, April 20, 1963.

19. Jacques Loeb: *The Mechanistic Conception of Life* (Chicago, University of Chicago, 1912), p. 31.

20. Loeb: *The Organism as a Whole* (New York, Putnam, 1916), p. 299.

21. Irene and Allen Cleaton: *Books and Battles* (Boston, Houghton Mifflin, 1937), p. 61.

22. Powys: *The Verdict of Bridlegoose,* p. 131.

23. Burton Rascoe: *Theodore Dreiser* (New York, McBride, 1926), p. 68.

24. Boyd: *Portraits Real and Imaginary,* p. 222.

25. *New York Evening Mail,* March 10; also, *New York Telegram,* March 4, 1923 (UP).

26. Manuel Komroff told Swanberg, Dec. 10, 1963.

27. TD to Beach, May 5, 1923.

28. *New York Telegraph,* May 19, 1923 (UP).

29. TD to Burgess, after May 19, 1923.

30. To TD, May 31, 1923.

31. Claude Bowers: *My Life* (New York, Simon & Schuster, 1962), p. 154.

32. The same, p. 156.

33. The same.

34. Liveright to TD, March 27, 1923.

35. *Boston Transcript,* Aug. 4, 1923 (UP).

36. Alice Phillips to TD, Feb. 6, 1923.

37. Miss Kusell told Swanberg, March 14, 1964.

38. Helen Dreiser: *My Life* . . . , p. 85.

39. To Miss Kusell, Aug. 10, Aug. 16 and July 29, 1923 (property of Miss Kusell).

40. Liveright to TD, Aug. 7, 1923.

41. The same.

42. Mencken to TD, Aug. 9, 1923.

43. Helen Dreiser: *My Life* . . . , p. 88.

44. The same, p. 89.

45. To Bettina, Sept. 8, 1923.

46. To W. W. Hamm, Sept. 26, 1923.

47. Moody to TD, Nov. 1, 1923.

48. TD to Ettinge, Oct. 7, 1923.

49. *The New York Times,* Dec. 23, 1923, III, pp. 6–7.

50. Miss Feld told Swanberg, Oct. 5, 1962.

51. *The New York Times,* cited Note 49 above.

52. Alexander Klein (ed.): *Grand Deception* (New York, Lippincott, 1955), p. 116.

53. Sept. 14, 1924.

54. TD to Mencken, Jan. 13, 1924.

55. Mencken to TD, Jan. 14, 1924.

56. Helen Dreiser: *My Life* . . . , pp. 90–91.

CHAPTER 2

1. TD to Helen, March 23, March 24 and March 30, 1924.

2. TD to Helen, Aug. 4, 1924; quoted in Helen Dreiser: *My Life* . . . , p. 99.

3. To Helen, March 24, March 28, April 3 and July 16, 1924.

4. Helen Dreiser: *My Life* . . . , p. 97.

5. To Helen, May 3 and March 31, 1924.

6. Undated April, June 2, June 17 and June 18, 1924.

7. June 1 and June 17, 1924.

8. April 4, 1924, in Louise Campbell: *Letters to Louise* (Philadelphia, University of Pennsylvania, 1959), p. 19.

9. To Helen, April 21, April 26, June 2 and April 12, 1924.

10. Tom Smith to TD, Aug. 8, 1924.

11. To Miss McCoy, July 9, 1924.

12. To Amy Parsons, Sept. 2, 1924. "Amy Parsons" is necessarily a fictitious name.

13. To Miss Parsons, Oct. 7, 1924.

14. To Miss Parsons, Nov. 6, 1924.

15. To Helen, Sept. 26, 1924.

16. Miss Kusell told Swanberg, March 14, 1964.

17. To Helen, March 28 and March 31, 1924.

18. Liveright to TD, May 6, 1924.

19. Komroff told Swanberg, Dec. 10, 1963.

20. TD to Helen, April 16, May 24, April 3 and July 16, 1924.

21. Undated Mencken letter.

22. TD to Helen, March 28, April 21, May 11 and May 26, 1924.

23. Bowers: *My Life*, p. 158.

24. To Helen, June 26, 1924.

25. Bowers: *My Life*, p. 157.

26. To Helen, June 5, 1924.

27. To Mrs. Campbell, June 14, 1924.

28. Bowers: *My Life*, p. 159.

29. To Helen, July 16 and Aug. 25, 1924.

30. Esherick told Swanberg, June 25, 1962.

31. TD to Helen, Aug. 25, 1924.

32. Helen Dreiser: *My Life* . . . , p. 96.

33. To Helen, Oct. 17, 1924.

34. Helen Dreiser: *My Life* . . . , pp. 96–97.

35. To Miss Parsons, Nov. 24, 1924.

36. Helen: *My Life* . . . , p. 106.

37. To Mencken, Nov. 14, 1924.

38. To Miss Parsons, Jan. 25, 1925.

39. TD to Upton Sinclair, Dec. 18, 1924 (Indiana).

CHAPTER 3

1. Mencken to TD, May 7, 1925.

2. Huebsch told Swanberg, Oct. 31, 1962.

3. Miss Boyd told Swanberg, Nov. 7, 1962; also, Edith M. Stern: "The Man Who Was Unafraid," *Saturday Review*, June 28, 1941; Lester Cohen: "And the Sinner—Horace Liveright," *Esquire*, Dec., 1960; Donald Friede told Swanberg, Jan. 11, 1963.

4. Helen to Miss Piercy, Feb. 24, 1925 (Indiana).

5. Miss Kusell told Swanberg, March 14, 1964.

6. See two unpublished M.A. theses, Emil Greenberg: ". . . Theodore Dreiser's *An American Tragedy*," New York University, 1936; and Ida Blacksin: "Dreiser and the Law," N.Y.U., 1940.

7. Esherick told Swanberg, June 25, 1962.
8. Gene Fowler: *Beau James* (New York, Viking, 1949), p. 37.
9. Quoted in Lacosky to TD, Nov. 1, 1925.
10. Mrs. Campbell told Swanberg, Jan. 24, 1963.
11. Tom Smith to Dreiser, June 3, 1925.
12. Tom Smith to TD, June 3, 1925.
13. TD to Mencken, Nov. 4, 1925; also, TD told Elias, Aug. 15, 1941 (RHE).
14. Quoted in Mencken to TD, Oct. 7, 1925.
15. Bowers: *My Life*, pp. 161–62.
16. Undated Nov., 1925.
17. To TD, Nov. 28, 1925.
18. To Mencken, same date.
19. TD to Mencken, Dec. 3, 1925. See also James W. Barrett: *Joseph Pulitzer and his World* (New York, Vanguard, 1941), pp. 382–83.
20. Dell told Swanberg, May 19, 1963.
21. Mencken to Helen Dreiser, Jan. 30, 1946.
22. TD Florida diary (UP), entry Dec. 12, 1925.
23. Miss Kusell to TD, Dec. 16, 1925.
24. TD diary entries, Dec. 18, 19, 20, 24 and 16, 1925.
25. Entries, Dec. 30 and 31, 1925, and Jan. 3, 1926.
26. To Lengel, Jan. 6, 1926.
27. To Mrs. Campbell, Jan. 14, 1926.
28. Diary, Jan. 4 and 5, 1926.
29. Tom Smith to TD, Jan. 9, 1926.
30. Helen Dreiser: *My Life . . .* , p. 119.
31. Diary, Jan. 18, 1926.

CHAPTER 4
1. *The Nation*, Feb. 10, 1926.
2. *Saturday Review*, Jan. 9, 1926.
3. *New York Herald Tribune Books*, Jan. 3, 1926.
4. Constable & Co. advertising brochure, 1926.
5. *London Evening Standard*, Dec. 30, 1926 (UP).
6. Quoted in Maxwell Geismar: *Rebels and Ancestors* (New York, Hill & Wang, 1963), p. 257 *fn*.
7. *American Mercury*, March, 1926.
8. Charles Angoff: *H. L. Mencken* (New York, Yoseloff, 1956), p. 101.
9. To Miss Kusell, Feb. 13, 1926 (Miss Kusell's property).
10. Postmarked Feb. 18, 1926.
11. Liveright to TD, March 8, 1926.
12. *New York World*, March 7, 1926 (UP).
13. Helen: *My Life . . .* , p. 123.
14. Wanger told Swanberg, Jan. 14, 1963.
15. Liveright to TD, March 26, 1926.
16. TD to Liveright, March 23, 1926.
17. To TD, April 2, 1926. Other sources on the coffee incident: Manuel

Komroff told Swanberg, Dec. 10, 1963; Louis Cline told Swanberg, April 30, 1963; Lester Cohen told Swanberg, Oct. 3, 1962.

18. April 3, 1926.
19. To Lengel, March 27, 1926.
20. Dr. Vera Dreiser Scott to Swanberg, May 4, 1964.
21. Jug to TD, March 31, 1926.
22. Jug to TD, April 7, 1926.
23. Undated, April, 1926 (CU).
24. Jug to TD, April 19, 1926.
25. Hemley to Malone, May 12, 1926 (UP).
26. Draft, after April 12, 1926.
27. Agreement dated June 21, 1926.
28. *Vanity Fair*, May–July, 1926.
29. Dwight Taylor: *Joy Ride* (New York, Putnam, 1959), pp. 229–32.
30. June 9, 1926.
31. Liveright to TD, June 21, 1926.
32. Memo of agreement dated June 2, 1926.
33. *Ekstra Bladet* (Copenhagen), July 31, 1926 (UP). Translated by Eva Svendsen.
34. *Politiken* (Copenhagen), Aug. 5, 1926 (UP). Translated by Eva Svendsen.
35. *New York World*, Nov. 7, 1926 (UP).
36. *Chicago Tribune*, Paris edition, Sept. 29, 1926 (UP).
37. Emma Goldman: *Living My Life* (New York, Knopf, 1931), II, p. 986.
38. Emma Goldman to TD, Sept. 29, 1926.
39. Quoted in *New York Herald Tribune*, Sept. 7, 1926.
40. *Paris New York Herald*, undated (UP).
41. *New York Herald Tribune*, Sept. 9, 1926. I find no real Dreiser lift from Ade's work.
42. *The New York Times*, Sept. 10, 1926.
43. To Kirah Markham (Miss Markham to Swanberg, Oct. 26, 1963).
44. *New York Herald Tribune*, Oct. 23, 1926.
45. The same.
46. Louis Cline told Swanberg, April 30, 1963.
47. Donald Friede: *The Mechanical Angel* (New York, Knopf, 1948), p. 43.

CHAPTER 5

1. Esherick told Swanberg, June 25, 1962.
2. Helen Dreiser: *My Life . . .* , p. 139.
3. TD to Carl Van Doren, Jan. 12, 1927.
4. Komroff told Swanberg, Dec. 10, 1963. The name of the pianist, "Kovacs," is fictitious.
5. Nathan: *Intimate Notebooks*, pp. 45–46; also, Mary Jane Matz: *The Many Lives of Otto Kahn* (New York, Macmillan, 1963), pp. 141, 268; Bowers: *My Life*, pp. 163–66; Van Vechten told Swanberg, April 20, 1963.
6. Dreiser tax figures (UP).

7. Dated May 5, 1927.

8. To Mr. Van Valkenburgh, June 19, 1927.

9. Friede told Swanberg, Jan. 11, 1963.

10. Dinamov to TD, Dec. 10, 1926.

11. TD to Dinamov, Jan. 5, 1927.

12. Louise Campbell: *Letters to Louise*, p. 38.

13. Private source.

14. Helen Dreiser: *My Life* . . . , p. 150.

15. The same, p. 143.

16. To Miss Kusell, March 25, 1927.

17. To Helen, same date.

18. Helen Dreiser: *My Life* . . . , p. 146.

19. To Helen, March 28 and 31, 1927.

20. To Pell, April 9, 1927.

21. To Mrs. Campbell, April 14, 1927.

22. Helen Dreiser: *My Life* . . . , pp. 149–50.

23. The same, p. 152.

BOOK FIVE

CHAPTER 1

1. Edward Smith to TD, Feb. 21, 1927.

2. TD's Russian diary, entry Oct. 11, 1927 (UP).

3. The same.

4. TD's Russian diary, entries Oct. 14 and 18, 1927.

5. Helen Dreiser: *My Life* . . . , p. 169.

6. *Paris New York Herald*, Oct. 27, 1927 (UP).

7. Diary, Oct. 24, 1927. See also, Bertram Wolfe: *Diego Rivera—His Life and Times* (New York, Knopf, 1939), p. 236 ff.

8. To Boyd, Oct. 27, 1927 (Yale).

9. Diary, Oct. 25, 1927.

10. *Paris New York Herald*, Oct. 27, 1927.

11. Diary, Oct. 26.

12. The same.

13. Huebsch told Swanberg, Oct. 31, 1962.

14. TD diary entries, Oct. 28 and 29, 1927.

15. Entries Nov. 3 and 4, 1927.

16. Deming Brown: *Soviet Attitudes Toward American Writing* (Princeton, Princeton University, 1962), p. 20 ff.

17. Diary, Nov. 5, 1927.

18. Diary, Nov. 7, 1927.

19. Vincent Sheean: *Dorothy and Red* (Boston, Houghton Mifflin, 1963), p. 60 (letter dated Nov. 8, 1927).

20. Quotations from diary, Nov. 14 to 22, 1927.

21. *Providence Tribune*, July 27, 1930 (UP).

22. To Bye, Nov. 25 (?), 1927.

23. Diary, Nov. 24, 1927.

24. Deming Brown: *Soviet Attitudes* . . . , p. 259.

25. Mark Schorer: *Sinclair Lewis*, p. 496; also, Vincent Sheean: *Dorothy and Red*, p. 79.

26. Robert Elias: *Theodore Dreiser* . . . , p. 233.

27. Diary, Dec. 10, 1927.

28. Entries Dec. 20, 17, 18, 19 and 23, 1927.

29. Helen Dreiser: *My Life* . . . , pp. 171–72.

30. Diary entries, Jan. 1 to 13, 1927.

31. Copy of statement, dated Jan. 13, 1928 (CU).

32. Added to diary, undated.

33. Helen Dreiser: *My Life* . . . , p. 180.

34. The same, p. 181.

35. *New York Herald Tribune*, Feb. 22, 1928.

36. George Jean Nathan: *Intimate Notebooks*, p. 52.

37. *New York Evening Post*, Feb. 21, 1928 (UP).

38. *The New York Times*, March 4, 1928.

39. TD to Strunsky, March 11, 1928.

40. TD to Louise Campbell, Feb. 20, 1928.

CHAPTER 2

1. Undated clipping (UP).

2. March 18 to 28, 1928, inclusive.

3. Nathan: *Intimate Notebooks*, p. 46.

4. March 18, 1928, unidentified news clipping (UP).

5. To Wylie, April 11, 1928.

6. Margaret Szekely (now Mrs. Kenneth Clark) told Swanberg, Oct. 16, 1963.

7. William Woodward: *The Gift of Life*, p. 315.

8. Claude Bowers: *My Life*, p. 167.

9. Boris Sokoloff: *The Crime of Dr. Garine* (New York, Covici-Friede, 1928), p. viii.

10. Lina Goldschmidt to TD, June 1, 1928.

11. Woods Hole data: *The Collecting Net*, July 21, 1928 (UP); Marguerite Tjader Harris told Swanberg, Oct. 9, 1962; Helen Dreiser: *My Life* . . . , p. 189 ff.

12. Mrs. Whitman's ms., p. 128.

13. Mrs. Whitman told Swanberg, Nov. 11, 1962.

14. Mrs. Campbell to Swanberg, Oct. 15, 1963.

15. *New York Evening Post*, Nov. 14, 1928.

16. The same.

17. The same.

18. Ernst, Fox & Cane to Liveright (UP), Nov. 27, 1928.

19. Both in Hays to Liveright (UP), Nov. 27, 1928.

20. Robert Elias note dated March 15, 1938 (RHE).

21. Lester Cohen told Swanberg, Oct. 3, 1962; also, Esther McCoy told Swanberg, March 4, 1963.

22. *Dreiser Looks at Russia* (New York, Liveright, 1928), p. 9.

23. The same, pp. 115, 116, 118 and 119.

24. Mrs. Woodward told Swanberg, Jan. 23, 1964.

25. Henry Varnum Poor to Swanberg, June 1, 1964.

26. Esherick told Swanberg, June 25, 1962.

27. Miss McCoy told Swanberg, March 4, 1963.

28. Esherick told Swanberg, June 25, 1962.

29. Margaret Szekely told Swanberg, Oct. 17, 1963.

30. Miss Van Dresser told Swanberg, Dec. 2, 1962.

31. Excerpt in Helen Dreiser: *My Life* . . . , p. 80. See also Jacob Zeitlin and Homer Woodbridge: *Life and Letters of Stuart P. Sherman* (New York, Farrar & Rinehart, 1929), II, p. 799.

32. Emma Goldman to TD, Jan. 7, 1929.

33. Nathan: *Intimate Notebooks*, p. 46.

34. Dated Feb. 11, 1929 (UP).

35. Undated.

36. TD to Liveright, Feb. 15, 1929.

37. To Kyllmann, Feb. 12, 1929.

38. To Kyllmann, March 19, 1929.

39. Undated *Jewish Day* clipping (UP); also, Miss Ish-Kishor told Swanberg, July 10, 1963.

40. Bowers: *My Life*, p. 168; also, *New York World*, March 29, 1929 (UP).

41. Nathan: *Intimate Notebooks*, p. 47.

42. "Commonwealth *v.* Donald S. Friede—Before Hayes, J. and a Jury, Suffolk County, 1929"; also, Friede told Swanberg, Jan. 11, 1963.

43. TD to Bowers, May 27, 1929.

44. May 8, 1929.

45. To Mrs. Clayburgh, Aug. 8, 1929. Ballet data also from: Hy Kraft told Swanberg, April 20, 1963; Esther Van Dresser told Swanberg, Dec. 2, 1962.

CHAPTER 3

1. *Bookman*, Sept., 1928.

2. Gold to TD, before Sept., 1928.

3. Fabri told Swanberg, Dec. 23, 1962.

4. Oct. 28, 1929.

5. Miss Markham to Swanberg, Jan. 9, 1964.

6. Fabri diary, entry Sept. 22, 1929.

7. Fabri diary, July 26, 1929.

8. The same, Sept. 21, 1929.

9. The same, Oct. 25, 1929.

10. The same, Oct. 28 and 29, 1929.

11. To TD, Oct. 25, 1929.

12. Daphne Walters to TD, Oct. 25, 1929.

13. Louise Campbell: *Letters to Louise*, p. 63.
14. Fabri told Swanberg, July 24, 1963.
15. The same.
16. Dr. Vera Dreiser Scott to Swanberg, May 4, 1964.
17. Esherick told Swanberg, June 25, 1962.
18. In Paul Palmer to TD, Oct. 14, 1929.
19. TD to Palmer, Oct. 25, 1929.
20. TD to Evelyn Scott, Aug. 1, 1929.
21. Fabri to Swanberg, Dec. 26, 1962.
22. Margaret Szekely told Swanberg, Oct. 16, 1963.
23. Dinamov to TD, June 22, 1928.
24. To TD, Oct. 4, 1929.
25. Frau Goldschmidt to TD, Dec. 19, 1929.
26. To TD, Aug. 19, 1929.
27. TD to Frau Goldschmidt, Nov. 20, 1929.
28. Miss Van Dresser told Swanberg, Dec. 2, 1962.
29. To Fabri, March (?), 1930.
30. *Tucson Daily Citizen*, April 6, 1930 (UP).
31. *New Mexico State Journal*, April 19, 1930 (UP).
32. *Albuquerque Journal*, April 19, 1930 (UP).
33. *El Paso Herald*, April 25, 1930 (UP).
34. *El Paso Evening Post*, April 26, 1930 (UP).
35. The same, April 30 (UP).
36. *Tucson Daily Citizen*, April 30, 1930 (UP).
37. *Dallas Morning News*, May 18, 1930 (UP).
38. *San Francisco Daily News*, May 30, 1930 (UP).
39. Mrs. Fremont Older diary, entry May 31, 1930.
40. *San Francisco Chronicle*, May 31, 1930 (UP).
41. Hearst to TD, May 31, 1930.
42. *San Francisco Jewish Journal*, June 4, 1930 (UP).
43. *Portland Oregonian*, June 13, 1930 (UP).
44. The same, July 15, 1930 (UP).
45. June 10, 1930, leaflet: "John Reed Club Answer" (UP).
46. Helen Dreiser: *My Life . . .* , p. 206.
47. To TD, June 30, 1930.
48. Nathan; *Intimate Notebooks*, p. 47.
49. *New York Herald Tribune*, July 8, 1930.
50. *New York Telegram*, July 9, 1930 (UP).
51. Quoted in *Literary Digest*, July 26, 1930.
52. July 16, 1930.

CHAPTER 4
1. Fabri told Swanberg, Dec. 23, 1962.
2. TD to John Reed Club, Oct. 28, 1930.
3. Kearney to Paramount, Sept. 26, 1930 (UP).
4. TD to Liveright, Oct. 27, 1930.
5. Liveright to TD, Oct. 31, 1930.

6. To C.B.S., July 5, 1930.

7. Miss Van Dresser told Swanberg, Dec. 2, 1962.

8. Sally Kusell told Swanberg, April 5, 1964.

9. TD to Madeleine Boyd, Nov. 7, 1930.

10. *The New York Times*, Dec. 13, 1930.

11. Fabri told Swanberg, Dec. 23, 1962.

12. Helen Dreiser: *My Life* . . . , p. 211.

13. Eisenstein: "An American Tragedy," *Close Up*, June, 1933 (UP). See also Edmund Wilson: *The American Earthquake* (Garden City, Doubleday Anchor, 1958), pp. 398–400; Arthur Knight: *The Liveliest Art* (New York, Macmillan, 1957), pp. 80–82.

14. Contract dated Jan. 2, 1931 (UP).

15. To James D. Mooney, March 14, 1931.

16. Swarts to TD, Feb. 13, 1931.

17. Hoffenstein to TD, Feb. 17, 1931.

18. TD to Hoffenstein, Feb. 18, 1931.

19. To TD, Feb. 20, 1931.

20. To Hoffenstein, Feb. 20, 1931.

21. TD to Hoffenstein, Feb. 26, 1931.

22. *The New York Times*, March 3, 1931.

23. Eleanor McFeary to TD, March 20, 1931.

24. To Lasky, March 10, 1931.

25. To Lasky, March 17, 1931.

26. *The New York Times*, March 21, 1931.

27. Lengel told Swanberg, March 2, 1962; also, TD's account to Elias, dated March 15, 1938 (RHE).

28. Undated.

29. *New York Herald Tribune*, March 25, 1931.

30. Kraft told Swanberg, April 20, 1963.

31. H. S. Kraft: "Dreiser's War in Hollywood," *The Screen Writer*, March, 1946.

32. Kraft told Swanberg, April 20, 1963.

33. *New York American*, April 12, 1931 (UP).

34. Cowley told Swanberg, June 28, 1963.

35. The same; also, Louis Adamic: *My America* (New York, Harper, 1938), p. 110.

36. Frank told Swanberg, Jan. 22, 1964.

37. Kraft told Swanberg, April 20, 1963.

38. Helen Dreiser: *My Life* . . . , pp. 213–14.

39. Fabri diary, May 14, 1931.

40. The same.

41. Clark to TD, June 16, 1931.

42. Long to TD, same date.

43. Brill to TD, same date.

44. *The New York Times*, July 23, 1931.

45. *New York Herald Tribune*, Aug. 2, 1931 (UP).

46. *Mt. Kisco Times*, July 24, 1931 (UP).

47. Fabri told Swanberg, July 24, 1963.
48. Croy told Swanberg, Oct. 30, 1962.

CHAPTER 5

1. Dorothy Van Doren to TD, Oct. 30, 1930.
2. TD to Anna North, Jan. 17, 1931.
3. *Daily Worker*, May 9, 1931 (UP).
4. TD telegram to Charles H. Dennis, July 2, 1931.
5. Browder to TD, Oct. 20, 1931.
6. Dreiser: "Running the Railroads," *Liberty*, Nov. 7, 1931.
7. Daniel Willard: "I Am Only a Railroad Man," *Liberty*, Nov. 14, 1931.
8. Emma Goldman to TD, Oct. 4, 1931.
9. *Pittsburgh Press*, June 25, 1931 (UP).
10. United Press dispatch, June 26, 1931 (UP).
11. Green to TD, July 1, 1931.
12. Browder to TD, Aug. 4, 1931.
13. TD to Sarah Millin, Aug. 24, 1931.
14. All in *New Masses*, Sept., 1931 (UP).
15. *New York World-Telegram*, Aug. 27, 1931 (UP).
16. To Morrison, Sept. 17, 1931.
17. Mrs. Campbell told Swanberg, June 21, 1962.
18. To Helen, July 6, 1931.
19. Anonymous: *Harlan Miners Speak* (New York, Harcourt Brace, 1932), p. 7.
20. Dos Passos to Swanberg, Nov. 11, 1962.
21. *The New York Times*, Nov. 6, 1931.
22. Cohen told Swanberg, Oct. 3, 1962.
23. Dos Passos to Swanberg, Nov. 11, 1962.
24. Cohen told Swanberg.
25. Testimony from *Harlan Miners Speak*, pp. 217, 200, 280–81.
26. Cohen told Swanberg.
27. Undated *Life* magazine clipping (UP).
28. Testimony from *Harlan Miners Speak*, pp. 183, 187–88.
29. *Knoxville News-Sentinel*, Nov. 9, 1931 (UP).
30. Nov. 6, 1931.
31. "Judge Jones, the Harlan Miners and Myself"—TD press release (before Nov. 12, 1931, UP).
32. Bowers: *My Life*, p. 170.
33. Nov. 11, 1931.
34. To TD, Nov. 13, 1931.
35. Mencken to F. H. Garrison, Nov. 6 and 12, 1931 (PC).
36. Nov. 12, 1931.
37. Nov. 27, 1931.
38. To TD, Sept. 29, 1933.
39. Undated.
40. Cameron to John W. Davis, Nov. 20, 1931 (UP).
41. Same date.

42. To TD, Dec. 26, 1931.
43. Wells to TD, April 9, 1931.

CHAPTER 6

1. *New Masses,* Jan., 1932 (UP).
2. Thomas review in *The Nation,* April 6, 1932 (UP).
3. Dinamov in *International Literature,* No. 2–3, 1932 (UP).
4. *New York Herald Tribune Books,* Jan. 24, 1932.
5. (New York) *Catholic News,* Feb. 6, 1932 (UP).
6. Browder told Swanberg, April 10, 1964; see also TD to Dallas Mc-Kown, June 9, 1932.
7. TD to Fisher C. Baily, April 6, 1932.
8. The same.
9. TD's secretary to Bryan Goldsmith, April 11, 1932.
10. TD to Fisher C. Baily, April 6, 1932.
11. Dudley: *Forgotten Frontiers,* pp. 467–68.
12. Arthur C. Hume to TD, June 16, 1931, and Dec. 1, 1932.
13. To Sackin, Feb. 8, 1932.
14. Kraft told Swanberg, April 20, 1963.
15. William Targ (who talked with Helen) told Swanberg, Jan. 11, 1963.
16. To Louise Campbell, April 15, 1932.
17. To Hume, March 19, 1932.
18. To Mrs. Campbell, April 15, 1932.
19. Quoted in TD to *The New York Times,* April 6, 1932.
20. The same.
21. Cochrane to TD, April 12, 1932.
22. Forrest Bailey to TD, April 19, 1932. Kearney committed suicide in 1933.
23. TD to Fort, Aug. 27, 1930.
24. Evelyn Light to TD, April, 1942; also, *The New York Times,* May 5, 1932.
25. To Mrs. Campbell, June 10, 1932.
26. To Helen, May 15, 1932.
27. June 9, 1932.
28. To Bettina, June 20, 1932.
29. To Sackin, June 15, 1932.
30. *New York Herald Tribune,* July 10, 1932 (UP).
31. To Mrs. Campbell, July 23, 1923.
32. To Pass, Aug. 17, 1932.
33. To Mr. Weinstone, Oct. 3, 1932.
34. To Pass, Oct. 14, 1932.
35. Dr. A. A. Brill script (property of Dr. E. R. Brill), passim; also, Dr. E. R. Brill told Swanberg, Dec. 10, 1963.
36. Orrick Johns: *Time of Our Lives,* p. 329.
37. Edgar Gleeson to Swanberg, Jan. 3, 1964.
38. Johns: *Time of Our Lives,* pp. 327 and 260–61; also, *San Francisco Examiner,* Nov. 7, 1932 (UP).

39. *Los Angeles Daily News*, Nov. 10, 1932 (UP).
40. Bettina to TD, Nov. 17, 1932.
41. To Hoagland, Dec. 14, 1932 (DC).
42. To Dinamov, Oct. 11, 1932.

CHAPTER 7

1. To Dinamov, Sept. 22, 1932.
2. Dinamov to TD, Jan. 3, 1933.
3. To Bogdanov, Jan. 13, 1933.
4. To Nathan, Jan. 7, 1933.
5. Memo to Nathan-Boyd, Dec. 5, 1932.
6. Kraft told Swanberg, April 20, 1963.
7. Feb. 16, 1933.
8. To Anna Tatum, March 7, 1933.
9. To Martha Aldrich, May 5, 1933.
10. Jotted on TD memo to Nathan-Boyd, March 29, 1933.
11. To Boyd, March 31, 1933.
12. *New York Daily News*, March 20, 1933 (UP).
13. To Schulberg, April 7, 1933.
14. Schulberg to TD, same date.
15. To Schulberg, April 10, 1933.
16. *Variety*, May 16, 1933 (UP).
17. To Hume, undated May. Hume reply, May 25, 1933.
18. To Anderson, May 12, 1933 (CC).
19. Powys to TD, undated 1933.
20. To V. F. Calverton, June 6, 1933.
21. Quoted in Joseph Freeman to TD, Jan. 21, 1933.
22. Jan. 20, 1933.
23. Eastman to TD, April 23, 1933.
24. To Eastman, April 26, 1933.
25. To Eastman, May 26, 1933.
26. TD to Miss McCoy, March (?) and April 11, 1933.
27. Henry Varnum Poor to Swanberg, June 1, 1964; also, Woodward: *The Gift of Life*, p. 367.
28. Draft wire, June 2, 1933.
29. To Rascoe, July 12, 1933.
30. Mrs. Ficke told Swanberg, Sept. 26, 1963.
31. *New York Daily Mirror*, Aug. 1, 1933 (UP).
32. Komroff to TD, Aug. 27, 1933.
33. TD memo to Nathan, Jan. 7, 1933.
34. To Miss McCoy, June 21, 1933.
35. To Benjamin Goldstein, Aug. 23, 1933.
36. *American Spectator*, Sept., 1933.
37. To Hapgood, Oct. 10, 1933.
38. Draft wire, Sept. 5, 1933.
39. To Boeing, Oct. 26, 1933.

40. To Isobel Sperry, Nov. 14, 1933 (RHE). "Isobel Sperry" is necessarily a fictitious name.

41. *Autobiography of Upton Sinclair* (New York, Harcourt, Brace & World, 1962), p. 249.

42. This number included shorter works and oddments, such as *My City* and *The Songs of Paul Dresser*.

43. Evelyn Light to Ullstein Verlag, Berlin, Nov. 23, 1933.

44. To Nathan, Oct. 7, 1933.

45. To TD, Sept. 15, 1933.

46. TD to Isobel Sperry, Dec. 25, 1933 (RHE).

47. Douglas to TD, Dec. 23, 1933.

48. To Goldwyn, March 13, 1934.

49. To Isobel, Jan. 22, 1934 (RHE).

50. Dated Jan. 6, 1934.

51. Fabri diary, entry Jan. 1, 1934.

52. To Isobel, Jan. 27, 1934 (RHE).

53. *Evansville Press*, Jan. 21, 1934 (UP).

54. TD to Eastman, June 14, 1933.

55. To Dos Passos, Feb. 27, 1934.

56. To Isobel Sperry, Feb. 27, March 2 and March 7, 1934 (RHE).

57. To Morrison, Feb. 27, 1934.

58. To Miss Sperry, March 26, 1934 (RHE).

59. To Lengel, April 3, 1934.

60. To Miss Sperry, May 16, 1934 (RHE).

61. To Miss Sperry, May 31, 1934 (RHE).

62. TD told Elias, Sept. 10, 1945 (RHE).

CHAPTER 8

1. TD to John Cowper Powys, March 17, 1934.

2. Miss Ish-Kishor told Swanberg, July 10, 1963.

3. TD to Morrison, April 24, May 3 and May 21, 1934.

4. To Mrs. Campbell, after June 30, 1934.

5. Draft wire, May 31, 1934.

6. Mrs. Sherwood Anderson told Swanberg, Oct. 30, 1962.

7. The same; also, Esherick told Swanberg, Jan. 26, 1963.

8. To Cherniavsky, July 6, 1934.

9. To Hume, July 10, 1934.

10. To Rolland Holbrook, July 16, 1934.

11. To Mendel Feder, Aug. 30, 1934.

12. To *Izvestia*, after July 24, 1934.

13. Script dated Aug. 21, 1934 (UP).

14. *New York World-Telegram*, Aug. 9, and *The New York Times*, Aug. 28, 1924 (UP).

15. TD to Erich Posselt, Sept. 7, 1934.

16. To Milton Goldberg, Sept. 5, 1934.

17. To *New York World-Telegram*, Aug. 25, 1934. In TD's copy, the last line was crossed out.

18. To Hume, July 5, 1934.

19. Willard S. McKay to Hume, Sept. 7, 1934.

20. *New York Post*, Oct. 5, 1934.

21. Lengel to Monica McCall, Sept. 19, 1934.

22. TD to Miss ———, Sept. 24, 1934.

23. Contract with Simon & Schuster dated Sept. 28, 1934.

24. To TD, Oct. 21, 1934.

25. To Schuster, Oct. 26, 1934.

26. Guest list at UP.

27. *The Nation*, Oct. 19, 1932.

28. Fabri diary, Oct. 28, 1934.

29. Knopf to TD, Nov. 19, 1934 (Rascoe quote attached).

30. To Rascoe, Nov. 20, 1934.

31. Mencken to TD, Nov. 21, 1934.

32. To Mencken, Nov. 24, 1934.

33. To TD, Nov. 29, 1934.

34. Gingrich told Swanberg, April 2, 1964.

35. Mencken to TD, Dec. 8, 1934.

36. Canby to TD, Jan. 2, 1935.

37. To Mencken, Jan. 3, 1935.

38. Mencken to TD, Jan. 4, 1935.

39. To Mencken, Jan. 14, 1935.

40. *The Nation*, April 17, 1935.

41. Kunitz told Swanberg, Jan. 23, 1964.

42. Lawson told Swanberg, Oct. 16, 1963.

43. *New Masses*, April 30, 1935 (UP).

44. *New Masses*, May 7, 1935. See also Daniel Aaron: *Writers on the Left* (New York, Harcourt, Brace & World, 1961), pp. 267–68.

45. To Bruce Crawford, Jan. 15, 1935.

46. Miss Halsey to TD, Jan. 25, 1935.

47. TD to Miss Halsey, Jan. 28, 1935.

48. Simon to TD, Jan. 31, 1935.

49. To Simon, Feb. 5, 1935.

50. To George Douglas, March 16, 1935.

51. TD to Charles E. Yost, May 17, 1935.

52. Angoff to TD, Dec. 26, 1934.

53. To Douglas, Jan. 11, 1935 (CU).

54. To Lal, Jan. 16; to Millikan, March 16; to Bridges, March 16, 1935.

55. Gingrich told Swanberg, April 2, 1964.

56. From Bettina, April 17, 1935.

CHAPTER 9

1. To George Vaughan, Sept. 13, 1933. See also Neda Westlake: "Theodore Dreiser's Notes on Life," pamphlet (UP).

2. In *American Mercury*, March, 1934, and *Esquire*, Nov., 1934, respectively.

3. To Brill, May 18, 1935 (property of Dr. E. R. Brill).

4. To Milton Goldberg, May 30, 1935.

5. Blum to TD, Sept. 27, 1934.

6. To Flexner, June 1, 1935.

7. To Mrs. Eric Knight, July 29, 1935.

8. Schuster to TD, July 11, 1935.

9. To Schuster, July 20, 1935.

10. To Schuster, Aug. 7, 1935.

11. Schuster to TD, Aug. 20, 1935.

12. TD to Schuster, Aug. 27, 1935.

13. Dinamov to TD, Aug. 15, 1935.

14. TD to Joel Stebbins, Aug. 30, 1935.

15. *Los Angeles Times,* July 29, 1935 (UP).

16. To Laemmle, Aug. 23, 1935.

17. Helen Dreiser: *My Life . . .* , p. 253.

18. The same, p. 254.

19. Oct. 30, 1935.

20. To Gingrich, Oct. 31, 1935.

21. To Miss Monash, Nov. 8, 1935.

22. TD to Langmuir, Dec. 30, 1935.

23. To Sherwood Anderson, Jan. 2, 1936 (Newberry).

24. Jan. 12, 1936. In Howard Mumford Jones and Walter B. Rideout (eds.): *Letters of Sherwood Anderson* (Boston, Little Brown, 1953), pp. 344–45.

25. TD to Anderson, Jan. 28, 1936 (Newberry).

26. To Esther McCoy, undated.

27. To *Pravda,* Dec. 30, 1935.

28. Schuster to TD, Dec. 21, 1935, and Jan. 5, 1936.

29. To Richard L. Simon, Jan. 27, 1936.

30. TD to Upton Sinclair, Dec. 27, 1935 (Indiana).

31. To George Douglas, Jan. 28, 1936.

32. Jan. 2, 1936. In Horace Gregory (ed.): *The Portable Sherwood Anderson* (New York, Viking, 1949), p. 608.

33. To Elinore Harrison, Feb. 6, 1936.

34. To Yost, Feb. 11, 1936.

35. Blum to TD, Feb. 10, 1936.

36. Feb. 10, 1936.

37. Mrs. Douglas to TD, Feb. 16, 1936.

38. Feb. 11, 1936.

39. Mrs. Baker to TD, Feb. 25, 1936.

40. To Mrs. Baker, March 7, 1936.

41. John Wentz: "The Piscator Dramatization," *Modern Drama,* Feb., 1962, pp. 371–73.

42. TD to Mrs. Campbell, Feb. 11, 1936.

43. After March 13, 1936 (Newberry).

44. To Mrs. Goodman, Feb. 28, 1936.

45. To Getts, April 7, 1936.

46. Schuster to TD, April 22, 1936.

47. To Chambers, March 20, 1936.
48. To Miss McCoy, April 3, 1936.
49. To Vladimir Romm, after April 23, 1936.
50. Before May 15, 1936 (Newberry).
51. Miss McCoy told Swanberg, Sept. 13, 1963.
52. To Lark-Horovitz, July 22, 1936.
53. To Miss McCoy, June 22, 1936.
54. TD to Paul Schwarz, Sept. 11, 1936.
55. Mencken to TD, May 26 and May 30, 1936.
56. To Mencken, July 25, 1936.
57. To Bruce Bliven, Sept. 9, 1936.
58. To TD, Aug. 26, 1936.

CHAPTER 10

1. To Mencken, Aug. 9, 1936.
2. To Mencken, Jan. 12, 1937.
3. O'Neill to TD, Dec. 3, 1936.
4. Undated 1937 news clipping (UP). *The New York Times*, June 30, 1937.
5. Letter to V. F. Calverton, after Feb. 11, 1937.
6. Miss Hurst told Swanberg, Aug. 12, 1964.
7. *New York Herald Tribune*, Aug. 25, 1937.
8. Elias: *Theodore Dreiser . . .* , pp. 289–90.
9. To TD, Aug. 31, 1937.
10. To Elias, Oct. 2, 1937 (RHE).
11. Elias notes dated Oct. 24, 1937 (RHE); also, Elias told Swanberg, May 10, 1962.
12. TD to Helen, Dec. 7, 1937.
13. To McCord, Jan. 5, 1938.
14. To Eisenstein, Jan. 3, 1938.
15. To Helen, Dec. 19, 1937.
16. "A Conversation," *Direction I*, Jan., 1938, pp. 351–52.
17. Masters to TD, Feb. 4, 1938.
18. Alice Davis diary, March 9, 1938; also, Mrs. Alice Davis Tibbetts told Swanberg, Oct. 16, 1963.
19. Lengel to TD, Feb. 8, 1938.
20. To Bostock, March 1, 1938.
21. TD told Elias, Aug. 26, 1941.
22. To Fabri, May 15, 1938.
23. To Golden, June 17, 1938.
24. To Evelyn Scott, June 17, 1938.
25. To Dr. Eugen Kerpel, June 20, 1938.
26. Helen to Fabri, undated 1938 (Fabri property).
27. Marguerite Tjader Harris told Swanberg, Nov. 26, 1962.
28. Elias notes, dated July 12–13, 1938 (RHE).
29. Daniel Aaron: *Writers on the Left*, p. 361.
30. To Mrs. Harris, July 15, 1938.

31. Two letters to Miss Bissell, July 15 and July 26, 1938.

32. Paris edition, *New York Herald Tribune*, July 24, 1938.

33. To Miss Bissell, July 26, 1938.

34. To Miss Bissell, Aug. 2, 1938; also, Theodore Dreiser: "Barcelona in August," *Direction*, Nov.–Dec., 1938.

35. Hughes to Folsom, Aug. 16, 1938 (CU).

36. To Miss Bissell, Aug. 8, 1938.

37. To J. C. Powys, Aug. 9, 1938.

38. To Powys and companion, April 12, 1939.

39. To McCord, Aug. 18, 1938.

40. Helen to Fabri, Aug. 5, 1938 (Fabri property).

41. TD to President Roosevelt, Aug. 23, 1938 (FDR).

42. To Roosevelt, Sept. 1, 1938 (FDR).

43. *The New York Times*, Aug. 27, 1938.

44. Gerhard Friedrich: "The Dreiser-Jones Correspondence," *Bulletin of the Friends Historical Association*, spring, 1957. But Dreiser while in Paris spoke of resuming *The Bulwark*.

45. In Lengel to TD, Oct. 17, 1938.

46. To Dr. Donald McCord, Oct. 18, 1938.

47. To Ernest Briggs, Nov. 2, 1938.

48. To Elias, Oct. 26, 1938 (RHE).

49. Mencken to TD, Oct. 31, 1938.

50. To Mencken, Nov. 3, 1938.

51. Harriet Bissell to Elias, undated 1953 (CU).

52. To Bye, Nov. 11, 1938.

53. To Mencken, Nov. 10, 1938.

54. Undated, 1938.

BOOK SIX

Chapter 1

1. May 11, 1939 (Fabri property).

2. Helen Dreiser: *My Life . . .* , p. 263.

3. Schuster to TD, Dec. 28, 1938.

4. To Mrs. Sinclair, Jan. 5, 1939 (Indiana).

5. To Masters, Feb. 6, 1939.

6. Gerhard Friedrich: "Dreiser's Debt to Woolman's *Journal*," *American Quarterly*, winter, 1955.

7. TD to Mary Elizabeth Thompson, Jan. 18, 1939.

8. Mencken to TD, Jan. 11, 1939.

9. TD to Yost, Jan. 17 and 27, 1939; also, *Autobiography of Upton Sinclair*, pp. 246–47.

10. Mrs. Smith told Swanberg, March 13, 1963.

11. Jan. 6, 1939 (Fabri property).

12. Jan. 5, 1939 (FDR).

13. To John F. Reich, Feb. 28, 1939.

14. Masters to TD, Aug. 4, 1939.

15. To Briggs, March 1, 1939; also, *San Francisco Chronicle*, Feb. 15; *Morning Oregonian*, Feb. 16; *Salt Lake Tribune*, Feb. 20; *Salt Lake Telegram*, Feb. 20, 1939 (all UP).

16. To Folsom, April 1, 1939.

17. Two letters to Lengel, May 6 and May 13, 1939.

18. To Stoddart, May 10, 1939.

19. To Barrymore, June 1, 1939.

20. To Mencken, June 16, 1939.

21. To Stoddart, June 22, 1939.

22. June 23, 1939. In Helen Dreiser: *My Life* . . . , pp. 267–68.

23. To Lorna Smith, June 7, 1939 (LAPL).

24. June 6, 1939.

25. Chaliapin told Swanberg, Sept. 12, 1963.

26. To Lengel, Oct. 30, 1939.

27. To Otvos, April 19, 1939.

28. TD to Sol Lesser, July 25, 1939.

29. Leaflet, "The Dawn Is in the East," undated; published in *Common Sense*, Dec., 1939.

30. To Mencken, Oct. 3, 1939.

31. Helen to Fabri, May 31, 1939 (Fabri property).

32. To Mrs. Manning, Aug. 29, 1939 (Huntington). "Estelle Manning" is necessarily a fictitious name.

33. TD to Lorna Smith, Oct. 17, 1939.

34. *New York Journal-American*, Nov. 22, and *Los Angeles Herald & Express*, Nov. 23, 1939 (UP).

35. TD to Steinbeck, Jan. 24, 1940. Steinbeck replied Jan. 28, saying, "It isn't the first time my hand writing has got me into trouble," and inviting him to call at the Steinbeck ranch.

36. To Shimkin, Dec. 21, 1939.

37. Esther McCoy told Swanberg, July 28, 1964.

38. To Fred Smith, Jan. 9, 1940.

39. To *New Masses*, Feb. 23, 1940.

40. Folsom to TD, June 10, 1940.

41. TD to Huebsch, June 19, 1940.

42. TD to Helen, June 14, 1940.

43. Lorna Smith told Swanberg, March 13, 1963.

44. To Mrs. Manning, June 28, 1940 (Huntington).

45. TD to Lengel, July 17, 1940.

46. To Lengel, July 31, 1940.

47. Belfrage to Swanberg, Dec. 6, 1963.

48. TD to Mencken, Aug. 22, 1940.

49. Belfrage to Swanberg, Dec. 6, 1963.

50. To Otvos, April 14, 1940.

51. Mencken to TD, Aug. 19, 1940.

52. Lengel to TD, Aug. 16, 1940.

53. To Lengel, Aug. 22, 1940.

54. Lengel to TD, Sept. 19, 1940.

55. Leaflet, "Editor & Publisher," Sept., 1940.

56. TD spoke over KHJ, Los Angeles, Oct. 29, 1940; script at UP.

CHAPTER 2

1. Nov. 9, 1940, radio speech; script at UP.

2. TD to Robinson, Dec. 16, 1940.

3. TD to Bruce Crawford, Dec. 23, 1940.

4. To Oumansky, Feb. 14, 1941. Dreiser later sent a copy to President Roosevelt.

5. To Clifford Welch, Jan. 2, 1941.

6. *New York Sunday Worker*, March 2, 1941 (UP); also, Elias told Swanberg, May 10, 1962.

7. Louis Budenz: *Men Without Faces* (New York, Harper, 1950), pp. 244–45.

8. *The New York Times*, March 5, 1941.

9. *The New York Times Book Review*, March 16, 1941.

10. Helen to Louis Street, Feb. 19, 1941.

11. *Philadelphia Public Ledger*, March 7, 1941 (UP).

12. Mencken to TD, Feb. 25, 1941.

13. To Mrs. Roosevelt, April 25, 1941.

14. Irving Howe and Lewis Coser: *The American Communist Party* (New York, Praeger, 1962), p. 395.

15. Draft telegram, July 2, 1941.

16. TD to *New Masses*, after June 26, 1941.

17. To Mencken, March 28, 1943.

18. Jug to Elias, Sept. 14, 1939.

19. Mrs. Goodman told Swanberg, Sept. 25, 1963.

20. To Seldes, Jan. 9, 1942.

21. From Kyllmann, July 23 and 25, 1941.

22. TD to Kyllmann, Aug. 12, 1941.

23. To Mrs. Helen Arnold, Sept. 27, 1941.

24. Unidentified news clipping, undated (UP).

25. Nov. 23, 1941 (Huntington).

26. Balch to TD, Nov. 25, 1941.

27. To Helen, Dec. 2, 1941.

28. Lengel to TD, Oct. 28, 1941.

CHAPTER 3

1. TD to Mrs. Roosevelt, March 19, 1942.

2. Two letters to Mrs. Manning, Feb. 23 and March 2, 1942 (Huntington).

3. Mencken to TD, March 27, 1942.

4. TD to Fabri, April 3, 1942.

5. TD to Mencken, April 2, 1942.

6. To Balch, May 1, 1942.

7. TD to Timofei Rokotov, May 20, 1942.

8. From Mencken, July 23, 1942.

9. To Lengel, July 1, 1942.

10. Mrs. Tobey told Swanberg, Sept. 13, 1963.

11. Sylvia Bradshaw to Swanberg, Aug. 7, 1963. "Sylvia Bradshaw" is necessarily a fictitious name.

12. The same.

13. TD to Balch, Aug. 11, 1942.

14. TD to Joseph North, July 24, 1942.

15. *Toronto Evening Telegram*, Sept. 21, 1942 (UP).

16. Unidentified Toronto news clipping, Sept. 21 (UP).

17. Oct. 3, 1942 issue (UP).

18. *New York PM*, Sept. 27, 1942 (UP).

19. Undated *PM* clipping (UP).

20. Leaflet, Oct. 6, 1942 (Fabri property).

21. To Miss Bradshaw, Nov. 23 [1942].

22. Mrs. Goodman told Swanberg, Sept. 25, 1963.

23. To Lengel, March 2, 1947.

24. Helen to Fabri, Nov. 12, 1942 (Fabri property).

25. Powys to TD, Oct. 14, 1942.

26. TD to Norman Cowan, Oct. 22, 1942.

27. Manuel told Swanberg, March 4, 1963.

28. Mr. and Mrs. Edgar Ward told Swanberg, March 8, 1963.

29. To Miss Bradshaw, Jan. 5 [1943].

30. Mencken to TD, March 19, 1943.

31. TD to Mencken, March 27, 1943.

32. Mencken to TD, April 1, 1943.

33. TD to Dr. Perceval Gerson, May 3, 1943.

34. Helen to Fabri, March 25, 1943 (Fabri property).

35. Esther Tobey told Swanberg, March 4, 1963.

36. Miss Bradshaw to Swanberg, Aug. 7, 1963.

37. Moffat to Helen, Sept. 22, 1943.

38. Helen to Moffat, Sept. 24, 1943.

39. Quoted in Helen Dreiser: *My Life . . .*, pp. 291–92.

40. TD to Mencken, Nov. 25, 1943.

41. Mencken to TD, Dec. 13, 1943.

42. Dies told Swanberg, June 19, 1963.

43. TD to Gingrich, Oct. 29, 1943; also, TD to Louise Campbell, Jan. 6, 1944; Miss Bradshaw to Swanberg, Aug. 7, 1963.

44. To Miss Bradshaw, undated, 1944.

45. Academy to TD, Jan. 4, 1944.

46. Schorer: *Sinclair Lewis*, p. 709.

47. TD to Damrosch, Jan. 10, 1944.

48. To Miss Bradshaw, Feb. 13, 1944.

CHAPTER 4

1. Mencken to TD, March 27, 1944.

2. TD to Mencken, April 22, 1944.

3. To Mencken, May 5, 1944.

4. Mencken to TD, May 9, 1944.

5. Letters to Miss Geffen, Feb. 19 and April 22, 1944.

6. Myrtle (Mrs. C. A. Butcher) told Swanberg, March 19, 1963.

7. Helen Dreiser: *My Life* . . . , p. 296.

8. Helen to Fabri, April 26, 1944 (Fabri property).

9. Fabri told Swanberg, Dec. 23, 1962.

10. TD to Helen, May 19, 1944.

11. TD to Helen, May 14, 1944.

12. TD to Helen, May 19, 1944.

13. TD to Mencken, May 14, 1944.

14. *Philadelphia Record,* May 22, 1944 (CU).

15. Marguerite Tjader Harris: "Dreiser's Last Visit to New York," *Twice A Year,* fall–winter, 1946–47, pp. 219–20.

16. "Broadcast by Theodore Dreiser," *Direction,* July, 1944 (UP).

17. Copy of Tinker citation (CU).

18. Untermeyer told Swanberg, Dec. 11, 1962; also, James T. Farrell to Swanberg, July 30, 1964.

19. Mrs. Harris: "Dreiser's Last Visit . . ."

20. Mrs. Harris told Swanberg, Sept. 18, 1963.

21. Dreiser's meetings with his relatives were described to me by Dr. Vera Dreiser Scott (to Swanberg, May 22, 1964).

22. Fabri diary, June 2, 1944.

23. Mencken to Farrell, June 5, 1944 (PC).

24. Mrs. Harris: "Dreiser's Last Visit . . ." *op. cit.,* p. 227.

25. Helen Dreiser: *My Life* . . . , p. 299.

26. Helen to Fabri, June 12, 1944 (Fabri property).

27. Helen Dreiser: *My Life* . . . , p. 300. Also, Myrtle Patges (Mrs. C. A. Butcher) told Swanberg, March 19, 1963.

28. To Mrs. Harris, June 15, 1944.

29. To Miss Bradshaw, June 20, 1944.

30. *Esquire* records—Gingrich to Swanberg, April 7, 1964.

CHAPTER 5

1. Lawson told Swanberg, Oct. 16, 1963.

2. Manuel told Swanberg, March 4, 1963.

3. June 27, 1944.

4. To Dr. Vera Dreiser Scott, July 17, 1944.

5. TD to Mme. Chiang, July 3, 1944.

6. To Mrs. Campbell, July 15, 1944. The sketch was "Ethelda," *Esquire,* Jan., 1945.

7. Esther Tobey told Swanberg, Sept. 13, 1963.

8. Helen to Fabri, Aug. 25, 1944 (Fabri property).

9. Aug. 8, 1944 (Huntington).

10. To Miss Bradshaw, Sept. 1, 1944.

11. To Browder, Sept. 28, 1944.

12. Mrs. Harris told Swanberg, Oct. 9, 1962, and Sept. 18, 1963; also, *Book Find News*, March, 1946, p. 7.

13. Lawson told Swanberg, Oct. 16, 1963.

14. Undated (Huntington).

15. Helen Dreiser: *My Life . . .* , p. 302.

16. Elias: *Theodore Dreiser . . .* , p. 298.

17. TD to Stalin, May 16, 1945.

18. TD to Russian consul in Los Angeles, Aug. 23, 1944.

19. Helen Dreiser: *My Life . . .* , p. 294.

20. To Mrs. Campbell, March 4, 1945.

21. Helen to Mrs. Campbell, May 9, 1945.

22. Mrs. Campbell told Swanberg, June 21, 1962.

CHAPTER 6

1. Quoted in Helen Dreiser: *My Life . . .* , pp. 321-22.

2. TD to Odets, May 10, 1945.

3. Lawson told Swanberg, Oct. 16, 1963.

4. Private source.

5. TD to Foster, July 20, 1945.

6. Foster to TD, Aug. 7, 1945. Details on TD's joining of the party have been gathered from: Helen Dreiser to Elias, Sept. 3, 1946, and Sept. 22, 1947 (RHE); TD told Elias, Sept. 10, 1945 (RHE); Lawson told Swanberg, Oct. 16, 1963; Browder told Swanberg, April 10, 1964; Howe and Coser: *The American Communist Party*, pp. 442-48.

7. To Mrs. Harris, Aug. 14, 1945.

8. Helen Dreiser: *My Life . . .* , p. 308.

9. To Miss Bradshaw, July 15, 1945.

10. To Mrs. Harris, Aug. 25, 1945.

11. Helen Dreiser: *My Life . . .* , p. 309.

12. Masters to TD, Jan. 31, 1945.

13. TD to Mencken, Sept. 2, 1945.

14. Mencken told Elias, Nov. 2, 1944 (RHE).

15. TD told Elias, Sept. 10, 1945 (RHE).

16. The same.

17. Mrs. Harris told Swanberg, Sept. 18, 1963.

18. But he grew uncertain, writing Farrell on Dec. 14, 1945, "Would you prefer, personally, to see the chapters on yoga come out of the book? If so, what would be your idea of a logical ending?"

19. But the book as published largely followed Mrs. Campbell's editing.

20. Elias: *Theodore Dreiser . . .* , p. 307; also, Helen Dreiser: *My Life . . .* , p. 308.

CHAPTER 7

1. Two letters, Mrs. Manning to Lengel, March 2, 1947, and Dec. 13, 1946 (Lengel property).

2. Helen Dreiser: *My Life . . .* , p. 309.

3. To Miss Bradshaw, Dec 20, 1945.

4. TD to Farrell, Dec. 24, 1945.

5. Helen Dreiser: *My Life* . . . , p. 315. Helen to Elias, Feb. 7, 1946 (RHE).

6. Details of Dreiser's death from: Esther Tobey to Swanberg, May 14, 1963; Mrs. Goodman told Swanberg, March 5, 1963; Helen Dreiser: *My Life* . . . , pp. 311–17.

7. Mrs. Manning to Lengel, March 2, 1947 (Lengel property).

8. *Indianapolis Star*, Dec. 31, 1945.

9. *Twice A Year*, fall–winter, 1946–47, p. 216.

10. Mencken statement, undated, 1946 (UP).

11. Harold J. Dies told Swanberg, June 19, 1963.

12. Helen to Elias, Feb. 7, 1946 (RHE).

13. Dreiser: *Moods, Philosophical and Emotional* (New York, Simon & Schuster, 1935), pp. 240–41.

14. Helen to Elias, Feb. 7, 1946 (RHE).

Index

tour (1939), predicts war, 461; seems in straits—blames Simon & Schuster and seeks new publisher, 462–63; perhaps exaggerates his "poverty," 462; suspects a "Jewish plot" against him, 462; his sympathy for Hitler, 465; last meeting with Sherwood Anderson, 465–66; publishers uninterested in TD, 466–67; inflamed by social causes, 467; works on *America is Worth Saving,* 468–70; excessive drinking, 470; supports Browder in 1940 election, 472; "saved" by sale of *Sister Carrie* to films, 472; moves to Kings Road, Hollywood, 473; on 1941 trip to New York, makes speech while tipsy, 474; rendered ill by Nazi invasion of Russia, 476–77; reporters shun him at 70th birthday, 477; now dependent on Helen despite other affairs, 478; his Anglophobia shocks Otto Kyllmann, 478–80; speaks in Indianapolis—confers with Putnam in New York, 481; contracts to finish *The Bulwark* and resumes it, 483–85; his slow progress and new romantic involvements, 485; visits Toronto (1942), creates international furore, 486–87; in a confusion of activities, he quits *The Bulwark,* 488–92; makes 1944 trip to New York to accept Academy award and seek another publisher, 494–502; decides to marry Helen after 25 years, 496–97; finds publishers uninterested in him, 498; Academy award ceremony, 499–500; Mencken, angered at his acceptance, breaks off friendship, 496, 498–99, 502; TD visits Masters, 499–500; explains his "writing block"—feels that his genius has fled, 500; visits the Ed Dreisers, 501–502; returns west and marries Helen in some secrecy, 503; finishes *The Bulwark,* 505–10; his 73rd birthday party, 507; deigns to attend church, 505–506, 509–10; writes protesting letter to Stalin —receives $34,600 in royalties from Russia, 510; quits Putnam, signs with Doubleday, 510; his "White Christ" theory, 510; joins Communist Party (1945)—the forces impelling him, 513–15; resumes *The Stoic* with Helen's help, 515–16; his last birthday party, 516; mind sometimes clouded, irrational, 517–18; denounces Helen, calls himself "the loneliest man in the world," 520; illness and death, 521–22; many thought him long since dead, 523; appraisals of him, 523–24; surprising hoard found at his bank, 524; expensive funeral, 525–26; leaves comfortable estate, 527; Mencken's final appraisal of, 527; his great vogue in Russia, 528

HIS TRAITS, HABITS, ACTIVITIES:

Sex worship: 15, 20–21, 27, 28, 34, 42, 44, 49, 56–59, 72, 99, 126, 152, 160, 246, 279, 409–16, 484–85

Religious questioning: 38, 42, 47, 60–61, 342, 433, 459–60, 476, 493, 502, 518

Hypochondria: 78, 124–25, 199, 260

Naïveté: 39, 72, 181, 183, 234, 248, 288, 436, 502

Superstitions: 32, 68, 87, 182, 191, 196–97, 198, 201, 202, 221, 227, 242, 358, 463

Mood fluctuations: 40, 41, 53, 152, 154, 198, 200, 202, 356

Sense of social protest: 55, 169, 189, 225, 238, 274, 366, 370, 384 ff.

Need for encouragement, a "helper": 84, 159, 216, 217, 276, 429, 436, 502, 503

Deep fear of poverty: 78, 155–56, 428, 462